A Special Edition of

BUSINESS STATISTICS

A Decision-Making Approach

VOLUME TWO

EDITED BY PAUL E. TIX

SIMON & SCHUSTER
CUSTOM PUBLISHING

Excerpts taken from:
Business Statistics: A Decision-Making Approach
by David F. Groebner and Patrick W. Shannon

A Simon & Schuster Company
Englewood Cliffs, NJ 07632

This special edition published in cooperation with Simon & Schuster Custom Publishing

Printed in the United States of America

10 9 8 7 6 5 4 3 2 1

ISBN 0-536-59466-X
BA 96064

SIMON & SCHUSTER CUSTOM PUBLISHING
160 Gould Street/Needham Heights, MA 02194
Simon & Schuster Education Group

Preface

Statistics has become increasingly relevant for business decision-making activities in all organizations. The statistical techniques described in an introductory course are used in all the functional areas of an organization, including accounting, finance, marketing, production, and personnel management. We continue to believe students will best understand why statistical topics are important if the subjects are approached from a user's perspective and this edition uses the same basic applications orientation as the previous editions.

The first three editions of *Business Statistics: A Decision-Making Approach* represented our evolving effort to provide a meaningful text for those who are interested in learning not only how statistical techniques are used, but also why decision makers need to use them. The feedback we have received from both faculty and student users has reinforced our belief that teaching business statistics from a decision-making perspective is the key to making the course both meaningful and enjoyable.

The fourth edition of *Business Statistics: A Decision-Making Approach* contains several major changes from the previous editions. The changes were based on our use of the text and comments from students and the many faculty members who critiqued the third edition. The most significant changes include:

1. Numerous scenarios used to introduce statistical topics were changed or rewritten. All applications discussed in topic development are now either based on actual data or, if confidentiality is an issue, based on disguised data but an actual situation.

2. The emphasis on quality has been increased. We believe the statistical relationship with quality control is best presented if the topic is included in relevant chapters and so we have added quality control sections to numerous chapters instead of adding a single new chapter on quality.
3. The discussion of nonparametric statistics has been increased. Several tests have been added, and coverage of small-sample statistical techniques is now presented.
4. The cases at the end of each chapter have been rewritten and either updated or replaced. All cases are now based on either actual data or disguised data from actual situations.
5. The use of computerized statistical tools has been increased. The computer application sections have been retained from the previous edition. We continue to present examples of MINITAB and SPSS-X output. However, we have added output from GB-STAT, a personal computer software package written for student use with significant capability and extensive graphical output.
6. As part of the emphasis on computer use, additional databases are supplied with the text for interested instructors and a set of database problems is included at the end of each appropriate chapter.
7. New application problems have been added at the end of each chapter. The problems have been mixed and are no longer identified with specific sections of the chapter. We believe students will benefit from identifying the correct tool in addition to applying the tool correctly.

Along with the improvements over the third edition, the fourth edition is accompanied by a wide range of supplementary materials. A comprehensive study guide written by Susan Fry is available. This guide has a complete set of notes for each chapter in the text and worked-out solutions to each of the odd-numbered problems. This study guide is ideally suited to the student who wishes to obtain the maximum knowledge from the statistics course.

For the instructor, the fourth edition offers an instructor's manual that contains worked solutions to all the problems and cases in the text. In addition, a set of transparency masters is available. These masters are designed to be used as the basis for the course lectures from each chapter in the text. The databases contained in both the text and the computer supplements are available in ASCII format on IBM/PC diskette form. Finally, a test bank of more than 1,000 objective test questions with correct answers is included.

The fourth edition of *Business Statistics: A Decision-Making Approach* contains many changes and improvements. Many of these are the result of the comments and constructive criticisms we received from the following individuals: Professor Serge Fotopoulos, Washington State University; Professor Michael Mays, West Virginia University; Professor Joe Sutka, Moraine Valley Community College.

In writing the previous editions of *Business Statistics: A Decision-Making Approach*, we learned a great deal about ourselves and our attitude toward education. We have been surprised at the dynamic nature of statistical education. The use of computer statistical packages and the emphasis on statistical quality control are the two most recent examples of this dynamic nature. Working on the fourth edition has extended our learning process. We know that we are better teachers for having written this text. We hope that after students have taken the course they will consider themselves better off for the experience. We hope they will understand the importance of statistics as a decision-making tool.

D.F.G.
P.W.S.

Contents

Volume II

BUSINESS STATISTICS

Tests of Variances and an Introduction to ANOVA

WHY DECISION MAKERS NEED TO KNOW

As we have continually emphasized, the reason to know statistical techniques is that they assist decision makers. The previous four chapters have introduced some of the more commonly used decision-making aids. An advantage to using both statistical estimation and hypothesis testing is not that they allow decision makers to always make correct decisions, but that they will increase the likelihood of the decisions being correct. The techniques will not eliminate the uncertainty a decision maker faces, but they will allow the uncertainty to be incorporated into the process. However, you may be able to think of decision-making situations that cannot be addressed using the techniques introduced to this point. For instance:

1. Almco Fabricated Parts has just signed a contract to supply parts for the power windows in Ford Thunderbirds. Each part has specified dimensions, including a tolerance: i.e., 10 ± 0.003 in. Almco wishes to know whether its production output meets the standard.
2. Elko Electronics is designing a ground-sensing radar unit to be used when landing newly built jumbo jets. The unit must be able to sense the ground and report the distance to within 6 inches. The design lab has developed two designs and wants to know whether both meet the specifications and which of the two is more accurate.
3. Farber Rubber Products makes a household product line at each of six manufacturing facilities across the country. It has just recently started receiving an excessive number of cus-

tomer complaints about poor quality. The question is whether the problem lies in all six plants or is confined to one or two facilities.

4. Biotech, Inc., a genetic engineering company, has just developed a new strain of soybeans. Although the product is clearly superior to present strains of soybeans, Biotech scientists have been asked which of eight possible levels of fertilizer to recommend to farmers buying the product.

The statistical tools introduced in previous chapters will not help in any of these situations. Both the hypothesis testing and estimation techniques we have considered so far are limited to dealing with measures of the location of a distribution, such as μ, $\mu_1 - \mu_2$, p, and $p_1 - p_2$. In situations 1 and 2, the decision makers are interested in the spread in a distribution. Therefore, we need tools for dealing with population variances (or standard deviations). In addition, the tools considered up to now were limited to dealing with one or two populations. Decision makers often need a way to consider more than two populations.

With the increasing emphasis on quality control applications of statistical tools, it has become increasingly important to be able to consider population variances and comparisons of more than two populations. Much of the emphasis of quality control techniques is to reduce the variation associated with the outcome of physical processes. Therefore, decision makers must be able to determine when a decrease or an increase in a measure of variation is statistically significant. In addition, trainers in many organizations are talking about developing skills in the general work force in the techniques of "experimental design." This is often a valuable procedure that is needed to make valid comparisons of samples taken from more than two populations.

CHAPTER OBJECTIVES

This chapter introduces methods for testing hypotheses involving a single population variance. The test procedure uses the chi-square distribution, a new statistical distribution introduced in this chapter. A method of testing hypotheses that involve the difference between two population variances is also considered. The F distribution is introduced as the needed distribution for the two-population test. Finally, the chapter also introduces an important statistical technique called analysis of variance and shows how it can be used by business decision makers to test hypotheses involving three or more population means. For cases when the analysis of variance leads us to conclude that population means are not all equal, three techniques are introduced to help you decide which population means are different.

STUDENT OBJECTIVES

After studying the material in this chapter, you should be able to do the following:

1. Recognize applications that require a hypothesis test of a single population variance and perform the test correctly.

2. Realize when an application calls for a hypothesis test involving the difference between two population variances and perform the test correctly.
3. Discuss why using multiple two-sample t tests is not an appropriate alternative to analysis of variance.
4. Describe what is meant by partitioning the sum of squares.
5. Perform an analysis of variance for a one-way experimental design.
6. List the assumptions necessary to use analysis of variance.
7. Apply Tukey's method for pairwise comparisons of population means.
8. Apply Scheffé's method for pairwise comparisons of population means.
9. Perform two-way analysis of variance tests and apply the least significant difference test to determine which populations have different means.
10. Recognize business applications for which analysis of variance is the appropriate statistical tool.

12-1 HYPOTHESES ABOUT A SINGLE POPULATION VARIANCE

The discussions in Chapters 9, 10, and 11 concentrated on the population center as the value of interest. As shown, the population center is often of interest when a decision is made. However, in some cases decision makers are more interested in the spread of a population than in its central location. For instance, military planes designed to penetrate enemy defenses have a ground-following radar system. The radar tells the pilot exactly how far the plane is above the ground. A radar unit that is correct *on the average* is useless if the readings are distributed widely around the true value. As a second example, many automatic transporation systems have stopping sensors to deposit passengers at the correct spot in a terminal. An automated stopping sensor that *on the average* lets passengers off at the correct point could leave many irritated people long distances up and down the track. Therefore, many product specifications involve both an average value and some limit on the dispersion these values can have. These specifications are called *tolerances*. For example, the specification for a steel push-pin may be an average length of 1.78 inches plus or minus 0.01 inch. The manufacturer using these pins would be interested in both the average length and how much these pins vary in length.

A recent survey of sources of consumer dissatisfaction indicated that one of the primary problems is scheduling a service call, only to have the service person be late for the appointment time. H & L Machines provides service for all types of copy machines in the San Antonio area. Based on past records and manufacturer recommendations, the company determines that the average service call for a Xerox Model 1075 computer should be 2 hours. However, scheduling calls every 2 hours, plus required travel time, has led to delays and customer complaints. Nina Ray, the person in charge of service scheduling, realizes she must consider the variation in these service times, in addition to their average.

Based on a discussion with a group of service representatives, Nina thinks the variability of the distribution of service times should have a standard deviation of 0.5 hour or less. She is now ready to gather information to see if it will support her contention. Using the methods introduced in previous chapters, she is interested in testing the following null and alternative hypotheses:

$$H_0: \quad \sigma \leq 0.5$$
$$H_A: \quad \sigma > 0.5$$

There is no statistical technique for directly testing hypotheses about a population standard deviation. However, a test is available for testing about a population variance. Thus, the previous hypotheses must be converted to:

$$H_0: \quad \sigma^2 \leq 0.25$$
$$H_A: \quad \sigma^2 > 0.25$$

As with all the hypothesis tests introduced in Chapters 9, 10 and 11, the decision to reject or accept the null hypothesis will be based on the statistic computed from a sample. In testing hypotheses about a single population variance, the appropriate statistic is S^2, the sample variance, given in equation 12-1:

$$S^2 = \frac{\Sigma(X - \overline{X})^2}{n - 1} \qquad \textbf{12-1}$$

To test a null hypothesis about a population variance, we compare S^2 with the hypothesized population variance, σ^2. To do this, we need to be able to standardize the distribution of sample variances in much the same way we used the Z distribution and the t distribution when hypothesizing about population means. The standardized distribution for sample variances is a *chi-square distribution.* The standardized chi-square variable is computed by equation 12-2:

$$\chi^2 = \frac{(n - 1)(S^2)}{\sigma^2} \qquad \textbf{12-2}$$

where

χ^2 = Standardized chi-square variable

n = Sample size

S^2 = Sample variance

σ^2 = Hypothesized variance

FIGURE 12-1

Chi-square Distributions

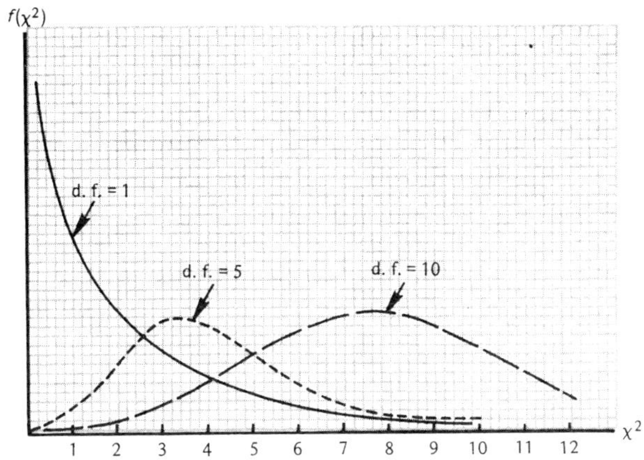

The shape of the standardized chi-square distribution depends on the hypothesized variance and the degrees of freedom, $n - 1$. Figure 12-1 illustrates chi-square distributions for various degrees of freedom. Note that as the degrees of freedom increase, the chi-square distribution approaches a normal distribution.

Returning to the H & L Machines example, suppose Nina Ray took a sample of twenty service calls and found a variance of 0.33 hour squared. Figure 12-2 presents the hypothesis test at an alpha level of 0.10.

FIGURE 12-2

Chi-square Test for One Population Variance for the H & L Machines Example

Hypotheses:

H_O: $\sigma^2 \leq 0.25$

H_A: $\sigma^2 > 0.25$

$\alpha = 0.10$

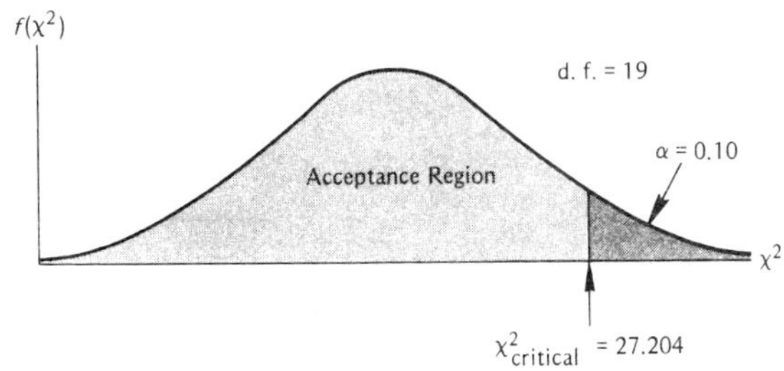

Decision Rule:

If $\chi^2 > \chi^2_{\text{critical}} = 27.204$, reject H_0.
Otherwise, do not reject H_0.

The chi-square test is as follows:

$$\chi^2 = \frac{(n-1)(S^2)}{\sigma^2} = \frac{19(0.33)}{0.25}$$

$$= 25.08$$

Since $\chi^2 = 25.08 < \chi^2_{\text{critical}} = 27.204$, accept H_0.

Appendix E contains a table of chi-square values for various probabilities and degrees of freedom. The chi-square table is used in a manner similar to the use of the *t*-distribution table. For example, to find $\chi^2_{critical}$ for the H & L Machines example, we first determine the degrees of freedom, $n - 1 = 20 - 1 = 19$, and the desired alpha level, 0.10. Now we go to the chi-square table under the column headed "0.10" (corresponding to the desired alpha) and find the χ^2 value in this column that intersects the row corresponding to the appropriate degrees of freedom. Table 12-1 illustrates how the chi-square table is used to find $\chi^2_{critical} = 27.204$. If the calculated χ^2 exceeds $\chi^2_{critical}$, the null hypothesis should be rejected.

TABLE 12-1

Finding Critical Values in the Chi-square Table

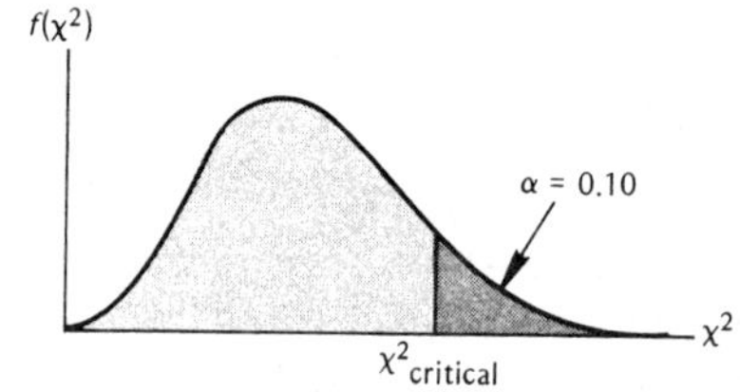

d.f.	Probabilities (Or Areas under χ^2 Distribution Curve above Given χ^2 Values)								
	0.90	0.70	0.50	0.30	0.20	0.10	0.05	0.02	0.01
	Values of χ^2								
1									
2									
.									
.									
.									
.									
.									
.									
.									
17					21.615	24.769			
18					22.760	25.989			
19						**27.204**	30.144		
20							31.410		
21									
.									
.									
.									
.									
.									
.									
.									
.									

As you can see in Figure 12-2, the sample variance is not significantly larger than the hypothesized variance as to cause the manager to reject the null hypothesis. She will conclude, based on these results, that the service representatives do complete their service calls according to a distribution with a standard deviation of 0.5 hour or less.

In most applications, decision makers are concerned about the variance being too large. However, there are instances in which decision makers are concerned with knowing whether the variance is *higher* or *lower* than a specified level. For instance, the Acme Assembly Company assembles clock radios. The number assembled from day to day varies because of several factors, such as parts availability and employee attitudes. From past records, the production supervisor knows that the assembly variance should be 50. He has selected 25 days at random from this year's production reports and found a sample variance of 20. Figure 12-3 shows the statistical test using an alpha level of 0.20. As the test indicates, this sample information is so different from past information that the production supervisor should infer that the true variance has decreased. Based on this conclusion, the supervisor would, no doubt, try to find out what caused the improved consistency in an effort to ensure that it continues. Of course he would also want

FIGURE 12-3

Chi-square Test for One Population Variance for the Acme Assembly Company Example

Hypotheses:

H_0: $\sigma^2 = 50$
H_A: $\sigma^2 \neq 50$
$\alpha = 0.20$

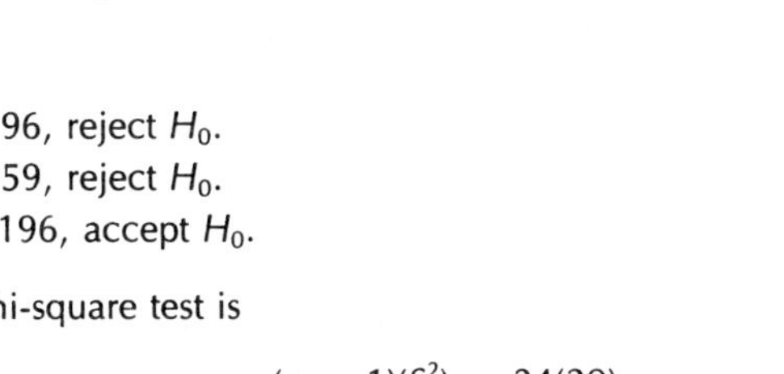

Decision Rule:

If $\chi^2 > \chi^2_{\text{critical}} = 33.196$, reject H_0.
If $\chi^2 < \chi^2_{\text{critical}} = 15.659$, reject H_0.
If $15.659 \leq \chi^2 \leq 33.196$, accept H_0.

The chi-square test is

$$\chi^2 = \frac{(n-1)(S^2)}{\sigma^2} = \frac{24(20)}{50}$$
$$= 9.6$$

Since calculated $9.6 < 15.659$, reject H_0.

*Since the hypothesis test is two-tailed, the lower critical value is found from the chi-square table under the column for an area $1 - \alpha/2 = 1 - 0.10 = 0.90$. The upper critical value is found from the chi-square table under the column for an area $\alpha/2 = 0.10$.

to determine whether the assembly process is meeting the standard for average output.

SKILL DEVELOPMENT PROBLEMS FOR **SECTION 12-1**

The following set of problems is meant to test your understanding of the material in this section.

1. Find the value of chi-square when $n = 10$ and the upper tail area (alpha) of the distribution is 0.05.

2. Find the value of chi-square when $n = 20$ and the upper tail area (alpha) of the distribution is 0.10.

3. Find the value of chi-square when $n = 22$ and the upper tail area (alpha) of the distribution is 0.20.

4. Find the value of chi-square when $n = 18$ and the upper tail area (alpha) of the distribution is 0.05.

5. Given the following null and alternative hypotheses:

$$H_0: \ \sigma^2 \leq 40$$
$$H_A: \ \sigma^2 > 40$$

   a. Test if $n = 10$, $S = 7$, and $\alpha = 0.05$. Be sure to show the decision rule.
   b. Test if $n = 30$, $S^2 = 54$, and $\alpha = 0.10$. Show the decision rule.

6. Given the following null and alternative hypotheses:

$$H_0: \ \sigma^2 \leq 300$$
$$H_A: \ \sigma^2 > 300$$

   a. Test if $n = 20$, $S = 20$, and $\alpha = 0.05$. Be sure to show the decision rule.
   b. Test if $n = 15$, $S^2 = 420$, and $\alpha = 0.10$. Show the decision rule.

7. Given the following null and alternative hypotheses:

$$H_0: \ \sigma^2 \leq 12$$
$$H_A: \ \sigma^2 > 12$$

   a. Test if $n = 13$, $S = 4$, and $\alpha = 0.10$. Be sure to show the decision rule.
   b. Test if $n = 30$, $S^2 = 21$ and $\alpha = 0.05$. Show the decision rule.

8. The Haglund Corporation manufactures paint and stain products for interior and exterior home and commercial applications. The new "Apple Wood Stain" product is thought to be a real improvement over some of the company's previous products. One criterion of a quality stain is the consistency of coverage per gallon. Haglund hopes that the standard deviation in coverage will not exceed 20 square feet per gallon. To test this, they have

selected a random sample of twelve gallons and found the following coverage in square feet:

245	302	240	280	255	300	290	240	300	270	230	300

a. State the null and alternative hypotheses.
b. State the decision rule, assuming an $\alpha = 0.05$.
c. Perform the test and write a one-paragraph conclusion for the Haglund manager.

9. The National Football League is in the process of renegotiating its television contracts with the networks. At issue is concern over what happens if a game goes too long and runs into the time slot reserved for other programs. As part of the negotiations, the NFL commissioner claimed that the game-time standard deviation does not exceed 8 minutes. To test this claim, a random sample of fifteen past games was selected, with the following times (in minutes) recorded:

145	136	123	109	145
125	137	134	140	138
120	146	129	135	134

a. State the appropriate null and alternative hypotheses.
b. Determine the decision rule, assuming an alpha level of 0.10.
c. Test the null hypothesis and comment on the result.

12-2 HYPOTHESES ABOUT TWO POPULATION VARIANCES

Just as decision makers are often interested in testing hypotheses regarding two poulation means, they are often faced with decision problems involving *two population variances*. For example, the Midlands Asphalt and Grading Company is considering purchasing a new paving machine. The company has two machines from which to choose. Midlands has decided to select the paver that provides the lesser variation in paving thickness. Variations in asphalt depth can have effects on both material cost and road strength. In addition, penalties are often assessed if testers find the road too thin.

One machine is considerably less expensive than the other, and, although Midlands will buy the more expensive model if necessary, the company does not want to miss out on a good deal if the less expensive machine will spread asphalt with a comparable variation.

The purchasing agent at Midlands has arranged to sample eleven surfaces paved by machine 1 and thirteen surfaces paved by machine 2 to see whether he can detect a difference in thickness variation between the two. The hypotheses are

Hypotheses:

$$H_0: \sigma_1^2 = \sigma_2^2$$
$$H_A: \sigma_1^2 \neq \sigma_2^2$$

Since the population variances are not known, they must be estimated from the sample variances S_1^2 and S_2^2. Intuitively, you might reason that if the two population variances are actually equal, the sample variances should be nearly equal also.

If the samples are selected from two normally distributed populations with σ_1^2 equal to σ_2^2, the ratio of the sample variances, S_1^2/S_2^2, has a probability distribution known as an F distribution. The F statistic is given in equation 12-3:

$$F = \frac{S_1^2}{S_2^2} \tag{12-3}$$

Because S_1^2 and S_2^2 have $n_1 - 1$ and $n_2 - 1$ degrees of freedom, respectively, the F distribution formed by the ratio of sample variances has $D_1 = n_1 - 1$ and $D_2 = n_2 - 1$ degrees of freedom.

The calculated F value gets larger if S_1^2 is greater than S_2^2. Since we have control over which population we label as "1" and which we label as "2" in a two-tailed test, we always select as population 1 the population with the larger sample variance. Therefore, if the calculated F gets too large, we conclude that the two populations have unequal variances.

Suppose the samples for the two paving machines yield variances of $S_1^2 = 0.025$ and $S_2^2 = 0.017$. Figure 12-4(a) presents the test of the hypothesis that the two machines have equal variances. As was the case with the normal, t, and chi-square distributions, the F distribution has been tabulated. The F-distribution values for upper-tail areas of 0.05 and 0.01 are provided in Appendix F.

The relationship between the specified alpha level and the appropriate F table is important. Two situations can occur:

1. If the hypothesis test is two-tailed (that is, H_0: $\sigma_1^2 = \sigma_2^2$), the appropriate F table is the one with an upper-tail area (area above the critical value) equal to one-half alpha. For example, if you have a two-tailed test with an alpha level of 0.10, you should use the F-distribution table containing values of F for the upper 5% of the distribution. If the alpha level is 0.02, you should use the F table containing values of F for the upper 1%.
2. If the hypothesis test is one-tailed (that is, H_0: $\sigma_1^2 \leq \sigma_2^2$), the appropriate F table is the one with the upper-tail area equal to alpha. For example, if the alpha level is 0.05, use the F table containing values of F for the upper 5% of the distribution.

Thus, to determine which F table to use, you must know the alpha level and also whether the test is one- or two-tailed. We can illustrate this concept with two examples. First, take the case of a two-tailed test with a stated alpha level of 0.10

FIGURE 12-4

***F* Test for Two Population Variances for the Midlands Asphalt and Grading Company Example**

(a) Two-Tailed Test

Hypotheses:

H_0: $\sigma_1^2 = \sigma_2^2$
H_A: $\sigma_1^2 \neq \sigma_2^2$
$\alpha = 0.10$

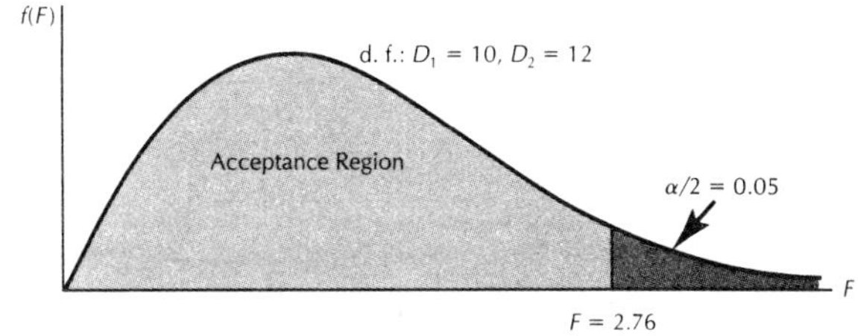

Decision Rule:

If $F \leq F_{\text{critical}} = 2.76$, accept H_0.
If $F > F_{\text{critical}}$, reject H_0.

The F test is

$$F = \frac{S_1^2}{S_2^2} = \frac{0.025}{0.017}$$
$$= 1.47$$

Since $F = 1.47 < F_{\text{critical}} = 2.76$ with $D_1 = 10$ and $D_2 = 12$ degrees of freedom, accept H_0.
Note: The right-hand tail of the F distribution always contains an area of $\alpha/2$ if the hypothesis test is two-tailed.

(b) One-Tailed Test

Hypotheses:

H_0: $\sigma_1^2 \leq \sigma_2^2$
H_A: $\sigma_1^2 > \sigma_2^2$
$\alpha = 0.01$

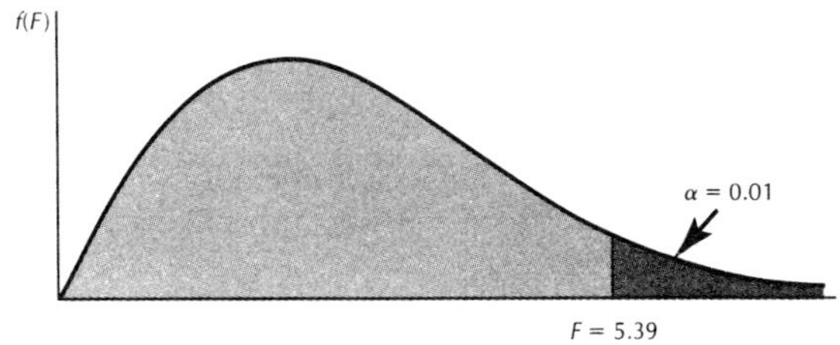

Decision Rule:

If $F \leq F_{\text{critical}} = 5.39$, accept H_0.
If $F > F_{\text{critical}} = 5.39$, reject H_0.

The F test is

$$F = \frac{S_1^2}{S_2^2} = \frac{0.035}{0.015} = 2.33$$

Since $F = 2.33 < F_{\text{critical}} = 5.39$ with $D_1 = 6$ and $D_2 = 10$ degrees of freedom, accept H_0.

TABLE 12-2

Finding Critical Values in the F Table (Values of F for Upper 5%)

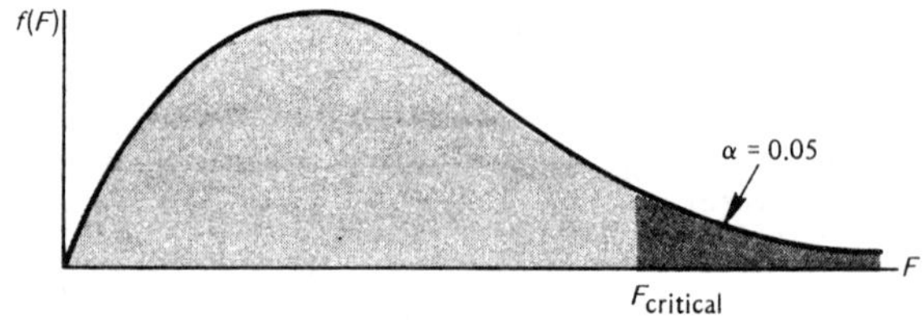

D_2 \ D_1	1	2	3	4	5	6	7	8	10	12
1										
2										
3										
4										
5										
6										
7										
8										
10								3.07	2.97	
12								2.85	**2.76**	
14									2.60	2.53
16										
20										
24										
⋮										

and degrees of freedom D_1 equal to 10 and D_2 equal to 12. We can use Table 12-2 to illustrate how $F_{critical}$ is determined. First, because it is a two-tailed test, go to the F table having an upper-tail area equal to one-half alpha (in this case, $0.10/2 = 0.05$). Next, go to the column corresponding to $D_1 = 10$ and read down to the row corresponding to $D_2 = 12$. The value at the intersection of the row and column is the desired $F_{critical}$ (2.76).

One-tailed tests involving two population variances are performed in a similar manner to the two-tailed tests. To illustrate, suppose the managers at Midlands decided to test two other paving machines. In this instance, prior research indicated that machine 1 should produce greater variation in pavement thickness than machine 2. The managers have sampled seven surfaces paved by machine 1 and eleven surfaces paved by machine 2 with the following results:

$$S_1^2 = 0.035$$
$$S_2^2 = 0.015$$

Figure 12-4(b) illustrates the one-tailed hypothesis test using an alpha = .01 level. Recall that in a two-tailed test, the F ratio is formed by placing the larger sample variance in the numerator and the smaller variance in the denominator. In a one-tailed test, we look to the alternative hypothesis to determine which sample variance should go in the numerator. If, as in this example, population 1 is thought to have the larger variance, then the sample variance from population 1 forms the numerator regardless of the size of the sample variances. In another example, if population 2 is thought to have the larger variance, the sample variance from population 2 would form the numerator in the F ratio calculation.

It is important that the F ratio be formed correctly for two reasons. First, the correct F ratio is computed. Second, the correct degrees of freedom will be used to determine the critical value to test the null hypothesis. In the Midlands one-tailed example, the numerator represents population 1 and the denominator represents population 2. The F ratio is

$$F = \frac{.035}{.015} = 2.33$$

Thus, the degrees of freedom are $D_1 = 7 - 1 = 6$ and $D_2 = 11 - 1 = 10$. Table 12-3 (page 592) shows how to locate the appropriate critical value of 5.39 for this one-tailed test with alpha = .01.

As shown in Figure 12-4(b), the calculated F ratio falls in the "acceptance" region so the null hypothesis is not rejected. Based on the sample data, there is no reason to believe that machine 1 produces higher variation than machine 2.

SKILL DEVELOPMENT PROBLEMS FOR **SECTION 12-2**

The following set of problems is meant to test your understanding of the material in this section.

10. Find the appropriate F value from the F-distribution table for each of the following:
    a. $D_1 = 10,\ D_2 = 14,\ \alpha = 0.05$
    b. $D_1 = 8,\ D_2 = 8,\ \alpha = 0.01$
    c. $D_1 = 14,\ D_2 = 10,\ \alpha = 0.05$

11. Find the appropriate F value from the F-distribution table for each of the following:
    a. $D_1 = 16,\ D_2 = 14,\ \alpha = 0.01$
    b. $D_1 = 5,\ D_2 = 12,\ \alpha = 0.05$
    c. $D_1 = 16,\ D_2 = 20,\ \alpha = 0.01$

TABLE 12-3

Finding Critical Values in the *F* Table (Values of *F* for Upper 1%)

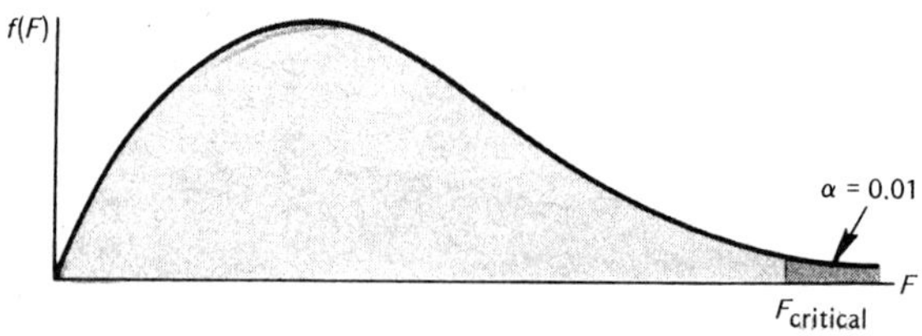

D_2 \ D_1	1	2	3	4	5	6	7	8	10	12
1										
2										
3										
4										
5										
6										
7										
8						6.37				
10					5.64	**5.39**	5.21			
12					5.06	4.82				
14										
⋮										

12. Given the following null and alternative hypotheses:

$$H_0: \ \sigma_1^2 = \sigma_2^2$$
$$H_A: \ \sigma_1^2 \neq \sigma_2^2$$

and the following sample information:

Sample 1	*Sample 2*
$n = 11$	$n = 21$
$S = 19$	$S = 23$

a. If $\alpha = 0.02$, state the decision rule for the hypothesis.

b. Test the hypothesis and indicate whether the null hypothesis should be rejected.

13. Given the following null and alternative hypotheses:

$$H_0: \sigma_1^2 = \sigma_2^2$$
$$H_A: \sigma_1^2 \neq \sigma_2^2$$

and the following sample information:

Sample 1	*Sample 2*
$n = 15$	$n = 11$
$S = 230$	$S = 210$

a. If $\alpha = 0.10$, state the decision rule for the hypothesis.
b. Test the hypothesis and indicate whether the null hypothesis should be rejected.

14. Given the following null and alternative hypotheses:

$$H_0: \sigma_1^2 \leq \sigma_2^2$$
$$H_A: \sigma_1^2 > \sigma_2^2$$

and the following sample information:

Sample 1	*Sample 2*
$n = 13$	$n = 21$
$S^2 = 1{,}450$	$S^2 = 1{,}320$

a. If $\alpha = 0.05$, state the decision rule for the hypothesis.
b. Test the hypothesis and indicate whether the null hypothesis should be rejected.

15. Given the following null and alternative hypotheses:

$$H_0: \sigma_1^2 \geq \sigma_2^2$$
$$H_A: \sigma_1^2 < \sigma_2^2$$

and the following sample information:

Sample 1	*Sample 2*
$n = 21$	$n = 13$
$S^2 = 345.7$	$S^2 = 745.2$

a. If $\alpha = 0.01$, state the decision rule for the hypothesis.
b. Test the hypothesis and indicate whether the null hypothesis should be rejected.

16. The McBurger Company operates fast-food stores throughout the United States and in fourteen other countries. Management is very concerned about

making sure that a standard quality of service is achieved. For instance, they are interested in whether there is a difference in variance in service times for customers who use the drive-up window versus those who go inside to the service counter.

The McBurger store in Knoxville, Tennessee, recently was the subject of evaluation. A sample of thirteen drive-through customers was selected and a sample of nine inside-counter customers was selected. The time (in minutes) it took each customer to be serviced was recorded. The following statistics were computed from the sample data:

Drive-Through	*Walk-In*
$\overline{X} = 4.5$	$\overline{X} = 4.0$
$S = 2.0$	$S = 1.2$

a. State the appropriate null and alternative hypotheses for testing about equality of variances.
b. Based on an alpha level of 0.10, determine the appropriate decision rule and test the null hypothesis.
c. Suppose the managers are also interested in testing whether there is a difference in average time it takes to service the two types of customers. State the appropriate null and alternative hypotheses and test at an $\alpha =$ 0.05 level.

17. A national TV telethon committee is interested in determining whether males give donations that have greater variability in amount than do those of females. To test this, random samples of twenty-five males and twenty-five females were selected from people who donated during last year's telethon. The following statistics were computed from the sample data:

Males	*Females*
$\overline{X} = \$12.40$	$\overline{X} = \$8.92$
$S = \$2.50$	$S = \$1.34$

a. State the null and alternative hypotheses to be tested.
b. Based on an alpha level of 0.05, determine the decision rule and test the null hypothesis.
c. Suppose the committee is also interested in determining whether there is a difference in average donations between men and women. State the appropriate null and alternative hypotheses and test at the $\alpha = 0.05$ level.

12-3 ANALYSIS OF VARIANCE—ONE-WAY DESIGN

The Hudson Company is a diversified manufacturer of electronics products, both for the consumer and manufacturing segments of the economy. The company has always tried to develop numerous small plants as opposed to a few, huge operations. Consequently, it has plants in North America, Asia, and Europe. The company has always maintained a decentralized management style, but does set some corporate goals. A recent goal is to increase the "local content" of goods and services each plant purchases. The purpose of this goal is to add to the stability of the local economy.

The North American division of the Hudson Company is divided into four areas. At the yearly strategic planning meeting, the four regional supervisors decided to determine whether any of the regions were doing better than the others in their efforts to increase the local content. Since "local content" is a difficult value to measure, the supervisors decided to form a working group and sample eight manufacturing sites in each area. Since the working group would expect variation to exist among the sites, it formulated the following null and alternative hypotheses:

$$H_0: \quad \mu_1 = \mu_2 = \mu_3 = \mu_4$$
$$H_A: \quad \text{Not all means are equal.}$$

It also established an alpha level of 0.05 for this test.

WHY TWO-SAMPLE *t* TESTS WILL NOT WORK

One method to test the null hypothesis involving four population means would be to use the two-sample *t* test discussed in Chapter 11. The working group could set up a series of null and alternative hypotheses involving *all* possible pairs of sales regions. The two-sample *t* test could be used to test each null hypothesis. With four populations, there are

$$\begin{aligned} {}_4C_2 &= \frac{4!}{2!(4-2)!} \\ &= 6 \end{aligned}$$

separate pairs of regions. Thus, to test the null hypothesis that all four population means are equal would require six separate *t* tests of the form

$$H_0: \quad \mu_1 = \mu_2$$
$$H_A: \quad \mu_1 \neq \mu_2$$

with the test statistic as in equation 12-4:

$$t = \frac{(\overline{X}_1 - \overline{X}_2) - 0}{S_{\text{pooled}}\sqrt{\dfrac{1}{n_1} + \dfrac{1}{n_2}}} \qquad \textbf{12-4}$$

If the six separate t tests are performed, and the null hypothesis is accepted in each case, we could conclude that all four population means are equal. However, the problem with using a series of two-sample t tests is that although each test has an alpha level of 0.05, the true alpha level for all tests combined is greater than 0.05. If we consider the six tests to be independent, the probability of committing at least one Type I error in six tests is given by equation 12-5:

$$\begin{aligned}\alpha_{\text{actual}} &\leq [1 - (1 - \alpha_1)(1 - \alpha_2)(1 - \alpha_3)\cdots(1 - \alpha_6)] \\ &\leq [1 - (0.95)(0.95)(0.95)(0.95)(0.95)(0.95)] \\ &\leq 1 - 0.7351 \\ &\leq 0.2649\end{aligned} \quad \textbf{12-5}$$

Thus, the probability of committing one or more Type I errors using a series of six t tests, each with an alpha level of 0.05, is, at most, 0.2649. The logic behind this increase in alpha is that *as more tests are performed, the risk of rejecting at least one true hypothesis is increased.*

Due to this problem, a series of two-sample t tests is not generally considered adequate to test hypotheses involving more than two populations. However, a statistical tool known as *analysis of variance* (ANOVA) can be used without "compounding" the probability of committing a Type I error.

THE RATIONALE OF ONE-WAY ANALYSIS OF VARIANCE

In the Hudson Company example, the working group needs to determine whether the average local content is equal among the four North American regions. Analysis of variance is a statistical procedure that, as its name implies, is used to examine population variances to determine whether the population means are equal.

Three assumptions (the same ones as for a two-sample t test) must be satisfied before analysis of variance can be applied.

1. The samples must be independent random samples.
2. The samples must be selected from populations with normal distributions.
3. The populations must have equal variances (that is, $\sigma_1^2 = \sigma_2^2 = \cdots = \sigma_k^2 = \sigma^2$).

The rationale behind analysis of variance might best be understood by studying Table 12-4, which presents the data the working group has collected. You should notice several things about the data. First, the plants in the sample do not all have the same percentage of local content in goods and services purchased. Thus, variation exists in the content percentage of the thirty-two plants. This is

TABLE 12-4

Local Content Data for the Hudson Company Example (Values Given as Percentages)

Plant	Region 1	Region 2	Region 3	Region 4
1	4	7	5	12
2	6	9	11	8
3	10	13	6	7
4	12	8	8	9
5	5	9	4	11
6	8	14	9	10
7	4	7	10	6
8	7	5	11	9
Total	56	72	64	72
	$\overline{X}_1 = 7$	$\overline{X}_2 = 9$	$\overline{X}_3 = 8$	$\overline{X}_4 = 9$

Grand total = 264

$$\text{Grand mean} = \overline{\overline{X}} = \frac{264}{32} = 8.25$$

called the **total variation** in the data. Second, within any particular region, not all plants have the same percentage of local content. Thus, variation exists within regions. This variation is called **within-sample variation.** Finally, the sample means for the four regions are not all equal. Thus, variation exists between the regions. As you might have guessed, this is called **between-sample variation.**

The basic principle of one-way analysis of variance is that

$$\text{Total sample variation} = \text{Between-sample variation} + \text{Within-sample variation}$$

From our discussion of variance in Chapter 3, we know that the variability in a set of measurements is proportional to the sum of the squared deviations of the measurements from the mean, as given by expression 12-6:

$$\Sigma(X - \overline{X})^2 \qquad \text{(12-6)}$$

Therefore, the total sample variation in the data shown in Table 12-4 is proportional to the sum of the squared deviations of the thirty-two figures around the *grand mean.* This is called the *total sum of squares* (TSS) and is calculated by equation 12-7:

$$\text{TSS} = \sum_{i=1}^{K} \sum_{j=1}^{n_i} (X_{ij} - \overline{\overline{X}})^2 \qquad \textbf{12-7}$$

where

TSS = Total sum of squares

K = Number of populations (columns)

n_i = Sample size from population i

X_{ij} = jth measurement from population i (in the present example, the thirty-two different measurements)

$\overline{\overline{X}}$ = Grand mean (here, the mean of all thirty-two measurements)

The total sum of squares for the Hudson Company example is

$$\begin{aligned}\text{TSS} &= (4 - 8.25)^2 + (6 - 8.25)^2 + (10 - 8.25)^2 + \cdots + (9 - 8.25)^2 \\ &= 226\end{aligned}$$

As was stated earlier, total variation equals the between-sample variation plus the within-sample variation. Equation 12-8 states this:

$$\underbrace{\sum_{i=1}^{K} \sum_{j=1}^{n_i} (X_{ij} - \overline{\overline{X}})^2}_{\text{TSS}} = \underbrace{\sum_{i=1}^{K} n_i(\overline{X}_i - \overline{\overline{X}})^2}_{\text{SSB}} + \underbrace{\sum_{i=1}^{K} \sum_{j=1}^{n_i} (X_{ij} - \overline{X}_i)^2}_{\text{SSW}} \qquad \textbf{12-8}$$

Equation 12-8 shows that TSS can be *partitioned* into two parts: the *sum of squares between* (SSB) and the *sum of squares within* (SSW).[1] For this example,

$$\begin{aligned}\text{SSB} &= 8(7 - 8.25)^2 + 8(9 - 8.25)^2 + 8(8 - 8.25)^2 + 8(9 - 8.25)^2 \\ &= 22\end{aligned}$$

$$\begin{aligned}\text{SSW} &= \text{TSS} - \text{SSB} = 226 - 22 \\ &= 204\end{aligned}$$

The working group wants to determine whether the mean local contents in the four regions are equal. However, it must decide this based on a sample from

[1] The chapter glossary contains calculation formulas for each of the sum of squares formulas contained in this section.

FIGURE 12-5

Normal Populations with Equal Means and Equal Variances

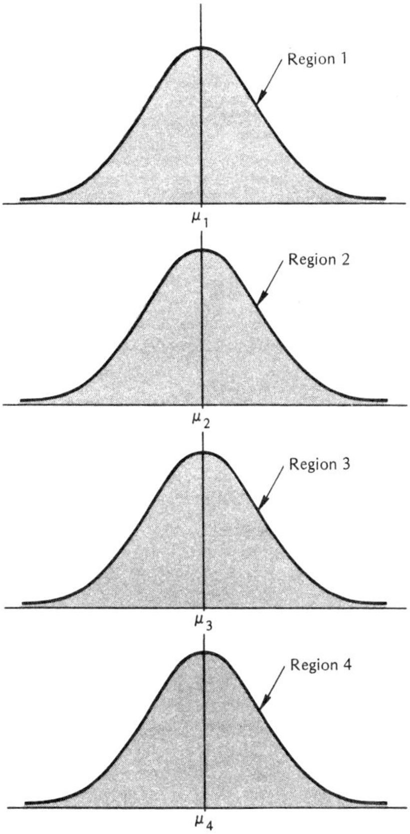

each region. The group wants to know whether the four distributions shown in Figure 12-5 best describe the distributions, or whether Figure 12-6 (page 600) applies. If Figure 12-5 applies, a null hypothesis that all means are equal should be accepted. If Figure 12-6 applies, the null hypothesis should be rejected. Note that these figures illustrate the assumptions of normal populations and equal population variances.

To determine whether to accept or reject the null hypothesis using analysis of variance, we perform the following:

1. Establish the null hypothesis to be tested:

$$H_0: \quad \mu_1 = \mu_2 = \mu_3 = \cdots$$
$$H_A: \quad \text{Not all means are equal.}$$

2. Make two estimates of the population variance, one based on individual regions and one based on differences in regional averages.
3. If the two estimates are about the same, we conclude that Figure 12-5 applies and that the means are equal. If the variance-estimates are sub-

FIGURE 12-6

Normal Populations with Unequal Means and Equal Variances

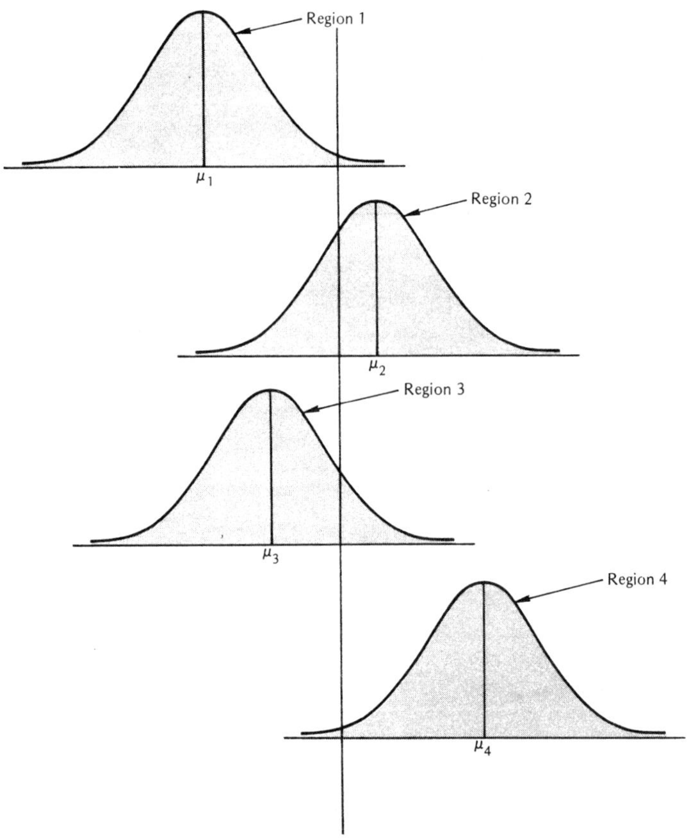

stantially different, we conclude that the population means are not all equal and reject H_0.

The computational procedures necessary to make the variance estimates are not complicated if we remember that any variance is a sum of squares divided by degrees of freedom. The first estimate is given by equation 12-9:

$$\text{MSW} = \frac{\text{SSW}}{N - K} = \text{Unbiased estimate of } \sigma^2 \tag{12-9}$$

where

MSW = Mean square within

SSW = Sum of squares within

N = Total number of measurements from all samples

K = Number of groups (here, four regions)

Also, if the region means are truly equal (the null hypothesis is true), the second estimate is given by equation 12-10:

$$\text{MSB} = \frac{\text{SSB}}{K - 1} = \text{Unbiased estimate of } \sigma^2 \qquad \textbf{12-10}$$

where

MSB = Mean square between

SSB = Sum of squares between

K = Number of groups

Thus, if the null hypothesis is true (that is, all means are equal), MSW and MSB are both estimates of the population variance, σ^2, and we would expect MSW and MSB to be nearly equal.

However, because of the way SSB is calculated, the more the sample means differ, the *larger* SSB becomes. As SSB is increased, MSB begins to differ from MSW. When this difference gets too large, our conclusion will be that the population means are not all equal. Therefore we would reject the null hypothesis. But how do we determine what "too large" is?

Recall the test of two population variances presented in Section 12-2. There we saw that the ratio of two unbiased estimates of the same variance, σ^2, forms an F distribution with D_1 and D_2 degrees of freedom. If the population means are equal, MSW and MSB are both unbiased estimates of σ^2. Their ratio should produce a statistic that is F-distributed when H_0 is true, as shown in equation 12-11:

$$F = \frac{\text{MSB}}{\text{MSW}} \qquad \textbf{12-11}$$

The calculated F comes from an F distribution with $D_1 = K - 1$ and $D_2 = N - K$ degrees of freedom, if H_0 is true.

A common means of illustrating analysis of variance calculations is in table format. The Hudson working group has formulated Table 12-5 (page 602). Notice that it has listed the null and alternative hypotheses, and has shown the F distribution and the decision rule for an alpha level of 0.05.

The ratio of MSB to MSW for this example is 1.0065. This value is smaller than the critical F value of approximately 2.92 found in the F-distribution table in

TABLE 12-5

ANOVA for the Hudson Company Example

Hypotheses:

H_0: $\mu_1 = \mu_2 = \mu_3 = \mu_4$
H_A: Not all means are equal.

$\alpha = 0.05$

Source of Variation	*SS*	*d.f.*	*MS*	*F Ratio*
Between samples	22	$K - 1 = 3$	MSB = 7.33	MSB/MSW = 1.0065
Within samples	204	$N - K = 28$	MSW = 7.29	
Total	226	$N - 1 = 31$		

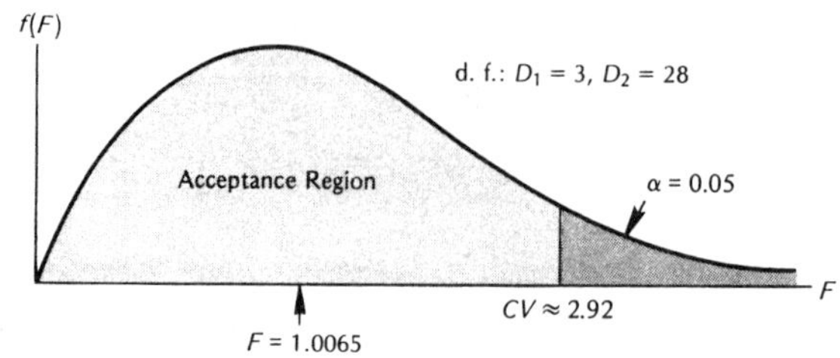

Decision Rule:

If $F > F_{critical} \approx 2.92$, reject H_0.
Otherwise, do not reject H_0.

Since $1.0065 < 2.92$, do not reject H_0.

Appendix F. Note that we have used degrees of freedom $D_1 = 3$ and $D_2 = 30$ to obtain an approximation for the critical F value. The exact F value could be found from an F table that contains entries for degrees of freedom $D_1 = 3$ and $D_2 = 28$. Since the calculated F value is smaller than the critical F value, the working group should *not* reject the null hypothesis. It would conclude that the average local area contents in the four regions could, in fact, be equal.

The analysis of variance has allowed the Hudson Company to test a null hypothesis involving four population means without compounding alpha above the 0.05 level.

ONE-WAY ANALYSIS OF VARIANCE—A SECOND EXAMPLE

A city in Arizona has recently received a federal grant to purchase two new fire trucks and hire six additional firefighters. The city manager, in compliance with the grant, will assign the trucks and firefighters to the two busiest fire districts in the city. However, the city manager does not know which districts are the busiest or, for that matter, if there is a difference among the city's three districts.

The city manager develops the following null hypothesis:

H_0: There is no difference in the average number of responses per day among the three fire districts.

To test this hypothesis (and help determine which districts will get the firefighters and equipment), the city manager selected a random sample of 10 days during the current year. He asked the district fire marshals to supply the number of responses made in their districts on each day. These data are shown in Table 12-6.

Assuming the populations are normally distributed, with equal variances, analysis of variance can be used to test the hypothesis of equal means. Table 12-7 (page 604) shows the null and alternative hypotheses, as well as the analysis of variance calculations and decision rule for this example.

Based on the analysis of variance shown in Table 12-7, the city manager should conclude that the average number of responses is not equal for the three districts.

TABLE 12-6

Response Data by Fire District (Number of Responses)

Day	District 1	District 2	District 3
1	3	4	2
2	2	4	2
3	1	4	1
4	0	4	0
5	0	3	0
6	0	5	0
7	2	4	3
8	2	4	0
9	1	4	2
10	4	4	0
Total	15	40	10
	$\overline{X}_1 = 1.5$	$\overline{X}_2 = 4$	$\overline{X}_3 = 1$

$$\text{TSS} = \sum_{i=1}^{K} \sum_{i=1}^{n_i} (X_{ij} - \overline{\overline{X}})^2 = (3 - 2.1667)^2 + (2 - 2.1667)^2 + \cdots + (0 - 2.1667)^2$$

$$= 82.17$$

$$\text{SSB} = \sum_{i=1}^{K} n_i(\overline{X}_i - \overline{\overline{X}})^2 = 10(1.5 - 2.1667)^2 + 10(4 - 2.1667)^2 + 10(1 - 2.1667)^2$$

$$= 51.67$$

$$\text{SSW} = \text{TSS} - \text{SSB}$$

$$= 30.50$$

TABLE 12-7

ANOVA for the Arizona Fire Districts Example

Hypotheses:

H_0: $\mu_1 = \mu_2 = \mu_3$
H_A: Not all means are equal.

$\alpha = 0.05$

Source of Variation	*SS*	*d.f.*	*MS*	*F Ratio*
Between districts	51.67	2	25.84	22.87
Within districts	30.50	27	1.13	
Total	82.17	29		

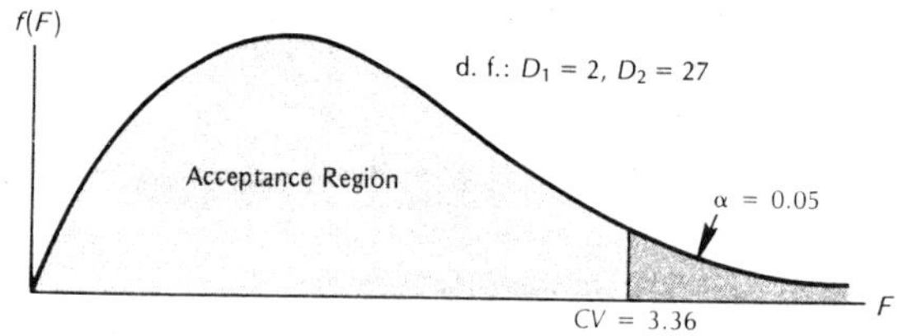

Decision Rule:

If $F > F_{critical} = 3.36$, reject H_0.
Otherwise, do not reject H_0.

Since $F = 22.87 > 3.36$, reject H_0.

*The critical F value, denoted CV, is found by interpolating the F distribution for values of F between degrees of freedom: $D_1 = 2$, $D_2 = 24$ and $D_1 = 2$, $D_2 = 30$.

Given this conclusion, the next logical step is to determine which means are different. Several statistical procedures exist to help the city manager accomplish this and decide which districts get the trucks and firefighters. In the next section we will introduce two of these techniques: *Tukey's method* and *Scheffé's method.*

COMPUTER OUTPUT—ANALYSIS OF VARIANCE

Because analysis of variance is such a common statistical technique, all computer packages will perform the calculations necessary to complete the ANOVA output table. Figure 12-7 shows the output for the Hudson Company example given by

FIGURE 12-7

GB-STAT Output for the Hudson Company Example

ANOVA SUMMARY TABLE

SOURCE	SUM SQRES	DF	MEAN SQRES	F-RATIO	PROB
BETWEEN GRPS	22	3	7.33333	1.0065	.4045
WITHIN GRPS	204	28	7.28571		
TOTAL	226	31			

the GB-STAT package. Notice that the output contains a *p*-value (PROB) that should be compared with the alpha in the hypothesis. Since the *p*-value is greater than the 5% level established by the working group in that example, the null hypothesis is not rejected.

SKILL DEVELOPMENT PROBLEMS FOR **SECTION 12-3**

Several exercises and problems designed to help you understand the material presented in Section 12-3 follow.

18. Given the following sample data:

Item	*Group 1*	*Group 2*	*Group 3*
1	10	8	13
2	9	6	12
3	11	8	12
4	12	9	11
5	13	10	13
6	12	10	15

a. State the appropriate null and alternative hypotheses for determining whether a difference exists in the average value for the three populations.
b. Compute the sum of squares between for the above sample data.
c. Compute the sum of squares within for the above sample data.
d. Based on the computations in parts **b** and **c**, develop the ANOVA table and test the null hypothesis using an $\alpha = 0.05$.

19. Given the following sample data:

Item	*Group 1*	*Group 2*	*Group 3*	*Group 4*
1	20	28	17	21
2	27	26	15	23
3	26	21	18	19
4	22	29	20	17
5	25	30	14	
6	30	25		
7	23			

a. State the appropriate null and alternative hypotheses for determining whether a difference exists in the average value for the four populations.
b. Compute the sum of squares between for the above sample data.
c. Compute the sum of squares within for the above sample data.
d. Based on the computations in parts **b** and **c**, develop the ANOVA table and test the null hypothesis using an $\alpha = 0.05$.

20. Given the following sample data:

Item	*Group 1*	*Group 2*	*Group 3*
1	100	98	113
2	69	96	102
3	110	88	120
4	112	99	110
5	55	100	100

a. State the appropriate null and alternative hypotheses for determining whether a difference exists in the average value for the three populations.
b. Compute the sum of squares between for the above sample data.
c. Compute the sum of squares within for the above sample data.
d. Based on the computations in parts **b** and **c**, develop the ANOVA table and test the null hypothesis using an $\alpha = 0.01$.

21. The Green-Checker Cab Company operates twelve taxis in Seattle, Washington. The manager is interested in determining whether there is a difference in average fares collected for the day, swing, and graveyard shifts. To test whether a difference exists, she has collected a random sample of ten observations from each shift. The following summary values have been computed from the sample data:

$$TSS = 156{,}764 \qquad SSB = 55{,}600$$

a. State the appropriate null and alternative hypotheses.
b. Develop the appropriate ANOVA table and test the hypotheses using an $\alpha = 0.01$.

22. The American Beef Growers Association is trying to promote the consumption of beef products. The organization performs numerous studies, the results of which are often used in advertising campaigns. One such study involved a quality perception test. Three levels of beef gradings—choice, standard, and economy—were involved. A random sample of people was provided a piece of choice-grade beefsteak and asked to rate its quality on a scale of 1 to 100. A second sample of people was given a piece of standard-grade beefsteak and a third sample was given a piece of economy-grade beefsteak, with instructions to rate the beef on the 100-point scale. The following data were obtained.

Choice	*Standard*	*Economy*
78	67	65
87	80	62
90	78	70
87	80	66
89	67	70
90	70	73

Based on the sample data, is there sufficient evidence to conclude that there is a difference in perceived quality for the three grades of beefsteak? Test at an $\alpha = 0.05$ level; make sure to state the null and alternative hypotheses and provide the ANOVA table.

12-4 TUKEY'S AND SCHEFFÉ'S METHODS OF MULTIPLE COMPARISONS

Once the analysis of variance leads to rejecting the null hypothesis of equal means, decision makers need a method to determine which means are not equal and that will not compound the alpha error. (Remember that t tests are not acceptable; they compound the probability of Type I errors.) One method, developed by John W. Tukey, can be used when the samples from the populations are the same size. Tukey's method involves establishing a *T range* according to equation 12-12:

$$T \text{ range} = T\sqrt{\text{MSW}} \qquad \textbf{12-12}$$

where

$$T = \frac{1}{\sqrt{n}}q$$

q = Value from the Studentized range table (Appendix G), given the alpha level and $D_1 = K$ and $D_2 = N - K$ d.f.

n = Common sample size

If any pair of sample means has an *absolute difference,* $|\overline{X}_1 - \overline{X}_2|$, greater than the T range, we can conclude that the population means are not equal. For example, our Arizona city has three fire districts. The possible *pairwise* comparisons (formally referred to as *contrasts*) are

$$|\overline{X}_1 - \overline{X}_2| = |1.5 - 4.0| = 2.5$$
$$|\overline{X}_1 - \overline{X}_3| = |1.5 - 1.0| = 0.5$$
$$|\overline{X}_2 - \overline{X}_3| = |4.0 - 1.0| = 3.0$$

The calculated T range for this example with an alpha level of 0.05 is

$$T \text{ range} = T\sqrt{\text{MSW}}$$

where

$$T = \frac{1}{\sqrt{n}} q_{(1-\alpha),\, D_1=K=3,\, D_2=N-K=27}$$

$$= \frac{1}{\sqrt{10}} 3.51$$

$$= 1.110$$

Note that q is from the Studentized range table in Appendix G (value interpolated).

Then

$$T \text{ range} = 1.110\sqrt{1.13}$$
$$= 1.180$$

Thus

$$|\overline{X}_1 - \overline{X}_2| = |1.5 - 4.0| = 2.5 > 1.180$$
$$|\overline{X}_2 - \overline{X}_3| = |4.0 - 1.0| = 3.0 > 1.180$$
$$|\overline{X}_1 - \overline{X}_3| = |1.5 - 1.0| = 0.5 < 1.180$$

Therefore, based on Tukey's method, the city manager can conclude that the mean number of responses for district 1 is *not* equal to the mean for district 2 and that the mean for district 2 is *not* equal to the mean for district 3. However, he does not have enough statistical evidence to conclude that the means of district 1 and district 3 are different.

By examining the sample means, the city manager can infer that district 2 has more responses on the average than district 1 and more than district 3. Thus, district 2 should receive some new firefighters and at least one truck. However, based on this study, the city manager has no statistical basis for assigning a truck or crew to a second district. He cannot conclude that districts 1 and 3 differ with respect to average responses. Some other factor will have to be used to make the final decision.

Tukey's method of multiple comparisons allows decision makers to determine which population means are not equal once analysis of variance leads to rejecting the null hypothesis of equal population means. This method does not compound the alpha level, but applies only when the sample sizes are equal.

The main restriction of Tukey's method is that it requires equal sample sizes. In some controlled applications, managers can guarantee equal sample sizes from each population. However, in many other applications equal sample sizes are not possible. When decision makers have unequal sample sizes, the analysis of variance equations still apply, as does the interpretation of results. But, since Tukey's method does not apply, decision makers need a method of multiple comparisons that allows for unequal sample sizes. H. Scheffé has developed such a procedure.

The Zero Defects Corporation has recently begun bidding on contracts to assemble printed circuit boards. It has received a contract to assemble the main control board for a popular fish finder (a sonar-like unit that locates fish in lakes). The contract is for a fixed cost per board, so the more efficiently the boards can be assembled, the more profitable the contract will be.

While the company has recently purchased an automatic soldering machine, putting the required components on the boards is presently an entirely manual operation. Eduardo Martez, the production manager, is experimenting with five different assembly sequences. To determine which sequence is most effective, he selected a random sample of fifty workers. Ten workers were randomly assigned to each sequence. At the end of a 1-day training period, the workers began assembling circuit boards using their assigned sequence. Table 12-8 shows the average number assembled during a 2-week period for each worker for each sequence. As might be expected for a study of this kind, several workers missed work or had other training scheduled and had to be eliminated from the study. Therefore, unequal sample sizes resulted.

Table 12-9 (page 610) presents the analysis of variance results, the null and alternative hypotheses, and the decision rule. The null hypothesis that the five assembly sequences are equal with respect to the average number of circuit boards assembled is clearly rejected. Eduardo Martez should conclude that not all assembly sequences will produce equal average outputs.

TABLE 12-8

Printed Circuit Board Assembly Data for the Zero Defects Corporation Example (Number of Boards Assembled)

Sequence 1	Sequence 2	Sequence 3	Sequence 4	Sequence 5	
47	86	65	58	49	
52	85	63	62	51	
46	81	67	63	47	
49	90	64	64	55	
53	84	59	59	54	
39	88	67	55	42	
51	77	70	70	53	
	79	59	59	57	
	82		60	59	
			61	58	
$n_1 = 7$	$n_2 = 9$	$n_3 = 8$	$n_4 = 10$	$n_5 = 10$	$N = 44$
$\bar{X}_1 = 48.14$	$\bar{X}_2 = 83.56$	$\bar{X}_3 = 64.25$	$\bar{X}_4 = 61.10$	$\bar{X}_5 = 52.50$	$\bar{\bar{X}} = 62.25$

$$\text{TSS} = \sum_{i=1}^{K}\sum_{j=1}^{n_i}(X_{ij} - \bar{\bar{X}})^2 = (47 - 62.25)^2 + (52 - 62.25)^2 + \cdots + (48 - 62.25)^2$$

$$= 7{,}264.25$$

$$\text{SSB} = \sum_{i=1}^{K} n_i(\bar{X}_i - \bar{\bar{X}})^2 = 7(48.14 - 62.25)^2 + \cdots + 10(52.50 - 62.25)^2$$

$$= 6{,}474.27$$

$$\text{SSW} = \text{TSS} - \text{SSB}$$

$$= 789.98$$

TABLE 12-9

ANOVA for the Zero Defects Corporation Example

Hypotheses:

H_0: $\mu_1 = \mu_2 = \mu_3 = \mu_4 = \mu_5$
H_A: Not all means are equal.

$\alpha = 0.05$

Source of Variation	SS	d.f.	MS	F Ratio
Between methods	6,474.27	4	1,618.57	79.91
Within methods	789.98	39	20.26	
Total	7,264.25	43		

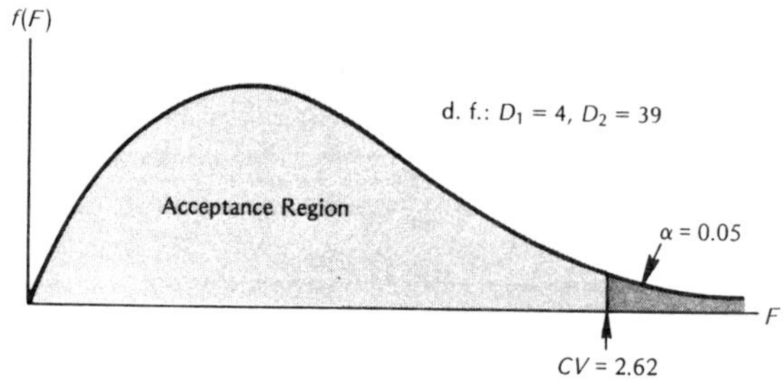

Decision Rule:

If $F > F_{\text{critical}} = 2.62$, reject H_0.
Otherwise, do not reject H_0.

Since $79.91 > 2.62$, reject H_0.

Once the analysis of variance indicates that the null hypothesis should be rejected, *Scheffé's method of multiple comparisons* can determine which means are different. Like Tukey's method, Scheffé's method produces a range to which the absolute differences in pairs of sample means (called contrasts) can be compared. This range is given in equation 12-13:

$$S \text{ range} = S\hat{\sigma} \qquad \textbf{(12-13)}$$

where

$$S = \sqrt{(K-1)(F_{\alpha, D_1=K-1,\, D_2=N-K})}$$

$$\hat{\sigma} = \sqrt{\left(\frac{1}{n_i} + \frac{1}{n_j}\right)(\text{MSW})}$$

One contrast for an alpha level of 0.05 is

$$|\overline{X}_1 - \overline{X}_2| = |48.14 - 83.56| = 35.42$$

If 35.42 is greater than the S range, Martez should conclude that sequences 1 and 2 differ significantly with respect to average output. In this case the S range is

$$S \text{ range} = S\hat{\sigma}$$

where

$$S = \sqrt{(K-1)(F_{\alpha,D_1,D_2})} = \sqrt{4(2.62)}$$
$$= 3.23$$

$$\hat{\sigma} = \sqrt{\left(\frac{1}{n_1} + \frac{1}{n_2}\right)(\text{MSW})} = \sqrt{\left(\frac{1}{7} + \frac{1}{9}\right)(20.26)}$$
$$= 2.27$$

Therefore,

$$S \text{ range} = 3.23(2.27) = 7.332$$

Since the absolute difference of 35.42 is greater than 7.332, Eduardo will conclude that the mean levels for these sequences do differ. Based on the sample means, he infers that assembly sequence 2 will give significantly higher average output than sequence 1.

The Scheffé method can be applied to any or all possible pairwise contrasts. The S range will differ slightly from contrast to contrast if the sample sizes differ. Table 12-10 shows all possible pairwise contrasts and their associated S ranges for our board assembly example. The only contrasts for which we can conclude that the population means are not different are μ_1 and μ_5, and μ_3 and μ_4. Based on the sample means, the production supervisor infers that sequence 2 will produce a higher average output than the other four sequences.

TABLE 12-10

Scheffé Test for the Zero Defects Corporation Example

Contrast	S Range	Significant?
$\lvert\bar{X}_1 - \bar{X}_2\rvert = \lvert 48.14 - 83.56\rvert = 35.42$	7.332	Yes
$\lvert\bar{X}_1 - \bar{X}_3\rvert = \lvert 48.14 - 64.25\rvert = 16.11$	7.524	Yes
$\lvert\bar{X}_1 - \bar{X}_4\rvert = \lvert 48.14 - 61.10\rvert = 12.96$	7.165	Yes
$\lvert\bar{X}_1 - \bar{X}_5\rvert = \lvert 48.14 - 52.50\rvert = 4.36$	7.165	No
$\lvert\bar{X}_2 - \bar{X}_3\rvert = \lvert 83.56 - 64.25\rvert = 19.31$	7.064	Yes
$\lvert\bar{X}_2 - \bar{X}_4\rvert = \lvert 83.56 - 61.10\rvert = 22.46$	6.680	Yes
$\lvert\bar{X}_2 - \bar{X}_5\rvert = \lvert 83.56 - 52.50\rvert = 31.06$	6.680	Yes
$\lvert\bar{X}_3 - \bar{X}_4\rvert = \lvert 64.25 - 61.10\rvert = 3.15$	6.896	No
$\lvert\bar{X}_3 - \bar{X}_5\rvert = \lvert 64.25 - 52.50\rvert = 11.75$	6.896	Yes
$\lvert\bar{X}_4 - \bar{X}_5\rvert = \lvert 61.10 - 52.50\rvert = 8.60$	6.502	Yes

COMPUTER OUTPUT—TUKEY AND SCHEFFÉ TESTS

While virtually all statistical packages will perform analysis of variance calculations, not all will perform the Tukey and Scheffé tests. Some recent PC packages,

FIGURE 12-8

GB-STAT Output for the Arizona Fire District Example

SAMPLE DESCRIPTIVE STATISTICS

N 1 = 10
N 2 = 10
N 3 = 10

MEAN GROUP 1 = 1.5
VAR. GROUP 1 = 1.83333
MEAN GROUP 2 = 4
VAR. GROUP 2 = .22222
MEAN GROUP 3 = 1
VAR. GROUP 3 = 1.33333

ANOVA SUMMARY TABLE

SOURCE	SUM SQRES	DF	MEAN SQRES	F-RATIO	PROB
BETWEEN GRPS	51.66669	2	25.83334	22.8689	<.0001
WITHIN GRPS	30.5	27	1.12963		
TOTAL	82.16669	29			

PROTECTED T-TESTS

	1 DIST 1	2 DIST 2	3 DIST 3
DIST 1	0	−5.2597**	1.0519
DIST 2	−5.2597**	0	6.3116**
DIST 3	1.0519	6.3116**	0

**p < .01 *p < .05

including GB-STAT, will perform both tests. These tests are found on the additional statistics menu after analysis of variance is selected. However, while the output for ANOVA tables is fairly consistent between packages, the output formats for the Tukey and Scheffé tests are not as consistent. Figure 12-8 shows the computer output for both the ANOVA table and Tukey (protected t) tests for the Arizona fire district example. Note that the Tukey output is in matrix format. The values in the matrix are equivalent to t values, and the double asterisks (**) found next to some values indicate that the means for the corresponding districts have differences significant at the 0.01 level.

Figure 12-9 shows the GB-STAT output for the Zero Defects example. Notice that the Scheffé output is also given in matrix form, with the double asterisks indicating significance at the 0.01 level.

FIGURE 12-9

GB-STAT Output for the Zero Defects Corporation Example

SAMPLE DESCRIPTIVE STATISTICS

N 1 = 7
N 2 = 9
N 3 = 8
N 4 = 10
N 5 = 10

MEAN GROUP 1 = 48.14286
VAR. GROUP 1 = 22.80952
MEAN GROUP 2 = 83.55556
VAR. GROUP 2 = 17.77778
MEAN GROUP 3 = 64.25
VAR. GROUP 3 = 15.07143
MEAN GROUP 4 = 61.1
VAR. GROUP 4 = 16.54445
MEAN GROUP 5 = 52.5
VAR. GROUP 5 = 28.5

ANOVA SUMMARY TABLE

SOURCE	SUM SQRES	DF	MEAN SQRES	F-RATIO	PROB
BETWEEN GRPS	6474.272	4	1618.568	79.9061	<.0001
WITHIN GRPS	789.9794	39	20.25588		
TOTAL	7264.251	43			

SCHEFFE COMPARISONS

	1 SEQ 1	2 SEQ 2	3 SEQ 3	4 SEQ 4	5 SEQ 5
SEQ 1	0	60.9435**	11.9543**	8.5321**	.9648
SEQ 2	60.9435**	0	19.4821**	29.4798**	56.384**
SEQ 3	11.9543**	19.4821**	0	.5443	7.5732**
SEQ 4	8.5321**	29.4798**	.5443	0	4.5641**
SEQ 5	.9648	56.384**	7.5732**	4.5641**	0

**p < .01 *p < .05

SKILL DEVELOPMENT PROBLEMS FOR **SECTION 12-4**

Several exercises and problems designed to help you understand the material presented in Section 12-4 follow.

23. Under what conditions would Tukey's method of multiple comparison be used and for what purpose is it used?

24. Under what conditions would Scheffé's method of multiple comparison be used and for what purpose is it used?

25. Given the following sample data:

Item	*Group 1*	*Group 2*	*Group 3*
1	12	8	16
2	15	5	12
3	21	7	12
4	15	8	14
5	17	10	15
6	12	10	15

a. State the appropriate null and alternative hypotheses for determining whether a difference exists in the average value for the three populations.
b. Compute the sum of squares between for the above sample data.
c. Compute the sum of squares within for the above sample data.
d. Based on the computations in parts **b** and **c**, develop the ANOVA table and test the null hypothesis using an $\alpha = 0.05$.
e. Employ the appropriate method for detecting which means are different, using an $\alpha = 0.05$.

26. Given the following sample data:

Item	*Group 1*	*Group 2*	*Group 3*	*Group 4*
1	20	28	17	21
2	27	26	15	23
3	26	21	18	19
4	22	29	20	17
5	25	30	14	
6	30	25		
7	23			

a. State the appropriate null and alternative hypotheses for determining whether a difference exists in the average value for the four populations.
b. Compute the sum of squares between for the above sample data.
c. Compute the sum of squares within for the above sample data.
d. Based on the computations in parts **b** and **c**, develop the ANOVA table and test the null hypothesis using an $\alpha = 0.05$.
e. Use the appropriate method of multiple comparison to determine which populations have different means. Use an $\alpha = 0.05$.

27. Given the following sample data:

Item	*Group 1*	*Group 2*	*Group 3*
1	105	88	113
2	69	86	102
3	110	88	120
4	112	99	110
5	55	90	100

a. State the appropriate null and alternative hypotheses for determining whether a difference exists in the average value for the three populations.
b. Compute the sum of squares between for the above sample data.
c. Compute the sum of squares within for the above sample data.
d. Based on the computations in parts **b** and **c**, develop the ANOVA table and test the null hypothesis using an $\alpha = 0.01$.
e. Using the appropriate method of multiple comparison, determine which populations have different means. Use an $\alpha = 0.01$.

28. The Green-Checker Cab Company (see Problem 21) operates twelve taxis in Seattle, Washington. The manager is interested in determining whether there is a difference in average fares collected for the day, swing, and graveyard shifts. To test whether a difference exists, she has collected a random sample of ten observations from each shift. The following summary values have been computed from the sample data:

$$TSS = 156{,}764 \qquad SSB = 55{,}600$$

a. State the appropriate null and alternative hypotheses.
b. Develop the appropriate ANOVA table and test the hypothesis using an $\alpha = 0.01$.

29. The American Beef Growers Association (see Problem 22) is trying to promote the consumption of beef products. The organization performs numerous studies, the results of which are often used in advertising campaigns. One such study involved a quality perception test. Three levels of beef gradings—choice, standard, and economy—were involved. A random sample of people was provided a piece of choice-grade beefsteak and asked to rate its quality on a scale of 1 to 100. A second sample of people was given a piece of standard-grade beefsteak and a third sample was given a piece of economy-grade beefsteak, with instructions to rate it on the 100-point scale. The following data were observed.

Choice	*Standard*	*Economy*
78	67	65
87	80	62
90	78	70
87	80	66
89	67	70
90	70	73

Based on the sample data, is there sufficient evidence to conclude that there is a difference in perceived quality for the three grades of beefsteak? Test at the $\alpha = 0.05$ level; make sure to state the null and alternative hypotheses and provide the ANOVA table. Also, if appropriate, determine which populations have different means, using a method of multiple comparison.

12-5 TWO-WAY ANALYSIS OF VARIANCE (OPTIONAL)

In the previous sections, you were introduced to the one-way analysis of variance statistical procedure for testing hypotheses involving three or more population means. One-way analysis of variance is appropriate as long as we are interested in analyzing one factor at a time and we select independent random samples from the populations. For instance, our example involving printed circuit board assembly at the Zero Defects Corporation (Table 12-8) illustrated a situation in which we were interested in only one factor—number of circuit boards assembled by different sequences. To test the hypothesis that the five assembly sequences were equal with respect to average number of circuit boards assembled in a 2-week period, five groups of people were assigned to each sequence independently. Thus, the one-way ANOVA design was appropriate.

There are, however, situations in which the one-way design may not be appropriate. Chapter 11 introduced you to the concept of paired samples and indicated that there are instances when it is desirable to test for differences in two population means by employing paired samples. The reason for using paired samples is to control for sources of variation that might adversely affect the analysis. For instance, in testing average lifetime for automobile shock absorbers, we might put one shock absorber of each type on a car and then repeat this for a sample of cars. We would be attempting to control for the variation in cars while testing the average lifetime of the shock absorbers.

The same kinds of concern can arise in hypothesis tests involving more than two population means. For instance, suppose we wish to test the hypothesis that there is no difference in the average house appraisal by three different appraising companies. We would likely want to control for the variation in size, quality, and location of homes that were appraised in order to fairly test that the three companies' appraisals are equal on the average. To do this, we would select a random sample of properties and have each company appraise the same properties. The properties are called blocks and the test design is called a blocked design. The

TABLE 12-11

Sample Data for Real Estate Appraisers Example (in Thousands of Dollars)

	Appraisers			
Property	1	2	3	$\bar{X}_j$
1	78.0	82.0	79.0	79.67
2	102.0	102.0	99.0	101.00
3	68.0	74.0	70.0	70.67
4	83.0	88.0	86.0	85.67
5	95.0	99.0	92.0	95.33
$\bar{X}_i$	85.2	89.0	85.2	

$\bar{\bar{X}} = 86.47$

blocked design is merely an extension of the paired-sample t test introduced in Chapter 11.

Table 12-11 illustrates appraisals for five properties by each appraisal company. We are interested in testing the following hypothesis:

H_0: $\mu_1 = \mu_2 = \mu_3$
H_A: Not all population means are equal.

Because we have chosen a blocked design, we must employ **two-way analysis of variance** to test the hypothesis. Two-way ANOVA is similar in concept to one-way ANOVA in that we can partition the total sum of squares into component parts. Once again, the total variation in the data is represented by equation 12-14:

12-14

$$\text{TSS} = \sum_{i=1}^{K} \sum_{j=1}^{r} (X_{ij} - \bar{\bar{X}})^2$$

where

K = Number of columns (appraisers)

r = Number of rows or blocks (properties)

X_{ij} = Individual appraisals

$\bar{\bar{X}}$ = Grand mean (86.47)

Then

$$\begin{aligned}\text{TSS} &= (78.0 - 86.47)^2 + (102.0 - 86.47)^2 + \cdots + (92.0 - 86.47)^2 \\ &= 1{,}829.73\end{aligned}$$

When discussing one-way ANOVA, we showed that

$$\text{TSS} = \text{SSW} + \text{SSB}$$

With two-way ANOVA, we partition the total sum of squares into three parts instead of two:

$$\text{TSS} = \text{SSB} + \text{SSBL} + \text{SSW}$$

where

TSS = Total sum of squares

SSB = Sum of squares between groups

SSBL = Sum of squares between blocks

SSW = Sum of squares within groups

Now, SSB is given by equation 12-15:

$$\text{SSB} = \sum_{i=1}^{K} r(\overline{X}_i - \overline{\overline{X}})^2 \qquad \textbf{12-15}$$

where

$\overline{X}_i$ = Mean of each group

Since r is the number of blocks (in this case properties):

$$\begin{aligned}\text{SSB} &= 5(85.2 - 86.47)^2 + 5(89.0 - 86.47)^2 + 5(85.2 - 86.47)^2 \\ &= 48.13\end{aligned}$$

Also, SSBL is given by equation 12-16:

$$\text{SSBL} = \sum_{j=1}^{r} K(\overline{X}_j - \overline{\overline{X}})^2 \qquad \textbf{12-16}$$

where

K = Number of groups

$\overline{X}_j$ = Mean for each block across groups

SSBL is the **between-blocks variation.** As you can see from equation 12-16, the SSBL value is the weighted sum of the difference between the block means and the grand mean. Then

$$\begin{aligned}\text{SSBL} &= 3(79.67 - 86.47)^2 + \cdots + 3(95.33 - 86.47)^2 \\ &= 1{,}759.07\end{aligned}$$

Finally, using equation 12-17,

$$\begin{aligned}\text{SSW} &= \text{TSS} - \text{SSB} - \text{SSBL} \\ &= 1{,}829.73 - 48.13 - 1{,}759.07 \\ &= 22.53\end{aligned} \qquad \textbf{12-17}$$

TABLE 12-12

Two-way Analysis of Variance Table

Source	SS	d.f.	MS	F
Between	SSB	$K - 1$	SSB/$(K - 1)$	MSB/MSW
Blocks	SSBL	$r - 1$	SSBL/$(r - 1)$	MSBL/MSW
Within	SSW	$(K - 1)(r - 1)$	SSW/$[(K - 1)(r - 1)]$	
Total	SST	$N - 1$		

Substituting numerical values yields the following:

Source	SS	d.f.	MS	F
Between	48.13	2	48.13/2 = 24.07	8.54
Blocks	1,759.07	4	1,759.07/4 = 439.77	155.95
Within	22.53	8	22.53/8 = 2.82	
Total	1,829.73	14		

Test for Blocking Effectiveness

H_0: $\mu_1 = \mu_2 = \mu_3 = \mu_4 = \mu_5$
H_A: Not all means are equal.
$\alpha = 0.05$

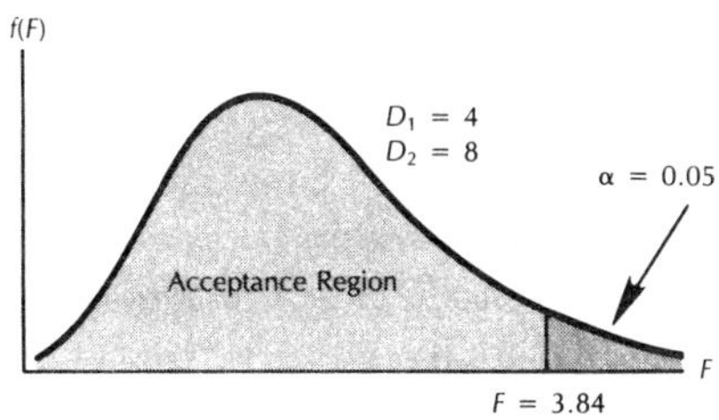

Since $F = 155.95 > 3.84$, reject H_0; conclude that blocking is effective.

Test for Difference between Companies

H_0: $\mu_1 = \mu_2 = \mu_3$
H_A: Not all means are equal.
$\alpha = 0.05$

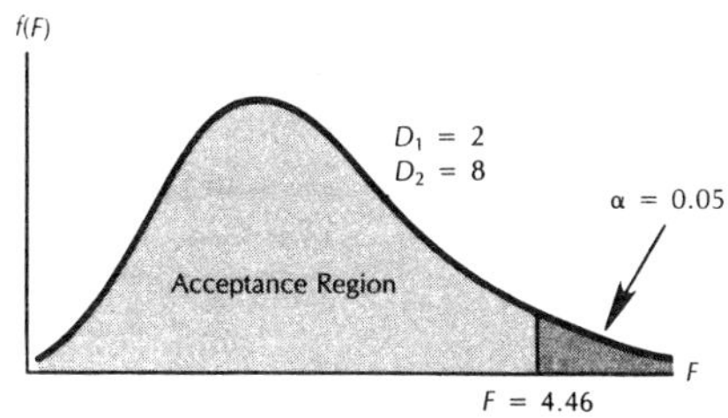

Since $F = 8.54 > 4.46$, reject H_0; conclude that not all population means are equal.

You should note that the computation for SSB is performed exactly as with one-way ANOVA. However, the within-group variation has been broken into two parts, SSBL and SSW. Table 12-12 shows the ANOVA table for the two-way analysis of variance.

Note that in Table 12-12 we have computed two F values. This is because there is a secondary hypothesis to be tested; this deals with the effectiveness of blocking.

Effective blocking in this case would mean that the property appraisals are in fact influenced by the property being appraised. The blocks then form a second factor of interest and we formulate a secondary hypothesis dealing with this factor as follows:

$$H_0: \mu_1 = \mu_2 = \mu_3 = \mu_4 = \mu_5$$
$$H_A: \text{Not all block means are equal.}$$

Thus, in performing the two-way ANOVA, we also test to see whether the average appraisals for each property are equal. If the null hypothesis is rejected, this means that blocking was effective and the block design was justified. Referring to Table 12-12, we see that the F ratio formed by

$$F = \text{MSBL/MSW} = 155.95$$

is substantially larger than the F_{critical} for $D_1 = 4$ and $D_2 = 8$ degrees of freedom of 3.84 at an alpha level of 0.05. Thus, we reject the secondary hypothesis and conclude that the blocking design was appropriate; now we go on to the primary hypothesis involving whether the companies appraise properties at equal values on the average. (Note that if we conclude that blocking is not effective and if the main hypothesis is not rejected, then we should begin again by selecting independent samples and analyze using one-way analysis of variance.)

The main factor of interest is whether the companies appraise properties at values that are equal on the average. Table 12-12 shows the F ratio formed as

$$F = \text{MSB/MSW} = 8.54$$

exceeds the F_{critical} for $D_1 = 2$ and $D_2 = 8$ degrees of freedom from the F-distribution table of 4.46 at an alpha level of 0.05. Thus, we should conclude that the mean appraisals by the three companies do differ, on the average.

As was the case with one-way ANOVA, once the null hypothesis is rejected we conclude that not all means are equal. The next step is to determine which means are not equal and which, if any, are equal. We earlier learned that Tukey's or Scheffé's method was useful for making such conclusions with one-way ANOVA. *Fisher's least significant difference* is a way for testing multiple comparisons when two-way ANOVA is used. This test also avoids the problem of compounding the Type I error probability.

If the null hypothesis has been rejected, then we can compare the absolute differences in sample means from any two populations to the *least significant difference* (LSD) and reject that the means for the two populations are equal if equation 12-18 is true:

$$|\overline{X}_i - \overline{X}_j| > \text{LSD} \qquad \textbf{12-18}$$

where

$$\text{LSD} = t\sqrt{\text{MSW}}\sqrt{\frac{1}{n_i} + \frac{1}{n_j}}$$

and where

t = t value for $\alpha/2$ and $(K - 1)(r - 1)$ degrees of freedom from the Studentized t distribution
MSW = Mean square within from the two-way analysis of variance
n_i and n_j: Sample sizes from populations i and j, respectively

Since we have equal sample sizes from all three populations, the common LSD is computed as follows:

$$\text{LSD} = t_{0.025,8}\sqrt{\text{MSW}}\sqrt{\frac{1}{5}+\frac{1}{5}}$$
$$= 2.306\sqrt{2.82}\sqrt{\frac{1}{5}+\frac{1}{5}}$$
$$= 2.449$$

Then we form the three possible comparisons as follows:

Absolute Difference $\lvert\overline{X}_i - \overline{X}_j\rvert$	*Conclusion*
$\lvert 85.2 - 89.0\rvert = 3.8$	$\mu_1 \neq \mu_2$
$\lvert 85.2 - 85.2\rvert = 0.0$	$\mu_1 = \mu_3$
$\lvert 89.0 - 85.2\rvert = 3.8$	$\mu_2 \neq \mu_3$

Therefore, from the sample data we can infer that the mean appraisals of company 1 and company 3 both differ significantly from that of company 2, but not from each other.

COMPUTER OUTPUT—TWO-WAY ANALYSIS OF VARIANCE

Statistical software packages will commonly perform two-way analysis of variance calculations. Figure 12-10 (page 622) shows the MINITAB output for the appraisal example just considered. In analyzing this output, consider the following:

1. The different property values were loaded into column 1 (C1), the property numbers were loaded into column 2 (C2), and the appraiser numbers were loaded into column 3 (C3).
2. The columns were renamed using the name convention, but "appraiser" is too long a word to use, so "person" was substituted.
3. The standard ANOVA table is printed out but MINITAB does not calculate F values, so you will have to determine these values manually. Other software programs will calculate F values for this table.

INTERACTIVE EFFECTS

This section has introduced two-way analysis of variance and showed how it is applied in a case where there are actually two factors of interest. The procedures presented rely on the basic assumption that the blocks are *additive*. This means that the difference between any two blocks' means is a constant amount regardless of which population we are considering.

For instance, consider again the example where we are testing about the mean appraisals for three appraisal companies. The additivity assumption implies, for example, that the average difference between assessments of property 3 and prop-

FIGURE 12-10

MINITAB Output for the Two-way Analysis of Variance Example

```
MTB > read into c1 c2 c3
DATA > 78 1 1
DATA > 82 1 2
DATA > 79 1 3
DATA > 102 2 1
DATA > 102 2 2
DATA > 99 2 3
DATA > 68 3 1
DATA > 74 3 2
DATA > 70 3 3
DATA > 83 4 1
DATA > 88 4 2
DATA > 86 4 3
DATA > 95 5 1
DATA > 99 5 2
DATA > 92 5 3
MTB > end
MTB > name c1 'value' c2 'property' c3 'person'
MTB > table 'property' by 'person';
SUBC > mean 'value'.
ROWS: property     COLUMNS: person

              1          2          3        ALL

 1       78.000     82.000     79.000     79.667
 2      102.000    102.000     99.000    101.000
 3       68.000     74.000     70.000     70.667
 4       83.000     88.000     86.000     85.667
 5       95.000     99.000     92.000     95.333
ALL      85.200     89.000     85.200     86.467

CELL CONTENTS—
              value: MEAN
MTB > twoway 'value' blocks 'property' treatment 'person'

ANALYSIS OF VARIANCE value
SOURCE      DF         SS         MS
property     4    1759.07     439.77
person       2      48.13      24.07
ERROR        8      22.53       2.82
TOTAL       14    1829.73
```

erty 5 by company 1 will be the same as the average difference in assessments for the same two properties if company 2 or company 3 did the assessment. Since each company made only one assessment of each property we have no choice but to make this assumption.

However, in many instances, instead of additivity there is **interaction** between the factors. For instance, suppose we have three types of glues that can be used in making plywood (Brand 1, Brand 2, and Brand 3). We are interested in determining whether there is a difference in the mean strength of the plywood. One factor thought to affect the strength of plywood in addition to glue type is the species of wood that is used to construct the plywood. If one species of wood tends to work better with one brand of glue while another species makes stronger plywood when a different glue is used, we call this *interaction* between the wood and the glue. If no interaction exists, then the species of wood that is superior for one type of glue will be superior for all types of glue and the degree of superiority on the average will be a constant when compared with other wood species.

Thus, when interaction is suspected, it is necessary to control for it when analyzing the main factor of study. We do this by employing two-way ANOVA with interaction. This topic, also referred to as factorial ANOVA, is beyond the scope of this text. However, if you take a course in experimental design or analysis of variance, substantial time will be spent interpreting the meaning when interaction is present in the analysis.

SKILL DEVELOPMENT PROBLEMS FOR **SECTION 12-5**

Several exercises and problems designed to help you understand the topics presented in Section 12-5 follow.

30. A two-way ANOVA experiment has been performed, with the following sample data resulting:

Case	*Group 1*	*Group 2*	*Group 3*
1	20	24	30
2	17	26	28
3	15	24	29
4	30	35	40
5	12	16	21
6	20	25	29
7	17	29	31

a. State the appropriate null and alternative hypotheses to be tested.
b. Compute TSS, SSBL, SSB, and SSW.
c. Develop the ANOVA table and test the hypotheses. Be sure to indicate whether blocking was effective. Use $\alpha = 0.05$.
d. If you concluded that the three population means are different, use the LSD method to determine which populations have different means. Use an $\alpha = 0.05$ level.

31. A two-way ANOVA experiment has been performed, with the following sample data resulting:

Case	*Group 1*	*Group 2*	*Group 3*	*Group 4*
1	10	7	16	21
2	12	3	13	26
3	10	9	17	23
4	9	10	20	25
5	10	5	22	30
6	13	8	17	24
7	11	7	16	22
8	14	12	23	21

a. State the appropriate null and alternative hypotheses to be tested.
b. Compute TSS, SSBL, SSB, and SSW.
c. Develop the ANOVA table and test the hypotheses. Be sure to indicate whether blocking was effective. Assume an $\alpha = 0.05$ level.
d. If you concluded that the four population means are different, use the LSD method to determine which populations have different means.

32. The *Buying Guide* is similar to other sales catalogs but instead of carrying a wide line of merchandise in one edition, each edition of *Buying Guide* contains many colors and styles of only a few brands of merchandise. Recently, the sales manager decided to perform a study to determine whether there is a difference in average purchases per order from three of the editions. Because she was concerned that the variability from customer to customer might mask a real difference between catalog editions, she set up the study as a two-way ANOVA problem. She sampled 100 customers and sent each one a copy of each of the three editions. The following data reflect the orders from those who placed orders (10 customers) from all three catalog editions:

Customer	*Edition 1*	*Edition 2*	*Edition 3*
1	$ 44	$ 27	$ 90
2	67	36	80
3	50	20	112
4	80	40	230
5	36	18	60
6	50	30	80
7	110	140	209
8	80	40	140
9	20	12	40
10	30	12	58

a. State the null and alternative hypotheses to be tested.
b. Develop the appropriate ANOVA table and test the hypotheses at the $\alpha =$ 0.01 level.

c. If you have concluded that there is a difference in mean order sizes for the three editions, use the LSD method to determine which editions have different means.

33. The Goodmonth Tire Company has four plants where they make the XG-99 all-season radial tire. The production control staff is concerned about whether the four plants are producing tires that will provide the same average mileage for the customers. To test this, they have selected a random sample of twenty car owners and mounted one tire from each plant on the car. The tires were then used for 12,000 miles (with rotation every 500 miles) and at the end of the period the amount of remaining tread was measured.

The following values were computed from the sample data:

$$TSS = 200 \qquad SSB = 50 \qquad SSBL = 70$$

a. State the appropriate null and alternative hypotheses.
b. Develop the ANOVA table and test the hypotheses at the $\alpha = 0.05$ level. Discuss the results of your test in terms of what they mean to the Goodmonth Tire Company.
c. Indicate why it was appropriate to use a two-way ANOVA design in this case.

12-6 COMPUTER APPLICATIONS

This chapter has introduced analysis of variance, which is used to test hypotheses involving means of three or more populations. The computations involved can be performed using a calculator, but when sample sizes become large, the effort required and the chance for error increase. Computers and statistical software are ideally suited to the task of performing analysis of variance calculations.

The purpose of this section is to illustrate the type of computer output you can expect when you use statistical software to perform one-way analysis of variance. As in earlier chapters, the examples presented use the MINITAB, GB-STAT, and SPSS-X software systems and the data for the examples come from the KIVZ-Channel 5 survey used in earlier chapters and which appear in Table 2-10.

Table 12-13 (page 626) shows the MINITAB output for a one-way analysis of variance for testing the null hypothesis that the average income (X_{18}) is equal for viewers regardless of which station they prefer for their national news coverage (X_1). The F ratio of 0.27 is so small that it falls in the acceptance region for any reasonable alpha level. (See Figure 12-11 for MINITAB commands.)

Table 12-14 (page 627) shows the SPSS-X computer output for a one-way analysis of variance for testing the hypothesis that mean hours of television watched (X_{19}) is equal for all categories of marital status (X_{11}). Note that the F Prob. value can be compared directly with the selected alpha level. If the F Prob. is smaller than alpha, the null hypothesis of equal means can be rejected. If the F Prob. exceeds the alpha level, the null hypothesis should not be rejected. In this case, the F Prob. is 0.2630. Assuming an alpha of 0.05, these results show that the

TABLE 12-13 MINITAB Computer Output: One-way ANOVA for KIVZ-Channel 5 Case Study

```
ANALYSIS OF VARIANCE

DUE TO          DF            SS      MS=SS/DF      F-RATIO
FACTOR           4     26511992.      6627998.          .27
ERROR           45   1102671872.     24503820.
TOTAL           49   1129183744.

LEVEL           N           MEAN      ST. DEV.
0               1         21100.            0.
1              13         25069.         4613.
2               9         24633.         4706.
3              21         24605.         4503.
4               6         26150.         7276.

POOLED ST. DEV. =          4950.
1

INDIVIDUAL 95 PERCENT C. I. FOR LEVEL MEANS
(BASED ON POOLED STANDARD DEVIATION)
        +---------+---------+---------+---------+---------+---------+
0                I***********************I************************I
1                                            I******I******I
2                                         I********I*******I
3                                            I*****I****I
4                                           I*********I**********I
        +---------+---------+---------+---------+---------+---------+
    8000.    12000.    16000.    20000.    24000.    28000.    32000.
```

television viewers in the KIVZ market area may watch television an equal number of hours, on average, regardless of marital status of the head of household. (Figure 12-12 on page 628 shows the SPSS-X program statements.)

Table 12-15 (page 629) shows the GB-STAT output for the hypothesis that the average years respondents have spent in the state (X_{15}) is equal for viewers,

FIGURE 12-11

```
MTB> READ 'KIVZ5' INTO C1-C19
MTB> OUTFILE = 'PRINTER'
MTB> ONEWAY C18 C1
```

MINITAB Commands: Analysis of Variance for Income by National News Station

TABLE 12-14 SPSS-X Computer Output: One-way ANOVA for KIVZ-Channel 5 Case Study and Database

```
- - - - - - - - - - - - - - - - - - - - - - - - - - - - - - - - - O N E W A Y - - - - - - - - - - - - - - - - - - - - - - - - - -

     Variable  VAR19      HOURS OF TV
  By Variable  VAR11      MARITAL STATUS

                                 ANALYSIS OF VARIANCE

                                 SUM OF           MEAN               F       F
        SOURCE          D.F.     SQUARES          SQUARES            RATIO   PROB.
BETWEEN GROUPS            2       50.3147         25.1574           1.3750   .2630
WITHIN GROUPS            46      841.6444         18.2966
TOTAL                    48      891.9592

                                 STANDARD     STANDARD
GROUP        COUNT       MEAN   DEVIATION        ERROR     MINIMUM     MAXIMUM        95 PCT CONF INT FOR MEAN
Grp 1            3     8.3333      2.8868       1.6667      5.0000     10.0000         1.1622 TO       15.5045
Grp 2            1    14.0000
Grp 3           45    12.4222      4.3301        .6455      4.0000     21.0000        11.1213 TO       13.7231
TOTAL           49    12.2041      4.3107        .6158      4.0000     21.0000        10.9659 TO       13.4423

- - - - - - - - - - - - - - - - - - - - - - - - - - - - - - - - - O N E W A Y - - - - - - - - - - - - - - - - - - - - - - - - - -
```

FIGURE 12-12

SPSS-X Program Commands: Analysis of Variance

```
UNNUMBERED
TITLE DESCRIPTIVE STATISTICS EXAMPLES
FILE HANDLE KIVZ NAME='KIVZ DATA C'
DATA LIST FILE=KIVZ LIST/VAR01 TO VAR19
VARIABLE LABELS
  VAR01 'NATIONAL NEWS STATION'
  VAR02 'LOCAL NEWS STATION'
  VAR03 'NEWS RATING'
  VAR04 'SPORTS RATING'
  VAR05 'WEATHER RATING'
  VAR06 'ANCHOR RATING'
  VAR07 'SPORTSCASTER RATING'
  VAR08 'OVERALL RATING'
  VAR09 'NATIONAL INFLUENCE'
  VAR10 'SEX'
  VAR11 'MARITAL STATUS'
  VAR12 'NUMBER EMPLOYED'
  VAR13 'HOME STATUS'
  VAR14 'YEARS AT RESIDENCE'
  VAR15 'YEARS IN STATE'
  VAR16 'EDUCATION'
  VAR17 'AGE'
  VAR18 'INCOME'
  VAR19 'HOURS OF TV'
VALUE LABELS
  VAR01 1 'CHANNEL 5' 2 'CHANNEL 3' 3 'CHANNEL 8' 4
        'UNDECIDED'/
  VAR02 1 'CHANNEL 3' 2 'CHANNEL 8' 3 'CHANNEL 5' 4
        'UNDECIDED'/
  VAR03 TO VAR08 1 'POOR' 2 'FAIR' 3 'GOOD' 4 'VERY GOOD' 5
        'EXCEL'/
  VAR09 1 'TRUE' 2 'FALSE' 3 'UNDECIDED'/
  VAR10 1 'MALE' 2 'FEMALE'/
  VAR11 1 'SINGLE' 2 'DIVORCED' 3 'MARRIED' 4 'OTHER'/
  VAR13 1 'RENTING' 2 'BUYING'/
  VAR16 1 'GRADE SCHOOL' 2 'SOME COLLEGE' 3 'VOTECH' 4 'HIGH
        SCHOOL'
        5 'COLLEGE GRAD' 6 'GRADUATE WORK'
ONEWAY VAR19 BY VAR11(1,3)
```

regardless of which station they prefer for their local news (X_2). As you can see under PROB, the p-value is 0.0533, indicating that the averages are not quite significant at the 5% level.

The computer output examples shown in Tables 12-13, 12-14, and 12-15 are indicative of the type of output you can expect from most statistical software packages for one-way analysis of variance. Programs such as MINITAB, GB-STAT, and SPSS-X also can be used to run two-way analysis of variance applications.

12-7 QUALITY CONTROL AND ANALYSIS OF VARIANCE

W. Edwards Deming tells the story of an American automobile manufacturer that did not have enough capacity in its plants to make enough automatic transmissions to meet current production schedules. The American company contracted with a Japanese affiliate to produce the transmissions. Later, the company had

TABLE 12-15

GB-STAT Output: One-way ANOVA for KIVZ-Channel 5 Case Study and Database

SAMPLE DESCRIPTIVE STATISTICS

N 1 = 9
N 2 = 25
N 3 = 11
N 4 = 5

MEAN GROUP 1 = 19
VAR. GROUP 1 = 290.75
MEAN GROUP 2 = 33.28
VAR. GROUP 2 = 399.7933
MEAN GROUP 3 = 17.63636
VAR. GROUP 3 = 164.8546
MEAN GROUP 4 = 28.4
VAR. GROUP 4 = 137.3

ANOVA SUMMARY TABLE

SOURCE	SUM SQRES	DF	MEAN SQRES	F-RATIO	PROB
BETWEEN GRPS	2533.794	3	844.5981	2.7518	.0533
WITHIN GRPS	14118.78	46	306.9301		
TOTAL	16652.58	49			

warranty problems with the transmissions, but discovered the problems were almost entirely with those made in the American plant. Engineers selected samples of both American- and Japanese-made transmissions and broke them down, looking for potential differences. They found that all the American-made transmissions contained parts that varied somewhat, but were all clearly within the design specifications. When the engineers started measuring the Japanese-made parts, they first thought their instruments had failed—all parts measured the same. They soon discovered that they could not measure variation in the parts because virtually no variation existed—the parts *were* all the same!

The Japanese company was following a procedure formulated by Genichi Taguchi, who took to heart Deming's teaching that sources of variation in a process should be identified and reduced using statistically valid methods. The Taguchi method is cited as a key to the quality of Japanese manufacturing and depends heavily on analysis of variance. It starts with gathering enough statistical data to formulate a valid baseline for the existing process and to identify important points of variation in the output. The next step is to formulate experiments, similar to the two-way analysis of variance procedure discussed in Section 12-5, to determine the relationship between important variation in the output and alternative actions in the process. The idea is always to select the alternative that minimizes the resulting variation in the output. If sources of variation in the output are continually identified, and alternatives that minimize this variation are selected, eventually all output appear virtually identical.

Two-way ANOVA—No interaction

$$\text{TSS} = \sum_{i=1}^{K} \sum_{j=1}^{r} (X_{ij} - \overline{\overline{X}})^2 = \sum_{i=1}^{K} \sum_{j=1}^{r} X_{ij}^2 - \frac{\left(\sum_{i=1}^{K} \sum_{j=1}^{r} X_{ij}\right)^2}{(K)(r)}$$

$$\text{SSB} = \sum_{i-1}^{K} r(\overline{X}_i - \overline{\overline{X}})^2 = \sum_{i=1}^{K} \frac{\left(\sum_{j=1}^{r} X_{ij}\right)^2}{r} - \frac{\left(\sum_{i=1}^{K} \sum_{j=1}^{r} X_{ij}\right)^2}{(K)(r)}$$

$$\text{SSBL} = \sum_{j=1}^{r} K(\overline{X}_j - \overline{\overline{X}})^2 = \sum_{j=1}^{r} \frac{\left(\sum_{i=1}^{K} X_{ij}\right)^2}{K} - \frac{\left(\sum_{i=1}^{K} \sum_{j=1}^{r} X_{ij}\right)^2}{(K)(r)}$$

SOLVED PROBLEMS

1. The plant manager of a small Midwest fishing-equipment manufacturing plant is convinced that he can come up with a method of determining why his workers are sometimes very accurate and at other times very careless. Although he has not had much success up to this point in determining causes, he has recently read a book dealing with biorhythms. This seems to be the final explanation, so he has biorhythm charts prepared for all assembly employees. He divides the employees into four groups according to their positions on their charts: high, low, going up, or going down. He monitors the error rate (number of errors per 100 items produced) for each employee and finds the following results:

High	*Low*	*Going Up*	*Going Down*
2.3	3.2	3.6	1.7
3.1	1.8	2.7	2.5
1.9	2.2	2.9	2.0
2.7	2.5	3.0	1.8
2.1	1.9	3.8	2.1
3.3	2.0	3.4	2.6

a. Formulate the null hypothesis and decision rule necessary to test this situation if you want to control Type I error probability at the 1% level.
b. How many degrees of freedom are associated with the between-group estimate? How do you determine this value?
c. How many degrees of freedom are associated with the within-group estimate?
d. Set up the appropriate analysis of variance table and formulate a conclusion about the possible relationship between error rate and biorhythm level.
e. What is meant by MSW and MSB? What do they estimate?

Solution

a. **Hypotheses:**

H_0: $\mu_{\text{high}} = \mu_{\text{low}} = \mu_{\text{up}} = \mu_{\text{down}}$

H_A: Not all means are equal.

Decision Rule:

If $F > F_{\text{critical}}$, reject H_0.

If $F \leq F_{\text{critical}}$, accept H_0.

where $F_{\text{critical}} = 4.94$ (from Appendix F).

b. The degrees of freedom for the between-group estimate equal the number of groups minus 1. In this problem,

$$\begin{aligned} \text{d.f.} &= K - 1 = 4 - 1 \\ &= 3 \end{aligned}$$

c. For the within-group estimate, the degrees of freedom equal the total sample size minus the number of groups. Here,

$$\begin{aligned} \text{d.f.} &= N - K = 24 - 4 \\ &= 20 \end{aligned}$$

d.

Source of Variation	*SS*	*d.f.*	*MS*	*F Ratio*
Between groups	4.411	3	1.470	6.504
Within groups	4.528	20	0.226	
Total	8.939	23		

Since $6.504 > F_{\text{critical}} = 4.94$, the null hypothesis is rejected.

e. MSW is the population variance estimate based on the variation found within the groups after partitioning. MSB is the population variance estimate based on the average values found for each group.

2. An equipment rental firm is trying out three new types of oil in the transmissions of its rental front-end loaders. The maintenance manager is interested in whether any of the oils increase the time before the transmissions have to be repaired. The oils were randomly distributed among a set of new loaders; however, the numbers with each type of oil are not equal. The following data show the hours of use until repair for each front-end loader:

Oil 1	*Oil 2*	*Oil 3*
314	401	426
423	307	377
298	267	450
267	217	479
298		503
		532

a. Formulate the appropriate null hypothesis and decision rule to test this situation. Assume an alpha level of 0.01.
b. Construct the analysis of variance table for this situation and either accept or reject your hypothesis.
c. If you conclude one or more oils are associated with a longer average time to repair, determine which oils result in different means.

Solution

a. **Hypotheses**

H_0: $\mu_1 = \mu_2 = \mu_3$

H_A: Not all means are equal.

Decision Rule

If $F \leq F_{\text{critical}}$, accept H_0.

If $F > F_{\text{critical}}$, reject H_0.

where $F_{\text{critical}} = 6.93$ (from Appendix F).

b.

Source of Variation	*SS*	*d.f.*	*MS*	*F Ratio*
Between groups	83,098.75	2	41,549.38	10.35
Within groups	48,164.85	12	4,013.736	
Total	131,263.60	14		

Since $F = 10.35 > 6.93$, the null hypothesis should be rejected.

c. Since the number of observations differs between groups, we have to use Scheffé's method, where

$$S \text{ range} = S\hat{\sigma}$$

$$S = \sqrt{(K-1)F_{\text{critical}}}$$

$$\hat{\sigma} = \sqrt{\left(\frac{1}{n_1} + \frac{1}{n_2}\right)(\text{MSW})}$$

We have

$$F_{\text{critical}} = 6.93$$

so

$$S = \sqrt{(3-1)(6.93)} = 3.723$$

For groups 1 *and* 2:

$$\hat{\sigma} = \sqrt{\left(\frac{1}{5} + \frac{1}{4}\right)(4{,}013.736)} = 42.50$$

$$S \text{ range} = 3.723(42.50) = 158.23$$

For groups 1 *and* 3:

$$\hat{\sigma} = \sqrt{\left(\frac{1}{5} + \frac{1}{6}\right)(4{,}013.736)} = 38.36$$

$$S \text{ range} = 3.723(38.36) = 142.81$$

For groups 2 *and* 3:

$$\hat{\sigma} = \sqrt{\left(\frac{1}{4} + \frac{1}{6}\right)(4{,}013.736)} = 40.89$$

$$S \text{ range} = 3.723(40.89) = 152.23$$

Also, $\overline{X}_1 = 320$, $\overline{X}_2 = 298$, and $\overline{X}_3 = 461.167$.

Contrasts	*S Range*	*Significant?*
$\lvert\overline{X}_1 - \overline{X}_2\rvert = \lvert 320 - 298\rvert = 22$	158.23	No
$\lvert\overline{X}_1 - \overline{X}_3\rvert = \lvert 320 - 461.167\rvert = 141.167$	142.81	No
$\lvert\overline{X}_2 - \overline{X}_3\rvert = \lvert 298 - 461.167\rvert = 163.167$	152.23	Yes

CONCEPTUAL QUESTIONS AND ASSIGNMENTS

34. Explain in your own terms why, in a two-tailed *F* test for equal population variances, the alpha level is divided by 2 before the *F* critical value is looked up in the *F*-distribution table.
35. Consider some decision-making situations in your major and describe two or more in which tests of one or more population variances are important.
36. Discuss in your own words each of the following:
    a. Within-group variation
    b. Between-group variation
    c. Total sum of squares
    d. Degrees of freedom
37. Discuss in your own words why decision makers should use analysis of variance rather than multiple two-sample *t* tests when testing hypotheses involving more than two populations.
38. Why is Tukey's procedure for multiple comparisons used instead of performing several *t* tests?
39. A one-way analysis of variance test has just been performed. The conclusion reached is that the null hypothesis stating that the population means are equal is to be accepted. What would you expect Scheffé's multiple comparison method to show if it were performed for all pairwise comparisons? Discuss.
40. Visit a manufacturing company in your area. Determine what sources of variation exist in its processes. What techniques does the company use to analyze this variation and what efforts does it make to reduce the variation?

ADDITIONAL PROBLEMS

41. The Cranston Company has a contract to provide ball bearings that average 1.25 inches in diameter, with a standard deviation not to exceed 0.04 inch.

To monitor their production, a random sample of ball bearings was selected and Cranston quality control people found the mean bearing to be 1.2552 inches with a standard deviation of 0.061 inch. If the sample size was twenty ball bearings, is Cranston meeting the requirements of the contract? Test the hypotheses using an alpha level of 0.05. Discuss your results.

42. The Phillips Company makes basketball rims used in most college arenas and professional facilities. The basketball standard calls for the rim diameters to have a standard deviation no greater than 0.10 inch. A random sample of twenty-four rims selected from the inventory in the Phillips warehouse showed a variance of 0.032. Given these sample data, what should be concluded about the variation of rim diameters? Be sure to specify the correct null and alternative hypotheses and test at an alpha level of 0.05.

43. The makers of a cattle feed supplement claim that if cattle feeders use the supplement as directed, cattle will gain an average of 1.2 pounds per day over a 30-day period. Further, they say that the range in weight gain will be 12 pounds per cow over this period.

A test situation has been developed where a random sample of cattle will be checked for weight gain at the end of 30 days. The results of the test involving ten cattle showed a mean gain of 37 pounds, with a standard deviation of 5.2 pounds. What conclusions should be reached with respect to the two claims made by the cattle feed supplement maker? Test at the alpha level of 0.10. (*Hint:* Recall that the standard deviation can be approximated by Range/4.) Discuss your answer.

44. Hospitals tend to build facilities to support peak demand for their services. Without proper scheduling of patients, these peak demand periods can prove excessive. To help reduce the propensity to overbuild, hospitals in Idaho must have a coefficient of variation in daily patient demand not exceeding 20%. Periodically, a state agency will select a sample of daily patient census figures to verify whether the hospital is meeting the coefficient of variation requirement.

At one hospital, average daily demand is 100 patients. A sample of 20 days showed a standard deviation of twenty-five patients. What should be concluded with respect to this hospital meeting the coefficient of variation requirement? Test at the alpha level of 0.10. (*Hint:* Review the section on coefficient of variation in Chapter 3.)

45. As purchasing agent for the Horner–Williams Company, you have primary responsibility for securing high-quality raw materials at the best possible price. One particular material that the Horner–Williams Company uses a great deal is aluminum. After careful study, you have been able to reduce the prospective vendors to two. It is unclear whether these two vendors produce aluminum that is equally durable.

To compare durability, the recommended procedure is to put pressure on the aluminum until it cracks. The vendor whose aluminum requires the greatest average pressure will be judged to be the one that provides the most durable product.

To carry out this test, fourteen pieces from vendor 1 and fourteen pieces from vendor 2 are selected at random. The following results in pounds per square inch were noted.

Vendor 1	*Vendor 2*
$n_1 = 14$	$n_2 = 14$
$\overline{X}_1 = 2{,}345$ psi	$\overline{X}_2 = 2{,}411$ psi
$S_1 = 300$	$S_2 = 250$

Before testing the hypothesis about difference in population means, suppose the purchasing agent for the company was concerned whether the assumption of equal population variances was satisfied. Based on the sample data, what would you tell him if you tested at the alpha level of 0.10? Would your conclusion differ if you tested at the alpha level of 0.02? Discuss.

46. Campbell Electronics has decided to place an advertisement on television to be shown three times during a live broadcast of the local university's football game. The sales for each of the 7 days after the ad was placed are to be compared with the sales for the 7 days immediately prior to running the ad. The following data, representing the total dollar sales each day, were collected:

Sales before the Ad	*Sales after the Ad*
$1,765	$2,045
1,543	2,456
2,867	2,590
1,490	1,510
2,800	2,850
1,379	1,255
2,097	2,255

a. State the appropriate null and alternative hypotheses to be tested.
b. What assumptions must be made about the population distributions in order to test the hypothesis using the t distribution?
c. Based on the sample data, what conclusions should be reached with respect to average sales before versus after the advertisement?
d. Suppose the Campbell Electronics Company wished to verify whether the assumption of equal population variances was satisfied when it performed the two-sample t test. Based on the sample data, what should it conclude if the alpha level 0.02 is used?

47. The Fister Corporation makes ribbons for computer printers. It is currently considering changing from the current model to a new model expected to last just as long on the average as the current model. However, the new model is thought to be more consistent in terms of how long the individual ribbons will last.

To test this claim, random samples of twenty-one current-model and seventeen new-model ribbons were selected and tested on the company's quality testing equipment. The following results (measured in tens of thousands of characters) were recorded.

Current	New
$n = 21$	$n = 17$
$S = 3.45$	$S = 2.87$

a. State the null and alternative hypotheses to be tested.
b. Test the hypotheses at the $\alpha = 0.05$ level. Be sure to state clearly the decision rule and also discuss the results.

48. The production control manager at Ashmore Manufacturing is interested in determining whether there is a difference in standard deviation of product diameter for part #XC-343 for units made at the Trenton, New Jersey, plant versus those made at the Atlanta, Georgia, plant. The Trenton plant is highly automated and thought to provide better quality control. Thus, the parts produced there should be less variable than those made in Atlanta.

    A random sample of fifteen parts was selected from those produced last week at Trenton. The standard deviation for these parts was 0.14 inch. A sample of thirteen parts was selected from those made in Atlanta. The sample standard deviation for these parts was 0.202 inch.

    Based on these sample data, is there sufficient evidence to conclude that the Trenton plant produces parts that are less variable than those of the Atlanta plant? Test at the $\alpha = 0.05$ level.

49. Bach Photographs is a large regional photography business with studios in two locations. The owner is interested in monitoring business activity closely at the two locations. Among the factors in which he is interested is the variation in customer orders per day for the two locations. A random sample of 11 days' orders for the two locations showed the following data:

Location A			Location B		
\$444	\$478	\$501	\$233	\$127	\$230
200	400	350	299	250	300
167	250	300	800	340	400
300	600		780	370	

a. State the appropriate null and alternative hypotheses.
b. Based on the sample data, test the hypotheses, using an $\alpha = 0.02$ level. Be sure to state clearly the decision rule.

50. You are responsible for installing emergency lighting in a series of state office buildings. You have bids from four manufacturers of battery-operated emergency lights. The costs are about equal, so you decide to base your decision to buy on which type lasts the longest. You receive a sample of four lights from each manufacturer, turn on the lights, and record the time before each light fails. You find the following values in hours:

Type A	Type B	Type C	Type D
24	27	21	23
21	25	20	23
25	26	25	21
22	22	22	21

Based on this evidence, can you conclude that the mean times to failure of the four types are equal? You will have to specify an alpha level.

51. A large metropolitan police force is considering changing from full-size cars to intermediates. The force purchases fifteen cars, five from each of three manufacturers. Each car is driven for 5,000 miles, and the operating cost per mile computed. Unfortunately, one car is involved in an accident, one is run into a river during a high-speed chase, and one is "lost" due to a paperwork mix-up. The operating costs for the remaining twelve cars are distributed as follows in cents per mile:

Car A	*Car B*	*Car C*
13.3	12.4	13.9
14.3	13.4	15.5
13.6	13.1	14.7
12.8		14.5
14.0		

Perform an analysis of variance on these data. Assume an alpha level of 0.01. Do the experimental data provide evidence that the operating costs per mile for the three types of police cars are different?

52. A nationwide moving company is considering three different types of nylon tie-down straps. The purchasing department randomly selects straps of each type and determines their breaking strengths. The following values are found, in pounds:

Type 1	*Type 2*	*Type 3*
1,950	2,210	1,820
1,870	2,300	1,730
1,900	1,990	1,760
1,880	2,190	1,700
2,010	2,250	1,810

a. Construct the analysis of variance table for this set of data.
b. Based on your analysis, with a Type I error rate of 0.05, can you conclude that a difference exists among the types of nylon ropes?

53. A leading manufacturer of beer is considering five different types of advertising displays for a new low-calorie beer. The displays are each tested in five different randomly selected stores. A total of twenty-five stores are in the sample. The average monthly sales (in cases) and variances for the first 3 months for each type of display are as follows:

Display Type	*Mean*	*Variance*
A	98	10
B	77	8
C	84	8
D	103	11
E	91	9

Can the manufacturer conclude that it really does not matter which type of display is used? Assume an alpha level of 0.01.

54. Channel 9 television in Bextfort, Washington, recently conducted a study of television news viewers. One item of interest to Channel 9 management was whether the average age of viewers watching Channel 9 was the same as for the other two stations in Bextfort. The sample included twenty-four viewers of each station, with the following results: TSS = 2,900 and SSW = 700.

Using an alpha level of 0.05, what should Channel 9 conclude about the average ages of news viewers of the three stations? Why?

55. Ajax Mountain Ski Company operates a small snow-skiing operation with two chair lifts. Recently some customers have complained that the lines at chair 1 are too long. The Ajax manager has collected the following data, which represent the number of people in line at the two chair lifts at randomly observed times during a week:

Chair 1	*Chair 2*
10	14
3	13
14	19
7	7
19	11
33	9
28	12
11	13
26	15

a. Use a two-sample t test to determine whether there is a significant difference in the average numbers of people waiting at the two lifts. Test this at the alpha level of 0.05.

b. Use analysis of variance to test the null hypothesis that the average numbers waiting at the two chair lifts are equal.

c. What observations can you make about the relationship between the two-sample t test and two-sample analysis of variance?

56. The Savouy Corporation recently purchased a bicycle manufacturing plant formerly owned by the American Traveling Company. American had been outfitting its bikes with tires produced by the Leach Corporation. Savouy management is considering whether to stay with Leach tires or to change to another brand. Three other brands are being considered, all of which cost about the same as the Leach tire. The criterion for tire selection will be average tread life.

Samples of twenty have been selected from the Leach tires and from brands A, B, and C. The following results were found:

$$\overline{X}_{\text{Leach}} = 111 \text{ h} \qquad \overline{X}_A = 126 \text{ h} \qquad \overline{X}_B = 100 \text{ h} \qquad \overline{X}_C = 105 \text{ h}$$

$$\text{TSS} = 19{,}620$$

(Note that $\overline{X}$ indicates the average hours of use until the tread was reduced to a specified level.) Using an alpha level of 0.05, test that there is no difference in average tread life for the four brands.

57. A ski resort in Idaho has been charged with discriminating against some nationalities of ski instructors in the wages that they are allowed to earn from private lessons. Instructors of three nationalities teach at this resort: Canadians, Austrians, and Germans. Random samples of six Canadians, eight Austrians, and seven Germans were selected. The following statistics were recorded:

$$\overline{X}_{\text{Canadian}} = \$3{,}111 \qquad \overline{X}_{\text{Austrian}} = \$2{,}005 \qquad \overline{X}_{\text{German}} = \$3{,}511$$
$$\text{TSS} = 18{,}328{,}128$$

Based on these values, what do you conclude about average salaries for ski instructors at this ski resort? Use an alpha level of 0.05.

58. A recent study performed by a marketing consultant hired by State University to determine the best use for empty space in the student union surveyed fifty students selected at random from the student body. Among other questions, the consultant asked the students to indicate how much money they spent in the school bookstore the last month on items other than textbooks. The following data represent the sample results broken down by student class ranks. (Note that the data have been rounded to the nearest dollar.)

Freshman	*Sophomore*	*Junior*	*Senior*	*Graduate*
$12	$15	$13	$27	$14
9	13	15	19	10
12	14	17	23	7
14	15	14	23	26
12	13	21	25	14
14	11	19	16	10
5	12	15	32	16
10	14	17	26	17
13	17	20	23	19
13	16	19	27	19

a. Based on these sample data, what can be concluded with respect to the average purchases at the bookstore by students with these class rankings? Test using an alpha level of 0.05.

b. If the conclusion is reached that the population means are not all equal, perform the appropriate method of multiple comparison to determine which pairs of populations have different means. Discuss the results of your test in a short memo to the vice-president of operations at the university.

59. The Xerox Company makes a wide variety of office products, including a line of copying machines. Recently, the marketing directors at Xerox did a study of governmental users of Xerox copiers. They selected a random sample of

twelve clients each from city, county, and state government units. Data were collected on the number of copies made each month by the agencies sampled. The following calculation results were reported to the director of marketing services:

$$\text{TSS} = 204{,}500{,}000$$
$$\overline{X}_{\text{county}} = 16{,}900 \text{ copies}$$
$$\overline{X}_{\text{city}} = 21{,}300 \text{ copies}$$
$$\overline{X}_{\text{state}} = 18{,}700 \text{ copies}$$

a. Based on these sample results, what can you conclude about the average number of copies made by units in the three government sectors? Base your analysis on an alpha level of 0.01.

b. Which pairs of populations have different means? Discuss.

60. Referring to Problem 59, suppose Xerox decided to expand its study to include private-sector companies with 200 or more employees. The company uses the same government data collected earlier and combines this with the sample data collected from a sample of twelve private companies. In addition to those means found in Problem 59, the following values are now available:

$$\text{TSS} = 267{,}333{,}780$$
$$\overline{X}_{\text{private}} = 20{,}000 \text{ copies}$$

a. What should Xerox conclude about the average number of copies made per month for these four classes of organizations? Test using an alpha level of 0.05.

b. Which pairs of populations have different means based on the sample data? Show the appropriate calculations.

61. The Environmental Protection Agency (EPA) performs various tests on automobiles for mileage analysis. Recently, the EPA selected a random sample of people who had purchased a new car within the previous 6-month period. Of the twenty-four people surveyed, eight had purchased big luxury cars, eight medium-sized cars, and eight compact cars. The following data represent the difference between these car owners' mileage compared with the EPA mileage rating as posted on the car window when the car was bought:

Luxury Cars	*Medium-Sized Cars*	*Compact Cars*
3.5	3.8	1.5
7.4	4.5	2.3
5.0	3.5	0.5
2.0	3.0	−2.0
3.6	2.7	2.5
5.8	4.0	−3.0
8.0	5.0	3.0
7.0	−1.5	−2.0

Note that positive values indicate that the actual mileage was lower than advertised by the sticker on the car window; negative values indicate the actual mileage exceeded the EPA rating on the sticker.

a. Based on an alpha level of 0.05, what can you conclude about the three types of cars with respect to the average differences between actual mileage and EPA-sticker mileage ratings?
b. If a difference in means is indicated by the test performed in part **a**, which populations of cars have different means? Discuss.

62. A Midwestern U.S. city has four radio stations. Radio stations run a fine line between having enough commercial time versus having too much. A study was conducted in which a random sample of hours was selected for each station over a 1-month period. The actual minutes of commercial time in each of these hours were recorded. The following values represent calculations that were performed on the raw data:

$$\overline{X}_1 = 14.6 \qquad \overline{X}_2 = 9.7 \qquad \overline{X}_3 = 13.5 \qquad \overline{X}_4 = 7.9$$

$$TSS = 3{,}456.80$$

a. What can you conclude about the average minutes per hour of commercial time for the four stations if the sample size was 20 hours for each station? Test at the alpha level of 0.05.
b. Based on the appropriate method for multiple comparisons, what can be determined with respect to the mean commercial time for the four stations? Discuss.

63. The Wicks Advertising Agency recently ran a coupon marketing campaign for one of its retail clients in Denver. Coupons were mailed to several thousand households. In addition, coupons were placed in two daily papers. The coupon offered a 15% discount on any purchases made with the coupon. The Wicks Agency is interested in knowing whether the volume of purchases differs on the average depending on the source from which the customer obtained the coupon. The marketing executive in charge of this client had one of her staff personnel select a random sample of coupons from each source and keep track of the volume of the purchases that accompanied that coupon. The following data represent the dollar amounts rounded to the nearest dollar:

Mailing	*Paper 1*	*Paper 2*
38	20	14
27	19	16
33	20	11
12	10	9
33	15	
21	14	
13		
25		

a. Based on the sample data, what can be concluded about the average purchase amounts by customers using coupons from the three sources? Test using an alpha level of 0.05.

b. Which pairs of coupon sources have different population means? Use the appropriate method of multiple comparisons to answer this question.

64. Referring to Problem 63, form the *S* range using Scheffé's method of multiple comparison and compare this with the *T* range computed in Problem 63. Which method is appropriate to use and why? Also compare the values of the *T* range and the *S* range and comment on what the difference means.

65. The National Basketball Association (NBA) recently performed a survey of fans attending a Celtics game at the Boston Garden Arena. The survey collected data on money spent on concessions at the game. Four types of respondents were identified by the survey: students under 18 years, students over 18 years, professional people, and blue-collar workers. These people, who were selected at random, were observed and the dollar volume spent on concessions at the game recorded. These data are shown as follows:

Under 18	*Over 18*	*Professional*	*Blue-Collar*
\$3.10	\$2.40	\$2.80	\$4.20
2.45	2.70	1.25	3.75
3.00	1.75	0.00	5.90
4.50	2.00	2.30	4.20
3.00	0.00	1.50	2.80
	3.00	1.20	6.20
	2.30	0.00	3.00
		2.10	4.00
		0.00	1.25
		4.10	

a. Based on these data, what should the NBA conclude about the average expenditures on concessions by the four groups represented? Test at the alpha level of 0.05.

b. If the test performed in part a concluded that there is a difference in the mean amount spent on concessions among the four groups, which groups have different means? Perform the appropriate pairwise test method. Discuss.

66. The Blainville Police Department has four patrol regions in which officers are assigned for traffic detail. The chief is interested in whether the average dollar amounts in traffic fines were different among the four regions during the previous year. To answer his question, a random sample of court records was selected for tickets issued in each of the four regions. The following data represent the dollar amounts of the fines:

Region 1	*Region 2*	*Region 3*	*Region 4*
$25.00	$18.00	$45.00	$30.00
10.00	25.00	36.00	29.00
14.50	22.00	26.00	33.00
13.00	15.00	26.00	27.00
14.00	20.00	75.00	40.00
15.00	15.00	40.00	80.00
14.00	20.00	60.00	
	10.00	30.00	
	14.00	28.00	
	17.00		
	24.00		

a. Based on the sample data, what should the chief conclude about the average fines per ticket in the four regions? Test using an alpha level of 0.05.

b. Use the appropriate method of multiple comparisons to determine which regions have different means. Write a short report to the chief describing your results and offering some explanations for the findings.

67. Weekly cash sales records have been collected for four drive-in restaurants in Topeka, Kansas, for a 6-week period, and the following data were collected.

	Drive-in			
Week	*1*	*2*	*3*	*4*
1	$1,430	$ 980	$1,780	$2,300
2	2,200	1,400	2,890	2,680
3	1,140	1,200	1,500	2,000
4	880	1,300	1,470	1,900
5	1,670	1,300	2,400	2,540
6	990	550	1,600	1,900

a. Assuming that the assumptions of a one-way ANOVA design are satisfied in this case, what should be concluded about the average sales at the four drive-in restaurants in Topeka? Use an alpha level of 0.05.

b. Discuss whether you think the assumptions of a one-way ANOVA test are satisfied in this case and indicate why or why not. If they are not, what design is appropriate? Discuss.

68. Referring to Problem 67, perform a two-way analysis of variance test using an alpha level of 0.05 to determine whether the mean sales for the four drive-ins are equal. Comment on the difference in any of the results.

69. With reference to Problem 68, determine whether the blocking on week was effective. Test at the alpha level of 0.05 and discuss what is meant by effective blocking.

70. With reference to Problems 68 and 69, use Fisher's least significant difference procedure to determine which, if any, drive-ins have different true average weekly sales.

71. The Felton City Automobile Dealers Association recently authorized an independent testing firm to study the four Felton City dealers' service facilities. One of the tests the firm conducted involved the selection of seven vehicles at random that needed repairs of various kinds. The vehicles were taken to each of the dealers, and estimates for repair costs were made without the service department knowing that the vehicle was part of the test. The following data were collected. The values represent the dollar estimates rounded to the nearest dollar for each of the seven vehicles at each of the four dealers.

Car	*Dealer 1*	*Dealer 2*	*Dealer 3*	*Dealer 4*
1	114	156	65	126
2	224	203	156	188
3	430	379	290	290
4	55	103	30	120
5	240	133	110	190
6	500	490	300	609
7	160	200	80	195

a. Based on these sample data, was the testing agency justified in using a two-way analysis of variance? Test at the alpha level of 0.05.
b. What should the testing agency conclude about the average service costs at the four dealers? State the appropriate null and alternative hypotheses and test at the alpha level of 0.05.
c. Use the LSD approach to determine which pairs of dealers have different average service costs. Write a short memo explaining your results.

72. There are three commercial tax preparing offices in Benboe, Minnesota. The local Better Business Bureau has been receiving some complaints that one of the offices does not understand tax law well enough to provide expert advice. The complaints state that to safeguard itself, the preparing office overstates the tax due by the payer and thus avoids later problems.

The Better Business Bureau has decided to invest several hundred dollars in grant money to test the claim. It has selected eight people at random and asked that they allow each of the three offices to prepare their taxes using the same information. The following data show the tax bills as figured by each preparer:

Return	*Office 1*	*Office 2*	*Office 3*
1	$ 4,376.20	$ 5,100.10	$ 4,988.03
2	5,678.45	6,234.23	5,489.23
3	2,341.78	3,342.60	2,121.90
4	9.875.33	10,300.30	9,845.60
5	7,650.20	8,002.90	7,590.88
6	1,324.80	1,450.90	1,356.89
7	2,345.90	2,356.90	2,345.90
8	15,468.75	16,080.78	15,376.70

a. Assuming that the data meet the assumptions of the one-way analysis of variance, what conclusions should be made about the difference in average taxes figured by the three offices? Test at the alpha level of 0.05.
b. Recognizing that the design is a blocked design, determine whether blocking was effective. Test at the alpha level of 0.05.
c. What conclusions should be reached with respect to the average tax computed by the three offices? Test using an alpha level of 0.05. Discuss.
d. Determine which, if any, of the offices have different mean tax computations and write a short report outlining the position the Better Business Bureau should take in this case.

DATABASE PROBLEMS

The following questions and problems pertain directly to the State Department of Transportation case study and database introduced in Chapter 1. The questions and problems were written assuming that you will have access to a computer and appropriate statistical software. The database containing 100 observations and seventeen variables is shown in Table 1-1 in Chapter 1. *Assume that the data were collected using a simple random sampling process.*

1. Herb Kriner attended a conference last fall that indicated that female drivers tended to be relatively less variable in the number of convictions (X_5) than male drivers. He would like you to test this claim at the $\alpha = 0.05$ level and prepare a short letter confirming or rejecting the claim based on the sample information from this state. Indicate whether your conclusion can be applied to other states and indicate why or why not.

2. Herb Kriner would like you to test the hypothesis that there is no difference in average years of education for drivers with various employment statuses. Test using an $\alpha = 0.05$ level.

3. Use analysis of variance to test whether there is a difference in average age of male versus female drivers in this state. Then do the same test using a two-sample t test. Compare the results and write a short memo that discusses the relationship between the two approaches.

4. Considering only those drivers who have insured vehicles, is there a difference in average years lived in the state depending on their knowledge of the law? Test at the $\alpha = 0.05$ level and discuss your results.

ADDITIONAL DATABASE PROBLEMS

The questions and problems in this section reference the various databases that accompany this text and which are described in Chapter 1. Your instructor has been provided a diskette with these databases. It is expected that you will be using computer software to access these data and to perform the required calculations and graphs.

DATABASE: **CITIES** *(Refer to the database description in Chapter 1.)*

1. Create a new variable, X_9, which is coded 1 if the labor market stress index is between 100 and 110 inclusive, 2 if the index is between 111 and 120 inclusive, and 3 if it is higher than 120.
   a. Test the hypothesis that there is no difference in average 1989 unemployment rates for cities with the three different labor market stress index levels. Use an $\alpha = 0.05$ level to test the hypothesis. Make sure you state the null and alternative hypotheses and show the appropriate test results.
   b. If it is appropriate, use either Tukey's or Scheffé's (you determine which one) multiple comparison procedure to determine which populations have different means.
2. Suppose it has been claimed that the annual earnings for manufacturing workers is more variable than the earnings for white-collar workers. Assuming that the data represent random samples from the two populations, test the appropriate null and alternative hypotheses at the $\alpha = 0.05$ level. Discuss your conclusions.

DATABASE: **FAST100** *(Refer to the database description in Chapter 1.)*

1. Use the sample data in this database to determine whether there is any difference in the average total sales over the previous four quarters for companies trading on the three stock exchanges. State the appropriate null and alternative hypotheses. If the null hypothesis is rejected, use the appropriate method of multiple comparison to determine which populations have different means. Discuss your results. Test at the $\alpha = 0.05$ level.
2. Based on these sample data, is there a difference in average stock price as of 9/6/91 for companies trading on the three stock exchanges? Assume that these data reflect random samples from the three stock exchanges. Test at the $\alpha = 0.10$ level. If the null hypothesis is rejected, use the appropriate multiple comparison test to determine which populations have different means.
3. Based on these sample data, is there a difference in average price earnings ratio over the past four quarters for companies trading on the three stock exchanges? Assume that these data reflect random samples from the three stock exchanges. Test at the $\alpha = 0.05$ level. If the null hypothesis is rejected, use the appropriate multiple comparison test to determine which populations have different means.

DATABASE: **PACRIM** *(Refer to the database description in Chapter 1.)*

1. Based on these sample data, can it be concluded that there is a difference in average 1989 annual sales (X_2) for companies located in Japan, South Korea, or Australia? Test the appropriate null and alternative hypotheses at the $\alpha = 0.05$ level. Be sure to discuss your conclusions. If the null hypothesis is

rejected, use the appropriate method of multiple comparison to determine which countries have different average sales in 1989.

2. Based on these sample data, can it be concluded that there is a difference in average year-end stockholder's equity for companies located in Japan, South Korea, and Australia? Test the appropriate null and alternative hypotheses at the $\alpha = 0.05$ level. Be sure to discuss your conclusions. If the null hypothesis is rejected, use the appropriate method of multiple comparison to determine which countries have different means.
3. Group the data from Taiwan, Malaysia, and New Zealand together. Can these data be used to show that there is a significant difference in average number of employees for companies in Japan, Australia, South Korea, or the combined countries? Test at the $\alpha = 0.05$ level. Use the appropriate method of multiple comparison to determine which countries have different population means. Discuss your results.

DATABASE: **TRUCKS** (*Refer to the database description in Chapter 1.*)

1. Based on the sample data, is there a difference in average WIM gross weight for trucks weighed in the different months? State the appropriate null and alternative hypotheses and test at the $\alpha = 0.05$ level.
2. Break the data into three groups based on vehicle speed, as follows:

   Group 1: Under 35 mph
   Group 2: 35–45 mph
   Group 3: 46–55 mph
   Group 4: Over 45 mph

   Based on these sample data, can it be concluded that there is no difference in mean POE gross weight for trucks traveling at the four different speeds? Test using an $\alpha = 0.05$ level. If a difference is detected through the ANOVA test, then use the appropriate method of multiple comparison to determine which groups have different means.
3. Suppose it has been stated by representatives of the Idaho transportation department that there is no difference in the variation of gross vehicle weights on the WIM scale or the POE scale. Based on these sample data, can this statement be supported or refuted? State the appropriate null and alternative hypotheses and test at the $\alpha = 0.05$ level. Discuss your results.

CASES

12-A Consumer Information Association

Yolanda Carson is a newly hired research assistant for the Consumer Information Association. The association is a nonprofit group whose major purpose is to supply information necessary to help consumers make better-informed decisions. Yolanda has been assigned to work with the group studying consumer practices in the banking industry.

Yolanda is aware of studies that indicate that the interest banks charge for loans is related to demographic factors such as the size of the city in which the banks are located and whether the state allows branch banks. She has been asked to determine whether there is a difference in consumer loan charges between major sections of the country.

Yolanda has been assured the cooperation of the American Banking Institute and has been given access to any data the institute has. However, she knows that loan charges may depend on many factors and feels compelled to study banks firsthand. In particular, she has decided to randomly select banks in all parts of the country and apply for an automobile loan at each bank selected. She has decided to make the test during two time periods 6 months apart.

Since consumer interest rates have been changing rapidly lately, Yolanda has recorded all rates in terms of the prime rate plus a certain percentage. (The prime rate is the rate large banks charge their largest corporate customers.) In the first test, Yolanda found the following values charged:

Northeast	*Southeast*	*Midwest*	*West*
Prime + 3.2%	Prime + 2.7%	Prime + 3.4%	Prime + 3.7%
2.9	2.9	3.5	3.6
2.8	3.0	2.9	3.6
3.5	2.9	3.7	3.9
3.4	2.8	3.4	4.0
4.0	2.5	3.5	3.8
3.2	2.7	3.0	3.4
	2.9		3.8

The executive director of the Consumer Information Association is going to be holding a news conference in a few days to discuss the work the organization has been doing. He would like to be able to cite Yolanda's study as an example of its services.

12B West Coast Bell System

James Todd is the recently appointed Director of Employee Benefits for West Coast Bell, a regional telephone system. The West Coast Bell medical benefits system insures over 60,000 employees and dependents and over the last 5 years its medical costs have been increasing by over 20% annually. James knows that many companies, when facing these annual increases, have tried to pass some of the medical costs to their employees, generally by increasing the deductible allowance for each treatment visit. He has decided to look into the possibility of developing a managed-care network.

Managed-care networks are a recent development in health care. They involve a company contracting with a group of physicians and hospitals to provide a variety of health care services. The company monitors the cost of the care provided to its employees and holds discussions with those whose costs are high. In some cases, the relationship between the company and either a hospital or physician will be terminated. Some companies using managed-care networks have held their health care cost increases to less than one-third of the previous levels.

James Todd has recently read a study that reported on the cost of an operation to clear a patient's heart arteries. One hospital in Kansas City charged over $5,000 for the operation while a second, also in Kansas City, charged less than $3,000. James decided to use this operation to determine whether categories of hospitals tended to charge less for procedures. The four categories of hospitals he identified were as follows: university-related, religious affiliated, municipally owned, and profit-making. He contacted ten hospitals on the West Coast in each category, asking what they charged for this operation. Not all responded, and some who did provided data that could not readily be compared with that provided by the majority of respondents. The reported costs are shown, as follows:

University-Related	*Religious Affiliated*	*Municipally Owned*	*Profit-Making*
$6,120	$4,010	$4,320	$5,100
5,960	3,770	4,650	4,920
6,300	3,960	4,575	5,200
6,500	3,620	4,440	5,345
6,250	3,280	4,900	4,875
6,695	3,680	4,560	5,330
6,475	3,350	4,610	5,415
6,250	3,250	4,850	5,150
6,880	3,400		5,380
6,550			

Several coworkers have told James they would prefer going to a university hospital since they think the staff is more up-to-date on new medical procedures. While James may agree with that concensus for some newer treatments, he does not agree with it for established procedures. He is wondering whether his recently gathered cost data should lead him to consider one group of hospitals over the other for certain categories of procedures.

12C American Testing Services

When P. T. Miller formed American Testing Services he anticipated that there was a market for consulting services in the market-research area. By the amount of work that his firm has had during the past 3 years, he is sure he was correct.

Recently P. T. was approached by the Convestal Corporation to perform an analysis of the five running shoes Convestal makes. The basic research question to be answered was whether people who own Convestal running shoes share an equal opinion (on the average) of the shoes without regard to the particular type or style of Convestal shoe they own. If not, then the company wants to determine which styles seem to be most liked, and which seem to be most disliked, by the customers.

P. T. suggested that Convestal ask a random sample of shoe customers to rate their shoes on a scale of 1 to 100, with 100 being the highest. The following data represent the results of the sampling:

Style 1	*Style 2*	*Style 3*	*Style 4*	*Style 5*
84	67	78	60	88
54	56	79	64	79
88	70	89	60	84
90	67	84	72	78
88	59	78	77	68
76	66	84	70	70
	70	90	66	80
	56	85	70	80
	70		59	78
	67		70	84
				75

What should P. T. Miller conclude?

REFERENCES

Berenson, Mark L., and Levine, David M. *Basic Business Statistics Concepts and Applications,* 5th edition. Englewood Cliffs, New Jersey: Prentice-Hall, 1992.

Bowerman, Bruce L., and O'Connell, Richard T. *Linear Statistical Models,* 2nd edition. Boston: PWS-Kent, 1990.

Daniel, Wayne W., and Terrell, James C. *Business Statistics for Management and Economics,* 6th edition. Boston: Houghton Mifflin, 1992.

Iman, Ronald L., and Conover, W. J. *Modern Business Statistics,* 2nd edition. New York: Wiley, 1989.

Levin, Richard I., and Rubin, David S. *Statistics for Management,* 5th edition. Englewood Cliffs, New Jersey: Prentice-Hall, 1991.

Chapter 12

Hand-In Exercises

1. Problem 22 in chapter 12 provides the following data on consumers rating of beef-steak samples from their grades of beef. Use ANOVA to test the hypothesis that means of the three samples are equal.

a. State the null and alternative hypotheses.

b. Complete calculations in the following table to test the hypothesis at the 5% level. State your decision and conclusion at the end of the problem.

Choice	Standard	Economy
78	67	65
87	80	62
90	78	70
87	80	66
89	67	70
90	70	73

ANOVA Summary Table

Source	S.S.	D.F.	M.S.	F

2. Referring to Problem 55 in Chapter 12 we observe the following data:

Step a. Perform a two sample test of means on the data using the 5% level. Show calculations in part (a) below.

Step b. Perform an ANOVA test of means on the same data, also using the 5% level.
Show calculations in part (b) below.

Step c. Are results from the two methods consistent? Answer "yes" or "no" and elaborate on your answer in part (c) below.

Chair Lift 1	Chair Lift 2
10	14
3	13
14	19
7	7
19	11
33	9
28	12
11	13
26	15

a. To complete part (a) show each step in a two sample hypothesis test.

b. To complete part (b) do the ANOVA Summary Table and state a decision and conclusion.

ANOVA Summary Table

Source	S.S.	D.F.	M.S.	F

c. Comment on the consistency of the two methods.

Simple Linear Regression and Correlation Analysis

WHY DECISION MAKERS NEED TO KNOW

The statistical techniques discussed thus far have all dealt with a single variable. For example, in Chapter 8, where the fundamentals of statistical estimation were introduced, decision makers were interested in estimating values such as the average weight of a can of corn or the average income of families in a certain geographical area. Chapters 9 through 12 introduced the basic concepts of hypothesis testing. Again the hypothesis involved a single variable from one or more populations.

Although many business applications involve only one variable, in other instances decision makers need to consider the relationship between two or more variables. For example, the sales manager for a tool company may notice his sales are not the same each month. He also knows that the company's advertising expenditures vary from month to month. This manager would likely be interested in learning whether a relationship exists between tool sales and advertising. If he could successfully define the relationship, he might use this information to improve predictions of monthly sales and, therefore, do a better job of planning for his company.

This chapter introduces simple linear regression and correlation analysis. These techniques are important to decision makers who need to determine the relationship between two variables. Regression and correlation analysis are two of the most often applied statistical tools for decision making.

CHAPTER OBJECTIVES

This chapter will introduce simple linear regression and correlation techniques. Examples will be used to demonstrate the uses of regression analysis for prediction and description.

This chapter will also show how decision makers can determine whether a significant linear relationship exists between two variables. It shows how to determine whether regression analysis is actually useful in a practical decision-making situation. In addition, it shows how to develop confidence intervals for the estimates made using regression analysis.

Finally, this chapter will introduce the assumptions behind regression analysis and discuss some problems that might occur if regression analysis is incorrectly used.

STUDENT OBJECTIVES

After studying the material in this chapter, you should be able to do the following:

1. Calculate the simple correlation between two variables.
2. Determine whether the correlation is significant.
3. Calculate the simple linear regression equation for a set of data and know the basic assumptions behind regression analysis.
4. Determine whether a regression model is significant.
5. Develop confidence intervals for the regression coefficients.
6. Interpret the confidence intervals for the regression coefficients.
7. Recognize regression analysis applications for purposes of prediction and description.
8. Recognize some potential problems if regression analysis is used incorrectly.
9. Recognize several nonlinear relationships between two variables and be able to introduce the appropriate transformation to apply linear-regression analysis.

13-1 STATISTICAL RELATIONSHIPS BETWEEN TWO VARIABLES

Carl Markowitz has just completed his first year as director of personnel for Software Accessories, a company that specializes in developing and marketing computer packages for small businesses, such as dry cleaners and gas service stations. These smaller companies have mostly been neglected by the larger software development firms. While Software Accessories has been profitable, Carl has been concerned about the rapid turnover in its sales force and has implemented an exit interview procedure for departing sales men and women. In the course of these interviews, he discovered a major concern with the perceived fairness of the wage structure.

Software Accessories has a two-part wage structure, a base salary and a commission based on quarterly sales. On the average, about half of the total wages paid come from the base salary but some people do much better with commissions than others. The idea behind having such a large percentage of total wages associated with commissions is to allow people who want to sell to make the most money. The concern expressed by departing employees is that the training provided on the company's products is so minimal that starting employees cannot make an adequate wage for several years until they learn the product line through experience. Consequently, those with family responsibilities are forced to look for other opportunities.

Carl has decided to look at the relationship between total yearly sales and years with the company. He gathers data from a sample of twelve sales representatives. These data are shown in Table 13-1. By looking at the sample data, Carl is convinced that a relationship exists between total sales and years with the company. He needs to determine what the relationship will tell him.

Figure 13-1 (page 656) shows **scatter plots** that depict several potential relationships between a dependent variable, *Y*, and an independent variable, *X*. A **dependent variable** is the variable whose variation we wish to explain. An **independent variable** is a variable used to explain variation in the dependent variable. For the Software Accessories example, years with the company is the independent variable and total sales the dependent variable. Figures 13-1(a) and (b) are examples of *linear* relationships between *X* and *Y*. This means that as the independent variable, *X*, changes, the dependent variable, *Y*, tends to change systematically in a straight-line manner. Note that this systematic change can be positive (*Y* increases as *X* increases) or negative (*Y* decreases as *X* increases). Also notice that the points do not need to fall exactly on a straight line for a linear relationship to be exhibited.

TABLE 13-1

Sales Representative Data for the Software Accessories Example

Years With Company	Total Sales ($ thousands)
3	487
5	445
2	272
8	641
2	187
6	440
7	346
1	238
4	312
2	269
9	655
6	563

FIGURE 13-1

Two-Variable Relationships

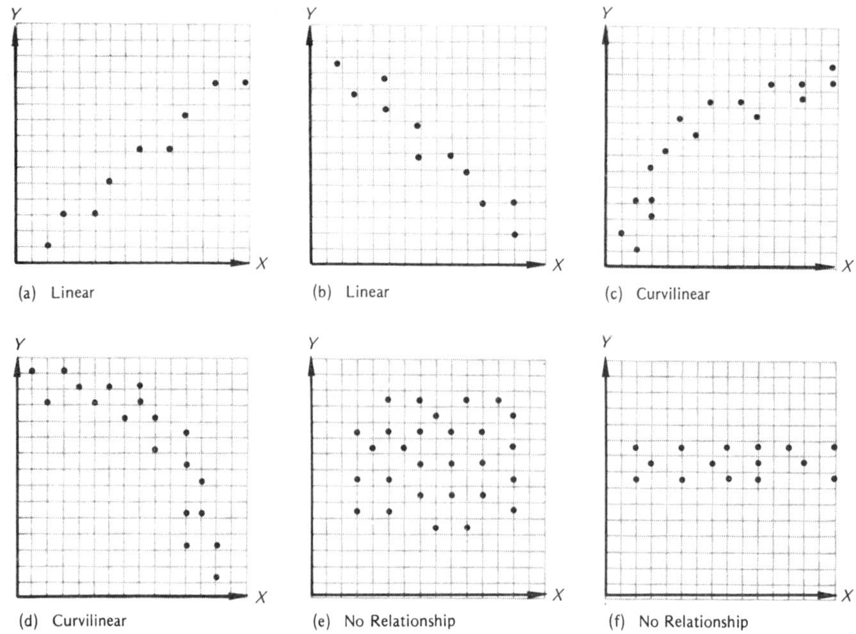

Figures 13-1(c) and (d) are examples of *curvilinear* statistical relationships between variables X and Y. Figures 13-1(e) and (f) are examples showing *no relationship* between X and Y. That is, when X increases, sometimes Y decreases and other times Y increases.

The three situations shown in Figure 13-1 are all possibilities for describing the relationship between sales and advertising for Software Accessories. The first step in determining the appropriate relationship is to plot the data shown in Table 13-1. This plot, shown in Figure 13-2, indicates that total sales and years with the company are related. However, the strength of this relationship is questionable.

FIGURE 13-2

Plot of Sales Versus Years with the Company for the Software Accessories Example

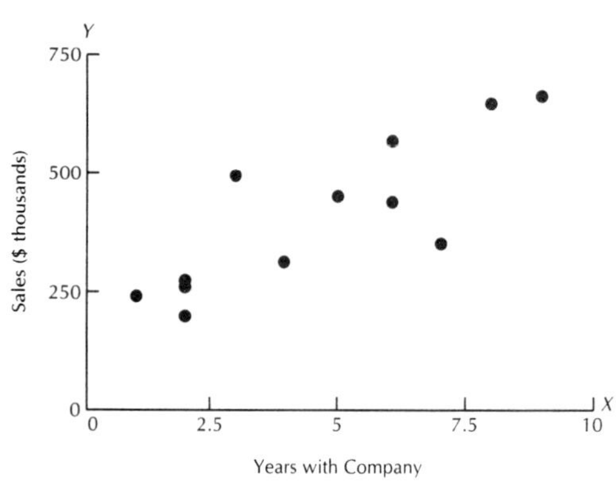

That is, how close do the points come to falling on a straight line? The scatter plot provides a visualization for the answer to this question, but we also need a quantitative measure of the strength of the linear relationship between two variables. The next section introduces a measure called the *correlation coefficient.*

SKILL DEVELOPMENT PROBLEMS FOR **SECTION 13-1**

The following exercises will help you learn the concepts presented in Section 13-1.

1. Develop a scatter plot for the following data:

Y	X
100	88
200	120
150	200
75	100
140	100
160	90
230	125

Based on the scatter plot, describe what, if any, relationship exists between these two variables.

2. Develop scatter plots for the variable Y against variables X_1 and X_2.

Y	X_1	X_2
25	4	7
29	3	9
40	1	13
20	6	6
24	5	8
18	7	5
30	3	11
25	3	5

Describe what, if any, relationship is present in each of the scatter plots.

3. If two variables have a negative linear relationship, what will the value of X tend to do when the corresponding value of Y increases substantially? Show with an example.

4. If the scatter plot of two variables shows a weak positive linear relationship, what will be the general change in Y associated with a downward change in X? Show with an example.

5. If a scatter plot shows that two variables have a curvilinear relationship showing Y increasing at a decreasing rate as X increases, what might the scatter plot look like? Can you think of two variables that might exhibit such a relationship?

13-2 CORRELATION ANALYSIS

The quantitative measure of strength in the linear relationship between two variables is called the **simple correlation coefficient.** The correlation coefficient for two variables (in the case of Software Accessories, sales and years with the company) can be estimated from sample data using equation 13-1:

$$r = \frac{\Sigma(X - \overline{X})(Y - \overline{Y})}{\sqrt{[\Sigma(X - \overline{X})^2][\Sigma(Y - \overline{Y})^2]}} \tag{13-1}$$

or by using an algebraic equivalent formula (equation 13-2) more suited to calculators:

$$r = \frac{n\Sigma XY - \Sigma X\Sigma Y}{\sqrt{[n(\Sigma X^2) - (\Sigma X)^2][n(\Sigma Y^2) - (\Sigma Y)^2]}} \tag{13-2}$$

where

r = Simple correlation coefficient

n = Sample size

X = Value of the independent variable

Y = Value of the dependent variable

The correlation coefficient can range from a perfect positive correlation, +1.0, to a perfect negative correlation, −1.0. If two variables have no linear relationship, the correlation between them is 0. Consequently, the more the correlation differs from 0, the stronger the linear relationship between the two variables. The sign of the correlation coefficient indicates the direction of the relationship, but does not aid in determining the strength.

Figure 13-3 illustrates some possible correlations between two variables. Note that for the correlation coefficient to equal plus or minus 1.0, all the (X, Y) points must be perfectly aligned. The more the points depart from a straight line, the weaker (closer to 0.0) the correlation between the two variables.

The scatter plot of sales and years with company for Software Accessories (Figure 13-2) indicates a *positive* linear relationship, but *not* a *perfect* linear relationship. Table 13-2 lists the calculations necessary to determine the correlation coefficient. The calculated correlation coefficient, r, is 0.8325.

FIGURE 13-3

Correlations Between Two Variables

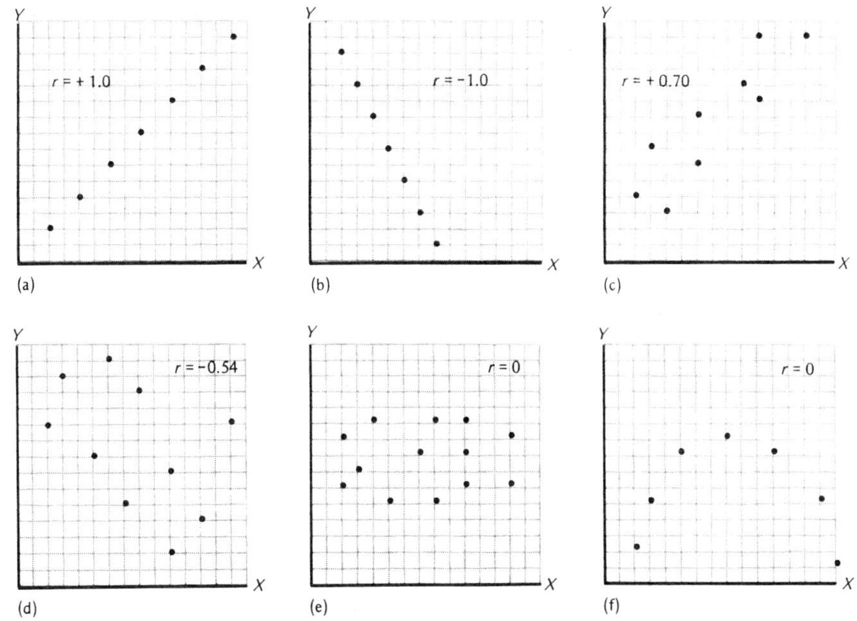

TABLE 13-2

Correlation Coefficient Calculations for the Software Accessories Example

Sales Y	Years X	YX	Y^2	X^2
487	3	1,461	237,169	9
445	5	2,225	198,025	25
272	2	544	73,984	4
641	8	5,128	410,881	64
187	2	374	34,969	4
440	6	2,640	193,600	36
346	7	2,422	119,716	49
238	1	238	56,644	1
312	4	1,248	97,344	16
269	2	538	72,361	4
655	9	5,895	429,025	81
563	6	3,378	316,969	36
$\Sigma = 4{,}855$	$\Sigma = 55$	$\Sigma = 26{,}091$	$\Sigma = 2{,}240{,}687$	$\Sigma = 329$

$$r = \frac{n\Sigma XY - \Sigma X \Sigma Y}{\sqrt{[n(\Sigma X^2) - (\Sigma X)^2][n(\Sigma Y^2) - (\Sigma Y)^2]}}$$

$$= \frac{12(26{,}091) - (55)(4{,}855)}{\sqrt{[12(329) - (55)^2][12(2{,}240{,}687) - (4{,}855)^2]}}$$

$$= 0.8325$$

Although a correlation coefficient of 0.8325 seems quite high (relative to 0), remember that this value is based on a sample of twelve data points and there is always a chance that the sample may provide misleading information due to extreme sampling error. To determine whether the linear relationship between sales and years with the company is significant, we must test whether the sample data support or refute the hypothesis that the population correlation coefficient, ρ, is 0. The hypothesis that the population correlation coefficient is 0 is tested by computing the t statistic, using equation 13-3:

$$t = \frac{r}{\sqrt{\frac{1 - r^2}{n - 2}}} \quad \text{(13-3)}$$

where

t = Number of standard deviations r is from 0

r = Simple correlation coefficient

n = Sample size

The degrees of freedom for this test are $n - 2$.

Figure 13-4 shows the test for an alpha level of 0.05. Based on these sample data, we should conclude there is a significant linear relationship between years of experience and total sales for Software Accessories sales representatives.

The t test for determining whether the population correlation is significantly different from 0 assumes that the data are interval or ratio level and that two variables (Y and X) are distributed as a *bivariate normal.* Although the formal mathematical representation is beyond the scope of this text, *two variables are bivariate normal if their joint distribution is normally distributed.* Although the t test assumes a bivariate normal distribution, it is robust—that is, correct inferences can be reached even with slight departures from the normal-distribution assumption. (See Neter and Wasserman's *Applied Linear Statistical Models* for further discussion of bivariate normal distributions.)

CAUSE-AND-EFFECT INTERPRETATIONS

Care must be used when interpreting the correlation results. Even though we found a significant linear relationship between years experience and sales for the Software Accessories sales force, the correlation does not imply cause and effect.

FIGURE 13-4

Correlation Significance Test for the Software Accessories Example

Hypotheses:

H_0: $\rho = 0$
H_A: $\rho \neq 0$

$\alpha = 0.05$

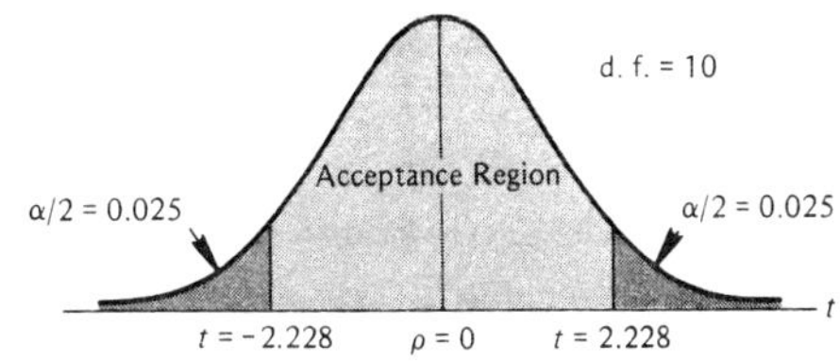

Decision Rule:

If $t > t_{\text{critical}} = 2.228$, reject H_0.
If $t < t_{\text{critical}} = -2.228$, reject H_0.
Otherwise, do not reject H_0.

Since $4.752 > 2.228$, reject H_0.
The calculated t value is

$$t = \frac{r}{\sqrt{\dfrac{1 - r^2}{n - 2}}} = \frac{0.8325}{\sqrt{\dfrac{1 - 0.6931}{10}}}$$
$$= 4.752$$

Although a change in experience may, in fact, cause sales to change, simply because the two variables are correlated does not guarantee a cause-and-effect situation. Two seemingly unconnected variables will often be highly correlated. For example, over a period of time, teachers' salaries in North Dakota might be highly correlated with the price of grapes in Spain. Yet, we doubt that a change in grape prices will *cause* a corresponding change in salaries for teachers in North Dakota, or vice versa. When a correlation exists between two seemingly unrelated variables, the correlation is **spurious.** You should take great care to avoid basing conclusions on spurious correlations.

Carl Markowitz has a logical reason to believe that years experience with the company and total sales are related. That is, sales theory and customer feedback hold that product knowledge is a major component in successfully marketing a product. However, a statistically significant correlation alone does not prove that this cause-and-effect relationship exists.

SKILL DEVELOPMENT PROBLEMS FOR **SECTION 13-2**

The following exercises will help you learn the concepts presented in Section 13-2.

6. You are given the following data for variables X and Y:

X	Y
20	16
18	12
24	18
20	17
22	21
14	10
18	10

a. Plot these variables in scatter plot format. Based on this plot, what type of relationship appears to exist between the two variables?
b. Compute the correlation coefficient for these sample data. Indicate what the correlation coefficient measures.
c. Test to determine whether the population correlation coefficient is 0. Use the $\alpha = 0.05$ level to conduct the test. Be sure to state the null and alternative hypotheses and show the test and decision rule clearly.

7. You are given the following data for variables X and Y:

X	Y
3.0	1.5
2.0	0.5
2.5	1.0
3.0	1.8
2.5	1.2
4.0	2.2
1.5	0.4
1.0	0.3
2.0	1.3
2.5	1.0

a. Plot these variables in scatter plot format. Based on this plot, what type of relationship appears to exist between the two variables?
b. Compute the correlation coefficient for these sample data. Indicate what the correlation coefficient measures.
c. Test to determine whether the population correlation coefficient is 0. Use the $\alpha = 0.05$ level to conduct the test. Be sure to state the null and alternative hypotheses and show the test and decision rule clearly.

8. You are given the following data for variables X and Y:

X	Y
100	80
110	90
90	75
100	90
110	80
80	60
90	90
90	70

a. Plot these variables in scatter plot format. Based on this plot, what type of relationship appears to exist between the two variables?
b. Compute the correlation coefficient for these sample data. Indicate what the correlation coefficient measures.
c. Test to determine whether the population correlation coefficient is 0. Use the $\alpha = 0.05$ level to conduct the test. Be sure to state the null and alternative hypotheses and show the test and decision rule clearly.

9. A sample of thirty-two people was randomly selected and height and weight measurements were made for each person. The correlation coefficient for the two variables was 0.80.
a. Discuss in your own words what the $r = 0.80$ means with respect to the variables height and weight.
b. Using an $\alpha = 0.10$ level, test to determine whether the population correlation coefficient is significantly different from 0. Be sure to state the null and alternative hypotheses.

10. A random sample of fifty bank accounts was selected from a local branch bank. The account balance and the number of deposits and withdrawals during the past month were the two variables recorded. The correlation coefficient for the two variables was -0.23.
a. Discuss what the $r = -0.23$ measures. Make sure to frame your discussion in terms of the two variables discussed here.
b. Using an $\alpha = 0.05$ level, test to determine whether there is a significant linear relationship between account balance and the number of transactions to the account during the past month. State the null and alternative hypotheses and show the decision rule.

11. Suppose it has been determined that the number of new workers hired per week in your county has a high positive correlation with the average weekly temperature. Is it safe to conclude that an increase in temperature causes an increase in the number of the new hires? Discuss.

13-3 SIMPLE LINEAR REGRESSION ANALYSIS

Carl Markowitz has determined that the relationship between years experience with Software Accessories and total sales is linear, and statistically significant, based on the correlation analysis performed in the previous section. Since hiring and training costs have been increasing, he would like to use this relationship to help formulate a more acceptable wage package for the sales force.

The statistical method Carl uses to analyze the relationship between years experience and total sales is *regression analysis.* Where there are only two variables, a dependent variable such as sales and an independent variable such as years with the company, the technique is **simple regression analysis.** When the relationship between the dependent variable and the independent variable is linear, the technique is *simple linear regression.*

The objective of simple linear regression (which we shall call regression analysis) is to represent the relationship between X and Y with a model of the form shown in equation 13-4:

$$Y_i = \beta_0 + \beta_1 X_i + e_i \qquad \text{(13-4)}$$

where

Y_i = Value of the dependent variable

X_i = Value of the independent variable

β_0 = Y-intercept

β_1 = Slope of the regression line

e_i = Error term, or residual (i.e., the difference between the actual Y value and the value of Y predicted by the model)

The simple linear regression model described in equation 13-4 has four assumptions:

1. Individual values of the dependent variable, Y, are statistically independent of one another.
2. For a given X value, there can exist many values of Y. Further, the distribution of possible Y values for any X value is normal.
3. The distributions of possible Y values have equal variances for all values of X.

FIGURE 13-5

Graphical Display of Linear Regression Assumptions

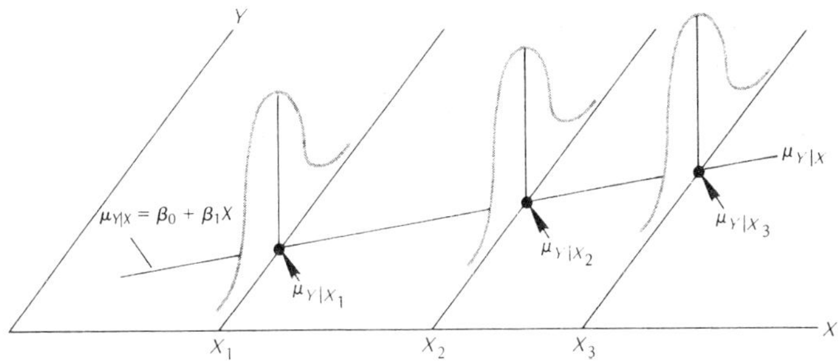

4. The means of the dependent variable, Y, for all specified values of the independent variable, ($\mu_{Y|X}$), can be connected by a straight line called the *population regression model.*

Figure 13-5 illustrates assumptions 2, 3, and 4. The regression model (straight line) connects the averages of Y for each level of the independent variable, X. The regression line (like any other straight line) is determined by two values, β_0 and β_1. These values are the **regression coefficients.** Value β_0 identifies the Y-intercept and β_1 the slope of the regression line. Under the regression assumptions, the coefficients define the true population model. For each observation, the actual value of the dependent variable, Y, for any X, is the sum of two components, as shown by equation 13-5:

$$Y_i = \underbrace{\beta_0 + \beta_1 X_i}_{\text{Linear component}} + \underbrace{e_i}_{\text{Random error component}} \quad (13\text{-}5)$$

The random error component, e_i, may be positive or negative, depending on whether a single value of Y for a given X falls above or below the regression line.

MEANING OF THE REGRESSION COEFFICIENTS

Coefficient β_1, the slope of the regression line, measures the average change in the dependent variable, Y, for each unit change in X. The slope can be either positive or negative, depending on the relationship between X and Y. For example, a positive slope of 12 ($\beta_1 = 12$) means that for a one-unit increase in X, we can expect an average twelve-unit increase in Y. Correspondingly, if the slope is negative 12 ($\beta_1 = -12$), we can expect an average decrease of twelve units in Y for a one-unit increase in X.

The Y-intercept, β_0, indicates the mean value of Y when X is 0. However, this interpretation holds only if the population could have X values of 0. When this cannot occur, β_0 does not have a meaningful interpretation in the regression model.

Carl Markowitz of Software Accessories has a sample of twelve sales representatives' data available, and he has been able to establish a significant linear relationship between years experience and total sales using correlation analysis. Now he would like to estimate the *true* linear relationship between years experience and sales by determining the regression model for the twelve data points.

Figure 13-6 shows the scatter plot for years with the company and sales. Carl needs to use the sample points to estimate β_0 and β_1, the true intercept and slope of the line representing the relationship between the two variables. Statistical theory shows that the best estimates for β_0 and β_1 are the intercept and slope formed from the available sample data. Thus, the *regression line* through the sample data is the estimate of the population regression line. However, there are an infinite number of possible regression lines for a set of points. For example, Figure 13-7 shows three different lines that pass through Software Accessories sales representative experience and sales points. These are but a few of the lines that could have been drawn. Which line should be used to estimate the true regression model?

FIGURE 13-6

Plot of Sales Versus Years with Company for the Software Accessories Example

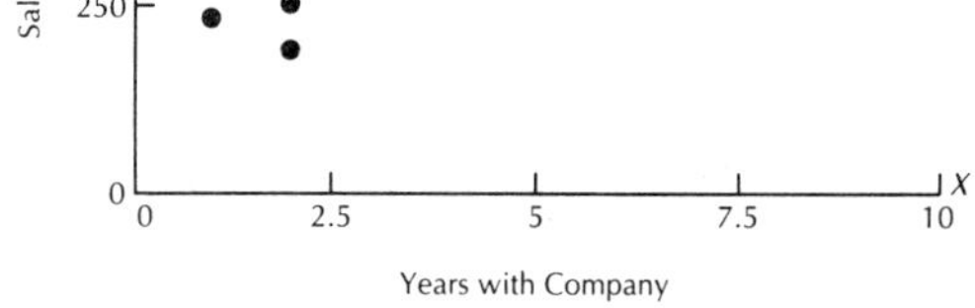

Since so many possible regression lines exist for a sample of data, we must establish a criterion for selecting the best line. The criterion used is the *least squares criterion.* According to the **least squares criterion,** the best regression line is the one that minimizes the sum of squared distances between the observed (X, Y) points and the regression line. Note that the distance between an (X, Y) point and the regression line is called the *residual* or error.

FIGURE 13-7

Potential Regression Lines for the Software Accessories Example

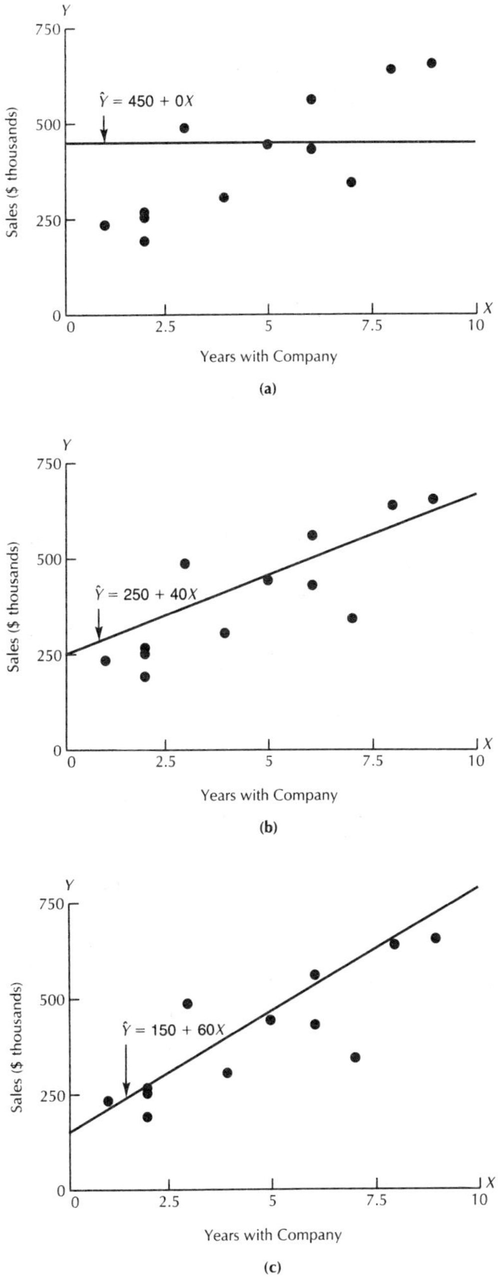

FIGURE 13-8

Computation of Regression Error for the Software Accessories Example

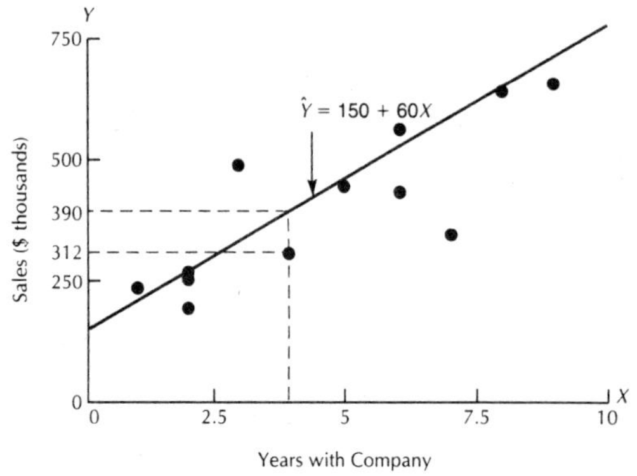

Figure 13-8 shows how the error is calculated when X equals 4 years and the regression line is $\hat{Y} = 150 + 60X$ (where $\hat{Y}$ is the estimated sales value). Notice that when $X = 4$, the difference between the regression line value, $\hat{Y} = 390$, and the observed, $Y = 312$, is 78. Thus, the residual for this line when $X = 4$ is 78.

Table 13-3 shows the calculated errors and sum of squared errors for each of the three regression lines shown in Figure 13-7. Of these three potential regression models, the line with the equation $\hat{Y} = 150 + 60X$ has the smallest sum of squared errors. However, is this line the best of all possible lines? That is, would

$$\sum_{i=1}^{n} (Y_i - \hat{Y}_i)^2 = 97{,}667$$

be smaller than for any other line? One way to determine this is to calculate the sum of squared errors for other regression lines. However, since there are an infinite number of these lines, this approach is not feasible. Fortunately, through the use of calculus, equations can be derived to directly determine the slope and intercept estimates such that $\Sigma(Y_i - \hat{Y})^2$ is minimized.

Let the estimated regression model be of the form shown in equation 13-6:

$$\hat{Y}_i = b_0 + b_1 X_i \qquad \textbf{(13-6)}$$

where

$\hat{Y}_i$ = Estimated, or predicted, Y value

b_0 = Unbiased estimate of the regression intercept

b_1 = Unbiased estimate of the regression slope

X_i = Value of the independent variable

TABLE 13-3

Sum of Squared Errors for Three Linear Equations for Software Accessories Example

From Figure 13-7(a): $\hat{Y} = 450 + 0X$

X	$\hat{Y}$	Y	$Y - \hat{Y}$	$(Y - \hat{Y})^2$
3	450	487	37	1,369
5	450	445	−5	25
2	450	272	−178	31,684
8	450	641	191	36,481
2	450	187	−263	69,169
6	450	440	−10	100
7	450	346	−104	10,816
1	450	238	−212	44,944
4	450	312	−138	19,044
2	450	269	−181	32,761
9	450	655	205	42,025
6	450	563	113	12,769
				Σ = 301,187

From Figure 13-7(b): $\hat{Y} = 250 + 40X$

X	$\hat{Y}$	Y	$Y - \hat{Y}$	$(Y - \hat{Y})^2$
3	370	487	117	13,689
5	450	445	−5	25
2	330	272	−58	3,364
8	570	641	71	5,041
2	330	187	−143	20,449
6	490	440	−50	2,500
7	530	346	−184	33,856
1	290	238	−52	2,704
4	410	312	−98	9,604
2	330	269	−61	3,721
9	610	655	45	2,025
6	490	563	73	5,329
				Σ = 102,307

From Figure 13-7(c): $\hat{Y} = 150 + 60X$

X	$\hat{Y}$	Y	$Y - \hat{Y}$	$(Y - \hat{Y})^2$
3	330	487	157	24,649
5	450	445	−5	25
2	270	272	2	4
8	630	641	11	121
2	270	187	−83	6,889
6	510	440	−70	4,900
7	570	346	−224	50,176
1	210	238	28	784
4	390	312	−78	6,084
2	270	269	−1	1
9	690	655	−35	1,225
6	510	563	53	2,809
				Σ = 97,667

Then the values of b_0 and b_1 are calculated by equations 13-7, 13-8, and 13-9:[1]

$$b_1 = \frac{\Sigma (X - \overline{X})(Y - \overline{Y})}{\Sigma (X - \overline{X})^2} \qquad \text{13-7}$$

$$b_1 = \frac{\Sigma XY - \dfrac{\Sigma X \Sigma Y}{n}}{\Sigma X^2 - \dfrac{(\Sigma X)^2}{n}} \qquad \text{13-8}$$

and

$$b_0 = \overline{Y} - b_1\overline{X} \qquad \text{13-9}$$

Table 13-4 shows the calculations necessary to estimate the population line for Software Accessories. In this case, the best regression line, given the least squares criterion is

$$\hat{Y}_i = 175.8289 + 49.9101X_i$$

Table 13-5 shows the predicted sales values and the errors and squared errors associated with this best regression line. The errors are called **residuals.** From Table 13-5, the sum of the squared residuals is 84,834.29. This is the smallest sum of squared residuals possible. Any other regression line through these twelve (X, Y) points will produce a larger sum of squared residuals.

Figure 13-9 (page 672) shows the scatter plot of sales and years experience and the least squares regression line for Software Accessories.

LEAST SQUARES REGRESSION PROPERTIES

Table 13-5 and Figure 13-9 illustrate several important properties of least squares regression:

1. The sum of the residuals from the least squares regression line is 0 (equation 13-10):

$$\sum_{i=1}^{n} (Y_i - \hat{Y}_i) = 0 \qquad \text{13-10}$$

[1] The derivation of these least squares regression values for b_0 and b_1 is presented in a technical appendix at the end of this chapter.

TABLE 13-4

Calculations for Least Squares Regression Coefficients for the Software Accessories Example

Y	X	YX	X^2
487	3	1,461	9
445	5	2,225	25
272	2	544	4
641	8	5,128	64
187	2	374	4
440	6	2,640	36
346	7	2,422	49
238	1	238	1
312	4	1,248	16
269	2	538	4
655	9	5,895	81
563	6	3,378	36
Σ = 4,855	Σ = 55	Σ = 26,091	Σ = 329

$$b_1 = \frac{\Sigma XY - \dfrac{\Sigma X \Sigma Y}{n}}{\Sigma X^2 - \dfrac{(\Sigma X)^2}{n}} = \frac{26{,}091 - \dfrac{(55)(4{,}855)}{12}}{329 - \dfrac{(55)^2}{12}}$$

$$= 49.9101$$

Then,

$$b_0 = \overline{Y} - b_1\overline{X} = 404.5833 - 49.9101(4.5833)$$
$$= 175.8289$$

The least squares regression line is, therefore,

$$\hat{Y} = 175.8289 + 49.9101X$$

TABLE 13-5

Residuals and Squared Residuals for the Software Accessories Example

X	$\hat{Y}$	Y	$Y - \hat{Y}$	$(Y - \hat{Y})^2$
3	325.5592	487	161.4408	26,063.13
5	425.3794	445	19.6206	384.9679
2	275.6491	272	−3.6491	13.31593
8	575.1097	641	65.8903	4,341.532
2	275.6491	187	−88.6491	7,858.663
6	475.2895	440	−35.2895	1,245.349
7	525.1996	346	−179.2	32,112.5
1	225.739	238	12.261	150.3321
4	375.4693	312	−63.4693	4,028.352
2	275.6491	269	−6.6491	44.21053
9	625.0198	655	29.9802	898.8124
6	475.2895	563	87.7105	7,693.132
			Σ = 0.0	Σ = 84,834.29

FIGURE 13-9

Least Squares Regression Line for Software Accessories Example

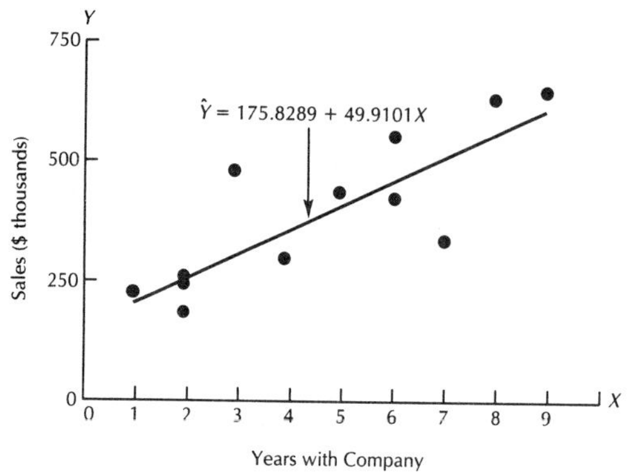

2. The sum of the squared residuals is a minimum (equation 13-11):

$$\sum_{i=1}^{n} (Y_i - \hat{Y}_i)^2 = \text{Minimum} \qquad \textbf{13-11}$$

This property provided the basis for developing the equations for b_0 and b_1.

3. The simple regression line always passes through the mean of the Y variable, $\overline{Y}$, and the mean of the X variable, $\overline{X}$. This is illustrated in Figure 13-9. Thus, to draw any simple linear regression line, all you need to do is connect the least squares Y-intercept with the $(\overline{X}, \overline{Y})$ point.
4. The least squares coefficients are unbiased estimates of β_0 and β_1. Thus, the expected values of b_0 and b_1 are β_0 and β_1, respectively.

SKILL DEVELOPMENT PROBLEMS FOR **SECTION 13-3**

The following exercises and problems will help you learn the concepts presented in Section 13-3.

12. You are given the following sample data for variables Y and X:

Y	140	120	80	100	130	90	110	120	130	130	100
X	5	3	2	4	5	4	4	5	6	5	4

a. Develop a scatter plot for these data and describe what, if any, relationship exists.

b. Compute the correlation coefficient. Test to determine whether the correlation is significant at the $\alpha = 0.05$ level.

c. Compute the regression equation based on these sample data and interpret the regression coefficients.

13. You are given the following sample data for variables Y and X:

Y	12.5	9.0	13.0	7.5	9.0	6.2	3.5	14.0	15.0
X	100	120	100	90	110	160	200	95	80

a. Develop a scatter plot for these data and describe what, if any, relationship exists.
b. Compute the correlation coefficient. Test to determine whether the correlation is significant at the $\alpha = 0.05$ level.
c. Compute the regression equation based on these sample data and interpret the regression coefficients.

14. The Apex Telephone Company recently performed a study in which ten households were surveyed to determine the number of phone calls made per week (Y) and the number of people living at the residence (X). The sample data were determined as follows:

Calls (Y)	37	23	67	21	10	33	46	67	44	38
People (X)	4	2	3	1	2	3	4	5	3	4

a. Develop a scatter plot for these data and describe what, if any, relationship exists.
b. Compute the correlation coefficient. Test to determine whether the correlation is significant at the $\alpha = 0.05$ level.
c. Compute the regression equation based on these sample data and interpret the regression coefficients.

15. At a recent Beach Boys concert, a survey was conducted that asked those sampled their age (X) and how many concerts they have attended since the first of the year (Y). The following data were collected with eleven respondents:

Age (X)	24	21	34	45	23	34	47	29	20	37	42
Concerts (Y)	3	2	1	3	5	2	1	3	5	2	3

a. Develop a scatter plot for these data and describe what, if any, relationship exists.
b. Compute the correlation coefficient. Test to determine whether the correlation is significant at the $\alpha = 0.05$ level.
c. Compute the regression equation based on these sample data and interpret the regression coefficients.
d. Compute the residuals and the sum of squared errors. Also compute the sum of squares for the Y variable and compare the sum of squared errors to this sum. Why do you suppose the sum of squared errors is smaller? Discuss.

16. At State University, a study was done to establish whether a relationship existed between student graduating GPA and the SAT score when the student originally entered the university. The sample data are reported as follows:

GPA (*Y*)	2.5	3.2	3.5	2.8	3.0	2.4	3.4	2.9	2.7	3.8
SAT (*X*)	640	700	550	540	620	490	710	600	505	710

a. Develop a scatter plot for these data and describe what, if any, relationship exists.
b. Compute the correlation coefficient. Test to determine whether the correlation is significant at the $\alpha = 0.05$ level.
c. Compute the regression equation based on these sample data and interpret the regression coefficients.
d. Compute the residuals and the sum of squared errors. Also, compute the sum of squares for the Y variable and compare the sum of squared errors to this sum. Why do you suppose the sum of squared errors is smaller? Discuss.

13-4 SIGNIFICANCE TESTS IN REGRESSION ANALYSIS

If you recall, Carl Markowitz found that sales varied for the Software Accessories sales force, depending on how many years of experience people had with the company. The statistical measure for total variation in a dependent variable (sales) is TSS (total sum of squares). TSS is computed using equation 13-12:

$$\text{TSS} = \sum_{i=1}^{n} (Y_i - \overline{Y})^2 \qquad \textbf{13-12}$$

where

TSS = Total sum of squares

n = Sample size

Y_i = ith value of the dependent variable

$\overline{Y}$ = Average value of the dependent variable

The total sum of squares for sales is calculated in Table 13-6. As you can see, the total variation in sales that needs to be explained is 276,434.9.

TABLE 13-6

Calculation of Total Sum of Squares for the Software Accessories Example

Person	Sales Y	$(Y - \overline{Y})^2$
1	487	6,792.562
2	445	1,633.534
3	272	17,578.25
4	641	55,892.99
5	187	47,342.36
6	440	1,254.364
7	346	3,431.968
8	238	27,749.9
9	312	8,571.612
10	269	18,382.75
11	655	62,708.67
12	563	25,095.95
$TSS = \Sigma(Y - \overline{Y})^2 = 276{,}434.9$		

The least squares regression line minimized the sum of squared residuals. This value (see Table 13-5) is called the *sum of squares error* (SSE) and is calculated by equation 13-13:

$$SSE = \sum_{i=1}^{n} (Y_i - \hat{Y}_i)^2 \tag{13-13}$$

where

n = Sample size

Y_i = ith value of the dependent variable

$\hat{Y}_i$ = Least squares estimated value for the average of Y for each given X value

The SSE represents the amount of variation in the dependent variable that is not explained by the least squares regression line. For Software Accessories, the amount of unexplained variation is 84,834.29. The amount of variation in the dependent variable that is explained by the regression line is called the *sum of squares regression* (SSR) and is calculated by equation 13-14:

$$SSR = TSS - SSE \quad \text{(13-14)}$$

where

SSR = Sum of squares regression

TSS = Total sum of squares

SSE = Sum of squares error

For the Software Accessories example, the least squares regression line calculated in Table 13-4 produces a sum of squares regression of

$$\begin{aligned} SSR &= 276{,}434.9 - 84{,}834.29 \\ &= 191{,}600.61 \end{aligned}$$

The percentage of the total variation in the dependent variable that is explained by the independent variable is called the **coefficient of determination** or R^2. We compute R^2 by equation 13-15, 13-16, or 13-17:

$$R^2 = 1 - \frac{\Sigma(Y - \hat{Y})^2}{\Sigma(Y - \overline{Y})^2} \quad \text{(13-15)}$$

$$R^2 = 1 - \frac{SSE}{TSS} \quad \text{(13-16)}$$

or, alternatively,

$$R^2 = \frac{SSR}{TSS} \quad \text{(13-17)}$$

Then, for the Software Accessories example, the percentage of variation in sales that can be explained by the level of advertising is

$$\begin{aligned} R^2 &= 1 - \frac{84{,}834.29}{276{,}434.9} \\ &= 1 - 0.3069 \\ &= 0.6931 \end{aligned}$$

This means that 69.31% of the variation in the sales data for this sample can be explained by knowing the number of years of experience that accompanied the sales amount.

R^2 can be a value between 0 and 1.0. If there is a perfect linear relationship between two variables, the coefficient of determination, R^2, will be 1.0. This would correspond to a situation in which the least squares regression line would pass through each of the points in the scatter plot.

R^2 is the measure used by many decision makers to indicate how well the linear regression line fits the (X, Y) data points. The better the fit, the closer R^2 will be to 1.0. R^2 will be close to 0 when there is a weak linear relationship or no linear relationship at all.

Finally, when you are employing *simple linear regression* (one independent variable in the model), there is an alternative way of computing R^2, as shown in equation 13-18:

$$R^2 = r^2 \tag{13-18}$$

where

R^2 = Coefficient of determination

r = Simple correlation coefficient

Thus, by squaring the correlation coefficient we can get R^2 for the simple regression model. Table 13-2 shows the correlation calculation giving $r = 0.8325$. Then using equation 13-18, we get R^2 as follows:

$$\begin{aligned} R^2 &= r^2 \\ &= 0.8325^2 \\ &= 0.6931 \end{aligned}$$

SIGNIFICANCE OF THE REGRESSION MODEL

Before Carl Markowitz uses the regression model to analyze the relationship between sales and years experience, he should find out if the model itself is statistically significant. To test the model, he uses analysis of variance as shown in Figure 13-10 (page 678). Based on the analysis of variance F test, he concludes that the proportion of sales variation explained by the least squares regression line is greater than 0. The analysis of variance test has shown that the sample coefficient of determination is significantly greater than 0. This means that the regression model he has developed is statistically significant. That is, predicting sales based on years sales experience using the least squares model would be generally preferable to just using the overall average sales value, $\overline{Y}$.

FIGURE 13-10 Significance Test of the Regression Model for the Software Accessories Example

Hypotheses:

H_0: The regression model does not explain any of the total variation in the dependent variable.
H_A: The regression model does explain a proportion of the total variation in the dependent variable greater than 0.0.

$\alpha = 0.05$

Source of Variation	*SS*	*d.f.*	*MS*	*F Ratio*
Regression	SSR = 191,600.61	$K = 1$	SSR/1 = 191,600.61	MSR/MSE* = 22.59
Unexplained (error)	SSE = 84,834.29	$n - 2 = 10$	SSE/10 = 8,483.43	
Total	TSS = 276,434.9	$n - 1 = 11$		

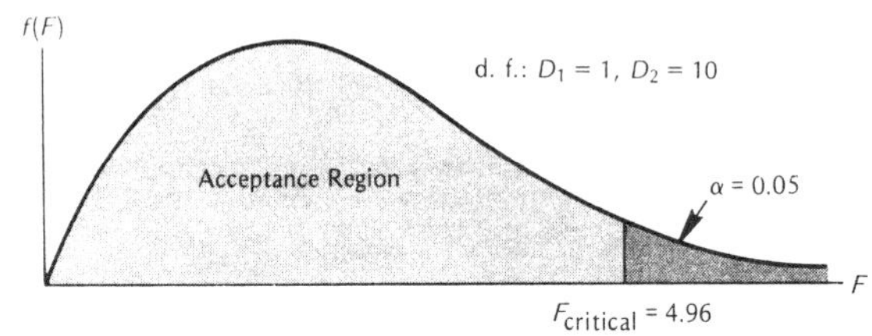

Decision Rule:

If $F > F_{critical} = 4.96$, reject H_0.
Otherwise, do not reject H_0.

Since $22.59 > 4.96$, we reject H_0 and conclude that the regression model explains a significant amount of variation in the dependent variable.

*MSR = mean square regression; MSE = mean square error.

SIGNIFICANCE OF THE SLOPE COEFFICIENT

To test the significance of the simple linear regression model, we test whether the true regression slope is 0. A slope of 0 would imply that the X variable is of no use in explaining the variation in Y. If the X variable is useful, then we should reject that the regression slope is 0. Because the b_1 value is calculated from a sample, it is subject to sampling error. Thus, even though b_1 is not 0, we must determine whether its difference from 0 is greater than would generally be attributed to sampling error.

If we selected several samples from the same population, and for each sample determined the least squares regression line, we would likely get lines with different slopes and different Y-intercepts. This is analogous to getting different sample means from different samples. Just as the distribution of possible sample means has a standard deviation, the possible regression slopes have a standard deviation, which is given in equation 13-19:

$$\sigma_{b_1} = \frac{\sigma_e}{\sqrt{\Sigma(X - \overline{X})^2}} \qquad \text{(13-19)}$$

where

σ_{b_1} = Standard deviation of the regression slope (called the **standard error of the slope**)

σ_e = **Standard error of the estimate**

Because we are sampling from the population, we estimate σ_{b_1} as shown in equation 13-20:

$$S_{b_1} = \frac{S_e}{\sqrt{\Sigma(X - \overline{X})^2}} = \frac{S_e}{\sqrt{\Sigma X^2 - \frac{(\Sigma X)^2}{n}}} \qquad \text{(13-20)}$$

where

S_{b_1} = Estimate of the standard error of the least squares slope

$S_e = \sqrt{\frac{\text{SSE}}{n - 2}}$ = Sample **standard error of the estimate** (the measure of deviation of the actual Y values around the regression line)

For Software Accessories, the estimate of the standard error of the slope is

$$S_{b_1} = \frac{\sqrt{\frac{84{,}834.29}{10}}}{\sqrt{329 - \frac{(55)^2}{12}}}$$

$$= 10.5021$$

If the standard error of the slope is large, the value of b_1 will be quite variable from sample to sample. On the other hand, if S_{b_1} is small, the slope will be less variable. However, regardless of the standard error, the average value of b_1 will

FIGURE 13-11

Standard Error of the Slope

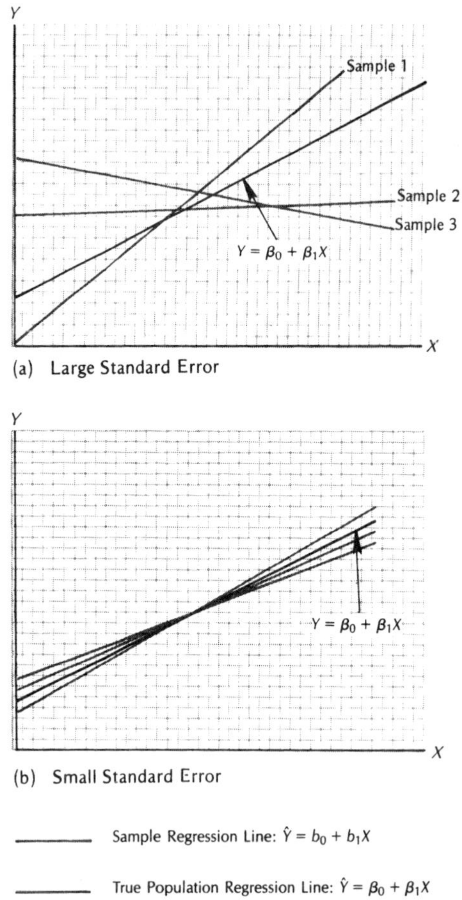

equal β_1, the true regression slope, if the assumptions of the regression analysis are satisfied. Figure 13-11 illustrates what this means. Notice that when the standard error is large, the sample slopes can take on values *much* different from the true population slope. As Figure 13-11(a) shows, a sample slope and the true population slope can even have different signs. However, when S_{b_1} is small, the sample regression lines will cluster closely around the true population line (Figure 13-11(b)).

Because the sample regression slope will most likely not equal the true population slope, we must test to determine whether the true slope could possibly be 0. A slope of 0 in the linear model means that the independent variable will not explain any variation in the dependent variable. To test the significance of a slope coefficient, we use the t test of equation 13-21:

$$t = \frac{b_1 - \beta_1}{S_{b_1}} \quad (13\text{-}21)$$

where

t = Number of standard errors b_1 is from β_1

b_1 = Sample regression slope coefficient

β_1 = Hypothesized slope

S_{b_1} = Estimate of the standard error of the slope

This test has $n - 2$ degrees of freedom. Figure 13-12 illustrates this test for the Software Accessories example and indicates that we should reject the hypothesis that the true regression slope is 0. Thus, years of experience can be used to help explain the variation in individual representatives' sales.

FIGURE 13-12

Significance Test for the Regression Slope for the Software Accessories Example

Hypotheses:

H_0: $\beta_1 = 0$
H_A: $\beta_1 \neq 0$

$\alpha = 0.05$

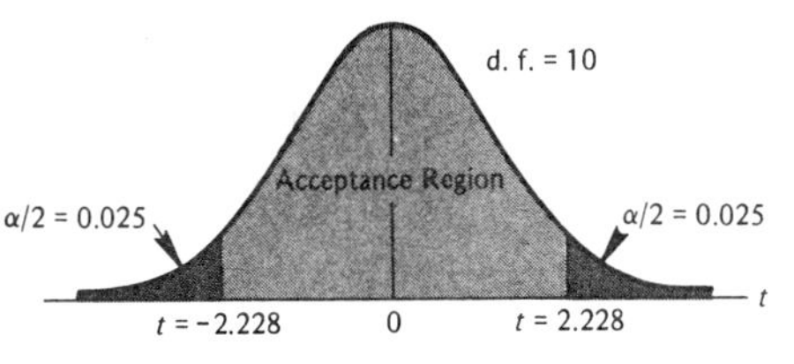

The calculated t is

$$t = \frac{b_1 - \beta_1}{S_{b_1}} = \frac{49.9101 - 0}{10.5021}$$
$$= 4.7524$$

Decision Rule:

If $t > t_{critical} = 2.228$, reject H_0.
If $t < t_{critical} = -2.228$, reject H_0.
Otherwise, do not reject H_0.

Since $4.7524 > 2.228$, we should reject the null hypothesis and conclude that the true slope is not zero.

FIGURE 13-13

Summary of Simple Regression Steps

Step 1. Develop a scatter plot of Y and X. You are looking for a linear relationship between the two variables.

Step 2. Calculate the correlation coefficient, r. This measures the strength of the linear relationship between the two variables.

Step 3. Test to see whether r is significantly different from 0. The test statistic is

$$t = \frac{r}{\sqrt{\frac{1 - r^2}{n - 2}}}$$

Step 4. Calculate the least squares regression line for the sample data.

Step 5. Calculate the simple coefficient of determination, r^2. This value measures the proportion of variation in the dependent variable explained by the independent variable.

Step 6. Test to see whether the model is significant. The test statistic is

$$F = \frac{\frac{\text{SSR}}{1}}{\frac{\text{SSE}}{n - 2}} = \frac{\text{MSR}}{\text{MSE}}$$

Step 7. Test to determine whether the true regression slope is 0. The test statistic with d.f. $= n - 2$ is

$$t = \frac{b_1 - \beta_1}{S_{b_1}}$$

Note: Steps 3, 6, and 7 are equivalent tests for the simple regression model. Only one of these tests needs to be performed.

Based on the results of his analysis, Carl Markowitz can conclude that a significant relationship exists between sales generated and years of sales experience with Software Accessories. He can also conclude that each year of experience should lead to an increase of about $50,000 in sales. The knowledge generated by this model should help him analyze the present wage scale for sales representatives.

Figure 13-13 outlines the steps involved in developing a simple linear regression model and reviews the various tests of significance. You should recognize that the three tests used thus far to test the significance of the linear relationship between X and Y are actually equivalent. Therefore, the decision maker needs to perform only one of these tests, since they will all lead to the same conclusion. However, you should be familiar with all three since they are each used. When we introduce multiple regression analysis in Chapter 14, the three tests serve different purposes.

COMPUTER APPLICATION

The calculations required to develop a simple linear regression model can be performed with a calculator. However, many computer programs have been developed that will perform the calculations quickly and with great accuracy. These computer programs will also calculate the values necessary to test the significance of the regression model. Table 13-7 (page 684) shows two sample regression outputs for the Software Accessories example. As in previous chapters, one output is for MINITAB (Table 13-7a) and the second is for GB-STAT (Table 13-7b).

As you look at the computer outputs you will see that each labels values a little differently than the text has been doing. For instance, in MINITAB the standard error of the estimate on the printout is s = 92.11, the standard error of the regression slope is Stdev = 10.50, and the intercept is shown on the printout as Constant = 175.83.

Other software packages will use still different labels for the regression values. However, the documentation that accompanies the various packages will indicate what the output labels mean.

SKILL DEVELOPMENT PROBLEMS FOR **SECTION 13-4**

The following exercises are included to help you gain a firm understanding of the concepts presented in this section.

17. You are given the following results from computations pertaining to a simple linear regression application:

$$\hat{Y} = 23.0 + 1.45X$$
$$SSE = 45{,}000$$
$$n = 25$$
$$\Sigma(X - \overline{X})^2 = 4{,}000$$

a. Based on the statistics supplied, can you conclude that there is a significant linear relationship between X and Y? Test at the $\alpha = 0.05$ level.
b. Interpret the slope coefficient.

18. The following data have been collected by an accountant who is performing an audit of parts inventory for a machinery company. The dependent variable, Y, is the actual number of units counted by the accountant. The independent variable, X, is the number of units on the computer inventory record.

Y	233	10	24	56	78	102	90	200	344	120	18
X	245	12	22	56	90	103	85	190	320	120	23

a. Develop a scatter plot for these data.
b. Compute the correlation coefficient and test to determine whether a significant linear relationship exists between the two variables. Test at an $\alpha = 0.05$ level.
c. Compute the regression model based on the sample data. Compute also the standard error of the estimate. Test to determine whether the regression slope is significantly different from 0. Use an $\alpha = 0.05$ level.

TABLE 13-7

a. MINITAB Output for the Software Accessories Example

```
MTB > name c1 'years' c2 'sales'
MTB > print c1-c2

ROW   years   sales
  1     3      487
  2     5      445
  3     2      272
  4     8      641
  5     2      187
  6     6      440
  7     7      346
  8     1      238
  9     4      312
 10     2      269
 11     9      655
 12     6      563

MTB > regress c2 on 1 predictor c1

The regression equation is
sales = 176 + 49.9 years

Predictor     Coef    Stdev   t-ratio      p
Constant    175.83    54.99      3.20   0.010
years        49.91    10.50      4.75   0.000

s = 92.11    R-sq = 69.3%    R-sq(adj) = 66.2%
Analysis of Variance

SOURCE       DF       SS       MS       F       p
Regression    1   191601   191601   22.59   0.000
Error        10    84834     8483
Total        11   276435
```

b. GB-STAT Output for the Software Accessories Example

```
Y = 175.8289 + 49.9101 · X

UNADJUSTED R^2            = .6931
CORRELATION COEFFICIENT = .8325

ANOVA FOR PREDICTION F  = 22.5853
CHANCE PROBABILITY    P = .0008

STD ERROR OF ESTIMATE   = 92.1056
VARIANCE OF ESTIMATE    = 8483.445

DEGREES OF FREEDOM      = 1 AND 10

WITH X = YEARS      AND Y = SALES
```

Note that MINITAB and GB-STAT provide output with slightly different results due to the number of decimal places printed by the software.

d. Referring to parts **b** and **c**, comment on the relationship between the two hypothesis tests.

19. The Skelton Manufacturing Company recently did a study of its customers. A random sample of $n = 50$ customer accounts was pulled from the computer records. Two variables were observed:

$$Y = \text{Total dollar volume of business this year}$$

$$X = \text{Miles customer is from corporate headquarters}$$

The following statistics were computed:

$$\hat{Y} = 2{,}140.23 - 10.12X$$

$$S_b = 3.12$$

a. Interpret the regression slope coefficient.
b. Using an $\alpha = 0.05$ level, test to determine whether the true regression slope is different from 0. Discuss the conclusions.

20. The National Football League is concerned about the injuries suffered by its players. A sample of players was selected prior to last season. At the end of the year, two variables were measured:

$$Y = \text{Number of days out with an injury}$$

$$X = \text{Weight of the player}$$

The data observed were as follows:

Y	17	9	0	3	26	18	2	8	19	38	20	0	2
X	221	198	234	256	278	197	206	224	234	278	220	199	234

a. Develop a scatter plot for these data.
b. Compute the correlation coefficient and test to determine whether a significant linear relationship exists between the two variables. Test at an $\alpha = 0.05$ level.
c. Compute the regression model based on the sample data. Compute also the standard error of the estimate. Test to determine whether the regression slope is significantly different from 0. Use an $\alpha = 0.05$ level.
d. Referring to parts **b** and **c**, comment on the relationship between the two hypothesis tests.

13-5 REGRESSION ANALYSIS FOR DESCRIPTION

Regression and correlation analysis is often used as a descriptive tool. For example, one of the most critical issues in many retail operations is shelf space allocation. All suppliers want their products to receive the "best" store location and the "maximum" shelf space. However, retailers should make shelf allocation decisions based on what is most profitable for the store, not the supplier.

Traditionally, measures such as gross margin, the difference between the product's selling price and its unit cost, have been used in making this allocation decision. A more recently developed measure, direct product profitability, which compares selling price to all costs related to the product, may be a more effective measure. Unfortunately, direct product profitability is more difficult to determine than is gross margin. Anna Gibson, manager of the Cloverdale store of the Riley's Supermarket chain, has been asked to determine whether a significant relationship exists between gross margin and direct product profitability. If a significant relationship exists, gross margin can be used to estimate the value of direct product profitability for each product.

A descriptive analysis using linear regression requires the same steps described in Figure 13-13. Using regression for description, the decision maker concentrates on the significance of the regression slope coefficient, and its sign, size, and standard error. For her study, Anna sampled ninety grocery products, and determined both the gross margin and direct product profitability. She found the following information:

$$\begin{aligned} Y &= \text{Direct product profitability} \\ X &= \text{Gross margin} \\ \Sigma(X - \overline{X})^2 &= 0.08138 \\ b_0 &= -0.5424 \\ b_1 &= 0.7968 \\ \text{SSE} &= 0.5045 \\ \text{d.f.} &= 90 - 2 = 88 \end{aligned}$$

In performing the descriptive analysis, Anna might first test to see whether the slope coefficient is significantly different from 0.

$$\begin{aligned} t &= \frac{b_1 - \beta_1}{S_{b_1}} = \frac{b_1 - \beta_1}{\sqrt{\dfrac{\text{SSE}/(n-2)}{\Sigma(X - \overline{X})^2}}} \\ &= \frac{0.7968 - 0}{\sqrt{\dfrac{0.5045/88}{0.08138}}} \\ &= 2.999 \end{aligned}$$

For any reasonable level of alpha, $t = 2.999$ will exceed the critical value from the t table. Thus, Anna Gibson can reject the hypothesis that the true regression slope is 0. Further, since the sign on the regression slope is positive, she can infer that there is a positive linear relationship between a product's gross margin and the associated direct product profitability.

Since the purpose of the regression analysis is to determine whether the gross margin value can be used to calculate the appropriate direct product profitability, the slope coefficient has a definite economic interpretation. For each \$1 increase in gross margin, direct product profitability will increase \$0.7968. However, since this value is based on sample information, it is subject to sampling error and a confidence interval estimate should be made for the slope coefficient. This estimate would be made using equation 13-22:

$$b_1 \pm t_{\alpha/2} S_{b_1}$$

or, equivalently,

$$b_1 \pm t_{\alpha/2} \sqrt{\frac{\frac{\text{SSE}}{n-2}}{\Sigma(X - \overline{X})^2}}$$

with d.f. $= n - 2$

13-22

So, for a 95 percent confidence interval, she would arrive at

$$0.7968 \pm 1.99 \sqrt{\frac{\frac{0.5045}{88}}{0.08138}}$$

$$0.7968 \pm 1.99(0.2656)$$

$$0.7968 \pm 0.5285$$

$$0.2683 \text{ \_\_\_\_ } 1.3253$$

The supermarket manager would be quite confident that, if the gross margin of a product increased by \$1, the direct product profitability would increase between \$0.2683 and \$1.3253. Whether this wide a range in values makes this a useful tool for shelf space allocation would be a managerial judgment. Therefore, even though the model is statistically significant, it may not be useful for managerial decision making. We will expand on this point in later chapters.

There are many other situations where the prime purpose of regression analysis is description. Economists use regression analysis for descriptive purposes as they search for a means of explaining the economy. Market researchers also use regression analysis, among other techniques, in an effort to describe the factors that influence the demand for products.

Consider again the Software Accessories example. The regression equation developed between the dependent variable, Y = sales, and the independent variable, X = years experience, is

$$\hat{Y} = 175.8289 + 49.9101X$$

We would interpret the slope coefficient to mean that for a one-unit (1-year) increase in experience, we would expect an average increase in sales of 49.9101 units (\$49,910.10). However, the slope coefficient is a *point estimate* for the true regression slope. In Section 13-4 we found that the potential variation in the value of the regression slope coefficient from sample to sample is measured by the *standard error of the slope*. This is

$$S_{b_1} = 10.5021$$

Then, to develop a 90% confidence interval estimate for the true regression slope, we use equation 13-22 as follows:

$$49.9101 \pm 1.812(10.5021)$$

$$49.9101 \pm 19.0298$$

$$30.8803 \ \_\_\_\_ \ 68.9399$$

SKILL DEVELOPMENT PROBLEMS FOR **SECTION 13-5**

The following exercises are included to help you gain a firm understanding of the concepts presented in this section.

21. You are given the following results from computations pertaining to a simple linear regression application:

$$\hat{Y} = 5{,}723.0 + 145X$$
$$n = 25$$
$$S_{b_1} = 10.80$$

a Based on the statistics supplied, can you conclude that there is a significant linear relationship between X and Y? Test at the $\alpha = 0.05$ level.

b. Interpret the slope coefficient.

c. Develop a 95% confidence interval estimate for the true regression slope and interpret the estimate.

22. The following data have been collected by an accountant who is performing an audit of paper products at a large office supply company. The dependent variable, Y, is the actual number of units counted by the accountant. The independent variable, X, is the number of units on the computer inventory record.

Y	23	100	242	56	178	10	94	200	44	128	180
X	24	120	228	56	190	13	85	190	32	120	230

a. Develop a scatter plot for these data.

b. Compute the regression model based on the sample data. Compute also the standard error of the estimate. Test to determine whether the regression slope is significantly different from 0. Use an $\alpha = 0.05$ level.

c. Develop a 90% confidence interval estimate for the true regression slope and interpret this interval estimate.

23. The Shelton Manufacturing Company (see Problem 19) recently did a study of its customers. A random sample of $n = 50$ customer accounts was pulled from the computer records. Two variables were observed, namely,

Y = Total dollar volume of business this year

X = Miles customer is from corporate headquarters

The following quantities were computed:

$$\hat{Y} = 2{,}140.23 - 10.12X$$
$$S_{b_1} = 3.12$$

a. Interpret the regression slope coefficient.
b. Develop a 95% confidence interval estimate for the true slope and interpret this interval.

24. The State Department of Transportation has conducted a study of 100 randomly selected vehicles in which they measured the speed of the vehicle and age of the driver. A regression model was developed, with vehicle speed as the dependent variable and age as the independent variable. The results obtained were as follows:

$$\hat{Y} = 56.78 + 0.124X$$
$$S_{b_1} = 2.88$$

a. Develop a 95% interval estimate for the true regression slope and interpret.
b. Based on your response to part **a**, can you conclude that age and speed are linearly related? Discuss.

13-6 REGRESSION ANALYSIS FOR PREDICTION

One of the main uses of regression analysis is *prediction*. In the Software Accessories sample, Carl Markowitz wanted to know whether years of sales experience was a helpful variable to use to predict sales. As another example, your state government may use regression to forecast annual tax revenues so that elected officials can establish state department budgets.

Using a regression model to predict the dependent variable is quite straightforward once the model has been found. The regression model for Software Accessories individual sales is

$$\hat{Y} = 175.8289 + 49.9101X$$

where

$\hat{Y}$ = Point estimate for the average sales in thousands of dollars, given X

X = Years of experience

To find $\hat{Y}$, the point estimate of expected sales, we substitute the specified years of experience into the regression model. For example, suppose Carl

Markowitz is analyzing the performance of someone with 6 years of sales experience. The point estimate for sales becomes

$$\begin{aligned}\hat{Y} &= 175.8289 + 49.9101(6)\\ &= 475.2895\end{aligned}$$

Converting back to dollars, we find the point estimate for sales when $X = 6$ to be \$475,289.50.

CONFIDENCE INTERVAL FOR THE AVERAGE *Y*, GIVEN *X*

In Chapter 8, we stated that decision makers cannot be confident of the accuracy of any point estimate. In fact, the best they can hope for is that the point estimate is close to the true value being estimated.

In some cases, only a point estimate of the expected value of the dependent variable is required. However, in many other cases the decision maker will want a *confidence interval estimate.* For example, Carl Markowitz might like a 95% confidence interval estimate for average sales, given that a sales representative has 6 years of experience. The prediction interval for the expected value of a dependent variable, given a specific level of the independent variable, is determined by equation 13-23:

$$\hat{Y} \pm t_{\alpha/2}\sqrt{\frac{\text{SSE}}{n-2}}\sqrt{\frac{1}{n}+\frac{(X_p-\overline{X})^2}{\Sigma X^2-\dfrac{(\Sigma X)^2}{n}}} \quad \textbf{13-23}$$

where

$\hat{Y}$ = Point estimate of the dependent variable

t = Interval coefficient with $n - 2$ d.f.

n = Sample size

X_p = Value of the independent variable used to arrive at $\hat{Y}$

$\overline{X}$ = Mean of the independent variable observations in the sample

Thus, if X_p equals 6, we get

$$475.2895 \pm 2.228\sqrt{\frac{84{,}834.29}{10}}\sqrt{\frac{1}{12}+\frac{(6-4.583)^2}{329-\dfrac{55^2}{12}}}$$

$$475.2895 \pm 67.8868$$

$$407.4027 \text{ ——— } 543.1763$$

Therefore, Carl Markowitz can state, at the 95% confidence level, that average sales for a representative with 6 years of experience will be between \$407,402.70 and \$543,176.30. This information would be useful in determining commission levels.

CONFIDENCE INTERVAL FOR A SINGLE *Y*, GIVEN *X*

The prediction interval just calculated is for the expected, or average, sales level, given a sales representative with 6 years of experience with Software Accessories. Carl Markowitz would also be interested in predicting the actual sales for individual sales representatives with 6 years of experience, not the average of the sales for all representatives with 6 years of experience. Developing the interval within which he can be 95% confident that sales will fall requires only a slight modification of equation 13-23. This predictive interval is given by equation 13-24:

$$\hat{Y} \pm t_{\alpha/2}\sqrt{\frac{SSE}{n-2}}\sqrt{1+\frac{1}{n}+\frac{(X_p-\overline{X})^2}{\Sigma X^2-\frac{(\Sigma X)^2}{n}}} \qquad \text{(13-24)}$$

For Software Accessories, the 95% confidence interval estimate for yearly sales for a representative with 6 years of experience is

$$475.2895 \pm 2.228\sqrt{\frac{84{,}834.29}{10}}\sqrt{1+\frac{1}{12}+\frac{(6-4.583)^2}{329-\frac{55^2}{12}}}$$

$$475.2895 \pm 216.1486$$

$$259.1409 \;\_\_\_\_\; 691.4381$$

Thus, the 95% confidence level estimate for yearly sales for a sales representative with 6 years of experience is from \$259,140.90 to \$691,438.10. As you can see, this estimate has extremely poor precision. Although the regression model explains a significant proportion of variation in the dependent variable, it is relatively imprecise for predictive purposes. To improve the precision, Carl might decrease his confidence requirements or increase the sample size and redevelop the model.

Note that the prediction interval for a single value of the dependent variable is wider (less precise) than the interval for predicting the average value of the dependent variable. This will always be the case, as seen in equations 13-23 and 13-24. From an intuitive viewpoint, we should expect to come closer to predicting an average value than a single value. For example, although the average weight of the U.S. population will not be above 250 pounds, many people weigh more than that.

FIGURE 13-14

Regression Lines, Illustrating the Increase in the Potential Variation in Y as X_p Moves Farther from $\overline{X}$

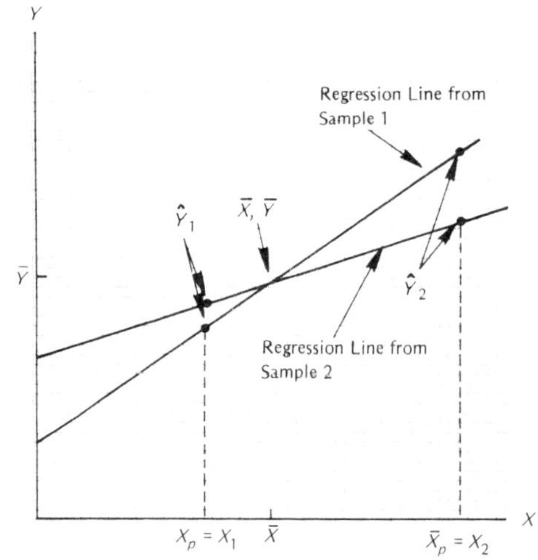

Note that the term $(X_p - \overline{X})^2$ has a particular effect on the confidence interval determined by both equations 13-23 and 13-24. The farther X_p (the value of the independent variable used to predict Y) is from $\overline{X}$, the greater $(X_p - \overline{X})^2$. Figure 13-14 shows two regression lines developed from two samples with the same set of X values. We have made both lines pass through the same $(\overline{X}, \overline{Y})$ point; however, they have different slopes and intercepts. At $X_p = X_1$, the two regression lines give predictions of Y that are close to each other. However, for $X_p = X_2$, the predictions of Y are quite different. Thus, when X_p is close to $\overline{X}$, the problems caused by variations in regression slopes are not as great as when X_p is far from $\overline{X}$. Figure 13-15 shows the prediction intervals over the range of possible X_p values. The band around the estimated regression line bends away from the regression line as X_p moves in either direction from $\overline{X}$.

SKILL DEVELOPMENT PROBLEMS FOR **SECTION 13-6**

The following exercises will help you better understand the materials presented in this section.

25. You are given the following summary statistics from a regression analysis:

$$\hat{Y} = 200 + 150X$$

$$SSE = 25.25$$

$$SSX = \text{Sum of squares } X = \Sigma X^2 - \frac{(\Sigma X)^2}{n} = 99{,}645$$

$$n = 18$$

$$\overline{X} = 52.0$$

a. Determine the point estimate for Y if $X_p = 48$ is used.

FIGURE 13-15

Confidence Intervals for $Y|X_p$ and $\overline{Y}|X_p$

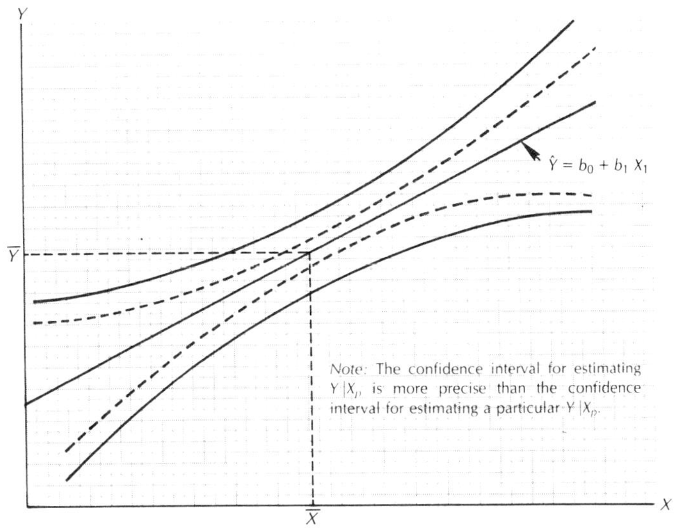

——— $\hat{Y} \pm t_{\alpha/2}\sqrt{\dfrac{SSE}{n-2}}\sqrt{1 + \dfrac{1}{n} + \dfrac{(X_p - \overline{X})^2}{\Sigma X^2 - \dfrac{(\Sigma X)^2}{n}}}$

Confidence Interval for the Estimate of a Particular Value of $Y|X_p$

- - - - - $\hat{Y} \pm t_{\alpha/2}\sqrt{\dfrac{SSE}{n-2}}\sqrt{\dfrac{1}{n} + \dfrac{(X_p - \overline{X})^2}{\Sigma X^2 - \dfrac{(\Sigma X)^2}{n}}}$

Confidence Interval for the Estimate of $\overline{Y}|X_p$

b. Provide a 95% prediction interval estimate for the average Y, given X_p = 48. Interpret this interval.

c. Provide a 95% prediction interval estimate for a particular Y, given X_p = 48. Interpret.

d. Discuss the difference between the estimates provided in parts **b** and c.

26. You are given the following summary statistics from a regression analysis:

$$\hat{Y} = 9{,}784 - 345.50X$$

$$SSE = 800.25$$

$$SSX = \text{Sum of squares } X = \Sigma X^2 - \frac{(\Sigma X)^2}{n} = 145{,}789$$

$$\overline{X} = 67.20$$

$$n = 20$$

a. Determine the point estimate for estimating Y if X_p = 48 is used.

b. Provide a 90% prediction interval estimate for the average Y, given X_p = 80. Interpret this interval.

c. Provide a 90% prediction interval estimate for a particular Y, given X_p = 80. Interpret.

d. Discuss the difference between the estimates provided in parts **b** and **c**.

27. You are given the following summary statistics from a regression analysis:

$$\hat{Y} = 1{,}200 + 0.878X$$

$$\text{SSE} = 145.40$$

$$\text{SSX} = \text{Sum of squares } X = 134{,}679$$

$$\overline{X} = 40{,}000$$

$$n = 8$$

a. Determine the point estimate for Y if $X_p = 48$ is used.

b. Provide a 95% prediction interval estimate for the average Y, given X_p = 40,000. Interpret this interval.

c. Provide a 95% prediction interval estimate for a particular Y, given X_p = 40,000. Interpret.

d. Discuss the difference between the estimates provided in parts **b** and **c**.

e. What would happen to the precision of the estimate if the value of X_p were increased to 43,000? Discuss.

28. The following data have been collected by an accountant who is performing an audit of account balances for a major retail company. The population from which the data were collected represented those accounts for which the customer had indicated the balance was incorrect. The dependent variable, Y, is the actual account balance as verified by the accountant. The independent variable, X, is the computer account balance.

Y	233	10	24	56	78	102	90	200	344	120	18
X	245	12	22	56	90	103	85	190	320	120	23

a. Prepare a regression analysis where Y is the dependent variable and X is the independent variable. Show the following results:

Regression equation $\quad \text{SSX} = \Sigma X^2 - \dfrac{(\Sigma X)^2}{n} \quad S_e$

b. Determine the point estimate for Y, given $X_p = 100$.

c. Develop a 95% prediction interval estimate for the average value of Y, given $X_p = 100$. Interpret.

d. Develop a 95% prediction interval estimate for the particular value of Y, given $X_p = 100$. Interpret.

13-7 COMMON PROBLEMS USING REGRESSION ANALYSIS

Regression is perhaps the most widely used statistical tool beyond descriptive statistical techniques. Since it is so widely used, decision makers need to be aware of the common problems found when the technique is employed.

Always remember that the conclusions and inferences made from a regression line apply only over the range of the data contained in the sample used to develop the regression line.

For instance, in the Software Accessories example, Carl Markowitz was analyzing the performance of sales representatives with 1 to 9 years of experience. Therefore, predicting sales levels of representatives not in the sample, but with 1 to 9 years of experience, would be justified assuming the sample Carl selected was representative of the population. However, if Carl were to try to predict the sales performance of someone with more than 9 years of experience, he should understand that the relationship between sales and experience may be different. Since no observations were taken for experience levels beyond the 1- to 9-year range, Carl has no information about what might happen outside that range. Figure 13-16 shows a case where the true relationship between sales and experience reaches a peak value at about 20 years and then starts to decline. If a linear regression line were used to predict sales based on experience levels beyond the relevant range of data, large overpredictions would occur.

A second important consideration, one that was discussed earlier, involves correlation and causation. The fact that a significant linear relationship exists between two variables does not imply that one variable causes the other. Although there may be a cause-and-effect relationship, decision makers should not infer such a relationship is present based only on regression and/or correlation analysis. Decision makers should also recognize that a cause-and-effect relationship between two variables is not necessary for regression analysis to be an effective tool. What matters is that the regression model accurately reflects the relationship between the two variables and that the relationship remains stable.

Finally, many users of regression analysis mistakenly believe that a high coefficient of determination (R^2) guarantees that the regression model will be a good predictor. You should remember that R^2 measures the percentage of variation in the dependent variable explained by the independent variable. While the least squares criterion assures us that R^2 will be maximized, the R^2 applies only to the sample data used to develop the model. Thus, R^2 measures the fit of the regression line to the sample data. There is no guarantee that there will be an equally good fit

FIGURE 13-16

Graph for a Sales Peak at 20 Years

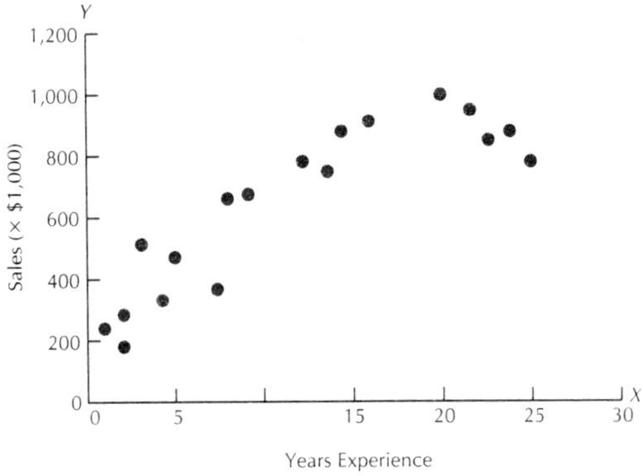

with new data. The only true test of a regression model's predictive ability is how well the model actually predicts.

13-8 REGRESSION ANALYSIS FOR CURVILINEAR RELATIONSHIPS (OPTIONAL)

Section 13-1 showed that there are a variety of ways in which two variables can be related. Correlation and regression analysis techniques are tools for modeling linear relationships between variables. Many situations in business have linear relationships between two variables, and regression equations that model that relationship will be appropriate to use in these situations.

However, there are also many instances where the relationship between two variables will be curvilinear rather than linear. For instance, demand for electricity has grown at an almost exponential rate relative to the population growth in some areas. Advertisers believe that a diminishing-returns relationship will occur between sales and advertising if advertising is allowed to grow too large. These two situations are shown in Figures 13-17 and 13-18, respectively. They represent just two of a great many possible curvilinear relationships that could exist between two variables.

FIGURE 13-17

Exponential Relationship of Increased Demand for Electricity Versus Population Growth

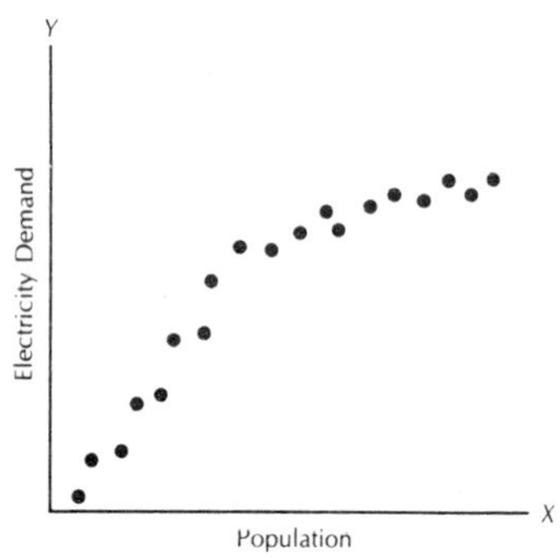

FIGURE 13-18

Diminishing Returns Relationship of Advertising Versus Sales

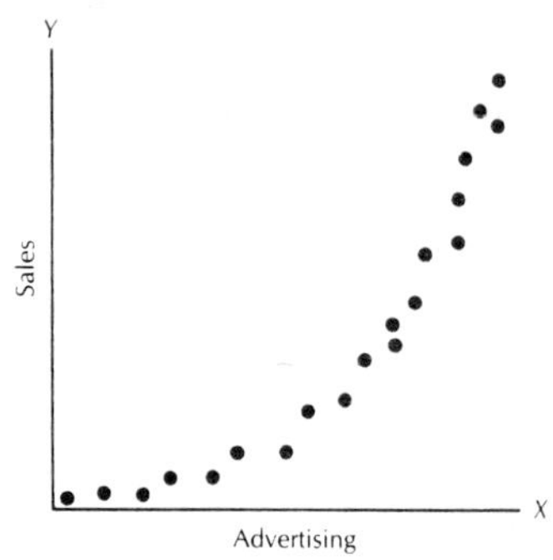

This section shows how linear regression analysis can be used in dealing with curvilinear relationships. The following examples illustrate two of the most common instances where curvilinear relationships can be used in decision making. They should give you an idea of how to approach similar situations.

Ashley Investment Services has been severely shaken by the recent downturn in the stock market. To maintain profitability and save as many jobs as possible, everyone has been expected to increase the time spent analyzing new investment opportunities. Harold Baines, the director of personnel, has noticed an increased number of people suffering from what appears to be "burnout," where physical and emotional fatigue affect job performance. While Harold cannot do anything about pressures on the job, he has read that burnout can also be influenced by the amount of time off the job people spend socializing with co-workers. With the help of the human resources lab at the local university, Harold has administered a questionnaire that measures both burnout and outside socialization. Sample data from questionnaires filled out by twenty investment advisors are shown in Table 13-8.

Figure 13-19 (page 698) presents a scatter plot of the data with the dependent variable, burnout, on the vertical axis and the independent variable, socialization, on the horizontal axis. Looking at Figure 13-19, there appears to be a linear relationship between the two variables. We used GB-STAT to fit a linear regression model to the data. Table 13-9 (page 698) shows the output from the linear regression module.

TABLE 13-8

Questionnaire Data for Ashley Investment Services Example

Burnout Index	Socialization Measure
100	20
525	60
300	38
980	88
310	59
900	87
410	68
296	12
120	35
501	70
920	80
810	92
506	77
493	86
892	83
527	79
600	75
855	81
709	75
791	77

FIGURE 13-19

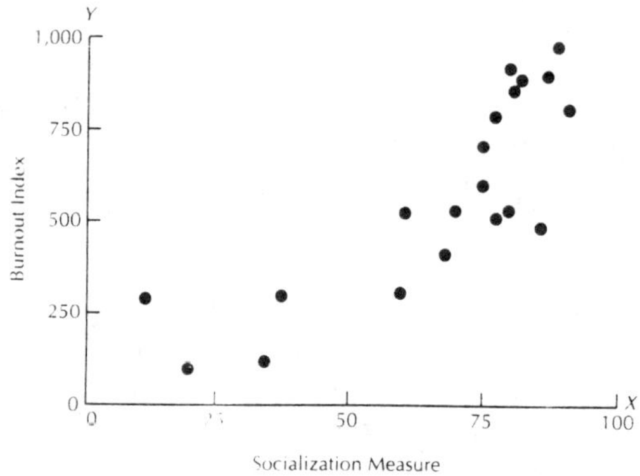

Scatter Plot for the Ashley Investment Services Example

We see from Table 13-9 that the correlation between the two variables is 0.8181. Recall that the correlation coefficient measures the strength of the linear relationship between the two variables. The t test to determine whether this correlation is significant is

$$t = \frac{r}{\sqrt{\frac{1 - r^2}{n - 2}}}$$

$$= \frac{0.8181}{\sqrt{\frac{1 - 0.6693}{18}}}$$

$$= 6.036$$

With 18 degrees of freedom, the critical t value with an alpha level of 0.05 is 2.101. Since 6.036 is greater than 2.101, we conclude there is a significant linear relationship between the two variables.

TABLE 13-9

Simple Linear Regression Output for Ashley Investment Services

```
Y = −66.164 + 9.5889 · X

UNADJUSTED R^2              =   .6693
CORRELATION COEFFICIENT     =   .8181

ANOVA FOR PREDICTION F      =   36.4299
CHANCE PROBABILITY        P = <.0001

STD ERROR OF ESTIMATE       =   159.9916
VARIANCE OF ESTIMATE        =   25597.31

DEGREES OF FREEDOM          =   1 AND 18

WITH X = SOCIALIZATION MEASURE AND Y = BURNOUT INDEX
```

FIGURE 13-20

Plot of Regression Line for the Ashley Investment Services Example

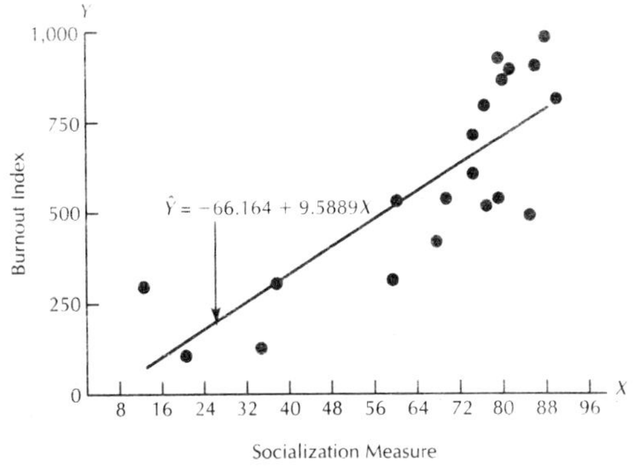

As you will recall from earlier discussions, analysis of variance can also be used to test whether the regression line explains a significant amount of variation in the dependent variable. From the computer output, $F = 36.4299$, which is significant at the 0.0001 level with 1 and 18 degrees of freedom. We could also test the regression slope coefficient for significance, but remember that all tests are the same for simple regression models.

The linear regression model shown in Table 13-9 is

$$\hat{Y} = -66.164 + 9.5889X$$

The sample data and the regression line are plotted in Figure 13-20. The line appears to fit the data. However, a closer inspection reveals instances where several consecutive points lie above or below the line instead of having the points randomly dispersed around the regression line, as we would expect given the regression analysis assumptions.

Finding instances of nonrandom patterns in the residuals for a regression model indicates the possibility of using a curvilinear relationship rather than a linear one. Looking again at the scatter plots in Figures 13-19 and 13-20, an exponential relationship between burnout and degree of socialization appears likely; that is, as socialization increases, burnout is increasing at an exponential rate.

While several methods exist to analyze curvilinear relationships, such as transforming the data, modern computer packages make these relationships as easy to analyze as linear models. The simple regression module of GB-STAT automatically fits an exponential model of the form

$$\hat{Y} = Ae^{BX}$$

to the sample data, where

A = Intercept point, or value of Y when $X = 0$

e = Base of natural logarithm (approx. 2.7183)

B = Coefficient of X in least squares model

TABLE 13-10

Exponential Regression Model for Ashley Investment Services Example

```
Y = 101.0621 * EXP(.0237 * X)
UNADJUSTED R^2            =   .7272
CORRELATION COEFFICIENT =   .8527
ANOVA FOR PREDICTION F =   44.4961
CHANCE PROBABILITY    P = <.0001
STD ERROR OF ESTIMATE   =   .3444
VARIANCE OF ESTIMATE    =   .1186
DEGREES OF FREEDOM      =   1 AND 18
WITH X = SOCIALIZATION MEASURE AND Y = BURNOUT INDEX
```

Table 13-10 shows the results from the exponential regression option using GB-STAT. Comparing these results with those of Table 13-9, we see that the new model provides a better fit to the sample data. The correlation coefficient has increased from 0.8181 to 0.8527 and the ANOVA F value has increased from 36.4299 to 44.4961. The new regression equation is

$$\hat{Y} = 101.0621e^{0.0237X}$$

Figure 13-21 shows the plot of this regression equation against the original data. Note the exponential regression equation gives a curve that appears to fit the data more closely than the straight line in Figure 13-20. The higher R^2 value supports this observation.

While the exponential model found in the previous example provided a good fit to the data, this is not the only nonlinear regression model that could be considered. The required transformation depends on the relationship between the two variables. For instance, the Four Winds Vacation Resort is considering changing its advertising campaign. The question is whether to concentrate on the segment of the vacation market that looks at stays of less than 1 week or more

FIGURE 13-21

Plot of Exponential Regression Line for the Ashley Investment Services Example

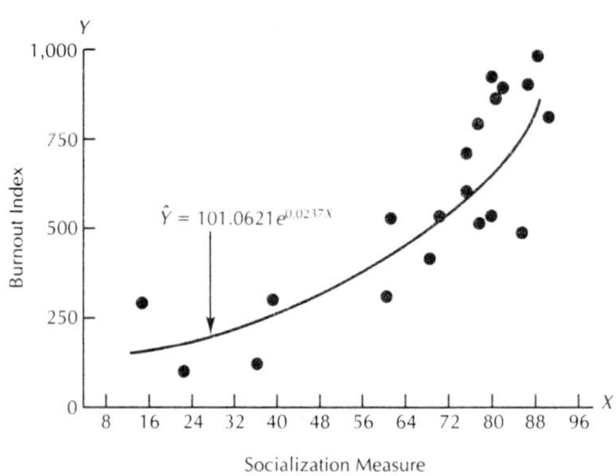

TABLE 13-11

Length of Stay and Amount Spent for the Four Winds Resort Example

Days	Amount Spent
2	$ 225
9	1,080
11	1,310
10	1,150
6	1,070
8	1,115
14	1,560
12	1,450
3	330
6	1,010
7	965
14	1,620
10	1,670
7	1,060
3	290

than 1 week. If the relationship between the time spent at the resort and the total money spent is linear—that is, if staying 2 weeks will cause a person to spend twice as much as staying 1 week—then having either guest will be equally profitable. But what if the relationship is not linear?

The resort's controller has randomly sampled fifteen guests and has data on the total amount spent at the resort and the time stayed. These data are shown in Table 13-11.

Figure 13-22 shows the scatter plot of these data and the least squares regression line. Table 13-12 (page 702) shows a summary of the regression results that were computed using the MINITAB package. These results indicate a significant linear relationship between the two variables, and thus a significant linear regression model can be developed. The model explains 85.8% of the variation in expenditures.

FIGURE 13-22

Plot of Regression Line (Linear) for Four Winds Resort Example

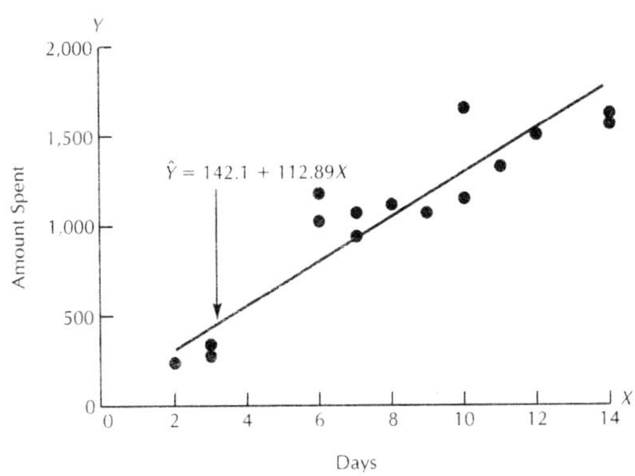

TABLE 13-12

MINITAB Output for Four Winds Resort Example

```
MTB > NAME C1 'DAYS' C2 'AMTSPENT'
MTB > PRINT C1 C2

ROW    DAYS    AMTSPENT
  1       2         225
  2       9        1080
  3      11        1310
  4      10        1150
  5       6        1070
  6       8        1115
  7      14        1560
  8      12        1450
  9       3         330
 10       6        1010
 11       7         965
 12      14        1620
 13      10        1670
 14       7        1060
 15       3         290

MTB > REGRESS C2 ON 1 PREDICTOR C1

The regression equation is
AMTSPENT = 142 + 113 DAYS

Predictor      Coef     Stdev    t-ratio      p
Constant      142.1     113.6       1.25  0.233
DAYS         112.89     12.74       8.86  0.000

s = 180.9      R-sq = 85.8%     R-sq(adj) = 84.7%

Analysis of Variance

SOURCE        DF        SS        MS        F        p
Regression     1   2571069   2571069    78.57    0.000
Error         13    425405     32723
Total         14   2996474
```

Although the linear regression results are significant, a closer look at Figure 13-22 illustrates the same problems we saw with the Ashley Investment Services example. The points do not seem to be randomly scattered around the regression line. The relationship between length of stay and total expenditures might be better modeled as a curvilinear relationship showing the diminishing expenditures that seem to take place as length of stay is increased.

A transformation that is often appropriate to indicate decreasing returns is to take the logarithm of the independent variable and regress this value against the

TABLE 13-13

Regression Model for Logarithmic Transformation in Four Winds Resort Example

```
MTB > LET C3 = LOGE(C1)
MTB > PRINT C1 - C3
```

ROW	DAYS	AMTSPENT	LOGEDAYS
1	2	225	0.69315
2	9	1080	2.19722
3	11	1310	2.39790
4	10	1150	2.30259
5	6	1070	1.79176
6	8	1115	2.07944
7	14	1560	2.63906
8	12	1450	2.48491
9	3	330	1.09861
10	6	1010	1.79176
11	7	965	1.94591
12	14	1620	2.63906
13	10	1670	2.30259
14	7	1060	1.94591
15	3	290	1.09861

```
MTB >

MTB > REGRESS C2 ON 1 PREDICTOR C3
```

The regression equation is
AMTSPENT = −415 + 753 C3

Predictor	Coef	Stdev	t-ratio	p
Constant	−415.2	129.9	−3.20	0.007
C3	752.60	63.62	11.83	0.000

s = 140.0   R-sq = 91.5%   R-sq(adj) = 90.8%

Analysis of Variance

SOURCE	DF	SS	MS	F	p
Regression	1	2741769	2741769	139.94	0.000
Error	13	254704	19593		
Total	14	2996474			

dependent variable values. MINITAB will easily perform the data transformation. Table 13-13 shows the commands necessary to perform this data transformation, the new data set including the transformed variable, and the results of the new regression analysis. If you compare the results shown in Table 13-13 with those shown in Table 13-12, you will see the transformation improves the regression results. The value of R^2 has increased from 0.858 to 0.915 and the mean square error has decreased from 32,723 to 19,593.

FIGURE 13-23

Plot of Regression Line (Curvilinear) for Four Winds Resort Example

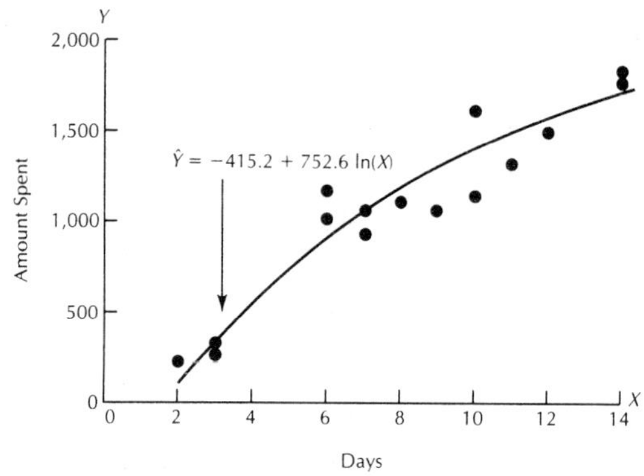

The improved regression model is plotted against the original data in Figure 13-23. Note that the transformed model gives a curved regression line and more accurately reflects the relationship between the two variables.

The preceding examples demonstrated just two of many possible transformations. As you build regression models you will encounter situations where the relationship between two variables is not linear. You will need to try different transformations to determine which is the most appropriate for the situation you are modeling.

13-9 COMPUTER APPLICATIONS

This chapter has introduced simple linear regression analysis. We manually worked through an example to show how the regression model was developed and how various statistics were computed. Although regression analysis can be performed by hand, using a computer and appropriate statistical software is obviously preferred. In this section, we provide several computer applications based on the KIVZ-Channel 5 data presented in Table 2-10. As in previous chapters, we will use the MINITAB, SPSS-X, and GB-STAT software packages.

Figure 13-24 shows the SPSS-X output produced when the SCATTERGRAM command is used with INCOME as the dependent variable and YEARS IN THE STATE as the independent variable. Both a scatter plot and regression results are shown.

The scatter plot shows little relationship between the two variables. This is confirmed by the regression output at the bottom of Figure 13-24, which shows a correlation of 0.02202 and an R^2 value of 0.00049. The regression line itself has an intercept of 24,692.41115 and a slope of 5.73521. The stated significance of 0.43967 means that the regression model would be significant if alpha were this value or greater. Figure 13-25 (page 706) shows the SPSS-X commands that produced the output in Figure 13-24.

FIGURE 13-24

SPSS-X Output: Scatter Plot and Regression

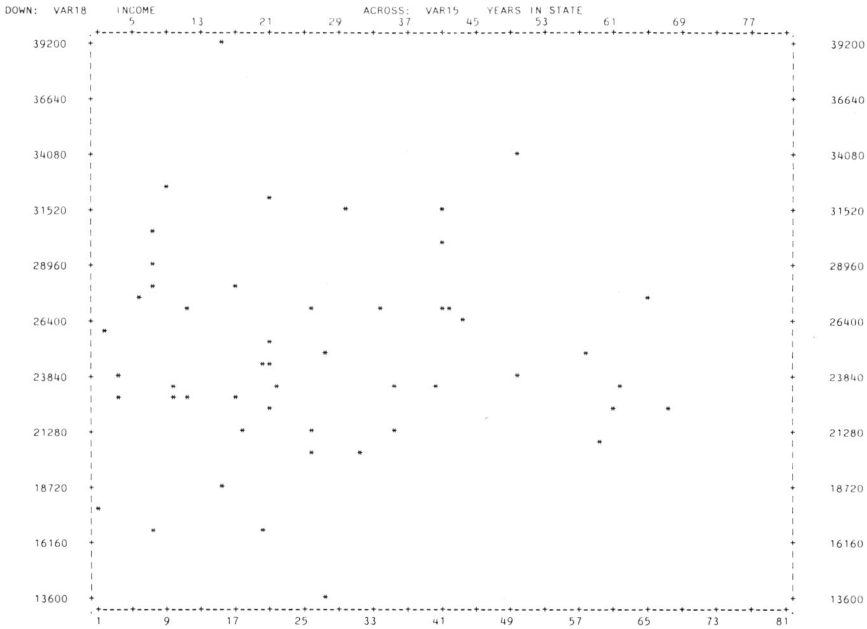


```
STATISTICS..
CORRELATION (R)-        .02202   R SQUARED       -       .00049   SIGNIFICANCE   -    .43967
STD ERR OF EST -    4849.04727   INTERCEPT (A)   -  24692.41115   SLOPE (B)      -   5.73521
PLOTTED VALUES -        50       EXCLUDED VALUES-       0         MISSING VALUES -   0
```

Table 13-14 (page 706) shows the MINITAB regression results when INCOME is used as the dependent variable and AGE is the independent variable. The regression line, with an intercept of 26,233 and a slope of −31.5, explains only 1% of the variation in the dependent variable. This can be seen by looking at either the R^2 value or the sum of squares column in the analysis of variance table. Figure 13-26 (page 707) shows the MINITAB commands necessary to produce this output.

Table 13-15 (page 707) shows the GB-STAT regression output when hours of TV watched is used as the independent variable and income is used as the dependent variable. Here, the linear regression model is significant at the 0.0154 level. This would be a good place to reiterate our previous statement about the difference between correlation and causation. The negative correlation between these two variables indicates that as TV watching decreases income increases. However, this does not mean that watching less television, by itself, will lead to greater incomes, despite what many parents have said. You have to do other things with this extra time—like read statistics books.

If you have access to a statistical package, you can do many of the homework problems in this chapter on the computer. This frees you from the computational burden and allows you to focus on interpretation of results.

FIGURE 13-25

SPSS-X Commands: Scattergram

```
UNNUMBERED
TITLE DESCRIPTIVE STATISTICS EXAMPLES
FILE HANDLE KIVZ NAME='KIVZ DATA C'
DATA LIST FILE=KIVZ LIST/VAR01 TO VAR19
VARIABLE LABELS
  VAR01 'NATIONAL NEWS STATION'
  VAR02 'LOCAL NEWS STATION'
  VAR03 'NEWS RATING'
  VAR04 'SPORTS RATING'
  VAR05 'WEATHER RATING'
  VAR06 'ANCHOR RATING'
  VAR07 'SPORTSCASTER RATING'
  VAR08 'OVERALL RATING'
  VAR09 'NATIONAL INFLUENCE'
  VAR10 'SEX'
  VAR11 'MARITAL STATUS'
  VAR12 'NUMBER EMPLOYED'
  VAR13 'HOME STATUS '
  VAR14 'YEARS AT RESIDENCE'
  VAR15 'YEARS IN STATE'
  VAR16 'EDUCATION'
  VAR17 'AGE'
  VAR18 'INCOME'
  VAR19 'HOURS OF TV'
VALUE LABELS
  VAR01 1 'CHANNEL 5' 2 'CHANNEL 3' 3 'CHANNEL 8' 4
        'UNDECIDED'/
  VAR02 1 'CHANNEL 3' 2 'CHANNEL 8' 3 'CHANNEL 5' 4
          'UNDECIDED'/
  VAR03 TO VAR08 1 'POOR' 2 'FAIR' 3 'GOOD' 4 'VERY GOOD' 5
        'EXCEL'/
  VAR09 1 'TRUE' 2 'FALSE' 3 'UNDECIDED'/
  VAR10 1 'MALE' 2 'FEMALE'/
  VAR11 1 'SINGLE' 2 'DIVORCED' 3 'MARRIED' 4 'OTHER'/
  VAR13 1 'RENTING' 2 'BUYING'/
  VAR16 1 'GRADE SCHOOL' 2 'SOME COLLEGE' 3 'VOTECH' 4 'HIGH
        SCHOOL'
SCATTERGRAM VAR18 VAR15
OPTIONS 4 7
STATISTICS ALL
```

TABLE 13-14 MINITAB Output: Regression Analysis

```
The regression equation is
INCOME = 26233 - 31.5 AGE

Predictor       Coef      Stdev     t-ratio
Constant       26233       2074       12.65
AGE           -31.47      44.44       -0.71

s = 4825     R-sq = 1.0%     R-sq(adj) = 0.0%

Analysis of Variance

SOURCE          DF            SS            MS
Regression       1      11673632      11673632
Error           48    1117510400      23281468
Total           49    1129184000

Unusual Observations
Obs.      AGE    INCOME      Fit      Stdev.Fit     Residual     St.Resid
  8      58.0     13600    24407            922       -10807      -2.28R
 11      81.0     31600    23683           1778         7917       1.76 X
 18      45.0     39200    24816            684        14384       3.01R

R denotes an obs. with a large st. resid.
X denotes an obs. whose X value gives it large influence.
```

FIGURE 13-26

MINITAB Commands: Regression Analysis

```
MTB> READ 'KIVZ5' into C1-C19
MTB> NAME C17 'AGE'
MTB> NAME C18 'INCOME'
MTB> OUTFILE = 'PRINTER'
MTB> REGRESS C18 1 C17
```

TABLE 13-15

GB-STAT Output: Regression Analysis for Income Versus Hours of TV Watched

```
Y = 29383.2 + -375.5958 * X

UNADJUSTED R^2             =     .1161
CORRELATION COEFFICIENT =    -.3408

ANOVA FOR PREDICTION F =    6.3075
CHANCE PROBABILITY    P =     .0154

STD ERROR OF ESTIMATE   = 4559.864
VARIANCE OF ESTIMATE    =    2.079236E+07

DEGREES OF FREEDOM      = 1 AND 48

WITH X = HRSTV AND Y = INCOME
```

13-10 CONCLUSIONS

This chapter has introduced the fundamental concepts of simple linear regression and correlation analysis. The techniques of regression and correlation analysis are widely used in business decision making and data analysis. Regression analysis can be applied as a tool for prediction, description, and control within an organization.

Correlation measures the strength of the linear relationship between two variables. The closer the correlation coefficient is to ±1.0, the stronger the linear relationship between the two variables. When a dependent and an independent variable are highly correlated, the resulting simple linear regression model will tend to explain a substantial proportion of the variation in the dependent variable.

A wide variety of statistical tests has been presented in this chapter. As indicated, many of these tests are equivalent. This chapter has limited discussion to the simple regression model. The next chapter introduces multiple regression analysis (more than one independent variable).

CHAPTER GLOSSARY

coefficient of determination The square of the correlation coefficient. A measure of the percentage of variation in the dependent variable explained by the independent variable in the regression model.

correlation coefficient A quantitative measure of the linear relationship between two variables. The correlation ranges from +1.0 to −1.0. A correlation of ±1.0 indicates a perfect linear relationship, whereas a correlation of 0 indicates no linear relationship.

dependent variable The variable to be predicted or explained in a regression model. This variable is assumed to be functionally related to the independent variable.

independent variable A variable related to a dependent variable in a regression equation. The independent variable is used in a regression model to estimate the value of the dependent variable.

least squares criterion The criterion for determining a regression line that minimizes the sum of squared residuals.

regression coefficients In the simple regression model, there are two coefficients: the intercept and the slope.

regression slope coefficient The average change in the dependent variable for a unit increase in the independent variable. The slope coefficient may be positive or negative, depending on the relationship between the two variables.

residual The difference between the actual value of the dependent variable and the value predicted by the regression model.

scatter plot A two-dimensional plot showing the (X, Y) value for each observation. The scatter plot is used as a picture of the relationship between two variables.

simple regression analysis A regression model that uses one independent variable to explain the variation in the dependent variable. The model takes the form

$$Y_i = \beta_0 + \beta_1 X_i + e_i$$

spurious correlation Correlation between two variables that have no known cause-and-effect connection.

standard error of the estimate A measure of the dispersion of the actual Y values around the regression line.

CHAPTER FORMULAS

Correlation coefficient

$$r = \frac{n\Sigma XY - \Sigma X\Sigma Y}{\sqrt{[n(\Sigma X^2) - (\Sigma X)^2][n(\Sigma Y^2) - (\Sigma Y)^2]}}$$

Test statistic for significance of the correlation coefficient

$$t = \frac{r}{\sqrt{\dfrac{1 - r^2}{n - 2}}}$$

Coefficient of determination

$$R^2 = \frac{\text{SSR}}{\text{TSS}} = 1 - \frac{\text{SSE}}{\text{TSS}}$$

Least squares estimate of the regression slope coefficient

$$b_1 = \frac{\Sigma XY - \dfrac{\Sigma X \Sigma Y}{n}}{\Sigma X^2 - \dfrac{(\Sigma X)^2}{n}} = \frac{\Sigma(X - \overline{X})(Y - \overline{Y})}{\Sigma(X - \overline{X})^2}$$

Least squares estimate of the regression intercept coefficient

$$b_0 = \overline{Y} - b_1\overline{X}$$

Standard error of the slope coefficient

$$S_{b_1} = \frac{S_e}{\sqrt{\Sigma(X - \overline{X})^2}}$$

Standard error of the estimate

$$S_e = \sqrt{\frac{\text{SSE}}{n - 2}}$$

Sum of squares error

$$\text{SSE} = \sum_{i=1}^{n} (Y_i - \hat{Y}_i)^2$$

Total sum of squares

$$\text{TSS} = \sum_{i=1}^{n} (Y_i - \overline{Y})^2$$

Test statistic for significance of the slope coefficient

$$t = \frac{b_1 - \beta_1}{S_{b_1}}$$

Test statistic for significance of the simple regression model

$$F = \frac{\dfrac{\text{SSR}}{1}}{\dfrac{\text{SSE}}{n - 2}}$$

Prediction interval for average Y, given X_p

$$\hat{Y} \pm t_{\alpha/2} \sqrt{\frac{\text{SSE}}{n-2}} \sqrt{\frac{1}{n} + \frac{(X_p - \overline{X})^2}{\Sigma X^2 - \frac{(\Sigma X)^2}{n}}}$$

Prediction interval for a particular Y, given X_p

$$\hat{Y} \pm t_{\alpha/2} \sqrt{\frac{\text{SSE}}{n-2}} \sqrt{1 + \frac{1}{n} + \frac{(X_p - \overline{X})^2}{\Sigma X^2 - \frac{(\Sigma X)^2}{n}}}$$

TECHNICAL APPENDIX

Derivation of Least Squares Equations

Objective:

$$\text{Min}\Sigma(Y_i - \hat{Y}_i)^2$$

where

$$\hat{Y}_i = b_0 + b_1(X_i)$$

Thus the objective is

$$\text{Min}\Sigma[Y_i - (b_0 + b_1X_i)]^2$$

Then let

$$Q = \Sigma[Y_i - (b_0 + b_1X_i)]^2$$

Then to minimize Q, we take partial derivatives with respect to b_0 and b_1, as follows:

$$\partial Q/\partial b_0 = -2\Sigma[Y_i - b_0 - b_1X_i]$$

and

$$\partial Q/\partial b_1 = -2\Sigma X_i[Y_i - b_0 - b_1X_i]$$

Then to determine b_0 and b_1 such that Q is minimized, we set the derivatives equal to 0 and formulate them as a system of two equations and two unknowns, as follows:

$$-2\Sigma(Y_i - b_0 - b_1X_i) = 0$$
$$-2\Sigma X_i(Y_i - b_0 - b_1X_i) = 0$$

Reformulating these equations, the −2 values cancel and we get

$$\Sigma Y_i - nb_0 - b_1\Sigma X_i = 0$$
$$\Sigma X_i Y_i - b_0\Sigma X_i - b_1\Sigma X_i^2 = 0$$

Then

$$\Sigma Y_i = nb_0 + b_1\Sigma X_i$$
$$\Sigma X_i Y_i = b_0\Sigma X_i + b_1\Sigma X_i^2$$

Solving for b_0 and b_1 we get

$$b_1 = \frac{\Sigma X_i Y_i - \dfrac{\Sigma X_i \, \Sigma Y_i}{n}}{\Sigma X_i^2 - \dfrac{(\Sigma X_i)^2}{n}} = \frac{\Sigma(X_i - \overline{X})(Y_i - \overline{Y})}{\Sigma(X_i - \overline{X})^2}$$

$$b_0 = \overline{Y} - b_1\overline{X}$$

SOLVED PROBLEMS

1. The Cal-Pit Water Company, located in Pittsburg, California, has selected a random sample of fifteen customers to see if it can develop a model for predicting water usage. Because of the short supply of water in the area, predicting water usage is an important part of the company's planning activities.

   The company wants to see whether a simple linear regression model, with family size as the independent variable and water used as the dependent variable, can be a valid predictive tool. The data based on the past month's water usage are as follows:

Customer	*Water Used (gals)* Y	*Family Size* X
1	1,100	3
2	1,425	5
3	785	2
4	950	3
5	1,200	4
6	1,152	4
7	973	3
8	1,525	5
9	1,600	4
10	700	3
11	1,100	5
12	1,414	4
13	700	2
14	953	2
15	1,063	2

Solution

The first step is to draw the scatter plot.

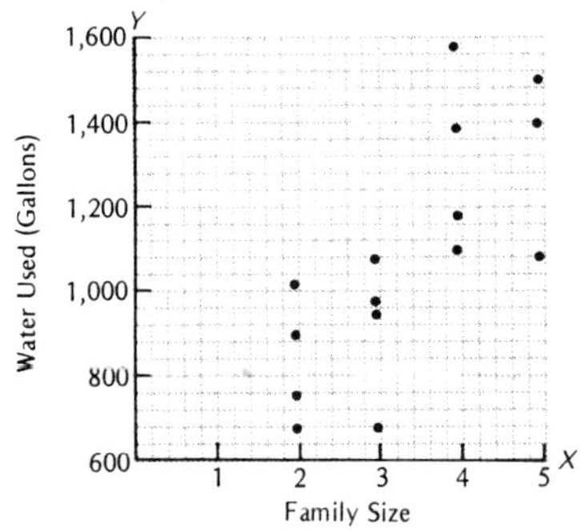

Although not perfect, there does appear to be a positive linear relationship between water used and family size. The next step is to calculate the correlation coefficient, r. Recall that r is a measure of the strength of the linear relationship between two variables and is calculated with the following equation:

$$r = \frac{n\Sigma XY - \Sigma X \Sigma Y}{\sqrt{[n(\Sigma X^2) - (\Sigma X)^2]\,[n(\Sigma Y^2) - (\Sigma Y)^2]}}$$

Instead of calculating this value by hand, a computer was used, and the resulting printout is

```
*****************************************************************
VARIABLE SELECTED IS.....X
SUM OF SQUARES REDUCED IN THIS STEP............622130
R-SQUARE...............................551986
CORRELATION COEFFICIENT................742958
F FOR ANALYSIS OF VARIANCE (D.F. = 1, 13)........16.1069
STANDARD ERROR OF ESTIMATE..........197.084
VARIABLE      REG. COEFF.      STD. ERR.-COEFF.      COMPUTED T
X                188.011               46.978              4.00212
INTERCEPT 470.094
*****************************************************************
```

The correlation coefficient in this computer output is $r = 0.743$. The test of significance is

$$H_0: \ \rho = 0$$
$$H_A: \ \rho \neq 0$$
$$\alpha = 0.05$$

$$t = \frac{r}{\sqrt{\dfrac{1 - r^2}{n - 2}}} = \frac{0.743}{\sqrt{\dfrac{1 - (0.743)^2}{13}}}$$

$$= 4.002$$

The critical t for an alpha level of 0.05 and 13 degrees of freedom is 2.160, and, since 4.002 is greater than 2.160, we conclude that there is a significant linear relationship between the two variables.

The next step is to calculate the regression coefficients. This was also done by the computer. The estimates are

$$\hat{Y} = 470.094 + 188.011X$$

The standard error of the estimate is 197.084. The table of residuals printed by the computer program is

OBS. NO.	Y OBSERVED	Y ESTIMATED	RESIDUAL
1	1100	1034.13	65.8713
2	1425	1410.15	14.8486
3	785	846.117	-61.1173
4	950	1034.13	-84.1287
5	1200	1222.14	-22.1401
6	1152	1222.14	-70.1401
7	973	1034.13	-61.1287
8	1525	1410.15	114.849
9	1600	1222.14	377.860
10	700	1034.13	-334.129
11	1100	1410.15	-310.151
12	1414	1222.14	191.860
13	700	846.117	-146.117
14	953	846.117	106.883
15	1063	846.117	216.883

Although our test of significance has indicated that family size has a positive linear relationship to water usage, note that family size explained only 55% of the variation in water usage for the sample data. Also, the standard error of the estimate, 197.084, is quite large, indicating that any prediction interval developed will be imprecise.

2. Referring to Solved Problem 1, suppose a family of five is going to be added to the Cal-Pit Water Company's customer list. Using the regression model developed in Problem 1, determine the 90% confidence interval for the number of gallons of water this family will use.

Solution

The desired prediction interval format is

$$\hat{Y} \pm t_{\alpha/2}\sqrt{\frac{\text{SSE}}{n-2}}\sqrt{1 + \frac{1}{n} + \frac{(X_p - \overline{X})^2}{\Sigma X^2 - \frac{(\Sigma X)^2}{n}}}$$

To obtain the value of $\hat{Y}$, we substitute 5 for X in the regression model.

$$\begin{aligned}\hat{Y} &= 470.094 + 188.011(5)\\ &= 1{,}410.149\end{aligned}$$

Thus, the point estimate of water used by this family of five is roughly 1,410 gallons.

To determine the confidence interval, you should recall that $\sqrt{SSE/(n-2)}$ is the standard error of the estimate. This value is 197.084 and appeared on the computer printout shown earlier. Thus, we have

$$1{,}410 \pm 1.771(197.084)\sqrt{1 + \frac{1}{15} + \frac{(X_p - \overline{X})^2}{\Sigma X^2 - \dfrac{(\Sigma X)^2}{n}}}$$

Our next step is to complete the calculations under the square root.

Family Size X	X^2	*Family Size* X	X^2
3	9	4	16
5	25	3	9
2	4	5	25
3	9	4	16
4	16	2	4
4	16	2	4
3	9	2	4
5	25		

$$\Sigma X = 51, \quad \Sigma X^2 = 191$$

Then

$$\overline{X} = \frac{51}{15} = 3.4$$

Thus the 90% prediction interval, given $X_p = 5$, is

$$1{,}410 \pm 1.771(197.084)\sqrt{1 + \frac{1}{15} + \frac{(5 - 3.4)^2}{191 - \dfrac{2{,}601}{15}}}$$

$$1{,}410 \pm 384.28$$

$$1{,}025.72 \text{ gal} \;\_\_\_\_\; 1{,}794.28 \text{ gal}$$

The Cal-Pit Water Company can be confident that this family of five will use between 1,026 and 1,794 gallons of water per month. Although this might be helpful information, the precision of the estimate is poor.

CONCEPTUAL QUESTIONS AND ASSIGNMENTS

29. Think of two variables that you believe would be negatively related in a somewhat linear manner. Describe what is meant by a negative linear relationship.

30. One statistics student was recently working on a class project that required him to compute a correlation coefficient for two variables. After careful work he arrived at a correlation coefficient of 2.45. Interpret this correlation coefficient for the student who did the calculations.

31. Referring to Problem 30, another student in the same class computed the correlation between the two variables to be −0.45 ($r = -0.45$). After trying several times and always coming up with the same result, she felt that she must be doing something wrong since the value was negative and she knew that this could not be right. Comment on this student's conclusion.

32. If we select a random sample of data for two variables and, after computing the correlation coefficient, conclude that the two variables may have zero correlation, can we say that there is no relationship between the two variables? Discuss.

33. Discuss why prediction intervals that attempt to predict a particular Y value are less precise than prediction intervals for predicting an average Y.

34. If you have tested for the significance of the correlation between two variables and found that the true correlation may be 0, is it feasible to develop a regression model using the same variables and data? Discuss.

ADDITIONAL PROBLEMS

35. The Farmington City Council recently commissioned a study of the park users. Data were collected on the age of the person surveyed and the number of times he or she has been to the park in the past month. The data collected were as follows:

Park Visits Y	*Age* X
7	16
3	15
6	28
5	16
1	29
2	38
4	48
8	18
4	24
5	33
1	56

Draw a scatter plot for these data and discuss what, if any, relationship appears to be present between the two variables.

36. Referring to Problem 35, compute the correlation between age and the number of visits to the park. Write a letter to the Farmington City Council explaining what the correlation measures. Test to determine whether the true correlation might actually equal 0. Use an α level of 0.10. Discuss.

37. A marketing research study performed by the marketing division of the Klondike Company surveyed the income levels and expenditures on recreation for a sample of twenty people. Measurements recorded Y, the expenditures on recreation during the previous year, and X, the total annual family income.

Y	X	Y	X
$1,425	$21,300	900	17,600
1,675	30,200	1,000	16,890
1,356	31,500	2,450	28,000
4,530	45,900	650	14,300
3,200	34,600	300	9,800
1,060	17,800	1,500	24,700
4,090	53,600	890	20,500
1,200	17,400	2,300	31,700
1,800	26,800	3,100	47,800
700	15,700	100	8,400

Draw a scatter plot for these data and discuss what, if any, relationship between the variables appears to exist based on the scatter plot.

38. Refer to Problem 37 and compute the correlation coefficient for the two variables *income* and *dollars spent on recreation.* Test to determine whether the true correlation is different from 0, using an alpha level of 0.05.

39. The Harris Corporation has recently done a study of homes that have sold in the Detroit area within the past 18 months. Data were recorded for the asking price (X) and the number of weeks (Y) the home was on the market before it sold. The data collected were as follows:

Y	X
23	$ 76,500
48	102,000
9	53,000
26	84,200
20	73,000
40	125,000
51	109,000
18	60,000
25	87,000
62	94,000
33	76,000
11	90,000
15	61,000
26	86,000
27	70,000
56	133,000
12	93,000

Draw a scatter plot for these data and indicate what, if any, relationship exists between the variables based on your analysis of the scatter plot.

40. Refer to Problem 39 and compute the correlation coefficient for the number of weeks the house has been on the market and the asking price of the house. Test at an alpha level of 0.10 to determine whether the sample data support or refute the null hypothesis that states that the true correlation is 0. Discuss your results.
41. Referring to Problem 39, develop a 90% confidence interval estimate for the true regression slope for the model using *asking price of a home* as the independent variable and *weeks on the market* as the dependent variable.
42. The Savemore Brokerage Firm of Spokane, Washington, recently studied a random sample of companies whose stock is sold on the New York Stock Exchange. Among other things, it collected data on stock price, *Y*, and previous years's profits, *X*. The following data were collected. (The *X* variable is measured in thousands of dollars.)

Y	X	Y	X
$18.70	$ 40,000	12.60	12,500
34.50	24,900	43.60	9,000
25.70	102,000	33.50	23,900
8.90	44,000	71.80	15,000
25.90	123,700	15.00	45,000
11.11	36,900	6.78	99,500
21.00	3,700	21.70	45,300
3.50	145,900	44.70	23,600

Draw a scatter plot for these data and discuss what, if any, relationship appears to exist between the two variables. Also comment on what other factors might be important to consider when studying stock price and earnings of the company.
43. The Penrose Consulting Company performs studies for universities that want to raise money through their alumni associations. As part of its work, it recently sampled eighteen universities across the United States and determined the number of alumni and the total dollars in gifts received from alumni during the previous academic year. The following data were recorded.

School	*Number of Alumni* X	*Gift Money* Y
1	987	$ 234,700
2	1,350	769,000
3	2,345	1,230,000
4	1,300	450,780
5	12,569	6,450,000
6	8,560	2,650,000
7	3,450	1,430,000
8	1,890	230,000
9	23,456	4,560,000
10	12,700	2,678,900

(continued)

School	Number of Alumni X	Gift Money Y
11	4,600	800,000
12	5,700	2,780,000
13	23,600	7,000,000
14	33,450	8,900,000
15	28,900	8,600,000
16	1,800	133,000
17	12,800	5,790,000
18	20,540	2,400,300

a. Draw a scatter plot of these two variables. Based on this plot only, does it appear that a linear relationship exists between the two variables?
b. Compute the correlation coefficient and discuss what it measures.
c. Test to determine whether the population correlation coefficient is actually 0, using an alpha level of 0.05.

44. A company that makes a cattle feed supplement has studied 335 cattle and found the correlation between the amount of supplement fed and the daily weight gain to be 0.104 ($r = 0.104$). Based on these results, what should be concluded about the true correlation between these two variables? Test using an alpha level of 0.05. Comment on the results.

45. The Smithfield Tobacco Company recently studied a random sample of thirty of its distributors and found the correlation between sales and advertising dollars to be 0.67. Can it conclude that there is a significant linear relationship between sales and advertising? If so, is it fair to conclude that advertising causes sales to increase?

46. The Grinfield Service Company marketing director is interested in analyzing the relationship between her company's sales and the advertising dollars spent. In the course of her analysis, she selected a random sample of 20 weeks and recorded the sales for each week and the amount spent on advertising. These data are shown as follows:

Sales	Advertising	Sales	Advertising
$2,050	$180	3,250	300
3,760	243	4,680	402
1,897	204	4,200	399
2,567	199	2,400	209
4,330	356	1,890	245
5,670	605	3,600	190
2,356	200	5,700	480
3,456	304	5,690	515
1,254	105	2,300	300
4,300	379	1,700	145

a. Identify the independent and dependent variables.
b. Draw a scatter plot with the dependent variable on the vertical axis and the independent variable on the horizontal axis.

c. Compute the correlation coefficient for these two variables and test to determine whether the true population correlation is different from 0 at the alpha level of 0.05.
d. Develop the least squares regression equation for these variables. Plot the regression line on the scatter plot.
e. Perform tests of significance on both the regression model and the slope coefficient.

47. The Rio-River Railroad, headquartered in Santa Fe, New Mexico, is trying to devise a method for allocating fuel costs to individual railroad cars on a particular route between Denver and Santa Fe. The railroad thinks that fuel consumption will increase as more cars are added to the train, but it is uncertain how much cost should be assigned to each additional car. In an effort to deal with this problem, the cost-accounting department has randomly sampled ten trips between the two cities and recorded the following data:

Rail Cars X	*Fuel (units/mile)* Y
18	55
18	50
35	76
35	80
45	117
40	90
37	80
50	125
40	100
27	75

a. Draw a scatter plot for these two variables and comment on the apparent relationship between fuel consumption and the number of rail cars on the train.
b. Compute the correlation coefficient between fuel consumption and train cars. Test statistically the hypothesis that the true correlation is 0, using an alpha level of 0.05. Comment on the results of this test. Do these results necessarily indicate that adding more cars will increase the fuel usage?
c. Develop the least squares regression model to help explain the variation in fuel consumption. Interpret the results and clearly show the least squares equation.

48. Henry Prince has served as a consultant to the federal government for several years. Recently, he was asked to make a study of high school students to obtain information about how television viewing habits are related to academic performance. Possibly because Henry is always paid by the hour, he has decided to perform two studies. In the first, he collected data from fifty randomly selected students for two variables: *hours of television watched per week* and *grade-point average during a given period.* In the second study, he

TABLE 13P-1 Study 1 Computer Printout

```
*****************************************************************************
CØRRELATIØN CØEFFICIENTS

                                        Y            X
                              Y    1.0000        -.4926
                              X    -.4926        1.0000
-----------------------------------------------------------------------------
DEPENDENT VARIABLE    Y   GRADE PØINT AVERAGE
INDEPENDENT VARIABLE   X   TV HØURS
-----------------------------------------------------------------------------
MEAN X   20.0
-----------------------------------------------------------------------------
R SQUARE                       .2426
STANDARD ERRØR ØF ESTIMATE     .5200
-------------------VARIABLES IN THE EQUATIØN---------------------------------
VARIABLE                               B       STD. ERRØR B      T VALUE
X                                   -.0015       .000382
(CØNSTANT)                          2.5300
*****************************************************************************
```

collected data from 100 students for two variables: *number of hours per week working at a paying job* and *grade-point average during a given period.*

Table 13P-1 shows a partial computer printout for the first study. Table 13P-2 shows a partial computer printout for the second study. Using the information in these printouts, and some insight of your own, answer Problems 48 through 52. Your responsibility in *this* problem is to fill in the missing values in Tables 13P-1 and 13P-2.

49. In his report, Henry Prince (see Problem 48) has indicated that the number of hours a student watches television each week is not a significant variable for explaining the variation in student grade-point average. He states that he tested this at the alpha level of 0.05. Based on the information provided, do you agree with Henry's conclusion? Discuss why or why not.

50. In the random sample of fifty students in study 1 (see Problem 48), the number of hours of television ranged from a low of eight to a high of forty per week. In his report, Henry states that based on the regression model, if no hours are spent watching television, students will have an average grade-point average of 2.530. Why do you suppose he came to this conclusion? Discuss whether you agree or disagree with him and indicate why.

TABLE 13P-2 Study 2 Computer Printout

```
*****************************************************************************
DEPENDENT VARIABLE   Y  GRADE PØINT AVERAGE

INDEPENDENT VARIABLE   X  HØURS WØRKED
-----------------------------------------------------------------------------
R SQUARE  .1600
-----------------------------------------------------------------------------
ANALYSIS ØF VARIANCE            D.F.    SUM ØF SQUARES      MEAN SQUARE     F

REGRESSIØN
RESIDUAL (UNEXPLAINED)          ___        _____
                                 99        550.0

------------------VARIABLES IN THE EQUATIØN------------------

VARIABLE                    B

X                         .0100

(CØNSTANT)               2.2500
*****************************************************************************
```

51. In study 2 (see Problem 48), where hours worked ranged from 0 hours to 20 hours, Henry Prince concluded that the independent variable, *hours worked,* and the dependent variable, *grade-point average,* are significantly correlated at the alpha level of 0.05. Therefore, he has stated that a student can increase his or her grade-point average by working at a paying job and should be encouraged to do so. Further, the more hours the student works, the higher the grade-point average will be. Support or refute Henry's statement.
52. In his report on study 2 (see Problem 48), Henry has indicated that he tested the significance of the model using the analysis of variance approach. However, he failed to include the results of the test in his report. Using the information in Table 13P-2, test the null hypothesis that the regression model is not significant, using the analysis of variance approach. Use an alpha level of 0.05. Discuss why a large F ratio should lead to the rejection of the null hypothesis. Also, using the information in the analysis of variance table, determine the standard error of the estimate and discuss briefly what it measures.
53. The American Airline Company recently performed a customer survey in which it asked a random sample of 100 passengers to indicate their income and the number of times they have flown on any airline for pleasure during the past year. A regression model was developed for the purposes of determining whether income could be used as a variable to explain the variation in number of times individuals fly on airlines in a year. The following regression results were obtained.

$$\hat{Y} = 0.25 + 0.0003X$$
$$S_e = 1.44$$
$$R^2 = 0.65$$
$$S_{b_1} = 0.0000222$$

a. Develop a 95% confidence interval estimate for the true regression slope and interpret this interval estimate.
b. Can the intercept of the regression equation be interpreted in this case, assuming that no one who was surveyed had an income of 0 dollars? Explain.
c. Use the information provided to perform an analysis of variance test of the significance of the regression model. Discuss your results, assuming the test is performed at the alpha level of 0.05.

54. A manager for a major manufacturing company recently delivered a speech to other managers from around the United States. During the course of the speech, he was explaining a study his company had done with respect to sales and price of a particular product. He said that it had developed a simple regression model and found the regression slope coefficient to be −3,456.98. He then said that this means that increasing price by 1 dollar will cause sales to drop by 3,456.98 units. Comment on this statement, indicating what, if anything, about the statement you agree with.

55. The Briggs Bank and Trust recently performed a study of its checking account customers. One objective of the study was to determine whether it is possible to explain the variation in average checking account balance by knowing the number of checks written per month. The sample data selected were as follows:

Average Account Balance	*Checks Written*
\$1,202	46
789	67
233	23
908	52
1,233	23
1,098	34
345	76
1,609	18
407	25
300	53
1,190	33

a. Draw a scatter plot for these data.
b. Develop the least squares regression equation for these data.
c. Develop the 90% confidence interval estimate for the true regression slope coefficient and interpret this interval.
d. Test to determine whether the true regression slope is different from 0. Use $\alpha = 0.05$. Comment on this result and the result of part c.

56. The Sanders Company production manager is in the process of performing a productivity study of the employees at the Black Hills plant. In the process of performing this study, he has selected a random sample of twenty employees who have worked for the company for 4 years or more. For each employee, he measured the number of hours of special training the employee has taken and the production rate for the employee in pieces per day produced. The following summary data are available:

$$Y = \text{Pieces produced per day}$$
$$X = \text{Hours of special training}$$
$$\overline{X} = 13.50$$
$$S_e = 11.0$$
$$\overline{Y} = 125.0$$
$$\hat{Y} = 88.5 + 1.5X$$
$$\Sigma(X - \overline{X})^2 = 1{,}245.0$$

a. Develop a 95% prediction interval for the average daily production for people who have taken 15.0 hours of training. Interpret this prediction interval estimate.
b. Develop a 95% prediction interval for a particular individual who has taken 8 hours of special training courses. Interpret these results.
c. Comment on whether you believe the prediction interval computed in part **b** is satisfactory for predicting productivity for individual employees with 8 hours of courses. Discuss.

57. A company is considering recruiting new employees from a particular college and plans to place a great deal of emphasis on college grade-point average. However, the company is aware that not all schools have the same grading standards, so it is possible that a student at this school might have a lower (or higher) grade-point average than a student from another school, yet really be on par with the other student. To make this comparison between schools, the company has devised a test that it has administered utilizing a sample size of 400. With the results of the test, it has developed a regression model which it uses to predict student grade-point average. The following equation represents the model:

$$\hat{Y} = 1.0 + 0.028X$$

The R^2 for this model is 0.88 and the standard error of the estimate is 0.20, based on the sample data used to develop the model. Note that the dependent variable is the grade-point average and the independent variable is test score, where this score can range from 0 to 100. For the sample data used to develop the model, the following values are known.

$$\overline{Y} = 2.76$$
$$\overline{X} = 68$$
$$\Sigma(X - \overline{X})^2 = 148{,}885.73$$

a. Based on the information contained in this problem, can you conclude that the regression slope coefficient is significantly different from 0, using an alpha level of 0.05?

b. Suppose a student interviews with this company, takes the company test, and scores 80% correct. What is the 90% prediction interval estimate for this student's grade-point average? Interpret the interval.

c. Suppose the student in part **b** actually has a 2.90 grade-point average at this school. Based on this evidence, what might be concluded about this person's actual grade-point average compared with other students at other schools with the same grade-point average? Discuss the limitations you might place on this conclusion.

58. Referring to Problem 57, suppose a second student with a 2.45 grade-point average took the test and scored 65% correct. What is the 90% prediction interval for this student's "real" grade-point average? Interpret.

59. Suppose the company that developed the test discussed in Problem 57 is interested in developing a 95% prediction interval estimate for the average grade-point average for students who score 88% correct on this test. Calculate this interval and interpret it.

60. An economist for the state government of Mississippi recently collected the following data on the percentage of people unemployed in the state and the interest rate of treasury bills offered by the federal government.

Unemployment Percentage	*Treasury Bill Interest Rate Percentage*
4.4	8.1
7.8	9.8
4.7	8.2
5.0	8.4
3.9	7.9
5.1	8.3
9.5	10.2
8.8	10.0
4.5	8.4
5.0	8.5
10.2	10.2
9.0	10.1
6.0	8.8
5.0	8.3
9.5	10.1
13.4	10.7
15.0	11.4
4.0	7.8

Assuming that these data were selected as a random sample of weeks from the past 5 years, develop a plot showing the relationship between the two variables. Describe the relationship as being either linear or curvilinear.

61. Referring to Problem 60:
   a. Develop a linear regression model with *unemployment rate* as the dependent variable. Write a short report describing the model and indicating the important measures. Can it be concluded that the linear regression model is statistically significant? Test at the alpha level of 0.05.
   b. Determine what appropriate transformation should be made to the independent variable to improve the regression results. Make this transformation and compute the new regression equation. Write a short report that compares the regression results obtained in part **a** with those obtained with this transformation. Perform any necessary statistical tests using an alpha level of 0.05.
   c. Substitute the values for the independent variable into each of the regression equations and plot these on a graph with Y on the vertical axis and X on the horizontal axis. Describes the two regression lines.

62. The Cooley Service Center polishes and cleans automobiles. It has major accounts such as the Bayview Taxi Service and Bayview Police Department. It also does work for the general public by appointment. Recently, the manager decided to survey customers to determine how satisfied they were with the work performed by the Cooley Service Center. He devised a rating scale between 0 and 100, with 0 being poor and 100 being excellent service. He selected a random sample of fourteen customers and asked the customers when they picked up their cars to rate the service. He also recorded the amount of time spent on each customer's car. These data are shown as follows:

Rating Y	*Time (in hours)* X
85	1.50
60	0.20
70	0.30
72	0.35
80	1.00
65	0.23
70	0.32
90	2.50
84	1.60
70	0.27
82	1.60
75	0.40
77	0.45
89	2.00

Draw a scatter plot showing these two variables, with the Y variable on the vertical axis and the X variable on the horizontal axis. Describe the relationship between these two variables.

63. Referring to Problem 62:
   a. Develop a linear regression model to explain the variation in the service rating. Write a short report describing the model and showing the results of pertinent hypothesis tests, using an alpha level of 0.10. Comment on whether you think the model could be improved by transforming the independent variable. Discuss.
   b. Determine what transformation to the independent variable might be appropriate. Then develop a regression model, using the transformed independent variable, and write a short report comparing this model to the one developed in part **a**. Discuss which model you prefer and why.

DATABASE PROBLEMS

The following questions and problems pertain directly to the State Department of Transportation case study and database introduced in Chapter 1. The questions and problems were written assuming that you will have access to a computer and appropriate statistical software. The database containing 100 observations and seventeen variables is shown in Table 1-1 in Chapter 1. *Assume that the data were collected using a simple random sampling process.*

1. Draw a scatter plot for the variables X_6 and X_9. Compute the correlation coefficient for these two variables and test statistically whether a significant linear relationship exists between these two variables. Use an $\alpha = 0.05$ level.
2. Draw a scatter plot and determine the correlation coefficient for the variables age, X_9, and total number of convictions, X_5. Test to determine whether there is a significant linear relationship between these two variables, using an $\alpha = 0.05$ level.
3. Referring to Problem 1, develop a simple linear regression model using X_6 as the dependent variable and X_9 as the independent variable. Test the significance of the slope coefficient and develop a 95% confidence interval estimate for the true regression slope coefficient. Indicate the R^2 and the standard error.
4. Determine the simple linear regression equation where variable X_{15} is the dependent variable and X_{13} is the independent variable. Make sure you test the appropriate hypotheses and that you develop a 90% confidence interval estimate for the regression slope. Indicate the R^2 and the standard error. Write a short letter describing the model and indicate whether it would be useful in predicting the number of years of formal education an individual would have. Test all hypotheses at the $\alpha = 0.10$ level.
5. Develop a simple linear regression model using X_5 as the dependent variable and X_{15} as the independent variable. Is the model statistically significant at the $\alpha = 0.05$ level? How much of the variation in X_5 has been explained by the model? Write a report that fully analyzes the regression results. Your report should include a scatter plot of the variables.

ADDITIONAL DATABASE PROBLEMS

The questions and problems in this section reference the various databases that accompany this text and which are described in Chapter 1. Your instructor has been provided a diskette with these databases. It is expected that you will be using computer software to access these data and to perform the required calculations and graphs.

DATABASE: **CITIES** (*Refer to the database description in Chapter 1.*)

1. Using X_2, estimated population growth, as the dependent variable and X_1, 1990 population, as the independent variable, do the following:
   a. Determine the correlation between the two variables. Interpret this value and test to determine whether the correlation is significant. Test at the $\alpha = 0.05$ level. Discuss your results.
   b. Develop the least squares regression model. Provide an interpretation of the regression slope coefficient. Test to determine whether the slope coefficient is significant at the $\alpha = 0.05$ level. Be sure to state the null hypothesis. Discuss your results.
   c. Compute the R^2 value and interpret it.
   d. Construct and interpret a 90% confidence interval estimate for the true population slope coefficient.
   e. Determine the predicted value for growth rate for a city having a population of 500,000 people. Also, determine a 95% prediction interval for this same city.
2. Using X_3, 1989 unemployment rate, as the dependent variable and X_8, labor market stress index, as the independent variable, do the following:
   a. Determine the correlation between the two variables. Interpret this value and test to determine whether the correlation is significant. Test at the $\alpha = 0.05$ level. Discuss your results.
   b. Develop the least squares regression model. Provide an interpretation of the regression slope coefficient. Test to determine whether the slope coefficient is significant at the $\alpha = 0.05$ level. Be sure to state the null hypothesis. Discuss your results.
   c. Compute the R^2 value and interpret it.
   d. Construct and interpret a 90% confidence interval estimate for the true population slope coefficient.
   e. Determine the predicted value for unemployment rate for a city having a labor market stress index of 125. Also, determine a 95% prediction interval for this same city. Interpret.

DATABASE: **FAST100** (*Refer to the database description in Chapter 1.*)

1. Using X_4, profits, as the dependent variable and X_2, total sales, as the independent variable, do the following:

a. Determine the correlation between the two variables. Interpret this value and test to determine whether the correlation is significant. Test at the $\alpha = 0.05$ level. Discuss your results.
b. Develop the least squares regression model. Provide an interpretation of the regression slope coefficient. Test to determine whether the slope coefficient is significant at the $\alpha = 0.05$ level. Be sure to state the null hypothesis. Discuss your results.
c. Compute the R^2 value and interpret it.
d. Construct and interpret a 95% confidence interval estimate for the true population slope coefficient.
e. Determine the predicted value for profits for a firm having total sales of $260 million. Also, determine a 90% prediction interval for this company. In addition, determine the 90% prediction interval for average sales for firms with $260 million in sales. Interpret.

2. As a decision maker, suppose you are interested in developing a linear regression model to explain the variation in stock price, X_5. Considering all variables, except X_8, as potential independent variables, which single variable would be the best to use? Discuss clearly why you selected that variable. Provide any statistical justification necessary to support your position. Discuss.
3. Using X_5, stock price, as the dependent variable and X_4, profits, as the independent variable, do the following:
   a. Determine the correlation between the two variables. Interpret this value and test to determine whether the correlation is significant. Test at the $\alpha = 0.05$ level. Discuss your results.
   b. Develop the least squares regression model. Provide an interpretation of the regression slope coefficient. Test to determine whether the slope coefficient is significant at the $\alpha = 0.05$ level. Be sure to state the null hypothesis. Discuss your results.
   c. Compute the R^2 value and interpret it.
   d. Construct and interpret a 95% confidence interval estimate for the true population slope coefficient.
   e. Determine the predicted value for stock price for a firm having total profits of $50 million. Also, determine a 90% prediction interval for this company. In addition, determine the 90% prediction interval for average stock prices for firms with $50 million in profits. Interpret.

DATABASE: **PACRIM** (*Refer to the database description in Chapter 1.*)

1. Placing yourself in the position of an analyst studying Pacific Rim countries, suppose you are interested in developing a regression model to explain the variation in 1989 after-tax profits for companies operating in the region. To do this, you plan to use year-end assets, X_5, as the independent variable of interest.

a. What is the correlation between these two variables? Test the significance at the $\alpha = 0.05$ level and discuss.
b. Develop the simple linear regression equation. Write a short statement that describes the model. What percentage of the variation in the dependent variable is explained by the model? Use the ANOVA approach to test whether the percentage explained is statistically significant at an $\alpha = 0.05$ level.
c. Interpret the slope coefficient (see part **b**) and then develop a 95% confidence interval estimate for the slope coefficient and interpret this estimate. Based on this estimate, can it be concluded that the true population slope is different from 0? Discuss.

2. Placing yourself in the position of an analyst studying Pacific Rim countries, suppose you are interested in developing a regression model to explain the variation in number of employees for companies operating in the region. To do this, you plan to use year-end stockholders' equity, X_7, as the independent variable of interest.
   a. What is the correlation between these two variables? Test the significance at the $\alpha = 0.05$ level and discuss.
   b. Develop the simple linear regression equation. Write a short statement that describes the model. What percentage of the variation in the dependent variable is explained by the model? Use the ANOVA approach to test whether the percentage explained is statistically significant at an $\alpha = 0.05$ level.
   c. Interpret the slope coefficient (see part **b**) and then develop a 95% confidence interval estimate for the slope coefficient and interpret this estimate. Based on this estimate, can it be concluded that the true population slope is different from 0? Discuss.

DATABASE: **TRUCKS** (*Refer to the database description in Chapter 1.*)

1. As an analyst for the Idaho Transportation Department (ITD), you have been given the assignment to develop a simple linear regression model that could be used to predict POE gross vehicle weight. The independent variable being proposed is WIM gross weight. Even if the POE and WIM scales do not provide identical weights, it is thought that there may be a linear relationship between the two that can be modeled.
   a. What is the correlation between these two variables? Test the significance at the $\alpha = 0.05$ level and discuss.
   b. Develop the simple linear regression equation. Write a short statement that describes the model. What percentage of the variation in the dependent variable is explained by the model? Use the ANOVA approach to test whether the percentage explained its statistically significant at an $\alpha = 0.05$ level.
   c. Interpret the slope coefficient (see part **b**) and then develop a 95% confidence interval estimate for the slope coefficient and interpret this

estimate. Based on this estimate, can it be concluded that the true population slope is different from 0? Discuss.

d. Write a short report that describes the model and discusses whether the ITD should use this model for prediction purposes. As part of your analysis, develop and interpret a 95% prediction interval for the particular POE gross weight for a truck weighing 75,000 pounds on the WIM scale.

2. As an analyst for the Idaho Transportation Department, you have been given the assignment to develop a simple linear regression model that could be used to predict POE gross vehicle weight. The independent variable being proposed is vehicle speed. It is thought that there may be a linear relationship between the two variables that can be modeled.

a. What is the correlation between these two variables? Test the significance at the $\alpha = 0.05$ level and discuss.

b. Develop the simple linear regression equation. Write a short statement that describes the model. What percentage of the variation in the dependent variable is explained by the model? Use the ANOVA approach to test whether the percentage explained is statistically significant at an $\alpha = 0.05$ level.

c. Interpret the slope coefficient (see part **b**) and then develop a 95% confidence interval estimate for the slope coefficient and interpret this estimate. Based on this estimate, can it be concluded that the true population slope is different from 0? Discuss.

d. Write a short report that describes the model and discusses whether the ITD should use this model for prediction purposes. As part of your analysis, develop and interpret a 95% prediction interval for the particular POE gross weight for a truck traveling 60 mph when it crosses the WIM scale.

CASES

13A Alamar Industries

While driving home in northern Kentucky at 8:00 P.M., Juan Alamar wondered whether his father had done him any favor retiring early and letting him take control of the family machine tool restoration business. When his father had started the business of overhauling machine tools, both for resale and on a contract basis, American companies dominated the tool manufacturing market. Over the last 30 years the original equipment industry had been devastated, first by competition from Germany and then from Japan. While foreign competition had not yet invaded the overhaul segment of the business, Juan had heard about foreign companies establishing operations on the West Coast.

The foreign competitors were apparently stressing the high quality service and operations that had been responsible for their great inroads into the original equipment market. Last week Juan had attended a day-long conference on total quality management, discussing the advantages of competing for the Baldrige Award, the national quality award established in 1987. Presenters from past Baldrige winners, including Xerox, Federal Express, Cadillac, and Motorola, stressed the positive effect on their company of winning, but said similar effects would be possible for any company. This assertion of only positive effects is what Juan questioned. He was certain that the effect on his remaining free time would not be positive.

The Baldrige Award considers seven corporate dimensions of quality. While the award is not based on a numerical score, an overall score is calculated. The maximum score is 1,000, with most recent winners scoring about 800. While Juan did not doubt the award was good for the winners, he wondered about the nonwinners. In particular, he wondered about any relationship between attempting to improve quality according to the Baldrige dimensions and company profitability. While individual company scores are not released, Juan was able to talk to one of the conference presenters to share some anonymous data, such as a company's score in the year applied, return on its investment in the year applied, and return on its investment in the year following. Juan decided to commit the company to a total quality management process, if the data provided evidence that it would lead to increased profitability.

Baldrige Score	*ROI Application Year*	*ROI Next Year*
470	11%	13%
520	10	11
660	14	15
540	12	12
600	15	16
710	16	16
580	11	12
600	12	13
740	16	16
610	11	14
570	12	13
660	17	19

13B Continental Trucking

Norm Painter is the newly hired cost analyst for Continental Trucking. Continental is a nationwide trucking firm, and, until recently, most of its routes were driven under regulated rates. These rates were set to allow small trucking firms to earn an adequate profit, leaving little incentive to work to reduce costs by efficient management techniques. In fact, the greatest effort was made to try to influence regulatory agencies to grant rate increases.

A recent rash of deregulation moves has made the long-distance trucking industry more competitive. Norm has been hired to analyze Continental's whole expense structure. As part of this study, Norm is looking at truck repair costs. Since the trucks are involved in long hauls, they inevitably break down. Up until now, little preventive maintenance has been done, and if a truck broke down in the middle of a haul, either a replacement tractor was sent or the haul was finished by an independent contractor. The truck was then repaired at the nearest local shop. Norm is sure this procedure has led to more expense than if major repairs had been made before the trucks failed.

Norm thinks that some method needs to be found for determining when preventive maintenance is needed. He believes that fuel consumption is a good indicator of possible breakdowns and that, as the trucks begin running badly, they will consume more fuel. Unfortunately, the major determinants of fuel consumption are the weight of the truck and head winds. Norm picks a sample of a single truck model and gathers data relating fuel consumption to truck weight. All trucks in the sample were in good condition. He separates the data by direction of the haul, realizing that winds tend to blow predominantly out of the west.

East–West Haul		*West–East Haul*	
Miles/Gallon	*Haul Weight*	*Miles/Gallon*	*Haul Weight*
4.1	41,000 lb	4.3	40,000 lb
4.7	36,000	4.5	37,000
3.9	37,000	4.8	36,000
4.3	38,000	5.2	38,000
4.8	32,000	5.0	35,000
5.1	37,000	4.7	42,000
4.3	46,000	4.9	37,000
4.6	35,000	4.5	36,000
5.0	37,000	5.2	42,000
		4.8	41,000

Although he can gather future data on fuel consumption and haul weight rapidly, now that Norm has these data, he is not quite sure what to do with them.

REFERENCES

Aaker, David. *Multivariate Analysis in Marketing: Theory and Applications.* 2d ed. Palo Alto, Calif: Science Press, 1981.

Berenson, Mark L., and Levine, David M. *Basic Business Statistics Concepts and Applications,* 5th edition. Englewood Cliffs, N.J.: Prentice-Hall, 1992.

Bowerman, Bruce L., and O'Connell, Richard T. *Linear Statistical Models,* 2d edition. Boston: PWS-Kent, 1990.

Draper, N. R., and Smith, H. *Applied Regression Analysis.* New York: Wiley, 1966.

Hair, Joseph F.; Anderson, Rolph E.; and Tatham, Ronald L. *Multivariate Data Analysis,* 2d edition. New York: Macmillan, 1987.

Kleinbaum, David G., and Kupper, Lawrence L. *Applied Regression Analysis and Other Multivariable Methods.* North Scituate, Mass.: Duxbury, 1978.

Neter, John, and Wasserman, William. *Applied Linear Statistical Models.* Homewood Ill.: Irwin, 1974.

Richards, Larry, and Lacava, Jerry. *Business Statistics: Why and When.* 2d ed. New York: McGraw–Hill, 1983

Wittink, Dick R. *The Application of Regression Analysis.* Needham Heights, Mass.: Allyn and Bacon, 1988.

Chapter 13

Hand-In Exercises

1. Data below for seven students show the credit hours carried in fall term and spring term of the same academic year.

a. Compute the correlation coefficient.

b. Test the hypothesis that the population correlation coefficient is 0 at the 5% level.

X = Fall credit load Y = Spring credit load

Student	X	Y
Adams	20	16
Baker	18	12
Clark	24	18
Dean	20	17
Evans	22	21
Flynn	14	10
Gill	18	10

2. A common use of regression analysis is to forecast changes in economic variables over time, using time as the predictor (independent) variable. The following data record changes in the price of a ride on a city bus over a ten year period. To simplify calculations the years are coded one through ten.

YEAR (X)	PRICE (Y)	XY	X^2	Y^2
1	7			
2	11			
3	15			
4	14			
5	18			
6	21			
7	23			
8	30			
9	32			
10	34			

a. Complete calculations in the third and fourth columns in the table and show the calculation of the slope coefficient here.

Introduction to Multiple Regression Analysis

WHY DECISION MAKERS NEED TO KNOW

Chapter 13 illustrated that decision makers often need to consider the relationship between two variables when analyzing a problem. Simple linear regression and correlation analysis provide a basis for analyzing two variables and their relationship to each other.

As you might expect, decision makers' problems are not limited to only two variables. Most practical situations involve analyzing the relationship among three or more variables. For example, a vice-president of planning for an automobile manufacturer would be interested in the relationship between her company's automobile sales and the variables that influence those sales. Included in her analysis might be such independent or explanatory variables as automobile price, competitors' sales, and advertising, as well as such economic variables as disposable personal income, the inflation rate, and the unemployment rate. The simple regression and correlation analysis techniques discussed in Chapter 13 do not allow analysis of more than two variables. This chapter introduces the extension of the simple regression methods—*multiple regression analysis.*

CHAPTER OBJECTIVES

This chapter will introduce multiple regression analysis. It will discuss how a multiple regression model is developed and how it should be applied and interpreted in a business setting.

It will also discuss how to incorporate both qualitative and quantitative variables in a multiple regression model. Finally, it will consider some potential problems in using multiple regression analysis and the possible consequences if a regression model is improperly developed.

STUDENT OBJECTIVES

After studying the material in this chapter, you should be able to do the following:

1. Recognize the need for multiple regression analysis in a decision-making situation.
2. Analyze the computer output for a multiple regression model and interpret the regression statistics.
3. Test hypotheses about the significance of a multiple regression model and test the significance of the independent variables in the model.
4. Recognize potential problems when using multiple regression analysis, including the problems of multicollinearity.
5. Incorporate qualitative variables into the regression model by using dummy variables.
6. Perform residual analysis to determine the aptness of the model.

14-1 DEVELOPING A MULTIPLE REGRESSION MODEL

Most states have provisions allowing the counties to raise revenue through property taxes. The amount of property taxes a real estate owner will pay depends on the class of property, the appraised value of the property, and the tax rate. Typically, the appraised value for tax purposes is supposed to be the market value for the property. The market value is the value the property would sell for if it were put on the open market. Usually, the county assessor is charged with the responsibility of making property appraisals. Obviously, making a correct property appraisal is important, but trying to determine how much each property would sell for if it were placed on the market is a difficult task, and many assessors are faced with irate taxpayers disputing their property taxes.

American County, located in the Midwest, is just now in the process of changing its appraisal system. The assessor has selected a sample of 531 residential properties that have sold recently in American County. Data for the following variables were obtained for each property:

$$Y = \text{Sales price}$$
$$X_1 = \text{Square feet}$$
$$X_2 = \text{Age of house}$$
$$X_3 = \text{Number of bedrooms}$$
$$X_4 = \text{Number of bathrooms}$$
$$X_5 = \text{Number of fireplaces}$$

The assessor has decided to develop an appraisal model based on multiple regression, an extension of the simple regression techniques discussed in the previous chapter.

You will remember from Chapter 13 that a simple regression model has the form shown in equation 14-1:

$$Y_i = \beta_0 + \beta_1 X_i + e_i \quad \text{(14-1)}$$

where

β_0 = Regression intercept

β_1 = Regression slope

e_i = Error

If we assume that the expected value of e_i equals 0, the regression model is given by equation 14-2:

$$E[Y] = \beta_0 + \beta_1 X \quad \text{(14-2)}$$

The simple regression model is characterized by two variables: Y, the *dependent variable,* and X, the *independent* or *explanatory variable.* The single independent variable explains some variation in the dependent variable, but unless X and Y are perfectly correlated, the proportion explained will be less than 100%. This means the error term, e_i, will be present. Recall that e_i is the *residual* and is the difference between the true regression line and the actual Y value (i.e., residual = $Y_i - \hat{Y}_i$). In Chapter 13, we assumed that these e_i values have a mean of 0 and a standard deviation called the **standard error of the estimate.** If this standard error is too large, the regression model may not be very useful for prediction.

In multiple regression analysis, additional independent variables are added to the regression model to explain some of the yet-unexplained variation in the dependent variable. Adding appropriate additional variables should thereby reduce the standard error of the estimate.

You will note as we proceed that multiple regression is merely an extension of simple regression analysis. However, as we expand the model from one independent variable to two or more there are some new considerations.

The general format of a **multiple regression model** is given by equation 14-3:

$$Y_i = \beta_0 + \beta_1 X_{1i} + \beta_2 X_{2i} + \cdots + \beta_K X_{Ki} + e_i \quad \text{(14-3)}$$

where

β_0 = Regression constant

β_1 = Regression coefficient for variable X_1

β_K = Regression coefficient for variable X_K

K = Number of independent variables

e_i = Error (residual)

There are three general assumptions of the linear multiple regression model:

1. The errors are normally distributed.
2. The mean of the error terms is 0.
3. The error terms have a constant variance, σ^2, for all combinations of values of the independent variables.

Since the error terms have a mean of 0, the expected value of Y for given values of $X_1, X_2, X_3, \ldots, X_K$ is given by equation 14-4:

$$E[Y] = \beta_0 + \beta_1 X_1 + \beta_2 X_2 + \beta_3 X_3 + \cdots + \beta_K X_K \quad \text{(14-4)}$$

This model is an extension of the simple regression model of Chapter 13 and equation 14-2. The principal difference is that, whereas equation 14-2 for the simple model is the equation for a straight line in a two-dimensional space (see Figure 14-1), the multiple regression model forms a *hyperplane* (or *response sur-*

FIGURE 14-1

Simple Regression Model (Dependent Variable: House Price; Independent Variable: Square Feet)

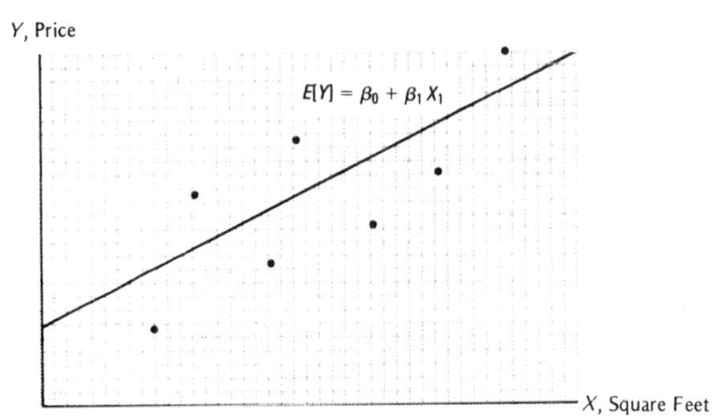

FIGURE 14-2

Illustration of a Regression Plane

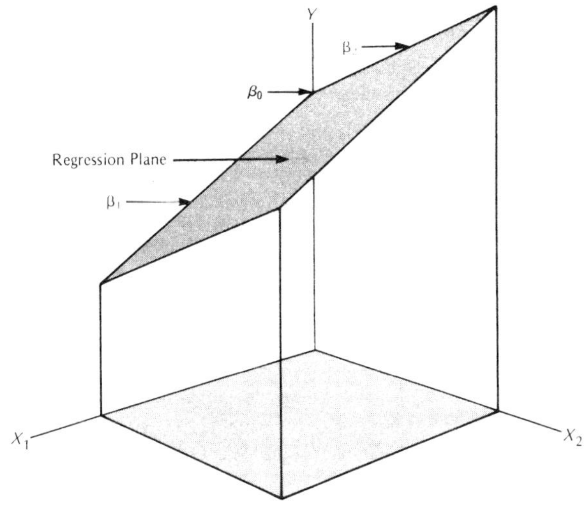

face) through multidimensional space. Each regression coefficient represents a slope. When there are only two independent variables, the **regression plane** can be drawn as shown in Figure 14-2. If there are more than two independent variables, the regression model cannot be visually represented, but the concept remains intact. The next section shows how a multiple regression model is developed.

When a decision maker has sample data available for the dependent variable and for K independent variables, the least squares regression coefficients are estimated, forming the sample regression model of the form shown in equation 14-5:

$$\hat{Y}_i = b_0 + b_1X_1 + b_2X_2 + \cdots + b_KX_K \quad \textbf{14-5}$$

where

b_0 = Y-intercept (constant)
$b_1, b_2, \ldots, b_K$ = Regression slope coefficients
$\hat{Y}_i$ = ith estimated value of the dependent variable
$X_1, X_2, \ldots, X_K$ = Independent variables

The estimates of the regression coefficients are determined mathematically so that $\Sigma(Y_i - \hat{Y}_i)^2$ is minimized. You should recall from Chapter 13 that this is referred to as the *least squares criterion*. The actual procedure for determining the values for the regression coefficients involves matrix algebra. The mathematical derivation is beyond the scope of this text, but equation 14-6 illustrates how the least squares regression coefficients are determined.

$$B = (X'X)^{-1}X'Y \quad \text{(14-6)}$$

where

$X = n \times (K + 1)$ matrix of values for the independent variables, with the first column all 1s

$Y = n \times 1$ matrix of the dependent variable values

$B = (K + 1) \times 1$ matrix of regression coefficients

(For a more complete treatment of the matrix algebra approach for estimating the multiple regression coefficients, consult *Applied Linear Statistical Models* by Neter and Wasserman.)

Almost exclusively, multiple regression analysis is performed with the aid of a computer and appropriate software. The following presentation of examples will be based on output from either GB-STAT or MINITAB. Note that each software package presents the results in a slightly different format; however, the same basic information will appear in all regression output.

Before a multiple regression analysis example is introduced, you should understand this important point: The sample size required to compute a regression model must be at least 1 greater than the number of independent variables. Thus, if we are thinking of developing a regression model with five independent variables, the absolute minimum number of cases required is six. Otherwise, the computer program will indicate an error has been made or will print out meaningless values.

As a practical matter, the sample size should be at least 4 times the number of independent variables. Thus, if we have five independent variables ($K = 5$), we would want at least twenty cases to develop the regression model.

14-2 AMERICAN COUNTY APPRAISAL MODEL

We indicated earlier that the assessor in American County wanted to use multiple regression to develop an appraisal model for residential property in the county.

The assessor gathered data on the following residential property variables for 531 houses:

Y = Sales price
X_1 = Square feet
X_2 = Age of house
X_3 = Number of bedrooms
X_4 = Number of bathrooms
X_5 = Number of fireplaces

TABLE 14-1

American County Data

Observation	Y	X_1	X_2	X_3	X_4	X_5
1	57,000	1,410	3.0	2.0	1.0	0
2	44,970	1,725	5.0	3.0	2.5	1
.	.	.	.	.	.	.
.	.	.	.	.	.	.
.	.	.	.	.	.	.
$n = 531$	110,790	2,250	1.0	4.0	2.75	2

TABLE 14-2

Means and Standard Deviations for Variables in the American County Example

Variable	Mean	Std. Dev.	Cases
Y	79,873.5619	28,034.4579	531
X_1	1,715.5273	588.1123	531
X_2	4.3936	7.7781	531
X_3	3.4038	0.0555	531
X_4	1.9143	0.6094	531
X_5	0.9209	0.5608	531

Note that sales price is the dependent variable and the other five variables are the independent variables. The assessor hopes to be able to use the variables to predict the market value (price) of residential properties in American County. Table 14-1 illustrates how the data would be arranged. Table 14-2 presents the mean and standard deviation for each variable. The standard deviation for the variable price is high, indicating a large variation in selling prices for houses.

CORRELATION MATRIX

The first step in developing the appraisal model is to examine the relationship between each independent variable and the dependent variable, *sales price.* As with simple regression analysis, we can measure the strength of the linear relationship between any two variables by calculating the correlation coefficient for each pair of (X, Y) variables using equation 14-7:

$$r = \frac{\Sigma(X_i - \overline{X})(Y_i - \overline{Y})}{\sqrt{\Sigma(X_i - \overline{X})^2 \Sigma(Y_i - \overline{Y})^2}} \qquad \textbf{14-7}$$

TABLE 14-3

Correlation Matrix Computer Output for the American County Example

	Y	X1	X2	X3	X4	X5
Y	1.000	.841	−.068	.494	.720	.599
X1	.841	1.000	.054	.644	.680	.589
X2	−.068	.054	1.000	.007	−.149	.086
X3	.494	.644	.007	1.000	.551	.338
X4	.720	.680	−.149	.551	1.000	.518
X5	.599	.589	.086	.338	.518	1.000

The **correlation matrix** found using GB-STAT is shown in Table 14-3. Note that the correlation between Y and each X variable is given, plus the correlation between each pair of independent variables. For example, the correlation between Y and X_2 is -0.068 and between X_3 and X_5 is 0.338. The correlation matrix is very useful for determining which independent variables are likely to help explain variation in the dependent variable. We look for correlations close to ± 1.0, since that indicates changes in one variable are linearly related to changes in the other variable.

Also, we can use the correlation matrix to determine the extent to which independent variables are correlated with one another. This can be useful in determining whether certain independent variables are redundant and not needed in the model.

Notice that the correlation matrix has 1.000s running down the main diagonal, indicating the variables are perfectly correlated with themselves. Finally, notice the matrix is symmetric about its diagonal. For example, the correlation between X_2 and X_5 (0.086) is the same as for X_5 and X_2 (0.086).

THE REGRESSION MODEL

The county assessor's goal is to develop a regression model to predict the appropriate selling price for a home, using certain measurable characteristics. The first attempt at developing the model will be to run a multiple regression computer program using all available independent variables except X_2, age. Age (X_2) was excluded in this run since the correlation between age and price was only -0.068 (see Table 14-3). The resulting output, using MINITAB, is shown in Table 14-4. Thus, the multiple regression model (rounding to two significant digits) is

$$Y = 20{,}494.98 + 29.17X_1 - 5{,}050.29X_3 + 11{,}710.94X_4 + 4{,}450.55X_5$$

These values come from the Coef column of the variables in the equation section of Table 14-4.

TABLE 14-4

MINITAB Output for American County Example

MTB > REGRESS 'Y' on 4 predictors 'X1' 'X2' 'X3' 'X4'

The regression equation is
Y = 20494.980 + 29.173X1 − 5050.290X3 + 11710.938X4 + 4450.552X5

Predictor	Coef	Stddev	t-ratio	p
Constant	20494.980			
X1	29.173	1.496	19.504	0.000
X3	−5050.290	1094.795	−4.613	0.000
X4	11710.938	1250.234	9.367	0.000
X5	4450.552	1210.376	3.677	0.000

s = 13600.502 R-sq = 76.7% R-sq(adj) = 76.5%

Analysis of Variance

SOURCE	DF	SS	MS	F	p
Regression	4	320033124448.934	80008281112.2334	432.538	0.000
Error	526	97296146146.6557	184973661.875771		
Total	530	417329270595.589			

To obtain a sales price point estimate for any house, we could substitute values for X_1, X_3, X_4, and X_5 into this regression model. For example, suppose a property with the following characteristics is considered:

$$X_1 = \text{Square feet} = 2{,}100$$
$$X_3 = \text{Number of bedrooms} = 4$$
$$X_4 = \text{Number of baths} = 1.75$$
$$X_5 = \text{Number of fireplaces} = 2$$

The point estimate for the sales price is

$$\hat{Y} = 20{,}494.98 + 29.17(2{,}100) - 5{,}050.29(4) + 11{,}710.94(1.75) + 4{,}450.55(2)$$
$$= 90{,}946.31$$

The computer output in Table 14-4 shows a number of other regression statistics. As we proceed, we will discuss these values. Our emphasis will be on interpreting the computer regression results.

INFERENCES ABOUT THE REGRESSION MODEL

Before the American County assessor actually uses this regression model to determine the value of a house, there are several questions that should be answered:

1. Is the overall model significant?
2. Are the individual variables significant?

3. Is the standard error of the estimate too large to provide meaningful results?
4. Is multicollinearity a problem?[1]

We shall answer each of these questions in order.

Is the Overall Model Significant?

Chapter 13 introduced the coefficient of determination, which measures the percentage of variation in the dependent variable that can be accounted for by the independent variable. With multiple regression, we also use *R-square*, which is calculated by equation 14-8:

$$R\text{-square} = R^2 = \frac{\text{Sum of squares regression}}{\text{Total sum of squares}} = \frac{\text{SSR}}{\text{TSS}} \quad (14\text{-}8)$$

The R-square (**multiple coefficient of determination**) for the appraisal model is given in the computer printout in Table 14-4 as 76.7%. Therefore, almost 77% of the variation in sales price can be explained by the four independent variables in the regression model.

Chapter 13 showed that an analysis of variance F test can be used to test whether the regression model explains a significant proportion of variation in the dependent variable. The computer printout in Table 14-4 provides the analysis of variance test for this example. To test the model's significance, we compare the calculated F value, 432.538, with a table F value for a given alpha level and 4 and 526 degrees of freedom. If we specify an alpha level of 0.01, the test is as shown in Figure 14-3.

Clearly, based on the analysis of variance F test, we should conclude that the regression model *does* explain a significant proportion of the variation in sales price.

The computer printout in Table 14-4 also provides a measure called the **adjusted R-square.** This is calculated by equation 14-9:

$$\text{Adjusted } R\text{-square} = R_A^2 = 1 - (1 - R^2)\left(\frac{n - 1}{n - K - 1}\right) \quad (14\text{-}9)$$

where

n = Sample size

K = Number of independent variables in the model

[1] **Multicollinearity** occurs when two independent variables are correlated with each other and therefore contribute redundant information to the model. When highly correlated independent variables are included in the regression model, they can affect the regression results.

FIGURE 14-3

Significance Test for American County Example

Hypotheses:

H_0: The regression model does not explain a significant proportion of the total variation in the dependent variable (model is not significant). ($\beta_1 = \beta_3 = \beta_4 = \beta_5 = 0$), $\rho^2 = 0$

H_A: The regression model does explain a significant proportion of the total variation in the dependent variable (model is significant). (At least one $\beta_j \neq 0$; $j = 1, 3, 4, 5$), $\rho^2 > 0$

$\alpha = 0.01$

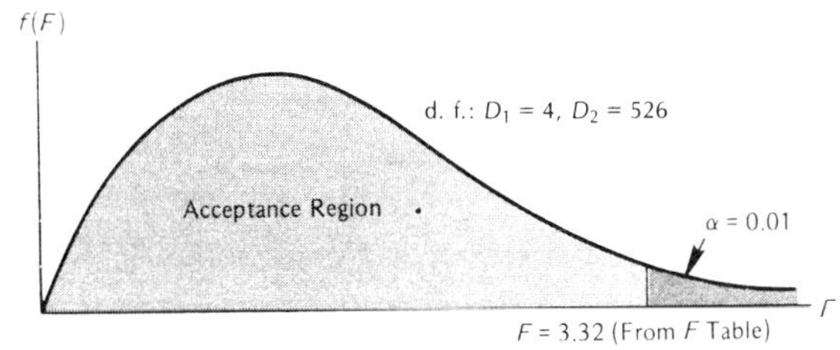

Decision Rule:

If $F > F_{\text{critical}} = 3.32$, reject H_0.
Otherwise, do not reject H_0.

The calculated F (see Table 14-4) is 432.54. Since 432.54 > 3.32, the null hypothesis should be rejected.

In the appraisal example,

$$R_A^2 = 1 - (1 - 0.767)\left(\frac{531 - 1}{531 - 4 - 1}\right)$$
$$= 0.765$$

Adding more independent variables to the regression model generally increases R^2. However, the cost in terms of losing degrees of freedom may not justify adding an additional variable. The R_A^2 value takes into account this cost and adjusts the R^2 value accordingly. Therefore, if a variable is added that does not contribute its fair share, the R_A^2 will actually decline.[2] R_A^2 is particularly important when the number of independent variables is large relative to the sample size. It takes into account the relationship between sample size and number of variables. R^2 may appear artificially high if the number of variables is high compared to the sample size.

Are the Individual Variables Significant?

We have concluded that the overall model is significant. This means that *at least* one independent variable explains a significant proportion of the variation in sales price. This does not mean that *all* the variables are significant.

[2] You might think of R_A^2 as similar to the net income on an income statement and R^2 as the total revenue. Thus R_A^2 is total revenue less expenses.

FIGURE 14-4

Significance Test for a Single Independent Variable in the American County Example

Hypotheses:

H_0: $\beta_i = 0$, given all other variables are already in the model
H_A: $\beta_i \neq 0$, given all other variables are already in the model

$\alpha = 0.01$

Decision Rule:

If $-2.576 \leq t \leq 2.576$, accept H_0.
Otherwise, reject H_0.

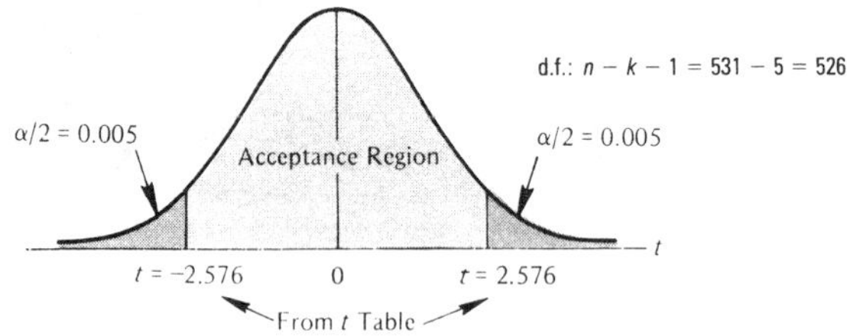

The test is:

For β_1: Calculated t (from printout) = 19.504.
Since $19.504 > 2.576$, reject H_0.

For β_3: Calculated $t = -4.613$.
Since $-4.613 < -2.576$, reject H_0.

For β_4: Calculated $t = 9.367$.
Since $9.367 > 2.576$, reject H_0.

For β_5: Calculated $t = 3.677$.
Since $3.677 > 2.576$, reject H_0.

Note: the degrees of freedom for the t-distribution is $n - k - 1$, where k is the total number of independent variables in the model.

We can test the significance of each independent variable using a t test, as discussed in Chapter 13. The calculated t value for each variable is provided on the computer printout in Table 14-4. Recall that the t statistic is determined by dividing the regression coefficient by the standard deviation of the regression coefficient. The test for each variable is performed in Figure 14-4. These t tests are *conditional* tests. This means the hypothesis that states that *the value of each slope coefficient is 0* is made recognizing that the other independent variables are already in the model.[3] Based on the t tests in Figure 14-4, we conclude that all four independent variables in the model are significant. When a regression model is to be used for prediction, the model should contain no insignificant variables. If insignificant variables are present, they should be dropped and the regression model rerun before it is used for prediction purposes.

[3]Note that the t tests may be affected if the independent variables in the model are themselves correlated. A procedure known as the *sum of squares drop F test*, discussed by Neter and Wasserman in *Applied Linear Statistical Models*, should be used in this situation. Each t test considers only the marginal contribution of the independent variables and may indicate that none of the variables in the model are significant even though the ANOVA procedure indicates otherwise.

Is the Standard Error of the Estimate Too Large?

The purpose of developing the American County regression model is to be able to determine values of the dependent variable when corresponding values of the independent variables are known. An indication of how good the regression model is can be found by looking at the relationship between the measured values of the dependent variable and those values that would be predicted by the regression model. The sample standard deviation of the regression model, often referred to as the **standard error of the estimate** (S_e), measures the dispersion of observed sale values, Y, around values predicted by the regression model. The standard error of the estimate, listed simply as s in Table 14-4, is found by

$$S_e = \sqrt{\frac{\text{SSE}}{n - K - 1}}$$

where

$$\begin{aligned} \text{SSE} &= \text{Sum of squares error} \\ n &= \text{Sample size} \\ K &= \text{Number of independent variables} \end{aligned}$$

Notice also in Table 14-4 that the standard error is the square root of the mean square error of the residuals found in the analysis of variance table.

Sometimes, even though the model has a high R^2, the standard error of the estimate will be too large to provide adequate precision for the prediction interval. A rule of thumb that we have found useful is to examine the range $\pm 2S_e$.[4] If this range is acceptable from a practical viewpoint, the standard error of the estimate might be considered acceptable.

In the American County example, as shown in Table 14-4, the standard error is 13,600.50. Thus, the rough prediction range is

$$\pm 2(13{,}600.50)$$
$$\pm \$27{,}201$$

From a practical viewpoint, this range is *not* acceptable. The error is over $27,000 in either direction. Not many homeowners would be willing to have their appraisal value set by a model with this possible error. The county assessor needs to take steps to reduce the standard error of the estimate. Subsequent sections of this chapter discuss some ways to reduce this value.

[4] The actual confidence interval for prediction of a new observation requires the use of matrix algebra as follows:

$$\hat{Y}_p \pm S_e\sqrt{1 + [(X_p')(X'X)^{-1}(X_p)]}$$

where

$\hat{Y}_p$ = Point estimate given values for the independent variables
X_p = Vector of independent variable values used to calculate $\hat{Y}_p$
X = Matrix of independent variable values used to develop the regression model

Refer to *Applied Linear Statistical Models* by Neter and Wasserman (1974) for further discussion.

Another measure of whether S_e is too large is the *coefficient of variation*, which is

$$CV = \frac{S_e}{\overline{Y}}(100)$$

where

$$\overline{Y} = \text{Mean of the } Y \text{ variable}$$

In this case,

$$CV = \frac{13{,}600.50}{79{,}873.56}(100)$$
$$= 17.03\%$$

As a rule, we like to see a CV of 10% or less. However, each application must be analyzed on an individual basis.

Is Multicollinearity a Problem?

Even if a regression is significant, and if each independent variable is significant, decision makers should still examine the regression model to determine whether it appears reasonable. That is, does any coefficient have an unexpected sign?

Before answering this question for our appraisal example, we should review what the regression coefficients mean. First, the constant term, β_0, is the model's Y-intercept. If the data used to develop the regression model contain values of X_1, X_3, X_4, and X_5 that are simultaneously 0 (such as would be the case for vacant land), the constant is the mean value of Y, given that X_1, X_3, X_4, and X_5 all equal 0. Under these conditions β_0 would equal the average value of a vacant lot. However, in the American County example, no vacant land was in the sample, so the constant has no particular meaning.

The coefficient for square feet, β_1, indicates the average change in sales price corresponding to a change in house size of 1 square foot, holding the other independent variables constant. The value shown in Table 14-4 for β_1 is 29.17. The coefficient is positive, indicating that an increase in house size is associated with an increase in sales price. This relationship is expected.

Likewise, the coefficients for X_4, number of bathrooms, and X_5, number of fireplaces, are positive, indicating that an increase in their numbers is also associated with an increase in price. This is also expected. However, the coefficient for variable X_3, number of bedrooms, is $-5{,}050.29$, meaning that, if we hold the other variables constant but increase the number of bedrooms by one, the average price will *drop* by \$5,050.29. This relationship may not be reasonable given the real estate market and buyers' attitudes.

Referring to the correlation matrix in Table 14-3, the correlation between variable X_3 and Y, the sales price, is $+0.494$. This indicates that, without considering the other independent variables, the linear relationship between number of bedrooms and sales price is positive. But why does the regression coefficient turn out negative? The answer lies in what is called *multicollinearity*. **Multicollinearity** occurs when the independent variables are themselves correlated. For example, X_3 and the other independent variables have the following correlations:

$$r_{X_3,X_1} = 0.644$$
$$r_{X_3,X_4} = 0.551$$
$$r_{X_3,X_5} = 0.338$$

In each case, the correlation is significant. Therefore, the other variables in the model are overlapping X_3; hence, to some extent, X_3 becomes unnecessary to the model once X_1, X_4, and X_5 are included. This overlapping is multicollinearity. Multicollinearity can cause problems like those we have seen in this example, where the regression coefficient sign is clearly opposite of what we would expect.

The problems caused by multicollinearity, and how to deal with them, continue to be of prime concern to theoretical statisticians. From a decision maker's viewpoint, you should be aware that multicollinearity can (and usually does) exist and recognize the basic problems it can cause. Some of the most obvious problems and indications of severe multicollinearity are the following:

1. Incorrect signs on the coefficients
2. A change in the values of the previous coefficients when a new variable is added to the model
3. The change to insignificant of a previously significant variable when a new variable is added to the model
4. An increase in the standard error of the estimate when a variable is added to the model

Mathematical approaches exist for dealing with multicollinearity and reducing its impact. Although these procedures are beyond the scope of this text, one suggestion is to eliminate the variables that are the chief cause of the multicollinearity problems. In the American County example, we would drop X_3 from the analysis. This variable is highly correlated with X_1, X_4, and X_5 and has low correlation with Y.

Dealing with multicollinearity problems requires a great deal of experience. This text simply aims to make you aware that such problems may exist and should be considered before the regression model is used.

SKILL DEVELOPMENT PROBLEMS FOR **SECTION 14-2**

The following exercises are included to help you gain a more complete understanding of the material presented in Section 14-2. If possible, use a computer and statistical software to solve the problems and exercises.

1. The Western State Tourist Association gives out pamphlets, maps, and other tourist-related information to people who call a toll-free number and request the information. The association orders the packets of information from a documents printing company and it likes to have enough available to meet

the immediate need without having too many sitting around taking up space. The marketing manager decided to develop a multiple regression model to be used in predicting the number of calls that will be received in the coming week. A random sample of 11 weeks is selected, with the following variables:

Y = Number of calls

X_1 = Number of advertisements placed this week

X_2 = Number of calls received last week

X_3 = Number of airline tour bookings into western cities for this week

The following data were collected.

i	Y	X_1	X_2	X_3
1	345	12	297	3,456
2	456	14	502	2,456
3	356	13	340	3,600
4	605	16	450	3,500
5	209	14	350	2,400
6	306	10	340	2,890
7	457	15	401	3,457
8	259	12	340	2,590
9	540	13	400	3,240
10	460	16	440	3,560
11	378	14	348	2,460

Develop a correlation matrix for these variables and write a short report describing the various correlations. Comment on whether you think a multiple regression model will be effectively developed from these data.

2. Referring to the data in Problem 1, compute three simple linear regression models, one for each of the independent variables. Write a report that fully describes each of the models. Indicate in your report which of these models is best.

3. Referring to the data in Problem 1 and to your work in Problem 2, develop a multiple regression model that contains all three independent variables.
   a. Indicate the regression equation.
   b. How much of the total variation in the dependent variable is explained by the three independent variables in the model?
   c. Test to determine whether the overall model is statistically significant. Use $\alpha = 0.05$ to conduct this test.
   d. Which, if any, of the independent variables is statistically significant? Test using $\alpha = 0.05$.
   e. Determine the adjusted R-square and comment on what it means.
   f. As the model stands, comment on whether it will be a useful model for predicting the number of calls to the Western State Tourist Association.

4. Referring to Problems 1–3, prepare a short report that addresses the following points:
   a. Define the term multicollinearity.
   b. Indicate the potential problems that multicollinearity can cause.
   c. Indicate what, if any, evidence there is of multicollinearity problems with this multiple regression model.

5. The athletic director of State University is interested in developing a multiple regression model that might be used to explain the variation in attendance at football games at his school. A sample of sixteen games was selected from home games played during the past ten seasons. Data for the following factors were determined.

$$Y = \text{Game attendance}$$
$$X_1 = \text{Team win/loss percentage to date}$$
$$X_2 = \text{Opponent win/loss percentage to date}$$
$$X_3 = \text{Games played this season}$$
$$X_4 = \text{Temperature at game time}$$

The following data were collected.

i	Y	X_1	X_2	X_3	X_4
1	14,502	33.3	80.0	6	47
2	12,459	25.0	50.0	4	56
3	15,600	80.0	66.6	5	55
4	16,780	75.0	100.0	8	60
5	14,600	60.0	80.0	10	55
6	19,300	100.0	60.0	10	49
7	14,603	66.6	25.0	3	67
8	15,789	50.0	50.0	6	55
9	17,800	80.0	40.0	10	53
10	19,450	75.0	100.0	8	48
11	13,890	20.0	75.0	5	65
12	15,097	70.0	70.0	10	56
13	17,666	83.3	66.6	6	60
14	12,500	20.0	20.0	5	59
15	16,780	80.0	100.0	8	46
16	17,543	80.0	70.0	10	50

Develop a correlation matrix for these variables and write a short report describing the various correlations. Comment on whether you think that a multiple regression model will be effectively developed from these data.

6. Referring to the data in Problem 5, compute four simple linear regression models, one for each of the independent variables. Write a report that fully describes each of the models. Indicate in your report which of these models is best.

7. Referring to the data in Problem 5 and to your work in Problem 6, develop a multiple regression model that contains all four independent variables.
   a. Indicate the regression equation.
   b. How much of the total variation in the dependent variable is explained by the four independent variables in the model?
   c. Test to determine whether the overall model is statistically significant. Use $\alpha = 0.05$ to conduct this test.
   d. Which, if any, of the independent variables is statistically significant? Test using $\alpha = 0.05$.
   e. Determine the adjusted R-square and comment on what it means.
   f. Develop 95% confidence interval estimates for the regression coefficients and interpret these intervals. Write a short report to the athletic director describing the regression model.

8. Referring to Problems 5–7, prepare a short report that addresses the following points:
   a. Define the term multicollinearity.
   b. Indicate the potential problems that multicollinearity can cause.
   c. Indicate what, if any, evidence there is of multicollinearity problems with this multiple regression model.

14-3 DUMMY VARIABLES IN REGRESSION ANALYSIS

In many cases decision makers may want to use a nominal or ordinal variable (see Chapter 1, Section 1-2) as an independent variable in a regression model. If so, the variable is called a *qualitative variable.* For example, in a model for predicting individual income, a potential variable might be sex—male or female. In another example with GNP (gross national product) as the dependent variable, an interesting independent variable might be the U.S. president's political party—Republican or Democrat. In still another example, where the dependent variable is the number of dollars spent by women on cosmetics, such independent variables as marital status (single, married, widowed, divorced, or separated) and employment status (full time, part time, retired, unemployed, or other) are variables that may help to explain the variation in the dependent variable.

The problem with qualitative variables in a regression analysis is in assigning values to the outcomes. What value should we assign to a male as opposed to a female? What about assigning values for Republican versus Democrat? These classifications do not have unique numerical values, and different decision makers might well assign different values that could affect the regression analysis.

To overcome this problem, qualitative variables are incorporated into a regression analysis by using **dummy variables.** For example, for the qualitative variable sex, which has two categories—male or female, a single dummy variable is created as follows:

$$\text{If sex} = \text{male},\ X_2 = 0.$$
$$\text{If sex} = \text{female},\ X_2 = 1.$$

For the political party variable, the dummy variable is

$$\text{If party} = \text{Republican}, X_2 = 1.$$
$$\text{If party} = \text{Democrat}, X_2 = 0.$$

Although the qualitative variable is coded (0, 1), it makes no difference which attribute is assigned 0 and which is assigned 1.

When the qualitative variable has more than two possible categories, a series of dummy variables must be used. For example, since marital status could have five categories—single, married, separated, divorced, and widowed, we would develop four (5 − 1 = 4) dummy variables as follows:

$$\text{If single}, X_2 = 1$$
$$\text{Otherwise}, X_2 = 0$$

$$\text{If married}, X_3 = 1$$
$$\text{Otherwise}, X_3 = 0$$

$$\text{If separated}, X_4 = 1$$
$$\text{Otherwise}, X_4 = 0$$

$$\text{If divorced}, X_5 = 1$$
$$\text{Otherwise}, X_5 = 0$$

For a widowed person, X_2, X_3, X_4, and X_5 would all be 0. By default, the person must belong to the remaining category, "widowed."[5]

To illustrate the effect of incorporating dummy variables into a regression model, consider the data displayed in the scatter plot in Figure 14-5 (page 754). The population from which these data were selected consists of executives between the ages of 24 and 60 who are working in U.S. manufacturing business. Data for the dependent variable, annual salary, and the independent variable, age, are available. Even though this model might be statistically significant, we would likely search for other independent variables that could help us to further explain the variation in annual salary.

Suppose we know which of the sixteen people in the sample had an MBA degree. Figure 14-6 (page 754) shows the scatter plot for these same data with the MBA data circled. We can create a new variable, X_2, which is a dummy variable coded

$$X_2 = 0, \text{ if no MBA}$$
$$X_2 = 1, \text{ if MBA}$$

Now we develop a two-variable multiple regression model of the form

$$\hat{Y} = b_0 + b_1X_1 + b_2X_2$$

[5]The mathematical reason that the number of dummy variables must be 1 less than the number of possible responses is called the **dummy variable trap.** Perfect multicollinearity is introduced and the least squares regression estimates cannot be obtained if the number of dummy variables equals the number of possible categories.

FIGURE 14-5

Income Versus Age

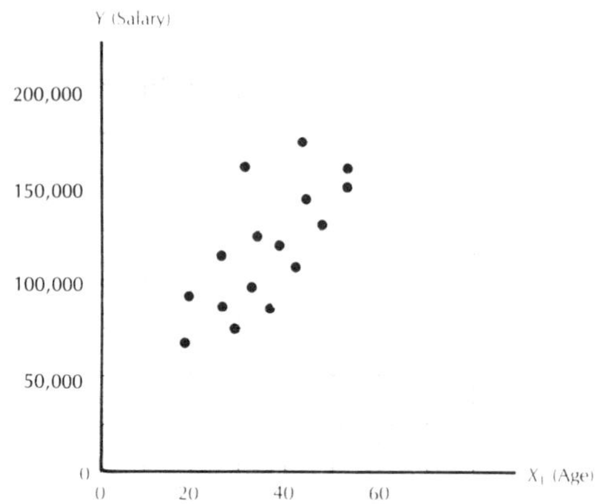

After employing a computer and statistical software, we get the following model:

$$\hat{Y} = 50{,}004 + 1{,}250X_1 + 14{,}246X_2$$

Since the dummy variable, X_2, has been coded 0 or 1 depending on degree status, incorporating it into the regression model is like having two simple linear regression lines with the same slopes, but different intercepts. For instance, when $X_2 = 0$, the regression equation is

$$\begin{aligned}\hat{Y} &= 50{,}004 + 1{,}250X_1 + 14{,}246(0)\\ &= 50{,}004 + 1{,}250X_1\end{aligned}$$

This line is shown in Figure 14-6.

However, when $X_2 = 1$ (the executive has an MBA), the regression equation is

$$\begin{aligned}\hat{Y} &= 50{,}004 + 1{,}250X_1 + 14{,}246(1)\\ &= 64{,}250 + 1{,}250X_1\end{aligned}$$

FIGURE 14-6

Impact of Dummy Variables on Regression Analysis

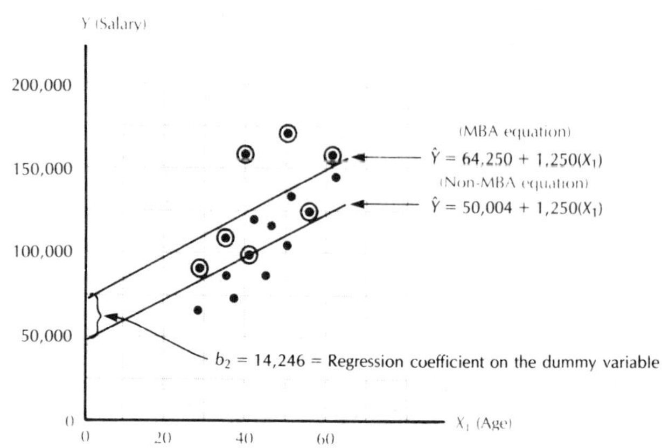

This regression line is also shown in Figure 14-6. As you can see, the effect of the dummy variable is on the regression intercept. In this case, the intercept for executives with an MBA degree is \$14,246 higher than for those without an MBA.

We interpret the regression coefficient on this degree dummy variable as follows: "Based on these data, on the average and controlling for age (X_1), executives with an MBA degree make \$14,246 per year more in salary than their non-MBA counterparts."

Of course, we could develop confidence interval estimates for this regression coefficient and test its significance just as we can with a quantitative variable.

We can also show the effect of including a dummy variable in the American County regression model by starting with the following simple regression equation:

$$\text{Sales price} = 17{,}590.59 + 36.28X_1$$

Figure 14-7 illustrates this regression line for sales price as a function of square feet, X_1.

Now, suppose a qualitative variable defining whether or not the house has central air conditioning is added. The variable would be

$$\text{If air conditioning, } X_6 = 1$$
$$\text{If no air conditioning, } X_6 = 0$$

Then the regression model would be

$$\hat{Y} = b_0 + b_1X_1 + b_6X_6$$

FIGURE 14-7

Simple Regression Line for the American County Example

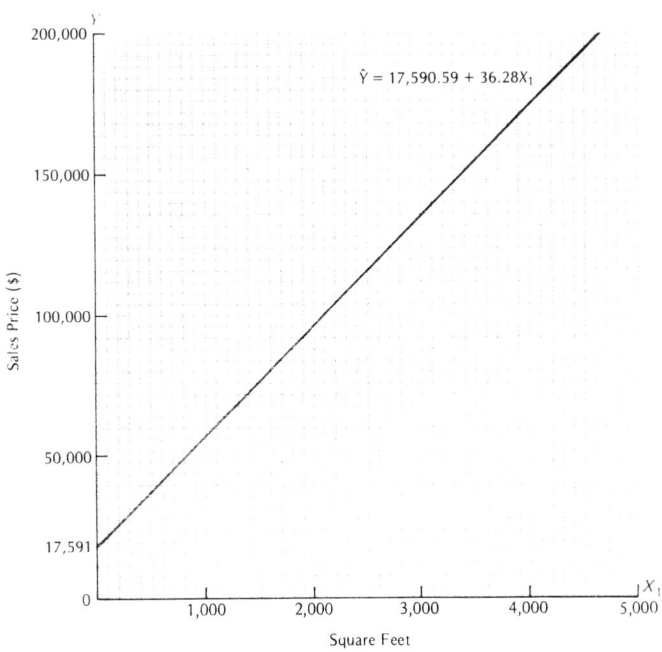

TABLE 14-5

MINITAB Output with Dummy Variable for the American County Example

```
MTB > REGRESS 'Y' on 2 predictors 'X1' 'X6'

The regression equation is
Y = 15503.336 + 32.138X1 + 4356.988X6
```

Predictor	Coef	Stddev	t-ratio	p
Constant	15503.336			
X1	32.138	1.247	25.78	0.000
X6	4356.988	1158.773	3.76	0.000

s = 13821.679   R-sq = 75.8%   R-sq(adj) = 75.7%

Analysis of Variance

SOURCE	DF	SS	MS	F	p
Regression	2	316460785892.635	158230392946.318	828.263	0.000
Error	528	100868484702.954	191038796.785898		
Total	530	417329270595.589			

Table 14-5 shows the computer output for the American County regression model with square feet and air conditioning as the independent variables. The model is

$$\hat{Y} = 15{,}503.34 + 32.14X_1 + 4{,}356.99X_6$$

Since variable X_6 can be only 0 or 1, incorporating a dummy variable is equivalent to finding two regression equations with *equal* slopes but *different* intercepts:

$$\hat{Y} = 15{,}503.34 + 32.14X_1 \qquad \text{if } X_6 = 0$$

and

$$\hat{Y} = 19{,}860.33 + 32.14X_1 \qquad \text{if } X_6 = 1$$

The impact of the dummy variable is illustrated in Figure 14-8. The difference in intercepts indicates that, holding square feet constant, the price of a house is on the average \$4,356.99 higher if it has central air conditioning.

IMPROVING THE AMERICAN COUNTY APPRAISAL MODEL

The real estate appraisal model we developed earlier was statistically significant, but because of the relatively large standard error of the estimate, the model was judged to be of little practical use. It might prove to be impossible to develop a regression appraisal model that is practically significant. However, before abandoning the idea, we might attempt to improve the model by *respecifying the model.* If a model is incorrectly specified, it is generally due to either of the following two factors:

1. Useful independent variables have been omitted from the model.
2. Independent variables have been included in the model that should not have been included.

FIGURE 14-8

Impact of a Dummy Variable on the Regression Model for the American County Example

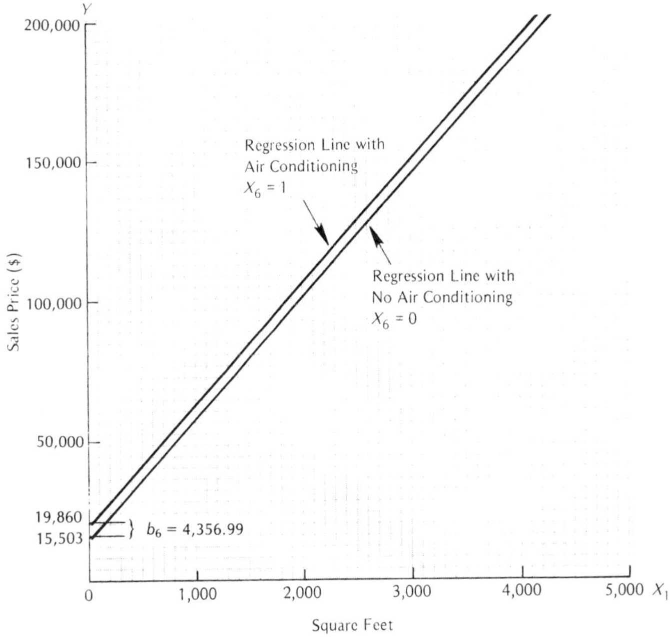

There is no sure way of determining the correct model specification. However, a recommended approach is for the decision maker to try adding new variables or removing variables from the model in an attempt to improve the results.

Two variables that might affect sales price of a residential property are the location and whether the house has central air conditioning. If we can identify whether a house has air conditioning, we can use the dummy-variable concept just discussed and code this variable

$$\text{If air conditioning, } X_6 = 1$$
$$\text{If no air conditioning, } X_6 = 0$$

Data for the location variable are more difficult to come by. There are two high schools in the county. We can determine in which high school district each house is located. This breakdown of location should improve the regression model. The location variable is coded

$$\text{If Douglas High, } X_7 = 1$$
$$\text{If Biltmore High (not Douglas High), } X_7 = 0$$

Table 14-6 (page 758) presents the computer output for the latest regression run with variables X_6 and X_7 included and variable X_3, number of bedrooms, excluded. Recall that X_3 was apparently giving rise to multicollinearity problems.

This latest regression model has a smaller standard error and higher R^2 than the original model shown in Table 14-4. However, the dummy variable for location, X_7, has a t value of -0.53. We must conclude that the regression coefficient

TABLE 14-6

MINITAB Output of Improved Model for the American County Example

```
MTB > REGRESS 'Y' on 5 predictors 'X1' 'X4' 'X5' 'X6' 'X7'

The regression equation is
Y = 20494.98 + 30.044X1 + 7372.015X4 + 3567.722X5 + 3499.685X6 - 1228.370X7
```

Predictor	Coef	Stddev	t-ratio	p
Constant	20494.980			
X1	30.044	1.456	20.63	0.000
X4	7372.015	1087.318	6.78	0.000
X5	3567.722	1230.249	2.90	0.002
X6	3499.685	1073.523	3.26	0.000
X7	−1228.370	2317.680	−.53	0.298

s = 12796.564 R-sq = 79.4% R-sq(adj) = 79.2%

Analysis of Variance

SOURCE	DF	SS	MS	F	p
Regression	5	331359440852.898	662718881706.580	404.709	0.000
Error	525	85969829742.691	163752056.653		
Total	530	417329270595.589			

on this variable is not different from 0, since −0.53 does not exceed the critical *t* value of −2.576 for an alpha level of 0.01 and 525 degrees of freedom. Therefore, the location variable (high school district) is not helpful in determining the sales price of houses. In fact, the model as it now stands is still of little use since the standard error is again large. However, the standard error of the estimate should be judged on a *relative* rather than an *absolute* basis. A standard error of the estimate that is too large in one situation may be quite acceptable in another. For instance, although $S_e = \$12,797.56$ may be too large in an appraisal model, this same value would be viewed as exceptional in a model where U.S. GNP was the dependent variable.

This example illustrates that although a regression model may pass the statistical tests of significance, it may not be functional. Good appraisal models can be developed using multiple regression analysis, provided more detail is available about such characteristics as finish quality, landscaping, location, neighborhood characteristics, and so forth. The cost and effort required to obtain these data can be relatively high.

Developing a multiple regression model is more an art than a science. The real decisions revolve around how to select the best set of independent variables for the model.

SKILL DEVELOPMENT PROBLEMS FOR **SECTION 14-3**

The following exercises are included to help you gain a better understanding of the material presented in this section.

9. A manager is considering incorporating a new variable into her regression model. This variable measures education level of the respondent. The variable has been measured on four levels as follows:

   1. No high school degree
   2. High school degree
   3. Some college courses
   4. College degree

   a. She is considering this variable and plans to use the codes 1, 2, 3, and 4 to determine which educational level the respondent has achieved. Comment on this.
   b. How many dummy variables would you set up to handle this situation? Describe each dummy variable.

10. The Polk Utility Corporation is developing a multiple regression model that it plans to use to predict customers' utility usage. It currently has three quantitative variables in the model, but is dissatisfied with the *R*-square and the standard error of the estimate. Two variables that it thinks might be useful are whether the house has a gas water heater or an electric water heater and whether the house was constructed after the 1974 energy crisis or before.

    Provide the utility with the proper means of including these qualitative variables in its analysis.

11. A study was recently performed by the American Automobile Association in which it attempted to develop a regression model to explain variation in EPA mileage ratings of new cars. At one stage of the analysis, the model took the following form:

$$\hat{Y} = 34.20 - 0.003X_1 + 4.56X_2$$

where

$$\begin{aligned} X_1 &= \text{Vehicle weight} \\ X_2 &= 1, \text{ if standard transmission} \\ &= 0, \text{ if automatic transmission} \end{aligned}$$

   a. Interpret the regression coefficient for variable X_1.
   b. Interpret the regression coefficient for variable X_2.
   c. Discuss the effect of a dummy variable being incorporated in a regression model like this one. Use a graph if it is helpful.

12. A recent study by the U.S. Department of Agriculture attempted to develop a multiple regression model to explain variation in farm income. At one stage of development, the model took the following form:

$$\hat{Y} = -23{,}200 + 4.2X_1 + 2{,}345X_2 + 4{,}670X_3$$

where

$$X_1 = \text{Number of acres farmed}$$
$$X_2 = 1, \text{ if land is row-irrigated}$$
$$= 0, \text{ if not}$$
$$X_3 = 1, \text{ if land is sprinkler-irrigated}$$
$$= 0, \text{ if not}$$

a. Interpret the regression coefficient for variable X_1.
b. Interpret the regression coefficient for variable X_2.
c. Interpret the regression coefficient for variable X_3.

13. The following data were collected by the Gilmore Accounting Firm in an effort to explain variation in client profitability:

Y	X_1	X_2
2,345	45	1
4,200	56	2
278	26	3
1,211	56	2
1,406	24	2
500	23	3
−700	34	3
3,457	45	1
2,478	47	1
1,975	24	2
206	32	3

where

Y = Net profit earned from the client
X_1 = Number of hours spent working with the client
X_2 = Type of client:
1, if manufacturing
2, if service
3, if governmental

a. Develop a plot of each independent variable against the client income variable. Comment on what, if any, relationship appears to exist.
b. Run a simple linear regression analysis using only variable X_1 as the independent variable. Describe this model fully.
c. Now, incorporate the client type variable into the regression analysis and describe the resulting multiple regression model. Test all appropriate hypotheses, using an $\alpha = 0.05$ level. (*Hint:* You will have to develop dummy variables.)
d. Holding the other factors constant, what is the average difference in profit if the client is governmental? Also state this in terms of a 95% confidence interval estimate.

14-4 STEPWISE REGRESSION ANALYSIS

In the American County example, we began with five independent variables plus the dependent variable, sales price. After examining the correlation matrix, we eliminated the age variable, X_2, since it had such a low correlation with price. Finally, we used a computer routine to develop the multiple regression model shown in Table 14-4. Once the model had been developed, we were left to analyze its statistical and functional validity. We use the term *ordinary regression* for this approach of bringing all independent variables into the model at one step.

Another method for developing a regression model is called *stepwise regression*. Stepwise regression, as the name implies, develops the least squares regression equation in steps, either through *backward elimination* or through *forward selection*.

BACKWARD ELIMINATION

The backward elimination stepwise method begins by developing an ordinary regression model using all independent variables. Then a t test for significance is performed on each regression coefficient at a specified alpha level. Provided at least one t value is in the acceptance region (H_0: $\beta_i = 0$ is accepted), the variable with the t value closest to 0 is removed, and another ordinary regression model is developed with the remaining independent variables. The backward elimination continues until all independent variables remaining in the model have coefficients that are significantly different from 0. The models at each step are printed by the computer routine.[6]

The advantage of backward elimination is that the decision maker has the opportunity to look at all the independent variables in the model before removing the variables that are not significant.

FORWARD SELECTION

Whereas the backward elimination procedure begins with a regression model containing all variables and eliminates insignificant variables in a stepwise fashion, the forward selection procedure works in the opposite direction. The forward selection procedure begins by selecting a single independent variable from all those available. The independent variable selected at step 1 is the variable that is most highly correlated with the dependent variable. At step 2, a second independent variable is selected based on its ability to explain the remaining unexplained variation in the dependent variable.

The independent variable selected at each step is the variable with the highest *coefficient of partial determination*. The coefficient of determination measures the proportion of variation explained by all the independent variables in the

[6] Most software packages allow the user to override the default and force variables from the model even though they may be statistically significant.

model. By contrast, the coefficient of partial determination measures the marginal contribution of a single independent variable, given that other independent variables are in the model.

Thus, after the first variable (say, X_1) is selected, R^2 will indicate the percentage of variation explained by this variable. The forward selection routine will then compute all possible two-variable regression models with X_1 included and determine the R^2 for each model. The coefficient of partial determination at step 2 is the proportion of unexplained variation (after X_1 is in the model) that is explained by the additional variable. The independent variable that adds the most to R^2, given the variables already in the model, is the one selected. This process continues until either all independent variables have been entered or the remaining independent variables do not add appreciably to R^2. This procedure is outlined in Figure 14-9.

FIGURE 14-9

Graphical Representation of the Forward Stepwise Procedure

(a) No independent variables in the model.

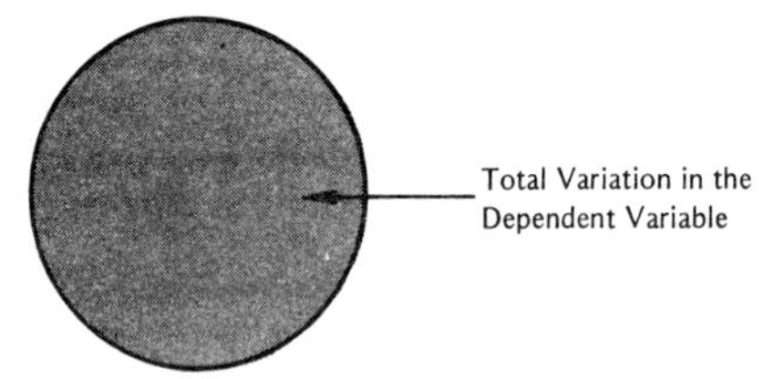

(b) Enter the variable with the highest correlation.

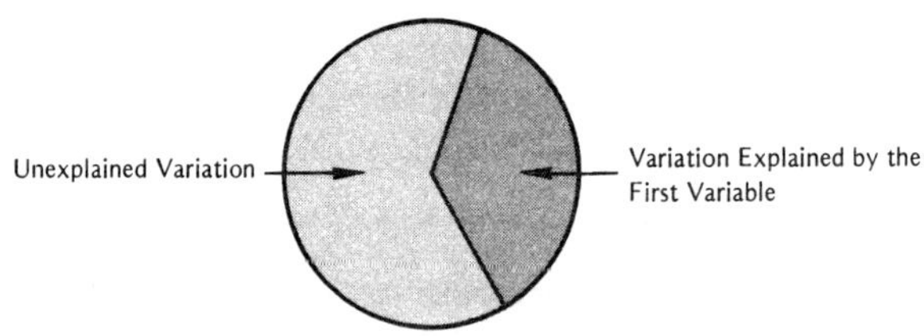

(c) Enter the variable that explains the most of the unexplained variation (has the highest coefficient of partial determination).

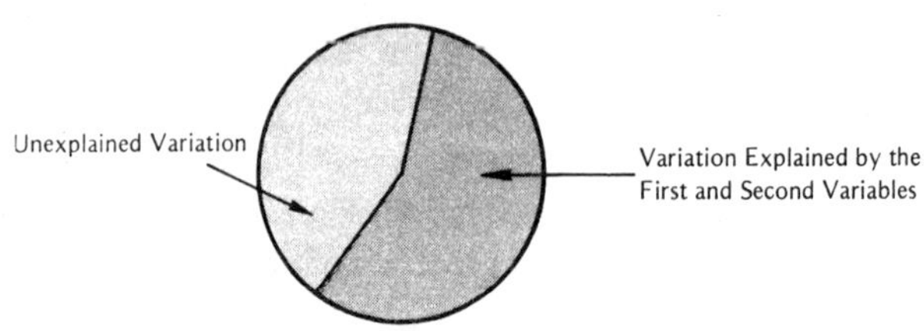

(d) Continue adding variables based on how much of the unexplained variation they account for until the next variable explains an insignificant proportion.

The forward selection stepwise method serves one more important function. If two or more variables overlap, a variable selected in an early step may become insignificant when other variables are added at later steps. The forward selection procedure will drop this insignificant variable from the model. Stepwise regression also offers a means of observing multicollinearity problems since we can see how the regression model changes as each new variable is added to the model.

The forward selection stepwise procedure is widely used in decision-making applications and is generally recognized as a useful regression method. However, care should be exercised when using this procedure since it is easy to rely too heavily on the automatic selection process. Remember, the order of variable selection is conditional, based on the variables already in the model. There is no guarantee that stepwise regression will lead you to the best set of independent variables from those available. Decision makers still must use common sense in applying regression analysis to make sure they have usable regression models.

A STEPWISE REGRESSION EXAMPLE

The B. T. Longmont Company operates a large retail department store in San Francisco. Like other department stores, Longmont has incurred heavy losses due to shoplifting and employee pilferage. The store's security manager wants to develop a regression model to explain the monthly dollar loss from these factors. The variables the security manager is interested in are

X_1 = Average monthly temperature (°F)

X_2 = Number of sales transactions

X_3 = Number of days per month the store is open

X_4 = Number of persons on the store's monthly payroll

Y = Monthly dollar loss due to shoplifting and pilferage

Table 14-7 (page 764) lists the data for these variables for a random sample of seventeen months. The correlation matrix of the data is presented in Table 14-8 (page 764).

Note that variable X_2, number of sales transactions, is most highly correlated with dollars lost. Using the forward stepwise selection procedure, X_2 will be the first variable selected. The GB-STAT output for the model at step 1 is shown in Table 14-9 (page 765).

At step 1, variable X_2, number of monthly sales transactions, explains 0.3978 of the variation in the dependent variable. The GB-STAT ANOVA output shows that the overall model is significant at the 0.0066 level at this point. This means that the probability of randomly finding a regression model with these slope and intercept values, explaining this much of the total variation in dollar loss for two unrelated variables, would be 0.0066.

Now, look at the bottom of Table 14-9 to the section, "Partial Correlations." The next variable added is the one that can contribute most to R^2, given that variable X_2 is already in the model. This variable will be the one with the highest

TABLE 14-7

Data for the B. T. Longmont Company Example

	Temperature X_1	No. Sales Made X_2	No. Days X_3	No. Employees X_4	Dollars Lost Y
1	58.8	7,107	21	129	3,067
2	65.2	6,373	22	141	2,828
3	70.9	6,796	22	153	2,891
4	77.4	9,208	20	166	2,994
5	79.3	14,792	25	193	3,082
6	81.0	14,564	23	189	3,898
7	71.9	11,964	20	175	3,502
8	63.9	13,526	23	186	3,060
9	54.5	12,656	20	190	3,211
10	39.5	14,119	20	187	3,286
11	44.5	16,691	22	195	3,542
12	43.6	14,571	19	206	3,125
13	56.0	13,619	22	198	3,022
14	64.7	14,575	22	192	2,922
15	73.0	14,556	21	191	3,950
16	78.9	18,573	21	200	4,488
17	79.4	15,618	22	200	3,295

partial correlation. As you can see, the variable selected in step 2 should be X_4, number of employees, since it is most highly correlated with the remaining variation in the dependent variable. Tables 14-10, 14-11 (page 766), and 14-12 (page 767) show the GB-STAT output for steps 2, 3, and 4 of the stepwise regression.

The model at step 4 explains 76.7% of the variation and is significant at the 0.0009 level ($F = 9.8761$). In analyzing the independent variables, using the t test, we find all four significant at the alpha level of 0.05. However, we find some evidence of multicollinearity in the model. For instance, at step 4 the coefficient of X_4, number of employees, is negative, yet the correlation matrix shows a positive correlation between dollar loss and number of employees. Also, as we move from step to step in the output, the regression coefficients change. In addition, the significance of variable X_1 improves when variable X_3 is added in the final step.

TABLE 14-8

Correlation Matrix for the B. T. Longmont Company Example

	X1	X2	X3	X4	Y
X1	1.000	−.024	.438	−.082	.286
X2		1.000	.096	.920	.628
X3			1.000	.032	−.089
X4				1.000	.413
Y					1.000

TABLE 14-9

GB-STAT Output: Step 1 of the Regression Model for the B. T. Longmont Example

FORWARD STEPWISE REGRESSION

CURRENT REGRESSION SUMMARY TABLE

DEPENDENT VARIABLE: Y

MULTIPLE R = .6307
STD ERR EST = 358.0108
F = 9.909

IND VAR	B COEF	STD ERR(B)	T-VALUE	PROB
X2	.079889	.025379	3.14786	.0066
CONSTANT				
2273.111				

ANOVA FOR CURRENT REGRESSION

	SUM SQUARES	DF	MEAN SQUARES	F-RATIO	PROB
REGRESSION	1270056	1	1270056	9.909	.0066
RESIDUAL	1922576	15	128171.7		
TOTAL	3192633	16	199539.5		

PARTIAL CORRELATIONS

PARTIALLED OUT: X2

Y WITH X1 = .38796
Y WITH X3 = −.20154
Y WITH X4 = −.54116

TABLE 14-10

GB-STAT Output: Step 2 of the Regression Model for the B. T. Longmont Example

CURRENT REGRESSION SUMMARY TABLE

DEPENDENT VARIABLE: Y

MULTIPLE R = .7577
STD ERR EST = 311.6242
F = 9.4383

IND VAR	B COEF	STD ERR(B)	T-VALUE	PROB
X2	.203437	.055863	3.641727	.0027
X4	−21.56773	8.957054	−2.407905	.0304
CONSTANT				
4600.81				

ANOVA FOR CURRENT REGRESSION

	SUM SQUARES	DF	MEAN SQUARES	F-RATIO	PROB
REGRESSION	1833098	2	916549.1	9.4383	.0025
RESIDUAL	1359534	14	97109.6		
TOTAL	3192633	16	199539.5		

PARTIAL CORRELATIONS

PARTIALLED OUT: X2 X4

Y WITH X1 = .3681
Y WITH X3 = −.3513

TABLE 14-11

GB-STAT Output: Step 3 of the Regression Model for the B. T. Longmont Example

CURRENT REGRESSION SUMMARY TABLE

DEPENDENT VARIABLE: Y

MULTIPLE R = .7949
STD ERR EST = 300.6813
F = 7.4377

IND VAR	B COEF	STD ERR(B)	T-VALUE	PROB
X1	8.037326	5.63064	1.427427	.177
X2	.193347	.054363	3.556626	.0035
X4	−19.67675	8.74347	−2.250451	.0424
CONSTANT				
3865.898				

ANOVA FOR CURRENT REGRESSION

	SUM SQUARES	DF	MEAN SQUARES	F-RATIO	PROB
REGRESSION	2017312	3	672437.3	7.4377	.0038
RESIDUAL	1175321	13	90409.27		
TOTAL	3192633	16	199539.5		

PARTIAL CORRELATIONS

PARTIALLED OUT: X1 X2 X4

X3 WITH Y = −.60589
Y WITH X3 = −.60589

These are all signs of correlation among the independent variables. We suggest the security manager be cautious about any conclusions he might reach based on this model.

This example has illustrated stepwise regression analysis and has shown what a computer output for such an analysis looks like. The model was developed using the forward selection procedure; however, the model at step 4 is exactly the same as it would be using the ordinary approach with all four independent variables. The order in which variables enter makes no difference as long as all variables are in the model.

SKILL DEVELOPMENT PROBLEMS FOR **SECTION 14-4**

The following exercises have been included to help you gain a solid understanding of the material discussed in this section.

14. Referring to the data collected by the Western State Tourist Association (see Problem 1), develop the multiple regression model for predicting the number of calls received, using stepwise regression.

a. At the final step of the analysis, how many variables are in the model?

TABLE 14-12

GB-STAT Output: Step 4 of the Regression Model for the B. T. Longmont Example

CURRENT REGRESSION SUMMARY TABLE

DEPENDENT VARIABLE: Y

MULTIPLE R = .8758
STD ERR EST = 248.9728
F = 9.8761

IND VAR	B COEF	STD ERR(B)	T-VALUE	PROB
X1	13.87032	5.159981	2.688056	.0197
X2	.21172	.045549	4.648154	.0006
X3	−126.7026	48.02445	−2.638294	.0216
X4	−21.81985	7.285272	−2.995063	.0112
CONSTANT				
6360.643				

ANOVA FOR CURRENT REGRESSION

	SUM SQUARES	DF	MEAN SQUARES	F-RATIO	PROB
REGRESSION	2448783	4	612195.8	9.8761	.0009
RESIDUAL	743849.5	12	61987.46		
TOTAL	3192633	16	199539.5		

MULTIPLE CORRELATION SUMMARY

	MULTIPLE R	R-SQUARE
UNADJUSTED	.8758	.767
ADJUSTED	.8303	.6893

STD ERROR OF ESTIMATE = 248.9728
SAMPLE SIZE = 17

b. Indicate the regression model by showing the intercept and regression coefficients.
c. Test to determine whether the overall regression model is statistically significant at the $\alpha = 0.05$ level.
d. Discuss why the variables entered the model in the order shown by the stepwise regression.

15. In Problem 5, the athletic director at State University was interested in developing a multiple regression model for explaining the variation in home-game football attendance. Use stepwise regression to develop the model.
    a. Which variable entered the model at step 1? Discuss why this variable entered.
    b. Indicate the order of variables entering the stepwise regression model. What happens to R-square and the standard error of the estimate for each variable entering?
    c. Indicate the regression model at the final step. Also indicate why the model stopped at this step.

d. Test the overall significance of the regression model at the final step. Also test whether each regression coefficient is statistically significant. Use an $\alpha = 0.05$ level.

16. Comment on the statement, "Stepwise regression is the way to go. It will always give you the best subset of independent variables from the original list of variables. R-square will be maximized by using stepwise regression."

17. We have four potential independent variables, X_1, X_2, X_3, and X_4, from which we wish to develop a multiple regression model. Using stepwise regression, X_2 and X_4 entered the model.
   a. Why did only two variables enter the model? Discuss.
   b. Suppose an ordinary regression with variables X_2 and X_4 had been run. Would the resulting model be different from the stepwise model? Discuss.
   c. Comment on the statement, "The stepwise regression with the two variables will have a higher R-square than an ordinary regression with all four variables included."

14-5 DETERMINING THE APTNESS OF THE MODEL (OPTIONAL)

When we develop a simple linear or multiple regression model, we cannot be sure that the model is proper for the application. That is, the model we have developed may not be suited to the available data. In Chapter 13, we outlined the assumptions associated with linear regression analysis. To summarize, the regression assumptions are as follows:

1. The relationship between the dependent and independent variables is linear.
2. The residuals are independent.
3. The variance of the residuals is constant over the range of the independent variables.
4. The residuals are normally distributed.

The degree to which the regression model satisfies the assumptions is called its *aptness*.

ANALYSIS OF RESIDUALS

The residual, the difference between the actual value of the dependent variables and the value predicted by the regression model, is defined by equation 14-10:

$$\text{Residual} = (Y_i - \hat{Y}_i) \quad \text{(14-10)}$$

A residual value can be computed for each observation in the data set. A great deal can be learned about the *aptness* of the regression model by analyzing the residuals. The principal means of residual analysis is study of residual plots. The following problems can be discovered through graphical analysis of residuals:

1. The regression function is not linear.
2. The residuals do not have a constant variance.
3. The residuals are not independent.
4. The error terms are not normally distributed.

We will address each of these in order.

The Regression Function Is Not Linear

A plot of the residuals (on the vertical axis) against the independent variable (on the horizontal axis) is useful for detecting whether a linear function is the appropriate regression function. Figure 14-10 illustrates two different residual plots. Figure 14-10(a) shows residuals that systematically depart from 0. When X_1 is small, the residuals are positive. When X_1 is in the midrange, the residuals are negative, and for large X_1 values, the residuals are positive again. This type of plot

FIGURE 14-10

Residual Plot—Linear Versus Nonlinear

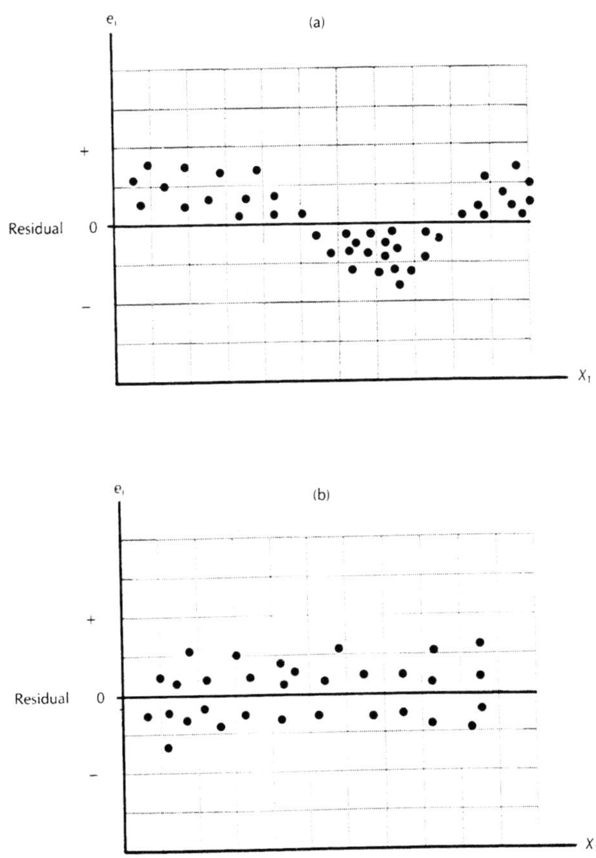

suggests that the relationship between Y and X_1 is nonlinear. Figure 14-10(b) shows a plot where the residuals do not show a systematic variation from 0, implying that the relationship between X_1 and Y is linear.

If a linear model is appropriate, we expect the residuals to band around 0 with no systematic pattern displayed.

The Residuals Do Not Have a Constant Variance

Residual plots can also be used to determine whether the residuals have a constant variance. Consider Figure 14-11, in which the residuals are plotted against the independent variable. The plot in Figure 14-11(a) shows an example in which, as X_1 increases, the residuals become less variable. Figure 14-11(b) shows the opposite situation. When X_1 is small, the residuals are tightly packed around 0,

FIGURE 14-11

Constant and Nonconstant Variance

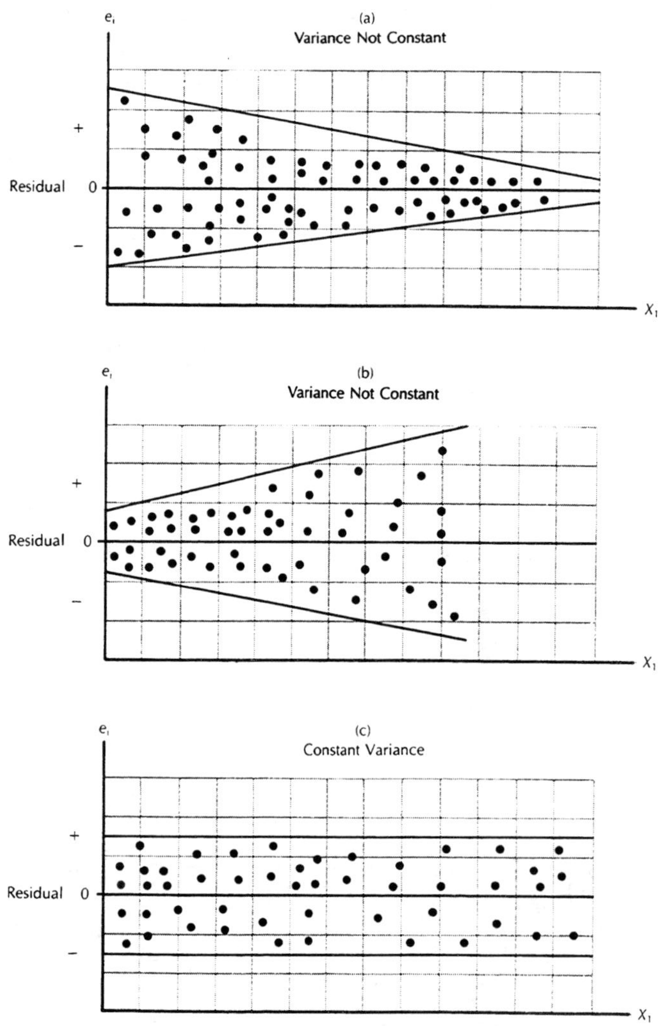

but as X_1 increases, the residuals become more variable. Figure 14-11(c) shows an example in which the residuals exhibit a constant variance around the zero mean.

When the residual plot is cone-shaped, as in either Figure 14-11(a) or 14-11(b), it suggests that the assumption of constant variance has been violated. When a multiple regression model has been employed, we can analyze the constant variance assumption by plotting the residuals against the predicted values, as shown in Figure 14-12 (page 772). Because the plot is cone-shaped, we conclude that the constant variance assumption has not been satisfied.

The Residuals Are Not Independent

If the data used to develop the regression model are measured over time, a plot of the residuals against time is used to determine whether the residuals are correlated. Figure 14-13(a) (page 772) shows an example where the residual plot against time suggests independence. The residuals in Figure 14-13(a) appear to be randomly distributed around the mean of zero over time. However, in Figure 14-13(b), the plot suggests that the residuals are not independent, since in the early time periods the residuals are negative and in later time periods the residuals are positive. This, or any other pattern in the residuals over time, indicates the assumption of independent residuals has been violated. Generally, this means some variable associated with the passage of time has been omitted from the model. Often, time is used as a surrogate for other time-related variables in a regression model. Chapters 17 and 18 will discuss time series data analysis and forecasting techniques in more detail and will address the issue of incorporating the time variable into the model.

The Error Terms Are Not Normally Distributed

The need for normally distributed residuals occurs when we want to test a hypothesis on the regression model. Small departures from normality do not cause serious problems. However, if the residuals depart dramatically from a normal distribution, there is cause for concern.

One method for graphically analyzing the residuals is to form a frequency histogram of the residuals to determine whether the general shape is normal. The chi-square goodness-of-fit test can be used to test whether the residuals fit a normal distribution. This test is discussed in Chapter 15.

Another method for determining normality is to calculate the **standardized residuals** (equation 14-11):

$$\frac{e_i}{\sqrt{\text{MSE}}} \tag{14-11}$$

where

$$e_i = i\text{th residual}$$
$$\text{MSE} = \Sigma(Y_i - \hat{Y}_i)^2/(n - K - 1)$$

FIGURE 14-12

Plot of Residuals Against $\hat{Y}$

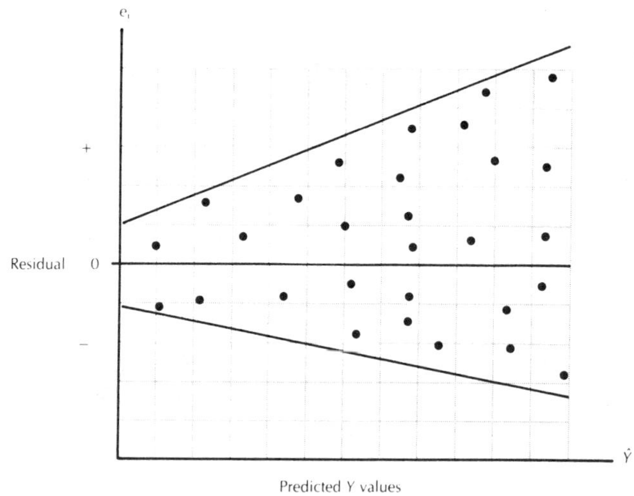

FIGURE 14-13

Plot of Residuals Against Time

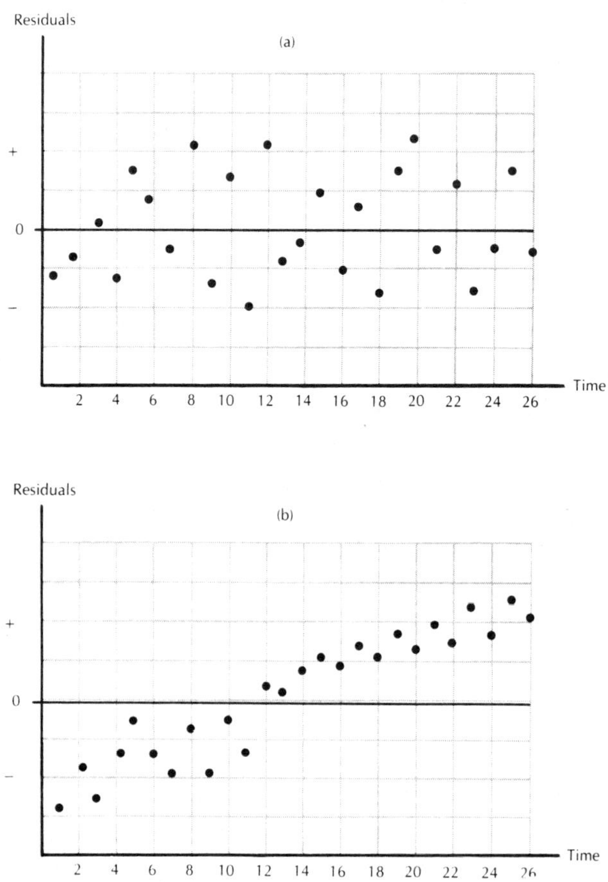

We then determine whether approximately 68% of the standardized residuals have values between +1 and −1 and whether about 95% of the standardized residuals fall between +1.96 and −1.96. If these criteria are satisfied, we can assume that no gross departures from normality have occurred. Most regression software packages have an option to print the standardized residuals.

Because other problems such as nonconstant variance and nonindependent residuals can result in residuals that seem to be nonnormal, it is usually appropriate to check these other factors before addressing the normality assumption.

CORRECTIVE ACTIONS

If, based on analyzing the residuals, you decide the model constructed is not appropriate, but still want a regression-based model, some corrective action may be warranted. There are two approaches that may work: transform some variables or use a different regression model.

Section 13-8 of Chapter 13 outlined the steps involved in variable transformation. The transformations of the independent variables (such as raising X to a power, taking the square root of X, or taking the log of X) are used to make the data conform to a linear relationship. If our model suffers from both nonlinearity and from the residuals having a nonconstant variance, it may be helpful to transform both the independent and dependent variables. In cases where the normality assumption is not satisfied, it is often helpful to try transformations of the dependent variable. In many instances, a log transformation is useful.

The alternative of using a different regression model means that we respecify the model to include new independent variables or remove existing variables from the model. In most modeling applications, we are in a continual state of model respecification. We are always seeking to improve the regression model by finding new independent variables.

SKILL DEVELOPMENT PROBLEMS FOR **SECTION 14-5**

The following exercises are included to help you gain a more complete understanding of the material presented in this section.

18. Listed below are data collected on an independent variable and a dependent variable:

Y	X
200	23.4
180	19.5
210	20.3
230	26.9
219	21.0
195	16.6
267	27.0
290	27.5
304	28.1
240	25.7

a. Develop a simple linear regression model using the above data. Show the regression equation, R-square, and the standard error of the estimate.
b. Compute the residuals for each observation.
c. Plot the residuals against the X variable. What conclusions could be reached about the aptness of the model based on this plot? Discuss.
d. Plot the residuals against the predicted values of Y and comment on what this plot says about the aptness of the model.

19. Referring to Problem 1 in Section 14-2, compute the residuals.
    a. Based on the appropriate residual plot, what can you conclude about the constant variance assumption?
    b. Based on the appropriate residual analysis, does it appear that the residuals are independent? Discuss.

20. Referring to Problem 5 in Section 14-2, compute the residuals.
    a. Based on the appropriate residual plot, what can you conclude about the constant variance assumption?
    b. Based on the appropriate residual analysis, does it appear that the residuals are independent? Discuss.

21. Discuss what is meant by the term *aptness of the model.* Use some examples to illustrate your answer.

22. Under what conditions is it desirable to plot the residuals against the predicted Y values? Discuss.

23. In a multiple regression model, if we wish to determine whether the residuals have a constant variance, is it appropriate to plot the residuals against each X variable individually? If not, what should be done?

14-6 COMPUTER APPLICATIONS

This chapter has presented an introduction to multiple regression analysis. Although multiple regression can be done manually, we doubt that anyone would attempt it in this age of computers. In fact, the examples presented in this chapter have been done using a computer and statistical software. In this section, we present some further computer applications of multiple regression analysis. The data used are the KIVZ-Channel 5 survey data originally introduced in Chapter 2. We suggest you refer to Tables 2-10 and 2-11 for a listing of the data and a description of the variables. The software used here include GB-STAT, MINITAB, and SPSS-X.

Table 14-13 shows the correlation matrix for several of the variables in the KIVZ-Channel 5 survey. This correlation matrix, which was developed using SPSS-X, shows the correlation between each pair of variables. Also shown are the p-values referred to earlier in this text. The p-values indicate the level of significance of the correlation coefficients. For instance, the correlation between X_{13} and X_{14} is 0.0856 and this is significant at the 0.277 level. This means that the correlation would be significant if our alpha level is more than 0.277. Figure 14-14 shows the SPSS-X commands used to generate the correlation matrix in Table 14-13.

TABLE 14-13 SPSS-X Output: Correlation Coefficients

-- - - - - - - PEARSON CORRELATION COEFFICIENTS - - - - - - - -

	VAR12	VAR13	VAR14	VAR15	VAR17	VAR18	VAR19
VAR12	1.0000	.0037	.0511	.0996	-.0615	-.0323	-.3307
	(0)	(50)	(50)	(50)	(50)	(50)	(50)
	P= .	P= .490	P= .362	P= .246	P= .336	P= .412	P= .009
VAR13	.0037	1.0000	.0856	.2189	.0692	-.1462	.0081
	(50)	(0)	(50)	(50)	(50)	(50)	(50)
	P= .490	P= .	P= .277	P= .063	P= .316	P= .156	P= .478
VAR14	.0511	.0856	1.0000	.5754	.4410	.2276	-.0104
	(50)	(50)	(0)	(50)	(50)	(50)	(50)
	P= .362	P= .277	P= .	P= .000	P= .001	P= .056	P= .472
VAR15	.0996	.2189	.5754	1.0000	.5199	.0220	-.1307
	(50)	(50)	(50)	(0)	(50)	(50)	(50)
	P= .246	P= .063	P= .000	P= .	P= .000	P= .440	P= .183
VAR17	-.0615	.0692	.4410	.5199	1.0000	-.1017	.1398
	(50)	(50)	(50)	(50)	(0)	(50)	(50)
	P= .336	P= .316	P= .001	P= .000	P= .	P= .241	P= .166
VAR18	-.0323	-.1462	.2276	.0220	-.1017	1.0000	-.3408
	(50)	(50)	(50)	(50)	(50)	(0)	(50)
	P= .412	P= .156	P= .056	P= .440	P= .241	P= .	P= .008
VAR19	-.3307	.0081	-.0104	-.1307	.1398	-.3408	1.0000
	(50)	(50)	(50)	(50)	(50)	(50)	(0)
	P= .009	P= .478	P= .472	P= .183	P= .166	P= .008	P= .

FIGURE 14-14 SPSS-X Commands: Correlation Matrix

```
UNNUMBERED
TITLE DESCRIPTIVE STATISTICS EXAMPLES
FILE HANDLE KIVZ NAME='KIVZ DATA C'
DATA LIST FILE=KIVZ LIST/VAR01 TO VAR19
VARIABLE LABELS
  VAR01 'NATIONAL NEWS STATION'
  VAR02 'LOCAL NEWS STATION'
  VAR03 'NEWS RATING'
  VAR04 'SPORTS RATING'
  VAR05 'WEATHER RATING'
  VAR06 'ANCHOR RATING'
  VAR07 'SPORTSCASTER RATING'
  VAR08 'OVERALL RATING'
  VAR09 'NATIONAL INFLUENCE'
  VAR10 'SEX'
  VAR11 'MARITAL STATUS'
  VAR12 'NUMBER EMPLOYED'
  VAR13 'HOME STATUS '
  VAR14 'YEARS AT RESIDENCE'
  VAR15 'YEARS IN STATE'
  VAR16 'EDUCATION'
  VAR17 'AGE'
  VAR18 'INCOME'
  VAR19 'HOURS OF TV'
 VALUE LABELS
  VAR01 1 'CHANNEL 5' 2 'CHANNEL 3' 3 'CHANNEL 8' 4
        'UNDECIDED'/
  VAR02 1 'CHANNEL 3' 2 'CHANNEL 8' 3 'CHANNEL 5' 4
        'UNDECIDED'/
  VAR03 TO VAR08 1 'POOR' 2 'FAIR' 3 'GOOD' 4 'VERY GOOD' 5
        'EXCEL'/
  VAR09 1 'TRUE' 2 'FALSE' 3 'UNDECIDED'/
  VAR10 1 'MALE' 2 'FEMALE'/
  VAR11 1 'SINGLE' 2 'DIVORCED' 3 'MARRIED' 4 'OTHER'/
  VAR13 1 'RENTING' 2 'BUYING'/
  VAR16 1 'GRADE SCHOOL' 2 'SOME COLLEGE' 3 'VOTECH' 4 'HIGH
        SCHOOL' 5 'COLLEGE GRAD' 6 'GRADUATE WORK'
 PEARSON CORR VAR12 TO VAR15, VAR 17 TO VAR19
```

TABLE 14-14 MINITAB Output: Regression Analysis

```
The regression equation is
INCOME = 24824 + 1844 SEX + 32.3 YEARS - 42.6 AGE

Predictor        Coef      Stdev      t-ratio
Constant        24824       2333        10.64
SEX              1844       1395         1.32
YEARS           32.31      43.92         0.74
AGE            -42.57      52.12        -0.82

s = 4819    R-sq = 5.4%    R-sq(adj) = 0.0%

Analysis of Variance

SOURCE          DF            SS          MS
Regression       3      60945584    20315196
Error           46    1068238592    23222580
Total           49    1129184256

SOURCE     DF       SEQ SS
SEX         1     42239232
YEARS       1      3217043
AGE         1     15489310

Unusual Observations
Obs.     SEX    INCOME      Fit    Stdev.Fit    Residual    St.Resid
  8     0.00     13600    23227         1227       -9627      -2.07R
 18     1.00     39200    25237         1040       13963       2.97R

R denotes an obs. with a large st. resid.
```

Table 14-14 shows a MINITAB multiple regression output where INCOME is the dependent variable and AGE, YEARS in the state, and SEX are the independent variables. Figure 14-15 shows the MINITAB commands used to generate the output. Note that the SEX variable was originally coded 1 = Male, 2 = Female. We have recoded it to be 0 = Male, 1 = Female, and it is used as a dummy variable in the regression model. (This recoding is not necessary except to be consistent with the presentation in this chapter.)

Table 14-15 shows the GB-STAT output for a multiple regression model with income as the dependent variable and age, years in the state, and hours spent watching T.V. as the independent variables. This output is generated using the multiple regression option from the statistics (F3) menu.

FIGURE 14-15

MINITAB Commands: Multiple Regression Analysis

```
MTB> READ 'KIVZ5' INTO C1-C19
MTB> NAME C18 'INCOME'
MTB> NAME C10 'SEX'
MTB> NAME C17 'AGE'
MTB> NAME C15 'YEARS'
MTB> SUBTRACT 1 C10 C10
MTB> OUTFILE = 'PRINTER'
MTB> REGRESS C18 3 C10 C15 C17
```

TABLE 14-15

GB-STAT Output: Regression Analysis

STRAIGHT MULTIPLE REGRESSION

CURRENT REGRESSION SUMMARY TABLE

DEPENDENT VARIABLE: INCOME

MULTIPLE R = .3453
STD ERR EST = 4649.885
F = 2.0751

IND VAR	B COEF	STD ERR(B)	T-VALUE	PROB
YRSTAT	2.708668	43.45617	.062331	.9506
AGE	−18.8249	51.7178	−.363993	.7175
HRSTV	−364.7278	158.6675	−2.298693	.0261
CONSTANT				
30008.8				

ANOVA FOR CURRENT REGRESSION

	SUM SQUARES	DF	MEAN SQUARES	F-RATIO	PROB
REGRESSION	1.345987E+08	3	4.486622E+07	2.0751	.1165
RESIDUAL	9.945857E+08	46	2.162143E+07		
TOTAL	1.129184E+09	49	2.304458E+07		

MULTIPLE CORRELATION SUMMARY

	MULTIPLE R	R-SQUARE
UNADJUSTED	.3453	.1192
ADJUSTED	.2485	.0618

STD ERROR OF ESTIMATE = 4649.885
SAMPLE SIZE = 50

14-7 COMMON PROBLEMS WITH MULTIPLE REGRESSION

As you continue your studies of business topics you will find multiple regression to be one of the most widely used statistical tools. You will find it applied particularly in production, finance, accounting, and economics. Because it is such a widely used tool, it is also widely misused. Following is a brief list of some of the most common mistakes we have found, some in student projects and others in business applications.

When we assign projects, students will sometimes come to ask questions about their "perfect" model. They know it is perfect because the R^2 value is 1.0. This commonly occurs for two reasons: either they have used the same measurement as both the dependent and an independent variable or they have the same number of variables as data points. In general, no statistical model is perfect. Anytime you have an R^2 of 1.0, look for a problem.

Because multiple regression is such a powerful tool, it is often used when its assumptions are not satisfied. For instance, the variables in the model must be measurable on an interval or ratio scale for correlations to be correctly determined. Many business-related data meet this restriction, but many do not. For instance, questionnaire data, where multiple responses are given for each question, do not meet this restriction. In some cases, we have seen numerical values assigned to marital status and this variable used in a regression analysis. Categorical variables would correctly be analyzed using analysis of variance or assigning dummy variables in a regression model.

Due to the high-speed data-gathering and analysis capabilities of modern computer systems, managers have more information available than at any time in the past. Multiple regression models can be built by just screening large data sets for variables that are highly correlated with a dependent variable. While we will say more about this in the chapter on forecasting, in general we suggest that independent variables in a regression model should "make sense" and not just be chosen because of a high correlation found in a data set.

We know a very good manager who claims that most proposed major actions must be supported by a detailed statistical analysis. His reasoning is that it will add credence to the proposal, even if it is not necessary. If your analysis is going to be used to support a major decision, make sure the model is as free of major errors as possible. In particular, be concerned about problems of multicollinearity and interaction caused by relationships among the independent variables. These sources of statistical error can cause totally erroneous relationships to be defined.

14-8 CONCLUSIONS

Multiple regression is an extension of simple regression analysis. In multiple regression, two or more independent variables are used to explain the variation in the dependent variable. Just as a manager searches for the best combination of employees to perform a job, the decision maker using multiple regression analysis searches for the best combination of independent variables to explain variation in the dependent variable.

The presentation of multiple regression analysis has largely been an analysis of computer printouts. As a decision maker, you will almost assuredly not be required to manually develop the regression model, but you will have to judge its applicability based on a computer printout. The programs we have used in Chapters 13 and 14 are representative of the many available. You no doubt will encounter printouts that look somewhat different from those shown in this text; some of the terms used may differ slightly. However, the basic information will be the same, as will be the inferences you can make from the model.

This chapter has discussed the difference between R^2 and adjusted R^2, as well as the difference between statistical significance and practical significance. As a decision maker, you must recognize that a regression model can be statistically significant yet have no practical use because the standard error of the estimate is too large or multicollinearity impacts too heavily.

CHAPTER GLOSSARY

adjusted *R*-square (R_A^2) A measure of the percentage of explained variation in the dependent variable that takes into account the relationship between the number of cases and the number of independent variables in the regression model. Whereas R^2 will generally increase when an independent variable is added, adjusted R^2 (R_A^2) will decrease if the added variable does not reduce the unexplained variation enough to offset the loss of degrees of freedom.

correlation matrix A table showing the pairwise correlations between all variables (dependent and independent).

dummy variables Variables in a regression model that have two categories, valued 0 and 1. If a qualitative variable has v multiple categories, $v - 1$ dummy variables are formed to represent the qualitative variable in the analysis.

multicollinearity Correlation among the independent variables. Usually the term is used when the intercorrelation is high.

multiple coefficient of determination (R^2) The percentage of variation in the dependent variable explained by the independent variables in the regression model.

multiple regression model A regression model having two or more independent variables with a regression equation of the form

$$Y_i = \beta_0 + \beta_1 X_{1i} + \beta_2 X_{2i} + \beta_3 X_{3i} + \cdots + \beta_K X_{Ki} + e_i$$

regression plane The multiple regression equivalent of the simple regression line. The plane has a different slope for each independent variable.

standard error of the estimate The square root of the mean square residual in the analysis of variance table for a regression model. The standard error measures the dispersion of the actual values of the dependent variable around the fitted regression plane.

standardized residual The residual divided by the standard error of the estimate.

CHAPTER FORMULAS

Standard error of the estimate

$$S_e = \sqrt{\text{MSE}} = \sqrt{\frac{\text{SSE}}{n - K - 1}}$$

Correlation coefficient

$$r = \frac{\Sigma(X_i - \overline{X})(Y_i - \overline{Y})}{\sqrt{\Sigma(X_i - \overline{X})^2 \Sigma(Y_i - \overline{Y})^2}}$$

Coefficient of multiple determination

$$R^2 = \frac{\text{SSR}}{\text{TSS}}$$

Adjusted R^2

$$R_A^2 = 1 - (1 - R^2)\left(\frac{n - 1}{n - K - 1}\right)$$

Standardized residual

$$\frac{e_i}{\sqrt{\text{MSE}}}$$

CONCEPTUAL QUESTIONS AND ASSIGNMENTS

24. Discuss in your own terms the similarities and differences between simple linear regression analysis and multiple regression analysis.
25. Discuss the assumptions associated with regression analysis.
26. Discuss what is meant by the least squares criterion as it pertains to multiple regression analysis. Is the least squares criterion any different for simple regression analysis? Discuss.
27. List the basic assumptions of regression analysis and discuss in your own terms what each means.
28. What does it mean if we have developed a multiple regression model and have concluded that the model is apt?
29. Go to the library and locate three articles using a regression model with more than one independent variable. For each article write a short summary covering the following points:

    Purpose for using the model

    How the variables in the model were selected

    How the data in the model were selected

    Any possible violations of the needed assumptions

    The conclusions drawn from using the model

30. Select a company in your area that you think might use a regression model and interview a decision maker in that company. If the company uses a regression model, outline its use. If the company does not use a regression model, discuss the alternate tools used.

ADDITIONAL PROBLEMS

The problems in this chapter are written with the assumption that you will be solving them with the aid of a computer and appropriate software.

31. A financial analyst for a Wall Street firm recently collected a random sample of twenty-four companies and recorded their year-end stock prices. She hopes to be able to develop a regression model that can be used to explain the variation in stock prices for these twenty-four firms. She plans on using financial ratios such as the debt/equity ratio as independent variables. What would you suggest to her as the maximum number of independent variables to use in the model? Discuss.

32. The managerial development director of a major corporation is trying to determine what personal abilities are necessary for a manager to move from middle- to upper-level management. Although she has been relatively successful predicting who will move rapidly from lower- to middle-management levels, she has had difficulty determining the characteristics necessary to move to the next major level. For a long time, the director has heard that the most glaring deficiency in college graduates entering the company is in communication skills, so she decides to measure whether these skills may be a determining factor.

    The director decides to try to develop a multiple regression relationship between job ratings and communication ability. She picks a random sample of middle-level managers who have been in their present positions less than 5 years but more than 1 year. These managers are given a series of cases to analyze and asked to present both written and oral recommendations. They are rated by a group of top-level managers on their analyses and on their written and oral presentations. These ratings are then compared with the latest employee rating. The data are as follows:

Employee	*Job Rating*	*Case Analysis Score*	*Written Presentation Score*	*Oral Presentation Score*
1	87	8.4	8.7	9.2
2	93	8.2	9.4	9.4
3	91	9.3	9.7	9.5
4	85	7.9	8.1	8.7
5	86	8.1	8.3	8.8
6	97	9.4	9.3	9.6
7	90	9.1	9.0	9.2
8	93	8.9	9.2	9.5
9	88	8.6	8.4	8.5
10	96	9.7	9.5	9.6
11	86	8.3	7.9	8.4
12	89	8.7	8.5	8.7
13	94	9.2	9.1	9.6
14	91	8.1	9.5	9.2
15	95	9.3	9.1	9.7

Use a computer routine available at your school to determine the multiple regression equation for these data.

Problems 33–40 refer to the data given in Problem 32.

33. One of the assumptions of multiple regression is that the independent variables are not correlated with each other. Is this assumption satisfied for these data? What do you check to see if multicollinearity is a problem? Use an alpha level of 0.05.
34. Does the multiple regression model you have estimated show a significant relationship between job ratings and the three independent variables measured? How did you measure this significance? Test with an alpha level of 0.05.
35. If you were a middle-level manager, would you be willing to have your job rating determined just on the basis of your performance on these three independent variables? Explain in statistical terms why or why not.
36. Discuss how much of the variation in job rating is explained by the three independent variables. How do you measure this factor?
37. Are all the independent variables significant in your multiple regression relationship? How can you tell?
38. As a test, the development director gives the same cases to a group of middle-level managers without knowing their job ratings. One of the managers received the following scores:

Case analysis	9.1
Written presentations	9.4
Verbal presentations	9.3

Based on these data, what is the best estimate of the job rating this manager received?
39. The personnel director comments that perhaps the regression model just developed would be a good tool to use before hiring new employees. What do you think of this idea?
40. One manager who participated in this study is concerned with his job rating and would like to know how much his job rating should change if his written presentation score increased by a full point. You are to develop a 95% confidence interval for the regression coefficient for the independent variable, written presentation. Be sure to interpret this interval.
41. A publishing company in New York is attempting to develop a model that it can use to help predict textbook sales for books it is considering for future publication. The marketing department has collected data on several variables from a random sample of fifteen books. These data are given in the accompanying table.

Use an available computer routine to develop the correlation matrix showing the correlation between all possible pairs of variables. Test statistically to determine which independent variables are significantly correlated with the dependent variable, book sales. Use an alpha level of 0.05.

Book	Volumes Sold Y	Pages X_1	Competing Books X_2	Advertising Budget X_3	Age of Author X_4
1	15,000	176	5	$25,000	49
2	140,000	296	10	83,000	57
3	75,000	483	7	40,000	29
4	100,000	811	14	29,000	37
5	26,000	302	9	52,000	35
6	33,000	411	15	33,000	43
7	59,000	333	7	19,000	51
8	103,000	602	4	37,000	62
9	88,000	504	12	51,000	33
10	10,000	204	3	30,000	50
11	9,000	376	4	19,000	26
12	77,000	600	7	41,000	40
13	59,000	400	3	26,000	44
14	183,000	597	8	51,000	59
15	16,000	126	1	27,000	38

42. Referring to Problem 41, develop a multiple regression model containing all four independent variables. Show clearly the regression coefficients.
43. Referring to Problems 41 and 42, how much of the total variation in book sales can be explained by these four independent variables? Would you conclude that the model is significant at the 0.05 level?
44. Referring to Problems 41 and 42, develop a 95% confidence interval for each regression coefficient and interpret these confidence intervals.
45. Referring to Problem 44, which of the independent variables can be concluded to be significant in explaining the variation in book sales? Test using an alpha level of 0.05.
46. The publishing company in Problems 41–45 recently came up with some additional data for the fifteen books in the original sample. Two new variables, production expenditures (X_5) and number of prepublication reviewers (X_6), have been added. These additional data are as follows:

Book	X_5	X_6	Book	X_5	X_6
1	$38,000	5	9	$51,000	4
2	86,000	8	10	34,000	6
3	59,000	3	11	20,000	2
4	80,000	9	12	80,000	5
5	29,500	3	13	60,000	5
6	31,000	3	14	87,000	8
7	40,000	5	15	29,000	3
8	69,000	4			

Calculate the correlation between each of these additional variables and the dependent variable, book sales. You will have to use the data from Problem 41.

47. Referring to Problem 46, test the significance of the correlation coefficients, using an alpha level of 0.05. Comment on your results.

48. Referring to Problems 41–47, develop a multiple regression model that includes all six independent variables. Which, if any, variables would you recommend be retained if this model is going to be used to predict book sales for the publishing company? For any statistical tests you might perform, use an alpha level of 0.05. Discuss your results.

49. Referring to Problem 48, use the analysis of variance approach to test the null hypothesis that all slope coefficients are 0. Test with an alpha level of 0.05. What do these results mean? Discuss.

50. Referring to Problems 41–49, does it appear that multicollinearity problems are present in the model? Discuss the potential consequences of multicollinearity with respect to the regression model.

51. Refer to the textbook data in Problems 41 and 46. Develop a multiple regression model using all six independent variables.
    a. Show the regression equation.
    b. Compute the residuals and print these out.
    c. Plot the residuals against the predicted value of Y and comment on what this plot means relative to the aptness of the model.
    d. Compute the standardized residuals and form these in a frequency histogram. What does this indicate about the normality assumption?
    e. Comment on the overall aptness of this model and indicate what might be done to improve the model.

The following information applies to Problems 52–62.

The J. J. McCracken Company has authorized its marketing research department to make a study of customers who have been issued a McCracken charge card. The marketing research department hopes to be able to identify the significant variables that explain the variation in purchases. Once these variables are determined, the department intends to try to attract new customers who would be predicted to have a high volume of purchases.

Twenty-five customers were selected at random and values for the following variables were recorded (see Table 14P-1):

Y = Average monthly purchases (in dollars) at McCracken

X_1 = Customer age

X_2 = Customer family income

X_3 = Family size

A computer program was used to perform the multiple regression analysis. Tables 14P-2 through 14P-5 (pages 785–787) show the results of the computer run.

TABLE 14P-1

Data for the McCracken Company Example

Purchase Volume Y	Age X_1	Family Income X_2	Family Size X_3
75	42	$29,000	4
129	36	25,000	2
105	38	25,000	2
42	54	17,000	3
17	49	15,000	5
26	55	19,500	3
144	25	24,000	2
100	24	14,000	1
92	30	11,000	1
58	35	12,000	2
111	27	29,000	3
146	29	38,000	2
93	38	19,500	4
68	40	24,000	3
11	36	22,500	2
50	22	10,200	1
55	25	14,000	3
88	69	19,200	4
100	54	52,000	4
86	48	21,400	3
105	30	26,000	2
121	27	18,250	3
14	62	10,250	3
37	50	18,100	2
43	26	24,500	4

52. A first step in regression analysis often involves developing a scatter plot of the data. Develop the scatter plots of all the possible pairs of variables and with a brief statement indicate what each plot says about the relationship between the two variables.
53. Table 14P-2 illustrates the correlation matrix. Develop the decision rule for testing the significance of each coefficient. Which, if any, correlations are not significant? Use an alpha level of 0.05.

TABLE 14P-2

Correlation Matrix for the McCracken Company Example

	Y	X1	X2	X3
Y	1.000	−.4057	.4591	−.2444
X1		1.000	.0512	.5037
X2			1.000	.2718
X3				1.000

TABLE 14P-3

Step 1 of Stepwise Regression for the McCracken Company Example

```
********************************************************************************
STEP NUMBER 1
VARIABLE ENTERED          X2
R SQUARE                .2107
ADJUSTED R SQUARE       .1763
STANDARD ERRØR        36.3553
--------------------------------------------------------------------------------
ANALYSIS ØF VARIANCE        D.F.    SUM ØF SQUARES    MEAN SQUARE       F
REGRESSIØN                   1         8118.48          8118.48        6.14
RESIDUAL (UNEXPLAINED)      23        30399.32          1321.70

----------------------- VARIABLES IN THE EQUATIØN ------------------------
VARIABLE                     B              STD. ERRØR B            T
X2  INCØME                 .00199            .000803              2.478
(CØNSTANT)               33.7544
********************************************************************************
```

54. At step 1 of the output (see Table 14P-3), the variable X_2, family income, was brought into the model. Discuss why this happened.
55. Test the significance of the regression model at step 1 of the computer printout. Justify the alpha level you have selected.
56. Develop a 95% confidence level for the slope coefficient for the family income variable at step 1 of the model. Be sure to interpret this confidence interval.
57. Describe the regression model at step 2 (see Table 14P-4) of the analysis. In your discussion, be sure to discuss the effect of adding a new variable on the standard error of the estimate and on R^2.
58. Suppose the manager of McCracken's marketing department questions the appropriateness of adding a second variable. How would you respond to her question? Use the information in Table 14P-4 in your response.
59. Table 14P-5 presents the third and final step in the regression analysis. Test statistically the significance of each independent variable in the model at an alpha level of 0.05. Also test the hypothesis that all slope coefficients are 0 at the alpha level of 0.05. Why can the overall model be significant while some individual variables are not significant?
60. If you look carefully at the results shown in Tables 14P-3 through 14P-5, you can see that the value of the slope coefficient for variable X_2, family income, changes each time a new variable is added to the regression model. Discuss why this change takes place.
61. Analyze the regression model at step 3 and the intermediate results at steps 1 and 2. Write a report to the marketing manager pointing out the strengths

TABLE 14P-4

Step 2 of Stepwise Regression for the McCracken Company Example

```
*****************************************************************************
STEP NUMBER 2
VARIABLE ENTERED          X1
R SQUARE               .3955
ADJUSTED R SQUARE      .3405
STANDARD ERRØR       32.5313
-----------------------------------------------------------------------------
ANALYSIS ØF VARIANCE        D.F.   SUM ØF SQUARES   MEAN SQUARE      F
REGRESSIØN                    2        15235.4         7617.7       7.19
RESIDUAL (UNEXPLAINED)       22        23282.4         1058.29
--------------------VARIABLES IN THE EQUATIØN -------------------------------
VARIABLE                       B            STD. ERRØR B          T
X2  INCØME                  .00208           .000717            2.899
X1  AGE                   -1.31807           .508267           -2.593
(CØNSTANT)                 82.8875
*****************************************************************************
```

TABLE 14P-5

Step 3 of Stepwise Regression for the McCracken Company Example

```
*****************************************************************************
STEP NUMBER 3
VARIABLE ENTERED          X3
R SQUARE               .4322
ADJUSTED R SQUARE      .3510
STANDARD ERRØR       32.2724
-----------------------------------------------------------------------------
ANALYSIS ØF VARIANCE        D.F.   SUM ØF SQUARES   MEAN SQUARE      F
REGRESSIØN                    3        16646.1         5548.6       5.33
RESIDUAL (UNEXPLAINED)       21        21871.7         1040.5
--------------------VARIABLES IN THE EQUATIØN -------------------------------
VARIABLE                       B            STD. ERRØR B          T
X2  INCØME                  .00233           .000745            3.132
X1  AGE                    -.97047           .586042           -1.655
X3  FAMILY                 -8.7233           7.49549           -1.163
(CØNSTANT)                 87.7897
*****************************************************************************
```

and weaknesses of the model. Be sure to comment on the department's goal of being able to use the model to predict customers who will purchase high volumes from McCracken.

62. Refer to the data in Table 14P-1. Develop a multiple regression model using the three independent variables.
    a. Show the regression equation.
    b. Compute the residuals and print these out.
    c. Plot the residuals against the predicted value of Y and comment on what this plot means relative to the aptness of the model.
    d. Compute the standardized residuals and form these in a frequency histogram. What does this indicate about the normality assumption?
    e. Comment on the overall aptness of this model and indicate what might be done to improve the model.

63. *Special Problem:* Refer to the textbook data in Problems 41 and 46. Take any and all steps necessary to develop the best possible regression model using these data. Show each step of your process in a clear and concise manner. Prepare a written narrative describing what steps you have taken.

    Once you have what you consider to be the best model, determine its aptness, using the appropriate methods of residual analysis. If corrective actions are warranted, take those actions. Remember to document all your efforts in your narrative report.

DATABASE PROBLEMS

The following questions and problems pertain directly to the State Department of Transportation case study and database introduced in Chapter 1. The questions and problems were written assuming that you will have access to a computer and appropriate statistical software. The database containing 100 observations and seventeen variables is shown in Table 1-1 in Chapter 1. *Assume that the data were collected using a simple random sampling process.*

1. Develop the best possible linear regression model using X_7, vehicle year, as the dependent variable and any or all of the other variables as potential independent variables. Assume that your objective is to develop a predictive model. Write a report that discusses the steps you took to develop the final model. Include a correlation matrix and all appropriate statistical tests. Use an $\alpha = 0.05$. If you are using a nominal or ordinal variable, remember that you must make sure it is in the form of one or more dummy variables. The number of dummy variables will be 1 less than the number of categories for the original variable.

2. Develop the best possible linear regression model using X_6, total cancellations and suspensions, as the dependent variable and any or all of the other variables as potential independent variables. Assume that your objective is to develop a predictive model. Write a report that discusses the steps you took to develop the final model. Include a correlation matrix and all appropriate

statistical tests. Use an $\alpha = 0.05$. If you are using a nominal or ordinal variable, remember that you must make sure it is in the form of one or more dummy variables. The number of dummy variables will be 1 less than the number of categories for the original variable.

3. Develop the best possible linear regression model using X_{15}, number of years of formal education, as the dependent variable and any or all of the other variables as potential independent variables. Assume that your objective is to develop a predictive model. Write a report that discusses the steps you took to develop the final model. Include a correlation matrix and all appropriate statistical tests. Use an $\alpha = 0.05$. If you are using a nominal or ordinal variable, remember that you must make sure it is in the form of one or more dummy variables. The number of dummy variables will be 1 less than the number of categories for the original variable.

ADDITIONAL DATABASE PROBLEMS

The questions and problems in this section reference the various databases that accompany this text and which are described in Chapter 1. Your instructor has been provided a diskette with these databases. It is expected that you will be using computer software to access these data and to perform the required calculations and graphs.

DATABASE: **CITIES** *(Refer to the database description in Chapter 1.)*

1. Assume that Art Lee has requested you to develop a multiple regression model that would allow him to predict the labor market stress index, X_8, based on the other variables in the database. (*Note:* Be careful about the SAT/ACT variables—see Chapter 1.)
   a. Develop a correlation matrix for all relevant variables and write a short report that discusses the correlation results. Be sure to indicate which potential independent variables appear to have the most promise in the model.
   b. Bring all the relevant independent variables into the model at one time. Show the model, including the intercept and regression coefficients. Look at the signs on the coefficients and indicate which, if any, seem to have inappropriate signs. Discuss.
   c. Is the overall model significant? State clearly the null and alternative hypotheses and show your test procedure. Test at the $\alpha = 0.05$ level. Discuss.
   d. What is the coefficient of determination? Does the model explain a significant proportion of the variation in the dependent variable? Test at an $\alpha = 0.05$ level.
   e. Test each of the regression slope coefficients individually to determine which variables are significant in the model. Test at an $\alpha = 0.05$ level. Write a short report describing your results.

2. Referring to Problem 1, use forward stepwise regression to develop the regression model using appropriate independent variables. Write a complete report describing step-by-step what took place as the variables were entered into the model. Be sure to indicate what, if any, evidences of multicollinearity are present in the model. In your analysis, perform any appropriate tests of significance. Would you recommend that this model be used to predict a city's labor stress market index? Explain.

DATABASE: **FAST100** (*Refer to the database description in Chapter 1.*)

1. The objective set forth in a recent staff meeting at D. L. Green & Associates is to develop a regression model for predicting company stock price. The database called FAST100 contains data on several potential independent variables. Construct a correlation matrix that shows the correlation between the independent variables and the dependent variable and between all possible pairs of independent variables. Write a report that discusses the correlation matrix. Which variables appear to have most promise as predictors of stock price? Discuss.
2. Referring to Problem 1, X_8 is a coded variable indicating on which stock exchange the company's stock is traded. Can this variable be used directly as it is or will you need to make some modification? If so, what is that modification, and why are you making it? Given that a modification is necessary, make the modification and determine the correlation between the new variable(s) and the dependent variable. Discuss.
3. Referring to Problems 1 and 2, develop a multiple regression model with stock price as the dependent variable. Bring in all appropriate independent variables.
   a. Identify the regression model including the intercept and slope coefficients. Comment on whether these coefficients look reasonable given the correlations in Problems 1 and 2. Discuss.
   b. Is the overall model significant? State clearly the null and alternative hypotheses and show your test procedure. Test at the $\alpha = 0.10$ level. Discuss.
   c. What is the coefficient of determination? Does the model explain a significant proportion of the variation in the dependent variable? Test at an $\alpha = 0.10$ level.
   d. Test each of the regression slope coefficients individually to determine which variables are significant in the model. Test at an $\alpha = 0.10$ level. Write a short report describing your results.
4. Referring to Problem 3, use forward stepwise regression to develop the regression model using appropriate independent variables. Write a complete report describing step-by-step what took place as the variables were entered into the model. Be sure to indicate what, if any, evidence of multicollinearity is present in the model. In your analysis, perform any appropriate tests of significance. Would you recommend that this model be used as a predictive tool? Explain.

DATABASE: **PACRIM** (*Refer to the database description in Chapter 1.*)

1. It has been suggested that you develop a model that might be used to explain the variation in stockholder's equity, X_7, for companies doing business in the Pacific Rim region. One of the variables that is under consideration is the country in which the company is headquartered. Discuss how you could incorporate this variable into the regression analysis. If new variables are required, go ahead and build the new variables. Discuss what you have done and why.
2. Referring to Problem 1, develop a correlation matrix that includes all independent and dependent variables. Discuss the correlations making note of the size and sign of the correlations.
3. Referring to Problems 1 and 2, develop a multiple regression model with stockholder's equity as the dependent variable. Bring in all appropriate independent variables.
   a. Identify the regression model, including the intercept and slope coefficients. Comment on whether these coefficients look reasonable given the correlations in Problems 1 and 2. Discuss.
   b. Is the overall model significant? State clearly the null and alternative hypotheses and show your test procedure. Test at the $\alpha = 0.10$ level. Dicuss.
   c. What is the coefficient of determination? Does the model explain a significant proportion of the variation in the dependent variable? Test at an $\alpha = 0.10$ level.
   d. Test each of the regression slope coefficients individually to determine which variables are significant in the model. Test at an $\alpha = 0.10$ level. Write a short report describing your results.
4. Referring to Problem 3, use forward stepwise regression to develop the regression model using appropriate independent variables. Write a complete report describing step-by-step what took place as the variables were entered into the model. Be sure to indicate what, if any, evidences of multicollinearity are present in the model. In your analysis, perform any appropriate tests of significance. Would you recommend that this model be used as a predictive tool? Explain.

CASE

14A Dynamic Scales, Inc.

In 1975, Stanley Ahlon and three financial partners formed Dynamic Scales, Inc. The company was based on an idea Stanley had for developing a scale to weigh trucks in motion and thus eliminate the need for every truck to stop at weigh stations along highways. This dynamic scale would be placed in the highway approximately one-quarter mile from the regular weigh station. The scale would have a minicomputer that would automatically record truck speed, axle weights, and climate variables, including temperature, wind, and moisture. Stanley Ahlon and his partners believed that state transportation departments in the United States would be the primary market for such a scale.

Like many technological advances, developing the dynamic scale has been difficult. When the scale finally proved accurate for trucks traveling 40 miles per hour, it would not perform for trucks traveling at higher speeds. However, 8 months ago, Stanley announced that the dynamic scale was ready to be field-tested by the Nebraska State Department of Transportation under a grant from the federal government.

TABLE 14C-1

Test Data for the Dynamic Scales, Inc., Example

Month	Front-Axle Static Weight	Front-Axle Dynamic Weight	Truck Speed	Temperature	Moisture
January	1,800 lb	1,625 lb	52 mi/h	21°F	0.00%
	1,311	1,904	71	17	0.15
	1,504	1,390	48	13	0.40
	1,388	1,402	50	19	0.10
	1,250	1,100	61	24	0.00
February	2,102	1,950	55	26	0.10
	1,410	1,475	58	32	0.20
	1,000	1,103	59	38	0.15
	1,430	1,387	43	24	0.00
	1,073	948	59	18	0.40
March	1,502	1,493	62	34	0.00
	1,721	1,902	67	36	0.00
	1,113	1,415	48	42	0.21
	978	983	59	29	0.32
	1,254	1,149	60	48	0.00
April	994	1,052	58	37	0.00
	1,127	999	52	34	0.21
	1,406	1,404	59	40	0.40
	875	900	47	48	0.00
	1,350	1,275	68	51	0.00
May	1,102	1,120	55	52	0.00
	1,240	1,253	57	57	0.00
	1,087	1,040	62	63	0.00
	993	1,102	59	62	0.10
	1,408	1,400	67	68	0.00
June	1,420	1,404	58	70	0.00
	1,808	1,790	54	71	0.00
	1,401	1,396	49	83	0.00
	933	1,004	62	88	0.40
	1,150	1,127	64	81	0.00

Stanley explained to his financial partners, and to Nebraska transportation officials, that the dynamic weight would not exactly equal the static weight (truck weight on a static scale), but that he was sure a statistical relationship between dynamic weight and static weight could be determined, which would make the dynamic scale useful.

Nebraska officials, along with people from Dynamic Scales, Inc., installed a dynamic scale on a major highway in Nebraska. Each month for 6 months, data were collected for a random sample of trucks weighed on both the dynamic scale and a static scale. Table 14C-1 presents these data.

Once the data were collected, the next step was to determine whether, based on this test, the dynamic scale measurements could be used to predict static weights. A complete report will be submitted to the U.S. government and to Dynamic Scales, Inc.

REFERENCES

Bowerman, Bruce L., and O'Connell, Richard T. *Linear Statistical Models,* 2nd edition. Boston: PWS-Kent, 1990.

Demmert, Henry, and Medoff, Marshall. "Game Specific Factors and Major League Baseball Attendance: An Econometric Study." *Santa Clara Business Review* (1977): 49–56.

Draper, N. R., and Smith, H. *Applied Regression Analysis.* New York: Wiley, 1966.

Gloudemans, Robert J., and Miller, Dennis. "Multiple Regression Analysis Applied to Residential Properties." *Decision Sciences* 7 (April 1976): 294–304.

Hair, Joseph F.; Anderson, Rolph E.; and Tatham, Ronald L. *Multivariate Data Analysis,* 2nd edition. New York: Macmillan, 1987.

Johnson, J. *Econometric Methods.* New York: McGraw–Hill, 1972.

Neter, John, and Wasserman, William. *Applied Linear Statistical Models.* Homewood, Ill.: Irwin, 1974.

Wittink, Dick R. *The Application of Regression Analysis.* Needham Heights, Mass.: Allyn and Bacon, 1988.

Chapter 14

Hand-In Exercises

1. In Table 14–4 is an equation for predicting the selling price of a house. Use the 5% level of significance when answering the following.

   a. Is square feet a valid predictor?

   b. Is number of bedrooms a valid predictor?

   c. Is number of bathrooms a valid predictor?

   d. Is number of fireplaces a valid predictor?

   e. Is the total regression estimating equation valid?

f. Predict a selling price for a home with 2000 square feet, 4 bedrooms, 2 bathrooms and a fireplace.

g. Do you think this is a good predicting equation on the basis of the standard error? Comment.

h. Do you think this is a good predicting equation on the basis of the coefficient of determination? Comment.

2. In Table 14–6 is an equation for predicting the selling price of a house with dummy variables included. Variables are evaluated at the 5% level.

a. Is the total equation valid?

b. Which predictor variable is not a valid predictor?

c. In this model, what is the effect on price of adding one square foot to the size of house?

d. How is the price effected by addition of air conditioning?

e. What is the value of an additional bedroom?

f. On the basis of the equation which school district seems to be preferred?

Contingency Tables and Goodness-of-Fit Tests

WHY DECISION MAKERS NEED TO KNOW

The estimation and hypothesis testing tools introduced in previous chapters are designed to be used with interval or ratio level data. For instance, a marketing manager may wish to estimate the average annual income of individuals in a particular region of his state. The variable of interest, income, is assumed to be measured on a ratio scale. A production manager might be interested in determining whether the average setup time on a machine has decreased after a training program was initiated. The variable, setup time, is measured on a continuous scale and is a ratio level variable. These are but two examples of the many you might encounter, where the large- and small-sample estimation and hypothesis-testing procedures introduced in previous chapters could be applied.

You will also encounter many business situations in which the level of data measurement for the variable of interest is either nominal or ordinal and the estimation and statistical procedures introduced thus far are not appropriate. For example, a bank may have data on its customers' automobile loan status that are represented by a code to indicate whether the customer is a poor risk or a good risk. The bank may also have data for these customers that indicate, by a code, whether each person is buying or renting a home. The loan officer may be interested in determining whether loan classification is independent of home ownership status. Since both variables are qualitative or categorical variables, their measurement level is nominal and a new statistical tool is needed to assist the manager in reaching an inference about the customer population. That statistical tool is contingency analysis. Contingency analysis is a widely used tool for analyzing the relationship between qualitative variables and one that decision makers in all business areas find helpful for data analysis.

Business decision makers also encounter situations in which they need to determine whether output data from a particular process can be described by a known distribution. For example, a food processing company uses an automated machine to fill packages of frozen vegetables. According to the machine's manufacturer, the distribution of individual package weights coming from the machine is normally distributed around a specified mean with a standard deviation of 0.10 pound. Periodically, the production control manager will weigh a sample of packages from the line and from these sample data infer whether the machine is functioning as specified by the manufacturer. To do this, she needs to utilize a statistical technique called goodness of fit. Goodness-of-fit tests are used in many business situations and you will find this tool very useful.

Thus, depending on the situation, as a decision maker you will need an ever-expanding array of statistical tools. The techniques of contingency analysis and goodness-of-fit tests are two additional techniques that will be important additions to tools presented in earlier chapters.

CHAPTER OBJECTIVES

This chapter introduces two important statistical tools: contingency analysis and goodness-of-fit testing. Contingency analysis is a useful tool for determining whether a relationship of statistical independence exists between two or more categorical variables. Goodness-of-fit tests are used to determine whether data coming from a process fit a specified distribution. This chapter will present a variety of real decision-making applications for which these statistical tools are helpful. Included in this discussion will be the introduction of the chi-square test for independence, the phi coefficient, the chi-square goodness-of-fit test, and the Lilliefors goodness-of-fit test.

STUDENT OBJECTIVES

After studying the material in this chapter, you should be able to do the following:

1. Set up a contingency analysis table and perform a chi-square test of independence.
2. Compute and interpret the phi coefficient for a contingency analysis application.
3. Utilize the chi-square goodness-of-fit test to determine whether data from a process fit a specified distribution.
4. Utilize the Lilliefors goodness-of-fit test to determine whether data from a process fit a normal distribution.

15-1 INTRODUCTION TO CONTINGENCY ANALYSIS

During the 1990–1991 academic year, Dalgarno Photo, Inc., undertook the task of surveying yearbook representatives at colleges and universities in its market area. A major part of Dalgarno Photo, Inc.'s business comes from taking photographs for college yearbooks in the eastern United States. A first-year MBA student was hired to develop a survey that would be administered as a mail questionnaire to the yearbook representatives at the colleges and universities.

The primary objective of the survey was to solicit objective views regarding a variety of issues related to the photography and publishing activities associated with yearbook development. For instance, the survey was designed to obtain information about what photographer and publisher services the schools currently use and what factors are most important in making these selections.

The respondents were unaware that Dalgarno Photo, Inc., originated the survey that was mailed to representatives at 850 colleges and universities. A total of 221 usable responses were returned. The survey instrument contained thirty questions, which were coded into 137 separate variables. A portion of the survey instrument is shown in Figure 15-1 (pages 798–799).

For our purposes here, we will focus on just four of the 137 variables obtained through the survey. They are as follows:

$$X_1 = \text{Source of university funding}$$
$$X_2 = \text{Total undergraduate enrollment}$$
$$X_3 = \text{Sex of the yearbook editor}$$
$$X_4 = \text{Yearbook budget}$$

Among his many interests in this study, Dalgarno's marketing manager has questioned whether funding source and sex of the yearbook editor are related in some manner. To analyze this issue, we examine variables X_1 and X_3 more closely. Variable X_1, source of university funding, is a categorical variable coded as follows:

$$1 = \text{Private funding}$$
$$2 = \text{State-funded}$$

Of the 221 respondents who provided data for this variable, 155 came from privately funded colleges or universities and 66 were from state-funded institutions.

Variable X_3, sex of the yearbook editor, is also a categorical variable with two response categories, coded as follows:

$$1 = \text{Male}$$
$$2 = \text{Female}$$

Of the 221 responses to the survey, 164 were from females and 57 were from males.

FIGURE 15-1

Dalgarno Photo, Inc., Market Survey

1. What type of institution is your college/university?
   1. Private   2. State-funded
2. What is the total undergraduate enrollment in your school?
   1. <400
   2. 400–2,000
   3. 2,000–4,000
   4. 4,000–8,000
   5. >8,000
3. What is your major course of study?
   1. Social science/Humanities
   2. Math/Science
   3. Journalism
   4. English
   5. Business/Economics
   6. Engineering/Computer
   7. Other ______________
4. What is your grade level?
   1. Sophomore
   2. Junior
   3. Senior
5. What is your gender?
   1. Male
   2. Female
6. What is your title?
   1. Editor-in-chief
   2. Photography editor
   3. Layout editor
   4. Faculty advisor
   5. Other ______________
7. What are your related publication experiences?
   1. Yearbook (dates and capacity) ______________
   2. Other publication(s) (dates and capacity) ______________
   3. No prior related experience
8. Who selected the editor-in-chief?
   1. Former editor-in-chief
   2. Former board of editors
   3. Faculty advisor
   4. Other ______________
9. How many people are on the yearbook staff?
   1. <5
   2. 5–10
   3. 10–20
   4. >20

⋮

21. How many rolls of film were shot last year? How many were in color?
22. What was your opinion of the quality of last year's yearbook?
    (Low) 1 2 3 4 5 6 7 8 9 (High)
23. When do you normally deliver the yearbook?
    1. Fall   2. Spring   3. Summer
24. Did you meet all your publication deadlines last year? If not, please give the reasons for and the extent of the lateness.
    1. Yes. All deadlines were met
    2. No. Reason(s) for lateness:
       Extent of lateness:

FIGURE 15-1

Dalgarno Photo, Inc., Market Survey (*Continued*)

25. What publication seminars or conventions are you or your staff planning to attend?
26. How active is your faculty advisor in the management of the yearbook?
    (Inactive) 1 2 3 4 5 6 7 8 9 (Active)
27. Who are your current publisher and photographer? How long have you been associated with them?

	Name	# of years of association
Publisher :		1 2 3 4 5 >6
Photographer:		1 2 3 4 5 >6

28. What are the important factors influencing your selection of the publisher and photographer? Please allocate 100 points among these factors, with the highest number of points for the most important factor.

	Publisher	Photographer
Quality	___	___
Service	___	___
Amount of discount revenue	___	___
Allowance for equipment (computers, cameras)	___	___
Previous experience with your school	___	___
Reputation	___	___
Location (local/national)	___	___
Other ______________	___	___
Total	100	100

29. Do you utilize a computer? If so, for what purpose?
    1. No
    2. Yes. a. Layout
       b. Design
       c. Word processing
       d. Accounting
       e. Other ______________
30. Please indicate the annual amount allocated to the yearbook budget.
    _____ Under $20,000 _____ $20,000–$40,000 _____ $40,000–$60,000
    _____ Over $60,000

In cases like this, where the variables of interest are both categorical and the decision maker is interested in determining whether a relationship exists between the two, a statistical technique known as **contingency analysis** is useful. To employ contingency analysis, we set up a two-dimensional table called a **contingency table.** A contingency table is nothing more than a table of the joint frequencies, also called a **crosstabulation** table (see Chapter 2). The contingency table for variables X_1 and X_3 is shown here:

	Source of Funding		
Sex	*Private*	*State*	
Male	14	43	57
Female	141	23	164
	155	66	221

This table shows that 14 of the respondents were males from schools that are privately funded. The numbers at the extreme right and along the bottom are called the **marginal frequencies.** For example, 57 respondents were males and 155 were from privately funded institutions.

The issue of whether there is a relationship between responses to these two variables is formally addressed through a hypothesis test where the null and alternative hypotheses are stated as follows:

H_0: Sex of yearbook editor is independent of source of college's funding.

H_A: Sex of yearbook editor *is not* independent of source of college's funding.

If the null hypothesis is true, the probability that a yearbook editor from a private institution is a male should be equal to the probability that an editor from a state-funded institution is a male. These two probabilities should also equal the probability that an editor is male without considering the school's funding source. To illustrate, we can find the probability (based on the sample data) of an editor being male as follows:

$$P(\text{male}) = \frac{\text{Number of male editors}}{\text{Number of respondents}} = \frac{57}{221}$$
$$= 0.258$$

Then, if the null hypothesis is true, we would expect

$$P(\text{male}|\text{private}) = P(\text{male}) = 0.258$$

and

$$P(\text{male}|\text{state}) = P(\text{male}) = 0.258$$

Thus, in this sample, we would expect 25.8% of the 155 privately funded schools, or 39.99 schools, to have a male yearbook editor. We would also expect 25.8% of the 66 state-funded schools, or 17.028, to have male yearbook editors. (Note, the expected numbers need not be integer values.) We can use this reasoning to determine the expected number of respondents in each cell of the contingency table:

	Source of Funding		
Sex	*Private*	*State*	
Male	Actual = 14 Expected = 39.99	Actual = 43 Expected = 17.028	57
Female	Actual = 141 Expected = 115.01	Actual = 23 Expected = 48.972	164
	155	66	221

Although sampling error will exist, we would expect, if the null hypothesis is true, the actual frequencies in each cell to closely match the corresponding expected cell frequencies. The greater the difference between the actual and the expected frequencies, the more likely the null hypothesis of independence is false and should be rejected. The statistical test to determine whether the sample data support or refute the null hypothesis is given by equation 15-1:

$$\chi^2 = \sum_{i=1}^{r} \sum_{j=1}^{c} \frac{(f_{A_{ij}} - f_{E_{ij}})^2}{f_{E_{ij}}} \quad \text{with d.f.} = (r-1)(c-1) \qquad \textbf{15-1}$$

where

f_A = Actual cell frequency

f_E = Expected cell frequency

r = Number of rows

c = Number of columns

Do not be confused by the double summation in equation 15-1; it merely indicates that all rows and columns must be used in calculating χ^2.

Figure 15-2 (page 802) presents the hypotheses and test results for this example. Note, the calculated chi-square statistic is compared to the tabled value of chi-square for an $\alpha = 0.05$ and degrees of freedom $= (2-1)(2-1) = 1$. Since $\chi^2_{\text{calculated}} = 76.15 > 3.841$, the null hypothesis of independence should be rejected and Dalgarno Photo representatives should conclude that the sex of the yearbook editor and the school's source of funding are not independent. The contingency table seems to indicate that males are proportionately underrepresented in privately funded schools and overrepresented in state-supported schools.

THE PHI COEFFICIENT FOR 2 × 2 CONTINGENCY TABLES

In Chapter 13, you were introduced to the correlation coefficient, a statistical measure of the strength of the linear relationship between two variables. Recall that if two variables are perfectly correlated, the correlation coefficient would be +1 or −1, depending on the direction of the relationship. However, the correlation coefficient is most applicable when the variables of interest are quantitative and measured by an interval or ratio scale. Thus, the correlation coefficient should not be used to measure the association between the sex variable and school-funding source variable in the Dalgarno Photo, Inc., example we have been discussing. An appropriate measure of association, however, does exist—the

FIGURE 15-2

Chi-Square Contingency Analysis Test for the Dalgarno Photo, Inc., Example

Hypotheses:

H_0: Sex of yearbook editor is independent of college's funding source.
H_A: Sex of yearbook editor *is not* independent of college's funding source.

$\alpha = 0.05$

	Private	*State*
Male	$f_A = 14$ $f_E = 39.99$	$f_A = 43$ $f_E = 17.028$
Female	$f_A = 141$ $f_E = 115.01$	$f_A = 23$ $f_E = 48.972$

Test Statistic:

$$\chi^2_{\text{calculated}} = \sum_{i=1}^{r}\sum_{j=1}^{c}\frac{(f_{A_{ij}} - f_{E_{ij}})^2}{f_{E_{ij}}} = \frac{(14 - 39.99)^2}{39.99} + \frac{(43 - 17.028)^2}{17.028}$$
$$+ \frac{(141 - 115.01)^2}{115.01} + \frac{(23 - 48.972)^2}{48.972}$$
$$= 76.152$$

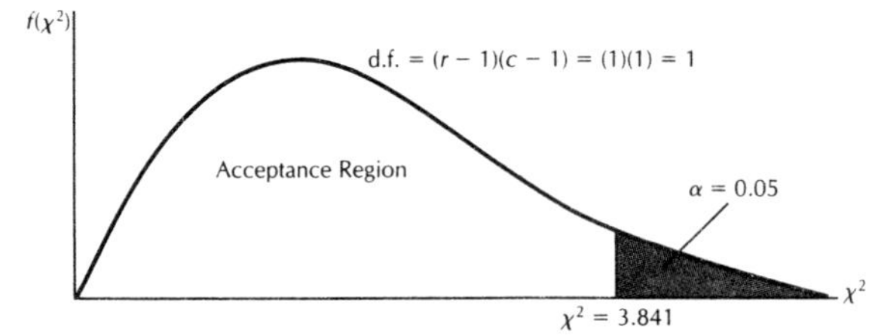

Decision Rule:

If $\chi^2_{\text{calculated}} > 3.841$, reject H_0.
Otherwise, do not reject H_0.

Since $76.152 > 3.841$, reject H_0.

phi coefficient. In this section, we introduce the phi coefficient for 2 × 2 contingency tables—those with 2 rows and 2 columns.

The **phi coefficient** is used to measure the row and column dependency in 2 × 2 contingency tables. In the contingency table, if all the items in row 1 are in one column, and all the items in row 2 are in the other column, the phi coefficient will equal +1 or −1. A phi coefficient of +1 or −1 then represents the most extreme case of dependency between the row and column variables. Values of phi close to 0 occur when there is independence between the row and column variables. Thus, the phi coefficient is a correlation coefficient computed on the observations in the contingency table.

The Greek symbol phi, ϕ, is used to represent the phi coefficient and is computed using equation 15-2:

$$\phi = \frac{ad - bc}{\sqrt{R_1 R_2 C_1 C_2}} \qquad \textbf{15-2}$$

where

a = Frequency count in row 1, column 1

b = Frequency count in row 1, column 2

c = Frequency count in row 2, column 1

d = Frequency count in row 2, column 2

R_i = Total frequency in row i

C_i = Total frequency in column i

Once again, consider the contingency table for Dalgarno Photo, Inc., with yearbook editor gender and college's funding source as the variables of interest:

	Source of Funding		
Sex	*Private*	*State*	
Male	14	43	57
Female	141	23	164
	155	66	221

We compute the phi coefficient using equation 15-2 as follows:

$$\phi = \frac{(14)(23) - (43)(141)}{\sqrt{(57)(164)(155)(66)}}$$
$$= -0.587$$

The phi coefficient shows a reasonably strong negative relationship between editor gender and the college's source of funding. In this case, the implication is that proportionally more editors at state-supported schools are males and proportionally more editors at private schools are females. This means that if an editor is from a state-supported school, it is more likely that the editor is male than female. Likewise, the probability is higher that, if an editor is from a privately funded institution, the editor is female.

Note that the negative sign on the phi coefficient in this example is a result of the order in which the rows and columns were arranged in the contingency table.

For example, if we had reversed the columns to show state schools in column 1 and private schools in column 2, the phi coefficient would be +0.587. Check this out for yourself.

USING PHI TO TEST FOR INDEPENDENCE

Previously, we used the chi-square test to determine whether the row and column variables are independent. The chi-square test is strictly a two-tailed test, meaning that, if the null hypothesis of independence is rejected, no direction of dependence is directly supported. However, an alternate test for independence based on the phi coefficient exists that allows the decision maker to use one-tailed tests when a direction of dependence is anticipated.

Consider the Dalgarno Photo example. Suppose the yearbook sales manager thought (before doing the survey) that private schools might favor women editors, while state-supported schools tended to have men editors. Then, given the previous row and column order, the null and alternative hypotheses that the manager wishes to test are as follows:

H_0: Sex of the editor is independent of college's source of funding.

H_A: There is a negative relationship between sex of editor and funding source.

Another way of stating the alternative hypothesis is

H_A: Proportionately more of the editors at private schools will be female and proportionately more editors at state schools will be males.

Testing the null hypothesis involves comparing the computed phi coefficient to a critical value determined as follows:

If H_A predicts a negative dependency, the critical value is $-Z_\alpha/\sqrt{n}$.

If H_A predicts a positive dependency, the critical value is $+Z_\alpha/\sqrt{n}$.

If H_A is nondirectional (two-tailed), the critical values are $\pm Z_{\alpha/2}/\sqrt{n}$.

Here Z_α is the Z value from the standard normal distribution with probability α in the tail of the distribution.

In this example, $\phi = -0.587$ and the alternative hypothesis predicts a negative dependency, so we need to compare $\phi = -0.587$ to $-Z_\alpha/\sqrt{n}$. Figure 15-3 illustrates the result of the test for an alpha level of 0.05. As is seen in Figure 15-3, the null hypothesis is rejected and we conclude that a significant negative relationship exists between the two variables.

The test of significance shown in Figure 15-3 using the phi coefficient is closely related to the chi-square test used in Figure 15-2. In fact, $\chi^2_{\text{calculated}} = n\,\phi^2$. Since the two tests are related in this manner, there is no need to compute both tests for a given application. The advantage of the phi coefficient is that it allows one-tailed tests to be performed, whereas the chi-square test is strictly two-tailed.

FIGURE 15-3

Test of Independence Using the Phi Coefficient for the Dalgarno Photo Example

Hypotheses:

H_0: Sex of the editor is independent of college funding source.
H_A: There is a negative relationship between sex of the editor and the college funding source.

$\alpha = 0.05$

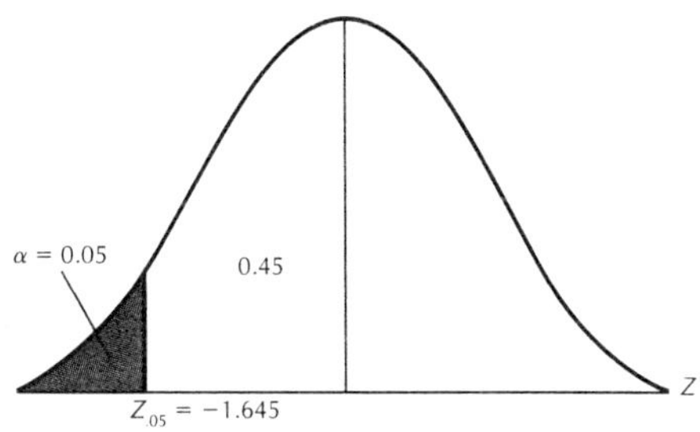

Test Statistic:

$\phi = -0.587$
Critical value $= -1.645/\sqrt{221} = -0.111$

Decision Rule:

If $\phi < -Z_\alpha/\sqrt{n}$, reject H_0.
Otherwise, do not reject H_0.

Since $-0.587 < -0.111$, reject H_0 and conclude that there is a negative relationship between the two variables.

This section has introduced the concept of contingency analysis, a very important statistical tool for analyzing categorical data. However, the applications in this chapter have been limited to 2×2 contingency tables. In the next section, we extend the topic of contingency analysis to applications with $r \times c$ tables (tables with r rows and c columns).

SKILL DEVELOPMENT PROBLEMS FOR **SECTION 15-1**

The following problems have been included to provide you with a chance to better understand the material presented in this section.

1. A survey has been conducted at a local company in which various questions about the workplace environment were asked. Two of the questions are listed as follows:

   1. Do you mind if people smoke in the office area? _____ Yes _____ No
   2. Do you smoke? _____ Yes _____ No

Shown are a subset of the responses that came back on these two variables. You are to construct a contingency analysis table from these data.

Respondent	Question 1	Question 2
1	Yes	No
2	Yes	Yes
3	No	Yes
4	No	Yes
5	No	No
6	Yes	No
7	Yes	No
8	Yes	Yes
9	No	No
10	Yes	No

2. Referring to Problem 1, suppose 200 people in the company responded to the survey and the following contingency table has been constructed from the responses.

	Do You Smoke?	
Do You Care About Smoking in the Office?	*Yes*	*No*
Yes	11	139
No	29	21

Based on these data, is attitude about smoking in the office independent of whether an individual smokes or not? Use the chi-square test and test at an $\alpha = 0.10$ level. Discuss the results.

3. Referring to Problems 1 and 2, compute the phi coefficient and interpret.

4. For the ten responses in Problem 1, use the code Yes = 1 and No = 2 for each variable. Then compute the correlation coefficient as discussed in Chapter 13. Also compute the phi coefficient. Compare the two coefficients and discuss.

5. Referring to Problems 1–3, suppose the claim has been made that proportionately more nonsmokers do not want smoking in the office. Thus, the expectation is that a negative relationship will exist between these two variables. Test this claim using the phi coefficient test at an $\alpha = 0.05$ level. Discuss.

6. A contingency analysis table has been constructed from data obtained in a phone survey of customers in a market area in which respondents were asked to indicate whether they owned a domestic or foreign car and whether they were a member of a union or not. The following contingency table is provided.

	Union	
Car	*Yes*	*No*
Domestic	155	470
Foreign	40	325

Use the chi-square approach to test whether type of car owned (domestic or foreign) is independent of union membership. Test using an $\alpha = 0.05$ level.

7. Referring to Problem 6, compute the phi coefficient and test the claim that proportionately more union workers will own domestic cars than will be true for nonunion people. Use $\alpha = 0.05$ and discuss.

8. Comment on the relationship between the chi-square statistic and the phi coefficient.

15-2 $r \times c$ CONTINGENCY TABLES

Although you will have occasion to work with 2×2 contingency tables, you will also encounter situations where the row and/or column variable has been divided into more than two categories. This section extends the previous discussion to encompass the general case of analysis involving $r \times c$ contingency tables.

Recall that in the Dalgarno Photo, Inc., example we selected four variables for potential analysis. One of these variables is total undergraduate enrollment, X_2. Variable X_2 could have been treated as a ratio level variable if the survey instrument had simply asked the respondent to record the school's enrollment. However, as can be seen in Figure 15-1, question 2 requires the respondent to indicate which category of enrollment size applies. The categories are as follows:

1: <400
2: 400–2,000
3: 2,000–4,000
4: 4,000–8,000
5: >8,000

(Note that the categories are not mutually exclusive. You should be careful to avoid this error when you construct response categories on survey instruments.)

As part of his analysis of the survey data, the yearbook manager at Dalgarno Photo, Inc., is interested in determining whether university enrollment is independent of source of school funding. The manager can use the sample data to test the following hypotheses:

H_0: Enrollment is independent of school funding source.

H_A: Enrollment *is not* independent of school funding source.

As with 2 × 2 contingency analysis, the test for independence can be made using the chi-square test, where the expected cell frequencies are compared to the actual cell frequencies using equation 15-1. The logic of the test says that if the actual and expected frequencies closely match, then the null hypothesis of independence is not rejected. However, if the actual and expected cell frequencies are substantially different overall, the null hypothesis of independence is rejected. The calculated chi-square statistic is compared to a tabled critical value for the desired alpha and degrees of freedom equal to $(r - 1)(c - 1)$. Figure 15-4 shows the hypothesis test process.

Note, the expected cell frequencies in Figure 15-4 are determined assuming the row and column variables are independent. This means, for example, that the probability that a school has enrollment under 400 students given that the school is privately funded is assumed to be the same as the overall probability that enrollment is under 400 students for all schools. An easy way to compute f_E, the expected cell frequencies, is given by equation 15-3.

$$f_E = \frac{\text{Row total} \times \text{Column total}}{\text{Total sample size}} \tag{15-3}$$

For row 1 and column 1,

$$f_E = \frac{18 \times 155}{221} = 12.62$$

and for row 3 and column 2,

$$f_E = \frac{41 \times 66}{221} = 12.24$$

Figure 15-4 shows that $\chi^2_{\text{calculated}} = 105.08 > \chi^2_{\text{critical}} = 9.488$ from the chi-square table in Appendix E. Therefore, the null hypothesis of independence is clearly rejected. Dalgarno's yearbook manager should conclude that there is a dependency relationship between source of a school's funding and undergraduate enrollment. A closer look at the contingency table in Figure 15-4 reveals that private schools tend to be overrepresented in the low enrollment categories and state schools tend to be overrepresented in the higher enrollment categories, relative to the expected frequencies.

Another analysis of variables based on the Dalgarno Photo example looks at the relationship between undergraduate enrollment and the yearbook budget, X_4, at the college. The survey questionnaire shown in Figure 15-1 indicates that question 30 requires the respondent to select a category for budget amount. Again, the survey has converted a quantitative variable into a qualitative variable with four

FIGURE 15-4

$r \times c$ Test of Independence for the Dalgarno Photo, Inc., Example

Hypotheses:

H_0: Enrollment is independent of school funding source.
H_A: Enrollment *is not* independent of school funding source.

$\alpha = 0.05$

Enrollment	*Source of Funding* Private	State	
<400	$f_A = 17$, $f_E = 12.62$	$f_A = 1$, $f_E = 5.38$	18
400–2,000	$f_A = 90$, $f_E = 66.63$	$f_A = 5$, $f_E = 28.37$	95
2,000–4,000	$f_A = 32$, $f_E = 28.76$	$f_A = 9$, $f_E = 12.24$	41
4,000–8,000	$f_A = 12$, $f_E = 25.95$	$f_A = 25$, $f_E = 11.05$	37
>8,000	$f_A = 4$, $f_E = 21.04$	$f_A = 26$, $f_E = 8.96$	30
	155	66	

Test Statistic:

$$\chi^2_{\text{calculated}} = \Sigma\Sigma \frac{(f_A - f_E)^2}{f_E} = \frac{(17 - 12.62)^2}{12.62} + \frac{(1 - 5.38)^2}{5.38} + \cdots + \frac{(4 - 21.04)^2}{21.04} + \frac{(26 - 8.96)^2}{8.96}$$

$$= 105.08$$

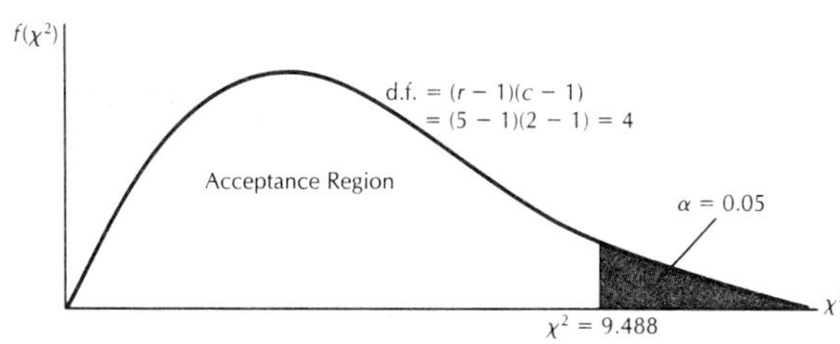

Decision Rule:

If $\chi^2_{\text{calculated}} > 9.488$, reject H_0.
Otherwise, do not reject H_0.

Since $\chi^2_{\text{calculated}} = 105.08 > 9.488$, reject H_0.
Row and column variable are *not* independent.

categories. The yearbook manager at Dalgarno is interested in testing the following null and alternative hypotheses:

H_0: The budget amount is independent of the school enrollment.

H_A: The budget amount *is not* independent of the school enrollment.

Figure 15-5 shows the 5 × 4 contingency table and the resulting test for independence using the chi-square test. This shows that $\chi^2_{\text{calculated}} = 100.94 > \chi^2_{\text{critical}} = 21.026$. Thus, the null hypothesis of independence is clearly rejected. We see in the contingency table that, generally, bigger schools have larger yearbook budgets.

CRAMER'S CONTINGENCY COEFFICIENT

In our discussion of 2 × 2 contingency tables, we introduced the phi coefficient. The phi coefficient is a measure of association between two categorical variables and is used when both variables have two categories. When we are working with larger contingency tables, there are a number of measures of association from which to choose. One of the most commonly used measures is called **Cramer's contingency coefficient.** The notation for Cramer's contingency coefficient is capital phi, Φ. As with the phi coefficient previously introduced, if the row and column variables are independent, Φ will be close to 0. Likewise, if all the observations in each row tend to be in one column but in a different column for each row, then Φ will be close to +1.0. The closer Φ is to +1.0, the stronger the association between the two variables. Note that, unlike the phi coefficient for 2 × 2 tables, Φ cannot be negative; it ranges between 0 and +1.0.

Cramer's contingency coefficient is computed using equation 15-4.

$$\Phi = \frac{\chi^2_{\text{calculated}}}{n(q-1)} \qquad \textbf{15-4}$$

where

$\chi^2_{\text{calculated}}$ = Calculated chi-square statistic using equation 15-1

q = Minimum of the number of rows and the number of columns

n = Overall sample size

To illustrate the application of Cramer's contingency coefficient, we will once again refer to the contingency table and hypothesis test shown in Figure 15-4, where the issue was whether there is an association between enrollment levels and the source of the school's funding. Recall, the chi-square test led us to conclude

FIGURE 15-5

$r \times c$ Test of Independence for the Dalgarno Photo, Inc., Example

Hypotheses:

H_0: Yearbook budget is independent of enrollment.
H_A: Yearbook budget *is not* independent of enrollment.

$\alpha = 0.05$

Budget

Enrollment	*Under $20,000*	*$20,000–$40,000*	*$40,000–$60,000*	*Over $60,000*	
<400	$f_A = 18$, $f_E = 7.82$	$f_A = 0$, $f_E = 6.92$	$f_A = 0$, $f_E = 2.04$	$f_A = 0$, $f_E = 1.22$	18
400–2,000	$f_A = 55$, $f_E = 41.27$	$f_A = 35$, $f_E = 36.54$	$f_A = 5$, $f_E = 10.75$	$f_A = 0$, $f_E = 6.44$	95
2,000–4,000	$f_A = 11$, $f_E = 17.81$	$f_A = 22$, $f_E = 15.77$	$f_A = 7$, $f_E = 4.64$	$f_A = 1$, $f_E = 2.78$	41
4,000–8,000	$f_A = 8$, $f_E = 16.07$	$f_A = 17$, $f_E = 14.23$	$f_A = 9$, $f_E = 4.19$	$f_A = 3$, $f_E = 2.51$	37
>8,000	$f_A = 4$, $f_E = 13.03$	$f_A = 11$, $f_E = 11.54$	$f_A = 4$, $f_E = 3.39$	$f_A = 11$, $f_E = 2.04$	30
	96	85	25	15	221

Test Statistic:

$$\chi^2_{\text{calculated}} = \sum\sum \frac{(f_A - f_E)^2}{f_E} = \frac{(18 - 7.82)^2}{7.82} + \frac{(0 - 6.92)^2}{6.92} + \cdots + \frac{(4 - 3.39)^2}{3.39} + \frac{(11 - 2.04)^2}{2.04}$$

$$= 100.94$$

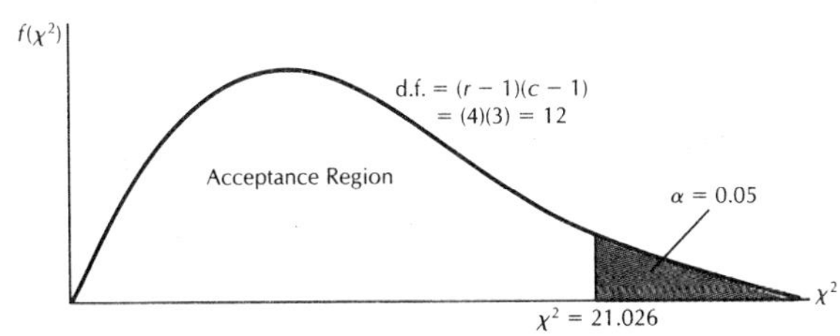

Decision Rule:

If $\chi^2_{\text{calculated}} > 21.026$, reject H_0.
Otherwise, do not reject H_0.

Since $\chi^2_{\text{calculated}} = 100.94 > 21.026$, we conclude that the row and column variables are not independent.

that there is an association. We will now use Cramer's contingency coefficient to measure the strength of that association as follows:

$$\Phi = \frac{\chi^2_{\text{calculated}}}{n(q - 1)}$$

where

$$\chi^2_{\text{calculated}} = 105.08$$
$$n = 221$$
$$q = 2$$

Then

$$\Phi = \frac{105.08}{(221)(2 - 1)} = 0.475$$

Thus, the relationship between these two variables is fairly strong based on Cramer's contingency coefficient.

As a second example, refer to the contingency analysis shown in Figure 15-5. The issue here is whether there is an association between enrollment and yearbook budget. The chi-square test indicated that a statistical relationship does exist. We can now use Cramer's contingency coefficient as a measure of the strength of the relationship as follows:

$$\Phi = \frac{100.94}{(221)(4 - 1)} = 0.152$$

Thus, there is a statistical association between the two variables, but not a very strong one, as evidenced by the 0.152 value for Cramer's contingency coefficient.

CHI-SQUARE TEST LIMITATIONS

You should be aware the chi-square distribution is only an approximation for the true distribution of $\chi^2_{\text{calculated}}$ for the previous examples. We use the chi-square approximation because the true distribution is impractical to compute in most instances. However, research has shown that the approximation (and therefore the conclusion reached) is quite good when all expected cell frequencies exceed 1.0. Further, if the number of degrees of freedom $[(r - 1)(c - 1)]$ is large, the approximation will still be good even though some expected cell frequencies dip below 1.0. However, if any expected cell frequencies drop below 0.5, the general advice is to group categories where appropriate or increase the overall sample size to increase the expected cell frequencies.

If you do decide to group categories together, there should be some logic behind the resulting categories, so you do not lose the meaning of the results through poor groupings. You will need to examine each application individually to determine whether the option of grouping classes to increase expected cell frequencies makes sense.

SKILL DEVELOPMENT PROBLMS FOR **SECTION 15-2**

The following problems have been included to help you better understand the material in this chapter.

9. In a recent study of college graduates, it was hypothesized that income was independent of number of different employers the person has worked for since graduation. The data collected were as follows:

	Number of Employers				
Income Level	*1*	*2*	*3*	*4*	*5 or more*
Under $20,000	3	4	3	2	3
20,000–30,000	5	3	7	3	2
30,000–40,000	2	5	3	6	1
40,000–50,000	1	7	9	3	4
Over 50,000	1	3	11	7	4

Assuming that these data reflect observed frequencies, what can be concluded about the hypothesis? Test at an $\alpha = 0.05$ level.

10. Compute Cramer's contingency coefficient for the Problem 9 data and provide an interpretation.

11. A study of automobile drivers was conducted to determine whether the number of traffic citations issued during a 3-year period was independent of the sex of the driver. The following data were collected.

	Sex of Driver	
Citations Issued	*Male*	*Female*
0	240	160
1	80	40
2	32	18
3	11	9
Over 3	5	4

Using an $\alpha = 0.05$ level, determine whether the two variables are independent.

12. Based on the information in Problem 11, determine the appropriate measure of association and interpret.

13. A bank in Midvale, Oregon, recently did a study of its customers to determine whether the number of transactions in a checking account was independent of the marital status of the customer. The following data were obtained.

	Number of Transactions				
Marital Status	*0–10*	*11–20*	*21–30*	*31–40*	*Over 40*
Single	13	23	19	20	11
Married	6	15	33	45	27
Divorced	4	19	22	20	15
Other	2	11	8	5	2

Based on these data, what should the bank conclude? Test at an $\alpha = 0.05$ level.

14. Compute the appropriate measure of association for the data provided in Problem 13 and interpret.

15. In a recent labor negotiation, the union officials collected data from a sample of union members regarding how long they had been with the company and how long they would be willing to stay out on strike if a strike were called. The following data were collected.

	Strike Length Toleration		
Time with Company	*Under 1 Week*	*1–4 Weeks*	*Over 4 Weeks*
Under 1 year	23	6	3
1–2 years	19	15	8
2–5 years	20	23	19
5–10 years	4	21	29
Over 10 years	2	5	18

Based on these data, can the union conclude that the strike length toleration is independent of time with the company? Test at the $\alpha = 0.05$ level.

16. Based on the results in Problem 15, determine the appropriate measure of the association between time with the company and strike length toleration. Comment on what this measure means in this application.

15-3 AN INTRODUCTION TO GOODNESS-OF-FIT TESTS

Gere Memorial Hospital is a privately owned hospital providing a wide range of services to people in a midwestern metropolitan community. Vickie Shelly was recently hired as operations manager from a similar position at a smaller hospital in New Mexico. One of her responsibilities is hospital staffing. A natural concern is that staffing level, consisting of nurses and other support personnel, be balanced appropriately with the patient load in the hospital.

Currently, the staffing level is balanced during the weekdays, Monday through Friday, with a reduced staffing level on Saturday and Sunday. The reasoning behind this, as explained by her predecessor, is that patient demand is fairly level throughout the weekday period and about 25% less on weekends. Although Vickie was willing to operate with this schedule for a while, discussions with other hospital staff soon convinced her to perform a study of patient demand to see whether the pattern may have changed.

To conduct the study, Vickie requested a sample of twenty days for each day of the week, showing the number of patients in the hospital on each of the sample days. A portion of the data that she received follows:

Day	*Patient Count*
Monday, May 6	325
Monday, October 7	379
Tuesday, July 2	456
Monday, July 15	323
Wednesday, April 3	467
⋮	⋮
etc.	etc.

For the 140 days observed, the total count was 56,000 patients. Vickie then computed the total patient count for each day of the week. These results are shown in Table 15-1 and are graphed in Figure 15-6.

TABLE 15-1

Patient Count Data for Gere Memorial Hospital Example

Day	Total Patient Count
Sunday	4,502
Monday	6,623
Tuesday	8,308
Wednesday	10,420
Thursday	11,032
Friday	10,754
Saturday	4,361
Total	56,000

FIGURE 15-6

Graph of Actual Frequencies

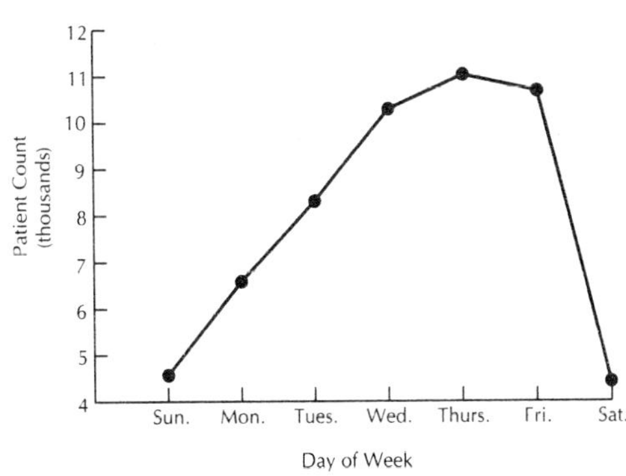

FIGURE 15-7

Actual and Expected Frequencies

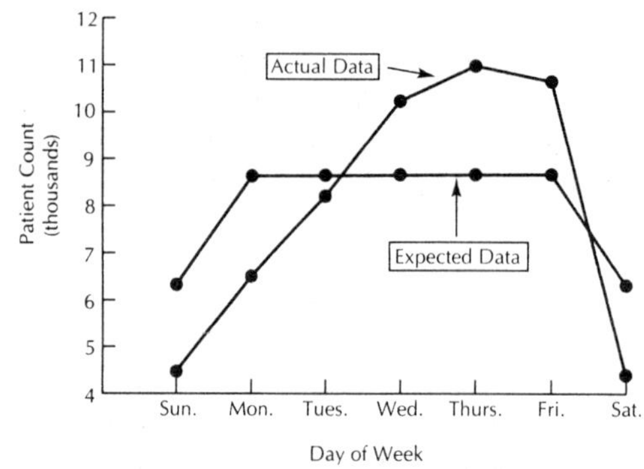

Recall that the previous operations manager at Gere Memorial based his staffing on the premise that from Monday to Friday the patient count remained essentially the same and then for Saturdays and Sundays went down 25%. If this is actually the case, how many of the 56,000 patients would have been expected on Monday? How many on Tuesday and so forth? To figure this out, Vickie determined weighting factors by allocating 4 units each to days Monday through Friday and 3 units each (representing the 25% reduction) to Saturday and Sunday. The total number of units is then $(5 \times 4) + (2 \times 3) = 26$ units. The percentage of total patients expected on a weekday is $4/26 = 0.154$ or 15.4% and the percentage expected on a weekend day is $3/26 = 0.115$ or 11.5%. The expected number of patients on a weekday is $0.154 \times 56{,}000 = 8{,}624$ and the expected number on each weekend day is $0.115 \times 56{,}000 = 6{,}440$.

Figure 15-7 shows a graph with both the actual sample data and the expected values. With the exception of what might be attributed to sampling error, if the distribution claimed by the previous operations manager is correct, the actual frequencies for each day of the week should fit quite closely with the expected frequencies. As you can see in Figure 15-7, the actual data and the expected data do not match perfectly. Is the difference enough to warrant a change in staffing patterns?

THE CHI-SQUARE GOODNESS-OF-FIT TEST

The situation facing Vickie is one for which a number of statistical tests have been developed. One of the most frequently used is the **chi-square goodness-of-fit test.** The term *goodness of fit* is very appropriate since what Vickie needs to examine is how well the sample data fit the hypothesized distribution. In fact, Vickie wishes to test the following null and alternative hypotheses:

H_0: The patient demand distribution is evenly spread through the weekdays and 25% lower on the weekend.

H_A: The patient demand follows some other distribution.

Equation 15-5 is the equation for the chi-square goodness-of-fit test statistic. You should notice that it is very similar in form to the chi-square contingency analysis test statistic shown earlier as equation 15-1. The difference is the data shown in Table 15-1 actually represent a contingency table with seven rows but only one column.

$$\chi^2_{\text{calculated}} = \Sigma \frac{(f_A - f_E)^2}{f_E} \qquad \textbf{15-5}$$

where

f_A = Actual cell frequency for row i
f_E = Expected cell frequency for row i

As was the case with contingency analysis, if the calculated chi-square statistic gets large this is evidence to suggest the fit of the actual data to the hypothesized distribution is not good, and the null hypothesis should be rejected.

Figure 15-8 (page 818) shows the hypothesis test process and results for this chi-square goodness-of-fit test. Note, the degrees of freedom for the chi-square test are $k - 1$, where k is the number of categories. In this example, we have seven categories corresponding to the days of the week. Thus, the degrees of freedom are $7 - 1 = 6$. The critical value for 6 degrees of freedom and an upper-tail test with $\alpha = 0.05$ is found in Appendix E to be 12.592.

As Figure 15-8 indicates, $\chi^2_{\text{calculated}} = 3{,}302.7 > 12.592$, so the null hypothesis is rejected and Vickie Shelly should conclude the demand pattern does not match the previously defined distribution. She would now most likely wish to make changes in the scheduling to more closely approximate current demand patterns.

GOODNESS-OF-FIT TESTS—A POISSON DISTRIBUTION EXAMPLE

Consider another example in which D. A. Weber and Associates, a computer service bureau, is involved in a study of the demand for its computer services. The customers have computer terminals, located at their own establishments, that are connected to the D. A. Weber and Associates mainframe computer by telephone data transmission lines.

When the mainframe computer was originally purchased, a study was done showing that during any given hour, the demand for an access port to the com-

FIGURE 15-8

Chi-Square Goodness of Fit Test for the Gere Memorial Hospital Example

Hypotheses:

H_0: Patient demand is evenly spread through the weekdays and 25% lower on weekends.

H_A: Patient demand follows some other distribution.

$\alpha = 0.05$

	Total Patient Count	
Day	*Actual* f_A	*Expected* f_E
Sunday	4,502	6,440
Monday	6,623	8,624
Tuesday	8,308	8,624
Wednesday	10,420	8,624
Thursday	11,032	8,624
Friday	10,754	8,624
Saturday	4,361	6,440
Total	56,000	56,000

Test Statistic:

$$\chi^2_{\text{calculated}} = \Sigma \frac{(f_A - f_E)^2}{f_E} = \frac{(4{,}502 - 6{,}440)^2}{6{,}440} + \frac{(6{,}623 - 8{,}624)^2}{8{,}624} + \cdots + \frac{(4{,}361 - 6{,}440)^2}{6{,}440}$$

$$= 3{,}302.7$$

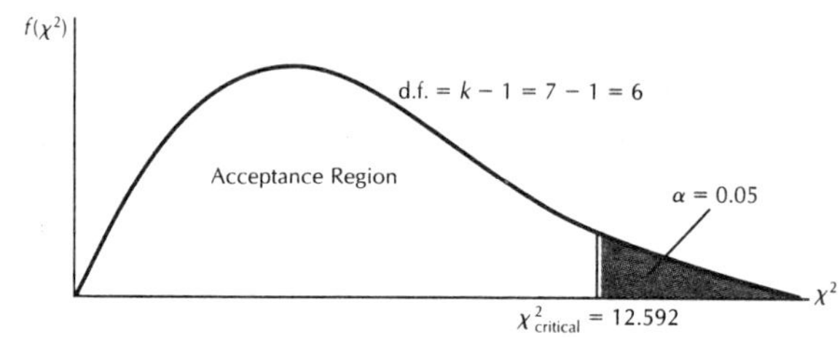

Decision Rule:

If $\chi^2_{\text{calculated}} > 12.592$, reject H_0.
Otherwise, do not reject H_0.

Since $3{,}302.7 > 12.592$, reject H_0.

puter was Poisson distributed, with an average of five users. Thus, D. A. Weber purchased a computer system that has eleven ports, ten of which are available to the service bureau customers. Wilson Farber, manager of customer service, recently indicated that there appears to be a problem since he often receives calls from customers claiming that they have attempted to access the computer, but found that a port was not available. He thinks that the demand distribution may be changing because the ten ports were sufficient to handle a Poisson-distributed demand with mean equal to 5 per hour.

To determine whether the demand distribution has changed, Wilson has collected data available from the phone company on the number of attempts to access the D. A. Weber computer during 200 randomly selected hours during the past 2 months. These data are shown in Table 15-2.

To test whether the demand distribution continues to be Poisson distributed with a mean equal to 5, the chi-square goodness-of-fit test can be used. Figure 15-9 (page 820) presents the chi-square goodness-of-fit test for the D. A. Weber and Associates example. As Figure 15-9 shows, Wilson Farber should reject the hypothesis that the demand distribution for his company's computer services is Poisson distributed with a mean equal to 5.

A point should be made with respect to employing the chi-square goodness-of-fit test. If the distribution and parameters are specified in the hypothesis, the degrees of freedom are the number of cells minus 1. This was the case in the D. A. Weber example since the null hypothesis involved the distribution type (Poisson) and the parameter, λ. However, if one or more parameters are left unspecified in the null hypothesis, they must be estimated from the sample data, and the degrees of freedom are reduced by 1 for each parameter estimated.

To illustrate, suppose Wilson Farber had originally hypothesized that the demand distribution was Poisson distributed, but did not specify the mean of the distribution. We shall again use the data in Table 15-2 to test this latest hypothesis. First, we must estimate the mean of the distribution from the sample data. Suppose from the raw data the sample mean equals 6.2. This estimated mean is then used to determine the probabilities in Figure 15-10 (page 821) from the Poisson table in Appendix B.

TABLE 15-2

Computer Access Data for the D. A. Weber and Associates Example

No. of Access Requests	Frequency
0	2
1	4
2	7
3	12
4	15
5	30
6	35
7	55
8	20
9 and over	20
Total	200 h

FIGURE 15-9

Chi-Square Goodness-of-Fit Test for the D. A. Weber and Associates Example

Hypotheses:

H_0: The demand distribution is Poisson distributed with a mean equal to 5.
H_A: The demand distribution is not Poisson distributed with a mean equal to 5.

$\alpha = 0.05$

No. of Access Attempts	f_A	*Probability**	f_E**	$(f_A - f_E)^2/f_E$
0	2	0.0067	1.34	0.325
1	4	0.0337	6.74	1.114
2	7	0.0842	16.84	5.750
3	12	0.1404	28.08	9.208
4	15	0.1755	35.10	11.510
5	30	0.1755	35.10	0.741
6	35	0.1462	29.24	1.135
7	55	0.1044	20.88	55.755
8	20	0.0653	13.06	3.688
9 and over	20	0.0681	13.62	2.989
Total	200	1.0000		$\chi^2 = 92.215$

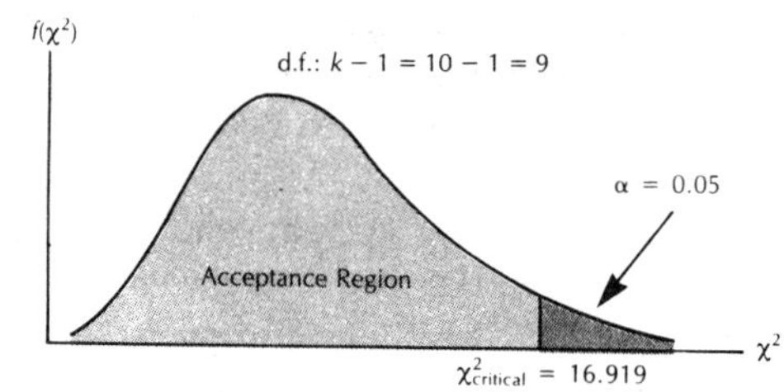

Decision Rule:

If $\chi^2 \leq \chi^2_{critical}$, accept H_0.
If $\chi^2 > \chi^2_{critical}$, reject H_0.

Since $92.215 > 16.919$, reject H_0.

*From Poisson table, $\lambda = 5$.
**f_E = Probability · 200.

The test results shown in Figure 15-10 indicate that Wilson Farber should conclude that the demand distribution is not Poisson distributed since the chi-square goodness-of-fit test indicates that the null hypothesis should be rejected. Note that in Figure 15-10 we have combined access requests 0 and 1 because the expected cell frequency for 0 requests, given a Poisson distribution with a mean equal to 6.2, is less than 1.0. Note also that degrees of freedom are computed as the number of cells less 2 in this case, since we estimated the mean of the distribution from the sample data. We lose an additional degree of freedom for each parameter we have to estimate.

FIGURE 15-10

Chi-Square Goodness-of-Fit Test: Parameter Estimated from Sample for the D. A. Weber and Associates Example

Hypotheses:

H_0: Demand distribution is Poisson distributed.
H_A: Demand distribution is not Poisson distributed.

$\alpha = 0.05$

No. of Access Requests	f_A	*Probability*	f_E	$(f_A - f_E)^2/f_E$
1 and under	6	0.0146	2.92	3.248
2	7	0.0390	7.80	0.082
3	12	0.0806	16.12	1.053
4	15	0.1249	24.98	3.987
5	30	0.1549	30.98	0.031
6	35	0.1601	32.02	0.277
7	55	0.1418	28.36	25.024
8	20	0.1099	21.98	0.178
9 and over	20	0.1742	34.84	6.321
Total	200	1.0000		$\chi^2 = 40.201$

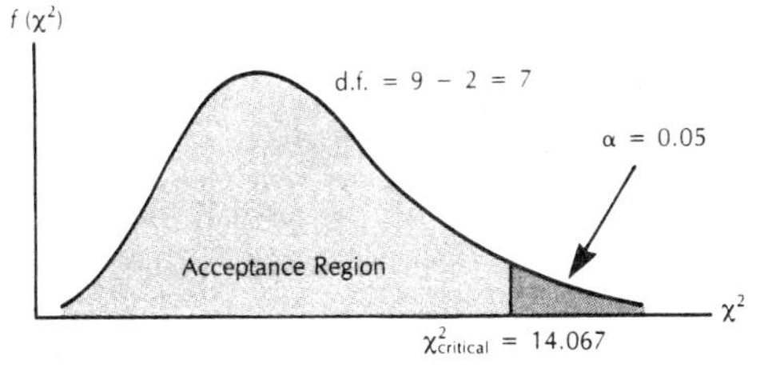

Decision Rule:

If $\chi^2 \le \chi^2_{critical}$, accept H_0.
If $\chi^2 > \chi^2_{critical}$, reject H_0.

Since $40.201 > 14.067$, reject H_0.

Note: Degrees of freedom are computed by the number of cells minus 2 since we estimated λ rather than specifying it as part of the null hypothesis.

The chi-square goodness-of-fit test can be employed to determine whether a set of sample data comes from any specified distribution. However, when the hypothesized distribution is the normal distribution, a goodness-of-fit test called the Lilliefors test is preferred. This test is discussed in the next example.

THE LILLIEFORS TEST FOR NORMALITY—A QUALITY CONTROL EXAMPLE

Woodtrim Products, Inc., a company based in southern Idaho, makes wood moldings, door frames, and wood frame window products. It purchases lumber from mills throughout Idaho, Washington, Oregon, and Montana. The lumber it purchases is called "dimension lumber" and comes in thicknesses measured as 5 quarter and 6 quarter, in widths ranging from 8 inches to 16 inches. The pieces have knots and other imperfections, such as warp.

The first step in the production process is to cut the dimension lumber into narrower strips ranging from $2\frac{3}{8}$ inches to $3\frac{7}{8}$ inches. A machine called a ripsaw is used for this purpose and is run by a highly skilled operator. The operator starts by aiming a light beam down the length of the board to mark where the saw will cut. The operator's judgment is required to determine what width of pieces to cut from each board to maximize the value to the company. Pieces with no knots or other imperfections can be made into the most profitable products. Each width goes into making a different product. For example, wider pieces with no imperfections are used to make door and window frames. Once the operator makes his decision by lining the light beam along the board, the decision is locked into a computer and when the board reaches the ripsaw a few feet away the saw is automatically adjusted to cut the board at the desired widths. The manufacturer claims that the saw will cut within ± 0.008 inch of the target width.

The company has recently become concerned that the ripsaw may not be cutting the boards at the exact dimension being indicated by the operator. Further downstream in the production process, operators at other machines are finding ripped pieces that are too wide or too narrow. The too wide boards have to be sent through a backripsaw, which trims the pieces to a narrower width. This results in waste and lost profit. The pieces that are too narrow cannot be back-ripped, so they are sent to a "hogger," which grinds the boards to make wood-chips, a low-profit by-product.

A "quality improvement team," QIT, has started to investigate the problem. In essence, it is doing a process capability study (see our earlier discussion in Chapter 3). This means that the QIT will collect data on boards coming off the ripsaw to determine just how capable the saw is of holding the cutting width. To do this, the members selected a random sample of twenty boards just as they came off the ripsaw. To provide a measure of control, the only pieces sampled in the initial study were pieces with stated widths of $2\frac{7}{8}$ inches. The piece was then measured for width at a point halfway between the ends. The difference between $2\frac{7}{8}$ and the measured width was computed. Ideally, the difference would be 0. However, as indicated previously, the manufacturer claims that the saw should cut within ± 0.008 inch and the distribution around 0 is normally distributed. As part of the process capability study, the team wishes to test whether the distribution is normal and then determine what percentage of the product will be within the ± 0.008 inch tolerance.

Table 15-3 shows the data for the sample of twenty boards. Note, the differences have been computed. The chi-square goodness-of-fit test introduced in the previous examples relied on the logic that if the actual sample data closely fit the hypothesized distribution, the null hypothesis would not be rejected. We could employ the chi-square test in this example too, but a better test exists when the hypothesized distribution is normal. This test is the Lilliefors test.

TABLE 15-3

Sample Data of Board Thicknesses for Woodtrim Products, Inc., Example

Sample #	Actual Width	Stated Width	Difference
1	2.870	2.875	−0.005
2	2.863	2.875	−0.012
3	2.885	2.875	0.010
4	2.872	2.875	−0.003
5	2.891	2.875	0.016
6	2.893	2.875	0.018
7	2.868	2.875	−0.007
8	2.861	2.875	−0.014
9	2.889	2.875	0.014
10	2.872	2.875	−0.003
11	2.879	2.875	0.004
12	2.876	2.875	0.001
13	2.869	2.875	−0.006
14	2.890	2.875	0.015
15	2.880	2.875	0.005
16	2.870	2.875	−0.005
17	2.867	2.875	−0.008
18	2.874	2.875	−0.001
19	2.873	2.875	−0.002
20	2.867	2.875	−0.008

The null and alternative hypotheses for this example are stated as follows:

H_0: The distribution of cut width error is normally distributed.
H_A: The distribution of cut width error is not normally distributed.

In order to use the Lilliefors test, we perform the following steps:

1. Compute the sample mean, $\overline{X}$, and the sample standard deviation, s, on the data in the differences column.
2. Find the Z score for each value in the sample, where $Z = (X - \overline{X})/s$. This is referred to as "standardizing" the data.
3. Arrange the Z scores in order from smallest to largest.
4. Find the probability of a Z value as small as or smaller than each Z score using the standard normal table in Appendix C.
5. Find the percentage of sample points at or below each Z score.
6. Compute the absolute difference between the values found in steps 4 and 5 for each sample value.
7. Compare the maximum absolute difference found in step 6 to the Lilliefors test statistic table in Appendix J for the appropriate sample size and $1 - \alpha$ value.

TABLE 15-4

Sample Data of Board Thicknesses for Woodtrim Products, Inc., Example

Sample #	Difference	Z Score
1	−0.005	−0.57
2	−0.012	−1.30
3	0.010	0.99
4	−0.003	−0.36
5	0.016	1.62
6	0.018	1.83
7	−0.007	−0.78
8	−0.014	−1.51
9	0.014	1.41
10	−0.003	−0.36
11	0.004	0.37
12	0.001	0.06
13	−0.006	−0.67
14	0.015	1.52
15	0.005	0.47
16	−0.005	−0.57
17	−0.008	−0.88
18	−0.001	−0.15
19	−0.002	−0.26
20	−0.008	−0.88

To demonstrate an application of the Lilliefors test, we first compute the mean and standard deviation for the sample differences in Table 15-3. These values are as follows:

$$\overline{X} = 0.00045$$
$$s = 0.0096$$

We next compute the Z score for each data point. The results are shown in Table 15-4. For example, the Z score for sample 1 difference is calculated as

$$Z = \frac{-0.005 - 0.00045}{0.0096} = -0.57$$

The next step is to arrange the Z scores from lowest to highest and to find the probability of a Z value as small as or smaller than each Z score using the standard normal distribution.

We also establish the cumulative relative frequencies for the sample values and take the absolute difference between the normal distribution probabilities and the cumulative frequencies. These results are shown in Table 15-5.

TABLE 15-5

Sample Data of Board Thicknesses for Woodtrim Products, Inc., Example

Z Score	Cumulative Probability Z	Cumulative Frequency	Difference
−1.51	0.0655	1/20 = 0.05	0.0155
−1.30	0.0968	2/20 = 0.10	0.0032
−0.88	0.1894	3/20 = 0.15	0.0394
−0.88	0.1894	4/20 = 0.20	0.0106
−0.78	0.2177	5/20 = 0.25	0.0323
−0.67	0.2514	6/20 = 0.30	0.0486
−0.57	0.2843	7/20 = 0.35	0.0657
−0.57	0.2843	8/20 = 0.40	0.1157
−0.36	0.3594	9/20 = 0.45	0.0906
−0.36	0.3594	10/20 = 0.50	0.1406
−0.26	0.3974	11/20 = 0.55	0.1526
−0.15	0.4404	12/20 = 0.60	0.1596
0.06	0.5239	13/20 = 0.65	0.1261
0.37	0.6443	14/20 = 0.70	0.0557
0.47	0.6808	15/20 = 0.75	0.0692
0.99	0.8389	16/20 = 0.80	0.0389
1.41	0.9207	17/20 = 0.85	0.0707
1.52	0.9357	18/20 = 0.90	0.0357
1.62	0.9474	19/20 = 0.95	0.0026
1.83	0.9664	20/20 = 1.00	0.0336

Note in Table 15-5 that the maximum difference is 0.1596. This figure is compared with the table value, w_p, for the Lilliefors test in Appendix J. The decision rule is as follows:

If $0.1596 > w_p$, reject H_0.
Otherwise, do not reject H_0.

For a sample of size twenty and $1 - \alpha$ level of 0.95, the critical Lilliefors value, w_p, is 0.190. Since the calculated value of $0.1596 \leq 0.190$, the null hypothesis is *not* rejected. Thus, based on the sample data, the Woodtrim quality improvement team will conclude that the cut width error distribution is normal.

The next step for the team is to determine, based on these sample data, the probability of cut widths being within 0.008 inch of the target width. Figure 15-11 (page 826) shows the computations. Thus, using $\overline{X} = 0.00045$ and $s = 0.0096$, and assuming the cut width error distribution is normal, the percentage of cuts within ± 0.008 inch is computed to be 0.5958, or almost 60% of all boards. This level of capability is probably not as good as the company would like

FIGURE 15-11

Process Capability Analysis for the Woodtrim Products, Inc., Example

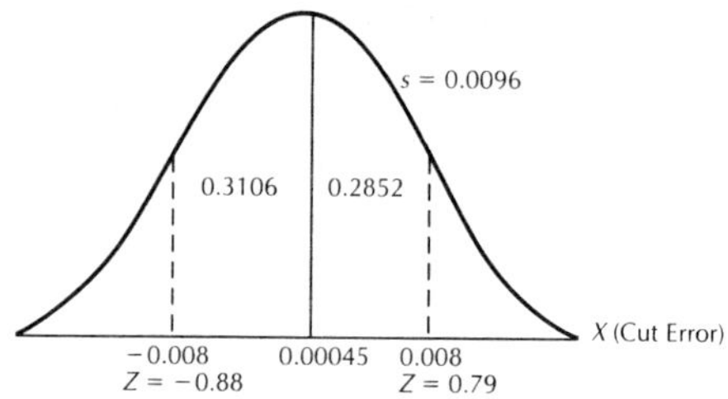

$$Z = \frac{X - \overline{X}}{s} = \frac{0.008 - 0.00045}{0.0096} = 0.79$$

$$Z = \frac{X - \overline{X}}{s} = \frac{-0.008 - 0.00045}{0.0096} = -0.88$$

From normal distribution table:

Probability for $Z = 0.79$: 0.2852
Probability for $Z = -0.88$: 0.3106

$P[-.008 \leq \text{Error} \leq .008] = 0.2852 + 0.3106 = 0.5958$

and the quality improvement team will want to begin looking for reasons that the cut width errors are so frequently outside the ± 0.008 range.

CHI-SQUARE VS LILLIEFORS TEST

The chi-square goodness-of-fit test is a very useful tool for testing whether sample data fit certain specified distributions. It is very versatile and can be used to test almost any distribution. However, if the variable of interest is continuous, the chi-square test requires that the data be grouped into classes. For example, Figure 15-12 shows the use of the chi-square test to determine whether the weight distribution of frozen french fry packages is normally distributed with mean equal to 5.0 pounds and standard deviation equal to 0.20 pound. A sample of 1,000 bags has been selected and each package weighed. The data have been grouped into six classes as shown in Figure 15-12. The expected frequencies in each class are determined by finding the probability of an item falling within the specified class limits, if the true distribution is as hypothesized, and multiplying this probability by the sample size of 1,000. As can be seen in Figure 15-12, $\chi^2_{\text{calculated}} = 400.3 > \chi^2_{\text{critical}} = 11.07$, so the null hypothesis is rejected. The distribution must be something other than a normal one with mean 5 and standard deviation 0.20.

Note that the chi-square test requires us to group the raw sample data into classes. The computed value of chi-square will change depending on how the grouping is performed. In fact, it is possible to reach different conclusions with the same data by just changing the way the classes are structured. Because of this,

FIGURE 15-12

Chi-Square Test of Normal Distribution for French Fry Package Example

Hypotheses:

H_0: Distribution of weights is normal with mean equal to 5 pounds and standard deviation equal to 0.20 pound.

H_A: Distribution of weights is not as hypothesized.

$\alpha = 0.05$

Weight Class	f_A *Actual Frequency*	f_E *Expected Frequency*	
Under 4.80	18	(0.1587 × 1,000) =	158.7
4.80 and under 4.90	102	(0.1498 × 1,000) =	149.8
4.90 and under 5.00	305	(0.1915 × 1,000) =	191.5
5.00 and under 5.10	360	(0.1915 × 1,000) =	191.5
5.10 and under 5.20	140	(0.1498 × 1,000) =	149.8
5.20 and over	75	(0.1587 × 1,000) =	158.7
	n = 1,000		1,000

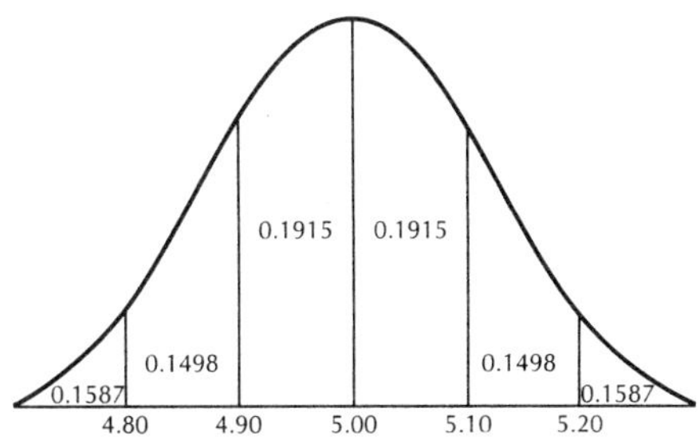

Test Statistic:

$$\chi^2_{\text{calculated}} = \Sigma \frac{(f_A - f_E)^2}{f_E} = \frac{(18 - 158.7)^2}{158.7} + \frac{(102 - 149.8)^2}{149.8} + \cdots + \frac{(75 - 158.7)^2}{158.7}$$

$$= 400.3$$

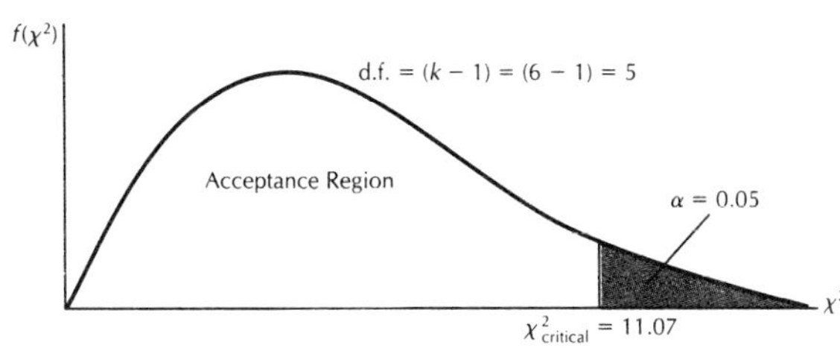

Decision Rule:

If $\chi^2_{\text{calculated}} > 11.07$, reject H_0.
Otherwise, do not reject H_0.

Since $\chi^2_{\text{calculated}} = 400.3 > 11.07$, reject H_0.

one could easily criticize the goodness-of-fit results on the basis of how the data were grouped.

The Lilliefors test, on the other hand, works with the actual raw data and does not require grouping. From that standpoint it is advantageous. It is also preferred to the chi-square for testing hypotheses about normal and exponential distributions because it is more powerful than the chi-square test. This means the Lilliefors test is more likely to reject the null hypothesis when it should be rejected than is the chi-square test using the same data. Thus, we recommend the Lilliefors test be used for normal and exponential distributions and the chi-square test be used for other applications.

SKILL DEVELOPMENT PROBLEMS FOR **SECTION 15-3**

The following problems have been included to help you better understand the material in this chapter.

17. Daily sales volumes in dollars have been grouped as follows. Can you conclude that the sales are uniformly distributed? Test at $\alpha = 0.05$.

Sales	*Frequency*
\$500 and under \$1,000	40
\$1,000 and under \$1,500	63
\$1,500 and under \$2,000	55
\$2,000 and under \$2,500	50
\$2,500 and under \$3,000	61

18. Use the chi-square goodness-of-fit test to determine whether the number of phone calls coming in to a radio talk show is Poisson distributed with a mean of 5 per hour. The following data, selected over a period of 100 hours, show the frequency distribution for the number of calls in a given hour. Test at the $\alpha = 0.05$ level.

Number of Calls	*Frequency*
0	0
1	2
2	4
3	10
4	7
5	14
6	11
7	13
8	5
9	10
10	5
11	5
12	7
13	4
14	3
	100

19. The Baltimore Steel and Pipe Company recently selected a random sample of twenty sections of pipe that was designed to measure 2.00 inches in diameter. Company representatives measured the diameter of each of the twenty sections. According to the product specifications, the diameters are supposed to be normally distributed. Based on the following sample data, can the company conclude that the pipe diameters are normally distributed? Use the Lilliefors test at an $\alpha = 0.05$ level.

Pipe Section	*Diameter (inches)*
1	2.04
2	2.13
3	2.07
4	1.99
5	1.90
6	2.06
7	2.19
8	2.01
9	2.05
10	1.98
11	1.95
12	1.90
13	2.10
14	2.02
15	2.11
16	1.96
17	1.89
18	1.99
19	2.13
20	1.90

15-4 COMPUTER APPLICATIONS

Both contingency analysis and goodness-of-fit tests require substantial computations for even the most elementary applications. As you might imagine, statistical software packages typically contain modules for performing these functions. In this section we demonstrate examples based on the KIVZ-Channel 5 data introduced in Chapter 2 (see Tables 2-10 and 2-11). The examples shown in this section demonstrate contingency analysis using SPSS-X and GB-STAT software.

Table 15-6 (page 830) shows a contingency analysis table developed using the CROSSTABS command in SPSS-X. This table shows SEX crossed with EDUCATION. The chi-square statistic is printed. In this example, eight of twelve cells have expected frequencies of 5 or less. This is too many and may result in an inflated chi-square statistic. However, since the calculated chi-square is only 2.459, with a significance level of 0.7827, we would "not reject" the hypothesis of independence. This means that collapsing the cells to reduce the occurrence of

TABLE 15-6 SPSS-X Output: Contingency Analysis

```
- - - - - - - - - - -   C R O S S T A B U L A T I O N   O F   - - - - - - - - - -
   VAR10      SEX                      BY  VAR16       EDUCATON
- - - - - - - - - - - - - - - - - - - - - - - - - - - - - - - - - - - PAGE 1 OF 1
                     VAR16
            COUNT
                    |GRADE    SOME      VOTECH     HIGH     COLLEGE  GRADUATE   ROW
                    |SCHOOL   COLLEGE              SCHOOL   GRAD      WORK      TOTAL
                    |  1.00  |  2.00  |     3.00 |  4.00  |  5.00  |   6.00|
VAR10       --------+--------+--------+---------+--------+--------+--------+
             1.00   |        |    7   |     2   |   3    |    7   |    3   |    22
   MALE             |        |        |         |        |        |        |   44.0
                   -+--------+--------+---------+--------+--------+--------+
   FEMALE    2.00   |   2    |    8   |     2   |   5    |    6   |    5   |    28
                    |        |        |         |        |        |        |   56.0
                   -+--------+--------+---------+--------+--------+--------+
           COLUMN       2        15         4        8       13        8         50
            TOTAL     4.0      30.0       8.0     16.0     26.0     16.0      100.0

CHI-SQUARE  D.F.  SIGNIFICANCE  MIN E.F.  CELLS WITH E.F. < 5
----------  ----  ------------  --------  -------------------
   2.45900     5      0.7827       0.880  8 OF    12 ( 66.7%)

NUMBER OF MISSING OBSERVATIONS =       0
```

FIGURE 15-13

SPSS-X Commands: CROSSTABS

```
UNNUMBERED
TITLE DESCRIPTIVE STATISTICS EXAMPLES
FILE HANDLE KIVZ NAME='KIVZ DATA C'
DATA LIST FILE=KIVZ LIST/VAR01 to VAR19
VARIABLE LABELS
   VAR01 'NATIONAL NEWS STATION'
   VAR02 'LOCAL NEWS STATION'
   VAR03 'NEWS RATING'
   VAR04 'SPORTS RATING'
   VAR05 'WEATHER RATING'
   VAR06 'ANCHOR RATING'
   VAR07 'SPORTSCASTER RATING'
   VAR08 'OVERALL RATING'
   VAR09 'NATIONAL INFLUENCE'
   VAR10 'SEX'
   VAR11 'MARITAL STATUS'
   VAR12 'NUMBER EMPLOYED'
   VAR13 'HOME STATUS '
   VAR14 'YEARS AT RESIDENCE'
   VAR15 'YEARS IN STATE'
   VAR16 'EDUCATION'
   VAR17 'AGE'
   VAR18 'INCOME'
   VAR19 'HOURS OF TV'
VALUE LABELS
   VAR01 1 'CHANNEL 5' 2 'CHANNEL 3' 3 'CHANNEL 8' 4
         'UNDECIDED'/
   VAR02 1 'CHANNEL 3' 2 'CHANNEL 8' 3 'CHANNEL 5' 4
         'UNDECIDED'/
   VAR03 TO VAR08 1 'POOR' 2 'FAIR' 3 'GOOD' 4 'VERY GOOD'
         5 'EXCEL'/
   VAR09 1 'TRUE' 2 'FALSE' 3 'UNDECIDED'/
   VAR10 1 'MALE' 2 'FEMALE'/
   VAR11 1 'SINGLE' 2 'DIVORCED' 3 'MARRIED' 4 'OTHER'/
   VAR13 1 'RENTING' 2 'BUYING'/
   VAR16 1 'GRADE SCHOOL' 2 'SOME COLLEGE' 3 'VOTECH' 4 'HIGH
         SCHOOL' 5 'COLLEGE GRAD' 6 'GRADUATE WORK'
CROSSTABS TABLES = VAR10 BY VAR16
STATISTICS 1
```

TABLE 15-7

GB-STAT Contingency Table Output for KIVZ-Channel 5 Example

CONTINGENCY TABLE—'Nat ns' X 'Loc ns'

COLS:'Nat ns' C1 BASE = 0, WIDTH = 1

ROWS:'Loc ns' R1 BASE = 1, WIDTH = 1

		1	2	3	4	5	Total
	1	0	5	4	0	0	9
	2	1	3	3	16	2	25
	3	0	5	1	5	0	11
	4	0	0	1	0	4	5
TOT		1	13	9	21	6	50

SUMMARY STATISTICS

D.F. = 12

CHI-SQUARE = 44.09455

PROB: <.0001

CRAMER'S V = .5422

CONTINGENCY COEF = .6846

small expected cell frequencies is not necessary. Figure 15-13 shows the SPSS-X commands for generating a contingency table.

Table 15-7 shows the GB-STAT output for the relationship between national news rating and local news rating. Since GB-STAT is a menu-driven package, the user accesses the statistics menu, selects the nonparametric statistics option, and then selects the chi-square contingency table option. The computer then prompts the user to identify the variables to form the rows and columns in the table. As seen in Table 15-7, the computed chi-square is 44.09, which is significant at any reasonable level of alpha. This implies that national news ratings are not independent of local news ratings. Note that Table 15-7 shows the actual joint frequencies for the two variables. GB-STAT will also print out the expected cell frequencies. Also, the Cramer's *V* shown in the output is the square root of Cramer's contingency coefficient discussed in Section 15-2.

15-5 CONCLUSIONS

This chapter has introduced two very useful statistical tools: contingency analysis and goodness-of-fit testing. Contingency analysis is a frequently used statistical tool that allows the decision maker to test whether responses to two variables are independent. Market researchers, for example, use contingency analysis in analyzing survey research data when at least one of the variables of interest is categorical. For instance, the marketer may be interested in determining whether attitude about the quality of her company's product is independent of whether the customer is male or female. By using contingency analysis and the chi-square contingency test, she can make this determination based on the sample of customers. If either or both of the variables are continuous in nature, they must be recoded before contingency analysis can be performed. Most software can facilitate this recoding process.

Goodness-of-fit testing is used when a decision maker wishes to determine whether sample data come from a population having specific characteristics. Two goodness-of-fit procedures were introduced in this chapter—the chi-square goodness-of-fit test and the Lilliefors test. Both tests rely on the idea that if the distribution of the sample data is substantially different from the hypothesized population distribution, then the population distribution from which these sample data came must not be what was hypothesized. The Lilliefors test is particularly useful for determining whether a population is normally distributed when the raw data from the sample are available. The chi-square goodness-of-fit test is most effective when the sample data have been organized into a grouped frequency distribution.

Both contingency analysis and goodness-of-fit tests are special examples of statistical procedures that, as a group, are known as nonparametric statistics. Chapter 16 will introduce you to several other very useful nonparametric statistical tools.

CHAPTER GLOSSARY

chi-square goodness-of-fit test This is a test utilizing the chi-square distribution to determine whether sample data come from a specific hypothesized population distribution.

contingency table A table used to classify sample observations according to two or more identifiable characteristics. This table is used as an intermediate step in performing contingency analysis.

Cramer's contingency coefficient A statistical measure of the strength of the relationship between responses to the row and column variables in an $r \times c$ contingency table. Values of the Cramer contingency coefficient close to 0 imply independence between the row and column variables.

Lilliefors test A goodness-of-fit test for testing whether sample data (in raw form) come from a population that is normally distributed.

phi coefficient A statistic computed from data in a 2×2 contingency table that is used to measure the row and column dependency. The phi coefficient ranges from -1 to $+1$. Values close to 0 imply independence between the rows and columns.

CHAPTER FORMULAS

Chi-square contingency coefficient

$$\chi^2 = \sum_{i=1}^{r} \sum_{j=1}^{c} \frac{(f_{A_{ij}} - f_{E_{ij}})^2}{f_{E_{ij}}}$$

Phi coefficient (2 × 2 tables)

$$\phi = \frac{ad - bc}{\sqrt{R_1 R_2 C_1 C_2}}$$

Cramer's contingency coefficient

$$\Phi = \frac{\chi^2_{\text{calculated}}}{n(q-1)}$$

Expected cell frequency

$$f_E = \frac{\text{Row total} \times \text{Column total}}{\text{Total sample size}}$$

Chi-square goodness-of-fit statistic

$$\chi^2_{\text{calculated}} = \Sigma \frac{(f_A - f_E)^2}{f_E}$$

SOLVED PROBLEMS

1. Burtco Incorporated designs and manufactures gears for heavy-duty construction equipment. One such gear, #9973, has the following specifications:

    1. Mean diameter 3 inches
    2. Standard deviation 0.001 inch
    3. Output normally distributed around the mean

    An assistant to the production control manager has selected a random sample of 500 gears from the inventory. The raw data are no longer available but the frequency distribution is as follows:

Gear Diameter (inches)	*Frequency*
Under 2.995	3
2.995 and under 2.996	4
2.996 and under 2.997	5
2.997 and under 2.998	19
2.998 and under 2.999	98
2.999 and under 3.000	146
3.000 and under 3.001	124
3.001 and under 3.002	83
3.002 and under 3.003	11
3.003 and over	7
Total	500

Based on this sample information, does gear #9973 meet specifications? Use a significance level of 0.05.

Solution

This is an example of a one-sample goodness-of-fit problem. We can hypothesize as follows:

H_0: The diameters of gear #9973 are normally distributed with a mean diameter of 3 inches and standard deviation 0.001 inch.

H_A: Gear #9973 is not within specifications.

$\alpha = 0.05$

Since the raw data are not available, an appropriate statistical procedure is the chi-square goodness-of-fit test. This test calculates the expected frequencies for each interval and compares the expected to the observed frequencies. If the calculated χ^2 gets too large, we will conclude that the fit is not good and reject the null hypothesis.

To determine the expected frequencies, we calculate the probability of a gear having a diameter in each of the intervals, assuming the gear meets the required specifications. Then we multiply the probability by 500 to obtain the expected frequency. The procedure is as follows:

$P(\text{less than } 2.995)$ = Area under normal curve to the left of 2.995

$$Z = \frac{X - \mu_x}{\sigma_x} = \frac{2.995 - 3}{0.001}$$
$$= -5.00$$

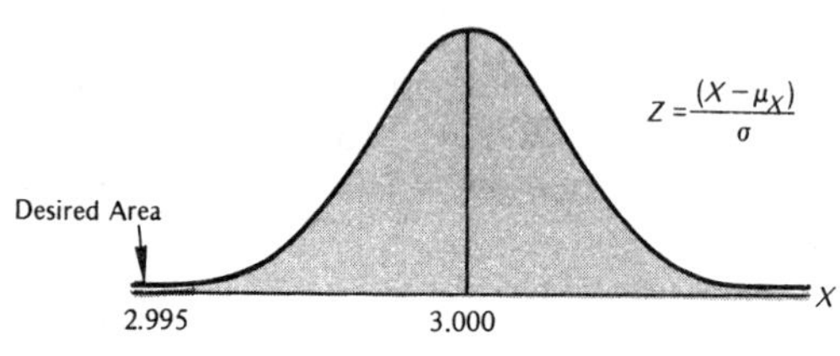

The area to the left of $Z = -5.00$ is essentially 0. Therefore, the expected frequency is $(0)(500) = 0$.

As another example,

$P(2.997 \leq X \leq 2.998)$ = Area under the normal curve between 2.997 and 2.998

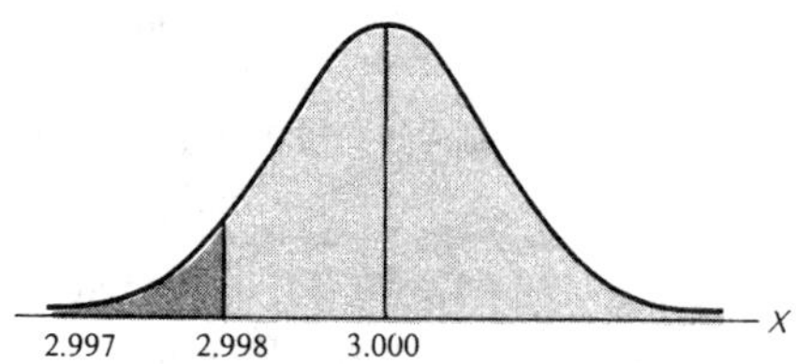

$$Z = \frac{2.997 - 3}{0.001} = -3; \text{ area to the right} = 0.4987$$

$$Z = \frac{2.998 - 3}{0.001} = -2; \text{ area to the right} = 0.4772$$

Therefore, the desired probability is 0.4987 − 0.4772 = 0.0215, and the expected frequency is (0.0215)(500) = 10.75.

In a like manner, we find the expected frequencies for each interval:

Gear Diameter (inches)	f_A	f_E
Under 2.997	12	0.650
2.997 and under 2.998	19	10.750
2.998 and under 2.999	98	67.950
2.999 and under 3.000	146	170.650
3.000 and under 3.001	124	170.650
3.001 and under 3.002	83	67.950
3.002 and under 3.003	11	10.750
3.003 and over	7	0.650

Because the chi-square goodness-of-fit test does not work well when more than 20% of the cells have expected cell frequencies below 5.0, as is the case in this example, we must combine the cells.

Gear Diameter (inches)	f_A	f_E	$(f_A - f_E)^2$	$(f_A - f_E)^2/f_E$
Under 2.998	31	11.4	384.16	33.70
2.998 and under 2.999	98	67.95	903.00	13.29
2.999 and under 3.000	146	170.65	607.62	3.56
3.000 and under 3.001	124	170.65	2,176.22	12.75
3.001 and under 3.002	83	67.95	226.50	3.33
3.002 and over	18	11.40	43.56	3.82
				$\chi^2 = 70.45$

$$\chi^2 = \sum_{i=1}^{k} \frac{(f_{A_i} - f_{E_i})^2}{f_{E_i}}$$

$$= 70.45$$

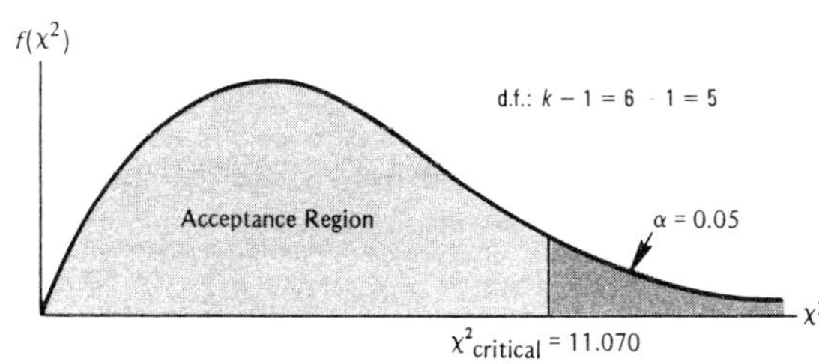

Since $\chi^2 = 70.45 > \chi^2_{\text{critical}} = 11.070$, we reject the null hypothesis and conclude that the gears are *not* within specifications. The production manager would most likely want to halt production and attempt to adjust the process to bring the gears within specifications. However, as often happens, he may discover that the specifications are unreachable with the machinery he has to work with, in which case either new machinery will be required or the specifications will have to be renegotiated.

2. Automobile insurance companies have long used age, sex, and marital status for determining rates. For example, single males under 25 years of age are considered the highest risk and are charged the highest premiums. Single females in the same age group are charged somewhat lower premiums.

Recently, the National Ranch Insurance Company studied 1,000 of its policyholders. The purpose of the study was to determine whether such factors as age, sex, and marital status are independent of whether the policyholder has filed an accident claim. With regard to age for all drivers, both male and female, National Ranch found the following:

	Age				
	Under 25	*25–40*	*40–55*	*Over 55*	
Reported Claim	93	72	53	63	281
No Claim	115	155	265	184	719
	208	227	318	247	1,000 = N

Based on these data, what should National Ranch conclude about age and claim status?

Solution

The basic question facing National Ranch is whether age is independent of claim status. Therefore, we set up our null and alternative hypotheses as follows:

H_0: Whether or not an insurance claim has been filed by a policyholder is independent of the policyholder's age.

H_A: Age and claim status are not independent.

$\alpha = 0.05$

An appropriate test is the chi-square test of independence.

$$\chi^2 = \sum_{i=1}^{r} \sum_{j=1}^{c} \frac{(f_{A_{ij}} - f_{E_{ij}})^2}{f_{E_{ij}}}$$

The expected frequencies are

$$f_{E_{11}} = \frac{281(208)}{1{,}000} = 58.45$$

$$f_{E_{12}} = \frac{281(227)}{1{,}000} = 63.79$$

$$f_{E_{13}} = \frac{281(318)}{1{,}000} = 89.36$$

$$\vdots$$

$$f_{E_{24}} = \frac{719(247)}{1{,}000} = 177.59$$

The completed contingency table is as follows:

	Age			
	Under 25	*25–40*	*40–55*	*Over 55*
Reported Claim	$f_A = 93.00$ $f_E = 58.45$	$f_A = 72.00$ $f_E = 63.79$	$f_A = 53.00$ $f_E = 89.36$	$f_A = 63.00$ $f_E = 69.41$
No Claim	$f_A = 115.00$ $f_E = 149.55$	$f_A = 155.00$ $f_E = 163.21$	$f_A = 265.00$ $f_E = 228.64$	$f_A = 184.00$ $f_E = 177.59$

Then

$$\chi^2 = \frac{(93.00 - 58.45)^2}{58.45} + \frac{(72.00 - 63.79)^2}{63.79} + \cdots + \frac{(184.00 - 177.59)^2}{177.59}$$
$$= 51.27$$

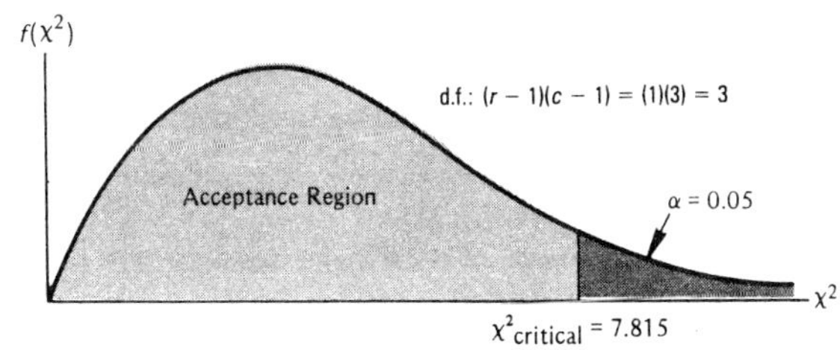

Since $\chi^2 = 51.27 > \chi^2_{critical} = 7.815$, National Ranch should reject the hypothesis of independence. Based on the data, the insurance company might infer that young drivers have more accident claims than expected, and therefore higher rates might be justified.

CONCEPTUAL QUESTIONS AND ASSIGNMENTS

20. Go to the library and locate a journal article using either contingency analysis or a goodness-of-fit test. Discuss the article, paying particular attention to the reasoning behind using the particular statistical test.
21. In the text we stated that the Lilliefors test is more powerful than the chi-square goodness-of-fit test. Formulate an example to demonstrate this point.
22. Assess the problems you would expect to find if a test that assumes interval or ratio data is used for variables with categorical data. You may want to spend some time in the library for this question.
23. Go to the library and find a marketing research book (or borrow one from a friend). Does it discuss either of the tests considered in this chapter? If yes, outline the discussion. If no, determine where in the text such a discussion would be appropriate.

ADDITIONAL PROBLEMS

24. Linda Stevens, the manager of Arlington Super Discount, always keeps four checkout stands open. However, she frequently notices lines for registers 1 and 2. She is not sure whether the layout of the store channels customers into these registers or whether the check-out clerks in these lines are simply slower than the other two.

    Linda kept a record of which stands 2,000 shoppers chose for checkout. The shoppers checked out of the four stands according to the following pattern:

Stand 1	*Stand 2*	*Stand 3*	*Stand 4*
677	550	402	371

    Based on these data, can Linda conclude that an equal number of shoppers are likely to use each of the stands? (Use an alpha level of 0.05.)
25. A manufacturer of packaged food has decided to market a new cake mix. This venture is rather risky since the new mix will compete with three established brands. The production manager argues that quality will sell the new mix. The marketing manager states that the average consumer cannot tell the difference between brands and that the critical factor in selling the mix will be the advertising campaign.

    To test the marketing manager's contention, the four types of cakes were baked under equal conditions. Shoppers were randomly stopped in several supermarkets and asked to sample each cake and indicate which of the four tasted the best. Which cake was tasted first was randomly determined, and the production manager and the marketing manager believe the process yielded representative results. The following data show how many shoppers rated each brand the tastiest:

Brand			
A	B	C	*New*
37	23	27	41

    Which contention do these data support? Use a Type I error rate of 0.01.

26. Cooper Manufacturing, Inc., of Dallas, Texas, has a contract with the U.S. Air Force to produce a part for a new fighter plane being manufactured. The part is a bolt that has specifications requiring that the length be normally distributed with a mean of 3.5 inches and a standard deviation of 0.15 inch. As part of the company's quality control efforts, each day Cooper's engineers select a random sample of 100 bolts produced that day and carefully measure the bolts to determine whether the production is within specifications. The following data were collected yesterday:

Length (inches)	*Frequency*
Under 3.30	5
3.30 and under 3.35	16
3.35 and under 3.40	7
3.40 and under 3.50	20
3.50 and under 3.60	36
3.60 and under 3.65	8
Over 3.65	8

Based on these sample data, what should Cooper's engineers conclude about the production output if they test using an alpha level of 0.01? Discuss.

27. The Cooper Company discussed in Problem 26 has a second contract with a private firm for which it makes fuses for an electronic instrument. The quality control department at Cooper periodically selects a random sample of five fuses and tests each fuse to determine whether it is defective. Based on these findings, the production process is either shut down (if too many defectives are observed) or allowed to run. The quality control department believes that the sampling process follows a binomial distribution and it has been using the binomial distribution to compute the probabilities associated with the sampling outcomes.

The contract allows for at most 5% defectives. The head of quality control recently compiled a list of the sampling results for the past 300 days in which five fuses were tested, with the following frequency distribution for the number of defectives observed. She is concerned that the binomial distribution with a sample size of 5 and a probability of defectives of 0.05 may not be appropriate.

Number of Defectives	*Frequency*
0	209
1	33
2	43
3	10
4	5
5	0

Using an alpha level of 0.10, what should the quality control manager conclude based on these sample data? Discuss.

28. Ralph Rogers has developed a highly successful practice as an acupuncture specialist. Ralph's success is built on his money-back guarantee. If his

treatment wears off, he will treat you again. His accountant, in trying to set up an allowance for future visits account, hypothesizes that whether or not a patient will demand a retreatment is related to the price of the original treatment. The following data show the relationship between price and return treatment:

		Price		
		High	*Medium*	*Low*
	In Less than 2 Years	46	53	56
Retreatment	*In 2–5 Years*	83	75	92
	None in 5 Years	127	119	149

a. What should the accountant conclude regarding the hypothesis? (Use an alpha level of 0.05.)
b. What factors that the accountant apparently has not considered might be important to the analysis?

29. A regional cancer treatment center has had success treating localized cancers with a linear accelerator. While admissions for further treatment nationally average 1.1 per patient per year, the center's director thinks that readmissions with the new treatment are Poisson distributed, with a mean of 1.2 per patient per year. He has collected the following data on a random sample of 300 patients:

Readmissions Last Year	*Patients*
0	139
1	87
2	48
3	14
4	8
5	1
6	1
7	0
8	2
	300

a. Formulate the null hypothesis to test the director's claim.
b. Calculate the test statistic to test this claim.
c. Assume the Type I error rate is to be controlled at 0.05. Do you agree with the director's claim? Why?

30. The J. Scholten CPA firm performed a study of last year's income-tax business. In one part of the study, the accountants collected data on their clients' gross taxable incomes and the associated tax payments. These data are shown in the following table, where, for example, there are fifty clients whose gross incomes were below $10,000 and who paid $3,000 or less in taxes.

	Taxes			
Gross Income	*\$0–\$3,000*	*\$3,001–\$5,000*	*\$5,001–\$10,000*	*Over \$10,000*
\$0–\$10,000	50	0	0	0
\$10,001–\$20,000	42	30	0	0
\$20,001–\$40,000	40	65	33	28
Over \$40,000	28	52	47	39

Based on these data, can Scholten conclude that its clients' gross incomes are independent of the income taxes paid? Test at the alpha level of 0.05. What comment would you have made had independence been concluded?

31. An instructor at a major university indicates that test scores in an introductory sociology class have been normally distributed since he started using a graduate student to grade his tests. To test this claim, a random sample of 300 test scores was selected from the previous academic year. These are shown as follows.

Test Score	*Frequency*
Under 30	20
30 and under 40	35
40 and under 50	40
50 and under 60	35
60 and under 70	105
70 and under 80	60
Over 80	5

Based on these sample data, can it be concluded that the test scores are normally distributed at an alpha level of 0.05? Note that you need to compute the sample mean and standard deviation.

32. Referring to Problem 30, Scholten also studied the time it took its accountants to complete each client's tax return, and related this time to the taxes paid by the client. Scholten managers were interested in determining whether a relationship exists between these two variables or whether they could consider the two variables independent. The following data are available:

		Taxes			
		\$0–\$3,000	*\$3,001–\$5,000*	*\$5,001–\$10,000*	*Over \$10,000*
No. Work Hours	*0–2*	52	55	30	27
	2–4	47	55	30	31
	Over 4	35	37	55	35

Based on these data, what should the Scholten firm conclude? Use an alpha level of 0.10.

33. Jack O'Connell, chief of officials for the National Basketball Association, reviews films of all games to evaluate calls made by the referees. Jack rates each call "good" or "bad." For games played during a 1-week period, Jack found the following distribution of calls for two officials:

Call	*Official A*	*Official B*
Good	463	518
Bad	51	38

a. Do these data indicate that the proportion of bad calls is the same for each official?
b. Test the data using a chi-square statistic with an alpha level of 0.05.
c. Compare the test in part **b** with the Z test for the difference between two population proportions.

34. Using an issue of *The Wall Street Journal* or a comparable source, select a random sample of 40 stocks that are traded on the New York Stock Exchange. For each stock, find the price as of Monday a week ago. Also find the price for each stock on Friday of that week. Use the Lilliefors test to determine whether the distribution of price changes is normally distributed for stocks traded on the New York Stock Exchange. Test using an $\alpha = 0.05$ level.

35. Develop a data collection form on which you can collect measurements for two variables from students in one of your other classes (not this statistics course). The two variables are GPA and number of hours per week spent working at a paying job. Obtain a sample size of at least twenty-five students and assume that these responses represent a random sample of all students at your college or university. Use the Lilliefors test to determine whether the two variables come from populations that are normally distributed. Test at an $\alpha =$ 0.05 level.

36. Using the sample data that you have collected for Problem 35, apply contingency analysis to determine whether GPA is independent of number of hours worked. Break GPA into four categories and hours worked into five categories. Test at an $\alpha = 0.05$ level. Compute Cramer's coefficient and interpret.

37. Referring to Problem 36, break the two variables into two categories each and test for independence. Compute the phi coefficient and interpret. Test at an $\alpha = 0.05$ level.

DATABASE PROBLEMS

The following questions and problems pertain directly to the State Department of Transportation case study and database introduced in Chapter 1. The questions and problems were written assuming that you will have access to a computer and appropriate statistical software. The database containing 100 observations and seventeen variables is shown in Table 1-1 in

Chapter 1. *Assume that the data were collected using a simple random sampling process.*

1. Herb Kriner is interested in determining whether seat belt status is independent of insurance status. Test this at the $\alpha = 0.05$ level. Show the contingency table and the test statistic.

2. Can Herb Kriner conclude that knowledge of the liability insurance law is independent of sex of the respondent? Test at the $\alpha = 0.05$ level.

3. Based on these sample data, can Herb Kriner conclude that the distribution of the time drivers have lived in Idaho is normally distributed? Test using an appropriate goodness-of-fit test at an $\alpha = 0.05$ level.

ADDITIONAL DATABASE PROBLEMS

The questions and problems in this section reference the various databases that accompany this text and which are described in Chapter 1. Your instructor has been provided a diskette with these databases. It is expected that you will be using computer software to access these data and to perform the required calculations and graphs.

DATABASE: **CITIES** (*Refer to the database description in Chapter 1.*)

1. Art Lee is preparing a speech for a trade conference and he intends to use information from the CITIES database that Phillis Rigg compiled. At one point in his speech, he would like to state that the estimate of population growth between 1990 and 1995 in percentage terms is normally distributed. Using an $\alpha = 0.10$ level, would Art be justified in making this statement? If so, what should he conclude that the mean should be? What about the standard deviation?
2. Using contingency analysis, can Art Lee consider the cities' labor market stress index to be statistically independent of 1989 unemployment rate? Break each variable into appropriate categories and conduct the hypothesis test using an $\alpha = 0.05$ level.
3. Referring to Problem 2, break the two variables into different categories and conduct the test again. Did the results change this time? Discuss why it is possible for the contingency analysis results to differ depending on how the categories are formed for a continuous random variable.

DATABASE: **FAST100** (*Refer to the database description in Chapter 1.*)

1. Based on the sample data, would it be appropriate to conclude that price earnings ratios are normally distributed? Test using an $\alpha = 0.05$.

2. Based on these sample data, can we conclude that stock price is independent of where the stock is traded? Break the stock price into three categories and test at an $\alpha = 0.10$ level.
3. Is the annual 3–5 year growth rate for companies in this study described by a uniform distribution? Test using an appropriate goodness-of-fit method at an $\alpha = 0.05$ level.

DATABASE: **PACRIM** (*Refer to the database description in Chapter 1.*)

1. Can it be concluded that profit ranking is independent of asset ranking based on these data for Pacific Rim companies? Break the rankings into four categories and test at an $\alpha = 0.05$ level.
2. Is it appropriate to conclude that the distribution of 1989 annual profits fits a normal distribution? Test using an $\alpha = 0.05$ level.
3. If your software allows you to test data for goodness of fit against several distributions, which of these best fits the data for year-end asset ranking? Discuss the thinking used to reach this conclusion.

DATABASE: **JOBAPPS** (*Refer to the database description in Chapter 1.*)

SPECIAL PROJECT

For each candidate, develop a contingency table that crosses the recommendation scale with the candidate's ranking. Write a paragraph that describes the table results for each candidate. Then test to determine whether the ranking is independent of the acceptability rating. Test each at an $\alpha = 0.05$ level. Finally, based on these faculty inputs and this analysis, which candidate(s) would you recommend? Write a short report justifying your selection.

DATABASE: **TRUCKS** (*Refer to the database description in Chapter 1.*)

1. Is the WIM gross weight normally distributed? Test this at the $\alpha = 0.05$ level.
2. Compute a variable that is the difference between WIM gross weight and POE gross weight. Then using contingency analysis, determine whether there is reason to support the belief that scale error is independent of the month the data were collected. Test at an $\alpha = 0.05$ level. Break the difference variable into five categories.
3. Referring to Problem 2, would your conclusion change if the difference variable was divided into more or fewer categories? Show two examples to justify your response.
4. Referring to Problem 2, can you conclude that the difference variable is normally distributed? Test this at the $\alpha = 0.05$ level.

CASE

15A American Oil Company

Chad Williams sat back in his airline seat to enjoy the hour flight between Los Angeles and Oakland, California. The hour would give him time to reflect upon his upcoming trip to Australia and the work he had been doing the past week in Los Angeles.

Chad is one man on a six-man crew for the American Oil Company who literally walks the earth searching for oil. His college degrees in geology and petroleum engineering landed him the job with American, but he never dreamed he would be doing the exciting work he now does. Chad and his crew spend several months in special locations around the world using highly sensitive electronic equipment for oil exploration purposes.

The upcoming trip to Australia is one that Chad has been looking forward to since it was announced that his crew would be going there to search the Outback for oil. In preparation for the Australia trip, the crew has been in Los Angeles at American's engineering research facility working on some new equipment that will be used in Australia in search of oil.

Chad's thoughts centered on the problem he was having with a particular component part on the new equipment. The specifications called for 200 of the components, each having a diameter of between 0.15 and 0.18 inch. The only available supplier of the component in New Jersey manufactures the components to specifications calling for normally distributed output with a mean of 0.16 inch and a standard deviation of 0.02 inch.

Chad faces two problems. First, he is unsure that the supplier actually does produce parts with the mean of 0.16 inch and standard deviation of 0.02 inch according to a normal distribution. Second, if that is the case, he needs to determine how many components to purchase if enough acceptable components are to be received to make two oil exploration devices.

The supplier has sent Chad the following data for 330 randomly selected components. Chad believes that the supplier is honest and that he can rely on the data.

Diameter (inch)	*Frequency*
Under 0.14	5
0.14 and under 0.15	70
0.15 and under 0.16	90
0.16 and under 0.17	105
0.17 and under 0.18	50
Over 0.18	10
Total	330

Chad needs to have a report ready for Monday indicating whether he believes the supplier delivers at its stated specifications and, if so, how many of the components American should order to have enough acceptable components to outfit two oil exploration devices.

REFERENCES

Berenson, Mark L., and Levine, David M. *Basic Business Statistics Concepts and Applications,* 5th edition. Englewood Cliffs, New Jersey: Prentice-Hall, 1992.

Daniel, Wayne W., and Terrell, James C. *Business Statistics for Management and Economics,* 6th edition. Boston: Houghton Mifflin, 1992.

Iman, Ronald L., and Conover, W. J. *Modern Business Statistics,* 2nd edition. New York: Wiley, 1989.

Levin, Richard I., and Rubin, David S. *Statistics for Management,* 5th edition. Englewood Cliffs, New Jersey: Prentice-Hall, 1991.

Sincich, Terry. *Business Statistics by Example,* 4th edition. New York: Dellen, 1992.

Chapter 15

Hand-In Exercises

1. Is political party affiliation conditioned by education? To answer this the data below were assembled. Use Chi-Square analysis and the 5% test level.

   a. Write a hypothesis of independence of education and political party affiliation. Also state the alternative hypothesis.

b. Calculate the test statistic for the following data.

	Republican	Democrat	Other
High School	20	30	20
College	30	60	20
Graduate Degree	20	20	20

Cell	Observed	Expected
1	20	
2	30	
3	20	
4	30	
5	60	
6	20	
7	20	
8	20	
9	20	

c. Determine degrees of freedom for the critical value.

d. Using degrees of freedom what is the critical value from the table at the 5% level?

e. What is the decision on the hypothesis?

f. What do you conclude about education and political party affiliation?

2. Use Chi-Square goodness of fit analysis to test if the data below fit a Poisson distribution, using the 5% level of significance. Include a statement of the hypothesis and show all calculations. These data are from Problem 29 in Chapter 15 on cancer treatment. A mean of 1.2 patients is assumed for calculations.

Readmission last year	Number of Patients	Probability
0	139	
1	87	
2	48	
3	14	
4	8	
5	1	
6	1	
7	0	
8	2	
	300	

3. Refer to Problem 31 in Chapter 15. Use a 5% level of significance and perform a test to see if these data on test scores fit a normal distribution.

Score	Frequency
Under 30	20
30 to under 40	35
40 to under 50	40
50 to under 60	35
60 to under 70	105
70 to under 80	60
80 and over	5

Introduction to Nonparametric Statistics

WHY DECISION MAKERS NEED TO KNOW

In previous chapters you have been introduced to a wide variety of inferential statistical techniques, some of which are large-sample hypothesis tests for one and two populations, small-sample estimation and hypothesis tests using the *t* distribution, analysis of variance, and correlation analysis. These tools are very powerful and heavily used by business decision makers. However, the use of these statistical tools is limited to the presence of those conditions for which they were originally developed. For example, the large-sample tests based on the standard normal distribution assume that the data can be measured at least at the interval level. The small-sample tests that use the *t* distribution assume that the sampled populations are normally distributed. Tests of significance using the correlation coefficient of Chapter 13 assume that the two variables are bivariate normally distributed.

While in many instances these conditions are satisfied, decision makers will encounter other situations where either the level of data measurement is too low or the distribution assumptions are clearly violated. In these cases, different statistical techniques are required, for which a class of statistical tools called **nonparametric statistics** has been developed. The chi-square goodness-of-fit test and the contingency analysis technique introduced in Chapter 15 are actually two special nonparametric techniques. While those techniques are important, you will encounter other situations that require different approaches. Consequently, you should become aware of the broader set of nonparametric statistical techniques and recognize when to apply these techniques in a business decision situation.

CHAPTER OBJECTIVES

This chapter introduces the category of statistical tools referred to as nonparametric statistics. Specifically, it will introduce several frequently used nonparametric statistical procedures and will show specific examples of how these techniques are used to aid in decision making. The nonparametric tests introduced in this chapter include the following: the runs test, the Mann–Whitney *U* test, the Wilcoxon signed rank test, Kruskal–Wallis one-way ANOVA, and the Spearman ranked correlation coefficient.

STUDENT OBJECTIVES

After studying the material in this chapter, you should be able to do the following:

1. Understand why nonparametric statistics are important to decision makers.
2. Recognize when and how to employ the runs test for testing for randomness.
3. Know when and how to perform a Mann–Whitney *U* test.
4. Recognize the situations for which the Wilcoxon signed rank test applies and be able to use it in a decision-making context.
5. Perform nonparametric analysis of variance using the Kruskal–Wallis one-way ANOVA procedure.
6. Compute the Spearman rank correlation coefficient and test whether the correlation is statistically significant.

16-1 INTRODUCTION TO NONPARAMETRIC STATISTICS

Chapters 1–15 of this text have presented a wide array of statistical tools both for describing data and for drawing inferences about a population based on sample information from that population. These tools are widely used in decision-making situations. However, you will soon run into situations for which the tools from Chapters 1–15 are either of limited use or not appropriate.

For instance, hypothesis tests involving small samples utilize the t distribution. However, the t distribution depends on the assumption that the population from which the sample is selected is normally distributed. If a small-sample application involves testing the difference between two population means, the t distribution is employed under the assumption that both populations are normally distributed and the populations have equal variances. The analysis of variance F test introduced in Chapter 12 is based on the assumption that all populations are normally distributed and the population variances are equal. In addition, each of these techniques requires that the variables of interest be interval or ratio level. In many situations, either these assumptions are satisfied or the departures from the assumptions are slight enough to warrant use of the technique. However, you will also encounter decision situations where major departures exist. For example, many populations, such as family income levels and house prices, are highly skewed. In other instances, the level of data measurement will be too low (ordinal or nominal) to warrant use of these techniques. The alternative is to employ a **nonparametric** statistical procedure which has been developed to meet specific inferential needs with fewer restrictive assumptions.

The contingency analysis and the goodness-of-fit tests introduced in Chapter 15 are actually examples of special-purpose nonparametric statistical tools. We devoted an entire chapter to those two topics because of their frequent use by decision makers. In this chapter, we introduce several additional nonparametric tests that are regularly applied in business decision-making situations. You should be aware that the nonparametric techniques introduced in this chapter are but a few of the many such techniques that exist. Several references listed at the end of this chapter, including books by Marascuilo and McSweeney, and Siegel, contain examples of a wide variety of available nonparametric tools.

The nonparametric tests introduced in this chapter include the following: the runs test, the Mann–Whitney *U* test, the Wilcoxon signed rank test, Kruskal–Wallis one-way ANOVA, and the Spearman ranked correlation coefficient. As has been the format in all previous chapters, we will introduce each of these five tools through a realistic decision-making situation.

16-2 THE RUNS TEST

All states regulate hunting and fishing through some government agency. Generally, a license is required to fish on the state's streams, rivers, and lakes. Likewise, a hunting license is required to hunt birds and big game. In some states, additional permits are required to hunt certain species of animals or to hunt female deer and elk. In Idaho and some other states, these permits are usually granted based on a random drawing from the list of those hunters that apply.

Idaho is a state of approximately 1 million people. Each year nearly 300,000 big-game hunting licenses are sold. Over half of these license holders pay an additional fee to be part of a drawing for special permits to hunt antelope, cow elk, mountain sheep, and mountain goats. The number of permits granted is far less than the number of applicants. The drawing each year is conducted by computer software at the Idaho Department of Fish and Game in Boise, Idaho.

Idaho is a relatively large state geographically. For several reasons, including the fact that the state capital and the headquarters of all government agencies for the state are located in Boise, most of the state's economic development occurs in and around Boise. As a result, there is an anti-Boise bias in other parts of the state. Possibly because of this anti-Boise feeling, a few years ago hunters from other parts of the state banded together to challenge the Idaho Fish and Game's system for allocating hunting permits. They charged that the system favored the Boise area hunters.

To answer these charges and to verify the validity of its software, the Fish and Game Department contracted with one of the authors to perform an independent

FIGURE 16-1

Permit Selection System for the Idaho Department of Fish and Game

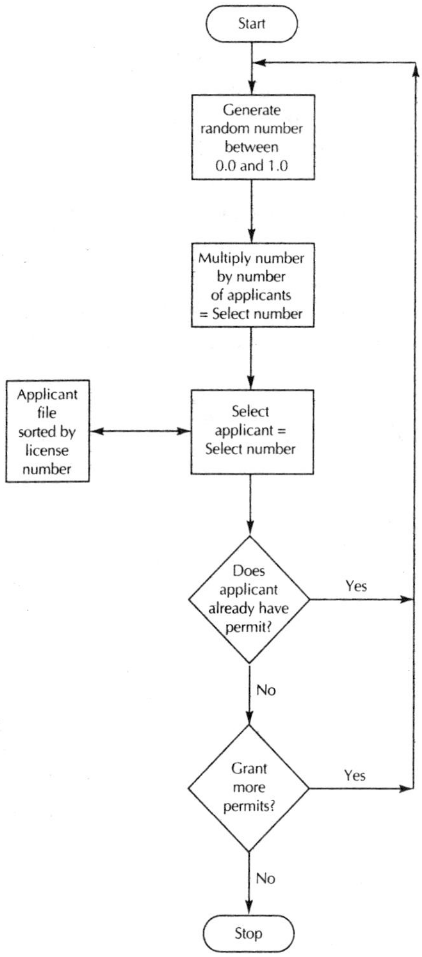

audit of the system. Figure 16-1 shows a flowchart of the steps involved in making the permit selections. For each class of permit, a file exists with applications ordered by hunting license number. The file typically contains applicants from around the state depending on the type of permit and the location for which it will be valid. The computer program uses an algorithm to generate a five-digit uniform random number between 0.0 and 1.0. This number is multiplied by the number of applicants in the file. The product, rounded to the nearest integer value, corresponds to an applicant in the file who will receive the hunting permit. For the purposes of this example, suppose 500 hunters applied for a certain permit and are arranged from 1 to 500 in the file, according to hunting license number. If the computer program generated a "random" number between 0.0 and 1.0 of 0.34509, the product of this number and 500 is

$$0.34509 \times 500 = 172.54500$$

The product is rounded to 173. Therefore, the 173rd person in the applicant file would receive the permit. If additional permits are available, a second uniform random number is generated and the process continues.

As long as the system generates random numbers between 0.0 and 1.0, the selection of hunters to receive permits would not favor hunters from any particular part of the state. The auditors needed a technique for testing whether the computer program generated numbers that will pass the test of randomness. One such technique is the **runs test.** The runs test utilizes a sample to test whether the population data are random by examining the number of runs in the sample. *A run is defined as a succession of occurrences of a certain type preceded and followed by occurrences of the alternate type.* Based on the logic of the runs test, if too few or too many runs are observed in the sample, the hypothesis of randomness is rejected. For example, suppose a coin is tossed twenty times, with H = head and T = tail, and the following sequence is observed:

Run 1 Run 2

T T T T T T T T T T H H H H H H H H H H

In this case, only two runs occurred in the twenty observations. Since we expect the occurrence of heads and tails to be random, these results suggest otherwise—there are too few runs! Suppose the following results occur for twenty tosses:

T H T H T H T H T H T H T H T H T H T H

This shows twenty runs, since tail and head alternated on every flip. This is probably too many runs and suggests that the coin does not produce heads and tails randomly. (Note that, in both cases, the number of heads in twenty flips was ten, the expected number.)

The runs test can be easily applied to the Idaho Fish and Game permit audit by assigning a "+" code to any random number greater than 0.50000 and a "−" code to any random number less than 0.50000. (Note that the chance of a number being exactly 0.50000 is very small, so we have not included it in the coding methodology.) The runs test can be used to determine whether the computer program generates too many or too few runs to pass the test of randomness.

SMALL-SAMPLE RUNS TEST

In employing the runs test, we select a statistical sample from the population and let n_1 equal the number of occurrences of one kind (e.g., the number of "+" signs corresponding to numbers >0.50000). We let n_2 equal the number of occurrences of the other kind (e.g., "−" signs corresponding to numbers <0.50000). If both n_1 and n_2 are less than 20, the **small-sample runs test** must be used.

To illustrate the application of the small-sample runs test, suppose a sample of 20 numbers was generated by the Idaho Fish and Game Department's computer software. These values are shown in Table 16-1 (page 852). Note that the sample items must be kept in the sequence in which they occur. In this example, the number of "+" signs is $n_1 = 9$ and the number of "−" signs is $n_2 = 11$. Both

TABLE 16-1

Idaho Department of Fish and Game "Random" Numbers

Sequence	Number	Code	Sequence	Number	Code
1	0.34561	–	11	0.67201	+
2	0.42789	–	12	0.23790	–
3	0.36925	–	13	0.24509	–
4	0.89563	+	14	0.01467	–
5	0.25679	–	15	0.78345	+
6	0.92001	+	16	0.69112	+
7	0.58345	+	17	0.46023	–
8	0.23114	–	18	0.38633	–
9	0.12672	–	19	0.60914	+
10	0.88569	+	20	0.95234	+

n_1 and n_2 are less than 20, so the small-sample runs test is used to test the following null and alternative hypotheses:

H_0: Computer-generated numbers are random between 0.0 and 1.0.

H_A: Computer-generated numbers are not random.

To perform the test, we count the number of runs of "+" and "–" over the sequence of 20 data points shown as follows:

	– – –	+	–	+ +	– –	+ +	– – –	+ +	– –	+ +
Runs:	1	2	3	4	5	6	7	8	9	10

There are $r = 10$ runs in these data. The question is whether 10 runs is considered too many or too few to support the null hypothesis of randomness. Thus, the runs test is two-tailed. For the small-sample runs test, this question can be answered by comparing $r = 10$ to a critical value in the runs table in Appendix K. The runs table is actually divided into two parts. Part (a) is used to locate the lower limit critical value and part (b) the upper limit critical value. Note that the runs table is for $\alpha = 0.05$.

To use the runs table, first go to part (a) and locate in the leftmost column a number corresponding to $n_1 = 9$, the number of "+" signs. Then locate in the top row the value $n_2 = 11$, the number of "–" signs. The value at the intersection of this row and column is 6. Thus:

If $r \leq 6$, we reject H_0.

Next, go to part (b) of the runs table and locate $n_1 = 9$ in the leftmost column and $n_2 = 11$ across the top row. The intersection of the row and column is at the critical value 16. Thus:

If $r \geq 16$, we reject H_0.

Since $r = 10$ falls between the critical values, these sample data do not refute the null hypothesis that the computer-generated numbers are random between

FIGURE 16-2

Small-Sample Runs Test for the Idaho Fish and Game Example

Hypotheses:

H_0: Computer-generated numbers are random between 0.0 and 1.0.
H_A: Computer numbers are not random.

$\alpha = 0.05$

Test Statistic:

$$r = 10 \text{ runs}$$

Critical Values from Runs Table in Appendix K:

Possible Runs:	1 2 3 4 5 6	7 8 9 10 11 12 13 14 15	16 17 18 19 20
	Reject H_0	Do not reject H_0	Reject H_0

Decision Rule:

If $r \leq 6$ or $r \geq 16$, reject H_0.
Otherwise, do not reject H_0.

Since $r = 10$ falls in acceptance region, we do not reject the null hypothesis. Based on the sample data, we cannot dispute the claim that the computer-generated numbers are random.

0.0 and 1.0 at the $\alpha = 0.05$ level. Figure 16-2 shows the runs test in summary form.

Thus, based in part on the runs test, the independent audit supported the Idaho Fish and Game Department's methodology for drawing hunting permits. There was no reason to believe that hunters from the Boise area received special consideration.

A QUALITY CONTROL EXAMPLE

Earlier in this text, we introduced a statistical quality control tool called the process control chart. We showed how this chart is used to assess whether a process is in control. A sample point falling outside the control limits is considered a signal that the process is out of control and an assignable cause of variation should be found. However, a point outside the control limits is not the only signal of control problems. A process may be operating with all points between the upper and lower control limits, yet be out of control. Since the area between the upper and lower control limits marks the inherent variation in the process, a process in control should yield observations that fall randomly above and below the center line within the control limits. If the process provides nonrandom sample points within this area, a signal indicating that the process is out of control is needed.

FIGURE 16-3

Childress Automotive Company $\overline{X}$ Control Chart

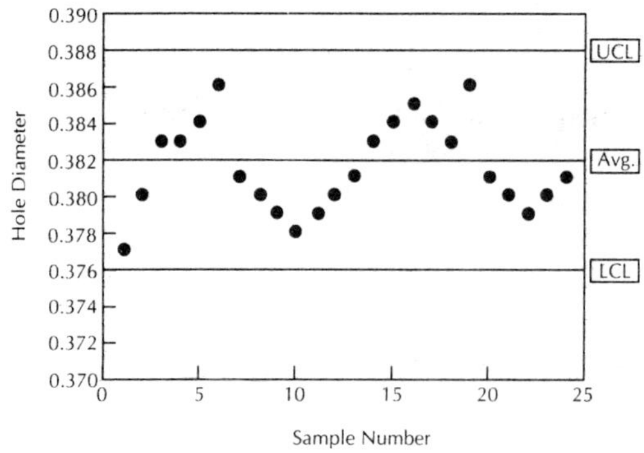

Note: Each point represents a sample mean hole diameter.
UCL = Upper control limit
LCL = Lower control limit

The runs test can be used to provide such a signal. Consider the Childress Automotive Company, which makes tire rims for a major automobile manufacturer. Figure 16-3 shows an $\overline{X}$ chart for the lug nut hole diameter for a particular tire rim made by the company. Note that these data show the last twenty-four subgroup means. As shown in Figure 16-3, no points fall outside a control limit. However, there appears to be a pattern in the data that might indicate a lack of randomness.

To use the runs test, we assign a code of "+" to any point above the center line and a code of "−" to any value below the center line. We then count the number of runs. From Figure 16-3, we get:

	−−	++++	−−−−−−−	++++++	−−−−−
Runs:	1	2	3	4	5

There are $r = 5$ runs in the data. Figure 16-4 shows the small-sample runs test for this example. As can be seen, $r = 5$ falls in the lower rejection region, indicating that this number of runs is too few to accept the hypothesis of randomness. Therefore, even though the control chart shows no points outside the control limits, the process can be considered out of control. Efforts should be made to determine why the process is not operating randomly around the center line.

LARGE-SAMPLE RUNS TEST

In using the runs test for randomness, if either n_1 or n_2 exceeds 20, the runs tables in Appendix K cannot be used. Instead, an approximation method utilizing the normal distribution has been developed. To demonstrate the large-sample runs test, consider the following production control example.

The Hillman Dairy Corporation processes a wide variety of dairy products including ice cream. All of Hillman's ice cream is made in its Salem, Oregon,

FIGURE 16-4

Childress Automotive Company Control Chart Runs Test

Hypotheses:

H_0: $\overline{X}$ values are randomly distributed around the center line.
H_A: $\overline{X}$ values are not randomly distributed around the center line.

$\alpha = 0.05$

n_1 = Number of "+" signs = 10
n_2 = Number of "−" signs = 14

Test Statistic:

$r = 5$ runs

Critical Values from Runs Table in Appendix K:

Possible Runs

1 2 3 4 5 6 7	8 9 10 11 12 13 14 15 16 17	18 19 20 21 22 23 24
Reject H_0	Do not reject H_0	Reject H_0

Decision Rule:

If $r \le 7$ or $r \ge 18$, reject H_0.
Otherwise, do not reject H_0.

Since $r = 5 \le 7$, we reject H_0 at the $\alpha = 0.05$ level and conclude that there are too few runs to justify the claim of randomness.

plant. The 32-ounce ice cream cartons are filled by a machine that inserts a mixture of ice cream product and air to reach the desired weight per carton. Ideally, each carton would contain exactly 32 ounces, but this is not the case. Instead, the filling machine produces ice cream cartons with weights varying around an average of 32 ounces. Kendall White, the production manager, is interested in determining whether the fill weights are randomly distributed around the 32-ounce average or whether there is some pattern or dependency relationship between successive cartons.

As a test, the fill machine operator selected 100 successive cartons from the day shift production. These data, coded "O" for over 32 ounces and "U" for under 32 ounces, are shown in Table 16-2. A careful check of these data shows that there are $n_1 = 53$ "O's," $n_2 = 47$ "U's," and a total of $r = 47$ runs.

TABLE 16-2

Hillman Dairy Products Ice Cream Data (in sequential order)

OOO	U	OO	U	O	UU	OO	UU	OOOO	UU	O	UU	OO	
U	O	UU	OOOO	UU	OO	UUU	O	UU	OO	UUUUU			
OOO	U	O	UU	OOO	U	OOOO	UUU	O	UU	OOO	U		
OO	UUU	O	U	OO	UUU	O	UU	OOOO	UUU	OOO			

The large-sample runs test is based on a normal approximation for the sampling distribution of r where the mean is given by equation 16-1 and the standard deviation by equation 16-2:

$$\mu_r = \frac{2n_1n_2}{n_1 + n_2} + 1 \quad \textbf{16-1}$$

$$\sigma_r = \sqrt{\frac{(2n_1n_2)(2n_1n_2 - n_1 - n_2)}{(n_1 + n_2)^2(n_1 + n_2 - 1)}} \quad \textbf{16-2}$$

Then the test statistic is given as equation 16-3:

$$Z = \frac{r - \mu_r}{\sigma_r} = \frac{r - \{[(2n_1n_2)/(n_1 + n_2)] + 1\}}{\sqrt{\frac{(2n_1n_2)(2n_1n_2 - n_1 - n_2)}{(n_1 + n_2)^2(n_1 + n_2 - 1)}}} \quad \textbf{16-3}$$

The derivation of these equations is beyond the scope of the text. However, we can quite easily substitute our values for n_1 and n_2 into equations 16-1 and 16-2 to solve for the mean and standard deviation as follows:

$$\mu_r = \frac{2 \times 53 \times 47}{53 + 47} + 1$$
$$= 50.82$$

$$\sigma_r = \sqrt{\frac{(2 \times 53 \times 47)(2 \times 53 \times 47 - 53 - 47)}{(53 + 47)^2(53 + 47 - 1)}}$$
$$= 4.95659$$

We see from these computations that for a sample of size 100 with 53 occurrences of one kind and 47 of the second kind, the expected, or mean, number of runs is 50.82 with a standard deviation of just under 5.0. Recall that we found $r = 47$ runs in the data in Table 16-2. Figure 16-5 shows the large-sample runs test based on the normal approximation approach. The calculated Z value of -0.771 is well within the acceptance region. Therefore, based on these sample data, the production manager has no basis for rejecting the premise that the process is filling ice cream cartons with randomly distributed weights on either side of 32 ounces.

FIGURE 16-5

Large-Sample Runs Test for the Hillman Dairy Company Example

Hypotheses:

H_0: Ice cream carton fill amounts are randomly distributed above and below the 32-ounce level.

H_A: Ice cream carton fill amounts are not randomly distributed above and below the 32-ounce level.

$\alpha = 0.05$

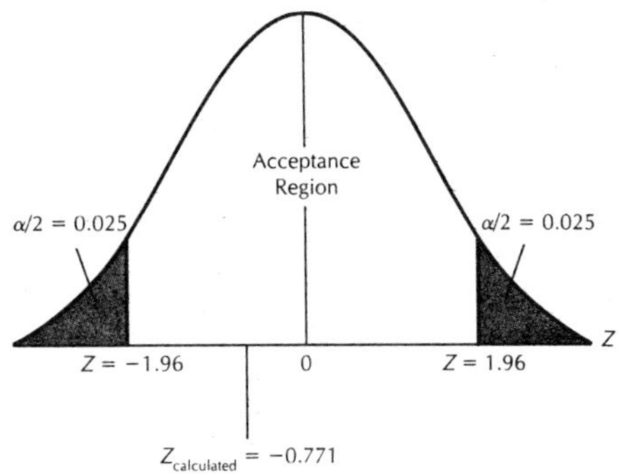

Test Statistic:

$$Z_{\text{calculated}} = \frac{r - \mu_r}{\sigma_r} = \frac{47 - 50.82}{4.95659}$$
$$= -0.771$$

Decision Rule:

If $Z_{\text{calculated}} \leq -1.96$ or $Z_{\text{calculated}} \geq 1.96$, reject H_0.
Otherwise, do not reject H_0.

Since $Z_{\text{calculated}} = -0.771$, we do not reject H_0.

SKILL DEVELOPMENT PROBLEMS FOR **SECTION 16-2**

The following problems have been included to help you better understand the materials presented in this section.

1. A store sells two brands of eggs, brand X and brand Y. Of interest is whether customer selection of brands is random. A sample of twenty customers yielded the following sequence of egg brand selection:

X X Y Y Y X Y X X Y Y Y X Y Y Y X Y X X

Based on these results:

a. How many runs are there in the data?
b. Using an $\alpha = 0.05$ level, test the hypothesis that egg brand selection is random between the two brands.

2. A daycare center operator is interested in determining whether children's preference for playing with trucks or dolls is random. To test this, she has observed fifteen individual children go into a room with a truck and a doll on the floor. The following represents the sequence of first toy selection:

T T T D T D T T D D D T T D T

   a. How many runs are present in these data?
   b. Test the hypothesis of randomness at the $\alpha = 0.05$ level. Discuss your results.

3. A department store operator is interested in determining whether the payment method for merchandise is randomly distributed between the store's credit card or a major bank card. He has observed 300 consecutive credit card sales and found 145 using the store card and 155 using a major credit card. The number of runs observed in the sample was 35. Based on these data, use the runs test to test for randomness at the $\alpha = 0.10$ level.

4. A bank operations manager has claimed that the arrivals of male and female customers to the drive-up window at a particular branch are random. To test this, she has observed 400 consecutive arrivals and recorded whether the driver was male or female. Of the 400, 302 were female and 98 were male. Further, there were 77 runs of male or female in the sample. Based on these data, what should the manager conclude? Use an $\alpha = 0.05$ level.

16-3 MANN–WHITNEY *U* TEST

The Ada County Highway District (ACHD) was recently formed to consolidate the street and highway maintenance and construction activities in Ada County. Formerly, the urban division took care of all the streets and roads in the county's largest city, and the rural division handled all street and road work outside that city. The urban and rural divisions had separate managements, and because of the perceived duplication of managerial activities, the consolidation was mandated by the Ada County commissioners. However, the working force of the ACHD at present remains divided between the divisions, rural and urban.

A few months following the consolidation, several rural division supervisors began claiming that the urban division employees waste gravel from the county gravel pit. They claimed that the urban division uses more gravel per mile of road maintenance than the rural division.

In response to these claims, Dennis Millier, the ACHD materials manager, decided to perform a test. He selected a random sample of weeks from the district's job cost records from work performed by the urban (U) division and a random sample of work performed by the rural (R) division. The data in Table 16-3 represent the yards of gravel used per mile of road for each week sampled.

Even though the data are of a ratio-level measurement, Dennis Millier is not willing to make the normality assumptions necessary to employ the two-sample t test discussed in Chapter 11. However, a nonparametric technique called the

TABLE 16-3

Yards of Gravel per Mile for the Ada County Highway District Example

Urban	Rural
460	600
830	652
720	603
930	594
500	1,402
620	1,111
703	902
407	700
1,521	827
900	490
750	904
800	1,400

Mann–Whitney *U* test will allow Dennis to compare the gravel use of the two divisions.

The Mann–Whitney *U* test is one of the most popular nonparametric tests and can be used to compare samples from two populations in those cases where the following assumptions are satisfied.

1. The two samples are independent and random.
2. The value measured is a continuous variable.
3. The measurement scale used is at least ordinal.
4. If they differ, the distributions of the two populations will differ only with respect to location.

The null hypothesis for the Mann–Whitney *U* test is always the same:

H_0: The two populations (A and B) have identical distributions.

The alternative hypothesis can take three different forms, depending on the situation.

H_A: The two populations differ with respect to location.

The values from population A tend to be smaller than the values from population B.

The values from population A tend to be larger than the values from population B.

In this situation Dennis has decided to test the following hypotheses:

H_0: The two divisions have equal gravel use distributions.

H_A: The urban division tends to use larger amounts of gravel than the rural division.

$$\alpha = 0.05$$

TABLE 16-4

Ranking of Yards of Gravel per Mile for the Ada County Highway District Example

Urban ($n_1 = 12$)		Rural ($n_2 = 12$)	
Yards of Gravel	Rank	Yards of Gravel	Rank
460	2	600	6
830	16	652	9
720	12	603	7
930	20	594	5
500	4	1,402	23
620	8	1,111	21
703	11	902	18
407	1	700	10
1,521	24	827	15
900	17	490	3
750	13	904	19
800	14	1,400	22
Sum of ranks_1 =	142	Sum of ranks_2 =	158

The first step in testing this hypothesis using the Mann–Whitney U test is to combine the raw data from the two samples into one set of numbers, then rank the numbers in this set from low to high, which leads to the rankings as shown in Table 16-4. The logic of the Mann–Whitney U test centers on the idea that if the sum of the rankings of one group differs greatly from the sum of the rankings of the second group, we should conclude that there is a difference in central locations of the populations.

We calculate a U value for each sample as shown in equations 16-4 and 16-5:

$$U_U = n_1 n_2 + \frac{n_1(n_1 + 1)}{2} - \text{Sum of ranks}_1 \tag{16-4}$$

$$U_R = n_1 n_2 + \frac{n_2(n_2 + 1)}{2} - \text{Sum of ranks}_2 \tag{16-5}$$

where n_1 and n_2 are the two sample sizes. Thus, for our example using the ranks in Table 16-4:

$$U_U = 12(12) + \frac{12(13)}{2} - 142$$

$$= 80$$

$$U_R = 12(12) + \frac{12(13)}{2} - 158$$

$$= 64$$

Note that $U_R + U_U = n_1n_2$. This is always the case and provides a good check on the correctness of the rankings in Table 16-4.

Now, we select the smaller U value and call this U_{test}. In this case, $U_{test} = 64$. When the larger of the two sample sizes is in the range 9 to 20, the null hypothesis can be tested by comparing U_{test} with the appropriate critical value given in the Mann–Whitney U table in Appendix N. We begin by locating the part of the table associated with the desired alpha. In this case, we have a one-tailed test with $\alpha = 0.05$.

Across the top of the Mann–Whitney U table, locate the value corresponding to the larger sample size. In our example, both sample sizes are 12, so we go over to the value 12. Then use the leftmost column to locate the value corresponding to the smaller sample size, also 12 in this example. The intersection of these column and row values gives a critical value of 42. We can now form the decision rule as follows:

If $U_{test} \leq 42$, reject H_0.
Otherwise, do not reject H_0.

Now since $U_{test} = 64 > 42$, we do not reject the null hypothesis. Therefore, Dennis Millier can conclude that the urban division is no more wasteful than the rural division in the use of gravel on construction jobs.

A QUALITY CONTROL EXAMPLE

An important part of an overall quality control program is customer feedback. Some organizations take a very passive approach and essentially wait until the customer chooses to provide feedback, usually in the form of a complaint. However, other companies actively seek customer feedback. First State Bank is a good example of a company that regularly seeks customer feedback to help management assess how the customer views its service.

We give an example of what the bank regularly does. Recently, Jeff Wilson, senior marketing vice-president, conducted two focus group sessions with two classes of customers. In the first session, a random sample of the bank's commercial customers met to provide feedback about loan processing service quality. At the close of the discussion, each of the seven customers was asked to assign a rating between 1 and 100 (1 is low and 100 is high) for the service provided by the bank. In the second session, Jeff met with a random sample of thirteen residential loan customers to discuss the same issues. They too were asked to provide a service quality rating on the 100-point scale. The data from both groups are presented in Table 16-5 (page 862).

Jeff's objective in collecting the sample data is to determine whether there is a difference in how the two groups rate the bank's loan processing service. Although Jeff has considered using a two-sample t test, he has concerns about the normality assumption and data level. Therefore, instead of the t test, he plans to use the Mann–Whitney U test. We begin by converting the ratings shown in Table 16-5 to rankings, with the lowest rating given the rank of 1. These rankings are shown in Table 16-6. Note also that the sum of the rankings for the two samples are shown in Table 16-6.

TABLE 16-5

First State Bank Service Quality Ratings

Commercial		Residential	
Customer	Rating	Customer	Rating
1	85	1	76
2	60	2	90
3	70	3	57
4	55	4	95
5	82	5	50
6	89	6	65
7	94	7	30
		8	74
		9	68
		10	61
		11	71
		12	77
		13	58

Figure 16-6 shows the hypothesis test using the Mann–Whitney U test. Notice that the critical value is obtained from the Mann–Whitney U table in Appendix N. As Figure 16-6 shows, the null hypothesis is not rejected since the U statistic exceeds the critical value of 20. Thus, these data do not indicate that the two classes of customers have differing perceptions of service quality.

TABLE 16-6

First State Bank Service Quality Ratings and Ranks

Commercial			Residential		
Customer	Rating	Rank	Customer	Rating	Rank
1	85	16	1	76	13
2	60	6	2	90	18
3	70	10	3	57	4
4	55	3	4	95	20
5	82	15	5	50	2
6	89	17	6	65	8
7	94	19	7	30	1
		Sum = 86	8	74	12
			9	68	9
			10	61	7
			11	71	11
			12	77	14
			13	58	5
					Sum = 124

FIGURE 16-6

Mann–Whitney U Test for First State Bank Example

Hypotheses:

H_0: There is no difference in average ratings by the two groups.
H_A: There is a difference in average ratings by the two groups.

$\alpha = 0.05$

Compute U_1 and U_2 based on the sample data:

$$U_1 = n_1 n_2 + [n_1(n_1 + 1)]/2 - \text{Sum of ranks}_1$$
$$= 7 \times 13 + [7(7 + 1)]/2 - 86$$
$$= 33$$

$$U_2 = n_1 n_2 + [n_2(n_2 + 1)]/2 - \text{Sum of ranks}_2$$
$$= 7 \times 13 + [13(13 + 1)]/2 - 124$$
$$= 58$$

Select the smaller U value and call it U_{test}. Then $U_{test} = 33$.

Since the larger of the sample sizes is between 9 and 20, the critical value for a two-tailed test with $\alpha = 0.05$ is found in the Mann–Whitney U table in Appendix N. Going across the top row to 13 and down the left-hand column to 7, we get the critical value at the intersection. The critical value is 20.

Decision Rule:

If $U_{test} \leq 20$, reject H_0.
Otherwise, do not reject H_0.

Since $U_{test} = 33 > 20$, we do not reject H_0.

MANN–WHITNEY U TEST—VERY SMALL SAMPLE SIZES

In Mann–Whitney U test applications where neither of the sample sizes exceeds 8, an alternative method is used to determine whether the null hypothesis should be rejected or not rejected. To illustrate this alternate method, consider an example involving an organization called Consumer's Check. This nonprofit organization performs product testing and publishes a monthly newsletter outlining its findings.

Recently, the testing department compared two brands of cellular phones. At issue was the number of minutes the phone could be used without having to recharge the battery. The engineers selected five phones of each brand at random. After the batteries were fully charged, the units were turned on and allowed to stay on until the batteries gave out. Table 16-7 (page 864) shows the time in minutes until each phone went dead. Table 16-8 shows the same data and the rankings from low to high.

We use equations 16-4 and 16-5 to compute U values for each sample as follows:

$$U_1 = n_1 n_2 + \frac{n_1(n_1 + 1)}{2} - \Sigma R_1$$

$$= 5 \times 5 + \frac{5(5 + 1)}{2} - 17$$

$$= 23$$

TABLE 16-7

Consumer's Check Cellular Phone Time Data

	Brand 1		Brand 2
	Time (min)		Time (min)
1	43	1	56
2	39	2	49
3	47	3	53
4	46	4	57
5	40	5	44

TABLE 16-8

Consumer's Check Cellular Phone Time Data and Rankings

	Brand 1			Brand 2	
	Time	Rank		Time	Rank
1	43	3	1	56	9
2	39	1	2	49	7
3	47	6	3	53	8
4	46	5	4	57	10
5	40	2	5	44	4
	Sum = 17			Sum = 38	

and

$$U_2 = n_2 n_1 + \frac{n_2(n_2 + 1)}{2} - \Sigma R_2$$

$$= 5 \times 5 + \frac{5(5 + 1)}{2} - 38$$

$$= 2$$

Recent advertisements by the makers of brand 2 state that it will outlast all other brands of cellular phones between charges. Thus, Consumer's Check's engineers plan to test the following null and alternative hypotheses:

H_0: There is no difference in usage time for the two phones.

H_A: Brand 2 will outlast brand 1.

They wish to test this using a one-tailed test at an $\alpha = 0.05$.

Since the larger of the sample sizes is less than 9, an alternate method of performing this test is required. The alternative approach utilizes a new table called the Mann–Whitney U probability table; it is shown in Appendix M. This table is actually made up of six subtables, corresponding to a larger sample size of 3 to 8. In our example, since both sample sizes are 5, the larger sample size is 5.

We go to the subtable for sample size of 5 in Appendix M. We then go across the top of this table to the sample size corresponding to the smaller sample, in our case 5. The values in the column below represent the cumulative probabilities of a given U value assuming H_0 is true.

In this example, the smaller U value is 2, which we denote as U_{test}. The probability of $U \leq 2$ from the table in Appendix M is 0.016. This is the p-value for U_{test}. Since this is smaller than $\alpha = 0.05$, we should reject H_0 and conclude that brand 2 does outlast brand 1, as claimed by the advertisements. If the probability from the table (the p-value) had exceeded our alpha level, the null hypothesis would not have been rejected.

If the test is two-tailed, the probabilities from the Mann–Whitney U probability table in Appendix M should be doubled and then compared to the alpha level.

One final point regarding the "very small sample" Mann–Whitney U test. Recall that we used equations 16-4 and 16-5 to compute U_1 and U_2. These equations are designed to be of special benefit when the sample sizes are larger. When we have very small samples, the U value can be determined in another way which may help to understand what U really means.

First, we list the rankings in order from Table 16-8, keeping track of the brand:

Ranking	1	2	3	4	5	6	7	8	9	10
Brand	1	1	1	2	1	1	2	2	2	2

Next, we find the U value by counting the number of times that a brand 2 rank precedes that of a brand 1 rank. This value is 2, since the rank of 4 associated with brand 2 exceeds the ranks of 5 and 6 associated with brand 1. In all other instances, brand 2's ranking exceeded brand 1 rankings. Thus, $U = 2$, which we found earlier as U_2.

We can also count the number of times brand 1 preceded brand 2 in the rankings. A careful count will yield a value of 23, which we found earlier as U_1. Thus, the U values represent the number of times a ranking for a given sample exceeds that of the second sample. Equations 16-4 and 16-5 represent easier ways of arriving at these values for larger samples.

TIED RANKINGS

In the examples we have used to illustrate the Mann–Whitney U test, the ranks contained no ties. That is, no two values in the raw data had the same value, so no two values had the same rank. However, in practice, you will likely encounter applications where ties will exist. For instance, suppose we have two samples of size 4 each with raw data shown as follows:

Group 1	*Group 2*
20	25
30	20
30	15
18	40

When we convert these raw data to ranks, the smallest value, 15, will receive a rank of 1, the value 18 will receive a rank of 2, but the next smallest value, 20, occurs twice. Since these two values would constitute ranks 3 and 4, we average these ranks as (3 + 4)/2 = 3.5 and assign the rank 3.5 to each value. Note also that there are two values equal to 30, which would be ranked 6 and 7. These ranks are averaged as (6 + 7)/2 = 6.5 and the rank of 6.5 is assigned to each number 30. The final rankings are shown as follows:

Group 1		*Group 2*	
Value	*Rank*	*Value*	*Rank*
20	3.5	25	5
30	6.5	20	3.5
30	6.5	15	1
18	2	40	8

When ties occur between values in the same group (as was the case with the value 30 in group 1), the computation of the U value is not affected. However, the U value is affected when the ties occur across the two samples. The effect is usually minor and typically does not alter the hypothesis test. However, if you encounter an application with a large number of tied observations, we suggest that you consult nonparametric references such as Siegel (see references at end of this chapter) for details on how to correct for tied rankings.

MANN–WHITNEY *U* TEST—LARGE SAMPLES

When you encounter an application with sample sizes in excess of 20, the previous approaches to the Mann–Whitney U test cannot be used because of table limitations. However, the U statistic approaches a normal distribution as the sample sizes increase. Therefore, the Mann–Whitney U test is conducted using a normal approximation approach where the mean and standard deviation are as given in equations 16-7 and 16-8, respectively:

$$\mu = \frac{n_1 n_2}{2} \qquad \text{16-6}$$

and

$$\sigma = \sqrt{\frac{(n_1)(n_2)(n_1 + n_2 + 1)}{12}} \qquad \text{16-7}$$

Equations 16-6 and 16-7 are used to form the test statistic in equation 16-8:

$$Z = \frac{U - \frac{n_1 n_2}{2}}{\sqrt{\frac{(n_1)(n_2)(n_1 + n_2 + 1)}{12}}} \tag{16-8}$$

Then, the Z value is computed and the standard normal distribution is applied as usual to test the null hypothesis.

SKILL DEVELOPMENT PROBLEMS FOR **SECTION 16-3**

The following exercises have been included to help you better understand the material in this section.

5. From a recent study we have collected the following data from two independent random samples:

Population 1	*Population 2*
405	300
450	340
290	400
370	250
345	270
460	410
425	435
275	390
380	225
330	210
500	395
215	315

   a. Based on these sample data, can it be concluded that the two populations have equal means? Use an $\alpha = 0.05$ and test using the t distribution. What assumptions are needed to use this distribution?
   b. Suppose we do not wish to make the assumptions indicated in part **a**. Use the appropriate nonparametric test to determine whether the populations have equal means. Test at the $\alpha = 0.05$ level.

6. The makers of the Plus 20 Hardcard, a plug-in hard disk unit on a PC board, have recently done a marketing research study in which they asked two independently selected groups to rate the Hardcard on a scale of 1 to 100,

with 100 being perfect satisfaction. The first group consisted of professional computer programmers. The second group consisted of home computer users. The company hoped to be able to say that the product would receive the same average ranking from each group. The following summary data were recorded.

Professionals	*Home Users*
$n = 10$	$n = 8$
Sum of ranks = 92	Sum of ranks = 79

Based on these data, what should the company conclude? Test at the $\alpha = 0.02$ level.

7. The Acme Speed Reading Company claims that graduates of its program have a higher average reading speed per minute than people who did not take the course. An independent agency conducted a study to determine whether this claim was justified. They selected a random sample of people who had taken the speed reading course and another random sample of people who had not taken the course. The agency was unwilling to make the assumption that the populations were normally distributed. Therefore, a nonparametric test was needed. The following summary data were observed:

With Course	*Without Course*
$n = 7$	$n = 5$
Sum of ranks = 42	Sum of ranks = 36

Assuming that higher ranks imply more words per minute being read, what should the testing agency conclude based on the sample data? Test at an $\alpha = 0.05$ level.

8. The Internal Revenue Service for a midwestern state recently conducted a study to determine whether there is a difference in average deductions taken for charitable contributions depending on whether the tax return was filed as a single or joint return. A random sample from each category was selected, with the following results:

Single	*Joint*
$n = 6$	$n = 8$
Sum of ranks = 43	Sum of ranks = 62

Based on these data, what should the IRS conclude? Use an $\alpha = 0.05$ level.

16-4 THE WILCOXON MATCHED-PAIRS SIGNED RANK TEST

The Mann–Whitney U test introduced in the previous section is a very useful nonparametric technique. However, its use is limited to those applications where the samples from the two populations are independent. As we discussed in Chapters 10 and 11, you will encounter decision situations in which the samples will be paired and are not independent. For example, a study may wish to compare quality attributes for two products. The decision maker may decide to have the same people rate both products to control for a source of variation that could affect her results. When the samples are paired in this manner, the Mann–Whitney U test cannot be employed.

A nonparametric test called the Wilcoxon matched-pairs test has been developed for situations where the decision maker has related samples and is unwilling or unable (due to data level limitations) to use the paired sample t test. To illustrate the Wilcoxon test, consider the following example.

SMALL-SAMPLE TEST

The Write-Perfect Corporation develops and markets word-processing software for personal computers. To differentiate its product from the many other fine word-processing packages on the market, Write-Perfect has built many macros into its software. Thus, according to Write-Perfect, once a user learns the macro keystrokes, many powerful writing tools available in all word processors become much easier to use.

As part of its product development testing program, software engineers at Write-Perfect have selected a focus group of seven people who frequently use a competitor's word-processing package. Each is given a task of preparing a lengthy document for publication using that software. This task will require that the subjects use many extensive features of the software. A systems program will monitor the subjects and count the number of times that each subject employs a "sophisticated tool" in the software. Then, these same seven individuals will get a training course in Write-Perfect software and macros. They will be given a similar task, to prepare a lengthy document for publication using the Write-Perfect software. Again the systems software will count the number of times that "sophisticated tools" are used. These data are shown in Table 16-9.

You should recognize that the samples in this application are not independent since the same subjects are used in both cases. If the software engineers performing the analysis are unwilling to make the normal distribution assumption re-

TABLE 16-9

Write-Perfect Corporation: Number of Sophisticated Tools Used

Subject	Before Training	After Training
1	11	24
2	18	20
3	23	19
4	15	20
5	16	13
6	22	28
7	8	15

quired of the paired-sample t test, they can use the Wilcoxon matched-pairs signed rank test. The hypothesis being tested in this application is as follows:

H_0: There is no difference in number of sophisticated tools used before vs. after the Write-Perfect training.

H_A: More sophisticated tools will be used after the Write-Perfect training.

To test this hypothesis using the Wilcoxon test, we convert the data in Table 16-9 to differences as shown in Table 16-10. Some explanation for Table 16-10 is needed. First, the column of differences, d, gives the "before" minus "after" differences. The next column is the rank of the d values from low to high. Note that the ranks are determined without considering the sign on the d value. However, once the rank is determined, the original sign on the d value is attached to the rank. For example, $d = -13$ is given a rank of -7, while $d = 4$ has a rank of 3.

To determine the values in the final column, we add the absolute values of the like-signed ranks. For instance, the ranks with plus signs add to 5 (2 + 3) and the ranks with a minus sign add to 23 (1 + 4 + 5 + 6 + 7). For the final column, we enter the ranks that give the smaller sum and label the sum, T. Thus, the values 3 and 2 are written in the final column. These values are summed to give $T = 5$.

Under the logic of the Wilcoxon test, if the null hypothesis is true, we would expect to find some large positive d values and some large negative d values. Thus, we would expect the sum of the positive ranks and the sum of the negative ranks to be about equal when H_0 is true. Thus, the value for T could just as easily come from either the positive or negative ranks if H_0 is true. Therefore, the null hypothesis should be rejected if the sum of the positive ranks is very much different from the sum of the negative ranks. The Wilcoxon test focuses on the T value. If it gets too small, the null hypothesis is rejected.

To determine whether T is too small, we consult the Wilcoxon table of critical T values in Appendix L. If the calculated T is less than or equal to the critical T

TABLE 16-10

Write-Perfect Corporation Ranked Data

Subject	Before Training	After Training	d	Rank of d	Rank with Less Frequent Sign
1	11	24	−13	−7	
2	18	20	−2	−1	
3	23	19	4	3	3
4	15	20	−5	−4	
5	16	13	3	2	2
6	22	28	−6	−5	
7	8	15	−7	−6	
					$T = 5$

from the table, the null hypothesis is rejected. For instance, with $\alpha = 0.025$ for our one-tailed test and $n = 7$, we get a critical value of 2. Since $T = 5 > 2$, we do not reject H_0. Thus, based on these sample data, the Write-Perfect Company has no basis for stating that its product will increase the number of sophisticated word-processing tools used in preparing documents.

TIES IN THE DATA

If the data for an individual case have the same values and therefore a d value of 0 is computed, that case is dropped from the analysis and the sample size is reduced accordingly. You should note that this procedure favors rejecting the null hypothesis since we are eliminating cases where the two samples have exactly the same values.

If two or more d values have the same absolute values, we assign the same rank to each one using the same approach as with the Mann–Whitney U test. For example, if we have two d values that tie for rank 4, we average them as $(4 + 5)/2 = 4.5$ and assign both a rank of 4.5. Studies have shown that this method of assigning ranks to ties has little effect on the Wilcoxon test results. For a more complete discussion of the effect of ties on the Wilcoxon matched-pairs signed rank test, please see the text by Marascuilo and McSweeney referenced at the end of this chapter.

LARGE-SAMPLE WILCOXON TEST

If the sample size (number of matched pairs) exceeds 25, the Wilcoxon table of critical T values cannot be used. However, statistical theory has shown that the distribution of T values is approximately normal with a mean and standard deviation given by equations 16-9 and 16-10, respectively:

$$\mu = \frac{n(n+1)}{4} \tag{16-9}$$

and

$$\sigma = \sqrt{\frac{n(n+1)(2n+1)}{24}} \tag{16-10}$$

The test statistic is given by equation 16-11:

$$Z = \frac{T - \frac{n(n+1)}{4}}{\sqrt{\frac{n(n+1)(2n+1)}{24}}} \quad \textbf{16-11}$$

Then, the Z value is compared to the critical value from the standard normal table in the usual manner.

SKILL DEVELOPMENT PROBLEMS FOR **SECTION 16-4**

The following exercises have been included to help you better understand the material in this section.

9. Consider the following data for two paired samples.

Case #	*Sample 1*	*Sample 2*
1	258	304
2	197	190
3	400	500
4	350	340
5	237	250
6	400	358
7	370	390
8	130	100

Test the following null and alternative hypotheses at an $\alpha = 0.05$ level:

H_0: There is no difference between the two population distributions.
H_A: There is a difference between the two populations.

10. Property taxes are based on assessed values of property. In most states, the law requires that assessed values be "at or near" market value of the property. In one Washington State county, a tax protest group has claimed that assessed values are higher than market values. To address this claim, the county tax assessor, together with representatives from the protest group, has selected fifteen properties at random which have sold within the past 6

months. Both parties agree that the sale price was the market value at the time of the sale.

The assessor then listed the assessed values and the sales values side-by-side as shown:

House	*Assessed Value*	*Market Value*
1	$102,000	$ 98,000
2	76,000	82,400
3	49,000	54,300
4	98,500	98,500
5	114,000	118,000
6	135,000	130,000
7	205,000	198,900
8	87,500	90,000
9	50,000	49,800
10	123,000	122,000
11	78,500	80,000
12	145,000	150,900
13	67,000	65,200
14	119,000	120,700
15	234,000	220,000

a. Assuming that the population of assessed values and the population of market values have the same shape distribution and that they may differ only with respect to means, state the appropriate null and alternative hypotheses.

b. Test the hypotheses using an $\alpha = 0.01$ level.

11. A decision maker has collected data for forty matched pairs of cattle showing weight gain on two different feed supplements. His purpose in collecting the data is to determine whether there is a difference in the distributions of weight gain for the two supplements. He has no preconceived idea about which supplement might produce higher weight gain. He wishes to test using an $\alpha = 0.05$ level.

a. State the appropriate null and alternative hypotheses.

b. Assuming that the T value for these data is 480, what should be concluded? Use the large-sample Wilcoxon matched-pairs signed rank test normal approximation.

12. Radio advertisements have been stressing the virtues of an audio tape program to help children learn to read. To test whether this tape program can have a quick improvement on reading ability, ten children were given a nationally recognized reading test that measures reading ability. The same ten children were then given the tapes to listen to for 4 hours spaced over a

2-day period. The children were then tested again. The test scores observed were as follows:

Child	*Before*	*After*
1	60	63
2	40	38
3	78	77
4	53	50
5	67	74
6	88	96
7	77	80
8	60	70
9	64	65
10	75	75

a. State the appropriate null and alternative hypotheses.
b. Use the Wilcoxon matched-pairs signed rank test to test the null hypothesis at the $\alpha = 0.025$ level.

16-5 KRUSKAL–WALLIS ONE-WAY ANALYSIS OF VARIANCE

Section 16-3 showed that the Mann–Whitney U test is a useful nonparametric procedure for determining whether two independent samples are from populations with the same mean. However, as discussed in Chapter 12, many decisions involve comparing more than two populations. That chapter introduced one-way analysis of variance and showed how, if certain assumptions are satisfied, the F distribution can be used to test the hypothesis of equal population means. However, what if the decision makers are not willing to assume normally distributed populations? In that case, they can turn to a nonparametric procedure to compare the populations. **Kruskal–Wallis one-way analysis of variance** is the nonparametric counterpart to the analysis of variance procedure presented in Chapter 12. It is applicable anytime the variable in question has a continuous distribution, the data are at least ordinal, the samples are independent, and the samples come from populations whose only possible difference is that at least one may have a different central location than the others.

The Bartholomew Company is considering acquiring a new computer system to handle its on-line data-processing activities, including inventory management, production scheduling, and general accounting and billing applications. Based on cost and performance standards, Gladys Coil, Bartholomew's data-processing manager, has reduced the possible suppliers to three. One critical factor for Gladys is down time (the time when the computer is nonoperational). When the computer goes down, the on-line applications are halted, and normal business activities are interrupted. Gladys has received, from each supplier, a list of firms that are using the computer system Bartholomew is considering. From these lists

TABLE 16-11

Computer Down Times for the Bartholomew Company Example (Hours/Month)

System A	System B	System C
4.0	6.9	0.5
3.7	11.3	1.4
5.1	21.7	1.0
2.0	9.2	1.7
4.6	6.5	3.6
9.3	4.9	5.2
2.7	12.2	1.3
2.5	11.7	6.8
4.8	10.5	14.1

Gladys selected random samples of nine users of each computer system. In a telephone interview, she found the number of hours of down time in the previous month for each system. The down times are shown in Table 16-11.

To use the Kruskal–Wallis analysis of variance here, we first replace each down-time measurement by its *relative ranking* within all groups combined. The smallest down time is given a rank of 1, the next smallest a rank of 2, and so forth, until all down times for the three systems have been replaced by their relative rankings. Table 16-12 shows these rankings for the twenty-seven observations. Notice that the rankings are summed for each computer system. The Kruskal–Wallis test will determine whether these sums are so different that it is not likely they came from populations with equal means.

If the samples actually do come from populations with equal means (that is, the three systems have the same per-month average down time), then the H statistic, calculated by equation 16-12 as follows, will be distributed as a chi-square

TABLE 16-12

Rankings of Computer Down Times for the Bartholomew Company Example

System A	System B	System C
11	19	1
10	23	4
15	27	2
6	20	5
12	17	9
21	14	16
8	25	3
7	24	18
13	22	26
Sum of ranks = 103	Sum of ranks = 191	Sum of ranks = 84

variable with $K - 1$ degrees of freedom, where K equals the number of samples under study:

$$H = \frac{12}{N(N+1)} \sum_{i=1}^{K} \frac{R_i^2}{n_i} - 3(N+1) \quad \text{(16-12)}$$

where

N = Total of all observations

K = Number of samples

R_i = Sum of the ranks in the ith sample

n_i = Size of the ith sample

If H is larger than χ^2_{critical}, the hypothesis of equal means is rejected, and Gladys would conclude that the populations from which the samples were selected have different means. Figure 16-7 presents the hypotheses and statistical

FIGURE 16-7

Kruskal–Wallis One-Way Analysis of Variance Test for the Bartholomew Company Example

Hypotheses:

H_0: The mean down times are equal for all three computer systems.
H_A: The mean down times are not equal for all three computer systems.

$\alpha = 0.10$

Using the rankings and sums in Table 16-12,

$$H = \frac{12}{N(N+1)} \sum_{i=1}^{K} \frac{R_i^2}{n_i} - 3(N+1)$$

$$= \frac{12}{27(27+1)}\left[\frac{(103)^2}{9} + \frac{(191)^2}{9} + \frac{(84)^2}{9}\right] - 3(27+1)$$

$$= 11.49$$

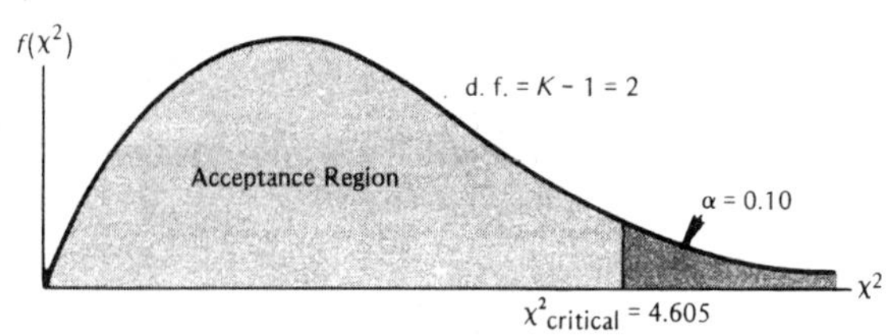

Decision Rule:

If $H \leq \chi^2_{\text{critical}}$, accept H_0.
If $H > \chi^2_{\text{critical}}$, reject H_0.

Since $H = 11.49 > \chi^2_{\text{critical}} = 4.605$, reject H_0.

test for the Bartholomew example. The Kruskal–Wallis one-way analysis of variance shows that Gladys Coil should conclude that the three computer systems *do not* have equal average down times. From this analysis, the supplier of computer system B would most likely be eliminated from consideration unless other factors such as price or service offset the apparent longer down times.

LIMITATIONS AND OTHER CONSIDERATIONS

The Kruskal–Wallis one-way analysis of variance does *not* require the assumption of normality and is therefore often used instead of the analysis of variance technique discussed in Chapter 12. However, the Kruskal–Wallis test as discussed here applies only if the sample sizes from each population are at least 5, the samples are independently selected, and each population has the same distribution except for a possible difference in location.

When ranking observations, decision makers will sometimes encounter ties. When ties occur, each observation is given the mean rank for which it is tied. The H statistic is influenced by ties and should be corrected by dividing equation 16-12 by equation 16-13.

$$1 - \frac{\sum_{i=1}^{g} (t_i^3 - t_i)}{N^3 - N} \qquad \text{16-13}$$

where

g = Number of different groups of ties

t = Number of tied observations in the tied group of scores

N = Total number of observations

Thus the correct formula for calculating the Kruskal–Wallis H statistic when ties are present is equation 16-14:

$$H = \frac{\dfrac{12}{N(N+1)} \sum_{i=1}^{K} \dfrac{R_i^2}{n_i} - 3(N+1)}{1 - \dfrac{\sum_{i=1}^{g} (t_i^3 - t_i)}{N^3 - N}} \qquad \text{16-14}$$

Correcting for ties increases H and thus makes rejecting the null hypothesis more likely than if the correction is not used. A rule of thumb is that if no more than 25% of the observations are involved in ties, the correction factor is not required. Solved Problem 1 at the end of this chapter illustrates the use of the correction for ties for the Kruskal–Wallis test.

SKILL DEVELOPMENT PROBLEMS FOR **SECTION 16-5**

The following exercises have been included to help you gain a better understanding of the material in this section.

13. A consumer testing agency has been contracted to test user ratings for the three leading brands of running shoes. The rating scale is 1 to 40, with 40 being perfect. The following results were recorded.

Shoe 1	*Shoe 2*	*Shoe 3*
21	17	29
25	15	38
36	34	28
35	22	27
33	16	14
23	19	26
31	30	39
32	20	36

a. What assumptions are required to employ the analysis of variance methods discussed in Chapter 12?

b. If the testing agency does not want to make the assumptions stated in your answer to part **a**, based on these sample data, what should the testing agency conclude about the average ratings for the three brands of shoes? Test at an $\alpha = 0.05$ level.

14. A study was conducted by the sports department of a national network television station in which the objective was to determine whether a difference exists between average annual salaries of NBA basketball players, NFL football players, and major league baseball players. The analyst in charge of the study believes that the normal distribution assumption is violated in this study. Thus, she thinks that a nonparametric test is in order.

The following summary data have been collected.

NBA	*NFL*	*Baseball*
$n = 20$	$n = 30$	$n = 40$
$R = 1{,}710$	$R = 1{,}100$	$R = 1{,}340$

Based on these data, what can be concluded about the average salaries for the three sports? Test at the $\alpha = 0.05$ level. Assume no ties.

15. Referring to Problem 14, suppose that there were forty ties at eight different salary levels. The following shows how many scores were ties at each salary level:

Level	*t*
1	2
2	3
3	2
4	4
5	8
6	10
7	6
8	5

Use the appropriate adjustment for ties and adjust the test conducted in Problem 14.

16-6 SPEARMAN RANK CORRELATION COEFFICIENT

Chapter 13 introduced you to a measure of the strength of the linear relationship between two variables called the *correlation coefficient.* Recall that the correlation coefficient ranges between ± 1.0, with a value of 0 indicating no linear relationship between the two variables. Recall also that Chapter 13 introduced a test for the statistical significance of the correlation coefficient. This test assumes that the data for the two variables are at least interval scaled and the joint distribution of the variables is bivariate normal. However, in cases where the level of data measurement is ordinal or when the bivariate normal distribution assumption seems not to be satisfied, an alternative nonparametric measure of correlation called **Spearman's rho** can be used.

Consider, for example, the Porter Company, which markets photocopiers in the eastern United States. Recently, the company's marketing department undertook a study of its clients to determine whether there is a significant correlation between the number of copies made per month and the number of employees working for the company. It hoped this information would be useful in helping clients evaluate their copier needs.

Table 16-13 (page 880) presents data collected by the marketing department from twelve clients selected at random. The individual in charge of the study wishes to determine whether there is significant correlation, but does not feel justified in making the assumption of bivariate normal distributions. Thus, he has decided to calculate the nonparametric Spearman correlation coefficient. The first step is to convert the data in Table 16-13 to ranks, as shown in Table 16-14. Note that the ranks are done separately for each variable.

TABLE 16-13

Sample Data for the Porter Company Example

No. Copies Used (000s) Y	Employees X
23.0	140
11.0	101
9.5	43
3.5	55
20.0	79
14.5	134
6.3	75
42.0	211
3.1	78
2.0	36
15.0	45
5.5	11

TABLE 16-14

Data in Ranked Form for the Porter Company Example

No. Copies Used (000s) Y	Employees X
11	11
7	9
6	3
3	5
10	8
8	10
5	6
12	12
2	7
1	2
9	4
4	1

The Spearman correlation coefficient is computed using equation 16-15.

$$\text{rho} = r_s = 1 - \frac{6 \sum_{i=1}^{n} d_i^2}{n^3 - n} \quad (16\text{-}15)$$

where

$d_i = Y_i - X_i$ (difference in ranks)

n = Sample size

TABLE 16-15

Spearman Correlation Coefficient Computation for the Porter Company Example

Y	X	d	d^2
11	11	0	0
7	9	−2	4
6	3	3	9
3	5	−2	4
10	8	2	4
8	10	−2	4
5	6	−1	1
12	12	0	0
2	7	−5	25
1	2	−1	1
9	4	5	25
4	1	3	9
		Sum of squared differences =	86

$$r_s = 1 - \frac{6\,\Sigma d^2}{n^3 - n}$$

$$= 1 - \frac{6(86)}{1{,}728 - 12}$$

$$= 1 - 0.301$$

$$= 0.699$$

Table 16-15 shows the calculations for the Spearman correlation coefficient. The correlation is positive 0.699 for these sample data. Now the question remains whether the true population correlation is 0. If the sample size exceeds 10, the test statistic is approximated by a t statistic with $n - 2$ degrees of freedom, as shown in equation 16-16:

$$t = r_s \sqrt{\frac{n - 2}{1 - r_s^2}} \qquad \text{(16-16)}$$

The hypotheses to be tested are

$$H_0: \quad \rho = 0.0$$
$$H_A: \quad \rho \neq 0.0$$

Thus, for the Porter Company example, we compute the test statistic as follows:

$$t = 0.699 \sqrt{\frac{12 - 2}{1 - 0.699^2}}$$

$$= 3.092$$

To test the null hypothesis using the t statistic, we go to the t-distribution table with $n - 2 = 10$ degrees of freedom for the appropriate level of alpha. Using an alpha level of 0.05, we get a critical t value equal to 2.228.

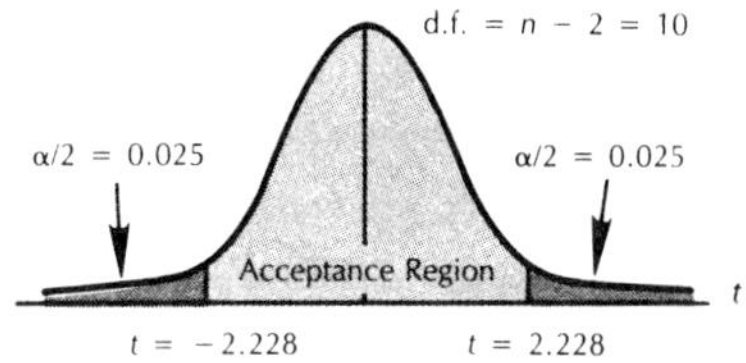

Decision Rule:

If $t > 2.228$, reject H_0.

If $t < -2.228$, reject H_0.

Otherwise, do not reject H_0.

Since $t = 3.092 > 2.228$, reject H_0 and conclude that there exists a significant positive correlation between the number of copies used and the number of employees working at the company.

Note that we have employed the t distribution to test the significance of the Spearman correlation coefficient. However, the assumption of bivariate normal populations is not necessary since we used rank data to compute the Spearman rho value.

Note also that the use of the t distribution for testing the significance of the Spearman correlation coefficient is limited to cases where the sample size is at least 10. Finally, ties are handled by giving each tied value the mean of the rank positions for which it is tied. Therefore, if the ranked observations were 10, 12, 12, 13, the rankings would be 1, 2.5, 2.5, 4.

SKILL DEVELOPMENT PROBLEMS FOR **SECTION 16-6**

The following exercises have been included to help you gain a better understanding of the material presented in this section.

16. The following data were collected for two variables, X and Y:

X	Y
112	3.8
98	2.7
123	3.5
146	4.1
130	3.4
100	2.9
110	3.7
113	3.9
133	4.0
149	4.4
90	2.5
146	4.5

a. Compute the Spearman correlation coefficient for these two sets of data. Indicate what it measures.
b. Test whether the correlation is significant at the $\alpha = 0.05$ level.

17. The State Golf Association recently performed a study in which data were collected on golfers' handicaps and the number of rounds played during the year. The following sample data were collected:

Handicap	*Rounds Played*
13	24
23	34
17	23
6	22
2	40
15	35
18	11
4	46
8	25
10	17
16	42

a. Based on these data, what is the Spearman correlation coefficient?
b. Test at the $\alpha = 0.05$ level whether the correlation is statistically significant.

18. Executives were asked to rate the Federal Reserve Board relative to its handling of monetary policy. These ratings were made on a scale of 1 to 20. The ratings were then to be correlated with the age of the executive. The sample data are shown as follows:

Rating	*Age*
11	35
17	47
11	29
15	53
16	45
13	30
17	50
19	62
12	32
10	34
13	41
14	50
19	55
17	45
18	63

a. Compute the correlation coefficient and explain what it means with respect to these data.

TABLE 16-17

SPSS-X Output: Mann–Whitney *U* Test

```
----- MANN–WHITNEY U - WILCOXON RANK SUM W TEST
      VAR18       INCOME
   BY VAR10       SEX
      MEAN RANK   CASES
          23.20   22 VAR10 = 1.00 MALE
          27.30   28 VAR10 = 2.00 FEMALE
                  --
                  50 TOTAL
                           CORRECTED FOR TIES
      U         W          Z          2-TAILED P
    257.5     510.5      -0.9871      0.3236
```

FIGURE 16-9

SPSS-X Commands: Mann–Whitney *U* Test

```
UNNUMBERED
TITLE DESCRIPTIVE STATISTICS EXAMPLES
FILE HANDLE KIVZ NAME='KIVZ DATA C'
DATA LIST FILE=KIVZ LIST/VAR01 to VAR19
VARIABLE LABELS
   VAR01 'NATIONAL NEWS STATION'
   VAR02 'LOCAL NEWS STATION'
   VAR03 'NEWS RATING'
   VAR04 'SPORTS RATING'
   VAR05 'WEATHER RATING'
   VAR06 'ANCHOR RATING'
   VAR07 'SPORTSCASTER RATING'
   VAR08 'OVERALL RATING'
   VAR09 'NATIONAL INFLUENCE'
   VAR10 'SEX'
   VAR11 'MARITAL STATUS'
   VAR12 'NUMBER EMPLOYED'
   VAR13 'HOME STATUS '
   VAR14 'YEARS AT RESIDENCE'
   VAR15 'YEARS IN STATE'
   VAR16 'EDUCATION'
   VAR17 'AGE'
   VAR18 'INCOME'
   VAR19 'HOURS OF TV'
VALUE LABELS
   VAR01 1 'CHANNEL 5' 2 'CHANNEL 3' 3 'CHANNEL 8' 4
         'UNDECIDED'/
   VAR02 1 'CHANNEL 3' 2 'CHANNEL 8' 3 'CHANNEL 5' 4
         'UNDECIDED'/
   VAR03 TO VAR08 1 'POOR' 2 'FAIR' 3 'GOOD' 4 'VERY GOOD' 5
         'EXCEL'/
   VAR09 1 'TRUE' 2 'FALSE' 3 'UNDECIDED'/
   VAR10 1 'MALE' 2 'FEMALE'/
   VAR11 1 'SINGLE' 2 'DIVORCED' 3 'MARRIED' 4 'OTHER'/
   VAR13 1 'RENTING' 2 'BUYING'/
   VAR16 1 'GRADE SCHOOL' 2 'SOME COLLEGE' 3 'VOTECH' 4 'HIGH
         SCHOOL' 5 'COLLEGE GRAD' 6 'GRADUATE WORK'
NPAR TESTS M-W = VAR18 BY VAR10 (1,2)
```

TABLE 16-18 MINITAB Output: Kruskal–Wallis One-Way ANOVA

LEVEL	NOBS	MEDIAN	AVE. RANK	Z VALUE
1	9	45.00	26.6	0.25
2	25	45.00	25.6	0.04
3	11	42.00	25.7	0.06
4	5	35.00	22.6	-0.47
OVERALL	50		25.5	

H = 0.2536
H(ADJ. FOR TIES) = 0.2539

FIGURE 16-10

MINITAB Commands: Kruskal–Wallis One-Way ANOVA

```
MTB> READ 'KIVZ5' into C1-C19
MTB> NAME C17 'AGE'
MTB> NAME C2 'LOCAL'
MTB> OUTFILE = 'PRINTER'
MTB> KRUSKAL-WALLIS C17 C2
```

The GB-STAT software contains a variety of nonparametric tests including several introduced in this chapter. Figure 16-11 shows the menu of nonparametric tools available in GB-STAT. To illustrate GB-STAT, we will use menu item number 8, the ONE SAMPLE RUNS test. The application relates to the Clark Fork Sand and Gravel Company, which supplies gravel and fill dirt for contractors in the Missoula, Montana, area.

Recently, Robert Gianchetta, operations manager at the main gravel site, asked the business research center at the local university to help him analyze his loading operation. As part of the analysis, the university is planning to develop a model of incoming trucks and the loading process to assess whether improvements can be made. The modelers plan to base the truck arrivals on the Poisson distribution if the actual truck arrivals meet the assumption of randomness. To test this, a sequential sample of forty trucks is observed and the time between arrivals (in minutes) has been recorded. These times are referred to as the interarrival times. The data are shown in Table 16-19 (page 888). These data are loaded into GB-STAT using its full screen data editing capability. Then we select the ONE SAMPLE RUNS option shown in Figure 16-11. GB-STAT provides us the option of dividing the data at the mean, the median, or a user-designated value. We have selected the mean interarrival rate.

FIGURE 16-11

GB-STAT Nonparametric Menu

```
GB-STAT Ver 2.0                    Statistics Options

                                    1. RANGE STATISTICS
                                    2. CHI-SQUARE (CROSSTABS)
                                    3. MANN-WHITNEY U
                                    4. WILCOXON SIGNED-RANK
                                    5. COCHRAN'S Q
                                    6. KRUSKAL-WALLIS ANOVA
                                    7. FRIEDMAN'S ANOVA
                                  > 8. ONE SAMPLE RUNS
                                    9. CORRELATION

<F1>: MAIN  <F2>: MANAGE  <F3>: STATS  <F4>: GRAPHS  <F5>: DATA  <CTRL-C>: ABORT
<F6>: SHELL  <F7>: PRINT  <F8>: DISK  <F9>: REPEAT  <F10>: QUIT  <CTRL-D>: DESCP
```

TABLE 16-19

Clark Ford Sand and Gravel Company Truck Interarrival Times

Truck	Interarrival Time	Truck	Interarrival Time
1	12	21	14
2	17	22	7
3	8	23	10
4	22	24	30
5	11	25	23
6	9	26	19
7	11	27	6
8	32	28	3
9	7	29	15
10	6	30	17
11	15	31	40
12	40	32	32
13	20	33	11
14	7	34	27
15	5	35	15
16	6	36	9
17	3	37	30
18	26	38	28
19	19	39	25
20	22	40	14

The resulting GB-STAT output is shown in Table 16-20. The output shows that there were 19 runs. Of the 40 trucks, 18 arrived at interarrival times exceeding the mean of 16.825 minutes and 22 trucks had interarrival times less than the mean. Because of the large sample size, the normal approximation approach described in Section 16-2 is employed. The output shows the expected number of runs to be 20.8 with a standard deviation of 3.0894 runs. The calculated Z value is -0.5826. The two-tailed p-value is computed to be 0.5601. Thus, at any alpha

TABLE 16-20

GB-STAT Output: Runs Test for the Clark Ford Sand and Gravel Company

ONE SAMPLE RUNS TEST

SAMPLE	CASES	TEST VALUE
TIME	40	16.825

OBSERVED RUNS	EXPECTED RUNS	GREATER THAN	LESS THAN	SD OF RUNS
19	20.8	18	22	3.0894

SIGNIFICANCE TEST FOR LARGE SAMPLES

Z VALUE	2-TAILED P
−.5826	.5601

less than 0.5601, these data would lead us to "accept" the null hypothesis that the truck interarrival rates are random. Thus, the assumption of randomness required for the Poisson distribution is not refuted by these sample data.

16-8 CONCLUSIONS

Many people make the mistake of learning one or two statistical techniques and then using these techniques in all situations. Surprisingly, some people even get emotional about being able to analyze a particular problem using their favorite technique. As future managerial decision makers, you cannot afford the luxury of defining a problem situation so you can apply your favorite technique. Statistics should be an aid to decision making, not an end in itself.

Many powerful statistical tools discussed in this book rest on the assumptions that the data being analyzed can be measured by at least an interval scale and that the underlying populations being analyzed are normal. If these assumptions come close to being satisfied, many of the tools discussed prior to this chapter apply and are useful. However, in many practical situations these assumptions just do not apply, in which case the tools discussed in this chapter may be appropriate. In any case, nonparametric statistical tests should be part of every decision maker's tools. There are many other nonparametric statistical techniques that have been developed for specific applications. Many are aimed at situations involving small samples. You should consult the references at the end of the chapter for further reading.

CHAPTER GLOSSARY

distribution-free test A statistical test for a null hypothesis, H_0, that provides a Type I error probability equal to alpha regardless of the underlying population(s).

hypothesis test The process of formulating and implementing a decision rule that, on the basis of the sample data, leads the decision maker either to "accept" or to reject the null hypothesis.

Kruskal–Wallis test A nonparametric test to determine whether three or more populations have equal means. The data must be at least ordinal level and the samples must be independent.

Mann–Whitney *U* test A nonparametric test, based on ranks, used to determine whether two populations have different means.

nonparametric statistical procedure A statistical procedure that has certain desirable properties that hold under relatively mild assumptions regarding the underlying populations.

rank order Observations that are ordered according to size and assigned numbers (called ranks) that correspond to their positions in the ordering. Most nonparametric techniques require that the rank order be lowest to highest.

Spearman's rank correlation coefficient A nonparametric measure of the strength of the linear relationship between two variables. The computation is based on ranks and the test of significance does *not* require that the populations be bivariate normal.

CHAPTER FORMULAS

Kruskal–Wallis H statistic

$$H = \frac{12}{N(N+1)} \sum_{i=1}^{K} \frac{R_i^2}{n_i} - 3(N+1)$$

Kruskal–Wallis adjustment factor

If 25% or more of the ranked observations are ties, divide H by

$$1 - \frac{\sum_{i=1}^{R} (t_i^3 - t_i)}{N^3 - N}$$

Mann–Whitney U

$$U_1 = n_1 n_2 + \frac{n_1(n_1+1)}{2} - \Sigma R_1$$

$$U_2 = n_2 n_1 + \frac{n_2(n_2+1)}{2} - \Sigma R_2$$

For large samples

$$\text{Mean} = \frac{n_1 n_2}{2}$$

$$\text{St. Dev.} = \sqrt{\frac{n_1 n_2(n_1 + n_2 + 1)}{12}}$$

$$Z = \frac{U_{\text{test}} - \frac{n_1 n_2}{2}}{\sqrt{\frac{n_1 n_2(n_1 + n_2 + 1)}{12}}}$$

Runs Test—Large Sample

$$\text{Mean} = \frac{2n_1 n_2}{n_1 + n_2} + 1$$

$$\text{St. Dev.} = \sqrt{\frac{(2n_1 n_2)(2n_1 n_2 - n_1 - n_2)}{(n_1 + n_2)^2(n_1 + n_2 - 1)}}$$

Spearman's rho

$$r_s = 1 - \frac{6 \sum_{i=1}^{n} d_i^2}{n^3 - n}$$

Wilcoxon Matched-Pairs—Large Sample

$$\text{Mean} = \frac{n(n + 1)}{4}$$

$$\text{St. Dev.} = \sqrt{\frac{n(n + 1)(2n + 1)}{24}}$$

SOLVED PROBLEM

1. The Bixby Company operates in three states. Its primary business is to give review seminars for individuals who plan to sit for the CPA (certified public accountant) examination. Bixby has three teams that put on the seminars, one for each state. Michelle Bixby is quite concerned that there be consistent performance by the three teams. She believes that she can measure the success of her teams by the CPA exam scores received by persons who have taken the seminars.

   Michelle wishes to determine whether the average score received by those who took the seminar is the same in the three states. Because of the way the test is scored, she is *not* willing to assume the populations are normally distributed. A sample of twelve scores from each state provided the following data:

Maine	*New York*	*New Jersey*
90	90	55
65	88	55
72	83	90
83	83	83
65	65	65
50	65	65
65	83	60
83	83	55
83	90	65
55	90	72
72	65	90
65	72	65

   Based on these data, what should Michelle conclude about the average scores of the three states? Use an alpha level of 0.10. Assume the population variances are equal.

Advertising Plan 1	*Advertising Plan 2*
1,711	2,100
1,915	2,210
1,905	1,950
2,153	3,004
1,504	2,725
1,195	2,619
2,103	2,483
1,601	2,520
1,580	1,904
1,475	1,875
1,588	1,943

24. Two small regional life insurance companies are being studied by the Triangle Life Insurance Company as candidates for a possible merger. Triangle can merge with only one of these regional companies at this time and, as part of its study, wishes to determine whether there is a difference in the average annual premiums received by the two regional companies. The following data represent sample policy premiums for each company:

Company 1	*Company 2*
$246	$300
211	305
235	308
270	325
411	340
310	295
450	320
502	330
311	240
200	360

Do these data indicate a difference in mean annual premiums for the two companies? Apply the Mann–Whitney U test with an alpha level of 0.10.

25. Referring to Problem 24, apply the t test to determine whether the data indicate a difference between annual premiums for the two regional companies. Use an alpha level of 0.10. Also indicate what assumptions must be made to apply the t test.

26. The Style-Rite Company of Spokane, Washington, makes windbreaker jackets for people who play golf and who are active outdoors during the spring and fall months. The company recently developed a new material and is in the process of test marketing jackets made from the material. As part of this test-marketing effort, ten people were each supplied with a jacket made from the original material and asked to wear it for 2 months, washing it at least twice during that time. A second group of ten people was given a jacket made from the new material and asked to wear it for 2 months with the same washing requirements.

Following the 2-month trial period, the individuals were asked to rate the jackets on a scale of 0 to 100, with 0 being the worst performance rating and 100 being the best. The ratings for each material are shown as follows:

Original Material	*New Material*
76	55
34	90
70	72
23	17
45	56
80	69
10	91
46	95
67	86
75	74

It is expected that, on the average, the performance ratings will be superior for the new material. Do the sample data support this belief at an alpha level of 0.05? Discuss.

27. A study was recently conducted by the Bonniville Power Association to determine attitudes regarding the association's policies in western U.S. states. One part of the study asked respondents to rate the performance of the BPA on its responsiveness to environmental issues. The following responses were obtained for a sample of twelve urban residents and ten rural residents. The ratings are on a 1 to 100 scale, with 100 being perfect:

Urban	*Rural*
76	55
90	80
86	94
60	40
43	85
96	92
50	77
20	68
30	35
82	59
75	
84	

Based on the sample data, should the BPA conclude that there is no difference between the urban and rural residents with respect to average environmental rating? Test using an alpha level of 0.02.

28. Referring to Problem 27, perform the appropriate parametric statistical test and indicate the assumptions necessary to use this test that were not required by the Mann–Whitney tests. Use an alpha level of 0.02.

29. The Miltmore Corporation performs consulting services for companies that think they have image problems. Recently, Miltmore was approached by the

Bluedot Beer Company. Bluedot executives were concerned that the company's image, relative to its two closest competitors', had diminished. Miltmore conducted an image study in which a random sample of eight people were asked to rate Bluedot's image. Five people were asked to rate competitor A's image, and ten people were asked to rate competitor B's image. The image ratings were made on a 100-point scale, with 100 being the best possible rating. The results of the sampling were

Bluedot	*Competitor A*	*Competitor B*
40	95	50
60	53	80
70	55	82
40	92	87
55	90	93
90		51
20		63
20		72
		96
		88

a. Based on these sample results, should Bluedot conclude that there is an image difference between the three companies? Select your own alpha level and justify it.
b. Should Bluedot infer that its image has been damaged by last year's federal government recall of its product? Discuss why or why not.
c. Why might the decision maker wish to use parametric analysis of variance rather than the corresponding nonparametric test? Discuss.

30. A major car manufacturer is experimenting with three new methods of pollution control. The testing lab must determine whether the three methods produce equal pollution reductions. Readings from a calibrated carbon monoxide meter are taken from groups of engines randomly equipped with one of the three control units. The following data are found:

Method 1	*Method 2*	*Method 3*
45	39	26
49	37	31
48	31	32
50	42	40
33	43	44
46	47	41
46	46	34
47	27	28
46	29	30
39	31	34
	36	35
		38

Use the Kruskal–Wallis test to determine whether the three pollution-control methods will produce equal results.

31. The Luguna Hills Golf Club recently conducted a study of its playing members to determine whether a linear relationship exists between frequency of play and golf handicap. Data were collected over a 3-month period for twelve golfers selected at random from the club's membership list. Variable Y is handicap at the end of the 3-month period and variable X is the number of times the member played golf during the 3-month period. All golfers started with a 20 handicap.

Y	X
22	13
18	30
15	19
20	24
13	33
29	15
16	20
12	31
17	44
21	10
23	12
14	28

a. Plot these data on a scatter plot and verbally describe what, if any, relationship is present in the data.

b. Referring to Chapter 13, compute the correlation coefficient and test for significance at the alpha level of 0.05. Indicate what assumptions are required to test for statistical significance.

32. Referring to Problem 31, suppose the decision maker in charge of the golf study is not willing to make the assumptions necessary to test the significance of the correlation coefficient. As an alternative, compute the Spearman correlation coefficient and test for statistical significance, using an alpha level of 0.05. Comment on the results.

33. The financial analyst for Shafer and Associates regularly attempts to correlate stock prices for companies trading on the New York Stock Exchange with various financial variables from the company's financial records. One such study involved a random sample of fourteen companies in which stock price was related to earnings per share. The data collected in that study are shown as follows:

Stock Price	*Earnings per Share*
8.125	1.43
11.500	2.08
33.375	4.19
21.125	1.90
55.625	4.78

(*continued*)

Stock Price	*Earnings per Share*
23.625	2.56
33.500	5.12
14.000	0.75
67.750	3.59
72.125	5.23
4.625	0.89
19.000	1.43
26.750	2.90
30.875	3.01

Plot the two variables on a scatter plot and describe the apparent relationship between them.

34. Referring to Problem 33, compute the Spearman correlation coefficient for the two variables and test to determine whether the true correlation is significantly different from 0. Use an alpha level of 0.10.

35. A group of ten financial experts was asked to select a company at random from those selling shares on the New York Stock Exchange. Each expert then was asked to rate on a scale from 1 to 100 the financial position of the company by looking at the company's financial statement for the year ended 1986. They were then asked to examine the same company's financial statements for the year ended 1988 and provide still another rating of the company's financial position but this time on a scale of 1 to 1,000. The ratings are shown as follows.

1986	*1988*
55	690
89	900
45	200
50	500
69	980
70	750
80	770
90	940
75	850
95	950

a. Develop a scatter plot for these data and describe the apparent relationship between the two variables based on what you see in the scatter plot.
b. Would it be appropriate to compute the parametric correlation coefficient based on these data? Discuss why or why not.
c. Compute the Spearman correlation coefficient for these two variables and indicate whether the two variables are significantly correlated using an alpha level of 0.05.

36. During the production of a textbook, there are many steps between when the author first begins preparing the manuscript and when the book is finally

printed and bound. Tremendous effort is made to minimize the number of errors of any type in the text. One type of error that is especially difficult to eliminate is the typographical error that can creep in when the book is typeset. The Prolythic Type Company does contract work for many publishers. As part of its quality control efforts, it charts the number of corrected errors per page in its manuscripts. In one book particularly difficult to typeset, the following data were observed for a sample of 15 pages (in sequence):

Page	1	2	3	4	5	6	7	8	9	10	11	12	13	14	15
Errors	2	4	1	0	6	7	4	2	9	4	3	6	2	4	2

Based on these sample data, can the operations manager conclude that the occurrence of errors is random? Test at the 5% alpha level and use the mean as the cut-off for determining the two groups.

37. The catering manager at a major league baseball park is interested in determining whether the requests for beer or soda pop follow some pattern or are random. He has observed twelve customers arrive at a concession stand and place their beverage order. Letting B = beer and S = soda, the following data are observed:

B B B S B B B B S S S S

Test for randomness at the 0.05 alpha level.

38. A computer components manufacturer maintains a wide variety of control charts. One particular chart seems to be in control according to the operator. Her reasoning is that none of the points fall outside the control limits. However, an internal quality consultant thinks that it would be wise to examine the control chart in more detail to see whether the points do in fact exhibit a random pattern around the center line. In doing this study, the consultant studied the 100 most recent points and found 21 runs. Of the 100 points, 44 were above the center line and 56 were below the center line.
   a. State the appropriate null and alternative hypotheses.
   b. Based on the sample data, what conclusion should be reached at an $\alpha =$ 0.01 level?

39. A local golf course has undertaken a service quality improvement effort. As one part of this effort, the professional would like to be able to satisfy more customers by giving them tee times as close as possible to their preferred times to play. One question is whether players' preferences for morning versus afternoon tee times are random from call to call. To study this, a sample of 200 consecutive calls was monitored. The callers were asked to indicate morning or afternoon preference. Out of the 200 calls, 94 indicated a preference for afternoon times and 106 wanted morning times. Further, the calls showed 130 runs.
   a. State the appropriate null and alternative hypotheses to be tested.
   b. Based on an $\alpha = 0.05$, what conclusion should be reached regarding time preferences? Discuss.

40. A business statistics instructor at State University has been experimenting with her testing procedure. This term, she has taken the approach of giving two tests over each section of material. The first test is a problem-oriented exam, where students have to set up and solve an applications problem. The exam is worth 50 points. The second test, given a day later, is a multiple-choice test, covering the concepts introduced in the section of the text covered by the exam. This exam is also worth 50 points.

In one class of fifteen students, the following test scores were observed over the first section of material in the course:

Student	*Test 1*	*Test 2*
1	42	34
2	36	34
3	44	45
4	27	30
5	40	45
6	34	32
7	40	40
8	50	44
9	29	32
10	43	40
11	42	34
12	22	32
13	26	30
14	45	40
15	41	39

If the instructor is unwilling to make the assumptions for the paired-sample t test, what should she conclude based on these data about the distribution of scores for the two tests if she tests at an $\alpha = 0.05$ level?

41. Referring to Problem 40, is there a significant linear relationship between the two test scores? Test at an $\alpha = 0.05$ level.

42. A computer chip manufacturer is experimenting with a new wafer-cleaning compound. In this business, the problem with any cleaning compound is that while it may remove dust particles from the wafers, the compound can also leave some of its own particles. To test the effectiveness of the new compound, the engineer in charge of the project selected a random sample of twenty-six wafers. He first used an electromagnetic process to count the number of particles on each wafer. He next used the new cleaner on each of the twenty-six wafers and recounted the particles on each wafer. He expects that there will be significantly fewer particles after the new cleaner is applied.

The engineer is unwilling to make the normality assumption required for the paired-sample t test. Instead, he has set the problem up to be tested using the Wilcoxon matched-pairs signed ranks test.

a. Indicate the appropriate null and alternative hypotheses to be tested.

b. If the difference in particles is in the predicted direction, T, the smaller of the sum of the like-signed ranks, will be the sum of the ranks of the wafers whose d values will be in the direction opposite to that predicted. In this case, that would be the negative d values. The calculated T for these data is 53. Based on this result, what decision should be made using an $\alpha = 0.05$ level? Discuss. (Note that there were no differences of 0.)

43. Two brands of tires are being tested for tread wear. To control for vehicle and driver variation, one tire of each brand is put on the front wheels of ten cars. The cars are driven under normal driving conditions a total of 15,000 miles. The tread wear is then measured using a very sophisticated instrument. The following data were observed (note that the larger the number, the less wear in the tread):

Car	*Brand 1*	*Brand 2*
1	1.578	1.457
2	1.434	1.569
3	1.809	1.789
4	1.234	1.456
5	1.378	1.267
6	1.599	1.903
7	1.472	1.582
8	1.234	1.160
9	1.402	1.578
10	1.734	1.730

a. State the appropriate null and alternative hypotheses to be tested.
b. What would be the possible objection in this case for employing the paired-sample t test? Discuss.
c. Assuming that the decision makers in this situation are not willing to make the assumptions required to perform the paired-sample t test, what decision should be reached using the appropriate nonparametric test if an $\alpha = 0.05$ level is used? Discuss.

DATABASE PROBLEMS

The following questions and problems pertain directly to the State Department of Transportation case study and database introduced in Chapter 1. The questions and problems were written assuming that you will have access to a computer and appropriate statistical software. The database containing 100 observations and seventeen variables is shown in Table 1-1 in Chapter 1. *Assume that the data were collected using a simple random sampling process.*

1. Herb Kriner is interested in determining whether seat belt status is independent of insurance status. Test this at the $\alpha = 0.05$ level. Show the contingency table and the test statistic.

2. Herb Kriner would like to determine whether the average age of drivers in this state is the same for males and females. Herb recognizes that he could test using a two-sample t test, but he is unwilling to make the necessary assumptions. Therefore, he would like you to use the appropriate nonparametric test at an $\alpha = 0.05$ level. Be sure to discuss your results and indicate what assumptions are required by the t test that are not required by the nonparametric test.

3. Can Herb Kriner conclude that knowledge of the liability insurance law is independent of sex of the respondent? Test at the $\alpha = 0.05$ level.

ADDITIONAL DATABASE PROBLEMS

The questions and problems in this section reference the various databases that accompany this text and which are described in Chapter 1. Your instructor has been provided a diskette with these databases. It is expected that you will be using computer software to access these data and to perform the required calculations and graphs.

DATABASE: **CITIES** (*Refer to the database description in Chapter 1.*)

1. Use the Spearman rank correlation coefficient to measure the strength of the linear relationship between the 1990 population and the 1990 unemployment rate. Test to see whether the correlation is statistically significant at the $\alpha = 0.05$ level. Discuss your results.
2. Based on the Spearman rank correlation coefficient, is there a significant linear relationship between 1987 average annual earnings for white-collar workers and 1987 average annual earnings of manufacturing workers?
3. Select only the cases in the database where the reported values for X_4 and X_5 reflect SAT scores. Use the appropriate nonparametric test to determine whether there is a difference between average city dweller SAT scores and suburb dweller SAT scores. Test at an $\alpha = 0.10$ level.

DATABASE: **FAST100** (*Refer to the database description in Chapter 1.*)

1. Use the appropriate nonparametric test to determine whether there is a significant difference between average stock prices for firms trading on the three stock exchanges. Test at an $\alpha = 0.05$ level. Discuss your results.
2. Is there a difference in average earnings per share for companies trading on the three stock exchanges based on these sample data? Use the appropriate nonparametric test and conduct the test using an $\alpha = 0.05$ level.

3. Is there a significant linear relationship between stock price on 9/6/91 and the stock price a year earlier? Show a plot of the two variables, test for significance at the $\alpha = 0.05$ level, and discuss your results.

DATABASE: **PACRIM** (*Refer to the database description in Chapter 1.*)

1. Looking at only those companies located in Japan, South Korea, and Australia, do the sample data provide sufficient evidence to conclude that a difference exists in average 1989 after-tax profits? Use the appropriate nonparametric test and an $\alpha = 0.05$ level. Discuss your results.
2. Use the appropriate nonparametric technique to determine whether there is a statistically significant linear relationship between 1989 after-tax profits and year-end assets. Test at an $\alpha = 0.05$ level and discuss your results. Use an appropriate graph to help in your discussion.
3. Is there a difference in average number of employees for companies located in Japan versus Australia? Test using an $\alpha = 0.05$ level using the appropriate nonparametric tool. Discuss your results.

DATABASE: **JOBAPPS** (*Refer to the database description in Chapter 1.*)

1. Is there a statistical difference in rankings for the twelve candidates? Use the appropriate nonparametric test to reach your conclusion. Write a short report discussing the conclusions and indicating why a nonparametric technique should be used to conduct the test.
2. Develop Spearman rank correlation coefficients between ranking of each candidate and the acceptance rating for each candidate. Thus, you will be computing twelve correlation coefficients. Test each of these at the $\alpha = 0.05$ level and discuss your results. Indicate why it would not be appropriate to compute the correlation coefficient introduced in Chapter 13.

DATABASE: **TRUCKS** (*Refer to the database description in Chapter 1.*)

1. Use the appropriate nonparametric technique to test whether there is a difference in average WIM gross weight versus average POE gross weight. Test at an $\alpha = 0.05$ level. Discuss your results and include in your discussion the rationale for selecting the particular nonparametric tool that you did choose.
2. Assuming that the trucks are in sequence order, can you conclude that the speeds of vehicles are random? Use an $\alpha = 0.05$ to test. Discuss your results.
3. Based on the sample data, is there a statistical difference in average speed of the vehicles depending on the month that the truck was weighed on the WIM scale? Test using an $\alpha = 0.05$ level. What would be the justification for using the Kruskal–Wallis ANOVA instead of the parametric ANOVA introduced in Chapter 12? Discuss.

CASES

16A Bentford Electronics, Part 1

On Saturday morning Jennifer Bentford received a call at her home from the production supervisor at Bentford Electronics Plant #1. The supervisor indicated that she and the supervisors from Plants #2, #3, and #4 had agreed that something must be done to improve company morale and, thereby, increase the production output of their plants. Jennifer Bentford, president of Bentford Electronics, agreed to set up a Monday morning meeting with the supervisors to see if, together, they could arrive at a plan for accomplishing these objectives.

By Monday each supervisor had compiled a list of several ideas, including a 4-day work week and interplant competition of various kinds.

After listening to the discussion for some time, Jennifer Bentford asked if anyone knew if there was a difference in average daily output for the four plants. When she heard no positive response, she told the supervisors to select a random sample of daily production reports from each plant and test whether there was a difference. They were to meet again on Wednesday afternoon with test results.

By Wednesday morning the supervisors had collected the following data on units produced:

Plant #1	*Plant #2*	*Plant #3*	*Plant #4*
4,306	1,853	2,700	1,704
2,852	1,948	2,705	2,320
1,900	2,702	2,721	4,150
4,711	4,110	2,900	3,300
2,933	3,950	2,650	3,200
3,627	2,300	2,480	2,975

The supervisors had little trouble collecting the data, but were at a loss as to how to determine whether there was a difference in the output of the four plants. Jerry Gibson, the company's research analyst, told the supervisors that there were statistical procedures that could be used to test hypotheses regarding multiple samples if the daily output was distributed in a bell shape (normal distribution) at each plant. The supervisors expressed dismay because none thought his or her output was normal. Jerry Gibson indicated that there were techniques that did not require the normality assumption, but he did not know what they were.

The meeting with Jennifer Bentford was scheduled to begin in 3 hours.

16B Bentford Electronics, Part 2

Following the Wednesday afternoon meeting (see Case 16A), Jennifer Bentford and her plant supervisors agreed to implement a weekly contest called the NBE Game of the Week. The plant turning out the most production each week would be considered the NBE Game of the Week winner and would receive ten points. The second-place plant would receive seven points, and the third- and fourth-place plants would receive three points and one point, respectively. The contest would last 26 weeks. At the end of that period, a $200,000 bonus would be divided among the employees in the four plants proportional to the total points accumulated by each plant.

The announcement of the contest created a lot of excitement and enthusiasm at the four plants. No one complained about the rules since the four plants were designed and staffed to produce equally.

At the close of the contest, Jennifer Bentford called the supervisors into a meeting, at which time she asked for data to determine whether the contest had significantly improved productivity. She indicated that she had to know this before she could authorize a second contest. The supervisors, expecting this response, had put together the following data:

Units Produced (4 plants combined)	*Before-Contest Frequency*	*During-Contest Frequency*
0– 2,500	11	0
2,501– 8,000	23	20
8,001–15,000	56	83
15,001–20,000	15	52
	105 days	155 days

Jennifer examined the data and indicated that it looked like the contest was a success, but she wanted to base her decision to continue the contest on more than just an observation of the data. "Surely there must be some way to statistically test the worthiness of this contest," Jennifer stated. "I have to see the results before I will authorize the second contest."

REFERENCES

Berenson, Mark L., and Levine, David M. *Basic Business Statistics,* 5th edition. Englewood Cliffs, New Jersey: Prentice-Hall, 1992.

Daniel, Wayne W., and Terrell, James C. *Business Statistics,* 6th edition. Boston: Houghton Mifflin, 1992.

Iman, R. L., and Conover, W. J. *Modern Business Statistics,* 2nd edition. New York: Wiley, 1989.

Marascuilo, Leonard A. and McSweeney, Maryellen. *Nonparametric and Distribution-free Methods for Social Sciences.* Pacific Grove, California: Brooks/Cole, 1977.

Siegel, S. *Nonparametric Statistics.* New York: McGraw-Hill, 1956.

Chapter 16

Hand-In Exercises

1. Refer to Problem 1 in Chapter 16. Use the 5% level and perform a runs test of the hypothesis that egg brand selection is random.

Brand Selection Sequence

xx yyy x y xx yyy x yyy x y xx

2. Refer to Problem 8 in Chapter 16. Use the Mann-Whitney U test for small samples and a 5% level of significance. Test to see if there is a difference in charitable deduction taken between joint and single returns.

Single	Joint
n=6	n=8
Sum of ranks = 43	Sum of ranks = 62

3. Refer to Problem 5 in Chapter 16. Use the Mann-Whitney U test and the 5% level of significance. Suppose the data represent college entrance exams scores for samples from two populations. Test the hypothesis that the populations have equal means.

Out of state	Metro
405	300
450	340
290	400
370	250
345	270
460	410
425	435
275	390
380	225
330	210
500	395
215	315

4. Refer to Problem 9 in Chapter 16. Use the Wilcoxon signed rank test for matched pairs and a 5% level of significance and perform the test of differences in the two populations. Suppose the data represent college entrance exam scores for the same eight students at two different colleges. Does either college use a tougher entrance exam?

	Score at	
Student	Yell University	Dork College
Anderson	258	304
Bates	197	190
Clark	400	500
Duff	350	340
Evan	237	250
Foley	400	358
Gill	370	390
Howe	130	100

5. Refer to Problem 11 in Chapter 16. Data for 40 observations has been summarized and a T value of 480 is given. Use the 5% level and the normal approximation to the Wilcoxon test to determine if there is a weight gain difference between the two feed supplements.

6. Refer to Problem 13 in Chapter 16. Use the Kruskal-Wallis One-Way Anova test at the 5% level. Perform the test to see if there is a rating difference between the three brands of running shoes.

HARE	TERRAPIN	WINGS
21	17	29
25	15	38
36	34	28
35	22	27
33	16	14
23	19	26
31	30	39
32	20	36

7. Refer to Problem 17 in Chapter 16. Compute the Spearman correlation coefficient and test at the 5% level to see if it is statistically significant.

Golfer	Handicap	Rounds Played
Albor	13	24
Baker	23	34
Clark	17	23
Duff	6	22
Evan	2	40
Finn	15	35
Gorp	18	11
Howe	4	46
Ines	8	25
Jerum	10	17
Kelly	16	42

Time Series Analysis and Index Numbers

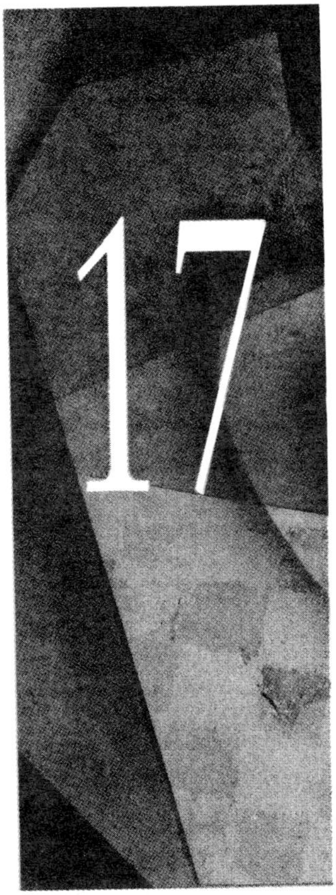

WHY DECISION MAKERS NEED TO KNOW

Forecasting the future of an organization is somewhat like forecasting the weather. What the weather will be like tomorrow is related to what it is like today. The corporate "weather" is generally measured as profit, earnings per share, price/earnings ratio, or some other quantitative characteristic of the industry within which the business functions. The historical record of a firm's performance can be charted to provide an indication of the past "weather" conditions as measured over time. Whether or not this historical record will provide insight about what the future holds depends on many factors. However, decision makers should understand how to analyze the past if they expect to incorporate past information into future decisions.

CHAPTER OBJECTIVES

This chapter will introduce the fundamentals of time series analysis. Time series analysis is the process by which a set of data measured over time is analyzed. The goals of this chapter include describing the four components of a time series, indicating how to recognize these components, and providing business examples of each component. In addition, the chapter will point out what the components mean to decision makers who intend to use information from the time series in decision making.

The chapter will also introduce the increasingly important subject of index numbers. We will discuss several different kinds of index numbers, demonstrate how they are calculated, and show how they can be used in decision-making situations.

STUDENT OBJECTIVES

After studying the material in this chapter, you should be able to do the following:

1. Define a trend component and recognize if a trend component is present in a time series.
2. Define a seasonal component and determine whether a seasonal component is present in a time series.
3. Define a cyclical component and determine whether the time series contains a cyclical component.
4. Define a random or irregular component.
5. Produce appropriate index numbers for applications requiring comparisons involving changes over time.
6. Discuss the general manner in which index numbers are constructed and their importance in managerial decision making.

17-1 TIME SERIES COMPONENTS

The world is filled with forecasters, ranging from business people and government officials who try to predict the future state of the national economy to homeowners who try to predict next weekend's weather. If the homeowner sprays weed killer on her yard just before an unexpected rain, the consequences are not devastating; she is just out a few dollars for weed killer. Unfortunately, the results of a poor managerial forecast are often more severe and cannot be rectified by an additional application of weed spray. When faced with trying to predict the future, a manager, like all of us, would like to connect what is going to happen with something that can be seen happening now.

A large number of factors can affect the outcome of any managerial decision. Identifying these factors, and then measuring them, is in many cases impossible since their importance changes and new factors are continually added. However, although the factors that affect the future are uncertain, often the past offers a good indication of what the future will hold.

If an organization has been gathering data on important measures, such as profits or sales levels, the decision maker may be able to use *time series analysis* to help analyze the future values of these measures. Past data, measured over time, are called *time series data.* The decision maker who plans to develop a quantitative forecasting model is often helped by analyzing the relevant time series data.

Before decision makers use past information to make a decision about the future, they must recognize how to extract the meaningful information from all the available past data. This chapter discusses the basic components of a **time series** and illustrates, through example, what each means.

All time series contain at least one of four time series components:

1. Long-term trend components
2. Seasonal components
3. Cyclical components
4. Irregular or random components

Time series analysis involves breaking down data measured over time into one or more of these components.

LONG-TERM TREND COMPONENT

The **trend component** is the long-term increase or decrease in a variable being measured over time. For example, 11 years of total sales data for the Kmart Corporation are shown in Figure 17-1. Figure 17-2 shows 11 years of total loan levels for Citicorp, the largest bank in the United States. In both cases, there is not much variation other than the overall upward trend. In other cases a strong trend component is evident, but variation exists around the long-term increase or decrease. Figure 17-3 (page 910) shows the last decade of sales for the Bird Corporation, a manufacturer of roofing products in the northeastern United States.

FIGURE 17-1

Kmart Yearly Sales

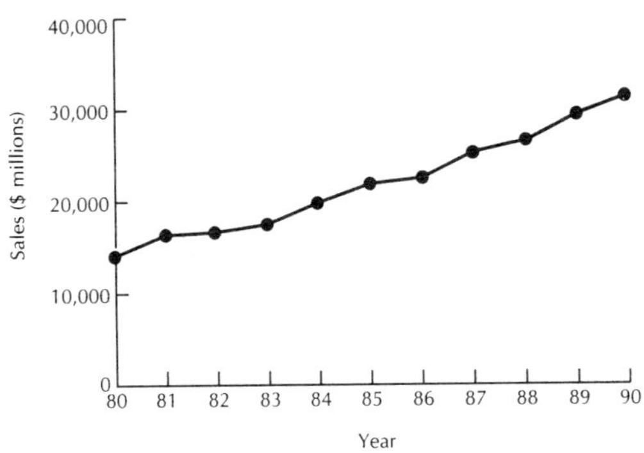

FIGURE 17-2

Citicorp Yearly Loan Levels

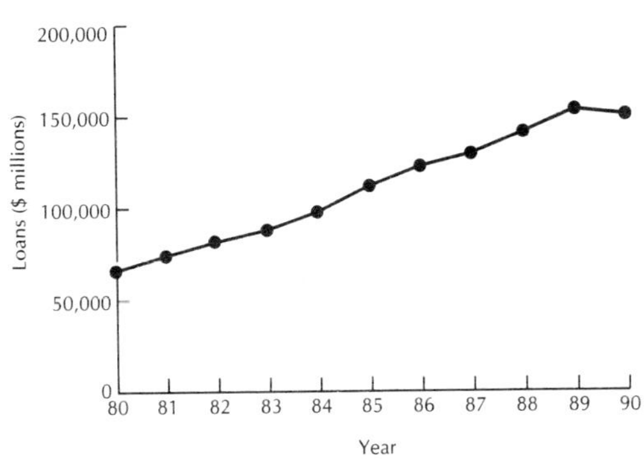

FIGURE 17-3

Bird Corp. Yearly Sales

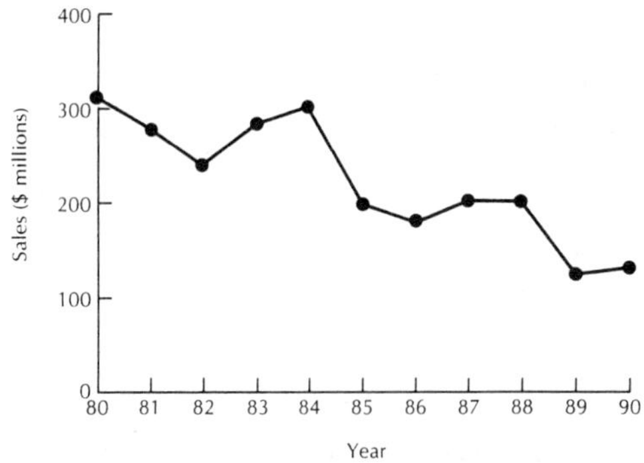

In today's world, organizations are facing increasing problems in planning, caused mainly by changing technology, complicated government regulations, and uncertain foreign competition. A combination of these and other factors has forced most organizations into increasing the time spans of their planning cycles. Most organizations, when considering capital expenditures, look at a time frame of from 3 to 7 years into the future. When you are planning to start spending money now to meet a demand existing in 3 to 7 years, you had better have a reason to believe the demand will be there. Because long-term forecasting is becoming increasingly important, the trend component in time series analysis is important to all organizations.

SEASONAL COMPONENT

Some organizations and industries are affected not only by long-term trends but also by *seasonal* variation. The **seasonal component** represents those changes in a time series that occur at the same time every year. Figure 17-4 shows the last 16 quarters of sales for the Marriott Corporation, the hotel and food service com-

FIGURE 17-4

Marriott Corp. Quarterly Sales

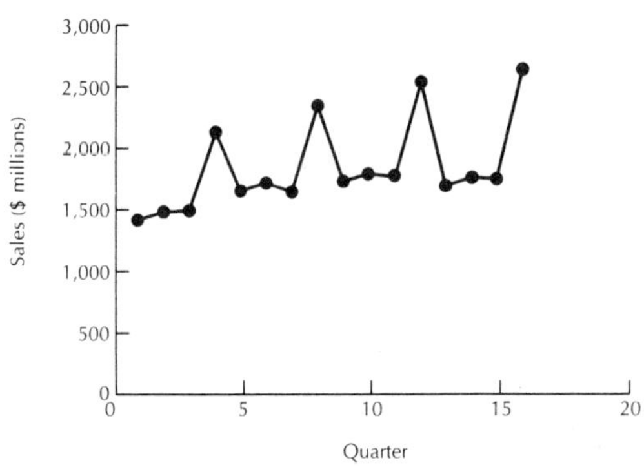

pany. The time series has yearly peaks in the quarter ending in December of each year.

Organizations facing seasonal variations, such as the motor vehicle industry, are often interested in knowing how well, or poorly, they are doing relative to the normal seasonal variation. For instance, while most retailers expect sales volume to be higher in December than November, they are interested in whether December sales are higher or lower than normal relative to November sales. The Bureau of Labor Statistics expects unemployment to increase in June because recent graduates are arriving on the job market and schools have dismissed for the summer. The question is whether the increase is more or less than expected.

Organizations that are affected by seasonal variation need to identify and measure this seasonality to help with planning for temporary increases or decreases in labor requirements, inventory, training, periodic maintenance, and so forth. In addition, these organizations need to know if the seasonal variation they experience occurs at more or less than the average rate.

CYCLICAL COMPONENT

Data collected annually obviously cannot have a seasonal component; however, they can contain certain *cyclical* effects. A **cyclical component** in a time series is represented by wavelike fluctuation around a long-term trend. In general, these fluctuations are thought to be caused by pulsations in factors such as interest rates, money supply, consumer demand, inventory levels, national and international market conditions, and other government policies. Cyclical fluctuations repeat themselves in a general pattern in the long term, but occur with differing frequencies and intensities. Thus they can be isolated, but not totally predicted. Figure 17-5 shows the change in business inventories in the United States, in 1982 dollars, from 1964 through 1989. Note the strong cyclical effect, with periods of high inventory growth and periods of net inventory reduction.

Firms affected by cyclical fluctuations are those particularly vulnerable to unexpected changes in the economy. Not only are cyclical effects generally unpredictable, but the overall effect of each cycle on individual organizations is differ-

FIGURE 17-5 Change in U.S. Business Inventories

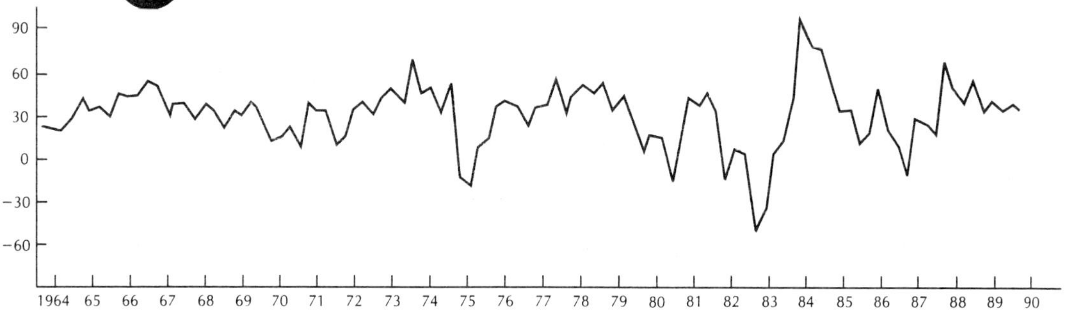

ent. Thus, even though you know what happened to your firm during the last cycle, you have no guarantee the effect will be the same the next time.

IRREGULAR OR RANDOM COMPONENT

The **irregular** or *random* **component** in a time series is that part of the series that cannot be attributed to any of the three previously discussed components. Random fluctuations can be caused by many factors, such as weather, political events, and other human and nonhuman actions. For example, severe winters affect vast segments of the economy, and political statements or actions of governments or regulatory agencies often introduce an unpredicted element into an organization's environment.

Two types of irregular fluctuations may exist in a time series. *Minor* irregularities show up as sawtoothlike patterns around the long-term trend. These minor irregular fluctuations are caused by many factors and, individually, are not significant in an organization's long-term operations. *Major* irregularities are significant one-time, unpredictable changes in the time series due to such external and uncontrollable factors as an oil embargo, war, droughts, and so forth. Figure 17-6 shows new private housing units authorized by building permits from 1964 through 1989, with 1967 as the base year. First, note the definite cyclical nature of these data, reflecting the nature of the housing industry. The irregular component is clearly seen as the seemingly random variations around the obvious cycles.

Almost all industries and organizations are affected by irregular components. Obviously organizations dealing with products that can be influenced by variations in the weather are interested in this component. This includes most agricultural and mining concerns. Some organizations, such as insurance companies and certain governmental agencies, are directly concerned with eliminating the risk to other organizations caused by unforeseen irregular factors.

FIGURE 17-6 New Private Housing Units Authorized by Building Permits

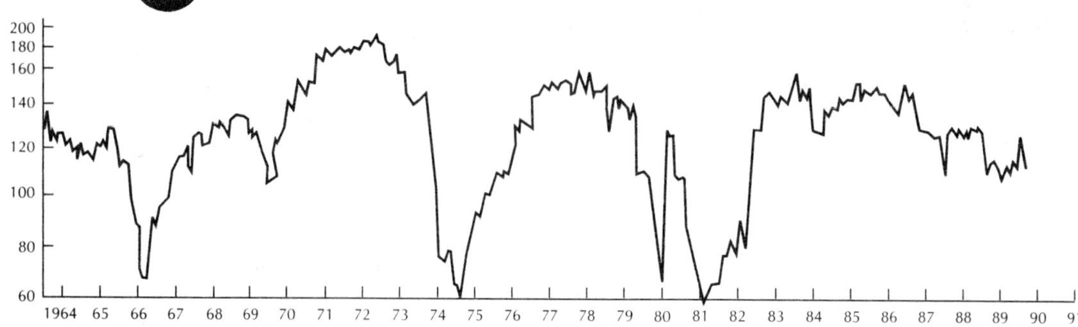

SKILL DEVELOPMENT PROBLEMS FOR **SECTION 17-1**

The following set of problems is included to test your understanding of the material in this section.

1. Consider the following set of sales data given in millions of dollars.

1988		*1990*	
1st quarter	152	1st quarter	217
2d quarter	162	2d quarter	209
3d quarter	157	3d quarter	202
4th quarter	167	4th quarter	221

1989		*1991*	
1st quarter	182	1st quarter	236
2d quarter	192	2d quarter	242
3d quarter	191	3d quarter	231
4th quarter	197	4th quarter	224

Plot these data and discuss which of the time series components you see.

2. Consider the following set of inventory data given in hundreds of thousands of dollars.

1988		*1990*	
1st quarter	109	1st quarter	118
2d quarter	95	2d quarter	103
3d quarter	115	3d quarter	126
4th quarter	108	4th quarter	120

1989		*1991*	
1st quarter	115	1st quarter	130
2d quarter	110	2d quarter	127
3d quarter	120	3d quarter	138
4th quarter	116	4th quarter	135

Plot these data and discuss which of the time series components you see.

3. José Gutierrez correctly predicted the increasing need for home health care services due to the country's aging population. Five years ago, he started a company offering meal delivery, physical therapy, and minor housekeeping services in the New Orleans area. Since that time he has opened offices in seven additional Gulf state cities. José is presently analyzing the revenue data from his first location for the first 5 years of operation.

	Revenue ($1,000s)				
	1987	*1988*	*1989*	*1990*	*1991*
January	23	67	72	76	81
February	34	63	64	75	72
March	45	65	64	77	71
April	48	71	77	81	83
May	46	75	79	86	85
June	49	70	72	75	77
July	60	72	71	80	79
August	65	75	77	82	84
September	67	80	79	86	91
October	60	78	78	87	86
November	71	89	87	91	94
December	76	94	92	96	99

Plot these revenue data and prepare a short report for José discussing which of the time series components you see.

17-2 ANALYZING THE VARIABILITY OF HISTORICAL DATA

Decision makers can think about time series analysis in much the same manner they can think about analysis of variance and regression analysis. The time series they are analyzing has some inherent variability, and they would like to explain as much of that variability as possible. The four types of components—long-term trend, seasonal, cyclical, and irregular—help explain that variability. The purpose of time series analysis is to use these components to explain the total variability in past data. This situation can be represented as shown in the following graph.

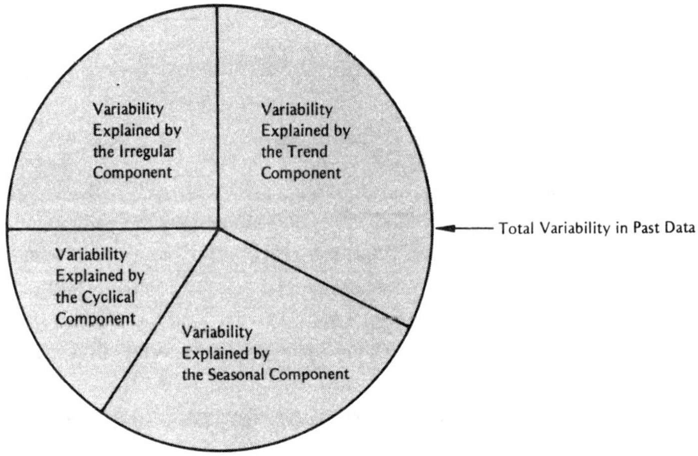

The problem is how to best separate each component from the others so that each can be analyzed. Some general approaches to this problem will be addressed in the remainder of this chapter. Only the most basic methods are presented. Refer to *Time Series Analysis* by Cryer (1986) for discussions of more sophisticated approaches to analyzing a time series.

17-3 ANALYZING THE TREND COMPONENT

The trend component identifies the long-term growth or decline in the time series. Long-term growth patterns have a wide variety of shapes. The *first-degree linear, exponential, modified exponential,* and *Gompertz curves* are some of the most common trend patterns. Figure 17-7 illustrates these curves and indicates some areas where these curves have been used to describe long-term trends.

Many methods are available to fit trend lines to a series of data. The easiest is simply to graph the data points and draw the trend line freehand. This approach often provides adequate information about the long-term trend.

Another way of fitting a trend line to a set of data is to use least squares regression, as discussed in Chapters 14 and 15. For example, suppose a financial analyst is comparing the performance of two of the nation's largest retailers, Sears and Kmart. The analyst has obtained data showing annual sales for the years 1980–1990. These data are shown in Table 17-1 (page 916).

The analyst can use simple regression analysis to measure the long-term trend of sales for each firm. The fitted model is

$$\hat{Y} = b_0 + b_1 t$$

FIGURE 17-7

Long-Term Trend Pattern Curves

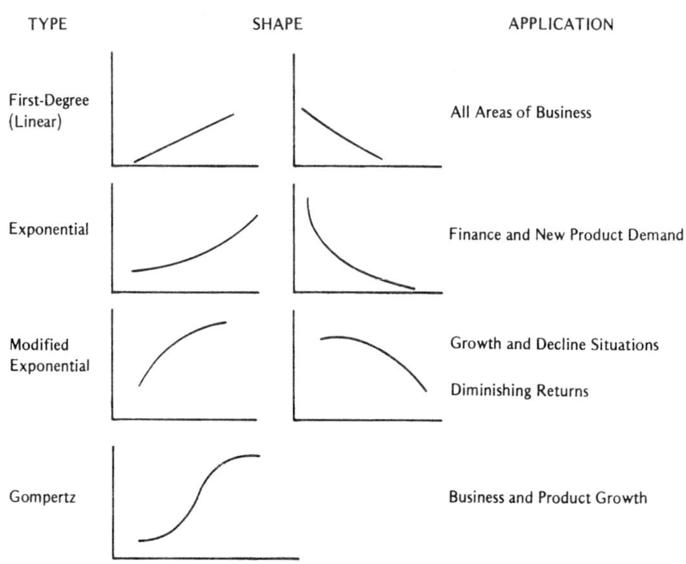

TABLE 17-1

Annual Sales for Sears and Kmart

Year	Sears	Kmart
1980	\$25,195 (million)	\$14,204 (million)
1981	27,357	16,527
1982	30,020	16,772
1983	35,883	18,598
1984	38,828	21,096
1985	40,715	22,420
1986	44,282	23,812
1987	48,440	25,626
1988	50,250	27,301
1989	53,974	29,533
1990	56,785	32,500

where

$\hat{Y}$ = Estimated annual sales

t = Time periods in years ($t = 1, 2, \ldots, 11$)

Note the independent variable in the regression analysis is time, t, where for 1980, $t = 1$, and for 1990, $t = 11$. The regression results, found using a statistical package, are as follows:

Sears	*Kmart*
$b_0 = 21{,}665.76$ (million)	$b_0 = 12{,}115.56$ (million)
$b_1 = 3{,}233.418$ (million)	$b_1 = 1{,}744.209$ (million)
$r^2 = 0.9943$	$r^2 = 0.9888$

The high r^2 values for both firms indicate the simple linear model, with time as the independent variable, fits the annual sales growth well. Figure 17-8 shows the time series plots for the two companies. As can be seen, the sales values show little cyclical or random fluctuation.

As the graphs show, not only does Sears presently have a larger sales volume than Kmart, but it has also been growing faster during the past 11 years.

SKILL DEVELOPMENT PROBLEMS FOR **SECTION 17-3**

The following set of problems is included to test your understanding of the material in this section.

4. Refer to the sales data given in Problem 1 in Section 17-1.
   a. Determine the least squares regression line describing these data.
   b. Discuss whether the regression line is a good fit to the data.

FIGURE 17-8

Annual Sales for Sears and Kmart

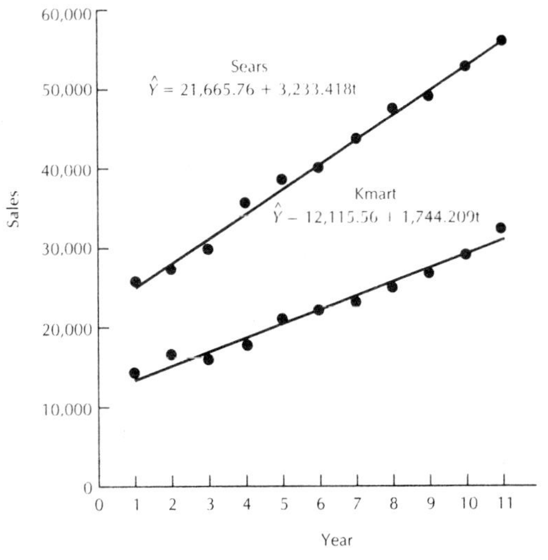

5. Refer to the inventory data given in Problem 2 in Section 17-1.
   a. Determine the least squares regression line describing these data.
   b. Discuss whether the regression line is a good fit to the data.

6. In Problem 3 in Section 17-1, we introduced José Gutierrez, who started a home health care service company in New Orleans. Refer to the revenue values given in that problem and prepare a short report for José discussing any trend you see in these data.

17-4 ANALYZING THE SEASONAL COMPONENT

Decision makers would have a much easier time if their operating environment contained no variation, but most often variation does exist. This is particularly true of industries and firms that are affected by a seasonal factor. For instance, although food processors would like to have a continual supply of fresh products, the supply is tied to the growing season. Lumber mill operators would like to have a continual supply of trees; however, tree harvesting is affected by snow depths and muddy ground during the winter and early spring. Toy store owners have a very seasonal business, with the majority of sales occurring in the 2 or 3 months immediately before Christmas.

For many organizations, either the demand for their product or service, or their source of supply, is highly dependent on the time of year. Since seasonal variation is considered normal in many businesses, the real questions are how this variation affects the planning process and whether the observed variation is more or less than expected.

The seasonal variation in a time series is considered by constructing a *seasonal index* for each month, or quarter, in the year. The **seasonal index** is determined by dividing the actual value for each month or quarter by some "normal" value for that period. Two methods are commonly used to find index values; one is known as the ratio to moving-average method and the other is the ratio to trend method. The ratio to moving-average method is considered superior if the time series data contain a cyclical component. However, constructing the moving average requires a loss of data and so the ratio to trend method is useful if a cyclical component is not present and a limited amount of data is available.

To demonstrate how a seasonal index is calculated, consider the past 4 years of quarterly revenues for JB's Restaurants, a chain of family restaurants located primarily in the southwestern United States. These data are shown in Table 17-2 and are graphed in Figure 17-9. Note that the data show an obvious seasonal pattern.

The ratio to trend method begins by assuming the time series can be represented by a multiplicative model.

$$Y = T \cdot S \cdot C \cdot I$$

where

Y = Value of the time series

T = Trend value

S = Seasonal value

C = Cyclical value

I = Irregular value

The multiplicative model assumes each time series value is determined by the relationships between the four components. The ratio to trend model removes the effect of the trend by finding Y/T for each observation. To find the trend value for each quarter we determine the regression line for the quarterly data:

$$\hat{Y} = 23.813 + 0.357t$$

The actual, forecast, and ratio to trend values are shown for each quarter in Table 17-3.

The ratio to trend values in Table 17-3 represent the effects of seasonal, cyclical, and irregular influences on revenues. Before proceeding with the analysis, we look to see whether the pattern shown by the index values is stable. For all 4 years, we see the third quarter revenues are larger than for any of the other quarters. We see that this pattern is stable, although the magnitudes of the indexes vary from year to year. If we are satisfied with the pattern's stability, we can

TABLE 17-2

Quarterly Revenues ($ millions) for JB's Restaurants

Year	Quarter			
	I	II	III	IV
1987	22.2	21.6	37.0	24.7
1988	21.9	21.8	31.1	24.9
1989	23.4	24.0	35.2	26.8
1990	24.2	24.5	37.1	29.2

FIGURE 17-9

Quarterly Revenues for JB's Restaurants

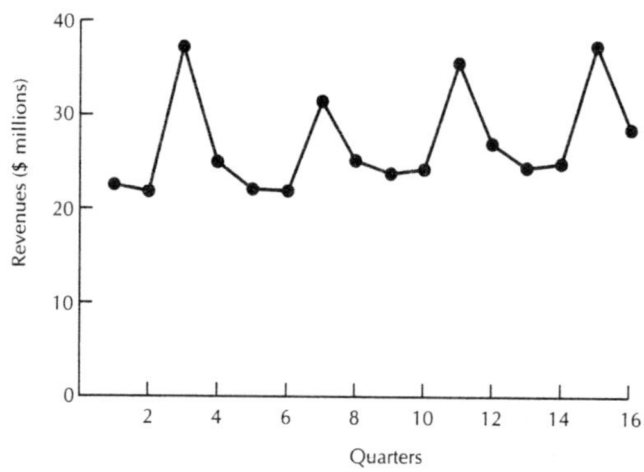

TABLE 17-3

Seasonal Indexes for JB's Restaurants Example

Quarter	Actual	Forecast	Ratio to Trend
1	22.2	24.17	0.918
2	21.6	24.53	0.881
3	37	24.88	1.487
4	24.7	25.24	0.979
5	21.9	25.60	0.856
6	21.8	25.96	0.840
7	31.1	26.31	1.182
8	24.9	26.67	0.934
9	23.4	27.03	0.866
10	24	27.39	0.876
11	35.2	27.74	1.269
12	26.8	28.10	0.954
13	24.2	28.46	0.850
14	24.5	28.82	0.850
15	37.1	29.17	1.272
16	29.2	29.53	0.989

TABLE 17-4

Computation of Seasonal Indexes

Year	Quarter			
	I	II	III	IV
1987	0.918	0.881	1.487	0.979
1988	0.856	0.840	1.182	0.934
1989	0.866	0.876	1.269	0.954
1990	0.850	0.850	1.272	0.989
Average	0.873	0.862	1.303	0.964
Normalized Average	0.8726	0.8616	1.3023	0.9635

average these ratios for corresponding quarters, as shown in Table 17-4. This will tend to smooth out the effect of both the irregular and cyclical components. Notice that we have both an average value in the table and a normalized average value. Since the index numbers represent the expected variation around the trend line each year, and we have quarterly data, the four values should sum to 4.0. The average values in Table 17-4 sum to 4.002. To normalize the index numbers, we simply multiply each average value by 4.0/4.002 = 0.9995. As you can see, for this problem, the adjustment is minimal.

While this example has looked at quarterly data, the same procedure would be followed for monthly data, except monthly index values would be determined.

SKILL DEVELOPMENT PROBLEMS FOR **SECTION 17-4**

The following set of problems is included to test your understanding of the material in this section.

7. Extract the seasonal component from the set of quarterly data given in Problem 1 in Section 17-1.

8. Extract the seasonal component from the following set of monthly data.

	1989	*1990*	*1991*
January	5.4	5.8	7.0
February	10.4	12.8	14.6
March	18.6	20.1	22.6
April	4.8	8.2	7.6
May	12.2	15.6	16.2
June	14.6	14.8	15.9
July	13.0	11.0	13.0
August	19.4	19.2	17.8
September	26.8	27.0	28.6
October	21.2	21.4	23.0
November	10.2	9.9	13.1
December	6.7	5.6	7.9

9. In the previous section, you analyzed the trend component of revenue data for José Gutierrez's health care business. (Also see Problem 3 in Section 17-1.) Now analyze the seasonal component of these data.

17-5 ANALYZING THE CYCLICAL COMPONENT

Cyclical variations in time series data do not repeat themselves in a regular pattern as do seasonal factors, but they cannot be considered random variations in the data either. Although cyclical variations generally show some recognizable pattern and are repetitious, they always differ in both intensity and timing. By *intensity* of a cycle, we mean the height from its crest to its trough. *Timing* is the frequency with which the crests and troughs occur. Therefore, cyclical components can be isolated and analyzed, but, unfortunately, cannot be accurately predicted.

Many industries are influenced by cyclical patterns in their environment. The most important cyclical factor for most organizations is the cycle of economic factors, generally referred to as the *business cycle.* While some economists previously thought governmental action could essentially eliminate cyclical swings in the economy, this component still apparently exists and is very important for many organizations. The organizations hardest hit by the cyclical component are those connected with items purchased with discretionary income (appliances, cars, travel, and so forth). These are items people can often postpone purchasing and, consequently, are those most affected by a downturn in the economy.

The cyclical component is isolated by first removing the trend and seasonal factors from the time series data. While many complicated methods exist to isolate the cyclical component, the general procedure can be demonstrated graphically by the sales data for the Apex Appliance Company in Figure 17-10 (page 922).

We will use the quarterly sales data for JB's Restaurants to demonstrate one method for isolating the cyclical component in a time series. Table 17-5 (page 923) shows the values involved in the calculations. The quarterly revenue data for years 1987–1990 are shown in column 2.

Column 3 contains the trend values determined by the least squares regression trend line,

$$\hat{Y} = 23.813 + 0.357t$$

where revenue is the dependent variable and $t = 1, 2, 3, \ldots, 16$.

Column 4 contains the seasonal index for each quarter, as determined in Table 17-4. Note that we have used the same index value, i.e., the normalized average, for all corresponding quarters.

The next step in separating the cyclical component from the trend and seasonal components is to calculate the statistical normal values ($T \cdot S$) by multiplying the trend value by the seasonal index values.

The cyclical component, which also contains the irregular fluctuations, is determined for each time period by dividing the statistical normal values into the

FIGURE 17-10

Isolating the Cyclical Component for the Apex Appliance Company Example

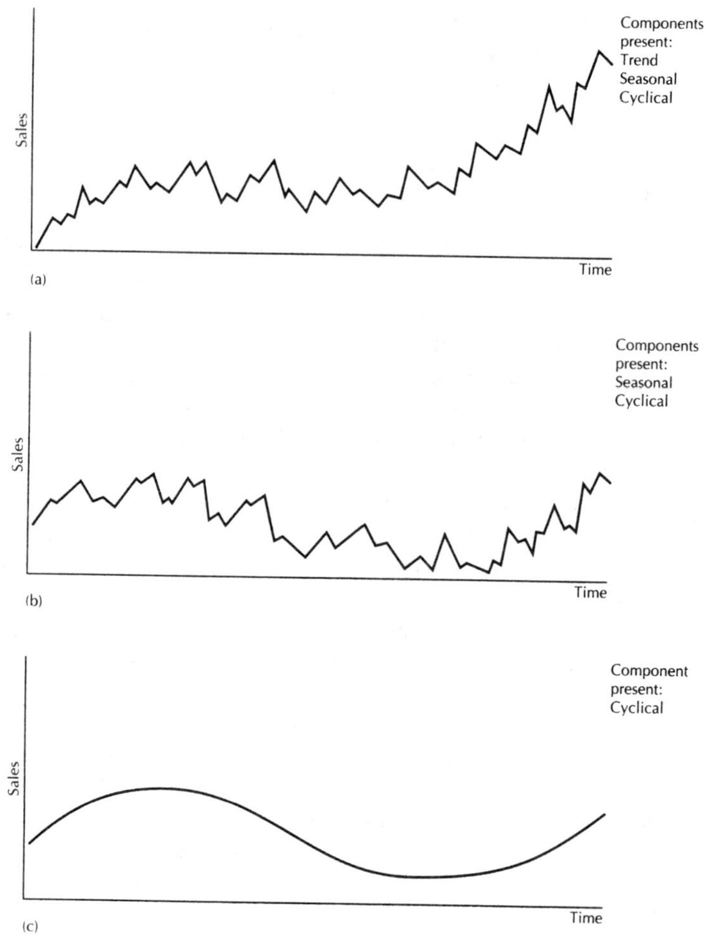

original actual revenue (column 2), $[Y/(T \cdot S)]$. To transfer this ratio to a percentage form, we multiply by 100. These percentages are shown in column 6 of Table 17-5. These values are also shown in Figure 17-11.

SKILL DEVELOPMENT PROBLEMS FOR **SECTION 17-5**

The following set of problems is included to test your understanding of the material in this section.

10. Refer to the sales data in Problem 8 in Section 17-4. Isolate the cyclical–irregular component of the sales data by constructing a table like Table 17-5.

TABLE 17-5

Determining the Cyclical Component for JB's Restaurants Example

Quarter	Actual Revenue	Trend Value T	Seasonal Index S	Statistical Normal $T \cdot S$	Cyclical–Irregular $\frac{Y}{T \cdot S} \cdot 100$
1	22.2	24.17	0.8726	21.09	105.3
2	21.6	24.53	0.8616	21.14	102.2
3	37	24.88	1.3023	32.40	114.2
4	24.7	25.24	0.9635	24.32	101.6
5	21.9	25.60	0.8726	22.34	98.0
6	21.8	25.96	0.8616	22.37	97.5
7	31.1	26.31	1.3023	34.26	90.8
8	24.9	26.67	0.9635	25.70	96.9
9	23.4	27.03	0.8726	23.59	99.2
10	24	27.39	0.8616	23.60	101.7
11	35.2	27.74	1.3023	36.13	97.4
12	26.8	28.10	0.9635	27.07	99.0
13	24.2	28.46	0.8726	24.83	97.5
14	24.5	28.82	0.8616	24.83	98.7
15	37.1	29.17	1.3023	37.99	97.7
16	29.2	29.53	0.9635	28.45	102.6

FIGURE 17-11

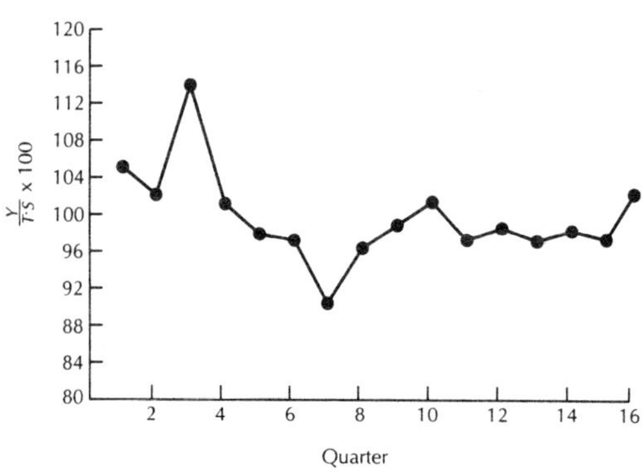

Cyclical–Irregular Component for JB's Restaurants Example

11. Isolate the cyclical–irregular component of the following quarterly inventory data given in hundreds of thousands of dollars by constructing a table like Table 17-5.

1988		*1989*	
1st quarter	218	1st quarter	250
2d quarter	190	2d quarter	220
3d quarter	236	3d quarter	265
4th quarter	218	4th quarter	241

(continued)

1990		*1991*	
1st quarter	244	1st quarter	229
2d quarter	228	2d quarter	221
3d quarter	263	3d quarter	248
4th quarter	240	4th quarter	231

12. If you have done Problems 6 and 9, you have analyzed the trend and seasonal data for José Gutierrez's health care business. Now find the cyclical–irregular component for the sales data from Problem 3, Section 17-1.

17-6 ANALYZING THE IRREGULAR COMPONENT

Irregular components are those fluctuations in a time series that cannot be attributed to any of the three previously discussed components. Irregular influences may be caused by any number of one-time factors. For instance, a severe winter, a summer drought, a civil war in a country supplying raw materials, and many other factors can cause irregular changes in the time series. These events would likely cause a large irregular fluctuation, but many small, unrelated events can combine to cause random variation around the time series.

Extreme irregular variations can cause organizations a great deal of trouble. In fact, if the irregularities are severe enough, they can cause the organization to go out of business. When possible, most organizations buy insurance against the monetary effects of severe irregular effects.

Small irregular variations cause lesser problems. One of these problems crops up when the time series is being analyzed. Decision makers will generally attempt to smooth out the minor irregularities, using a moving-average approach that will be discussed in some detail in the next chapter. The goal is to eliminate as much as possible the irregular influences, so that the true trend, seasonal, and cyclical components can be recognized.

17-7 PERCENTAGE PRICE INDEXES

"The dollar's not worth what it used to be" is a saying everyone has heard. The problem is that, for all organizations, nothing is worth what it used to be; sometimes it is worth more and other times it is worth less. For instance, a barrel of oil was worth less in both 1985 and 1975 than it was in 1980. The problem for decision makers is that, when evaluating data collected over time, they must often compare one figure or data point with others measured at different times. A common procedure for making relative comparisons is to construct a series of *index numbers*, using a base to which all other values can be compared.

The Armstrong Corporation is considering purchasing a small textile mill in Georgia. The present mill owners stress as a positive attribute the mill's rapid sales growth over the past 10 years. While conceding the sales growth, Ann Armstrong, who is negotiating the purchase, is concerned with the increase in per hour labor rates for production workers.

TABLE 17-6

Hourly Wage Rates for the Armstrong Corporation Example

Year	Hourly Wages
1982	$ 8.50
1983	9.10
1984	10.00
1985	10.80
1986	11.55
1987	12.15
1988	12.85
1989	13.70
1990	14.75
1991	15.45

Table 17-6 shows the mill hourly wage data for the years 1982 to 1991. Since she is dealing with price changes of a single item, Ann can construct an index number called a *percentage price relative.* To do this, she must first select a base year. Suppose she chooses 1982 as the base year. She will set the 1982 wage rate equal to 100, which means that 1982 hourly wages were 100 percent of 1982 hourly wages. Next, she can compute each subsequent year's wage rate as a percentage of the 1982 wage rate. To do this, divide each year's wage rate by the rate in the base period and multiply by 100, as shown in equation 17-1:

$$\text{Percentage price relatives index} = I_n = \frac{P_n}{P_b}100 \qquad \textbf{17-1}$$

where

P_b = Price (wage rate here) in the base year

P_n = Price (wage rate here) in a given year

The index numbers for the textile mill's wage rate are shown in Table 17-7.

By examining the index numbers in Table 17-7, Ann Armstrong can see that 1991 hourly wages are up 81.8% over 1982 hourly wages. However, she cannot compare two index numbers, such as those for 1990 and 1991, to each other. That is, wages were not up 8.3% between 1990 and 1991, simply because this is the difference between the index numbers for the 2 years. The true percentage increase between 1990 and 1991 is found by dividing the difference in index numbers by the earlier index number and then multiplying by 100.

$$\frac{181.8 - 173.5}{173.5}100 = 4.8\%$$

TABLE 17-7

Wage Rate Index for the Armstrong Corporation Example

Year	Hourly Wages	Index Numbers
1982	$ 8.50	100.0
1983	9.10	107.1
1984	10.00	117.6
1985	10.80	127.1
1986	11.55	135.9
1987	12.15	142.9
1988	12.85	151.2
1989	13.70	161.2
1990	14.75	173.5
1991	15.45	181.8

SKILL DEVELOPMENT PROBLEMS FOR **SECTION 17-7**

The following set of problems is included to test your understanding of the material in this section.

13. The following data represent United Way collections for a medium-sized southern city. Use 1978 as the base year to construct a relative index showing how donations have increased.

Year	*Donations (in millions)*
1978	$19.4
1979	22.6
1980	23.7
1981	25.5
1982	27.8
1983	28.1
1984	30.0
1985	32.2
1986	33.8
1987	35.3
1988	36.1
1989	38.9
1990	40.7

14. Analyze the donation data given in Problem 13, using 1983 as the base year.

17-8 AGGREGATE PRICE INDEXES

In the previous section, Ann Armstrong was analyzing the increase in hourly wage rates for production workers at a textile mill her company was interested in purchasing. She knows, however, that she should also consider office wage rates

TABLE 17-8

Hourly Wage Rates for the Armstrong Corporation Example

Year	Production Hourly Wages	Office Hourly Wages
1982	$ 8.50	$ 9.10
1983	9.10	9.45
1984	10.00	9.80
1985	10.80	10.25
1986	11.55	10.60
1987	12.15	10.95
1988	12.85	11.45
1989	13.70	11.90
1990	14.75	12.55
1991	15.45	13.45

in her analysis. Average hourly office wage rates and the same production worker rates are shown in Table 17-8.

Ann can use these two wage rates to calculate three common aggregate indexes.

THE UNWEIGHTED AGGREGATE INDEX

To find an unweighted index of wages, Ann would simply divide the sum of the wages in the two categories in each year by the sum of the wages in the base year. In notation form, this is given by equation 17-2:

$$I_n = \frac{\Sigma P_n}{\Sigma P_b} 100 \qquad \text{(17-2)}$$

The sum of the wages in the base year is P_{82} = \$8.50 + \$9.10 = \$17.60. The sum of the wages in 1983 is \$18.55, so I_{83} will be (18.55/17.60)100 = 105.4. The unweighted aggregate indexes for years 1982 through 1991 are shown in Table 17-9 (page 928).

The unweighted index may distort the true movement of wage rates. It assumes equal weighting for both groups, and to the extent to which this is not the case—for instance, if the company has more production employees than office employees—the index number will not represent actual wage movements. Two other common indexes—the Paasche and the Laspeyres—incorporate group weighting.

TABLE 17-9

Unweighted Aggregate Indexes for the Armstrong Corporation Example

Year	Production Hourly Wages	Office Hourly Wages	Index Numbers
1982	$ 8.50	$ 9.10	100.0
1983	9.10	9.45	105.4
1984	10.00	9.80	112.5
1985	10.80	10.25	119.6
1986	11.55	10.60	125.9
1987	12.15	10.95	131.3
1988	12.85	11.45	138.1
1989	13.70	11.90	145.5
1990	14.75	12.55	155.1
1991	15.45	13.45	164.2

THE PAASCHE INDEX

If Ann knew that the work force in 1991 was 60% office workers and 40% production workers, she could use these values to weight the index numbers constructed for all 10 years. She would be constructing a Paasche index, which is defined by equation 17-3:

$$I_n = \frac{\Sigma Q_n P_n}{\Sigma Q_n P_b} 100 \qquad \text{(17-3)}$$

where

P_b = Price (here wage rate) in the base year

P_n = Price in a given year

Q_n = Weighting percentages from a given year

Note that the percentages from the current period are used for all years in calculating the Paasche index.

In analyzing the wage rate increases using the Paasche index, the weighted wage rate for the base year, 1982, would be

$$0.6 \times \$9.10 + 0.4 \times \$8.50 = \$8.86$$

The weighted wage rate for 1983 would be

$$0.6 \times \$9.45 + 0.4 \times \$9.10 = \$9.31$$

TABLE 17-10

Paasche Indexes for the Armstrong Corporation Example

Year	Production Hourly Wages	Office Hourly Wages	Index Numbers
1982	$ 8.50	$ 9.10	100.0
1983	9.10	9.45	105.1
1984	10.00	9.80	111.5
1985	10.80	10.25	118.2
1986	11.55	10.60	123.9
1987	12.15	10.95	129.0
1988	12.85	11.45	135.6
1989	13.70	11.90	142.4
1990	14.75	12.55	151.6
1991	15.45	13.45	160.8

and the Paasche index for 1983 is (9.31/8.86)100 = 105.1. The Paasche indexes for the years 1982 through 1991 are shown in Table 17-10. Notice that the index numbers calculated using the 1991 weights in Table 17-10 are different from the unweighted indexes found in Table 17-9.

THE LASPEYRES INDEX

Ann Armstrong was able to use the percentage weights from 1991 to determine the appropriate values for the Paasche index. If she knew that the labor mix in the base year, 1982, was 60% production workers and 40% office workers she could construct a Laspeyres index, which is defined by equation 17-4:

$$I_n = \frac{\Sigma Q_b P_n}{\Sigma Q_b P_b} 100 \qquad \text{(17-4)}$$

where

P_b = Price (here wage rate) in the base year

P_n = Price in a given year

Q_b = Weighting percentages from the base year

Note that the percentages from the base year are used for all years in calculating the Laspeyres index.

The Laspeyres index is similar to the Paasche index, with the difference that percentages are found from the base year mix as opposed to the current year mix.

TABLE 17-11

Laspeyres Indexes for the Armstrong Corporation Example

Year	Production Hourly Wages	Office Hourly Wages	Index Numbers
1982	$ 8.50	$ 9.10	100.0
1983	9.10	9.45	105.7
1984	10.00	9.80	113.5
1985	10.80	10.25	121.1
1986	11.55	10.60	127.8
1987	12.15	10.95	133.5
1988	12.85	11.45	140.6
1989	13.70	11.90	148.5
1990	14.75	12.55	158.7
1991	15.45	13.45	167.6

The weighted wage rate for the base year, 1982, would be

$$0.4 \times \$9.10 + 0.6 \times \$8.50 = \$8.74$$

The weighted wage rate for 1983 would be

$$0.4 \times \$9.45 + 0.6 \times \$9.10 = \$9.24$$

and the Laspeyres index for 1983 is (9.24/8.74)100 = 105.7. The Laspeyres indexes for the years 1982 through 1991 are shown in Table 17-11. Notice that the index numbers calculated using the 1982 weights in Table 17-11 are different from those found in both Table 17-10 and Table 17-9.

The purpose of this section was to demonstrate how to determine three commonly used techniques to find index numbers for groups of values *and* to show that the same data can yield different index numbers depending on how they are analyzed. We will make more of this point in the next section.

SKILL DEVELOPMENT PROBLEMS FOR **SECTION 17-8**

The following set of problems is included to test your understanding of the material in this section.

15. The following values represent advertising rates paid by a regional catalog retailer which advertises either on radio or in newspapers.

Year	*30-Second Radio Advertisement*	*1/4-Page Newspaper Ad*
1985	150	200
1986	155	210
1987	165	230
1988	173	260
1989	181	290
1990	190	320
1991	198	330

Determine a relative index for each type of advertisement, using 1985 as the base year.

16. Using the values given in Problem 15, determine an unweighted aggregate index for the two types of advertisement.

17. In 1985 the retailer spent 30% of the advertisement budget on radio advertising and 70% on newspaper advertising. Use these values to construct a Laspeyres index for the data in Problem 15.

18. In 1991 the advertising had changed to 45% radio and 55% newspaper. Use these values to construct a Paasche index for the data in Problem 15.

17-9 COMMONLY USED INDEX NUMBERS

In addition to determining their own index numbers, decision makers will encounter a variety of index numbers in their normal activities. Federal and state governmental agencies produce index numbers that help measure such economic variables as retail prices, wholesale prices, stock market activity, production output, inventory levels, and the value of the dollar.

THE CONSUMER PRICE INDEX

To most of us, inflation has come to mean increased prices and less purchasing power for our dollar. The *Consumer Price Index* (CPI), constructed by the U.S. Department of Labor, Bureau of Labor Statistics, attempts to measure the overall change in retail prices for goods and services.

The consumer price index is a complicated attempt to provide a measure of changes in the relative price of a "market basket" of goods and services used by a typical wage earner living in a city. This compilation is so complicated that in 1977, two indexes were constructed. The first, the index for wage earners and clerical workers, was the same as had been constructed in previous years. The second, the index for all urban households, was a new index created to better represent this major segment of the economy. The purpose of having two indexes is to provide more useful economic information; however, changing consumption patterns will undoubtedly cause future revisions in the index. Therefore, any short discussion of the index will leave out important facts. The market basket consists of about 400 items a city dweller would purchase, grouped into seven major categories. The items in the basket are determined by sampling and are therefore subject to all the problems associated with sampling error. In addition, the basket of 400 items is a limited representation of the thousands of items households consume. On top of that, average prices for these goods and services are determined by measuring all large urban areas and a selected sample of smaller communities. The major categories used in determining this index are

Food and beverages

Housing

Apparel and upkeep

Transportation

Medical care

Entertainment

Other goods and services

The CPI was first published in 1913. Because the purpose of the index was to measure cost of living, the "market basket" has, of necessity, changed over the years as new consumer items such as televisions, stereos, and videocassette recorders have become available. Since 1945, the base period used in the index has been updated, using values in base periods of 1947–1949, 1957–1959, 1967, and 1982–1984.

Table 17-12 shows the percentage of the market basket devoted to the seven categories in June 1977 and December 1990. These percentages, or weighting factors, are periodically changed. Recently, the percentage of the market basket devoted to food and beverages has decreased while that devoted to housing has increased.

The consumer price index is similar to the Laspeyres index in that percentage weightings, once established, are used for future time periods. The percentage weightings may change between base periods; however, this would not happen with a true Laspeyres index. In addition, the CPI tries to consider product improvements and quantity decreases. For instance, if base model Pontiacs increase by $200 this year, but a stereo cassette player that was a $200 option becomes a standard feature this year, there would be no actual price increase. On the other hand, if the price of a Snickers candy bar remains the same this year, but the weight is decreased by 10%, there would be a price increase.

TABLE 17-12

Weightings for Major Categories in the Consumer Price Index for All Urban Consumers

Categories	June 1977 Percentage	December 1990 Percentage
Food and beverages	23.667	17.706
Housing	34.202	41.356
Apparel and upkeep	9.194	6.073
Transportation	13.548	17.796
Medical care*	9.288	6.387
Entertainment*	5.143	4.316
Other goods and services	4.582	6.367

*These categories changed between 1977 and 1990.

TABLE 17-13

End-of-Year Historical Consumer Price Index Values

Year	Index Values	Year	Index Values
1952	26.7	1972	42.5
1953	26.9	1973	46.2
1954	26.7	1974	51.9
1955	26.8	1975	55.5
1956	27.6	1976	58.2
1957	28.4	1977	62.1
1958	28.9	1978	67.7
1959	29.4	1979	76.7
1960	29.8	1980	86.3
1961	30.0	1981	94.0
1962	30.4	1982	97.6
1963	30.9	1983	101.3
1964	31.2	1984	105.3
1965	31.8	1985	109.3
1966	32.9	1986	110.5
1967	33.9	1987	115.4
1968	35.5	1988	120.5
1969	37.7	1989	126.1
1970	39.8	1990	133.8
1971	41.1		

The CPI values, determined using base years of 1982–1984, are shown in Table 17-13. Remember that you cannot determine the inflation rate simply by subtracting the values for 2 successive years. Instead, you must divide the difference by the value in the first of the 2 years.

WHOLESALE PRICE INDEX

The U.S. Department of Labor, Bureau of Labor Statistics, also constructs an index of prices of goods sold in U.S. primary markets. Primary markets are those where the first significant large-volume purchase for each item is made. Their measure determines the *Wholesale Price Index.*

Many groups—governmental, industrial, and academic—study the relationship between the Wholesale Price Index and the CPI. Generally, increases in the Wholesale Price Index are followed by a delayed increase in the CPI.

INDUSTRIAL PRODUCTION INDEX

The Federal Reserve Board constructs the *Industrial Production Index.* This index measures change in the volume of industrial production, including manufacturing, mining, and utilities. The purpose of this index is to keep us apprised of productivity levels through various groupings of products and materials.

STOCK MARKET INDEXES

Probably the best known stock market index is the *Dow Jones Industrial Average.* This index is computed each day the New York Stock Exchange is open and indicates the condition of the market in general. The Dow Jones Industrial Average is determined by the daily closing stock prices for thirty selected industrial companies, adjusted for any dividends or mergers that take place for these companies. Of course, stocks not included in the Dow may perform much differently than would be indicated by the index.

Another stock market index is the *Standard and Poor's 500.* This index is determined by stock prices of 500 industrials, not all of which are blue-chip companies. Many market analysts prefer the Standard and Poor's 500 to the Dow because they think it better represents the market as a whole.

17-10 USING INDEX NUMBERS TO DEFLATE A TIME SERIES

A common use of index numbers is to convert values measured at different times into more directly comparable measurements. For instance, if your wages increase, but at a rate less than inflation, you will in fact be earning less in "real terms." A company experiencing increasing sales at a rate of increase less than the inflation rate would actually be doing less well over time.

The Wyman–Gordon Company, located in Massachusetts, designs and produces forgings, primarily for internal combustion engines. The company has recently been experiencing some difficulty. It has also recently discontinued its agricultural and earthmoving equipment operations. Table 17-14 shows 11 years of

TABLE 17-14

Wyman–Gordon Yearly Sales

Year	Sales (in millions)
1980	$550.2
1981	610.3
1982	473.1
1983	383.5
1984	425.5
1985	384.1
1986	341.0
1987	310.3
1988	271.6
1989	371.6
1990	390.0

TABLE 17-15

Wyman–Gordon Yearly Sales (in Millions)

Year	Sales (Current $)	Sales (1982–1984 $)
1980	550.2	637.5
1981	610.3	649.3
1982	473.1	484.7
1983	383.5	378.6
1984	425.5	404.1
1985	384.1	351.4
1986	341.0	308.6
1987	310.3	268.9
1988	271.6	225.4
1989	371.6	294.7
1990	390.0	291.5

recent sales values. While these sales figures show a general decline, actual sales increases or declines can be masked by inflation. For instance, if inflation increases 5% in any year, a company should show at least a 5% sales increase. Otherwise, sales in real terms, or constant dollars, will have declined.

To convert the sales values to constant dollars, simply divide the current value by the appropriate index value found in Table 17-13 and then multiply by 100. So, in constant dollars, 1980 sales would be $(550.2/86.3) \times 100 = 637.5$. Table 17-15 shows sales in both current dollars and in 1982–1984 dollars. Notice, when the effect of inflation is accounted for by converting sales to a deflated value, the decline in sales seen by the company looks worse.

SKILL DEVELOPMENT PROBLEMS FOR **SECTION 17-10**

The following set of problems is included to test your understanding of the material in this section.

19. Use the consumer price index values given in Table 17-13 to deflate the following sales values:

Year	*Sales (in millions)*
1985	$10.4
1986	11.2
1987	12.1
1988	14.2
1989	15.0
1990	16.7
1991	18.3

20. Use the consumer price index values given in Table 17-13 to deflate the following inventory levels:

Year	*Inventory (×\$100,000)*
1975	4.3
1976	4.7
1977	5.1
1978	4.8
1979	6.2
1980	7.1
1981	6.6
1982	7.5
1983	8.2
1984	8.0
1985	7.7
1986	8.1

17-11 CONCLUSIONS

This chapter introduced the basics of time series analysis and defined the four components of a time series: long-term trend, seasonal component, cyclical component, and irregular component.

Decision makers need to examine variables measured over time in an effort to learn about the past. We study the past to make better decisions about the future. However, the future may or may not reflect the past, and care should be used in making conclusions about the future based solely on historical data.

We have illustrated some basic techniques for extracting the long-term trend, seasonal, and cyclical components from a time series. The techniques discussed here represent only a few of the many time series analytic procedures that have been developed and are applied in decision-making situations.

We can look backward by analyzing the time series data. This analysis will provide good information about the future as long as the future looks pretty much like the past. However, time series analysis is of little help if the future departs drastically from the past. No matter how sophisticated our analysis, we cannot use the past to foresee new and unusual events of the future. Decision makers should recognize both the strengths and weaknesses of time series analysis. If they do, they will find it a valuable tool in decision making.

In the past few decades, one of the disturbing factors on the decision-making scene has been the problem of inflation. A common method for trying to eliminate the effect of inflation when comparing data gathered in different time periods is to use an index number. This chapter has discussed how index numbers are constructed and has looked at some commonly used indexes.

CHAPTER GLOSSARY

cyclical component The periodic movements in a time series usually caused by economic factors. The frequency and intensity of the cyclical components are not totally predictable.

irregular component The changes in the time series that are unpredictable and cannot be attributed to a trend, seasonal, or cyclical factor.

seasonal component The increases and decreases in the time series that occur at predetermined times of the year with predictable intensities.

seasonal index The ratio found by dividing the observed value of a period by the value of an average period.

time series A series of measurements taken of a variable at different times. In most applications, the time periods are uniform.

trend component The long-run average increase or decrease in the time series.

CHAPTER FORMULAS

Paasche index

$$I_n = \frac{\Sigma Q_n P_n}{\Sigma Q_n P_b} 100$$

where

P_b = Price in the base year

P_n = Price in a given year

Q_n = Weighting percentages from a given year

Laspeyres index

$$I_n = \frac{\Sigma Q_b P_n}{\Sigma Q_b P_b} 100$$

where

P_b = Price in the base year

P_n = Price in a given year

Q_b = Weighting percentages from the base year

Percentage price relatives index

$$I_n = \frac{P_n}{P_b} 100$$

Unweighted aggregate index

$$I_n = \frac{\Sigma P_n}{\Sigma P_b} 100$$

CONCEPTUAL QUESTIONS AND ASSIGNMENTS

21. Identify three businesses in your community that might be expected to have sales that exhibit a seasonal component. Discuss.
22. If enrollments at a particular university have steadily declined over the past 10 years, which time series component would be illustrated if enrollments were graphed for this period of time? Discuss.
23. The Willow Manufacturing Company has been in operation for 20 years. Records of annual sales have been maintained over this time period. If we graphed the data, would it be likely that the data would contain a seasonal component? Discuss.
24. Discuss the difference between a cyclical component and a seasonal component.
25. Which component is more predictable, seasonal or cyclical? Discuss and illustrate with examples.
26. Discuss some of the advantages of using index numbers.

ADDITIONAL PROBLEMS

The following problems are all based on material covered in this chapter, but may not be presented to correspond with the order of the chapter.

Problems 27–30 refer to the Malcar Autoparts Company, which has started producing replacement control microcomputers for automobiles. This has been a growth industry since the first control units were introduced in 1976. Sales data since the control unit was introduced are as follows:

Year	*Sales*	*Year*	*Sales*
1976	$ 240,000	1984	$1,570,000
1977	218,000	1985	1,947,000
1978	405,000	1986	2,711,000
1979	587,000	1987	3,104,000
1980	795,000	1988	2,918,000
1981	762,000	1989	4,606,000
1982	998,000	1990	5,216,000
1983	1,217,000	1991	5,010,000

27. Graph these data and indicate whether they appear to have a linear trend.
28. Develop a simple linear regression model with *time* as the independent variable. Using this regression model, describe the trend and the strength of the linear trend over the 16 years. Is the trend line statistically significant? Plot the trend line against the actual data.
29. Does it appear that an exponential trend may be more descriptive of the sales pattern than a linear trend? Develop a least squares regression model using the square of time as the independent variable. Plot this regression line against the original data. Based on the regression statistics, would you conclude that the exponential trend is more representative of the sales data than the linear trend? Discuss. (*Hint:* See Chapter 14.)
30. Use the values given in Table 17-13 to deflate these sales data. Fit a linear regression line to both the original and deflated data. Discuss the differences between these two lines.

31. Sunrise Sports has experienced rapidly expanding retail sales. Its sales levels for the past 12 years are

Year	*Sales (millions)*	*Year*	*Sales (millions)*
1979	$1.9	1985	$ 8.6
1980	3.1	1986	9.3
1981	2.8	1987	11.0
1982	4.5	1988	13.9
1983	5.7	1989	16.6
1984	5.8	1990	19.4

Plot this series on ordinary graph paper and describe the trend in the data. Construct a least squares regression line to fit the data. How does this line explain the variation in past sales data? Comment on any patterns you see in the relationship between the actual sales values and those values predicted by the regression analysis.

32. Refer to Problem 31. Deflate this data using the CPI values given in Table 17-13. Then fit a simple linear regression line to both the original data and the deflated data. Discuss the differences between these two lines.

33. The following are birth rates (per 1,000) in the United States between 1930 and 1988. Develop a time series plot of the data.

Year	*Birth Rate*	*Year*	*Birth Rate*	*Year*	*Birth Rate*
1930	21.3	1950	23.9	1970	18.4
1931	20.2	1951	24.8	1971	17.2
1932	19.5	1952	25.0	1972	15.6
1933	18.4	1953	24.9	1973	14.8
1934	19.0	1954	25.2	1974	14.8
1935	18.7	1955	24.9	1975	14.6
1936	18.4	1956	25.1	1976	14.6
1937	18.7	1957	25.3	1977	15.1
1938	19.2	1958	24.5	1978	15.0
1939	18.8	1959	24.3	1979	15.6
1940	19.4	1960	23.7	1980	15.9
1941	20.3	1961	23.5	1981	15.8
1942	22.2	1962	22.6	1982	15.9
1943	22.7	1963	21.9	1983	15.5
1944	21.3	1964	21.2	1984	15.5
1945	20.4	1965	19.4	1985	15.8
1946	24.1	1966	18.4	1986	15.6
1947	26.5	1967	17.8	1987	15.7
1948	24.8	1968	17.5	1988	15.9
1949	24.5	1969	17.8		

Problems 34 and 35 refer to Sam Lamborn, who started Instisurv, a computerized service where clients could both find information and make purchases of items such as airline tickets, stereo equipment, and listed stocks, 4 years ago. Data on monthly calls for service for the time the company has been in business are shown.

Month		Calls	Month		Calls	Month		Calls
Jan	1	23,500		17	26,900		33	39,700
	2	21,700		18	29,700		34	42,400
	3	18,750		19	31,100		35	43,600
	4	22,000		20	32,400		36	47,400
	5	23,000		21	34,500	Jan	37	32,400
	6	26,200		22	35,700		38	35,600
	7	27,300		23	42,000		39	31,200
	8	29,300		24	42,600		40	34,600
	9	31,200	Jan	25	31,000		41	36,800
	10	34,200		26	30,400		42	35,700
	11	39,500		27	29,800		43	37,500
	12	43,400		28	32,500		44	40,000
Jan	13	23,500		29	34,500		45	43,200
	14	23,400		30	33,800		46	46,700
	15	21,400		31	34,200		47	50,100
	16	24,200		32	36,700		48	52,100

34. a. Consider the multiplicative time series model. Determine the trend associated with these data.
    b. Use the trend found in part **a** to isolate the effects of the other three components.
    c. Next isolate the $C \times I$ component in the data.

35. Use the methods discussed in Section 17-5 to extract the combined cyclical and irregular components from the time series. Plot these index values on a graph.

Problems 36 and 37 refer to Anna Chen, the personnel manager of Datatron Corporation. She is trying to determine whether a pattern exists for sick days by employees. She hopes to use this analysis to plan production schedules for the next year. Following are the data on sick days, by month, for the last 3 years.

Month		Days Sick	Month		Days Sick	Month		Days Sick
Jan	1	1,580	Jan	13	1,630	Jan	25	1,960
	2	1,608		14	1,700		26	1,880
	3	1,370		15	1,610		27	1,820
	4	1,260		16	1,590		28	1,750
	5	1,125		17	1,498		29	1,690
	6	1,306		18	1,540		30	1,730
	7	1,240		19	1,580		31	1,690
	8	1,340		20	1,680		32	1,780
	9	1,090		21	1,560		33	1,670
	10	980		22	1,520		34	1,560
	11	1,260		23	1,670		35	1,760
	12	1,680		24	1,920		36	2,040

36. a. Plot these data on a time series plot and describe in a short report what these 3 years of employee sick days have been like for Anna's company.
b. Determine whether a seasonal pattern exists for the 3 years of data.

37. Extract the combined cyclical and irregular components from the time series and plot these on a graph.

38. Ellial's Quality Discount Store has applied for a line of credit with the First National Bank. This line of credit is to be used primarily for financing inventory purchases. As part of the financial application, Ellial's has been asked to provide monthly inventory levels for the past 5 years. These levels (in millions of dollars) are

Month	*1987*	*1988*	*1989*	*1990*	*1991*
Jan	5.2	4.7	6.6	7.1	7.0
Feb	3.3	2.9	4.0	4.0	6.2
Mar	2.8	3.0	3.6	2.6	4.3
Apr	5.3	6.3	7.2	8.0	9.5
May	9.4	10.0	11.4	7.8	12.5
June	2.6	4.3	4.0	5.4	6.4
July	6.2	7.7	8.0	9.3	8.6
Aug	7.2	7.5	6.8	8.2	8.4
Sept	6.8	5.8	6.8	7.9	6.9
Oct	9.7	9.6	8.9	9.3	9.8
Nov	13.6	13.9	14.2	16.1	16.5
Dec	11.8	11.9	12.7	13.8	14.6

a. Determine the seasonal index number for each month.
b. Is there enough consistency between years to make you comfortable using seasonal index numbers?
c. Ellial's will finance 90% of its monthly inventory through bank borrowing. The company has been able to get money at the prime rate plus 2%. However, the interest must be paid monthly, and the value of the loan can change monthly. Estimate the value of interest payments for the next year.

39. Refer to the data for Ellial's Quality Discount Store in Problem 38. Determine the combined cyclical and irregular components using the approach discussed in Section 17-5.

40. The following data represent parking fines collected over the last 11 years by State University:

Year	*Fines*	*Year*	*Fines*
1981	$12,500	1987	$18,790
1982	14,600	1988	23,500
1983	16,250	1989	24,000
1984	19,800	1990	25,600
1985	23,700	1991	27,800
1986	22,700		

a. Construct a fines index for these data using 1981 as the base year. Write a short report analyzing this index.
b. Would it be appropriate to say that fines were up 31.2% between years 1984 and 1987? Discuss why or why not.
c. What percentage increase in parking fines took place between 1990 and 1991?

41. The Quarter-Tron Company is considering the acquisition of two companies to add to its already large list of holdings. Sales records are available for 7 years for company 1 and 5 years for company 2. These data are shown as follows:

Company 1		*Company 2*	
Year	*Sales*	*Year*	*Sales*
1985	$1,345,790	1987	$2,456,800
1986	1,468,900	1988	2,567,800
1987	1,780,000	1989	2,809,800
1988	1,906,700	1990	3,001,100
1989	2,178,000	1991	3,457,000
1990	2,345,600		
1991	2,569,900		

Develop a sales index for each company, using the first available year as the base year.

42. Referring to Problem 41, make the appropriate conversions so that the two indexes can be compared with respect to sales growth of the two companies.

Problems 43–46 refer to U.S. Homes, a major developer of housing communities in the New England area. The company has kept a record of the relative cost of labor (including fringe benefits) and materials in its market area since 1981. These data are as follows:

Year	*Average Hourly Wage for Labor*	*Average Material Cost per House*
1981	$20.10	$46,500
1982	20.50	48,900
1983	21.70	50,600
1984	22.50	50,900
1985	24.00	51,200
1986	24.50	51,700
1987	25.10	52,050
1988	25.05	53,700
1989	24.90	53,400
1990	23.80	54,100
1991	24.20	54,000

43. Using 1981 as the base year, construct a separate index for each component in the construction cost of a house.

44. Plot both series of data and comment on the trend you see in both plots. Then construct a trend line for each set of data. Are either of the trend lines significant at the 0.05 level?

45. Construct a Paasche index using the data, assuming that in 1991, 60% of the cost of a house was labor and 40% was materials. Use 1981 as the base year.

46. Construct a Laspeyres index using the data, assuming that in 1981, 40% of the cost of a house was labor and the rest materials.

47. Lamar Construction Materials has two divisions, the northwest region and the southwest region. Annual sales expenses for the two divisions since 1984 are as follows:

Year	*Sales Expense Northwest Region (×$100,000)*	*Sales Expense Southwest Region (×$100,000)*
1984	3.4	2.9
1985	3.7	3.4
1986	3.9	4.1
1987	4.4	4.8
1988	4.9	5.5
1989	5.2	5.9
1990	5.5	6.4
1991	5.9	7.1

Construct an unweighted aggregate index for Lamar's overall expenses.

48. In 1984 the northwest region accounted for 55% of Lamar Construction's total sales (see Problem 47). Use this percentage to construct a Laspeyres index for the sales expense.

49. In 1991 the southwest region accounted for 60% of Lamar Construction's total sales (see Problem 47). Use this percentage to construct a Paasche index for total sales expense.

CASE

17A Walroad, Wisconsin, Chamber of Commerce

Masao Sugiyama is the recently elected president of the Chamber of Commerce in Walroad, Wisconsin. He is the long-time owner of the only full-service hardware store in this small farming town. Being president of the Chamber has been considered largely a ceremonial post since business conditions have not changed in Walroad in as long as anyone can remember. However, Masao has just read an article in *The Wall Street Journal* that has made him think he needs to take a more active interest in the business conditions of his town.

The article concerned Wal-Mart, the largest retailer in the United States. Wal-Mart has expanded primarily by locating in small towns and avoiding large suburban areas. While the Walroad merchants have not had to deal with either Kmart or Sears since these companies have located primarily in large urban centers, Wal-Mart has recently entered the Wisconsin area. In addition, a supplier has recently told Masao that both Sears and Kmart are considering locating stores in smaller towns to prevent future expansion by Wal-Mart.

Masao has decided that he needs to know more about all three retailers and so has located the following sales data using the Value Line investment service.

Kmart	*Sales Values (million)*	*Sears*	*Sales Values (million)*	*Wal-Mart*	*Sales Values (million)*
1980	$14,204	1980	$25,195	1980	$1,643
1981	16,527	1981	27,357	1981	2,445
1982	16,772	1982	30,020	1982	3,376
1983	18,598	1983	35,882	1983	4,667
1984	21,096	1984	38,828	1984	6,401
1985	22,420	1985	40,715	1985	8,452
1986	83,218	1986	44,282	1986	11,909
1987	25,626	1987	48,440	1987	15,959
1988	27,301	1988	50,250	1988	20,649
1989	29,533	1989	53,794	1989	25,811
1990	32,500	1990	56,785	1990	32,520
1987		1987		1987	
Quarter 1	5,594	Quarter 1	10,480	Quarter 1	3,212
2	6,305	2	11,718	2	3,732
3	5,973	3	12,193	3	4,015
4	7,754	4	14,049	4	5,000
1988		1988		1988	
Quarter 1	5,842	Quarter 1	10,960	Quarter 1	4,282
2	6,684	2	12,160	2	4,845
3	6,358	3	12,567	3	4,991
4	8,417	4	14,563	4	6,531
1989		1989		1989	
Quarter 1	6,068	Quarter 1	12,160	Quarter 1	5,373
2	7,006	2	13,281	2	6,046
3	6,707	3	13,177	3	6,284
4	9,752	4	15,176	4	8,108
1990		1990		1990	
Quarter 1	7,044	Quarter 1	12,606	Quarter 1	6,768
2	7,785	2	13,852	2	7,605
3	7,200	3	14,225	3	7,897
4	10,471	4	16,102	4	10,250

Masao is interested in what all these data tell him. Which firm is growing faster? Are seasonal fluctuations an issue in these sales figures? Is there any evidence that one firm is more affected by the cyclical component than the others? He needs some help in analyzing these data.

REFERENCES

Bails, Dale G. and Peppers, Larry C. *Business Fluctuations: Forecasting Techniques and Applications.* Englewood Cliffs, New Jersey: Prentice-Hall, 1982.

Bowerman, Bruce L. and O'Connell, Richard T. *Time Series Forecasting: Unified Concepts and Computer Implementation,* 2d ed. Boston: Duxbury Press, 1987.

Cryer, Jonathan D. *Time Series Analysis.* Boston: Duxbury Press, 1986.

Granger, C. W. G. *Forecasting in Business and Economics,* 2d ed. New York: Academic Press, 1989.

Montgomery, Douglas C. and Johnson, Lynwood A. *Forecasting and Time Series Analysis,* 2d ed. New York: McGraw-Hill, 1990.

Willis, R. E. *A Guide to Forecasting for Planners.* Englewood Cliffs, New Jersey: Prentice-Hall, 1987.

Chapter 17

Hand-In Exercises

1. Problem 4 in Chapter 17 uses data from Problem 12 which are repeated here. Compute the regression equation and discuss whether it is a good fit. What trend seems to be present in these sales data?

Time Period	Sales
1	152
2	162
3	157
4	167
5	182
6	192
7	191
8	197
9	217
10	209
11	202
12	221
13	231
14	242
15	231
16	224

2. Problem 7 in Chapter 17 also relates to quarterly sales data given in Problem 1. Extract the seasonal component from these data.

	Sales '88	Sales '89	Sales '90	Sales '91
Q1	152	182	217	236
Q2	162	192	209	242
Q3	157	191	202	231
Q4	167	197	221	224

3. Use the results of your previous work from Hand In Exercises 1 and 2 to construct a table like Table 17–5 to isolate the cyclical—irregular component in the sales data.

4. Data given are for the cost of advertising by a catalog retailer who uses radio and newspaper ads. Treat 1985 as the base year and 1990 as a current year for which an index is to be constructed.

ITEM	1985 Price	1985 Quantity	1990 Price	1990 Quantity
Radio Ad	150	30	190	45
Newspaper Ad	200	70	320	55

a. Construct a Laspeyers index of ad costs for 1990 using 1985 as the base year.

b. Construct a Paasche index for 1990.

c. Construct an Edgeworth index for 1990.

d. Construct Fisher's Ideal index for 1990.

Introduction to Forecasting Techniques

WHY DECISION MAKERS NEED TO KNOW

No organization, large or small, can function effectively without a forecast for the goods and services it provides. A supermarket needs to forecast the demand for different types of dairy products. A farmer in Iowa must forecast the demand for corn when deciding what to plant in the spring. The concessionaire at Tiger Stadium in Detroit must forecast each game's attendance to determine how many soft drinks and hot dogs to have at hand. Your state's elected officials must forecast tax revenues in order to establish a budget each year. These are only a few instances in which business forecasting is required, but they should give you an idea of how important forecasting is in the decision-making process. In many cases, the success of the forecasting effort will play a major role in determining the general success of the organization.

CHAPTER OBJECTIVES

Although entire texts have been written about forecasting (see the books by Armstrong and others cited in the references), in this chapter we will introduce some of the most frequently used forecasting models. We will first consider the difference between judgmental and statistical forecasts, but will concentrate on statistical models. All statistical models use data gathered for past time periods to forecast future values. Many types of forecasting models may be used, but constructing a statistical model involves following a three-step procedure to be discussed in this chapter. The statistical models considered fall into four general categories. First, we will look at trend-based forecasting models. You will find these to be an extension of our time series discussion in Chapter 17. Second, we will introduce some simple regression-based forecasting models. These will extend the ideas considered in Chapters 13 and 14. Third, we will consider smoothing-based models, including a moving average, weighted moving average, and single and double exponential smoothing models. Finally, we will finish with a brief discussion of the Box–Jenkins forecasting model.

STUDENT OBJECTIVES

After studying the material in this chapter you should be able to do the following:

1. Discuss the differences between judgmental and statistical forecasts.
2. Discuss the steps needed to build a statistical forecasting model.
3. Extend the time series discussion of the previous chapter to make forecasts using the trend component of the time series.
4. Use both the trend and seasonal components of a time series to forecast future values of a variable of interest.
5. Construct and use autoregressive and indicator variable regression-based models.
6. Employ several kinds of smoothing models to make short-term forecasts.
7. Discuss the concepts involved in the Box–Jenkins forecasting model.

18-1 CATEGORIES OF FORECASTS

If you discuss forecasting with decision makers, they will often confuse forecasting and planning. **Planning** is the process of determining how to deal with the future. On the other hand, **forecasting** is the process of predicting what the future will be like. Forecasts are used as inputs for the planning process.

Experts agree that good planning is essential for an organization to be effective. Because forecasts are an important part of the planning process, decision makers need to be familiar with **forecasting methods.** In this section, we introduce some important terminology pertaining to forecasting and provide a basis for your study of the remaining sections in this chapter.

There are two broad categories of forecasting techniques:

1. Judgmental techniques
2. Statistical techniques

Judgmental forecasting techniques are based on expert opinion and judgment. **Statistical forecasting techniques** are based on statistical methods for analyzing historical data. In general, statistical forecasting techniques are employed when the following three conditions are satisfied:

1. Historical data relating to the variable to be forecasted exist.
2. The historical data can be quantified.
3. You can assume that the historical pattern will continue into the future.

If these conditions do not exist, judgmental forecasting techniques will be used.

In practice, the primary factor that determines the extent to which statistical and judgmental forecasts are used in a given situation seems to be how much uncertainty the decision maker sees in the future. When the decision maker sees the future as mostly an extension of the past, statistical models should be used. The more the future is expected to differ from the past, the more judgment should be incorporated into the decision. Many practical situations involve a combination of both techniques.

18-2 JUDGMENTAL FORECASTS

The advantage of judgmental forecasting is that it employs the experience base of the decision maker along with qualitative and quantitative data. A *judgmental forecast* has no specific data requirements and is not tied directly to the past. The major disadvantage of judgmental forecasting is that there are no statistical means to test the methodology used to arrive at the forecast.

Once a decision maker has decided that a judgmental forecast is needed, the question is whose judgment to use. Although many people have knowledge that will aid in making a forecast, most managers would like to base their decisions on the forecast of experts in a field. From an organizational point of view, these experts seem to fall into four main groups:

1. *Top Management* In many organizations, top-level managers are a good source of forecast information. This is particularly true if the manager has a lot of experience in the field or the organization.
2. *The Sales Force* All organizations ultimately exist because they supply a product or service to meet a demand. Since demand keeps changing, the sales force often develops a sense for this demand faster than any other group.
3. *Consumers* The people who ultimately buy the product or service of an organization are often the experts on their perceived future needs.
4. *Consultants* Often what is a new situation for one organization has been experienced already by another organization. Consultants are often familiar with what was tried, and often worked, someplace else and can provide the company with the necessary experience base.

This list is not all-inclusive. For many organizations, the expert chosen depends on the product or service being sold. Pharmaceutical manufacturers seek the judgment of physicians; electronics manufacturers seek the judgment of electrical engineers; textbook publishers seek the judgment of instructors; and so on. The point is, judgmental forecasting may be the best, or even the only, type of forecast that can be made.

In this section, we introduce two of the most commonly used qualitative forecasting methods. These are the *Delphi method* and *scenario projection.*

THE DELPHI METHOD

Decision makers who employ the **Delphi method** attempt to arrive at a consensus forecast from a group of experts through a systematic procedure involving a series of questionnaires. The experts are purposely kept separated throughout the process. This reduces the potential problems associated with interpersonal exchanges in which dominant personalities might sway the opinion of other experts. Although the precise steps in implementing the Delphi method depend on the situation, the following example demonstrates the general procedure.

1. An issue is identified and a study coordinator appointed. For instance, Artistic Energy Products has developed a process to convert plastic waste into an insulating material suitable for use as siding in new home construction. The new product will be more expensive than present alternatives and, while light, it is also bulky and is therefore hard to transport long distances. The company president is interested in forecasting total demand over the next 10 years within shipping distance of a potential manufacturing plant in Houston, Texas.
2. A group of experts with potential insight in this area would be hired to complete an initial questionnaire relating to the building industry and the prospects for this new product. Suppose three experts make up the panel. Their responses to two key questions are as follows:

   Question 1. What will the total number of new housing starts be over the next 10 years in the Artistic Energy Products market area?

Expert A	*Expert B*	*Expert C*
1,500,000	2,500,000	4,500,000

   Question 2. How many new houses would be likely to use the recycled, but more expensive, siding material over the next 10 years?

Expert A	*Expert B*	*Expert C*
150,000	40,000	500,000

3. Next, the panel of experts would be shown these responses without knowing which forecasts were associated with which expert. They would be given the opportunity to adjust their own responses to the questionnaire. Suppose the revised responses were as follows:

Question 1:

Expert A	*Expert B*	*Expert C*
2,000,000	2,700,000	3,200,000

Question 2:

Expert A	*Expert B*	*Expert C*
200,000	150,000	300,000

4. These results would be shared with the panel, along with responses to any other questions on the questionnaire, and the revision process would be repeated. Management would continue the process until either a general consensus is reached or until the experts cease to revise their forecasts. You should note that the objective is not to arrive at a single forecast value, but to achieve a reasonably narrow spread among the experts.

The Delphi method has some drawbacks, many of which are common to all judgmental forecasts. The most common complaint is the difficulty of evaluating the actual expertise of the "experts." The process may also be sensitive to the questionnaire. However, perhaps because of its structured nature, it is the most widely used qualitative forecasting technique.

SCENARIO PROJECTION

This technique is much less structured than the Delphi method. A company using **scenario projection** will take a set of well-defined and self-contained assumptions and develop a statement of what the future will likely be if these assumptions hold. In an actual application, many sets of assumptions would be formulated and a corresponding number of future scenarios would be determined. The decision maker would have to choose which set of assumptions is most likely and determine whether the related scenario is realistic.

Scenario projection is becoming an increasingly popular forecasting technique. Such leading companies as Royal Dutch/Shell, Southern California Edison, and Honeywell are reporting great success due to the flexibility this technique offers.

SKILL DEVELOPMENT PROBLEMS FOR **SECTION 18-2**

1. This problem must be done with a group. After forming a group of five or six, select one person to act as the forecast coordinator. The task is to use the Delphi method to forecast the skills you will need in order to be employable in the business workplace 25 years from now.

2. This problem is designed for a group. After selecting a forecast coordinator, use the Delphi method to prepare a forecast of significant changes in the

market for products of a locally important industry (e.g., steel, electronics, agriculture, oil, etc.).

3. Make three 20-year scenario projections for the steel industry in the United States. Prepare these scenarios for "best case," "worst case," and "most likely case" situations. For each of the three scenarios, discuss the kinds of companies you see as failing, surviving, and prospering.

4. Repeat Problem 3 for the U.S. computer industry.

18-3 BUILDING A STATISTICAL FORECASTING MODEL

Decision makers who are actively involved in forecasting will frequently say that forecasting is a mix of art and science. Determining the appropriate forecasting model is a challenging task but can be made manageable by employing a model-building strategy composed of the following three steps:

1. Model specification
2. Model fitting
3. Model diagnosis

Model specification, or model identification, involves selecting the forecasting technique to be used in the current application. As we will point out in later sections, guidelines exist for determining which techniques may be more appropriate than others for certain situations. However, it may be necessary to specify (and try) several model forms for a given application before determining an acceptable model.

Model fitting is the process of determining how well the specified model fits the past data. The idea is that if the future tends to look like the past, a model must adequately fit the past data to have a reasonable chance of forecasting the future. The forecaster will spend much time adjusting the model specification and estimating its *parameters* so as to reach an acceptable fit of the past data.

Model diagnosis relates to analyzing the quality of the model employed. You will determine how well the model fits the past data, how well it performs in mock forecasting trials, and how well the assumptions of the model appear to be satisfied. If the model fails on any count, you will be forced to revert to the model specification step and begin again.

An important consideration to keep in mind when you are developing a forecasting model is to use the simplest available model that will meet your forecasting needs. The objective of forecasting is to provide good forecasts. A sophisticated approach is not necessarily required if a simpler one will provide acceptable forecasts.

As in football, where some players specialize in defense and others in offense, forecasting techniques have been developed for special situations, generally dependent on the forecasting horizon. The **forecasting horizon** is the number of periods in the future covered by the forecast. This is referred to as *forecast lead time* by some forecasters. For the purpose of categorizing forecasting techniques, the horizon, or lead time, is typically divided into four categories:

1. **Immediate-term horizon**—less than 1 month
2. **Short-term horizon**—1 to 3 months
3. **Medium-term horizon**—3 months to 2 years
4. **Long-term horizon**—2 years or more

As we introduce different forecasting techniques, we will indicate the forecast horizon(s) for which each is best suited.

In addition to determining the desired forecasting horizon, the forecaster must determine the forecasting period. The **forecasting period** is the unit of time for which forecasts are made. For instance, the forecasting period might be a day, a week, a month, a quarter, or a year. Thus, the forecasting horizon is composed of one or more forecasting periods. If statistical forecasting techniques are to be used, historical data must be available on a forecast-period basis. If we want weekly forecasts, historical data must be measured on a weekly basis, and so forth.

The frequency with which new forecasts are prepared is called the **forecasting interval.** The forecasting interval is generally the same length as the forecast period. That is, if the forecast period is 1 week, then we will provide a new forecast each week.

18-4 TREND-BASED FORECASTING TECHNIQUES

As discussed in Chapter 17, some time series exhibit an increasing or decreasing trend, which may be a **linear trend** or a **nonlinear trend.** A plot of the data will usually help identify which, if any, trend exists.

In this section, we introduce trend-based forecasting techniques, which, as you will see, are based on the time series discussion of the last chapter. Once the *trend model* has been defined, it is used to provide forecasts for future time periods. Trend-based forecasts are very flexible and may be used for lead times ranging from immediate term to long term.

LINEAR TREND FORECASTING

HiRel Cables is a company, founded by a group of executives at a government research facility, that manufactures cables for linked computer systems. The company was founded 15 years ago, but started making a profit within the last 10 years. The founders are considering expanding their manufacturing facilities, since the land next to their plant has just been put up for sale. Table 18-1 (page 954) displays the last 10 years of sales data. A look at the time series plot shown in Figure 18-1 shows an increasing trend.

TABLE 18-1

Sales Values for the HiRel Cable Example

Year	Sales ($ 1,000s)
1982	9,157
1983	11,343
1984	13,419
1985	12,882
1986	10,587
1987	12,370
1988	14,750
1989	15,823
1990	13,890
1991	16,179

FIGURE 18-1

HiRel Cable Company Sales

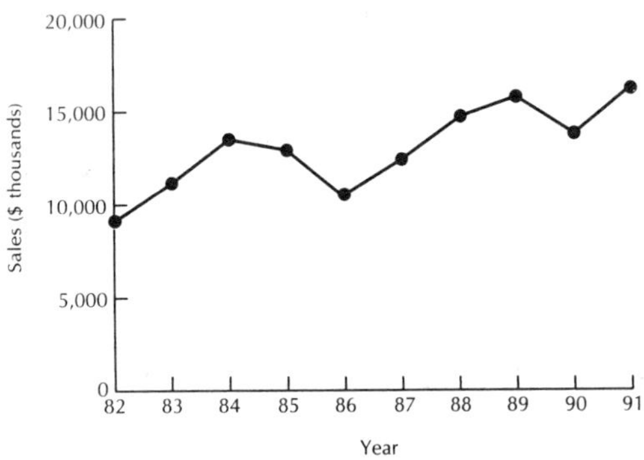

Recall that there are three steps in the forecasting process: model specification, model fitting, and model diagnosis. Model specification consists of identifying the appropriate forecasting technique for a given application; in the case of the HiRel Cable Company example, we propose a linear trend (straight-line) model. In the model-fitting step, the specified model is actually fit to the historical data. Since we have specified a linear trend model, fitting can be done by either "eyeballing" the trend line through the data or by least squares regression analysis.

To use the "eyeballing" method, the manager places a straight line through the data so as to "fit" the data. This method has great appeal since it requires no formal training and can be done quickly. But because different decision makers may well "eyeball" different trend lines, this method can lead to many possible trend lines, as shown in Figure 18-2. As you might expect, forecasts would differ depending on which trend line is selected. The "eyeball" approach is a "quick-and-dirty" method for modeling the trend; using *least squares regression* is gener-

FIGURE 18-2

Three "Eyeball" Trend Lines for the HiRel Cable Company Example

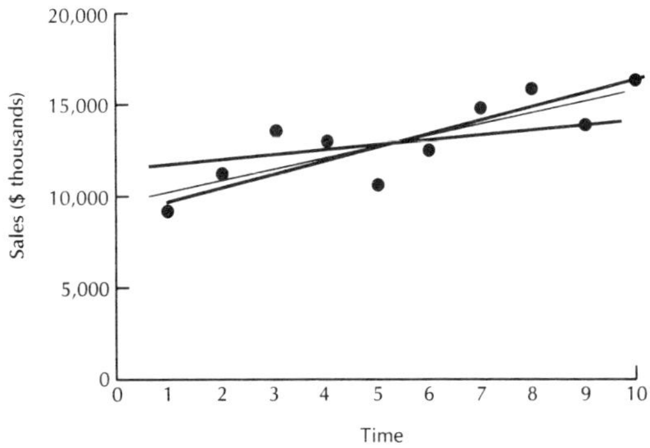

ally preferred. When the model specification calls for a linear trend model, a trend line can be described as a function of time, as shown by equation 18-1:

$$\hat{Y}_t = b_0 + b_1 t \qquad (18\text{-}1)$$

where

$\hat{Y}_t$ = Value of the trend at time t
b_0 = Y-intercept of the trend line
b_1 = Slope of the trend line
t = Time

We let the first period in the time series be $t = 1$, the second period be $t = 2$, and so forth.

Now, let's look at the time series sales data for the HiRel Cable Company in Table 18-1. The least squares equation for the trend line is determined in the following calculations. Note that the equation for b_1 is the same as indicated in Chapter 13, except that here we substitute t for X. Also, we will let Y = actual sales values and $\hat{Y}$ = forecast sales values.

Year	t	Y_t	tY_t	t^2
1982	1	9,157	9,157	1
1983	2	11,343	22,686	4
1984	3	13,419	40,257	9
1985	4	12,882	51,528	16
1986	5	10,587	52,935	25
1987	6	12,370	74,220	36
1988	7	14,750	103,250	49
1989	8	15,823	126,584	64
1990	9	13,890	125,010	81
1991	10	16,179	161,790	100
	55	130,400	767,417	385

FIGURE 18-3

Least Squares Linear Trend of Sales for the HiRel Cable Company

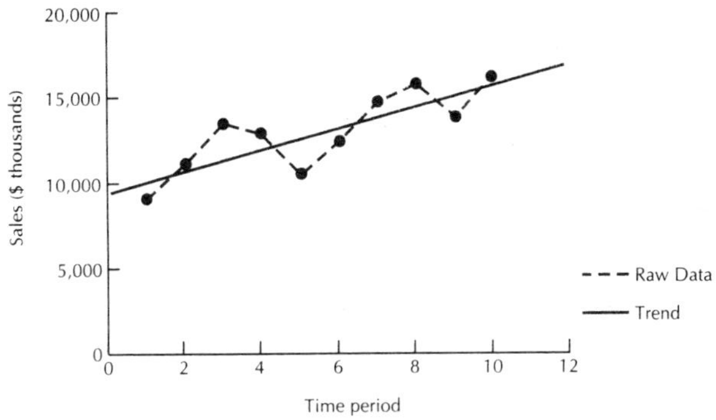

$$\bar{t} = \frac{55}{10} = 5.5$$

$$\bar{Y} = \frac{130{,}400}{10} = 13{,}040$$

$$b_1 = \frac{\Sigma t Y_t - \dfrac{\Sigma t \Sigma Y_t}{n}}{\Sigma t^2 - (\Sigma t)^2/n}$$

$$= \frac{767{,}417 - (55)(130{,}400)/10}{385 - 55^2/10}$$

$$= 608.691$$

$$b_0 = \bar{Y} - b_1\bar{t}$$

$$= 13{,}040 - 608.691(5.5)$$

$$= 9{,}692.2$$

The least squares trend line for the HiRel Cable Company is

$$\hat{Y} = 9{,}692.2 + 608.691t$$

The model has an $R^2 = 0.667$, which indicates the trend model explains 2/3 of the variation in sales values. The calculated F statistic, using a computer model, is 16.013 with 1 and 8 degrees of freedom, indicating the model is statistically significant. Figure 18-3 shows this trend line plotted against the actual sales data.

COMPARING THE TREND LINE WITH PAST DATA

The predicted sales values for periods $t = 1$ through $t = 10$ can be found by substituting for t in the forecast equation

$$\hat{Y}_t = 9{,}692.2 + 608.691t$$

TABLE 18-2

Forecast Values and Residuals ($ 1,000s) for the HiRel Cable Company Example

Year	t	Actual Sales Y_t	Forecast Sales $\hat{Y}_t$	Residual $(Y_t - \hat{Y}_t)$
1982	1	9,157	10,300.89	−1,143.89
1983	2	11,343	10,909.58	433.42
1984	3	13,419	11,518.27	1,900.73
1985	4	12,882	12,126.96	755.04
1986	5	10,587	12,735.65	−2,148.65
1987	6	12,370	13,344.35	−974.35
1988	7	14,750	13,953.04	796.96
1989	8	15,823	14,561.73	1,261.27
1990	9	13,890	15,170.42	−1,280.42
1991	10	16,179	15,779.11	399.89

For example, for $t = 1$ we get

$$\hat{Y}_1 = 9{,}692.2 + 608.691(1)$$
$$= 10{,}300.89$$

Note that the actual sales, Y_1, for period 1 (1982) was 9,157. The difference between the actual sales in time t and the values found using the trend model is called the **forecast error** or **residual.** You might review Section 14-5 for further discussion of residuals. Table 18-2 shows the predicted values for periods 1 through 10 and the residuals.

Finding the residuals by comparing the trend-line values with actual past data is an important part of the **model diagnosis** step. The residuals measure how close the model fits the actual data at each point. A perfect fit would lead to residuals of 0 each time. Beyond that, we would like to see "small" residuals and an "overall good fit." Two commonly used measures of fit based on the residual are available:

1. Mean squared residual or mean square error (MSE), equation 18-2:

$$\text{MSE} = \sum_{t=1}^{n} \frac{(Y_t - \hat{Y}_t)^2}{n} \qquad \textbf{18-2}$$

where

Y_t = Actual value at time t

$\hat{Y}_t$ = Predicted value at time t

n = Number of time periods

2. Mean absolute deviation (MAD), equation 18-3:

$$\text{MAD} = \sum_{t=1}^{n} \frac{|Y_t - \hat{Y}_t|}{n} \qquad \textbf{18-3}$$

Table 18-3 shows the MSE and MAD calculations for the HiRel Cable Company example. These measures are particularly helpful when comparing two or more forecasting techniques. We can compute the MSE and/or the MAD for each forecasting technique. The forecasting technique that gives the smallest MSE or MAD is generally considered to provide the best fit.

Once we are satisfied that the linear trend model provides acceptable predictions for the historical data, we can obtain forecasts for future time periods by substituting values of t into the trend equation. This is called **extrapolation.** For example, the forecast for 1992 is developed by substituting $t = 11$ into the trend equation as follows:

$$\begin{aligned}\hat{Y}_{11} &= 9{,}692.2 + 608.691(11) \\ &= 16{,}387.80\end{aligned}$$

You should be aware that forecasting techniques that use extrapolation work well only as long as the future tends to look like the past. If the future trend changes, the trend forecasting model may yield large forecast errors.

TABLE 18-3

MSE and MAD Computations for the HiRel Cable Company Example

Year	t	Residual $(Y_t - \hat{Y}_t)$	Squared Residual $(Y_t - \hat{Y}_t)^2$	Absolute Residual $\lvert Y_t - \hat{Y}_t\rvert$
1982	1	−1,143.89	1,308,484.3	1,143.89
1983	2	433.42	187,852.9	433.42
1984	3	1,900.73	3,612,774.5	1,900.73
1985	4	755.04	570,085.4	755.04
1986	5	−2,148.65	4,616,696.8	2,148.65
1987	6	−974.35	949,357.9	974.35
1988	7	796.96	635,145.3	796.96
1989	8	1,261.27	1,590,802.0	1,261.27
1990	9	−1,280.42	1,639,475.4	1,280.42
1991	10	399.89	159,912.0	399.89
			15,270,586.5	11,094.62

MSE = 15,270,586.5/10 = 1,527,058.65
MAD = 11,094.62/10 = 1,109.462

SPLIT SAMPLES

A model's true forecasting ability is determined by how well it forecasts future values, not how well it fits historical values. However, having to wait until after the forecast period to know how effective the forecast was does not help assess a model's effectiveness ahead of time. This problem can be partially overcome by using split samples.

Using **split samples** involves dividing the time series into two groups. We put the first (n_1) periods of historical data in the first sample. These n_1 periods will be used to develop the forecasting model. The second sample contains the remaining (n_2) periods of historical data, which will be used to test the model's forecasting ability. These data are called the holdout data. Usually, between three and five periods are held out, depending on the total number of periods in the time series.

In the HiRel Cable example, we have only 10 years of historical data, so we will hold out the last three periods and use the first seven periods to develop the linear trend model. The computations are performed as before, using equation 18-1. Note that since we are using a different data set to develop the linear equation, we get a slightly different trend line than when all ten periods were used. The new trend line is

$$\hat{Y}_t = 9{,}786.714 + 571.464t$$

This model is now used to provide forecasts for periods 8–10 by using trend projection. These forecasts, actual values, and residuals are as follows:

Year t	*Actual* Y_t	*Forecast* $\hat{Y}_t$	*Residual* $(Y_t - \hat{Y}_t)$
8	15,823	14,358.43	1,464.57
9	13,890	14,929.89	−1,039.89
10	16,179	15,501.35	677.65

Then we can compute the MSE and the MAD values for periods 8–10:

$$\text{MSE} = \frac{(1{,}464.57)^2 + (-1{,}039.89)^2 + (677.65)^2}{3} = 1{,}228{,}515.3$$

and

$$\text{MAD} = \frac{1{,}464.57 + |-1{,}039.89| + 677.65}{3} = 1{,}060.7$$

These values could be compared with those produced using other forecasting techniques or evaluated against the forecaster's own standards. Other factors should also be considered. For instance, a decision maker would be interested in whether a model would tend to overforecast or underforecast actual values. This will often happen if a linear model is used to model one of the nonlinear trends shown in Figure 17-7.

Forecasting models which tend to overforecast or underforecast are said to contain **bias.** The quantitative measure of bias is given by equation 18-4:

$$\text{Bias} = \frac{\Sigma(Y_t - \hat{Y}_t)}{n} \tag{18-4}$$

or

$$\text{Bias} = \frac{\Sigma(\text{Error})}{n}$$

Bias can be either positive or negative. A positive value indicates a tendency to underforecast. A negative value indicates a tendency to overforecast. The bias in the forecasts for periods 8–10 in our example is

$$\text{Bias} = \frac{1{,}464.57 - 1{,}039.89 + 677.65}{3} = 367.44$$

This means that, on average, the model underforecasts sales for the three periods by 367.44.

Suppose, in the judgment of the decision maker, the linear trend model has done an acceptable job in forecasting periods 8–10. All the available data (periods 1–10) would be used to develop a linear trend model, and the trend projection would be used to forecast for future time periods by substituting appropriate values for t into the trend model:

$$\hat{Y}_t = 9{,}692.2 + 608.691t$$

However, if the linear model is judged to be unacceptable, the forecaster will need to try a different technique.

ADJUSTING TREND-BASED FORECASTS FOR SEASONALITY

In Chapter 17 we discussed *seasonality* in a time series. The *seasonal component* represents those changes in the time series that occur at the same time every year. Most businesses connected with the tourist industry find that their sales are seasonal. For example, at Rocky Mountain Sports in Aspen, Colorado, business peaks at two times during the year: winter for skiing and summer for fishing and backpacking. These peaks can be identified in a time series if the sales data are measured on at least a quarterly basis. Figure 18-4 shows total sales in each quarter over the past 4 years. The data are displayed in Table 18-4. The time

FIGURE 18-4

Sales Time Series Plot for the Rocky Mountain Sports Example

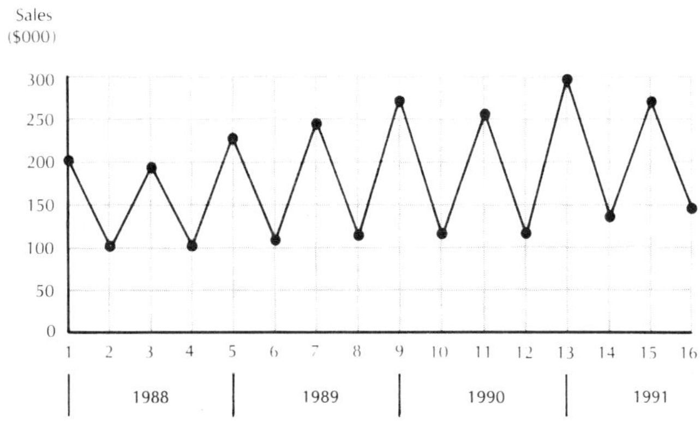

TABLE 18-4

Quarterly Sales for the Rocky Mountain Sports Example

Year	Quarter	t	Sales ($ 1,000s)
1988	Winter	1	205
	Spring	2	96
	Summer	3	194
	Fall	4	102
1989	Winter	5	230
	Spring	6	105
	Summer	7	245
	Fall	8	120
1990	Winter	9	272
	Spring	10	110
	Summer	11	255
	Fall	12	114
1991	Winter	13	296
	Spring	14	130
	Summer	15	270
	Fall	16	140

series plot clearly shows the summer and winter quarters are the busy times. There has also been an increasing linear trend in sales over the 4 years.

Suppose Rocky Mountain Sports wishes to forecast sales for each quarter of the upcoming year and hopes to use a linear trend model. If the data as given in Table 18-4 were used to construct the trend model, it would be

$$\hat{Y}_t = 155.075 + 2.962t$$

with an F statistic $= 0.5499$ and $R^2 = 0.038$—not a very good fit.

When the historical data reflect both a trend and seasonality, the trend-based forecasting model needs to be adjusted to incorporate the seasonality. As we saw in the last chapter, dealing with seasonality involves calculating **seasonal indexes.**

Since we have quarterly data, we can develop four seasonal indexes—winter, spring, summer, and fall. A seasonal index below 1.00 indicates the quarter has values typically below the normal values for the year. On the other hand, an index greater than 1.00 indicates the quarter is a higher than normal quarter.

COMPUTING THE SEASONALLY ADJUSTED FORECAST

Assuming the actual time series data can be represented as a product of the four time series components, as we did in the last chapter, we will use the ***multiplicative model*** to generate our forecast. The multiplicative model is represented by equation 18-5:

$$Y_t = T_t \cdot S_t \cdot C_t \cdot I_t \tag{18-5}$$

where

Y_t = Value of the time series at time t

T_t = Trend value at time t

S_t = Seasonal value at time t

C_t = Cyclical value at time t

I_t = Irregular, or random, value at time t

In the previous chapter we stated that two common methods are used to remove the seasonal component from a time series. These were the ratio to trend and ratio to moving-average methods. While both have advantages, we used the ratio to trend method in the example in that chapter. In this chapter, we will use the *ratio to moving-average* method.

The ratio to moving-average method begins by calculating consecutive four-period moving averages from the time series data (we would use a twelve-period moving average if we had monthly data). These averages are shown in Table 18-5. Notice we lose two periods of data at the beginning and end of the data set. This loss of data is a disadvantage of the ratio to moving-average procedure. The four-period moving averages are used to calculate the centered moving-average values which estimate the $T_t \cdot C_t$ part of the multiplicative model.

The ratio to moving-average value, $S_t \cdot I_t$, is found by dividing the actual sales value for each quarter by the corresponding centered moving average, as shown in equation 18-6:

$$S_t \cdot I_t = \frac{Y_t}{T_t \cdot C_t} \tag{18-6}$$

Table 18-5 also shows these values for the Rocky Mountain Sports data.

TABLE 18-5

Centered Moving Averages for the Rocky Mountain Sports Example

Year	Quarter	t	Sales ($ 1,000s)	4-Period Moving Average	Centered Moving Average $T \cdot C$	Ratio to Moving Average $S \cdot I$
1988	Winter	1	205			
	Spring	2	96			
				149.25		
	Summer	3	194		152.375	1.273
				155.50		
	Fall	4	102		156.625	0.651
				157.75		
1989	Winter	5	230		164.125	1.401
				170.50		
	Spring	6	105		172.750	0.608
				175.00		
	Summer	7	245		180.250	1.359
				185.50		
	Fall	8	120		186.125	0.645
				186.75		
1990	Winter	9	272		188.000	1.447
				189.25		
	Spring	10	110		188.500	0.584
				187.75		
	Summer	11	255		190.750	1.337
				193.75		
	Fall	12	114		196.250	0.581
				198.75		
1991	Winter	13	296		200.625	1.475
				202.50		
	Spring	14	130		205.750	0.632
				209.00		
	Summer	15	270			
	Fall	16	140			

The seasonal indexes for these data are shown as follows for each of the four quarters:

	Winter	*Spring*	*Summer*	*Fall*
1988			1.273	0.651
1989	1.401	0.608	1.359	0.645
1990	1.447	0.584	1.337	0.581
1991	1.475	0.632		
Total	4.323	1.824	3.969	1.877
Average	1.441	0.608	1.323	0.626
Normalized average	1.442	0.608	1.323	0.626

Thus, the seasonal index for winter is 1.442. This indicates that winter quarter sales at Rocky Mountain Sports are 44.2% above normal for the year. Likewise, sales in the spring quarter are only 60.8% of normal for the year.

The deseasonalized sales values are found by dividing Y_t by the appropriate seasonal index, S_t (equation 18-7):

$$\frac{Y_t}{S_t} = T_t \cdot C_t \cdot I_t \qquad \text{(18-7)}$$

TABLE 18-6

Deseasonalized Time Series Sales Data for the Rocky Mountain Sports Example

Year	Quarter	t	Y_t	$Y_t/S_t = T_t \cdot C_t \cdot I_t$
1988	Winter	1	205	142.16
	Spring	2	96	157.89
	Summer	3	194	146.64
	Fall	4	102	162.94
1989	Winter	5	230	159.50
	Spring	6	105	172.70
	Summer	7	245	185.19
	Fall	8	120	191.69
1990	Winter	9	272	188.63
	Spring	10	110	180.92
	Summer	11	255	192.74
	Fall	12	114	182.11
1991	Winter	13	296	205.27
	Spring	14	130	213.82
	Summer	15	270	204.08
	Fall	16	140	223.64

FIGURE 18-5

Deseasonalized Sales Data for the Rocky Mountain Sports Example

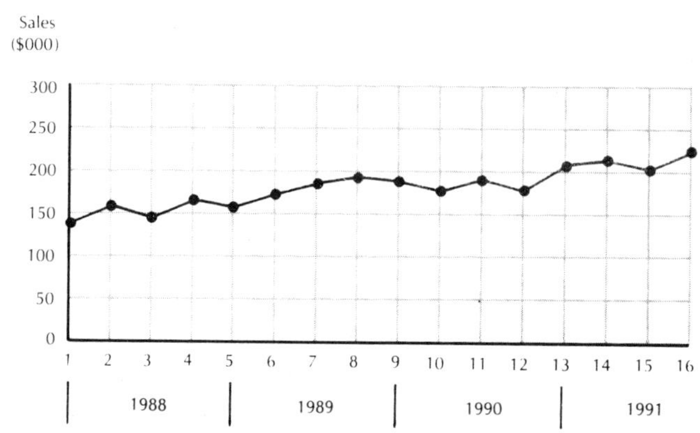

Table 18-6 contains the deseasonalized values for the Rocky Mountain Sports sales data. Figure 18-5 shows the graph of these deseasonalized sales data.

Once the data have been deseasonalized, the next step is to determine the trend of these deseasonalized data. As in previous examples, we use the least squares regression method to compute the linear trend equation:

$$\hat{Y}_t = b_0 + b_1 t$$

The resulting trend line equation is

$$\hat{Y}_t = 142.1128 + 4.685t$$

This model has an F statistic = 109.72 and $R^2 = 0.8868$. Obviously, deseasonalizing the data has improved the model.

We can use this trend line and the trend projection method to forecast period $t = 17$:

$$\hat{Y}_{17} = 142.1128 + 4.685(17)$$
$$= 221.76$$

This forecast is a **seasonally unadjusted forecast.** We need to adjust the forecast for period 17 to reflect the quarterly fluctuations. We do this by multiplying the unadjusted forecast by the appropriate seasonal index. In this case, period 17 corresponds to the winter quarter, so the adjusted forecast is

$$\hat{Y}_{17} = (221.76)(1.442)$$
$$= 319.78$$

The seasonally adjusted forecasts for each quarter in 1992 are as follows:

Year	*Quarter*	*t*	*Unadjusted Forecast*	*Seasonal Index*	*Adjusted Forecast*
1992	Winter	17	221.76	1.442	319.78
	Spring	18	226.44	0.608	137.68
	Summer	19	231.13	1.323	305.78
	Fall	20	235.82	0.626	147.62

REVIEW OF THE SEASONAL ADJUSTMENT PROCESS

We can summarize the steps required in performing a seasonal adjustment to a trend-based forecast as follows:

Step 1. Compute an n-period moving average where n is the number of periods in a year or season.

Step 2. Compute the centered moving averages.

Step 3. Isolate the seasonal component by computing the ratio to moving-average values.

Step 4. Compute the seasonal indexes by averaging the ratio to moving averages for comparable periods.

Step 5. Deseasonalize the time series by dividing the actual data by the appropriate seasonal index.

Step 6. Use least squares regression to develop the trend line, using the deseasonalized data.

Step 7. Develop the unadjusted forecasts, using trend projection.

Step 8. Seasonally adjust the forecasts by multiplying the unadjusted forecasts by the appropriate seasonal index.

You should use the seasonally adjusted trend model when the time series exhibits both a trend and seasonality. This process allows for a better identification of the trend and produces forecasts that are more sensitive to seasonality in the data.

AUTOCORRELATION

If the residuals, $Y_t - \hat{Y}_t$, resulting from a regression model constructed on time series data, are correlated, **autocorrelation** of the residuals exists. The statistical tests of significance for a regression-based forecasting model are based on the assumption that there is no autocorrelation. If autocorrelation exists, the least squares estimation techniques will not provide unbiased estimates of the regression coefficients and the sample standard error of the regression slope may seriously underestimate the standard deviation of the population regression slope. There is some controversy over the issue, but many statisticians believe forecasts should not be made using models that contain autocorrelated residuals.

A widely-used test for determining whether autocorrelation exists is the *Durbin–Watson test.* In most business and economics applications, if autocorrelation exists, it will be positive. Therefore, we will use the following null and alternative hypotheses to test for positive autocorrelation:

$$H_0: \quad \rho = 0$$
$$H_A: \quad \rho > 0$$

where

$$\rho = \text{True autocorrelation between adjacent residuals}$$

The Durbin–Watson test statistic is calculated by equation 18-8:

18-8

$$D = \frac{\sum_{t=2}^{n} (e_t - e_{t-1})^2}{\sum_{t=1}^{n} e_t}$$

where

e_t = Residual at time period t

e_{t-1} = Residual at time $t - 1$

The Durbin–Watson test is not an exact test, but instead provides lower and upper limits, d_l and d_u, to which we compare the calculated D value in equation 18-8. If D is less than d_l, we reject H_0 and conclude that we have positive autocorrelation. If D is greater than d_u, we accept H_0 and conclude that no autocorrelation exists. However, if D falls between d_l and d_u, no conclusion can be reached with respect to autocorrelation and a larger sample size is required.

A table of Durbin–Watson d_l and d_u values appears in Appendix I of this text. The limits are shown for different sample sizes and for regression models with different numbers of independent variables for alpha levels of 0.05 and 0.01.

TABLE 18-7

Revenue per Share for the Airborne Freight Example

Time period t	Year	Revenue/Share
1	1974	13.36
2	1975	13.86
3	1976	16.09
4	1977	17.92
5	1978	21.20
6	1979	28.54
7	1980	30.57
8	1981	29.81
9	1982	31.46
10	1983	29.20
11	1984	36.08
12	1985	39.89
13	1986	46.18
14	1987	45.80
15	1988	55.58
16	1989	60.16
17	1990	63.35
18	1991	75.80

One of the fastest-growing industries over the past decade has been overnight air carrier delivery. Airborne Freight Corporation operates the Airborne Express system, both in the United States and in other countries. Investors interested in buying stock in this company would be interested in the growth in revenues generated per share of stock. These values are shown, for 18 years, in Table 18-7.

Figure 18-6 shows the time series plot of these data. To provide a forecast of the revenue per share for the next 3 years, we could specify a linear trend model.

FIGURE 18-6

Revenue per Share for the Airborne Freight Example

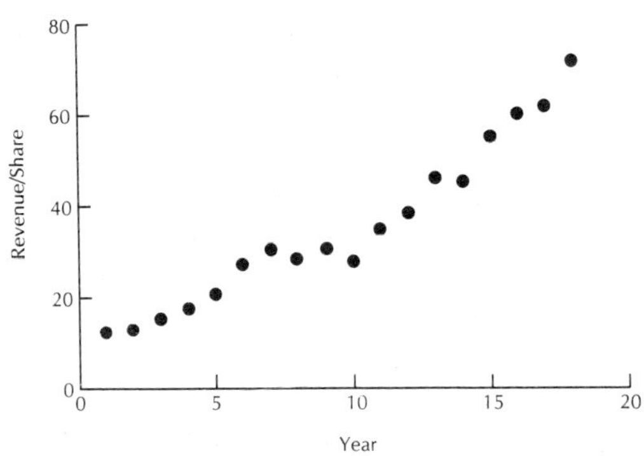

FIGURE 18-7

Linear Trend Line for Airborne Freight Example

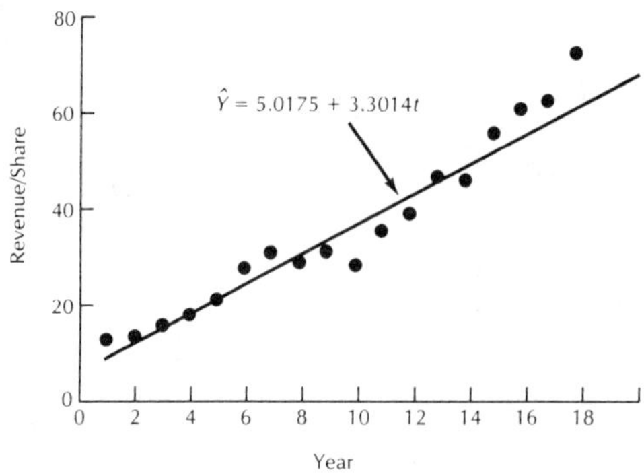

Fitting the eighteen data points with a least squares line, we find the following:

$$\text{Revenue per share} = 5.0175 + 3.3014t$$

The model has an $R^2 = 0.9352$, an F statistic $= 230.7564$, and a standard error of 4.78. The model explains a significant amount of variation in revenue per share over time. However, looking at a plot of the trend line shown in Figure 18-7, we see a pattern of actual values first above, and then below, the trend line. This pattern indicates possible autocorrelation among the residuals. We will test for autocorrelation by calculating the Durbin–Watson D statistic as shown in Table 18-8. (These calculations are tedious, but this is eased by the fact that most computer regression software prints out the Durbin–Watson D statistic as part of the regular output.)

From Table 18-8, we find that the D statistic is 0.661. We next go to the Durbin–Watson table in Appendix I and find the alpha level of 0.05, sample size 18, and number of independent variables equal to 1. The values from the table for d_l and d_u are

$$d_l = 1.16$$
$$d_u = 1.39$$

Since $D = 0.661$ is less than $d_l = 1.16$, we must reject the null hypothesis and therefore conclude that significant autocorrelation exists in the regression model. This means that the assumption of uncorrelated residuals has been violated in this case.

There are some techniques for dealing with the problem of autocorrelation that are beyond the scope of this text. (Refer to books by Nelson, and Wonnacott and Wonnacott.) However, one basic step might be taken in this case to potentially alleviate the autocorrelation problem. If we look closely at Figure 18-6, the relationship between revenue per share (Y) and the independent variable, time (t), appears nonlinear rather than linear. Chapter 13 introduced the idea of transforming the independent variable in certain circumstances when a curvilinear relationship appears to exist between the dependent and independent variables.

TABLE 18-8

Computation of Durbin–Watson *D* Statistic for Airborne Freight Example

t	Y	e_t	$(e_t - e_{t-1})$	$(e_t - e_{t-1})^2$	e_t^2
1	13.36	5.041			25.41168
2	13.86	2.24	−2.801	7.845601	5.0176
3	16.09	1.168	−1.072	1.149184	1.364224
4	17.92	−0.303	−1.471	2.163841	0.091809
5	21.2	−0.324	−0.021	0.000441	0.104976
6	28.54	3.714	4.038	16.30544	13.7938
7	30.57	2.442	−1.272	1.617984	5.963364
8	29.81	−1.618	−4.06	16.4836	2.617924
9	31.46	−3.27	−1.652	2.729104	10.6929
10	29.2	−8.831	−5.561	30.92472	77.98656
11	36.08	−5.253	3.578	12.80208	27.59401
12	39.89	−4.744	0.509	0.259081	22.50554
13	46.18	−1.755	2.989	8.934121	3.080025
14	45.8	−5.437	−3.682	13.55712	29.56097
15	55.58	1.042	6.479	41.97744	1.085764
16	60.16	2.321	1.279	1.635841	5.387041
17	63.35	2.209	−0.112	0.012544	4.879681
18	75.8	11.358	9.149	83.7042	129.0042
				$\Sigma = 242.1024$	$\Sigma = 366.142$

$$D = \frac{242.1024}{366.142}$$
$$= 0.661$$

One such transformation involves making the dependent variable, here revenue per share, an exponential function of the independent variable, time. The form of this regression model would be

$$\hat{Y} = b_0 e^{b_1 t}$$

With the aid of a computer and appropriate software, the new regression model is determined to be

$$\hat{Y} = 12.7753 e^{0.097t}$$

Figure 18-8 (page 970) shows a graph of this regression line against the original data for 18 years. The new model appears to provide a superior fit to the data and this is supported by an increased R^2 of 0.9687. However, the question remains as to whether transforming the variable eliminated the problem of correlated residuals.

A computer package was used to calculate a Durbin–Watson D value of 1.393 for the transformed model. From the Durbin–Watson tables for an alpha of 0.05, a sample size of 18, and number of independent variables equal to 1, the values of d_l and d_u are 1.16 and 1.39.

FIGURE 18-8

Airborne Freight Forecast Model with Transformed Independent Variable

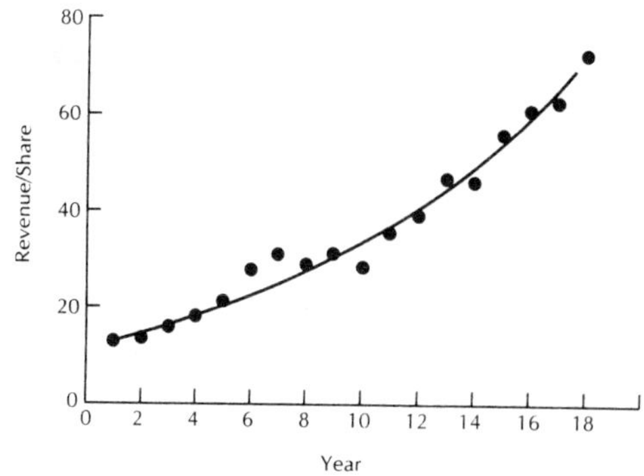

Since the calculated D value is greater than d_u, we can conclude that the transformation has cured the problem of autocorrelation. Remember that some statisticians believe models exhibiting autocorrelation should not be used for forecasting purposes; others stress that only the statistical hypotheses tests are affected and not the forecasting results. This text holds to the latter argument, but you should be careful any time a regression-based forecasting model is used. If the past does not reflect the future, the forecasts will almost certainly be in substantial error.

SKILL DEVELOPMENT PROBLEMS FOR **SECTION 18-4**

The following set of problems is meant to test your understanding of the material in this section.

5. Consider the following set of sales data, given in millions of dollars:

1988		*1990*	
1st quarter	242	1st quarter	307
2d quarter	252	2d quarter	299
3d quarter	257	3d quarter	292
4th quarter	267	4th quarter	311

1989		*1991*	
1st quarter	272	1st quarter	326
2d quarter	285	2d quarter	332
3d quarter	281	3d quarter	321
4th quarter	287	4th quarter	314

Fit a least squares regression line to these data and use the regression equation to forecast sales for the next four quarters. How much confidence would you have in this forecast?

6. Consider the following set of inventory data, given in hundreds of thousands of dollars:

1988		*1990*	
1st quarter	109	1st quarter	118
2d quarter	95	2d quarter	103
3d quarter	115	3d quarter	126
4th quarter	108	4th quarter	120
1989		*1991*	
1st quarter	115	1st quarter	130
2d quarter	110	2d quarter	127
3d quarter	120	3d quarter	138
4th quarter	116	4th quarter	135

Fit a least squares regression line to these data and use the regression equation to forecast the inventory level for the next four quarters. How much confidence would you have in this forecast?

7. Using the same data given in Problem 5, adjust the time series for seasonality. Prepare a new forecast for sales for the next four quarters. Do you think adjusting for seasonality improves your forecast? Why or why not?

8. Using the same data given in Problem 6, adjust the time series for seasonality. Prepare a new forecast for inventory for the next four quarters. Do you think adjusting for seasonality improves your forecast? Why or why not?

9. In the last chapter, we introduced José Gutierrez, who correctly predicted the increasing need for home health care services due to the country's aging population. Five years ago, he started a company offering meal delivery, physical therapy, and minor housekeeping services in the New Orleans area. Since that time, he has opened offices in seven additional gulf state cities. José is presently analyzing the revenue data from his first location for the first 5 years of operation.

	Sales Volume (×*1,000*)				
	1987	*1988*	*1989*	*1990*	*1991*
January	23	67	72	76	81
February	34	63	64	75	72
March	45	65	64	77	71
April	48	71	77	81	83
May	46	75	79	86	85
June	49	70	72	75	77
July	60	72	71	80	79
August	65	75	77	82	84
September	67	80	79	86	91
October	60	78	78	87	86
November	71	89	87	91	94
December	76	94	92	96	99

a. Use a least squares regression line to forecast sales for each month of the next year.
b. Determine the appropriate seasonal adjustment factors for these data and use them to prepare a monthly forecast for the next year.
c. Which forecast developed in parts **a** and **b** would you have most confidence in? Discuss in statistical terms, using the MSE, MAD, and coefficient of determination.

18-5 REGRESSION-BASED FORECASTING MODELS

Section 18-4 introduced trend-based forecasting where least squares regression was used to determine the trend. The trend-based forecasting models used two variables: a dependent variable, Y_t, and an independent variable, time. Regression analysis determined the trend line which "best fit" the time series data. An equation of the form

$$\hat{Y}_t = b_0 + b_1 t$$

was used. Forecasts were obtained by substituting the appropriate value for time into the trend equation.

This use of regression analysis is common, but regression analysis has a much broader application in forecasting. We will consider two additional regression model forms commonly used by forecasters: regression models with indicator variables and autoregressive models.

You should find the discussion in this section familiar since you have considered regression analysis extensively in Chapters 13 and 14. A brief review of Section 13-6 should make the following discussion easier to follow.

The major difference found in using regression analysis specifically for forecasting is in the relationship between the dependent and independent variables, not in the statistical techniques used. If a company is trying to forecast sales for next year, it will try to find a relationship between something measurable this year and sales next year. The company is specifically interested in finding variables that "lead" the dependent variable. These variables are often called **indicator variables.**

REGRESSION USING LEADING INDICATOR VARIABLES

Consider the Connelly Disk Drive Company, a maker of hard disk drives for IBM compatible personal computers. The company is trying to reduce its inventory levels and, consequently, the production manager needs to forecast weekly demand for disk drives. The manager has weekly sales data for production for the past 3 months (12 weeks). He also has data available on weekly expense account

TABLE 18-9

Sales Data for the Connelly Disk Drive Company Example

Week t	Demand ($\times$100) Y_t	Expense Spending ($ 1,000s) X_t
1	100	23
2	250	16
3	150	15
4	120	20
5	200	25
6	240	20
7	180	26
8	300	24
9	250	22
10	180	20
11	220	25
12	230	24

values from the company's technical sales force. These data are shown in Table 18-9. Notice that the company's demand, Y_t, varies from week to week. The marketing manager thinks the variation in expense account spending might be partially responsible for changes in demand the next week. Thus, in this example, expense account values would be considered a **leading indicator variable.**

A regression-based forecasting model could be specified in the form of equation 18-9:

$$\hat{Y}_t = b_0 + b_1 X_{t-1} \quad (18\text{-}9)$$

where

$\hat{Y}_t$ = Forecast value of sales for month t

b_0 = Regression intercept

b_1 = Regression slope

X_{t-1} = Expense account spending at time $t - 1$

We can use least squares regression to determine the "best" values for b_0 and b_1. Be careful when calculating the regression equation for an indicator variable model. In this case, the one-period lagged relationship means that demand in week 2 will be associated with expenses in week 1, and so forth. Therefore, we

TABLE 18-10

MAD Calculations for the Connelly Disk Drive Company Example

Month t	Demand (×100) Y_t	Expense Spending ($ 1,000s) X_1	Forecast (×100) $\hat{Y}_t$	Absolute Error $\|Y_t - \hat{Y}_t\|$
1	100	23		
2	250	16	230.5335	19.4665
3	150	15	141.6433	8.3567
4	120	20	128.9447	8.9447
5	200	25	192.4377	7.5633
6	240	20	255.9309	15.9303
7	180	26	192.4377	12.4377
8	300	24	268.6293	31.3707
9	250	22	243.2321	6.7679
10	180	20	217.8349	37.8349
11	220	25	192.4377	27.5633
12	230	24	255.9309	25.9309
				202.1675

$$\text{MAD} = 202.1675/11 = 18.3788$$

will have only eleven data pairs to build the model. Using these eleven data points, we find

$$\hat{Y}_t = -61.5343 + 12.6986X_{t-1}$$

This model has an F statistic = 39.40859, with 1 and 9 degrees of freedom and $R^2 = 0.8141$. Table 18-10 shows the MAD calculation when the indicator variable regression model output is compared with historical data.

To employ the model to forecast demand for period 13, the production manager would need to measure the level of expense spending for week 12. Suppose the company spends $24,000 ($X_{12} = 24$). Then the demand forecast for period 13 is

$$\hat{Y}_{13} = -61.5343 + 12.6986(24) = 243.23$$

Thus, the manager might plan on selling about 24,323 disk drives in week 13.

MULTIPLE REGRESSION MODELS WITH INDICATOR VARIABLES

Realistically, in forecasting applications like the Connelly Disk Drive example, there may be several potential explanatory variables that could be included in the model. A regression model with more than one independent (indicator) variable would be a **multiple regression forecasting model.** The forecast equation would take the form of equation 18-10:

$$\hat{Y}_t = b_0 + b_1 X_{1_{t-m1}} + b_2 X_{2_{t-m2}} + \cdots + b_k X_{k_{t-mk}} \quad \textbf{18-10}$$

where

$\hat{Y}_t$ = Forecast value for period t

b_0 = Regression intercept

mi = Number of periods ith variable is lagged

b_i = ith regression slope

$X_{i_{t-mi}}$ = Value of ith indicator variable measured at time $t - mi$

The model described in equation 18-10 shows the X_i variables measured with different lead times, $t - mi$, corresponding to when the dependent variable is measured. Thus, to forecast for time $t + 1$, we would need to know values for each variable at the appropriate lead points.

In some cases, we can use regression forecasting models without a lead time relationship between the independent and dependent variables. This would be possible when the indicator variable can be controlled. For instance, the manager of the Town Square Mall is looking for a model to forecast the daily traffic in the mall. Since she knows how many radio advertisements the mall is purchasing each day of the next month in the mall's market area, she could include this variable in a forecasting model for each day's traffic without a lagged relationship. However, when an explanatory variable cannot be controlled and its value is not known in advance, we must lag the data to have a viable forecasting equation.

AUTOREGRESSIVE FORECASTING MODELS

Another type of regression-based forecasting approach involves using indicator variables that are lagged values of the dependent variable. For instance, we might formulate a model like that of equation 18-11:

$$\hat{Y}_t = b_0 + b_1 Y_{t-1} + b_2 Y_{t-2} \quad \textbf{18-11}$$

where

$\hat{Y}_t$ = Forecast value in time t

Y_{t-1} = Value of the time series at time $t - 1$

Y_{t-2} = Value of the time series at time $t - 2$

Equation 18-11 illustrates a case where the two most recent time periods are used as independent variables. The success of an autoregressive model depends on how closely past data are related to current data.

OTHER REGRESSION-BASED MODELS

You should be aware that there are other regression-based forecasting models. For the most part, these are variations of those discussed in the previous sections. For instance, the trend-projection models that use time as the independent variable can be extended to a multiple regression model of the form of equation 18-12:

$$\hat{Y}_t = b_0 + b_1t + b_1t^2 + b_2t^3 \quad \textbf{18-12}$$

where

$\hat{Y}_t$ = Forecast value of the time series at time t

t = Value of time at time t

t^2 = Time squared

t^3 = Time cubed

This format could be appropriate for time series that exhibit nonlinear movements.

The distinguishing feature of each regression-based model is the form of the independent variable(s). We get a mixed regression model when the independent variables included in the model are mixed. For instance, we might determine a model of the following form:

$$\hat{Y}_t = b_0 + b_1Y_{t-1} + b_2t^2 + b_3X_{1t-1}$$

In this instance, we have a combined autoregressive, trend-projection, and indicator variable regression model.

The "art" of forecasting is to determine the most appropriate form for the forecasting model. Guard against the tendency to use the same model format in all applications. What worked well in one situation may not be appropriate in others.

SKILL DEVELOPMENT PROBLEMS FOR **SECTION 18-5**

The following set of problems is meant to test your understanding of the material in this section.

10. Consider the following data:

Period	*Dependent Variable*	*Independent 1*	*Independent 2*
1	101	19	202
2	120	18	210
3	129	17	208
4	122	20	210
5	126	22	212
6	131	23	211
7	133	22	215
8	139	21	214
9	136	24	218
10	140	26	219
11	141	27	220

a. If you were to construct a one-period leading indicator simple regression forecasting model to predict values of the dependent variable, which independent variable would you choose? Why?

b. Use the model you developed in part **a** to forecast the value of the dependent variable for the next period.

11. Refer to the sales data given in Problem 5 in section 18-4.

a. Construct autoregressive forecasting models with time lags of 1, 2, 3, and 4 periods.

b. If you were to forecast sales for the next four periods, which model would you choose? Why?

c. Use the model you picked in part **b** to forecast the next year's sales.

12. Refer to the inventory data given in Problem 6 in Section 18-4.

a. Construct autoregressive forecasting models with time lags of 1, 2, 3, and 4 periods.

b. Use the models you constructed in part **a** to forecast the next quarter's sales.

13. Let's return to the José Gutierrez example last considered in Problem 9 in Section 18-4. Refer to the 5 years of sales volume data given in that problem.

a. Prepare a 1-month and 12-month lag autoregressive model for these data. Which model do you think is best for forecasting?

b. Select the best model from part **a** to forecast next year's sales on a monthly basis.

18-6 FORECASTING USING SMOOTHING-BASED METHODS

Our earlier discussion of trend-based forecasting models applies to situations where the historical time series exhibits a trend. The least squares approach offers a method for modeling the trend and, by using trend projection, a forecast for future time periods can be developed. When the time series does not exhibit a trend, however, we need a different forecasting method.

If we are interested in forecasting one or two periods into the future, a class of forecasting techniques called *smoothing models* exists for situations in which there is no significant trend or cyclical or seasonal components in the time series data. These models attempt to "smooth out" the **random,** or irregular, **component** in the time series by an averaging process. In this section we discuss four smoothing techniques: moving average, weighted moving average, single exponential weighted smoothing, and double exponential weighted smoothing.

THE MOVING AVERAGE TECHNIQUE

You were actually introduced to a moving average earlier in this chapter when we discussed how to seasonally adjust the trend-based forecasting model using the ratio to moving-average value. To develop the procedure further, consider sixteen quarters of sales data for Jannock Ltd., a company that manufactures and distributes a variety of building and electrical equipment in Canada and the United States. Table 18-11 contains historical data for the last sixteen quarters. Figure 18-9 shows a graph of the time series. No apparent trend or seasonal components are present in these data.

An ***n*-period moving average** forecast model is developed as in equation 18-13:

$$\text{Moving average} = \frac{\text{Sum of } n \text{ consecutive } Y \text{ values}}{n} \quad \textbf{18-13}$$

For instance, in the Jannock Ltd. example, the first four-period moving average is found by averaging the values of Y_1 through Y_4:

$$\text{Moving average} = \frac{86.5 + 123.3 + 131.9 + 80.7}{4}$$
$$= 105.6$$

This becomes the forecast for period 5. The next moving average is determined by dropping Y_1 and picking up Y_5:

$$\text{Moving average} = \frac{123.3 + 131.9 + 80.7 + 58.6}{4}$$
$$= 98.625$$

TABLE 18-11

Quarterly Sales for the Jannock Ltd. Example

Sales ($ millions) Y_t	Quarter t
86.5	1
123.3	2
131.9	3
80.7	4
58.6	5
86.1	6
82.6	7
86.4	8
68.0	9
92.8	10
103.7	11
101.9	12
91.4	13
105.6	14
95.0	15
98.0	16

FIGURE 18-9

Quarterly Sales for the Jannock Ltd. Example

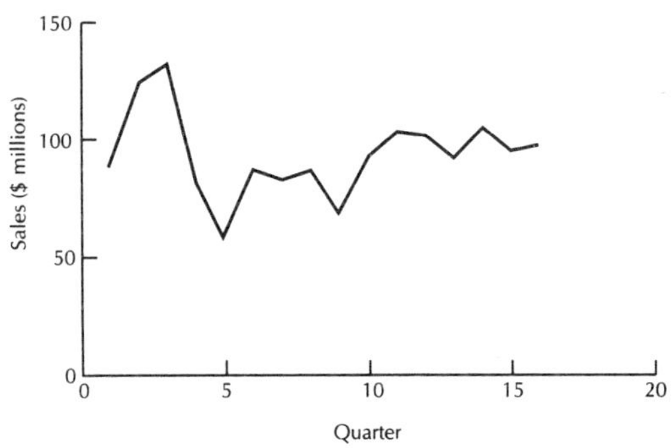

The forecast for period 6 is $98.625 (million). Table 18-12 (page 980) shows the four-period moving averages through period 16. Note that the forecast for period 17 is the average of the last four data values in the time series.

$$\hat{Y}_{17} = \frac{91.4 + 105.6 + 95 + 98}{4}$$
$$= 97.5$$

Figure 18-10 (page 980) shows a plot of the actual quarterly sales versus the forecast sales. The forecasts follow a much smoother pattern than do the original data.

TABLE 18-12

Four-quarter Moving Average for the Jannock Ltd. Example

Quarter t	Sales ($ millions) Y_t	Forecast $\hat{Y}_t$	Error $\lvert Y_t - \hat{Y}_t \rvert$
1	86.5		
2	123.3		
3	131.9		
4	80.7		
5	58.6	105.6	47
6	86.1	98.625	12.525
7	82.6	89.325	6.725
8	86.4	77	9.4
9	68.0	78.425	10.425
10	92.8	80.775	12.025
11	103.7	82.45	21.25
12	101.9	87.725	14.175
13	91.4	91.6	0.2
14	105.6	97.45	8.15
15	95.0	100.65	5.65
16	98.0	98.475	0.475
			Σ = 148.0

MAD = 148/12
= 12.333

FIGURE 18-10

Plot of Actual Sales versus Four-quarter Moving-Average Sales for the Jannock Ltd. Example

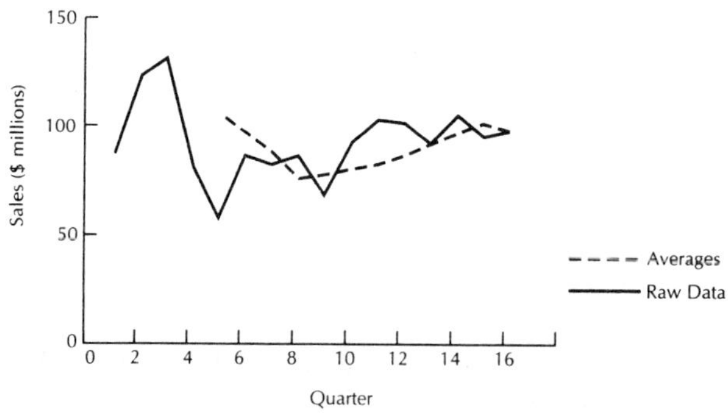

The basic question when using a moving-average model is how many periods to include in the moving average. We used four periods in the Jannock example. However, the forecast for quarter 17 will depend on how many periods are included. A five-period moving-average model will give a different forecast for quarter 17.

$$Y_{17} = \frac{101.9 + 91.4 + 105.6 + 95 + 98}{5}$$

$$= 98.38$$

This forecast, produced from the average of the last five periods in the time series, is higher than the forecast from a four-period moving average.

To determine the "best" number of periods to include in a moving average model, try various values and pick the one that gives the smallest MAD. Keep in mind that more smoothing will occur as the number of periods increases. Also be aware that the presence of trends, seasonal patterns, or cycles tends to diminish the effectiveness of the moving-average model.

WEIGHTED MOVING AVERAGE

The **weighted moving-average** model is a variation of the moving-average approach. The weighted moving-average method assigns different weights to the time series values. This might be practical if the decision maker believes that the more current values are more important in determining the forecast.

Consider again the Jannock Ltd. example. Suppose, in a four-period moving-average model, the managers believe the most recent value should be considered four times as important as the oldest value. Further, the next most recent value should be considered three times as important as the oldest, with the third most recent value weighted twice the oldest value. In forecasting for period 17, the weighted average for periods 13 through 16 is

$$\begin{aligned}\hat{Y}_{17} &= (1/10)91.4 + (2/10)105.6 + (3/10)95 + (4/10)98 \\ &= 97.96\end{aligned}$$

Note, the sum of the weights must be 1.0. Note also this model is simply an extension of the four-period moving-average model where the weights are actually 1/4 for each value.

EXPONENTIAL SMOOTHING

The trend-based forecasting methods discussed earlier are used in many applications. Least squares regression has the advantage of providing a trend line that "best fits" the historical data. As we showed, the trend line is computed using all available historical data. Each observation is given equal input in establishing the trend line. If the future pattern looks like the past, the forecast should be reasonably acceptable.

In many applications involving time series data, however, the more recent the observation, the more indicative it is of what the future values will be. For example, last month's sales are probably a better indicator of next month's sales than are sales of 20 months ago. However, with regression analysis, the data from twenty periods ago will have the same weight as data from this period in developing a forecasting model. This can be a drawback to the trend-based forecasting approach. A weighted moving-average forecast offers one means of overcoming this problem. **Exponential smoothing** is another.

We will introduce two classes of exponential smoothing models: **single exponential smoothing** and **double exponential smoothing.** Although the models are similar in some respects, the double smoothing model is used when the time series exhibits a linear trend. Single smoothing is used when no linear trend is present in the time series. Both single and double exponential smoothing are appropriate for *short-term* forecasting for one or two periods into the future.

Single Exponential Smoothing

Exponential smoothing gets its name from the manner in which the influence of past data is reduced. If the most recent observation is given a weight of 0.20, the observation just before that will have a weight of 0.20(1 − 0.20) = 0.16, and the observation before that a weight of 0.16(1 − 0.20) = 0.128, and so forth. As Figure 18-11 shows, the weight assigned to past observations declines exponentially. In the example shown in Figure 18-11, data from eight periods back have a weight of 0.03355 compared with the most current period's weight of 0.20. The weight assigned to the most recent observation is called the **smoothing constant,** or **alpha.** In single exponential smoothing, we use just one smoothing constant; double smoothing models use two smoothing constants.

Single exponential smoothing is given by equation 18-14:

$$\hat{Y}_{t+1} = \alpha Y_t + (1 - \alpha)\hat{Y}_t \qquad \textbf{18-14}$$

where

$\hat{Y}_{t+1}$ = Forecast value for period $t + 1$

Y_t = Actual value for period t

$\hat{Y}_t$ = Forecast value for period t

α = Alpha (smoothing constant) $(0 \leq \alpha \leq 1)$

FIGURE 18-11

Weighting of Past Observations in Exponential Smoothing ($\alpha = 0.20$)

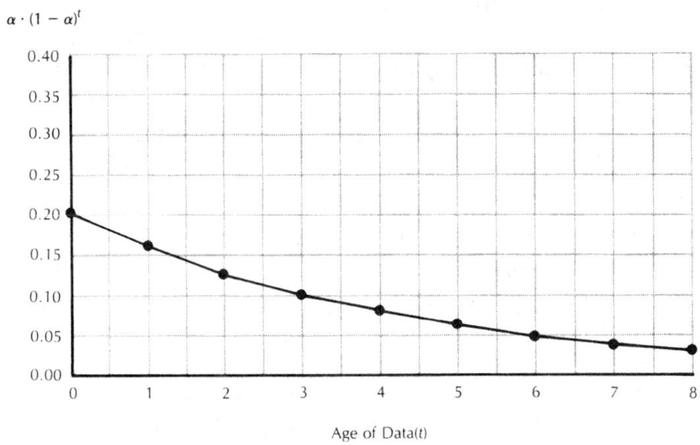

Note that the smoothing constant is between 0 and 1. The closer alpha is to 0, the less influence the current observation has in determining the forecast. Small alpha values will result in greater smoothing of the time series. Likewise, when alpha is close to 1, the current observations have greater impact in determining the forecast, and less smoothing will occur. There is no firm rule for selecting the appropriate value for the smoothing constant. However, in general, if the time series is quite stable, a small alpha should be used to lessen the impact of random or irregular fluctuations. If the time series contains increases and decreases that are not considered purely random, a larger alpha should be selected to allow the model to more quickly adapt to the changes in the time series.

To demonstrate how the single exponential smoothing model is used, consider the twelve weekly customer complaint levels from the Big Tree Inn in Monterey, California. These data are shown in Table 18-13 and are graphed in Figure 18-12. Suppose the current time period is the end of week 12 and we wish to

TABLE 18-13

Weekly Customer Complaints for the Big Tree Inn Example

Week t	Complaints Y_t
1	40
2	48
3	42
4	44
5	46
6	41
7	49
8	44
9	42
10	47
11	45
12	48

FIGURE 18-12

Weekly Customer Complaints for the Big Tree Inn Example

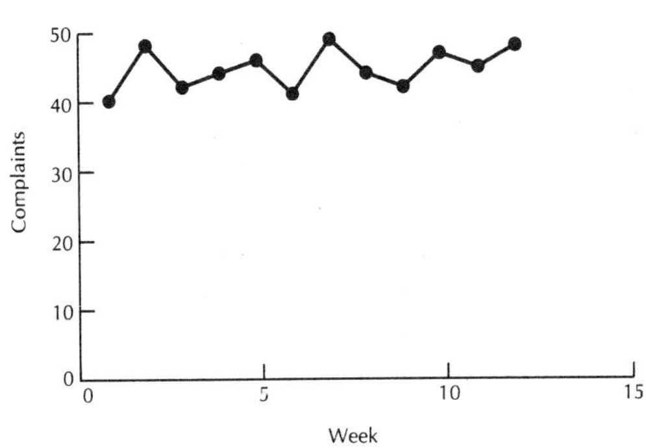

forecast complaints for week 13. We start by selecting an alpha smoothing constant value. We will use $\alpha = 0.20$ in this example.

The forecast value for period $t = 13$ is found using equation 18-14:

$$\hat{Y}_{13} = 0.20\ Y_{12} + (1 - 0.20)\hat{Y}_{12}$$

The forecast for period 13 is a weighted average of the actual sales in period 12 and the forecast for period 12. The forecast for period 12 is determined by

$$\hat{Y}_{12} = 0.20\ Y_{11} + (1 - 0.20)\hat{Y}_{11}$$

Again, this forecast is a weighted average of the actual sales in period 11 and the forecast sales for period 11. We would continue in this manner until we get

$$\hat{Y}_{2} = 0.20\ Y_{1} + (1 - 0.20)\hat{Y}_{1}$$

This requires a forecast for period 1. Since we have no sales data prior to week 1, we assume that $\hat{Y}_1 = Y_1$. This assumption is necessary to set the *starting value.* Because setting the starting value is somewhat arbitrary, you should obtain as many historical data as possible to *warm* the model and *dampen* the effect of the starting value. In our example, we have 12 periods of data to warm the model before the forecast for period 13 is made. Note that, because of the form of the exponential smoothing model, the effect of the initial forecast is reduced by $(1 - \alpha)$ in the forecast for period 2, then reduced again for period 3, and so on. After sufficient periods, any error due to the initial forecast will be very small.

Before we would actually use the forecast from the exponential smoothing for decision-making purposes, we would want to determine how successfully the model fits the historical data. Table 18-14 contains the results of using the single

TABLE 18-14

Single Exponential Smoothing Results ($\alpha = 0.2$) for the Big Tree Inn Example

Week t	Complaints Y_t	Forecast for This Period $\hat{Y}_t$	Forecast for Next Period $\hat{Y}_{t+1}$
1	40	40	40
2	48	40	41.6
3	42	41.6	41.68
4	44	41.68	42.14
5	46	42.14	42.92
6	41	42.92	42.53
7	49	42.53	43.83
8	44	43.83	43.86
9	42	43.86	43.49
10	47	43.49	44.19
11	45	44.19	44.35
12	48	44.35	45.08

exponential smoothing equation for weeks 1 through 12. The column headed $\hat{Y}_{t+1}$ represents the forecast from period t for the next period, $t + 1$. Thus, the last figure in that column, 45.08, is the forecast for week 13. The column headed $\hat{Y}_t$ contains the actual forecasts for periods 2 through 12. These two columns sometimes cause unneeded confusion. Simply, the 41.6 in week 2 of the $\hat{Y}_{t+1}$ column is the forecast made in week 2 *for* week 3. It is therefore the forecast value for week 3 in the $\hat{Y}_t$ column.

Table 18-15 shows the MAD computation for the forecast model with alpha = 0.20. Figure 18-13 shows the plot of the forecast values and the actual values. This plot shows that smoothing has occurred.

TABLE 18-15

MAD Computation of Single Exponential Smoothing Results ($\alpha = 0.2$) for the Big Tree Inn Example

Week t	Complaints Y_t	Forecast $\hat{Y}_t$	Absolute Forecast Error $\lvert Y_t - \hat{Y}_t \rvert$
1	40	40	0
2	48	40	8
3	42	41.6	0.4
4	44	41.68	2.32
5	46	42.14	3.86
6	41	42.92	1.92
7	49	42.53	6.47
8	44	43.83	0.17
9	42	43.86	1.86
10	47	43.49	3.51
11	45	44.19	0.81
12	48	44.35	3.65
			$\Sigma = 32.97$

$$\text{MAD} = 32.97/12 = 2.7475$$

FIGURE 18-13

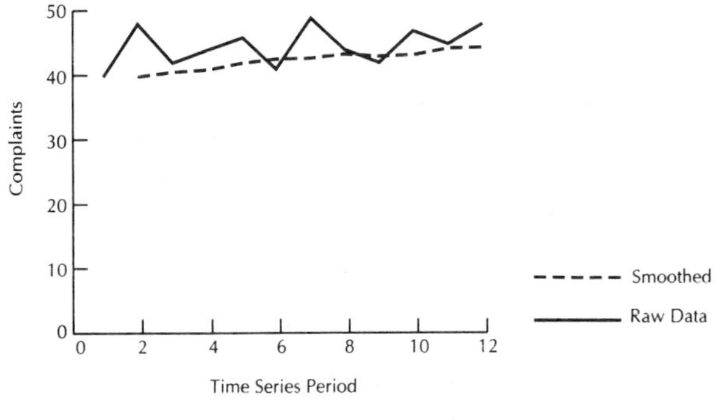

Plot of Forecast versus Actual Complaints Using Single Exponential Smoothing (α = 0.2) for the Big Tree Inn Example

TABLE 18-16

MAD Computation for Single Exponential Smoothing Results ($\alpha = 0.3$) for the Big Tree Inn Example

Week t	Complaints Y_t	Forecast $\hat{Y}_t$	Absolute Forecast Error $\lvert Y_t - \hat{Y}_t \rvert$
1	40	40	0
2	48	40	8
3	42	42.4	.4
4	44	42.28	1.72
5	46	42.80	3.20
6	41	43.76	2.76
7	49	42.93	6.07
8	44	44.75	.75
9	42	44.53	2.53
10	47	43.77	3.23
11	45	44.74	.26
12	48	44.82	3.18
			$\Sigma = 32.1$

$$\text{MAD} = 32.1/12 = 2.675$$

Our next step would be to try a different alpha and repeat the process. Table 18-16 shows the results of using single exponential smoothing, using an alpha = 0.30. Note that the MAD has been reduced from 2.7475 to 2.675 by changing the alpha from 0.20 to 0.30. Thus, if we use the smallest MAD as the selection criterion, alpha = 0.30 will be the better choice. The forecast for period 13, using this latest model, is

$$\begin{aligned}\hat{Y}_{13} &= 0.30(48) + (1 - 0.30)44.82 \\ &= 45.77\end{aligned}$$

This is slightly higher than the forecast produced by the exponential smoothing model with an alpha = 0.20 value.

In an actual application, you may want to try several different alphas and pick the one that fits the data best based on a MAD or MSE calculation. In fact, many commercial forecasting packages will try a range of alpha values and state which one fits the data best.

The exponential model is easy to update when new data become available. For instance, assume complaints for week 13 were actually 40. The forecast for week 14, using the model with alpha = 0.30, is

$$\begin{aligned}\hat{Y}_{14} &= 0.3(40) + 0.7(45.77) \\ &= 44.04\end{aligned}$$

As you can see, we do not need to go back and recompute the entire model as would have been necessary with a trend-based regression model.

Double Exponential Smoothing

When the time series has an increasing linear trend, forecasts developed using a single exponential smoothing model will constantly be lower than actual sales. When the trend is decreasing, the forecasts will exceed the actual values. A double exponential smoothing model will eliminate this problem.

In double smoothing, a second smoothing constant, **beta**, is included to account for the trend. Three equations are needed to provide the forecasts. These are equations 18-15, 18-16, and 18-17:

$$C_t = \alpha Y_t + (1 - \alpha)(C_{t-1} + T_{t-1}) \quad \textbf{18-15}$$

$$T_t = \beta(C_t - C_{t-1}) + (1 - \beta)T_{t-1} \quad \textbf{18-16}$$

$$\hat{Y}_{t+1} = C_t + T_t \quad \textbf{18-17}$$

where

Y_t = Actual value in time t

α = Constant process smoothing constant

β = Trend-smoothing constant

C_t = Smoothed constant process value for period t

T_t = Smoothed trend value for period t

$\hat{Y}_{t+1}$ = Forecast value for period $t + 1$

t = Current time period

Equation 18-15 is used to smooth the time series data. Equation 18-16 is used to smooth the trend, and equation 18-17 combines the two smoothed values to form the forecast for period $t + 1$.

The Boeing Company is one of the world's largest manufacturers and a leading exporter of passenger planes. Table 18-17 (page 988) presents 4 years of quarterly sales data. These data are graphed in Figure 18-14. Note that the sales show a definite upward trend and so we will use a double exponential smoothing model to forecast sales for quarter 17.

As was the case with single smoothing, we must select starting values for C_t and T_t and values for the smoothing constants α and β. With respect to C_t and T_t, initial values for period $t = 2$ are determined as follows:

$$C_2 = Y_1$$
$$= 3{,}763$$

TABLE 18-17

Quarterly Sales Data for the Boeing Company Example

Quarter t	Sales (million) Y_t
1	\$3,763
2	3,478
3	3,515
4	4,599
5	3,613
6	4,709
7	3,722
8	4,918
9	4,001
10	5,072
11	6,356
12	4,847
13	6,435
14	6,959
15	6,900
16	7,196

FIGURE 18-14

The Boeing Company Quarterly Sales

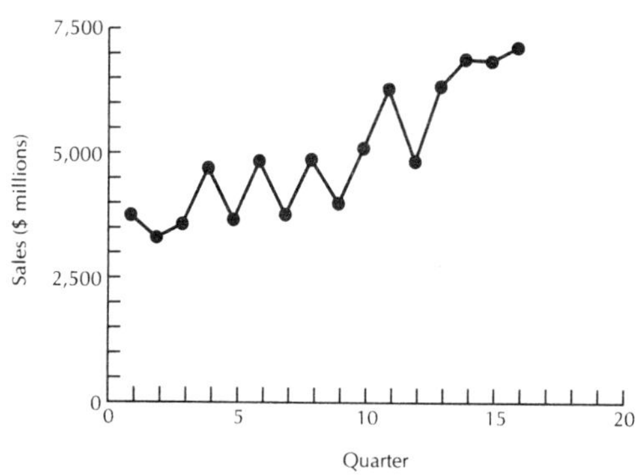

and

$$T_2 = Y_2 - Y_1 = 3{,}478 - 3{,}763 = -285$$

Then, the forecast for period 3 made at the end of period 2 is

$$\hat{Y}_3 = 3{,}763 - 285 = 3{,}478$$

The choice for smoothing constant values revolves around the same issues as discussed earlier with respect to single smoothing. That is, use smoothing constants closer to 1.0 when less smoothing is desired and values closer to 0.0 when more smoothing is desired. The larger the value, the more impact current data have on the forecast. Suppose, we use $\alpha = 0.20$ and $\beta = 0.30$ in this example.

At the close of quarter 3, in which actual sales were $3,515 million, the smoothing equations are updated as follows:

$$C_3 = 0.20(3{,}515) + (1 - 0.2)(3{,}478)$$
$$= 3{,}485.4$$

$$T_3 = 0.3(3{,}485.4 - 3{,}763) + 0.7(-285)$$
$$= -282.78$$

Then, the forecast for quarter 4 is

$$\hat{Y}_4 = 3{,}485.4 - 282.78$$
$$= 3{,}202.62$$

We then repeat the process through quarter 16 to find the forecast for quarter 17. Table 18-18 shows the results of the computations and the MAD value. Figure 18-15 (page 990) shows the actual time series and forecasts. The forecast for quarter 17 is

$$\hat{Y}_{17} = 7{,}407.61$$

Certainly, before settling on this forecast, anyone would want to try different smoothing constants to determine if a smaller MAD can be found. Notice that

TABLE 18-18

Double Exponential Smoothing ($\alpha = 0.2$, $\beta = 0.3$) for the Boeing Company Example

t	Y_t	$\hat{Y}_t$	$\lvert Y_t - \hat{Y}_t \rvert$
1	3,763		
2	3,478	3,763	285
3	3,515	3,478	37
4	4,599	3,202.620	1,396.380
5	3,613	3,282.899	330.101
6	4,709	3,169.728	1,539.272
7	3,722	3,390.748	331.252
8	4,918	3,390.038	1,527.962
9	4,001	3,720.349	280.651
10	5,072	3,818.036	1,253.964
11	6,356	4,185.624	2,170.376
12	4,847	4,866.717	19.717
13	6,435	5,108.608	1,326.392
14	6,959	5,699.304	1,259.696
15	6,900	6,352.244	547.756
16	7,196	6,895.660	300.340
			$\Sigma = 12{,}605.859$

MAD = 12,605.859/15 = 840.391

FIGURE 18-15

Plot of Actual Sales versus Forecast Sales for the Boeing Company Example

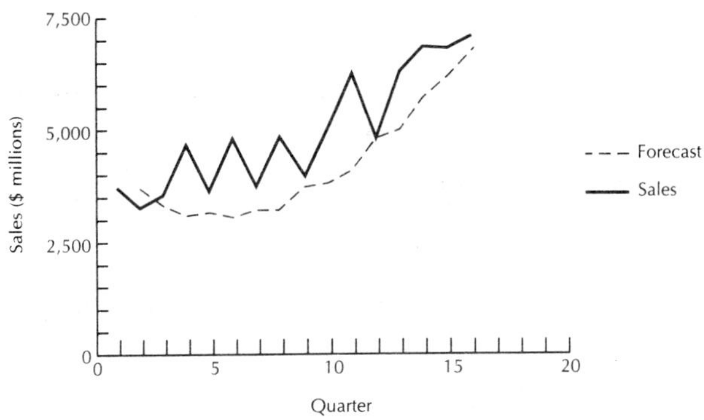

this set of coefficients consistently forecasts low, indicating the need for a higher trend smoothing constant. You would find that increasing the trend smoothing constant, β, to 0.6 would decrease the MAD to about 623.

DOUBLE EXPONENTIAL SMOOTHING OR LINEAR TREND ANALYSIS?

Double exponential smoothing is used when the time series data show an increasing trend. But earlier in this chapter we discussed linear trend analysis as a forecasting tool to use in the same situation. Is there a way to decide between the two forecasting techniques? Yes, but it is often an art. Some points for the decision maker to consider are as follows:

1. The best fit double exponential smoothing model can be compared, using the MAD or MSE, with the linear trend model. The model with the smaller MAD (or MSE) value has fit the past data better and *may* fit future data better.
2. If the environment in which the data were gathered in the past was stable, and no changes are foreseen in the immediate future, the linear trend model may be appropriate.
3. If the environment the decision maker is trying to forecast in is changing rapidly, more recent data may be more important than past data. In this case double exponential smoothing may be appropriate because it allows us to weight the more recent observations more heavily.

SKILL DEVELOPMENT PROBLEMS FOR **SECTION 18-6**

The following set of problems is meant to test your understanding of the material in this section.

14. Refer to the sales data given in Problem 5 in Section 18-4. You have worked with these data in each of the last two sections.
    a. Prepare a four-period moving-average forecast for the next quarter.

b. Prepare a weighted moving-average forecast for the next period, with successive weights being 0.1, 0.2, 0.3, and 0.4.
c. Prepare a single exponential smoothing model forecast for the next period with an alpha value of 0.25.
d. Use the MAD value to determine which of the forecasts prepared in parts **a**, **b**, and **c** is best.

15. Refer to the inventory data given in Problem 6 in Section 18-4. You have worked with these data in the last two sections.
   a. Prepare a four-period moving-average forecast for the next quarter.
   b. Prepare a weighted moving average forecast for the next period, with successive weights being 0.2, 0.2, 0.3, and 0.3.
   c. Prepare a single exponential smoothing model forecast for the next period, using an alpha value of 0.3.
   d. Prepare a double exponential smoothing model forecast for the next period, using an alpha of 0.2 and a beta of 0.3.
   e. Use the MAD value to determine which of the four forecasts prepared is best.

16. Let's return to the José Gutierrez example last considered in Problem 13. Refer to the 5 years of data in Problem 9, Section 18-4.
   a. Prepare single exponential smoothing models from these data, using alpha values of 0.2 and 0.3.
   b. Prepare double exponential smoothing models from these data, using an alpha of 0.25 and a beta of 0.3 and then an alpha of 0.4 and a beta of 0.5.
   c. Use the MAD value to determine which of the models developed in parts **a** and **b** best fits the sales data. (You might want to use a computer program to solve this problem.)

18-7 A BRIEF LOOK AT BOX–JENKINS FORECASTING

Several times in this chapter we have stated that forecasting is an art, not a science. Let's outline some factors that make it an art.

1. In any forecasting situation, choosing the model to use is generally a judgment call, as is the amount of past data to use and the forecasting period. Often, using different amounts of past data will lead to different forecasting models and someone must decide how much past data to use.
2. For many forecasting models, there is really no way to determine whether the model developed is optimal. Often model determination involves trial and error, with a little luck thrown in.
3. Those models that use regression analysis are generally used in situations that violate assumptions necessary to apply regression. In particular, there is no guarantee the underlying distributions of time series data are normal, which is required for regression analysis. In addition, the distri-

butions are probably not stable from one observation period to the next, which is also required for regression analysis. Finally, a regression model is valid only over the range contained in the observed data, and time series trend forecasts extend beyond this range.

4. In earlier chapters on estimation we emphasized that realistic estimates should contain an indication of how accurate the estimate is; therefore, we developed confidence interval estimates. Yet, so far in forecasting, we have been using only point estimates. The reason is that for the models considered up to now we have no guarantee the forecasting errors are normally distributed and thus cannot develop realistic interval estimates.

At this point you may be wondering, with all these problems with statistical models, why bother? The reason, of course, is that forecasts made using imperfect models are vastly superior to no forecasts at all. However, these problems with most statistical forecasting models caused enough worry that the Box–Jenkins model technique, introduced in 1970, caused widespread excitement.

A full development of Box–Jenkins modeling is beyond the scope of this book. However, since many organizations have begun to implement the Box–Jenkins approach, you should be generally aware of the model. In this section we will limit our discussion to considering its advantages and disadvantages and to outlining its general form.

ADVANTAGES OF BOX–JENKINS MODELS

Box–Jenkins models address many of the concerns raised in the last section about conventional time series models:

1. For any particular time series, the Box–Jenkins forecasting model will be optimal in terms of fitting the data pattern and minimizing the forecast error measured by MSE.
2. The Box–Jenkins approach allows for a systematic procedure for model development. It will determine the model that is best for any given set of time series data.
3. The forecasting errors generated by a Box–Jenkins model will be normally distributed, and, therefore, confidence interval estimates can be made.
4. The model can be extended to allow for forecasting in those cases where the time series distributions are not stationary.

As you can see, this forecasting technique has some impressive advantages.

DISADVANTAGES OF BOX–JENKINS FORECASTING

The disadvantages of Box–Jenkins forecasting models generally fall into two categories:

1. A wide variety of studies have shown that the forecasts generated by Box–Jenkins models are not, in all cases, significantly better than those generated by forecasting techniques considered earlier in this chapter.

2. A practical test of how useful a forecasting model is to operational organizations depends on whether the model is simple enough to be understood by those using it or the model is so good that people can simply use its output without understanding it.

A Box–Jenkins model will almost never be the simplest model available and is certainly difficult to understand. In addition, its forecasts are often not better than those generated by simpler models. Therefore, at this point in time, although organizations are beginning to employ the Box–Jenkins model, it is not the dominant forecasting technique for most of them.

TYPES OF BOX–JENKINS MODELS

Forecasting models generated by Box–Jenkins techniques can be placed into one of three categories: autoregressive models, moving-average models, and mixed autoregressive and moving-average models.

Autoregressive Models

The autoregressive model has the generalized form of equation 18-18:

$$Y_t = \phi_0 + \phi_1 Y_{t-1} + \phi_2 Y_{t-2} + \phi_3 Y_{t-3} + \cdots + \phi_k Y_{t-k} + E_t \quad \text{(18-18)}$$

where (similar to our previous regression models)

ϕ_0: Intercept value

ϕ_{t-i}: Slope coefficients for $i = 1$ to k

E_t: Error term

Moving-Average Models

The generalized moving-average model has the following form:

$$Y_t = \theta_0 + \theta_1 E_{t-1} + \theta_2 E_{t-2} + \theta_3 E_{t-3} + \cdots + \theta_k E_{t-k} + E_t$$

where

θ_0: Intercept value

θ_{t-i}: Slope coefficients for periods $t-1$ to $t-k$

E_{t-1} through E_{t-k}: Errors for the past k periods

E: Error term for the most recent period

Mixed Autoregressive and Moving-Average Models

As you might suspect, the mixed model has the following form:

$$Y_t = \phi_0 + \phi_1 Y_{t-1} + \phi_2 Y_{t-2} + \phi_3 Y_{t-3} + \cdots + \phi_k Y_{t-k} + \theta_1 E_{t-1} + \theta_2 E_{t-2} + \theta_3 E_{t-3} + \cdots + \theta_k E_{t-k} + E_t$$

where the previous intercept, coefficient, and error term definitions continue to hold.

IDENTIFYING THE APPROPRIATE MODEL AND ESTIMATING ITS PARAMETERS

Identifying the appropriate Box–Jenkins model to use in any situation is difficult and at present involves considerable judgment based on experience. However, the identification involves calculating correlations and partial correlations (you might want to review the discussion of correlation coefficients and partial correlation coefficients from Chapter 13). For instance, we could determine the correlation existing between all possible values of Y_t and Y_{t-1}, all possible values of Y_t and Y_{t-2}, and so forth. These correlations can be used to identify patterns in the time series data. If higher than average Y values are followed by higher than average values k periods later, the correlation will be positive. However, if higher than average Y values are followed by lower than average values k periods later, the correlation will be negative.

These correlation values are then graphed as an autocorrelogram. The pattern of correlations shown on the autocorrelogram indicates which of the three types of Box–Jenkins models should be used for a particular set of time series data. A hypothetical autocorrelogram is shown in Figure 18-16.

FIGURE 18-16

Hypothetical Autocorrelogram

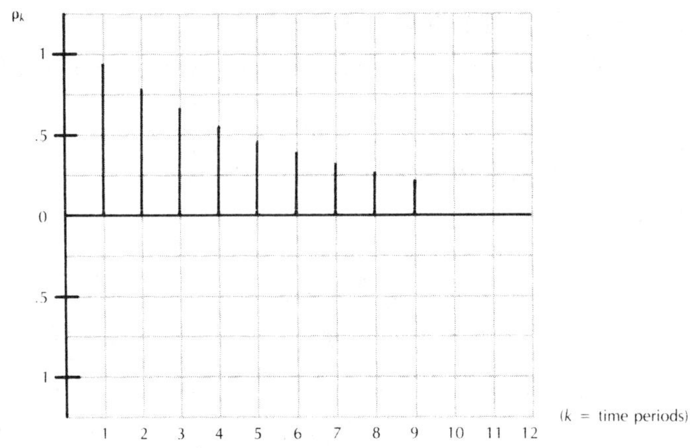

In a manner similar to that of determining the correlations between all values of Y_t and all possible lagged values of Y, partial correlations could be found for the same lagged relationships. These partial correlations are plotted as a partial autocorrelogram, which is also used in the model identification stage.

18-8 COMMON PROBLEMS USING FORECASTING MODELS

Since forecasting is such an important issue for all organizations, it is one of the most frequently used statistical tools discussed in this text. While the chance of error must be recognized whenever a forecasting model is used, the error should be associated with chance variation inherent in using any model—not *caused* by incorrect model use. Therefore, the decision maker should be aware of some common problems found when using forecasting models.

1. Often, managers forget the difference between forecasting and planning. Forecasting is attempting to determine what the organizational environment will look like in the future. Planning is an attempt to decide how to best take advantage of that forecasted environment. Often, managers will formulate a plan and expect everyone else to make it happen. A plan is not a forecast.
2. Probably the biggest problem is to recognize that statistical forecasting models rely on past data, and hence are effective only insomuch as the past represents the future. Statistical models have not done well historically in predicting the impact of unusual events. No statistical models, no matter how complex, did well predicting the impact of the rapid increase in energy prices during the 1970s. Likewise, they had trouble predicting the rapid decrease in inflation during the early 1980s.
3. Statistical forecasting models require valid data and extensive data. Often, organizations either skimp on data gathering or begin a very good effort and then slack off as the initial enthusiasm wanes. Any analytic model is only as good as the data used to construct the model.
4. Models are correctly used to help people in an organization make decisions. The models are not an end to themselves. Often organizations implement models that are not easy, or are impossible, for operational decision makers to understand. Since the most recent trend in organizations is to drive the decision-making authority to the lowest possible level, more and more people are required to use the results of the forecasting model. A model that cannot be understood does not receive the important "buy-in" from this increasingly large group of users and is then, in effect, ignored.

   For many organizations, the forecasting pendulum seems to be swinging toward less emphasis placed on quantitative forecasting models and more emphasis placed on simple scenario projections.
5. The last problem has become increasingly prevalent with the rapid increase of computer speed and decrease in computer cost. It involves at-

tempting to short-cut the model formulation stage by letting the computer pick the best forecasting model, based on maximizing a statistical measure, such as R^2. To be useful, a model should be understood by those using it and certainly by those developing it.

18-9 CONCLUSIONS

This chapter has introduced a variety of forecasting techniques, both judgmental and statistical; our discussion, however, is not complete. An entire semester or more could be devoted to the subject and still not do it justice. Our objective has been to provide insight into some of the more frequently used techniques and to acquaint you with some terminology pertaining to forecasting.

A number of statistical forecasting techniques were introduced, including

Trend projection (linear and nonlinear)

Seasonally adjusted trend projection

Moving average

Single exponential smoothing

Double exponential smoothing

Indicator variable regression models

Autoregressive regression models

Mixed autoregression models

Box–Jenkins forecasting models

Regardless of which model is considered, you should recognize that the success of the model is determined by two factors:

1. How well the model fits the historical time series
2. How much the future time series looks like the past

Ultimately, the best forecasting method is the one that provides the best forecasts.

We have observed that when a short-term forecast is needed on a fairly regular basis, a heavy reliance is placed on statistical techniques. For example, a company determining how many units of materials to purchase for its fabrication plant on a weekly basis will tend to use a statistical model such as exponential smoothing and may have the forecasting process tied in with the inventory system. A periodic review will be conducted to determine whether the model is performing satisfactorily. When the planning horizon is longer term, we have observed that decision makers tend to incorporate some qualitative judgment along with the statistical models. For instance, in the annual budgeting process, you will likely see a manager obtain a sales forecast from a technique such as a regression-based model and then adjust this forecast according to the judgment of his or her managers. When long-term forecasts of 5 or more years are involved, the tendency has been to place greater reliance on qualitative judgment methods and less reliance on statistical models.

Finally, regardless of the length of the planning horizon, our experience is that decision makers generally combine forecasting methods to arrive at a final forecast. This generally involves using some form of statistical forecasting to arrive at a base forecast, which is then adjusted through a qualitative judgment process. This practice is consistent with the premise we have set forth in this text that statistical models should be used to provide information for the decision process *but the decisions are made by people.*

CHAPTER **GLOSSARY**

alpha The smoothing constant used in exponential smoothing to indicate the relative weight placed on the most recent observations versus the historical observations.

autocorrelation Correlation between adjacent residuals in a time series regression model.

bias In forecasting, an indication of whether the model tends to overforecast or underforecast the actual values. A positive bias indicates a tendency to underforecast, whereas a negative bias indicates a tendency to overforecast.

deseasonalizing The process of removing the seasonal component from a time series.

double exponential smoothing An exponential smoothing forecasting model that incorporates a second smoothing statistic to account for the trend in the time series.

exponential smoothing A forecasting technique that weights the current data more heavily than the past data. The weights placed on the older observations decrease exponentially over time.

forecast error The difference between the actual value of a time series and the forecasted value. This is also referred to as the residual.

forecasting The process of predicting what the future will be like.

forecasting horizon The number of periods in the future covered by the forecasting model. Sometimes referred to as the forecast lead time.

forecasting interval The frequency with which new forecasts are prepared.

forecasting period The unit of time for which forecasts are made. The period may be a day, week, month, quarter, or year.

immediate-term horizon Less than 1 month into the future.

indicator variable An independent variable in a regression model measured at time $t - m$, used in forecasting the dependent variable in time t.

linear trend A long-term increase or decrease in a time series in which the rate of change is relatively constant.

long-term horizon Two years or more into the future.

mean absolute deviation The average of the absolute differences between the actual time series value and the forecast value.

medium-term horizon Three months to 2 years into the future.
model diagnosis The process of analyzing the quality of the model employed.
model fitting The process of determining how well a specified model fits past data.
model specification The process of selecting the forecasting technique to be used in a particular application.
moving average The average of n consecutive values of a time series.
nonlinear trend An increase or decrease in a time series where the rate of change is not constant.
random component Changes in the time series data that are unpredictable and cannot be associated with the trend, seasonal, or cyclical components.
ratio to moving average The actual value of the time series divided by the centered moving average. This is a step in the process of constructing seasonal indexes.
residual The difference between the actual value of the time series and the forecast value. This is also called the forecast error.
seasonal index A number used to quantify the effect of seasonality in time series data. Indexes exceeding 1.0 imply that the period has values higher than normal; values less than 1.0 imply values for the period are typically lower than normal.
seasonally unadjusted forecast A forecast, made for seasonal data, that does not include an adjustment for the seasonal component in the time series.
short-term horizon One to 3 months into the future.
smoothing constant The value (also called alpha) that determines the weight placed on the most current observation in an exponential smoothing model.
split samples An evaluation technique where the most recent data are not used in model construction but are used to test its forecasting ability.
weighted moving average A moving average with weights assigned to the time series values.

CHAPTER FORMULAS

Linear trend projection

$$\hat{Y}_t = b_0 + b_1 t$$

Multiplicative model

$$Y_t = T_t \cdot S_t \cdot C_t \cdot I_t$$

Deseasonalizing

$$Y_t/S_t = T_t \cdot C_t \cdot I_t$$

Nonlinear trend projection

$$\hat{Y}_t = b_0 + b_1 t + b_2 t^2 + b_3 t^3$$

Moving average

$$\text{Moving average} = \frac{\text{Sum of } n \text{ consecutive } Y \text{ values}}{n}$$

Single exponential smoothing

$$\hat{Y}_{t+1} = \alpha Y_t + (1 - \alpha)\hat{Y}_t$$

Double exponential smoothing

$$C_t = \alpha Y_t + (1 - \alpha)(C_{t-1} + T_{t-1})$$
$$T_t = \beta(C_t - C_{t-1}) + (1 - \beta)T_{t-1}$$
$$\hat{Y}_{t+1} = C_t + T_t$$

Indicator variable regression model—one variable

$$\hat{Y}_t = b_0 + b_1 X_{1t}$$

Indicator variable regression model—multiple variables

$$\hat{Y}_t = b_0 + b_1 X_{1t} + b_2 X_{2t} + \cdots + b_k X_{kt}$$

Autoregressive model

$$\hat{Y}_t = b_0 + b_1 Y_{t-1} + b_2 Y_{t-2}$$

SOLVED PROBLEMS

1. The annual sales for Safeway, the grocery retailing giant, for 17 years are as follows:

Year	*t*	*Sales (Y) (billions of dollars)*
1974	1	8.185
1975	2	9.717
1976	3	10.443
1977	4	11.249
1978	5	12.551
1979	6	13.718
1980	7	15.103
1981	8	16.580
1982	9	17.633
1983	10	18.585
1984	11	19.642
1985	12	19.651
1986	13	20.312
1987	14	18.301
1988	15	13.612
1989	16	14.325
1990	17	14.950

a. Plot the data and fit a least squares regression line, using time as the independent variable.
b. Discuss whether the linear regression line seems to be a good model to use on these data.
c. Use the regression line developed in part a to forecast sales for the next 2 years. How would you feel about using this as a forecasting model?

Solution

a. Using equations 13-8 and 13-9 to determine the slope and intercept of the regression line, we find

$$b_1 = \frac{\Sigma Y_t - (\Sigma Y \Sigma t)/n}{\Sigma t^2 - (\Sigma t)^2/n}$$
$$= \frac{2{,}491.589 - (254.557)(153)/17}{1{,}785 - 23{,}409/17}$$
$$= 200.576/408$$
$$= 0.49161$$
$$b_0 = \Sigma Y/n - b_1 \Sigma t/n$$
$$= 254.557/17 - 0.49161(153)/17$$
$$= 10.54947$$

The plot of this line is shown in Figure 18-17.

b. The R^2 associated with the model found in part **a** is 0.44 and the model is significant at the 5% level. However, the plot of the data indicates some unusual events must have taken place about 4 years ago. Those aware of Safeway's history know the company recently went through a restructuring after a leveraged buyout. This is a good example of using past data that are not related to the likely future environment of the company. We would not feel comfortable using this model to forecast sales for the next 2 years.

FIGURE 18-17

Least Squares Linear Trend of Sales

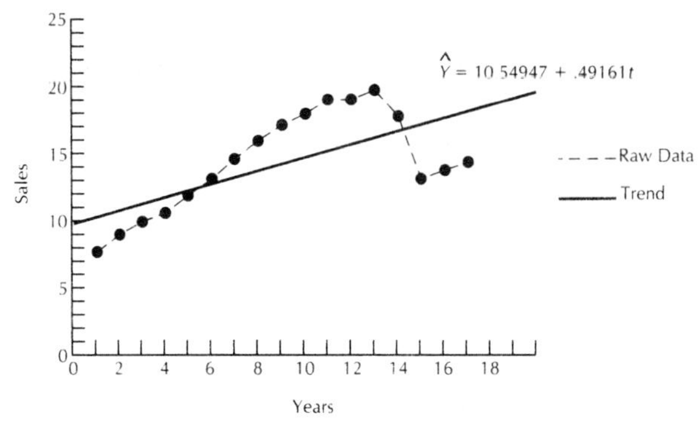

c. Assuming the model will work for the next 2 years, we would predict sales to be

$$\text{Sales (91)} = 10.54947 + 0.49161(18) = 19.4$$
$$\text{Sales (92)} = 19.9$$

This forecast would be subject to the concern expressed in part **b.**

2. Shown are the quarterly sales figures, in thousands, for keyboards the Datakey Company makes and sells to personal computer manufacturers. Datakey has decided to try exponential smoothing as a forecasting technique:

1989	1	14.7
	2	17.3
	3	15.5
	4	15.5
1990	1	21.2
	2	27.1
	3	25.9
	4	23.0
1991	1	33.1

a. Using an alpha of 0.2, use a single smoothing model to prepare a forecast for the next quarter. Assume your forecast for the first period is correct.
b. Use a double smoothing model with a trend smoothing constant of 0.3 and a process smoothing constant of 0.2 to prepare a forecast for the next period.
c. If you were to recommend one of the two models, which would you choose and why?

Solution

a. The forecast for the next quarter is found by using equation 18-14 and determining the values in the following table.

Period t	*Demand* Y_t	*Forecast for This Period* $\hat{Y}_t$	*Forecast for Next Period* $\hat{Y}_{t+1}$
89–1	14.7	14.7	14.7
–2	17.3	14.7	15.22
–3	15.5	15.22	15.28*
–4	15.5	15.28	15.32
90–1	21.2	15.32	16.50
–2	27.1	16.50	18.62
–3	25.9	18.62	20.08
–4	23.0	20.08	20.66
91–1	33.1	20.66	23.15

* Values from this point rounded to nearest 0.01.

b. Using equations 18-15, 18-16, and 18-17, with an alpha of 0.2 and a beta of 0.3, we find the following table of values:

t	Y_t	C_t	T_t	$\hat{Y}_t$
89–1	14.7	—	—	—
–2	17.3	14.7	2.6	—
–3	15.5	16.94	2.49*	17.3
–4	15.5	18.64	2.25	19.43
90–1	21.2	20.95	2.27	20.89
–2	27.1	24.00	2.50	23.22
–3	25.9	26.38	2.46	26.5
–4	23.0	27.67	2.11	28.84
91–1	33.1	30.44	2.31	29.78
				32.75

* Values from this point rounded to nearest 0.01.

c. When comparing the results of the two smoothing models, we see the single smoothing model lags the increasing sales. The double smoothing model does a much better job following the sales figures. This should not surprise you since the double smoothing model is designed to be used in situations where a trend exists.

CONCEPTUAL QUESTIONS AND ASSIGNMENTS

17. Assume your school's athletic department is in the process of developing a budget for next year and wants to forecast ticket sales for the football season. For this budget process, what is the forecast horizon?
18. What are the four categories of forecast lead times? Describe each one and give examples for which lead time would be appropriate.
19. If a company is interested in building a new manufacturing facility, its product-demand forecast model would need to cover a long lead time. Discuss why.
20. The Willow Manufacturing Company has been in operation for 20 years. Records of annual sales have been maintained for this time period. If we graphed the data, is it likely that the data would contain a seasonal component? Discuss.
21. Is it possible for a time series to have both a trend and a seasonal pattern? Discuss. If yes, provide an example that illustrates such a time series.
22. Go to the library and find data showing the state's population for the past 20 years. Plot these data and indicate which of the time-series components are present.
23. Contact the university registrar's office for enrollment data by quarter (or semester), including summer term, for the past 6 years. Graph the data and indicate which of the time-series components are present.

ADDITIONAL PROBLEMS

The following problems are all based on material presented in this chapter, but may not be presented to correspond to the order of the chapter.

24. EasyRide Stages has provided home-to-destination van service for 15 years for people restricted to wheelchairs in the Lexington, Kentucky, area. The following table shows revenues for each of the years.

Year	*Revenues*
1977	$ 266,000
1978	256,000
1979	404,000
1980	556,000
1981	776,000
1982	1,008,000
1983	1,226,000
1984	1,490,000
1985	1,950,000
1986	2,467,000
1987	2,671,000
1988	3,334,000
1989	2,463,000
1990	3,395,000
1991	4,660,000

a. Develop a linear trend forecasting model for these data. Use this model to forecast revenues for the next 3 years.
b. Develop a least squares regression model, with the square of time as the independent variable. Use this model to forecast revenues for the next 3 years.
c. Which of the two models just developed would you feel more comfortable with? Discuss.
d. Use the Durbin–Watson test statistic to determine whether either of the models shows signs of autocorrelation.

25. Refer to Problem 24.
a. Construct a 3-year moving-average model, using the same data, and use this model to forecast revenues for the next period.
b. Construct a first-order exponential smoothing model, using an alpha of 0.3, and use this model to forecast revenues for the next year.
c. Construct a second-order exponential smoothing model, with a beta of 0.2 and an alpha of 0.25, to forecast next year's revenues.
d. Use the MAD values for the three models to determine which has the best fit to the past data.

26. Fast-In-N-Out opened its breakfast and lunch restaurant near a midwestern university 15 years ago. Since that time the organization has been rapidly expanding by offering a limited menu of low-cost meals. Sales for the past 15 years are

Year	*Sales*	*Year*	*Sales*
1977	$2,400,000	1985	$11,300,000
1978	3,700,000	1986	12,400,000
1979	3,900,000	1987	14,000,000
1980	4,100,000	1988	15,900,000
1981	5,800,000	1989	18,600,000
1982	7,500,000	1990	23,400,000
1983	8,700,000	1991	25,200,000
1984	8,600,000		

a. Develop a linear trend forecasting model for these data. Use this model to forecast sales for the next 3 years.
b. Would you feel comfortable with the forecast made in part **a**? Discuss.
c. Use the Durbin–Watson test statistic to determine whether the model shows signs of autocorrelation.

27. Refer to the Fast-In-N-Out data from Problem 26.

a. Construct a 4-year moving-average model, using the same data, and use this model to forecast sales for the next period.
b. Construct a first-order exponential smoothing model, using an alpha of 0.4, and use this model to forecast sales for the next year.
c. Construct a second-order exponential smoothing model, with a beta of 0.3 and an alpha of 0.2, to forecast next year's sales.
d. Use the MAD values for the three models to determine which has the best fit to the past data.

28. Ned Thayer is the recently appointed service manager for Sundance Motors in Jacksonville, Florida. Ned has been told by the owner that the service department will be considered as a profit center and part of Ned's salary will be determined by just how profitable the department is. Ned reasons that forecasting the demand in his department will help him control costs, and therefore increase profits. Unfortunately, Ned can find records only on the number of cars repaired monthly for the last 3 years. These data are shown in the table.

	Month	*Cars Serviced*		*Month*	*Cars Serviced*		*Month*	*Cars Serviced*
Jan	1	2,691	Jan	13	2,740	Jan	25	2,960
	2	2,810		14	2,908		26	2,865
	3	2,260		15	2,780		27	2,810
	4	2,150		16	2,570		28	2,685
	5	2,035		17	2,390		29	2,560
	6	2,517		18	2,580		30	2,730
	7	2,245		19	2,730		31	2,620
	8	2,480		20	2,850		32	2,770
	9	2,076		21	2,640		33	2,650
	10	1,880		22	2,610		34	2,475
	11	2,465		23	2,890		35	2,905
	12	2,925		24	3,005		36	3,240

a. Determine the $T \cdot C$ portion of the multiplicative model for this time series by computing a 12-month and then a centered 12-month moving average.
b. Estimate the $S \cdot I$ portion of the multiplicative model by finding the ratio to moving-average for the time series. Indicate whether these values are stable from year to year.
c. Calculate the normalized monthly indexes for these data. Discuss the meaning of these indexes.
d. Use the values found in part **c** to adjust a trend forecast for next year's service demand. How much use do you think this forecast will be for Ned?

29. Refer to Problem 28.
a. Construct a 4-month moving-average model, using the same data, and use this model to forecast sales for the next period.
b. Construct a first-order exponential smoothing model, using an alpha of 0.2, and use this model to forecast sales for the next year.
c. Construct a second-order exponential smoothing model, with a beta of 0.2 and an alpha of 0.2, to forecast next year's sales.

Problems 30–37 refer to the following data on quarterly sales for Deere & Co., the manufacturer of farm and construction equipment.

Quarter	*Sales ($ millions)*
1	978
2	1,143
3	1,196
4	1,318
5	1,045
6	1,450
7	1,388
8	1,482
9	1,142
10	1,670
11	1,686
12	1,736
13	1,376
14	1,852
15	1,780
16	1,742

30. Plot the data and comment on any patterns you see.
31. Using a first-order exponential smoothing model with a smoothing constant of 0.10, develop a model to forecast sales for quarter 17. Evaluate the model by computing both the MSE and MAD.
32. Construct a four-period moving average to forecast sales for quarter 17. Find the MAD and MSE values for this forecasting model and compare them with the values found in Problem 31.

33. a. Determine the $T \cdot C$ portion of the multiplicative time series model by computing a four-quarter moving average and centered moving average.
b. Estimate the $S \cdot I$ portion of the multiplicative model by finding the ratio to moving-average for the time series. Indicate whether these values are stable from year to year.
c. Calculate the normalized quarterly indexes for these data. Comment on the stability you see in these indexes.
d. Use the values found in part c to adjust a trend forecast for sales for Deere for next year.

34. Analyze the time series data using a double exponential smoothing model with an alpha of 0.3 and a beta of 0.4. Find the MAD and MSE values for this model and compare them with the single exponential smoothing model found in Problem 31. Which model would you use for forecasting sales for quarter 17?

35. a. Analyze these data using a one-quarter lagged autoregressive model.
b. Analyze these data using a four-quarter lagged autoregressive model.
c. Use the MSE and MAD values to determine which of the above two models does a better job of matching actual past sales data.

36. Analyze the data using the two methods suggested in Problem 35, but hold-out the last four quarters of data and use them to measure the forecasting ability of the two models.

37. If you have worked all the problems associated with the Deere & Co. data, pick the model you consider the best forecasting tool. Justify your choice using MAD and MSE values.

Problems 38–45 refer to the following data on quarterly sales for Mattel, the manufacturer of Barbie Dolls and Hot Wheels.

Quarter	*Sales ($ millions)*
1	211.8
2	256.4
3	318.1
4	233.8
5	188.7
6	207.1
7	306.6
8	287.6
9	195.3
10	272.3
11	410.0
12	359.4
13	233.9
14	318.0
15	490.4
16	432.7

38. Plot the data and comment on any patterns you see.

39. Using a single exponential smoothing model with a smoothing constant of 0.10, develop a model to forecast sales for quarter 17. Evaluate the model by computing both the MSE and MAD.
40. Construct a four-period moving average to forecast sales for quarter 17. Find the MAD and MSE values for this forecasting model and compare them with the values found in Problem 39.
41. a. Determine the $T \cdot C$ portion of the multiplicative time series model by computing a four-quarter moving average and centered moving average.
    b. Estimate the $S \cdot I$ portion of the multiplicative model by finding the ratio to moving-average for the time series. Indicate whether these values are stable from year to year.
    c. Calculate the normalized quarterly indexes for these data. Comment on the stability you see in these indexes.
    d. Use the values found in part **c** to adjust a trend forecast for sales for Mattel for next year.
42. Analyze these time series data using a double exponential smoothing model with an alpha of 0.3 and a beta of 0.4. Find the MAD and MSE values for this model and compare them with the single exponential smoothing model found in Problem 39. Which model would you use for forecasting sales for quarter 17?
43. a. Analyze these data using a one-quarter lagged autoregressive model.
    b. Analyze these data using a four-quarter lagged autoregressive model.
    c. Use the MSE and MAD values to determine which of the above two models does a better job of matching actual past sales data.
44. Analyze the data using the two methods suggested in Problem 43, but hold out the last four quarters of data and use them to measure the forecasting ability of the two models.
45. If you have worked all the problems associated with the Mattel data, pick the model you consider the best forecasting tool. Justify your choice using MAD and MSE values.
46. The building permit section for a medium-size midwestern city has issued the following numbers of single-family building permits over the past 10 years:

Year	*Permits*	*Year*	*Permits*
1983	1,500	1988	1,350
1984	1,470	1989	1,180
1985	2,100	1990	1,550
1986	2,380	1991	2,000
1987	2,050	1992	2,040

    a. Construct single exponential smoothing models for these data, using alpha values of 0.2, 0.5, and 0.8. The city council is asking for a permit forecast for 1993. Which value would you use to forecast permits to be issued?
    b. Construct double exponential smoothing models, using the alpha values given in part **a** for the constant process smoothing values and trend

smoothing values of 0.2, 0.4, and 0.6. What conclusions can you draw about the relation between the two smoothing constants?

47. For the permit section data contained in Problem 46, if you had to forecast levels for 1993, would you use a single or double smoothing model? Discuss.

CASES

18A Medical Center Hospital

R. T. Trusty, the administrator of Medical Center Hospital, recently hired the U. R. Regis Consulting Firm to study the medical center's admissions and develop a model for predicting future admissions. Because of the emphasis on long-range planning, Mr. Trusty needs a good admissions forecasting model. U. R. Regis collected data for the past 10 years on the following variables:

VAR01	Admissions in year *t*
VAR02	Area population in year *t*
VAR03	Number of doctors in the area in year *t*
VAR04	Crime rate per 1,000 people in year *t*
VAR05	Average annual temperature in year *t*
VAR06	Number of vehicles registered in the county in year *t*
VAR07	Hospital capacity in year *t*
VAR08	Average daily patient cost in year *t*

U. R. Regis Consulting provided a printout of its work but no written report or evaluation of the model's usefulness.

Since Mr. Trusty is a little shaky on regression analysis, he would like you to write a short but accurate synopsis of the printouts in Tables 18C-1 through 18C-4. Be sure to indicate any attributes the model has relative to Medical Center Hospital's needs, as well as any potential problems with the model.

TABLE 18C1

Means and Standard Deviations

VARIABLE	MEAN	STD. DEV.	CASES
VAR01	5545.2000	2392.0319	10
VAR02	35860.0000	12655.9779	10
VAR03	22.8000	6.5625	10
VAR04	2.9700	1.0338	10
VAR05	65.6000	3.6878	10
VAR06	18563.5000	7398.9617	10
VAR07	6940.0000	2531.6661	10
VAR08	109.4000	23.3248	10

TABLE 18C2

Correlation Matrix

	VAR01	VAR02	VAR03	VAR04	VAR05	VAR06	VAR07	VAR08
VAR01	1.000	.948	.932	.280	.308	.945	.944	.962
VAR02	.948	1.000	.955	.175	.060	.922	.892	.913
VAR03	.932	.955	1.000	.191	.239	.836	.869	.905
VAR04	.280	.175	.191	1.000	.460	.207	.378	.298
VAR05	.308	.060	.239	.460	1.000	.167	.294	.387
VAR06	.945	.922	.836	.207	.167	1.000	.856	.893
VAR07	.944	.892	.869	.378	.294	.856	1.000	.940
VAR08	.962	.913	.905	.298	.387	.893	.940	1.000

18B University Registration

Dr. Ernesto Chavez, the vice-president for Student Affairs at Southeastern University has just completed a grueling 2-hour session with members of the faculty senate. He is not looking forward to tomorrow's meeting with the executive committee of the Associated Student Body. Both faculty and students have been upset with registration problems over the last several years. The major problems revolve around scheduling too few sections of courses that turn out to be exceptionally popular and too many sections of courses that no one wants to take. Ernesto had explained to the president of the school several times that course scheduling was certainly not his function, but had been asked to head a task force to consider better forecasting techniques.

Last spring, Dr. Chavez had hired two graduate students with a good background in statistical model building to work on an improved forecasting model. During several planning meetings the students had convinced him the project required a two-stage approach. The first stage would be model development, where the appropriate model would be developed, validated, and data gathered. The second stage would involve testing the model on trial data.

Ernesto is aware of the relationship between the complexity of the model and the amount of data required to develop the model. He is also aware that any statistical model is effective only if the future reflects the time period during which data were gathered. However, the last few semesters have generated so many complaints and course changes that the task force was of the opinion that any change would have to be for the better. Everyone eagerly awaits the results of the forecasting model.

18C Wagner Machine Works

Mary Lindsey has recently agreed to leave her upper-level management job at a major paper manufacturing firm and return to her home town to take over the

TABLE 18C3 Step 1 of the Regression Output

```
**************************** MULTIPLE REGRESSIØN ****************************

DEPENDENT VARIABLE   VAR01   ADMISSIØNS

VARIABLE(S) ENTERED ØN STEP NUMBER 1   VAR08   CØST

- - - - - - - - - - - - - - - - - - - - - - - - - - - - - - - - - - - - - - - - -

MULTIPLE R              .96258

R SQUARE                .92657

ADJUSTED R SQUARE       .91739

STANDARD ERRØR       687.51747

- - - - - - - - - - - - - - - - - - - - - - - - - - - - - - - - - - - - - - - - -

ANALYSIS ØF VARIANCE       D.F.   SUM ØF SQUARES     MEAN SQUARE        F

REGRESSIØN                  1     47714909.45544     47714909.45544   100.94542
RESIDUAL (UNEXPLAINED)      8      3781442.14456       472680.26807

- - - - - - - - - - - - - VARIABLES IN THE EQUATIØN - - - - - - - - - - - - -

VARIABLE                B                 STD. ERRØR B           F

VAR08                 98.71624              9.82529             100.945

(CØNSTANT)         -5254.35671

- - - - - - - - - - - - - VARIABLES NØT IN THE EQUATIØN - - - - - - - - - - - -

VARIABLE                      PARTIAL                  F

VAR02                          .62262                4.431
VAR03                          .53046                2.741
VAR04                        -.02570                  .005
VAR05                        -.25797                  .499
VAR06                          .70780                7.028
VAR07                          .43235                1.609
*********************************************************************************
```

family machine products business. The machine products industry in the United States had a strong position of world dominance until recently when the industry has been devastated by foreign competition, particularly from Germany and Japan. Among the many problems facing the American industry is that it is traditionally made up of many small firms and faces competition from major foreign industrial giants.

Wagner Machine Works, the company Mary is taking over, is one of the few survivors in its part of the state, but faces increasing competitive pressure.

TABLE 18C4 Step 2 of the Regression Output

```
******************************** MULTIPLE REGRESSIØN ********************************
VARIABLE(S) ENTERED ØN STEP NUMBER 2   VAR06   VEHICLES
--------------------------------------------------------------------------------
MULTIPLE R              .98151
R SQUARE                .96336
ADJUSTED R SQUARE       .95289
STANDARD ERRØR       519.20279
--------------------------------------------------------------------------------
ANALYSIS ØF VARIANCE         D.F.   SUM ØF SQUARES      MEAN SQUARE         F
REGRESSIØN                    2    49609350.84590    24804675.42295    92.01519
RESIDUAL (UNEXPLAINED)        7     1887000.75410      269571.53630

------------------------- VARIABLES IN THE EQUATIØN -------------------------
VARIABLE                    B               STD. ERRØR B          F
VAR08                  59.67294              16.49146            13.093
VAR06                    .13782                .05199             7.028
(CØNSTANT)          -3541.42269

------------------------- VARIABLES NØT IN THE EQUATIØN ---------------------
VARIABLE                        PARTIAL                 F
VAR02                           .36412                .917
VAR03                           .61276               3.607
VAR04                           .10130                .062
VAR05                           .07230                .032
VAR07                           .50339               2.036
********************************************************************************
```

Mary's father let the business slide as he approached retirement and Mary sees the need for an immediate modernization of their plant. Mary has arranged for a loan from the local bank, but now must forecast sales for the next 3 years to ensure the company has enough cash flow to repay the debt. Surprisingly, Mary has found her father has no forecasting system in place and she cannot afford the time, or money, to install a system like that used at her previous company.

Wagner Machine Works sales for the last 15 years, on a quarterly basis, are (in millions) as follows:

	Quarter			
Year	*1*	*2*	*3*	*4*
1977	10,490	11,130	10,005	11,058
1978	11,424	12,550	10,900	12,335
1979	12,835	13,100	11,660	13,767
1980	13,877	14,100	12,780	14,738
1981	14,798	15,210	13,785	16,218
1982	16,720	17,167	14,785	17,725
1983	18,348	18,951	16,554	19,889
1984	20,317	21,395	19,445	22,816
1985	23,335	24,179	22,548	25,029
1986	25,729	27,778	23,391	27,360
1987	28,886	30,125	26,049	30,322
1988	30,212	33,702	27,907	31,096
1989	31,715	35,720	28,554	34,326
1990	35,533	39,447	30,046	37,587
1991	39,093	44,650	32,035	40,877

While looking at these data, Mary wonders whether they can be used to forecast sales for the next 3 years. She wonders how much, if any, confidence she can have in a forecast made with these data. She also wonders if the increase seen in sales is due to growing business or just to inflationary price increases.

REFERENCES

Armstrong, J. S. *Long Range Forecasting: From Crystal Ball to Computer.* New York: Wiley, 1985.

Bowerman, Bruce L. and O'Connell, Richard T. *Time Series Forecasting: Unified Concepts and Computer Implementation.* 2d ed. Boston: Duxbury Press, 1987.

Box, G. E. P. and Jenkins, G. M. *Time Series Analysis, Forecasting and Control.* 2d ed. San Francisco: Holden-Day, 1976.

Cryer, Jonathan D. *Time Series Analysis.* Boston: Duxbury Press, 1986.

Granger, C. W. G. *Forecasting in Business and Economics.* 2d ed. New York: Academic Press, 1989.

Johnson, A. C. and Johnson, Marvin B. *Econometrics: Basic and Applied.* New York: Macmillan, 1987.

Montgomery, Douglas C. and Johnson, Lynwood A. *Forecasting and Time Series Analysis.* 2d ed. New York: McGraw-Hill, 1990.

Nelson, C. R. *Applied Time Series Analysis for Managerial Forecasting.* San Francisco: Holden-Day, 1983.

Willis, R. E. *A Guide to Forecasting for Planners.* Englewood Cliffs, New Jersey: Prentice-Hall, 1987.

Wonnacott, T. H. and Wonnacott, R. J. *Econometrics.* 2d ed. New York: Wiley, 1979.

Chapter 18

Hand-In Exercises

1. Refer to Problems 5 and 7 in Chapter 18. Use regression analysis to prepare a trend line forecast equation.

Time	Sales
1	242
2	252
3	257
4	267
5	272
6	285
7	281
8	287
9	307
10	299
11	292
12	311
13	326
14	332
15	321
16	314

2. Use the trend equation you computed in Exercise 1 to compute forecast sales for each quarter.

Time	Forecast Sales
1	
2	
3	
4	
5	
6	
7	
8	
9	
10	
11	
12	
13	
14	
15	
16	

3. Compute seasonal indices for each quarter by using Table 18–5 as a model for your calculations.

Time	Sales	4 Period M.A.	Centered M.A.	Ratio to M.A.

4. Use the results of Exercise 3 to deseasonalize the time series of sales data. Your results should look like Table 18-6.

5. Refer to Problem 14 in Chapter 18. Data to be used are from Problem 5 in Chapter 18.

a. Prepare a 4 period morning average and forecast for the next quarter. Also calculate MAD.

Time	Sales	Forecast	Error
1	242		
2	252		
3	257		
4	267		
5	272		
6	285		
7	281		
8	287		
9	307		
10	299		
11	292		
12	311		
13	326		
14	332		
15	321		
16	314		

MAD =

b. Prepare an exponential smoothing forecast for the next quarter on the same data. Also calculate MAD. Use an alpha of .25 for calculations.

Time	Sales	Forecast	Error
1	242		
2	252		
3	257		
4	267		
5	272		
6	285		
7	281		
8	287		
9	307		
10	299		
11	292		
12	311		
13	326		
14	332		
15	321		
16	314		

MAD =

c. On the basis of MAD which method gives the better forecast?

Additional Topics in Decision Analysis

WHY DECISION MAKERS NEED TO KNOW

Most decisions are made in an *uncertain* environment. Chapter 19 introduced some important tools of decision analysis, including decision trees. The expected-value criterion was introduced as the primary means of comparing decision alternatives. The advantage of the expected-value criterion is that it fully utilizes the decision maker's probability assessments about the uncertain events involved in a decision.

When probability assessments are based on subjective evaluation, they represent the decision maker's opinion, or state of mind, regarding the chances that an outcome will occur. The subjective assessments are based on personal experiences and all available information up to the point at which the probabilities are assessed. However, if new information becomes available, the decision maker should use the new information to revise his or her probability assessments. For instance, a sales representative for a national sporting goods manufacturer might have assessed the chances of making a sale to a particular client to be 0.60, given all available information. A day before her sales call, she learns that the client has just closed one of its stores in the city for financial reasons. This new information would seem to affect the chances of making a sale. The sales representative might then revise her probability estimate downward to 0.40.

Revising probability assessments is a normal part of decision making; people do it informally all the time. Think back to when you signed up for this course. You no doubt had formed some sort of expectation about the class and the instructor from comments by friends who had previously taken the class. Now think back to the first day of class. By then you probably had purchased this text and may have browsed through it to get an idea of the topics to be covered. As you listened to the instructor go over the course outline, explain the grading requirements, and so on, your expectations about the course were changing. Each person in the class began with different expectations and then processed the new information differently; however, you all went through the same revision of your expectations. (In fact, this process has no doubt continued throughout the term.)

Because the process of using new information to revise original probability assessments is a natural part of decision making, it is an important part of decision analysis. In this chapter, we introduce the Bayesian revision analysis technique, which is a formal means by which new information about events is incorporated into the decision process and used to revise the original probability assessments about those events. Bayesian revision is a very important component of decision analysis.

Regardless of the information available, not all decision makers view decisions the same way. Why do some people travel to Nevada or Atlantic City to gamble when they know that the odds are not in their favor? Why do some people pay \$10 a day for damage insurance when they rent a car and others choose not to? Why do some people buy lottery tickets? In most cases, the answers to all these questions relate to the individual's preference for risk.

People who purchase collision insurance on their automobiles are indicating their preference for paying an annual premium to protect them against having to pay for repairs in the unlikely event the vehicle is damaged in an accident. By paying the insurance premium, the individual is trading a relatively small insurance payment for the potentially large (but unlikely) cost of an accident. In most cases, the expected cost of the premium is greater than the expected cost of not buying the insurance.

Interestingly enough, often the same person who buys collision insurance when he or she rents a car will also be willing to gamble at a slot machine. Thus, a person may exhibit different attitudes toward risk in different decision-making situations.

Because of the way individuals incorporate preferences for risk into their personal decisions, attitudes toward risk are an important part of business decision making. This chapter will show you how to formally incorporate risk preference attitudes into the decision process as an extension of the decision-analysis techniques introduced in Chapter 19.

CHAPTER OBJECTIVES

This chapter introduces the Bayesian process for revising probability assessments to account for new information and discusses how to determine the value of this new information.

In this chapter we also introduce the concepts of risk-preference analysis and show how to incorporate attitudes toward risk into the decision-making process.

STUDENT OBJECTIVES

After reading this chapter you should be able to do the following:

1. Explain how to use the Bayesian revision process when the new information comes from a sample taken from a binomial process.
2. Identify risk-seeking or risk-avoiding behavior by examining the decision that has been made.
3. Construct an individual risk-preference function and use it in decision analysis.
4. Compute the risk premium for a risk avoider.
5. Recognize the importance of including attitudes toward risk in the decision-analysis process.

20-1 BAYES' RULE

Chapter 4 introduced the concept of conditional probabilities. **Conditional probabilities** are important in many decision-making situations. For instance, medical researchers are interested in determining the probability of a person getting cancer, given that the person was exposed to hazardous chemicals—that is,

$$P(\text{cancer}|\text{hazardous chemicals})$$

Educators are interested in the probability a student learns math skills, given that the student completed certain background work:

$$P(\text{learning skills}|\text{background work})$$

Managers are interested in the probability a worker will develop superior skills, given that the worker receives a certain job advancement sequence:

$$P(\text{work skills}|\text{advancement sequence})$$

Thus, conditional probability is the probability that event A will occur, *given* that a second event, B, has already occurred. In simple notation form, we can state this as:

$$P(A|B) = ?$$

where the symbol | represents *given*. For instance, you might recall the familiar problem of drawing a bead from an urn and the instructor posing a question like this one: If you have an urn with exactly 10 green beads and 10 white beads, what is the probability of getting a green bead on the second draw from the urn, *given* that the first bead drawn was also green and that it was not returned to the urn?

Using the above notation, we can restate the instructor's question as follows:

$$P(G_2|G_1) = ?$$

Since the beads are drawn without replacement, the probability of getting green on the second draw is *conditional* on the outcome of the first draw. For example, if the first draw produced a white bead, 10 of the remaining 19 beads are green and the chances of getting a green on the second draw are 10 in 19, or 10/19. However, if the first draw yielded a green bead, then 9 of the remaining 19 beads are green and the probability of getting a green on the second draw—*given* that the first bead drawn was green—is 9/19.

Earlier in this text, you used conditional probabilities each time you tested a hypothesis. The p-value associated with the test of a hypothesis is the conditional probability of observing the sample statistic, given that the null hypothesis is true.

Conditional probability can be used for making decisions in many types of business situations. Suppose a company has two production facilities, one in Ohio and one in Virginia. The Ohio facility makes 60% of the company's total output, and the remaining 40% is made by the Virginia plant. After extensive sampling, the quality assurance manager has determined that 5% of the items produced in Ohio and 10% of the items produced in Virginia are defective. All finished products from both facilities are sent to a central warehouse, but then are intermingled rather than being stored separately. When the company sells a defective product, it incurs not only the cost of replacing the item but also the loss of goodwill. The vice-president for production would like to allocate these costs fairly between the two plants. To do so, he knows that he must first determine the probability that a defective item was produced by a particular production line. Specifically, he needs to answer these questions:

1. What is the probability that an item was produced at the Ohio plant, given that the item is defective?
2. What is the probability that an item was produced at the Virginia plant, given that the item is defective?

In notation form, with D representing the occurrence of a defective item, what the manager wants to know is:

$$P(\text{Ohio plant}|D) = ?$$
$$P(\text{Virginia plant}|D) = ?$$

The general rule for determining conditional probability is given by equation 20-1:

$$P(A_1|B) = \frac{P(B \text{ and } A_1)}{P(B)} = \frac{P(A_1)P(B|A_1)}{P(B)} \quad \textbf{20-1}$$

The denominator in equation 20-1, $P(B)$, which is the probability of the event given to have occurred, is found using equation 20-2:

$$P(B) = \Sigma\, P(B \text{ and } A_i) = \Sigma\, P(A_i)\, P(B|A_i) \quad \textbf{20-2}$$

where A_i is a collection of mutually exclusive and collectively exhaustive events.

Another way of writing equation 20-1 is shown as follows in equation 20-3 and is called *Bayes' rule.*

Bayes' Rule

Let A_i ($i = 1, 2, 3 \ldots, n$) be a complete set of mutually exclusive events. Let B be another event which is preceded by an A_i event. Both $P(A_i)$ and $P(B|A_i)$ must be known. Then

$$P(A_1|B) = \frac{P(A_1)P(B|A_1)}{\sum_{i=1}^{n} P(A_i)P(B|A_i)} \tag{20-3}$$

We can use equation 20-3, known as Bayes' rule, for the manufacturing example. First, we are looking for:

$$P(\text{Ohio plant}|D) = \frac{P(\text{Ohio plant})\ P(D|\text{Ohio plant})}{P(D)}$$

$$P(\text{Virginia plant}|D) = \frac{P(\text{Virginia plant})\ P(D|\text{Virginia plant})}{P(D)}$$

We already know the probability that an item comes from the Ohio plant is $P(\text{Ohio plant}) = 0.60$. Likewise, we know the probability that an item comes from the Virginia facility is $P(\text{Virginia plant}) = 0.40$. We also know the chances of an item being defective, given its production facility:

$$P(D|\text{Ohio plant}) = 0.05 \qquad \text{and} \qquad P(D|\text{Virginia plant}) = 0.10$$

Thus, we can substitute into equation 20-1 as follows:

$$P(\text{Ohio plant}|D) = \frac{(0.60)(0.05)}{P(D)}$$

$$P(\text{Virginia plant}|D) = \frac{(0.40)(0.10)}{P(D)}$$

As you can see, we have values for everything but the overall probability of a defective item, $P(D)$. We can use equation 20-2 to find it, as follows:

$$\begin{aligned} P(D) &= P(\text{Ohio plant})\ P(D|\text{Ohio plant}) + P(\text{Virginia plant})\ P(D|\text{Virginia plant}) \\ &= (0.60)(0.05) + (0.40)(0.10) = 0.07 \end{aligned}$$

Now we can use equation 20-3, Bayes' rule, to find the conditional probabilities we originally sought:

$$P(\text{Ohio plant}|D) = \frac{(0.60)(0.05)}{0.07} = 0.428$$

$$P(\text{Virginia plant}|D) = \frac{(0.40)(0.10)}{0.07} = 0.572$$

Given that an item is found to be defective, there is a 0.428 chance that it came from the Ohio facility and a 0.572 chance that it came from the Virginia plant. Thus, 42.8% of the defective-item costs should be allocated to the Ohio plant and 57.2% to the plant in Virginia.

In the manufacturing example, in the absence of any additional information, we knew that the probability of an item being produced in Ohio was 0.60. This is called the *prior probability*. In more formal terms, **prior probability** is the probability that an event will occur (or a condition will exist), as assessed prior to the acquisition of any additional relevant information.

After learning that the item was defective, we used Bayes' rule (equation 20-3) to revise the probability downward to 0.428. Termed the **posterior probability**, this revised probability combined the *prior probability* and new information from the sample.

The importance of Bayes' rule to the study and application of decision analysis is that it gives decision makers a means of incorporating new information into the decision process. The *Bayesian revision analysis* procedures discussed in the remaining sections of this chapter provide a systematic method for using new information to revise prior opinions as well as a basis for determining the economic value of this new information.

20-2 USING BAYESIAN REVISION ANALYSIS

The Dexter Company supplies electrical lighting fixtures, bulbs, and replacement parts to office buildings in the Southeast. Replacement bulbs for fluorescent lights are a key product in Dexter's line and the firm's purchasing agents are always on the lookout for manufacturers whose bulbs will help Dexter keep its costs low.

Dexter currently buys its fluorescent bulbs from a Georgia company called Compu-Lite. This supplier produces a good product and, as determined from historical records of shipments to Dexter, has the following distribution of defective lights:

Proportion Defective	*Probability*
0.01	0.50
0.02	0.40
0.03	0.10
	1.00

Because of its emphasis on quality, Dexter guarantees its products and replaces any defective fluorescent items at no cost to the customer. Dexter's cost accountants have pegged the overall cost of each defective bulb, including lost goodwill, at $5.

The marketing department anticipates that Dexter will sell 100,000 fluorescent bulbs next year. If all 100,000 bulbs are purchased from Compu-Lite, the probability distribution for the number of defective bulbs and their overall cost is as follows:

Proportion Defective	*Number Defective*	*Overall Cost*	*Probability*
0.01	1,000	$ 5,000	0.50
0.02	2,000	10,000	0.40
0.03	3,000	15,000	0.10
			1.00

The expected replacement cost for Dexter, if all 100,000 bulbs are purchased from Compu-Lite, is

Cost x	*Probability* $P(x)$	$xP(x)$
$ 5,000	0.50	$2,500
10,000	0.40	4,000
15,000	0.10	1,500
		$8,000 = Expected cost

For the year, Dexter could expect to incur an $8,000 cost for replacing defective fluorescent lights purchased from Compu-Lite.

While attending the National Lighting Dealers Convention and Trade Show in Las Vegas recently, two Dexter managers were approached by representatives of a French manufacturer. The French sales reps offered to supply all the fluorescent lights Dexter would need at a cost of $.25 per unit less than Compu-Lite's price. This was an intriguing offer since, on 100,000 lights, an added profit of $25,000 was theoretically possible. The only uncertainty was the quality of the French lights.

After a number of phone calls to the French company and several of its customers, Dexter representatives subjectively developed the following probability distribution for the French manufacturer's defect rate:

Proportion Defective	*Subjective Probability*
0.01	0.10
0.02	0.20
0.03	0.40
0.10	0.20
0.15	0.10
	1.00

This probability distribution reflects the collective opinion of Dexter's quality engineers and thus reflects the state of mind of the decision makers regarding the quality of the French bulbs. The probability distribution indicates a good chance (0.70) that the defect rate will be 3% or less. However, the distribution also reflects Dexter's concern that the French company's products might have a defect rate of 10% or even 15%.

If the French company and Compu-Lite are the only suppliers under consideration by Dexter, which one should Dexter purchase from to minimize expected costs? To make this decision, Dexter managers must determine the expected cost of buying from the French company and compare it with the expected cost of buying from Compu-Lite.

The expected cost of replacing defective lights supplied by the French company is found as follows:

Proportion Defective	*Number Defective*	*Cost* x	*Probability* $P(x)$	$xP(x)$
0.01	1,000	$ 5,000	0.10	$ 500
0.02	2,000	10,000	0.20	2,000
0.03	3,000	15,000	0.40	6,000
0.10	10,000	50,000	0.20	10,000
0.15	15,000	75,000	0.10	7,500
			1.00	$26,000

If we compare only expected replacement costs, we obtain the following:

$$E(\text{Compu-Lite cost}) = \$8{,}000$$
$$E(\text{French company cost}) = \$26{,}000$$

Since $8,000 < $26,000, the choice based only on expected replacement costs would be to stay with Compu-Lite. This decision assumes no difference in the purchase price that Dexter pays per light. However, since the French company has quoted a price that is $.25 per unit less than Compu-Lite's price, this cost ($25,000 per 100,000 lights) must be added to the expected cost of replacing Compu-Lite's defective bulbs, as follows:

$$E(\text{Compu-Lite cost}) = \$8{,}000 + \$25{,}000 = \$33{,}000$$

Now, if we consider all the costs and base our decision solely on expected costs, the French company is the better alternative, since $26,000 < $33,000. The expected savings (and therefore higher profit earned) from changing suppliers is $7,000.

However, suppose the long-term business relationship that Dexter has enjoyed with Compu-Lite has caused Dexter's managers to give some more thought to their decision. They finally decide that before the relationship is severed, they need more information about the French product. Now Dexter requests that a random sample of fifty lights from the French manufacturer be tested by an independent testing service. Dexter officials plan to use the information from the sample tested, along with their prior probability distribution, in making the final decision. The technique of incorporating sample information into the decision process is called **Bayesian revision analysis.**

CONSTRUCTING A POSTERIOR PROBABILITY TABLE

A random sample of $n = 50$ lights was selected from the French manufacturer's inventory. We will assume a *binomial distribution* represents the sampling process in which a fluorescent bulb can be judged either good or defective. The Bayesian revision analysis for Dexter's decision is described in the following paragraphs.

First, recall that the possible outcomes in terms of the proportion of defectives and the associated prior probability distribution were subjectively assessed as:

Proportion Defective	*Subjective Probability*
0.01	0.10
0.02	0.20
0.03	0.40
0.10	0.20
0.15	0.10
	1.00

Next, in the second step, we determine the *conditional probability* of the sample result, given that the population of lights contains a particular proportion of defectives. Suppose the sample of fifty contains $X_1 = 6$ defectives. Remember that this is just one possible sample taken from the entire population of lights in the French manufacturer's inventory. The chances of seeing this sample result depend on what fraction of the total population actually is defective.

In the first step, the probability distribution indicated that the defect rate might be 0.01, . . . , 0.15. Now, for each possible defective rate, we must determine the conditional probability of finding six defectives in a sample of fifty lights. We have assumed that the process can be described by a binomial distribution and that the probabilities can be determined by using the tables in Appendix A, as follows: (1) Locate the binomial table for $n = 50$, (2) find the row for $X_1 = 6$, and (3) locate the p-value corresponding to a specific proportion defective. For instance, to find the probability for the first proportion defective, 0.01, we locate the intersection of the column headed $p = 0.01$ and the row for $X_1 = 6$. We find this value, 0.0000, which means there is essentially no chance that there would be six defectives in a sample of $n = 50$, given the proportion of defectives is 0.01.

TABLE 20-1

Conditional Probabilities for Dexter Example

Defect Rate (p)	Prior Probability	Conditional Probability
0.01	0.10	0.0000
0.02	0.20	0.0004
0.03	0.40	0.0030
0.10	0.20	0.1541
0.15	0.10	0.1419
	1.00	

Note: Conditional probability = $P(X_1, n|p)$, where $X_1 = 6$, $n = 50$.

Table 20-1 shows the conditional probabilities for all possible defect levels in the Dexter example. (Make sure you can find these probabilities. A common mistake is to set p = prior probability instead of p = proportion defective. Please do not do this!)

The third step in the Bayesian posterior analysis is to compute the joint probabilities. **Joint probability** is the probability of the simultaneous occurrence of two or more events. It represents the chances of observing both the sample information and a particular state of nature. In the Dexter example, it is the probability of a specific defective rate and the conditional probability of the sample information, given the defective rate. The joint probabilities, which form the numerator in Bayes' rule (equation 20-3), are calculated by multiplying the prior probability by the conditional probability. These values for the Dexter example are shown in Table 20-2.

The denominator in Bayes' rule is the sum of the joint probabilities; in this case, it is the overall probability of getting six defectives in a sample of fifty, given prior knowledge about the defective rate of the French products. Thus, there is a 0.04629 chance that we would get six defectives in a sample of fifty from this supplier.

The fourth step is to compute the *posterior probabilities* by dividing each joint probability by the sum of the joint probabilities. Table 20-3 shows the results of the completed Bayesian revision analysis.

The posterior probabilities reflect the combination of information from the prior probabilities and the sample data. Dexter now has a different view of the French company, since the posterior probabilities are quite different from the prior probabilities. Whereas before, Dexter officials thought there was a 70% chance that the defect rate would be 0.03 or less, the posterior probabilities indicate that the chance is actually slightly less than 3% (i.e., 0.00000 + 0.00173 + 0.02592 = 0.02765). Dexter officials now believe the French company is far more likely to supply a greater number of defective bulbs than they had estimated before the sample was tested. The fact that the sample contained 12% defectives was the key to this change in attitude. The posterior probabilities reflect Dexter officials' current state of mind about the French company's defect rate.

TABLE 20-2

Joint Probabilities for Dexter Example

Defect Rate (p)	Prior Probability	Conditional Probability	Joint Probability
0.01	0.10	0.0000	0.00000
0.02	0.20	0.0004	0.00008
0.03	0.40	0.0030	0.00120
0.10	0.20	0.1541	0.03082
0.15	0.10	0.1419	0.01419
	1.00		0.04629

Note:

$$\text{Joint probability} = \text{Prior probability} \times \text{Conditional probability} = P(X_1)P(X_1, n|p)$$

where

$$P(X_1) = \text{Prior probability}$$

$$P(X_1, n|p) = \text{Conditional probability}$$

and

$$X_1 = 6, n = 50$$

TABLE 20-3

Posterior Probabilities for Dexter Example

Defect Rate (p)	Prior Probability	Conditional Probability	Joint Probability	Posterior Probability
0.01	0.10	0.0000	0.00000	0.00000
0.02	0.20	0.0004	0.00008	0.00173
0.03	0.40	0.0030	0.00120	0.02592
0.10	0.20	0.1541	0.03082	0.66580
0.15	0.10	0.1419	0.01419	0.30655
	1.00		0.04629	1.00000

Note:

$$\text{Posterior probability} = \frac{\text{Joint probability}}{\text{Sum of joint probabilities}} = \frac{P(X_1)\,P(X_1, n|p)}{\sum_{i=1}^{k} P(X_i)\,P(X_i, n|p)}$$

where

$$P(X_1) = \text{Prior probability of state 1}$$

$$P(X_1, n|p) = \text{Conditional probability}$$

$$k = \text{Number of possible states}$$

and

$$X_1 = 6, n = 50$$

In the final step of the Bayesian revision analysis for the Dexter example, we use the posterior probabilities to reevaluate the decision situation. The revised cost distribution for the French supplier and the computation of expected cost of replacing defectives are given.

Proportion Defective	*Number Defective*	*Cost* x	*Probability* $P(x)$	$xP(x)$
0.01	1,000	\$ 5,000	0.00000	\$ 0
0.02	2,000	10,000	0.00173	17.30
0.03	3,000	15,000	0.02592	388.80
0.10	10,000	50,000	0.66580	33,290.00
0.15	15,000	75,000	0.30655	22,991.25
			1.00000	\$56,687.35

After incorporating the sample information with the prior probability distribution, we find that the expected cost of replacing defectives from the French company is \$56,687.35, which now exceeds the \$33,000 expected cost for Compu-Lite. Therefore, using the decision criterion of minimizing expected costs, the Dexter Company should continue to buy from Compu-Lite. The sample information caused this change from the initial decision.

SUMMARY OF THE BAYESIAN REVISION PROCESS

The Bayesian revision process applies Bayes' rule (equation 20-3) in a manner that allows new information to be included in the decision process. To review, the steps in the analysis are as follows:

1. Develop the prior probability distribution and evaluate the decision on the basis of the prior probabilities.
2. Collect new information and compute the conditional probabilities.
3. Compute the joint probabilities as the product of the conditional probability and the prior probability. The sum of the joint probabilities reflects the overall probability of observing the new information, given the prior state of knowledge about the population of interest.
4. Compute the posterior probabilities by dividing each joint probability by the sum of the joint probabilities.
5. Reevaluate the decision by computing the expected payoff, or cost, using the newly calculated posterior probabilities.

THE DEXTER EXAMPLE CONTINUES

You no doubt learned in your statistics course that the potential for sampling error exists whenever sampling is used. Sampling error is measured by the difference between a calculated sample value and the corresponding actual population value. The French supplier's production manager believes that his company has been a victim of bad luck and severe sampling error. He thinks the defect rate found in the sample of fifty is much higher than the actual defect rate in the bulbs this company produces. He is willing to pay for testing another sample of fifty lights in the hope that the new information will cause Dexter to decide to buy lights from his company. Since there is no cost to Dexter, its officials are happy to obtain more information. However, Dexter's managers inform the French production manager that they will not ignore the first sample and will use the newly formed posterior probabilities as the prior probabilities in their analysis after the second round of sampling.

What is about to take place in the Dexter example is very typical of business decision making. That is, we begin with a set of prior probabilities ("priors") which reflect our "current" state of mind. We observe information and revise our priors accordingly. The posterior probabilities become a new set of priors. We then review more information and revise the priors again. This revision process continues as long as new information is made available before the final decision must be made. Each time, *the posteriors become the priors for the next round of revisions.*

Suppose that the test of the second sample of fifty lights yielded only one defective bulb. Table 20-4 shows the results of the new Bayesian revision analysis,

TABLE 20-4

Posterior Probabilities Based on New Sample

Defect Rate (p)	Prior Probability	Conditional Probability	Joint Probability	Posterior Probability
0.01	0.00000	0.3056	0.00000	0.00000
0.02	0.00173	0.3716	0.00064	0.02190
0.03	0.02592	0.3372	0.00874	0.29911
0.10	0.66580	0.0286	0.01904	0.65161
0.15	0.30655	0.0026	0.00080	0.02738
	1.00000		0.02922	1.00000

Note:

$$\text{Posterior probability} = \frac{\text{Joint probability}}{\text{Sum of joint probabilities}}$$

$$= \frac{P(X_1)\,P(X_1, n|p)}{\sum_{i=1}^{k} P(X_i)\,P(X_i, n|p)}$$

where

$P(X_1)$ = Prior probability of state 1

$P(X_1, n|p)$ = Conditional probability

k = Number of possible states

and

$X_1 = 1,\ n = 50$

including the new posterior probabilities. (You should perform all the necessary calculations to be sure you fully understand the steps involved in computing the posterior probabilities using the new defect rate.)

Now we can compute a new expected cost, using the posterior probabilities from Table 20-4. Because the second sample of fifty had only one defective bulb, the probabilities now shift back somewhat, lowering the expected cost from \$56,687.35 to \$39,339.65. However, even after the new analysis, Dexter's best decision is to continue buying from Compu-Lite, since \$33,000 < \$39,339.15.

Proportion Defective	*Number Defective*	*Cost* x	*Probability* $P(x)$	$xP(x)$
0.01	1,000	\$ 5,000	0.00000	\$ 0
0.02	2,000	10,000	0.02190	219.00
0.03	3,000	15,000	0.29911	4,486.65
0.10	10,000	50,000	0.65161	32,580.50
0.15	15,000	75,000	0.02738	2,053.50
			1.00000	\$39,339.65

IS ONE BIG SAMPLE DIFFERENT FROM TWO SMALL SAMPLES?

After learning of Dexter's decision to stay with Compu-Lite, despite the favorable results of the second sample, the French company's managers lamented the fact that they had provided two samples of fifty instead of one sample of 100. Suppose that initially they had selected a random sample of 100 and found seven defective bulbs, the same total number of defectives found in the two fifty-bulb samples. Table 20-5 shows the revised probabilities based on the sample of $n = 100$ and $X_1 = 7$ defectives. With small differences for rounding, these posterior probabilities are equal to those in Table 20-4, which were computed after two successive samples of fifty each, with a total of seven defectives.

As you can see, the conclusions reached from the smaller samples and one larger sample are the same. The sum of the information in several small samples is exactly the same as the information in a large sample that is equal in size to the sum of the small samples. However, an argument is sometimes made for planning a series of small samples if the per unit cost of sampling is high, since the results of the first few small samples may be sufficient to make a decision.

SKILL DEVELOPMENT PROBLEMS FOR **SECTION 20-2**

The following exercises have been included to help you gain a better understanding of the material presented in this section.

1. The Skiwell Manufacturing Company gets materials for its cross-country skis from two suppliers. Supplier A's materials make up 40% of what is used, with supplier B providing the rest. Past records indicate that 15% of

TABLE 20-5

Posterior Probabilities Based on One 100-Unit Sample

Defect Rate (p)	Prior Probability	Conditional Probability	Joint Probability	Posterior Probability
0.01	0.10	0.0001	0.00001	0.00037
0.02	0.20	0.0031	0.00062	0.02263
0.03	0.40	0.0206	0.00824	0.30073
0.10	0.20	0.0889	0.01778	0.64890
0.15	0.10	0.0075	0.00075	0.02737
	1.00		0.02740	1.00000

Note:

$$\text{Posterior probability} = \frac{\text{Joint probability}}{\text{Sum of joint probabilities}}$$

$$= \frac{P(X_1)\,P(X_1, n|p)}{\sum_{i=1}^{k} P(X_i)\,P(X_i, n|p)}$$

where

$$P(X_1) = \text{Prior probability of state 1}$$

$$P(X_1, n|p) = \text{Conditional probability}$$

$$k = \text{Number of possible states}$$

and

$$X_1 = 7,\ n = 100$$

supplier A's materials are defective and 10% of B's are defective. Since it is impossible to tell which supplier the materials came from once they are in inventory, the manager wants to know which supplier most likely supplied the defective materials the foreman has brought to his attention.

2. Alpine Cannery is currently processing vegetables from the summer harvest. The manager has found a case of cans that has not been properly sealed. There are three lines that processed cans of this type and the manager wants to know which line is responsible for this mistake.

Line	*Contribution to Total*	*Proportion Defective*
1	0.40	0.05
2	0.35	0.10
3	0.25	0.07

3. Cascade Paint mixes paint in three separate plants and then ships the unmarked cans to a central warehouse. Plant A supplies 50% of the paint and past records indicate that the paint is incorrectly mixed 10% of the time. Plant B contributes 30% with a defective rate of 5%. Plant C supplies 20%

with paint mixed incorrectly 20% of the time. If Cascade guarantees its product and spent $10,000 replacing improperly mixed paint last year, how should the cost be distributed among the three plants?

4. The Chocolate House specializes in hand-dipped chocolates for special occasions. Recently, several long-time customers have complained about the quality of the chocolates. It seems there are several partially covered chocolates in each box. The defective chocolates should have been caught when the boxes were packed. The manager is wondering which of the three packers is not doing the job properly. Clerk 1 packs 40% of the boxes and usually has a 2% defective rate. Clerk 2 packs 30% with a 2.5% defective rate. Clerk 3 boxes 30% of the chocolates and her defective rate is 1.5%. Which clerk is most likely responsible for the boxes that have raised the complaints?

5. As the owner of the Union Nursery, Kelly is concerned about the quality of some of the plants purchased from a local wholesaler, but is not certain why the problem has suddenly cropped up. The company has been buying plants from this particular wholesaler for years and the quality has always been excellent. A new employee of Kelly's who worked for the wholesaler explains that just before he left his previous position, the wholesaler had started purchasing plants from a new grower in order to meet demand. The old grower has a good reputation and only 2% of his plants are unusable. The new grower's plants are of poor quality 30% of the time. The old grower currently supplies 80% of the wholesaler's plants. If Kelly receives another shipment of unsalable plants, which grower most likely supplied the plants?

20-3 RISK-PREFERENCE ATTITUDES

Not all people select the same alternative when faced with the same decision situation. For instance, managers often disagree over which course of action should be taken by a company facing the prospect of expansion. Decision makers might reach different conclusions about whether to hire an applicant for an important position. One important reason why the choices could be different is that the decision makers have different attitudes about taking a risk. Referred to as "risk preference," the decision maker's attitude toward risk influences his or her view of the potential outcomes associated with the various alternatives. In decision analysis, the risk-preference attitudes are commonly classified as follows:

1. Risk-neutral
2. Risk-averse
3. Risk-seeking

In this section, we will discuss these three types of decision behavior and show how a decision maker's risk preference can be incorporated into the decision-analysis model.

RISK-NEUTRAL

In Chapter 19, the expected-value criterion was used as the primary means for deciding between alternatives. This meant that we always selected the alternative with the highest expected payoff or the lowest expected cost. Decision makers who strictly apply the expected-value criterion and select the highest payoff or lowest cost are considered **risk-neutral.** For example, suppose a risk-neutral decision maker is given the following options:

1. Play a game consisting of tossing a fair coin one time. If a head turns up, the player will be paid \$10; if a tail turns up, the player will lose \$6.
2. Do not play the game.

This decision is diagrammed as follows:

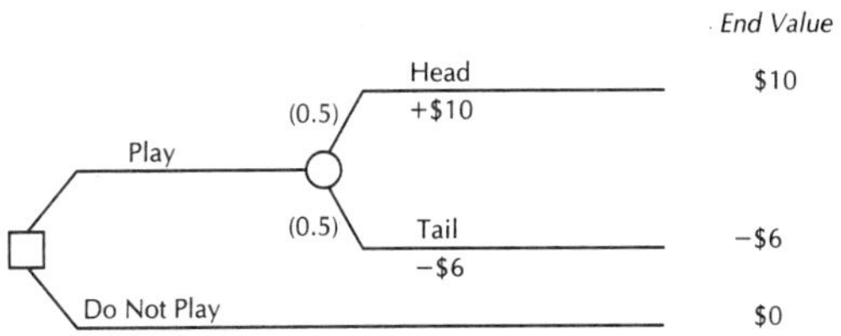

If the coin is fair, the chance of a head turning up is 0.5, the same as for a tail. The risk-neutral decision maker would compute the expected value of both alternatives as follows:

$$E(\text{play}) = \$10(0.5) + [-\$6(0.5)] = \$5 - \$3 = \$2$$
$$E(\text{do not play}) = \$0$$

Then, choosing strictly on the basis of expected value, the decision maker would select the "Play" alternative, since \$2 > \$0.

Consider a similar decision, diagrammed as follows:

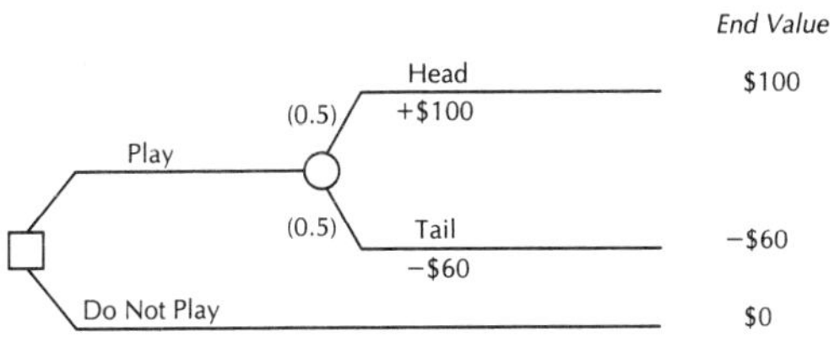

Now the expected values of the alternatives in this case are as follows:

$$E(\text{play}) = \$100(0.5) + [-\$60(0.5)] = \$20$$
$$E(\text{do not play}) = \$0$$

Deciding strictly on the basis of expected value, the risk-neutral decision maker will choose to play, since \$20 > \$0.

While most of us would like to win the $10 in the first example, our day would not be totally ruined if we lost and had to pay the $6. In the second example, we would very much like the $100 payoff, but the loss of $60 would hurt a bit. The risk-neutral decision maker does not let such thoughts affect the decision, and would make the same choice even if the game had payoffs of $10,000 and −$6,000, as follows:

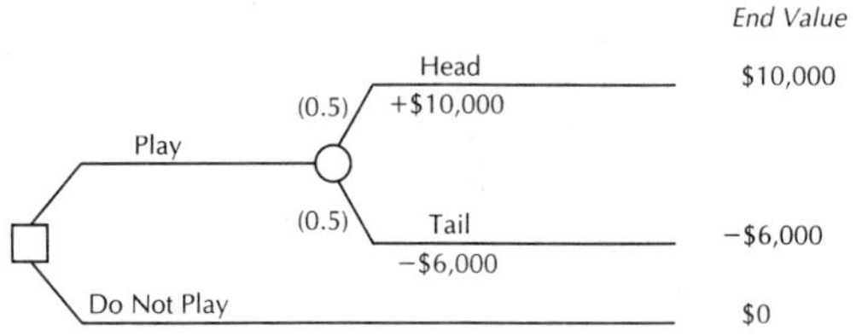

The expected value of the "Play" alternative is $2,000, which clearly makes the "best decision" to play the game. Right?

If you were faced with this latest decision situation, what would you do, given your current financial status? Just think how nice it would be to add $10,000 to your bank account—if a head turns up. However, how would you feel if a tail turns up and you suddenly *owe* $6,000? Most of us would tend to look at the values of the possible outcomes and balance our desire for the $10,000 gain versus our dislike of losing $6,000, before actually making our decision.

Considering end values and letting our attitude toward these values influence the decision means we are not risk-neutral. Further, when considering the end values in a decision situation, rarely will someone be risk-neutral over a wide range of decision situations. If a decision maker is not risk-neutral, then he or she is said to be either a *risk avoider* or a *risk seeker.* In either instance, the expected value of a decision alternative is not the sole decision criterion.

RISK-AVERSE

Consider the following situation. An investment option exists that will require you to invest $10,000. There is a 0.50 chance that you will walk away with $20,000; but there is also a 0.50 chance that you will end up with $0. The expected value is

$$E(\text{payoff}) = 0.5(\$20{,}000) + 0.5(\$0) = \$10{,}000$$

Thus, on average, you would break even. You would be paying $10,000 to earn back an average of $10,000. This is an *actuarially fair gamble.* Risk-neutral decision makers would be indifferent; they could take the investment option or leave it. A **risk-averse** individual would not take this investment option; in fact, a risk avoider would be willing to pay some certain amount, called a *certainty equivalent,* to get out of taking the gamble. Consider your own personal situation. If you were told that you had to ante up $10,000 for an investment option where the flip of a coin would determine whether you get either $20,000 or nothing, how would you feel? Would you be willing to pay some amount right now to get out of taking the gamble? How much would you pay? The more you would be willing to pay, the more risk-averse you are for this gamble.

Most people are risk avoiders, choosing to guard against the extreme "bad" outcome. Insurance companies rely on this fact. Consider the decision of whether to purchase health insurance for $600 per year. The policy has a $1,000-deductible clause, meaning you pay the first $1,000 in medical bills during each year, and it covers 90% of the costs over $1,000. Figure 20-1 shows the decision tree for this situation. Three possible outcomes are possible under each alternative. These outcomes and the subjectively assessed probabilities are as follows:

Medical Cost	*Probability*
$ 100	0.90
500	0.09
25,000	0.01

The probabilities reflect the decision maker's assessment of each possible outcome. There is a high chance that the medical costs during the year will be $500 or less and only 1 chance in 100 that a major medical problem costing $25,000 will occur.

Figure 20-1 shows that the expected cost is $385 for the "No insurance" alternative and $769 for the "Buy insurance" option. On the basis of expected

FIGURE 20-1

Decision Tree for Health Insurance Example

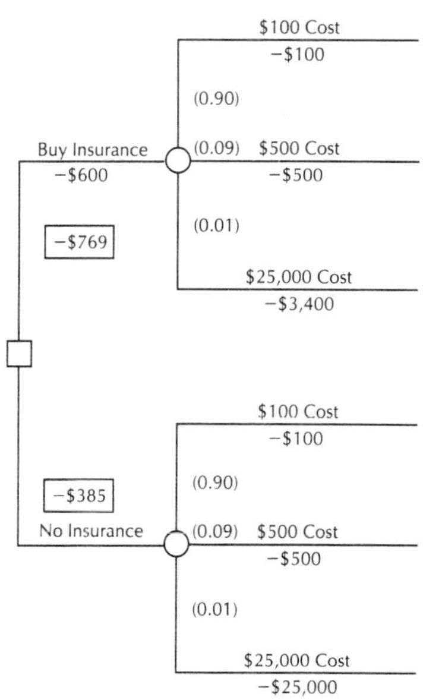

value, the "best decision" is not to buy insurance, since \$345 < \$769. However, most people will buy the insurance anyway, exhibiting a preference to avoid the risk of the potentially worst outcome.

Risk avoidance is also prevalent in business decision making. The reasons for this are at least twofold. First, since the individual is likely to be a risk avoider in many personal situations, this behavior will extend to business decisions, even though now it is the company's resources—not the decision maker's personal resources—that are at stake. Second, the reward structure in many organizations provides an incentive for people to avoid choosing alternatives with risky outcomes. While a good outcome may result in a bonus for the decision maker, often this bonus does not outweigh the possible consequences of an extremely negative outcome, such as being fired.

In practice, risk-avoiding behavior in an organization tends to be more prevalent at the lower and middle management levels. Often this runs somewhat counter to the desires of upper management which, publicly at least, talks about the need to take chances and be willing to fail.

RISK-SEEKING

Not everyone is a risk avoider. Clearly, there are many situations in which people exhibit **risk-seeking** behavior. For instance, consider another investment alternative which requires a \$10,000 investment. There is a 0.10 chance that you would walk away with \$80,000 and a 0.90 chance that you would lose your \$10,000 and end up with \$0. The expected payoff is:

$$E(\text{payoff}) = 0.10(\$80{,}000) + 0.90(\$0) = \$8{,}000$$

Thus, on average, an investor would leave with \$8,000 after making a \$10,000 investment. Since the expected loss is \$2,000, a risk-neutral decision maker would choose not to invest; so would a risk avoider. However, some people would want to invest to have the chance at \$80,000. These individuals are called risk seekers. In fact, if faced with the prospect of losing out on the investment option, a risk seeker might agree to pay some additional amount just to keep the investment opportunity open.

A good example of risk-seeking behavior is what happens when someone enters a "sweepstakes" contest sponsored by a magazine publishing company. For instance, in a contest held in 1990, the person who had the winning number would receive \$10 million. To be eligible to win, all a contestant had to do was mail in the entry form, which required spending \$0.25 for a stamp. The stated chance of winning was 1 in 100,000,000. The tree for this decision is shown in Figure 20-2. Even though the expected value was −\$0.15, millions of people entered this contest. They were willing to risk a \$0.25 stamp for the chance to make \$10 million.

Risk-seeking behavior is typically associated with situations in which one possible outcome is perceived by the decision maker to have the potential to

FIGURE 20-2

Decision Tree for Publisher's Sweepstakes

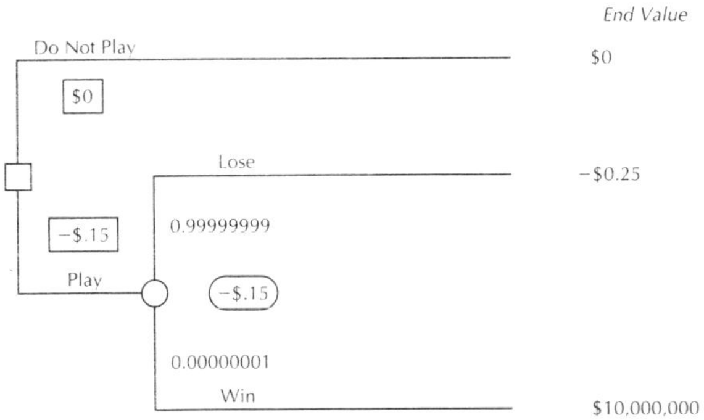

markedly change his or her life. Winning the contest and receiving $10 million is that type of outcome. States with government-run lotteries have found that they get more players if they offer a major prize of several million dollars instead of more, but smaller, prizes. People are more willing to take a risk in hopes of obtaining the big prize.

Business decision makers can also engage in risk-seeking behavior. About 5 years ago, a young accountant saw an advertisement in the Portland *Oregonian* newspaper offering for sale five franchises for a popular hamburger chain in the Eugene area. After reviewing the situation, assessing the possible gains and losses, and determining that the decision's expected value was negative, he invested anyway. The potentially high payoff meant more to him than a negative expected value.

The same person may be risk-averse in some situations and risk-seeking in others, depending on the range of outcomes. For example, if you were asked to spend $1 on a lottery ticket that offered a 1 in 1,000 chance of winning $500, you might consider it, even though the expected value is −$0.50. If you play, you are a risk seeker. On the other hand, if you were offered a chance to buy a $10,000 ticket in a lottery with a 0.25 chance of winning $100,000, you might refuse the offer, even though the expected value is $15,000. If you refuse, you are exhibiting risk-averse behavior. In the first case, the range of payoffs was −$1 to $500 and the worst outcome was to lose only $1. However, when the possible loss is greater, such as the −$10,000 in the second example, you might select an alternative that would protect you against this bad outcome.

20-4 DEVELOPING A RISK-PREFERENCE FUNCTION

The expected-value criterion suits the attitude of a risk-neutral decision maker. For this group of decision makers, the best decision is the one that maximizes the expected payoff or minimizes the expected cost. However, because not all (or even most) decision makers are risk-neutral, a method for formally incorporating risk-averse and risk-seeking attitudes into the decision process is needed.

The method used in decision analysis is to develop a **risk-preference function** that describes the decision maker's relative preferences for all outcomes within a specified range. (The preference function is commonly plotted as a line or curve on a graph.)

THE STANDARD GAMBLE APPROACH

Several methods can be used to establish a decision maker's risk-preference function. The method illustrated in this text, called the **standard gamble approach,** involves setting up a series of 50–50 gambles between two payoffs and determining the certainty equivalents. We begin by using a simple example to demonstrate how a standard gamble is used to develop risk-neutral, risk-averse, and risk-seeking preference functions. We will then follow with an example showing how preference functions are used in the decision-making process.

Risk-Neutral Preference Function

To develop a risk-preference function, we must have a range of possible outcomes measured in dollars. The outcomes typically range from the highest possible end value on a decision tree to the lowest possible end value. Suppose you are the decision maker analyzing a decision tree where the highest possible payoff is $10,000 and the lowest possible payoff is −$2,000. Further assume that you are risk-neutral.

The first step in developing your risk-preference function is to assign preference quotients to the highest and lowest possible outcomes. A **preference quotient** is a measure of the relative utility for the outcomes of a decision on a scale between 1.0 and 0.0. Let q represent the preference quotient. The higher the q value, the greater the relative preference for the dollar outcome. The highest possible payoff is assigned a value of $q = 1.0$, since that value is preferred over all other payoffs. The lowest possible payoff is assigned $q = 0.0$, indicating that you would prefer any other payoff over the lowest payoff. When dealing with costs instead of payoffs, we reverse this reasoning and assign a value of 1.0 to the lowest-cost alternative and 0.0 to the highest-cost alternative. For this example, we get

Payoff	q
$10,000	1.0
−2,000	0.0

The next step in developing the risk-preference function is to pose a series of *standard gambles*. The first one is diagrammed in Figure 20-3. The alternatives are either to play a game with a 0.50 chance of winning $10,000 and a 0.50 chance of losing $2,000 or not to play the game. The payoffs associated with the

FIGURE 20-3

Assessing the Risk-Preference Function: Standard Gamble 1

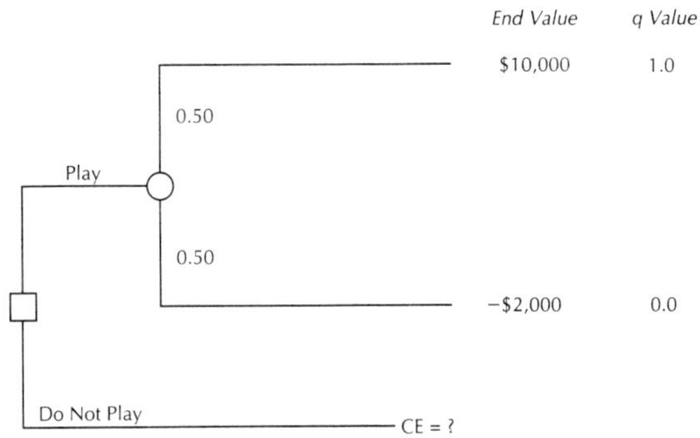

"Play" alternative are the same payoffs for which we have already assigned q values. This decision is referred to as a standard gamble because the chance of each payoff occurring is set at 0.50.

You must next determine what certain outcome for the "Do not play" branch would make you be indifferent toward playing or not playing. This value is termed the **certainty equivalent** (or CE value) of the gamble. You can think of it as the amount you would take to give up the opportunity to play the game.

The expected value of the "Play" branch is

$$EV = \$10{,}000(0.50) + -\$2{,}000(0.50) = \$4{,}000$$

This means that, on average, you would make $4,000 by selecting the "Play" alternative. A risk-neutral decision maker always selects the option with the highest expected payoff. If the payoff for the "Do not play" branch exceeds $4,000, then the choice would be not to play. If the payoff for the "Do not play" alternative is less than $4,000, then the "Play" branch would be selected. Thus, for a risk-neutral decision maker, the certainty equivalent for this standard gamble is the expected value, $4,000. If the "Do not play" branch had a certain payoff of $4,000, the risk-neutral decision maker would be indifferent toward the two alternatives.

Since we are assuming you are risk-neutral, the next step is to determine the q value for a payoff of $4,000. This is done by determining the expected q value for the "Play" branch based on the q values already assigned to the payoffs of $10,000 and −$2,000:

$$E(q) = 1.0(0.50) + 0.0(0.50) = 0.50$$

Thus, the preference quotient, q, for a payoff of $4,000 is 0.50. We now have the following q values:

Payoff	q
$10,000	1.0
4,000	0.5
−2,000	0.0

FIGURE 20-4

Assessing the Risk-Preference Function: Standard Gamble 2

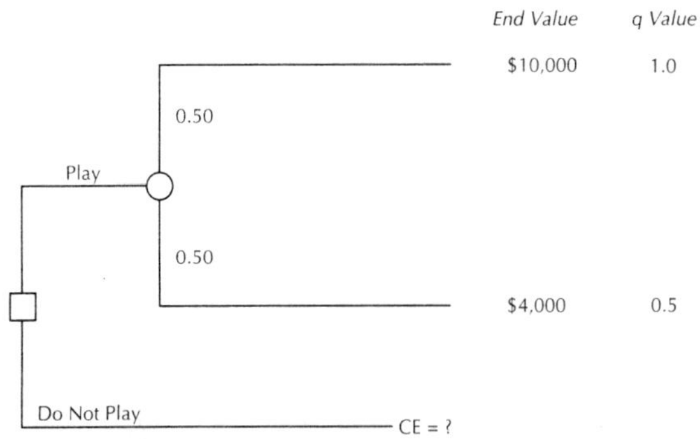

Note that the decision tree may not have an end value of $4,000; but this does not present a problem, since our objective is to develop a risk-preference curve which can be used to determine the relative preference for any value between $10,000 and −$2,000. We now have three points on this preference curve.

To determine additional points, we pose a second standard gamble, as shown in Figure 20-4. The "Play" alternative now shows a 0.50 chance at $10,000 and a 0.50 chance at $4,000. We have previously assigned q values to each of these outcomes and must now determine the CE value for this gamble. Remember, CE will be the point of indifference between playing and not playing.

The expected value of the "Play" branch is

$$EV = \$10{,}000(0.50) + \$4{,}000(0.50) = \$7{,}000$$

On average, the "Play" alternative will yield a $7,000 payoff. A risk-neutral decision maker would be indifferent toward playing or not playing if the "Do not play" alternative had a certain outcome of $7,000. Then, for a risk-neutral decision maker, CE = $7,000. We determine the q value for $7,000 by finding the expected q value for this standard gamble:

$$E(q) = 1.0(0.50) + 0.50(0.50) = 0.75$$

The preference quotient for a payoff of $7,000 is 0.75. We now have four values:

Payoff	*q*
$10,000	1.00
7,000	0.75
4,000	0.50
−2,000	0.00

We can pose still another standard gamble, as shown in Figure 20-5. The expected value of the "Play" branch is as follows:

$$EV = \$4{,}000(0.50) + [-\$2{,}000(0.50)] = \$1{,}000$$

A risk-neutral decision maker would be indifferent toward the alternatives if the certain outcome of the "Play" branch was $1,000. Thus, the CE for this standard

FIGURE 20-5

Assessing the Risk-Preference Function: Standard Gamble 3

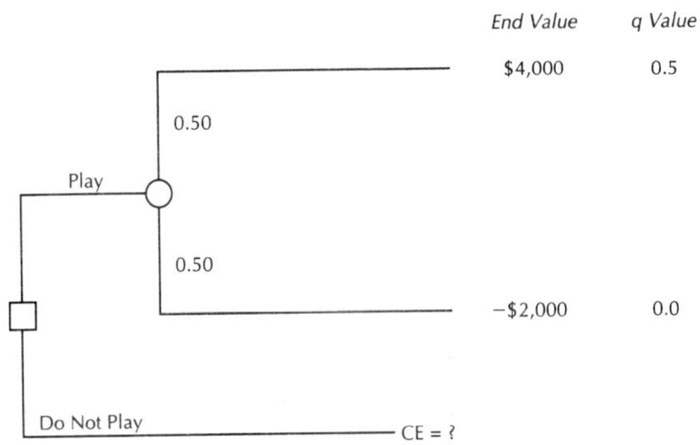

gamble is $1,000. We determine the q value for a $1,000 payoff as follows:

$$E(q) = 0.50(0.50) + 0.0(0.50) = 0.25$$

The preference quotient for a $1,000 payoff is 0.25, giving the following results so far:

Payoff	*q*
$10,000	1.00
7,000	0.75
4,000	0.50
1,000	0.25
−2,000	0.00

This process can be repeated as often as necessary until enough q values have been determined to allow us to graph the preference function. Let's use the five points we have so far to see how things look.

Figure 20-6 is a graph of this preference function. The horizontal axis shows the payoffs and the q values are shown on the vertical axis. As you can see, the

FIGURE 20-6

Risk-Neutral Preference Function Example

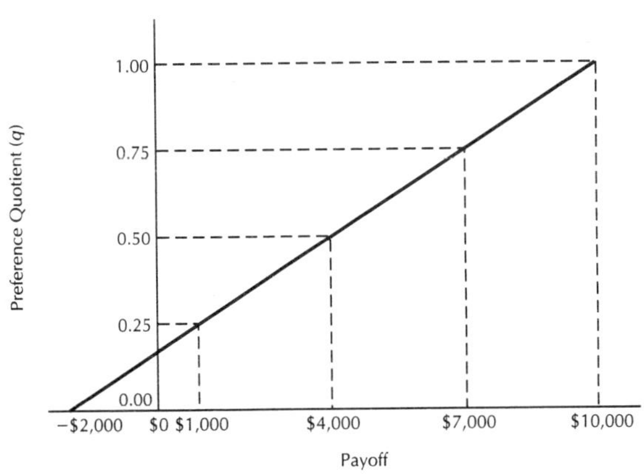

FIGURE 20-7

Risk-Neutral Preference Function for $5,000

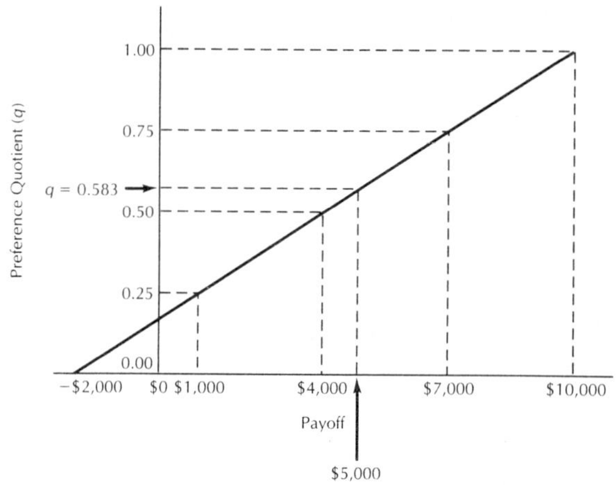

risk-neutral preference function is linear. You can use the preference function graphed in Figure 20-6 to determine the relative preference for any payoff between $10,000 and −$2,000 by going from the payoff number on the horizontal axis up to the preference-function line and then over to the vertical axis for the q value. Figure 20-7 shows how we found the q value of approximately 0.58 for a payoff of $5,000. Other q values can be determined in the same way.

Risk-Averse Preference Function

The linear preference function shown in Figure 20-6 is for a risk-neutral decision maker. The preference function is linear because the CE values for each standard gamble were always the expected value of the "Play" alternative. However, we indicated earlier that most decision makers are not risk neutral, but instead are risk-averse or risk-seeking. Let's reconsider the same decision problem as before, with the highest payoff of $10,000 and lowest payoff of −$2,000, but now suppose the decision maker is *risk-averse.*

A risk-averse decision maker will pick a certainty equivalent that is less than the expected payoff for a standard gamble. However, there are different degrees of risk aversion. The extent to which a person is risk-averse will be reflected in his or her risk preference function.

The steps in assessing a risk-averse decision maker's preference function are essentially the same as for a risk-neutral or risk-seeking decision maker. We begin by assigning $q = 1.0$ to the highest possible payoff, in this case $10,000, and assign $q = 0.0$ to the lowest possible payoff, −$2,000. This again gives

Payoff	q
$10,000	1.0
−2,000	0.0

Next, we pose the standard gamble shown earlier in Figure 20-3. Recall that the expected value for the "Play" alternative is \$4,000. A risk-neutral individual would set CE = \$4,000. But this will not be the case for a risk-averse decision maker. The CE (certainty equivalent) is the certain value associated with the "Do not play" branch that would make the decision maker indifferent toward the two options. A risk-averse person's indifference point will be less than \$4,000. How much less depends on how risk-averse he or she is.

Usually a decision maker has trouble directly assessing the CE for a standard gamble like the one shown in Figure 20-3. Someone helping assess the decision maker's risk-preference function might begin by asking, would he or she pay \$1,500 to avoid taking the play gamble? If the response is no, ask whether the decision maker would pay \$500 to get out of the gamble. As long as the decision maker prefers the gamble to the certain dollar figure, the point of indifference has not been reached.

Suppose that after several iterations the indifference point is determined to be \$0; that is, the decision maker would be indifferent toward playing or not playing if the "Do not play" alternative has a certain payoff of \$0. Then the CE for the standard gamble posed in Figure 20-3 is \$0. We next find the q for \$0, as follows:

$$E(q) = 1.0(0.50) + 0.0(0.50) = 0.50$$

This gives us the following three values:

Payoff	q
\$10,000	1.0
0	0.5
−2,000	0.0

You should note that this decision maker was willing to accept a \$0 payoff instead of the gamble with an expected payoff of \$4,000. The difference between the expected value and the CE is called the **risk premium.** Risk-averse decision makers have positive risk premiums. In effect, this decision maker is willing to pay a premium, in the form of a lost expected payoff, of \$4,000 to avoid the possibility of losing \$2,000. The risk premium is

$$\text{Risk premium} = \$4{,}000 - \$0 = \$4{,}000$$

Does this seem like an excessive premium to pay? Ask yourself whether today you would risk losing \$2,000 for the chance to win \$10,000 on the flip of a coin. If you would walk away from this gamble and take a \$0 payoff, you are at least as risk-averse as the decision maker in our example. If you would not give up the gamble so easily, then you are less risk-averse than this decision maker.

We now have three points on the preference function, but need more. Our next step is to pose still another standard gamble, like the one shown in Figure 20-8 (page 1090). Now the decision maker must determine the certain payoff of

FIGURE 20-8

Assessing the Risk-Preference Function: Standard Gamble 2

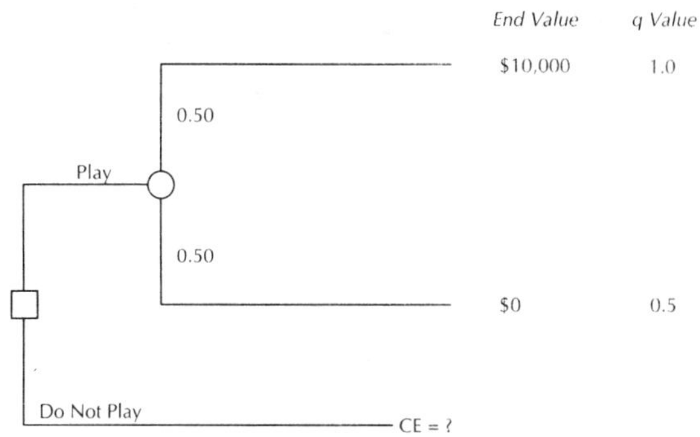

not playing that would make him or her indifferent toward playing or not playing. Using the same procedure as before, we would determine the indifference point. Assume the decision maker settles on $2,750 as the CE for this latest standard gamble. This means that he or she would be indifferent about taking the 50–50 gamble with payoffs of $10,000 or $0 versus the sure payoff of $2,750.

The expected payoff for the gamble is

$$\text{EV} = \$10{,}000(0.50) + \$0(0.50) = \$5{,}000$$

The difference between the expected value and the certainty equivalent is the risk premium. In this case, we get

$$\text{Risk premium} = \$5{,}000 - \$2{,}750 = \$2{,}250$$

This risk premium is less than the $4,000 risk premium associated with the earlier gamble. Therefore the decision maker is not as risk-averse over the range $10,000 to $0 as he or she was over the range $10,000 to −$2,000.

The q value for the $2,750 CE is

$$E(q) = 1.0(0.50) + 0.50(0.50) = 0.75$$

We have now determined four q values:

Payoff	*q*
$10,000	1.00
2,750	0.75
0	0.50
−2,000	0.00

You should determine as many q values as necessary to feel comfortable about drawing the risk-preference function. Let's find one more value, using the standard gamble diagrammed in Figure 20-9. Suppose the CE for this gamble is determined to be −$1,250. This decision maker would be willing to pay $1,250 to avoid a 50–50 chance of losing $2,000 or breaking even.

FIGURE 20-9

Assessing the Risk-Preference Function: Standard Gamble 3

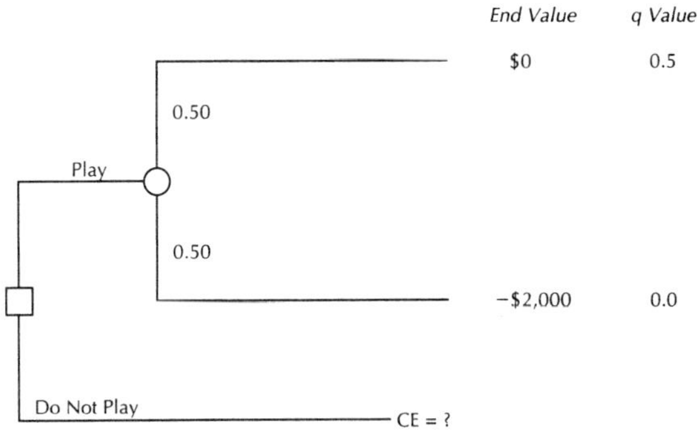

The expected value of the gamble shown in Figure 20-9 is −$1,000, and the risk premium is

$$\text{Risk premium} = -\$1{,}000 - (-\$1{,}250) = \$250$$

The q value for this −$1,250 CE is

$$E(q) = 0.50(0.50) + 0.0(0.50) = 0.25$$

We now have the following q values:

Payoff	q
$10,000	1.00
2,750	0.75
0	0.50
−1,250	0.25
−2,000	0.00

Figure 20-10 shows these five points connected to form the risk-preference function. Five is the minimum number of points to use for a risk-averse decision

FIGURE 20-10

Risk-Averse Preference Function

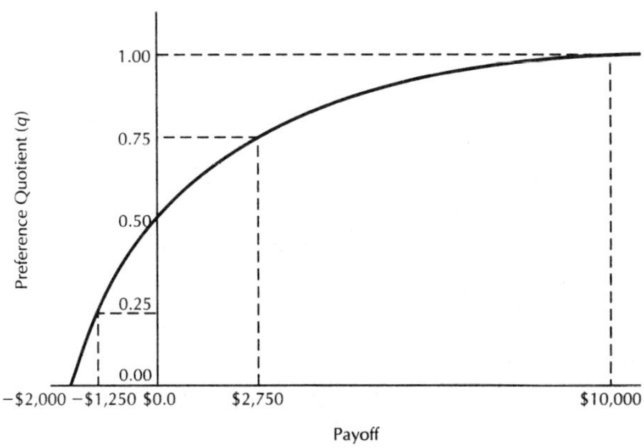

FIGURE 20-11

Risk-Averse Preference Function

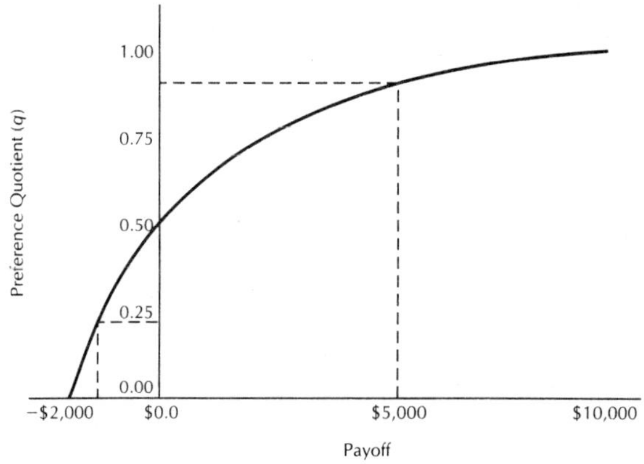

maker. We can use Figure 20-10 to determine the preference quotients for any value between $10,000 and −$2,000. For instance, Figure 20-11 shows that the q value for a payoff of $5,000 is approximately 0.91. Other q values would be determined in the same manner.

At this point, we can state three general conclusions regarding risk-preference functions. First, all risk-neutral preference functions are linear. Second, risk-averse preference functions are concave from the origin. You need only look at the general shape of the risk-preference function to determine whether the decision maker is risk-neutral or risk-averse. Third, the risk premium for a risk-averse decision maker will be positive, since the certainty equivalent will be less than the expected value of the standard gamble.

Risk-Seeking Preference Function

The steps required to assess the preference function of a risk seeker are the same as those for a risk avoider. The only difference is that a risk seeker will have a certainty equivalent that exceeds the expected value of the standard gamble. This means that the risk premium for a risk seeker is negative. An example will show what we mean.

Let's once again consider the decision with payoffs ranging from $10,000 to −$2,000. We again set $q = 1.0$ for the $10,000 payoff and $q = 0.0$ for the −$2,000 payoff. Now we propose the standard gamble shown in Figure 20-12. The gamble has an expected value of $4,000. A risk-neutral decision maker would set the CE at $4,000. We saw previously that a risk-averse decision maker would have a CE of less than $4,000 ($0 in the earlier example).

A risk seeker will demand a certain payoff in excess of $4,000 for not playing. This demand reflects his or her desire for the $10,000 payoff. The exact CE chosen will depend on how much of a risk taker the decision maker is. Suppose the "Do not play" branch would have to have a certain payoff of $6,500 to make

FIGURE 20-12

Assessing the Risk-Preference Function: Standard Gamble 1

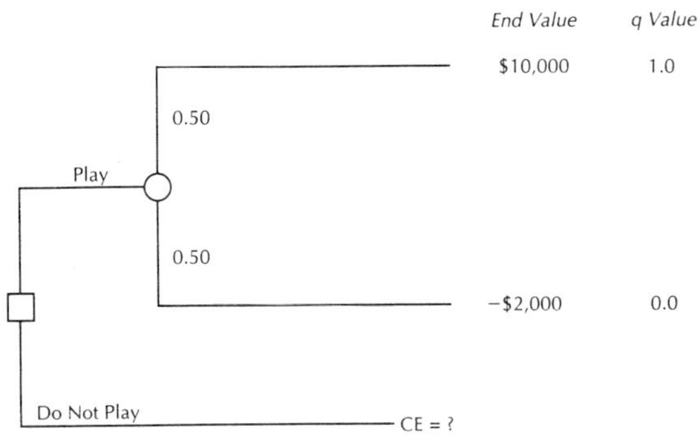

the decision maker indifferent toward the options of playing or not playing. Recall that the expected value of the "Play" option is $4,000; thus, CE > EV, indicating a negative risk premium:

$$\text{Risk premium} = \$4{,}000 - \$6{,}500 = -\$2{,}500$$

The preference quotient value for the CE of $6,500 is found as before:

$$E(q) = 1.0(0.50) + 0.0(0.50) = 0.50$$

We would continue proposing standard gambles to the risk-seeking decision maker and determine both the certainty equivalent and preference quotient for each gamble. After determining at least five preference quotients and certainty equivalents, we would be ready to determine the preference function. Figure 20-13 shows the completed risk-preference function for this risk seeker. This preference function can be used to determine q values for any payoff between $10,000 and −$2,000. Figure 20-13 also shows that the risk-preference function for a risk seeker is convex from the origin.

FIGURE 20-13

Risk-Seeking Preference Function

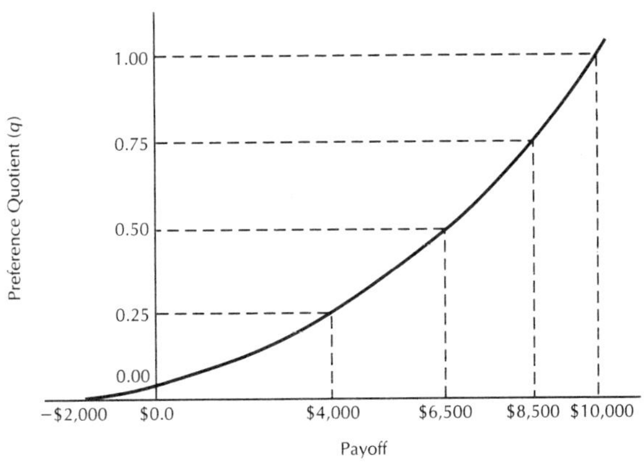

SKILL DEVELOPMENT PROBLEMS FOR **SECTION 20-4**

The following exercises have been included to help you gain a better understanding of the material presented in this section.

6. Use the standard gamble approach to develop your own risk-preference function for payoffs in the range of −$2,000 to $5,000. Based on the risk-preference function you have developed, indicate whether you are risk-averse or risk-seeking.

7. Based on the following standard gambles and certainty equivalents, develop the risk-preference function and indicate whether it describes a risk-averse, risk-neutral, or risk-seeking decision maker. (*Note:* The minimum payoff is $2,000 and the maximum is $100,000.)

Gamble 1	Payoffs: $2,000 and $100,000 Certainty equivalent = $55,000
Gamble 2	Payoffs: $55,000 and $100,000 Certainty equivalent = $79,000
Gamble 3	Payoffs: $2,000 and $55,000 Certainty equivalent = $37,000

8. Suppose a recent business school graduate has told you that she will be a risk seeker in business decisions. In preparation for an upcoming decision, you have worked with her using the standard gamble approach to assess her risk-preference function. During that effort, the following certainty equivalents and standard gambles were determined. Comment on the recent graduate's claim about being a risk seeker. (*Note:* The minimum and maximum payoffs are −$100,000 and $300,000, respectively.)

Gamble 1	Payoffs: −$100,000 and $300,000 Certainty equivalent = −$10,000
Gamble 2	Payoffs: −$10,000 and $300,000 Certainty equivalent = $20,000
Gamble 3	Payoffs: −$100,000 and −$10,000 Certainty equivalent = −$60,000

20-5 INCORPORATING RISK PREFERENCES INTO THE DECISION ANALYSIS

The previous section explained the steps involved in developing a risk-preference function for risk-neutral, risk-averse, and risk-seeking decision makers. In this section, we show how to incorporate risk preferences into the decision analysis. As you will see, once the preference function is developed, the method is very straightforward.

FIGURE 20-14

Decision Tree for the Investment Example

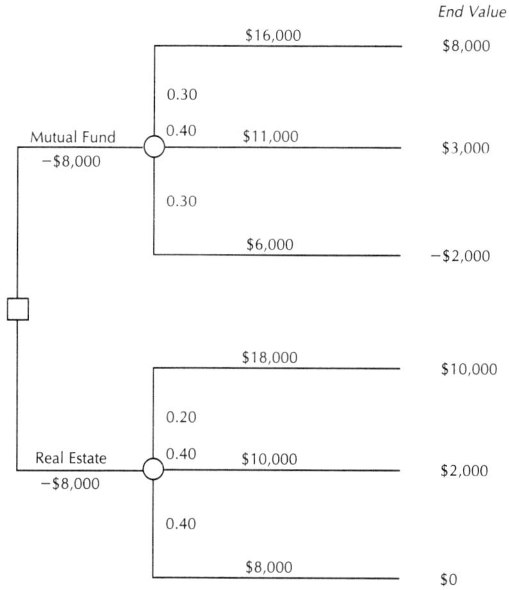

Betty Feeney has just received an $8,000 inheritance. Betty has decided to invest the money for 2 years until her oldest child enters college and then use it for tuition. She must decide between two alternative investments: a mutual fund and real estate. Figure 20-14 shows her completed decision tree. At the end of 2 years, Betty estimates her shares in the mutual fund could be sold for $16,000; $11,000; or $6,000, depending on how the stock market performs and how well the mutual fund is managed. The property could be sold at the end of the investment period for $18,000; $10,000; or $8,000, depending on the demand for real estate in the area.

Betty has subjectively assessed the following probability distributions:

Mutual Fund			Real Estate		
Selling Price	Net Cash Position	Probability	Selling Price	Net Cash Position	Probability
$16,000	$8,000	0.30	$18,000	$10,000	0.20
11,000	3,000	0.40	10,000	2,000	0.40
6,000	−2,000	0.30	8,000	0	0.40

The end values to the right of the decision tree in Figure 20-14 represent Betty's projected net cash position at the end of 2 years.

A RISK-NEUTRAL INVESTOR

In Chapter 19 you learned how to fold back a decision tree using end values. Figure 20-15 shows the result of this foldback process for Betty's decision. We see that the expected value of the mutual fund alternative is \$3,000, versus \$2,800 for the real estate. Thus, based on the expected values, Betty's "best decision" is to invest in the mutual fund.

The procedure of using the end values directly in the foldback process assumes that Betty is risk-neutral. Earlier, we indicated that a risk-neutral decision maker will make a decision strictly on the basis of expected value. Thus, for a risk-neutral decision maker, we can use an alternative method of decision-tree analysis. This method utilizes the risk-preference function.

We showed earlier that the preference function for a risk-neutral person is linear. Figure 20-6 illustrates a risk-neutral preference function that can be used for this example, since the preference function includes the same highest possible payoff (\$10,000) and lowest possible payoff (−\$2,000) as the investment decision. Incorporating the risk-preference function into the decision-tree analysis is quite easy. You begin by substituting the q value from the preference function for each end value on the decision tree. This is done by locating each end value on the horizontal axis on the preference-function graph. Then go up to the preference function and across to the vertical axis to find the preference quotient, q. Figure 20-16 shows this process for each end value on the decision tree for the investment example. For instance, the q value for a \$3,000 payoff is 0.43.

Figure 20-17 shows the decision tree with the q values to the right of the tree. The decision tree is now folded back, but we have used q values instead of dollar

FIGURE 20-15

Folding Back the Decision Tree for the Investment Example: Risk-Neutral

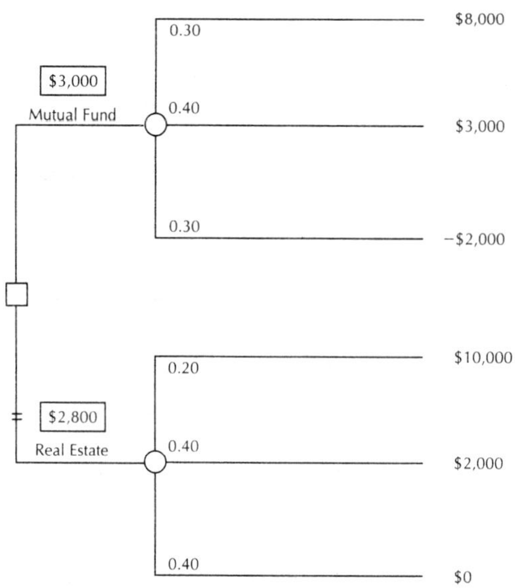

FIGURE 20-16

Risk-Neutral Preference Function for the Investment Example

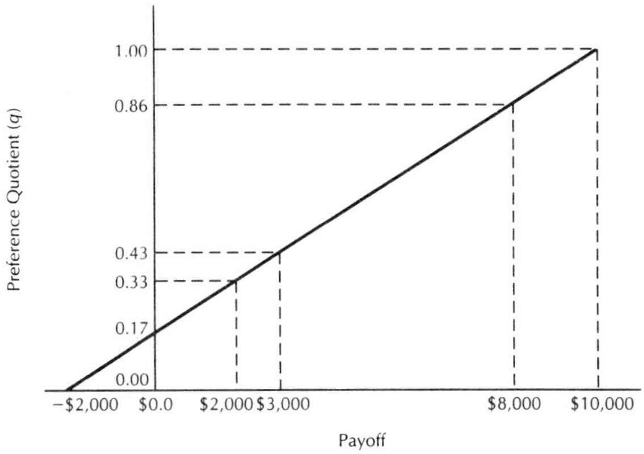

FIGURE 20-17

Folding Back the Decision Tree, Using *q* Values, for the Investment Example: Risk-Neutral

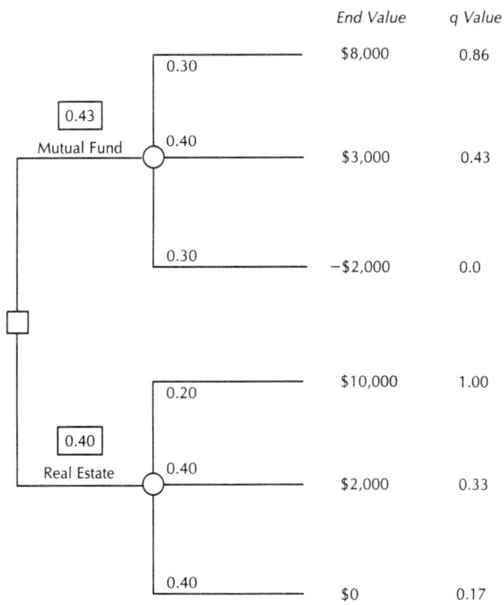

end values. We move from right to left, computing expected q values instead of expected payoffs. The "best decision" is the one that gives the highest expected q value. For this example, the expected q value for the mutual fund alternative is

$$E(q) = 0.86(0.30) + 0.43(0.40) + 0(0.30) = 0.43$$

and for the real estate alternative, it is

$$E(q) = 1.0(0.20) + 0.33(0.40) + 0.17(0.40) = 0.40$$

Then, since $0.43 > 0.40$, the "best decision" is to invest in the mutual fund.

Because a risk-neutral preference function is linear, a risk-neutral decision maker will make the same decision using dollar payoffs or q values. The q value for the \$3,000 expected value of the mutual fund alternative is 0.43, the same as the expected q value for this alternative in Figure 20-17. However, this equivalence holds only for risk-neutral decision makers.

A RISK-AVERSE DECISION MAKER

We just showed that for a risk-neutral person, using the actual dollar payoffs to fold back the decision tree leads to the same decision as using risk-preference quotients (q values). However, if the decision maker is not risk-neutral, a different decision can be reached.

Risk-averse decision makers are willing to pay a risk premium to avoid alternatives with undesirable outcomes. To illustrate how we incorporate risk-averse attitudes into the decision process, suppose that Figure 20-18 shows the risk-preference function for Betty's investment decision. We see that Betty is risk-averse, since the preference function is concave, curving up from the origin. Figure 20-18 shows the q values for each payoff level associated with the investment decision.

Figure 20-19 shows the decision tree with the q values on the right side; these q values, instead of the dollar payoffs, are folded back. The best decision at any decision fork is the one having the highest expected q value. For the mutual fund alternative:

$$E(q) = 0.98(0.30) + 0.79(0.40) + 0(0.30) = 0.61$$

For the real estate alternative:

$$E(q) = 1.0(0.20) + 0.71(0.40) + 0.50(0.40) = 0.684$$

FIGURE 20-18

Risk-Averse Preference Function for the Investment Example

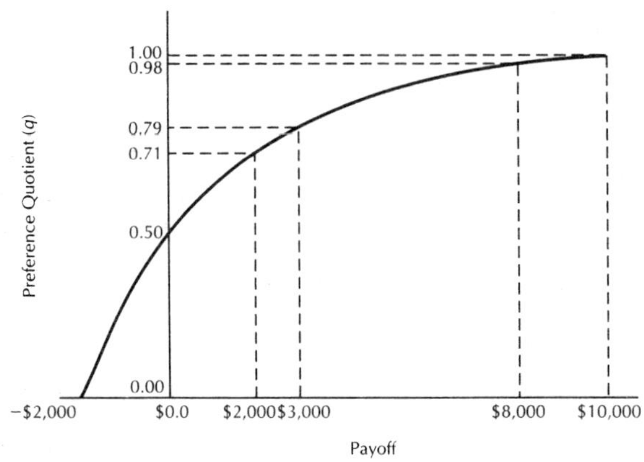

FIGURE 20-19

Folding Back the Decision Tree, Using q Values, for the Investment Example: Risk-Averse

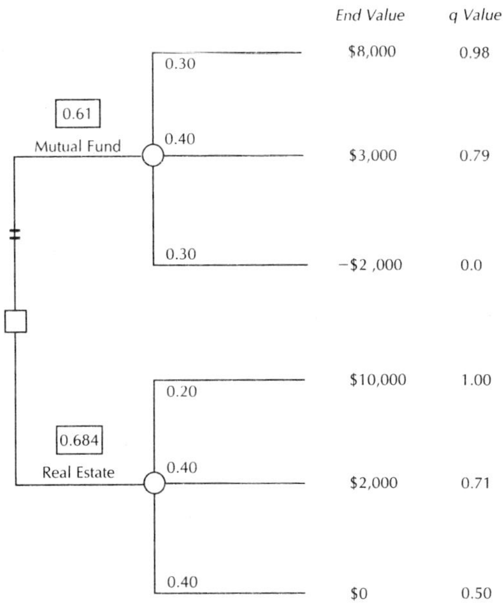

Since $0.6834 > 0.61$, the best decision for Betty, as a risk-averse decision maker, is to invest in real estate. This is a different choice than the risk-neutral decision maker would have made. The reason is that the decision shown in Figure 20-19 incorporates this risk-averse attitude. Being risk-averse, Betty is willing to take an alternative with a lower expected value ($2,800) rather than an alternative that has a higher expected value ($3,000), but also the possibility of losing $2,000.

In this example, the decision changed from mutual fund to real estate when Betty's risk-averse attitude was taken into account. However, decisions do not always change; in some instances, the alternative with the highest expected payoff will also be the least risky. In other cases, the decision maker's degree of risk aversion will not be sufficient to lead to a different decision. Each decision situation must be evaluated independently.

If the decision maker has a risk-seeking preference function, the process for incorporating his or her preferences into the decision analysis is the same as for a risk-averse individual. The tendency will be to select alternatives offering higher potential payoffs but with more risk of low or negative payoffs. We suggest that you use the risk-preference function in Figure 20-13 to analyze this investment decision.

SKILL DEVELOPMENT PROBLEMS FOR **SECTION 20-5**

The following exercises have been included to help you gain a better understanding of the material presented in this section.

9. The Chief Operations Officer for Steinbrenner Shipping in New York is contemplating sending a ship loaded with fruit to the Soviet Union and having it return with Soviet-made sunglasses. The problem is that the weather forecast is uncertain and there is a chance that the ship will have to take a roundabout route, causing the fruit to spoil. However, if the ship can make the trip on schedule, Steinbrenner stands to clear $30,000. If the fruit spoils, the company will lose $100,000. Based on weather forecasts, the chances are 0.10 that the weather will be bad enough to cause the delay, resulting in spoilage.

   The COO can purchase insurance for the shipment under these terms:

   a. Premium cost is $10,000.
   b. If the fruit spoils, Steinbrenner will be paid $90,000.

   Alternatively, he can purchase an insurance plan under the following terms:

   a. Premium cost is $4,500.
   b. If the fruit is spoiled, the insurance company will pay $45,000.

   The COO has considered his preference for risk and has developed the following risk-preference function:

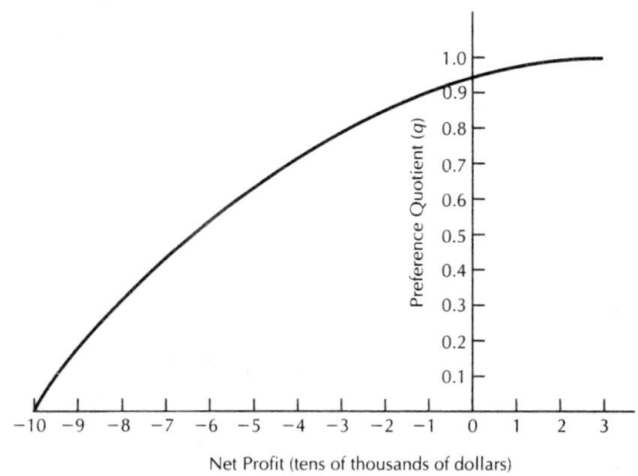

   a. Diagram the decision problem facing the Steinbrenner company.
   b. Based strictly on expected values, what decision should the COO make?
   c. Taking into account the COO's preference for risk, what decision should be made?

10. The CEO of Anderson Chemicals is faced with the decision regarding whether to market a new drug that has been developed by the company's research and development team. There are two sources of uncertainty: the actual production cost and the market size.

Based on discussions with the R & D people and the manufacturing manager, the per unit manufacturing cost is assessed as follows:

Units Produced	*Per Unit Cost*	*Probability*
5,000	$0.20	0.30
	0.25	0.40
	0.40	0.30
10,000	$0.10	0.25
	0.15	0.35
	0.20	0.30
	0.25	0.10
15,000	$0.05	0.40
	0.10	0.40
	0.15	0.20

The firm's marketing department has done some surveys and has concluded that the demand distribution is as follows:

Units Demanded	*Probability*
5,000	0.20
10,000	0.50
15,000	0.30

Any unsold pills are destroyed and are of no value to the company. Pills that are sold will have an average price of $1.50 each. Assuming that the CEO is risk-neutral, develop a decision tree for the problem and indicate what decision should be made.

11. Referring to Problem 10, use the standard gamble approach to develop a risk-averse preference function. Then apply this preference function to the decision problem and indicate what decision should be made. If your decision differs from that of a risk-neutral decision maker in Problem 10, discuss why. If the decision is the same, discuss how this came about.

12. Referring to Problem 10, if the CEO is a risk seeker, what decision should he make? Discuss how you arrived at this conclusion.

20-6 CONCLUSIONS

The idea of incorporating sample information into a decision-analysis problem has great intuitive appeal, since new information affects the decision maker's state of mind about the likelihood of uncertain outcomes. This chapter has presented a formal means for introducing new information into the decision process through the use of Bayes' rule. We showed how to merge the information in the prior probability distribution with the information in the sample to arrive at a posterior probability distribution. The Bayesian revision process is a central part of decision analysis and is a significant step toward making it more accessible to decision makers.

Not all decision makers are willing to make decisions strictly on the basis of the highest expected payoff or lowest expected cost. Many people will select an alternative that has a lower expected payoff than another alternative, if doing so reduces the possibility of a bad outcome. Another decision maker will pick an alternative with a lower expected value just for the chance of a high payoff. Thus, not all decision makers are risk-neutral; in fact, most are not. The majority tend to be risk avoiders and others are risk seekers.

This chapter has introduced the concept of risk preference and showed how attitudes toward risk are incorporated into the decision process. We explained how risk-preference functions are developed using the standard gamble approach and we discussed the concept of risk premium. We showed how to incorporate information from a risk-preference function into a decision-tree analysis; instead of folding back the dollar payoffs or costs, you fold back the q values for each payoff. Then, at each decision point, select the alternative with the highest q value.

A decision analysis is not complete, and does not accurately model the decision maker's state of mind, if it does not take into account his or her attitude toward risk. The basics introduced in this chapter will get you started in incorporating risk preferences into decision analysis. We suggest that you consult the chapter References for sources of information on risk-preference analysis.

CHAPTER **GLOSSARY**

Bayes' rule Let A_i ($i = 1, 2, 3, \ldots, n$) be a complete set of mutually exclusive events. Let B be another event which is preceded by an A_i event. Both $P(A_i)$ and $P(B|A_i)$ must be known. Then

$$P(A_1|B) = \frac{P(A_1)P(B|A_1)}{\sum_{i=1}^{n} P(A_i)P(B|A_i)}$$

certainty equivalent The value that would make a decision maker indifferent toward taking an uncertain gamble versus taking that value; the amount a decision maker would pay to give up the opportunity to take the gamble.

conditional probability The probability of event A occurring given that another event, B, has occurred. The conditional probability represents the chances of observing the sample information, given each possible state of nature.

joint probability The probability of the simultaneous occurrence of two or more events. For example, joint probability represents the likelihood of observing the sample information and each state of nature.

posterior probability The probability of an event modified in light of experimental evidence. Posterior probabilities are usually determined by employing Bayes' rule.

posterior table A table showing the states of nature, the prior probability of each state; the conditional probability of each state, given the sample information; the joint probability of each state, given the prior and conditional probabilities; and the posterior probability for each state.

preferencc quotient A measure of the relative utility for the outcomes of a decision on a scale between 1.0 and 0.0.

prior probability The probability of an event occurring before sample evidence relevant to the event has been observed.

risk-averse attitude The preference for risk under which the risk premium will be positive.

risk-neutral attitude The preference for risk under which the alternative with the highest expected payoff or lowest expected cost will be selected.

risk-preference function A graph of the decision maker's risk-preference quotients over the range of possible payoffs.

risk premium The difference between the expected value of an event and the certainty equivalent. The risk premium will be zero for a risk-neutral decision maker, positive for a risk-averse decision maker, and negative for a risk-seeking decision maker.

risk-seeking attitude The preference for risk under which the risk premium will be negative.

standard gamble approach The approach for assessing risk-preference functions which involves setting up a series of 50-50 gambles between two payoffs and determining the certainty equivalent for each gamble.

subjective conditional probability A probability that represents the chances of observing *A* given that *B* has occurred. It is assessed subjectively.

SOLVED PROBLEMS

1. The Batlow Newspaper Corporation is considering setting up a division to publish a weekly magazine that summarizes the major news stories of the previous week. Batlow estimates that the weekly fixed cost of establishing the division will be $300,000 and that the variable cost per magazine printed will be $0.50. The magazine will sell for $1.50. Further, the marketing department estimates that of Batlow's one million customers, the following possibilities exist with respect to the percentage who will buy this new magazine:

Proportion Buying	*Prior Probability*
0.20	0.10
0.30	0.30
0.40	0.40
0.50	0.20
	1.00

a. Based only on this prior information, should Batlow go ahead with the magazine if its goal is to maximize expected profits?
b. Suppose a random sample of twenty newspaper customers is selected and five indicate they will buy the new magazine if it is published. Assuming the binomial distribution applies, determine the revised or posterior probability for each possible proportion of customers who will buy the magazine.
c. Given the sample information, what should the Batlow Corporation do?

Solution

a. The first step is to determine the payoff for each possible level of demand as follows:

Proportion Buying	*Payoff*	*Probability*
0.20	−\$100,000	0.10
0.30	0	0.30
0.40	100,000	0.40
0.50	200,000	0.20
		1.00

The expected payoff, or profit, associated with publishing the new magazine is

$$\begin{aligned} E(\text{profit}) &= -\$100{,}000(0.10) + \$0(0.30) + \$100{,}000(0.40) \\ &\quad + \$200{,}000(0.20) \\ &= \$70{,}000 \end{aligned}$$

Since \$70,000 is greater than \$0, Batlow should publish the magazine if its objective is to maximize expected profits.

b. To revise the prior probabilities, we set up the following table and calculate the conditional probabilities using the binomial distribution:

Proportion Buying	*Prior Probability*	*Conditional Probability* $P(n = 20, X_1 = 5 \mid$ *proportion buying*)	*Joint Probability*	*Posterior Probability*
0.20	0.10	0.1746	0.01746	0.1680
0.30	0.30	0.1789	0.05367	0.5164
0.40	0.40	0.0746	0.02984	0.2871
0.50	0.20	0.0148	0.00296	0.0285
	1.00		0.10393	1.0000

c. To determine the best decision for Batlow using posterior analysis, we find the expected profit of the magazine alternative using the posterior probabilities.

$$\begin{aligned} E(\text{profit}) &= -\$100{,}000(0.1680) + \$0(0.5164) + \$100{,}000(0.2871) \\ &\quad + \$200{,}000(0.0285) \\ &= \$17{,}610 \end{aligned}$$

Although the Bayesian posterior analysis has produced a smaller expected profit, \$17,610 is greater than \$0, so the best decision is to publish the news summary magazine.

2. Use the standard gamble approach to construct a risk-preference function for the range of payoffs between \$100,000 and −\$50,000. Assume the decision maker is risk-averse.

Solution

We start by assigning preference quotients for the two extreme outcomes, as follows:

Payoff	*q*
\$100,000	1.0
−50,000	0.0

This indicates that the most preferred outcome is \$100,000 and the least preferred outcome is −\$50,000. Now we ask the decision maker what his or her certainty equivalent (CE) is for a 50-50 gamble at \$100,000 or −\$50,000. The expected value is

$$E(\text{payoff}) = 0.50(\$100{,}000) + 0.50(-\$50{,}000) = \$25{,}000$$

A risk-averse decision maker will have a CE less than \$25,000. Suppose that after careful discussion with the decision maker, we set the CE at −\$3,000. This means that the decision maker is indifferent about paying \$3,000 or taking the 50-50 gamble.

Now we determine the risk-preference quotient for the CE value by finding the expected q value for the gamble:

$$E(q) = 0.50(1.0) + 0.50(0.0) = 0.50$$

We now have the following:

Payoff	*q*
\$100,000	1.00
−3,000	0.50
−50,000	0.00

We continue by establishing another standard gamble between \$100,000 and −\$3,000. The expected value of a 50-50 gamble between these two values is

$$E(\text{payoff}) = 0.50(\$100{,}000) + 0.50(-\$3{,}000) = \$48{,}500$$

A risk-averse decision maker will have a CE lower than \$48,500. Suppose, after much discussion, the CE is set at \$40,000. The q value for this new CE is found by:

$$E(q) = 0.50(1.0) + 0.50(0.50) = 0.75$$

FIGURE 20-20

Preference-Function Curve

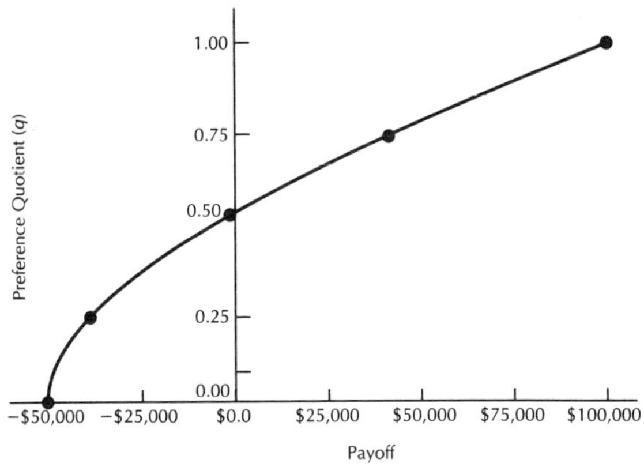

We now have

Payoff	q
\$100,000	1.00
40,000	0.75
−3,000	0.50
−50,000	0.00

We can continue by setting up a standard gamble for the payoffs −\$3,000 and −\$50,000. The expected value for this gamble is

$$E(\text{payoff}) = 0.50(-\$3{,}000) + 0.50(-\$50{,}000) = -\$26{,}500$$

A risk-averse decision maker will have a CE less than −\$26,500. Suppose this figure is −\$40,000. The q value for this value is found by:

$$E(q) = 0.50(0.50) + 0.50(0.0) = 0.25$$

We have now determined the following q values:

Payoff	q
\$100,000	1.00
40,000	0.75
−3,000	0.50
−40,000	0.25
−50,000	0.00

Although more points could be established, these five values are sufficient to develop a plot of the preference function, as shown in Figure 20-20.

CONCEPTUAL QUESTIONS AND ASSIGNMENTS

13. Discuss why the expected-value criterion is used in decision analysis for one-time decisions even though expected value represents the long-run average outcome.

14. The concept of *risk premium* is discussed in this chapter. Use an example of your own to illustrate what is meant by a risk premium.
15. Discuss the three types of risk-preference attitudes and present an example describing each one.
16. Could two people, one a risk avoider and the other a risk seeker, reach the same decision for a given application? Discuss. Formulate an example that supports your position.
17. Locate three or more articles that deal with using risk preferences for decision problems. Write a short paper discussing the situations described in these articles.
18. Contact a local business and meet with a lower-level manager. Construct a sample decision problem and show this manager the decision tree with the range of end values. Then use the standard gamble approach to construct his or her risk-preference function. Write a short report describing your experiences.
19. Referring to Problem 18, contact a higher-level manager in the same company, and go through the same process. Compare the preference functions for the two managers. Write a short report discussing the differences and/or similarities between the two.

ADDITIONAL PROBLEMS

20. A cement company has two suppliers of the raw materials used in making cement. Vendor 1 supplies 30% of the raw materials and vendor 2 supplies 70%. Tests have shown that 40% of vendor 1's materials are poor quality and 5% of vendor 2's materials are poor quality. The cement company's manager has just found some poor-quality materials in inventory. Which company most probably supplied these materials?
21. The Germaine L. Jones Manufacturing Company produces automobile windshields at three plants in the Detroit area. The windshields are sent to a centralized warehouse, where they are so mixed up that the identity of the particular plant is lost.

    Plant A makes 50% of the windshields, of which 10% contain some defect. Plant B accounts for 30% of the windshields, and of these 12% are defective. Finally, plant C makes 20% of the windshields, and of these only 5% are defective.

    Last year, the Germaine L. Jones Company incurred a replacement cost of \$400,000 on windshields produced. The cost accountants want to divide this cost between the three plants based on the ratio of defectives produced by each plant. Provide this breakdown in costs for the accountants.
22. The Upland Paving Company has three locations where it mixes its paving material. Forty percent of all material is mixed at plant A, 50% at plant B, and 10% at plant C. Although Upland would like to believe it has a good quality control system at each plant, sometimes bad batches do get mixed. For instance, in the past, 15% of plant A's batches, 10% of plant B's batches, and 25% of plant C's batches have been bad.

Suppose a bad batch has just been discovered at a construction project. Which plant most likely provided the bad batch?

23. The Telephone Company is considering whether to install a new computerized telephone system in Central City. The new system will offer several services such as call forwarding and conference call capability. The new computer can be leased for \$1 million per year, and the annual incremental cost per user is estimated at \$72. The Telephone Company will charge each customer served \$10 per month, or \$120 per year.

    There are currently 400,000 telephone customers in Central City, and for the Telephone Company to break even, 20,834 customers, or 5.2% of all customers, will have to purchase the extra services. The company's marketing department has assessed the following probability distribution for the proportion who will buy the service:

Proportion Buying	*Probability*
0.02	0.20
0.04	0.30
0.06	0.40
0.08	0.10
	1.00

    a. Determine the payoffs for each possible proportion buying.
    b. Analyze the problem facing the Telephone Company, using only prior information. Determine the "best" decision using the expected-value criterion.

24. The Internal Revenue Service (IRS) has selected an individual taxpayer at random for a basic audit from an area in which it is thought that 20% of the taxpayers have filed incorrect federal income tax returns. Basic audits are not perfect in that they sometimes indicate a problem when no problem exists and other times indicate no problem when, in fact, a problem does exist. The chance of the basic audit indicating no problem when, in fact, there is a problem is 90%. The probability that the basic audit indicates a problem when, in fact, no problem exists is thought to be 10%. Suppose that a basic audit reveals that there is a problem. What is the probability that there really will be a problem with this tax return?

25. As part of a camera company's quality control procedures, an inspector selects a sample of instant cameras to be thoroughly inspected. Past experience showed that 15% of all cameras are defective. The inspector judgmentally selects 25% of all cameras to go through a complete inspection. Past records show that of those items selected for inspection, 50% are actually good. This means that the inspector does provide some value in the selection process since proportionally fewer good cameras (50%) than the population as a whole (85%) actually get inspected needlessly. Suppose that a camera that was recently purchased proves to be good. What is the probability that the camera went through a complete inspection?

Problems 26–28 refer to the following situation.

When the Oliviera Milling and Frame Company has correctly set up its manufacturing process, only 5% of the products off the line are defective. When the process is set up incorrectly, 20% of the products are defective. Past experience indicates a 90% chance that the process will be set up properly.

26. Suppose a sample of ten items has been randomly selected and three have been found defective. Use this sample information to revise the probability that the process is set up correctly.
27. After the initial sample of ten taken in Problem 26, a second sample of fifteen yielded four defective products. Combine this new sample information with the revised probabilities found in Problem 26 to arrive at new posterior probabilities.
28. How would the posterior probabilities calculated in Problem 27 differ from the posterior probabilities that would be determined if one sample of twenty-five was selected and seven defectives were observed? Show the calculations to support your answer.
29. Executives of a cable TV network are considering forming an affiliated cable service to offer exclusive sporting events. They estimate that the monthly fixed cost of the affiliate will be $5,000,000 and the monthly variable cost per subscriber will be $2.50. The network will charge each subscriber $4.50 per month for the service. The marketing department estimates that of the network's present 10 million customers, the following possibilities exist with respect to the percentage who will subscribe to the new channel:

Proportion Subscribing	*Prior Probability*
0.10	0.10
0.20	0.30
0.30	0.40
0.40	0.20
	1.00

a. Considering only this prior information, should the network go ahead with the new service if its goal is to maximize expected profits?
b. Suppose a random sample of twenty present subscribers is selected and seven indicate they will take the new service if it is offered. Assuming the binomial distribution applies, determine the revised or posterior probability for each possible proportion of customers who will subscribe to the service.
c. Given the sample information in part **b**, what should the network do?

30. Western Bell is considering installing a new message recording system in its service area. The equipment necessary for the system can be leased for $6 million per year and the annual incremental cost per user is estimated at $60. Western Bell will charge each customer served $10 per month, or $120 per year.

There are currently 4 million telephone customers in Western Bell's area. The company's marketing department has assessed the following probability distribution for the proportion who will subscribe to the new service:

Proportion Subscribing	*Probability*
0.02	0.20
0.04	0.30
0.06	0.40
0.08	0.10
	1.00

a. Determine the payoffs for each possible proportion.
b. Analyze the problem facing Western Bell using only prior information. Determine the best decision using the expected-value criterion.

Problems 31–33 refer to the following situation.

Green Mountain Corporation has just developed a drug that may be effective in treating arthritis in hunting dogs. Because of the wide variety of genetic patterns in hunting dogs, the company realizes that no drug will be effective in all cases. However, if the drug is a "good" product, improvement will be shown by 80% of the dogs that are treated. If the drug is a "fair" product, 60% of the dogs will show improvement, and if it is a "poor" product, 30% will show improvement. On the basis of their laboratory studies, Green Mountain executives believe the following probabilities apply.

Effectiveness Level	*Probability*
Good	0.30
Fair	0.30
Poor	0.40
	1.00

31. Suppose a random sample of twenty-five hunting dogs takes the drug and fourteen show improvement. Determine the posterior probability for each effectiveness level.
32. Referring to Problem 31, two more samples of twenty-five dogs were given the drug, resulting in improvement for twelve dogs in one sample and fifteen dogs in the other. Determine the posterior probability for each effectiveness level.
33. Green Mountain has a policy of not marketing a drug unless the chance that its effectiveness will be at least "fair" exceeds 90%. Using the posterior probabilities determined in Problem 32, should the drug be marketed?

Problems 34–37 refer to the following situation.

Greg Williams, operations manager of a company that makes remote-controlled model cars, has to decide whether to lease a new assembly robot or have the current assembly line repaired at a cost of $30,000. Leasing the robot will cost $120,000, but it will decrease the assembly cost of each model car to $10 per unit. The current assembly line, after repair, will assemble the cars at a cost of $15 each. The finished model cars sell for $20 each. Because consumer buying habits are unpredictable, the demand for the cars is not known with certainty, but is expected to occur according to the following probability distribution:

Demand Level	*Probability*
10,000	0.05
15,000	0.15
20,000	0.20
30,000	0.40
50,000	0.20
	1.00

34. Construct a payoff table listing the decision alternatives and the payoff associated with each alternative for Greg's decision.
35. What decision should Greg make if his objective is to maximize the expected payoff? Provide a practical justification for your answer.
36. Suppose an independent market research firm has been hired by the model-car manufacturer. The market research report is based in part on sample information gathered by the firm and in part on the researchers' "expert analysis." The results of the marketing study are examined by Greg Williams. The report is basically optimistic, but Greg does not want to ignore the prior assessments, and, in fact, wants to include both the prior assessments and the market survey information in the decision. Greg assesses the conditional probability of observing the results of the market survey, given each possible demand level. These conditional probabilities are as follows:

Demand Level	*Conditional Probability* $P(\textit{optimistic survey}\mid\textit{demand})$
10,000	0.05
15,000	0.10
20,000	0.30
30,000	0.50
50,000	0.80

Use this information to determine the revised or posterior probability associated with each demand level.

37. Considering the posterior probabilities calculated in Problem 36, should Greg fix the current assembly line or lease the robot?

Problems 38–46 refer to the following situation.

Russell Smith is assessing his options as the planting season for his 1,000-acre farm nears. The problem is this has so far been a bad snow year and Russell's farm is dependent on irrigation water from the Magic Valley Reservoir. If the remaining spring snowfall in the mountains that feed the reservoir is below average, his farm will run out of irrigation water in August. If the spring snowfall is average, he will have water for the entire season, but at 75% of the normal level. If the snowfall is above average, Russell will have his normal allocation of water. Russell has three options: (1) not plant at all, and collect federal idle-land payments, (2) plant oats, and (3) plant potatoes. While not planting at all will guarantee a payment, the federal money will not cover the loan payment due at the bank. However, the money that is necessary to plant either of the two crops will be lost if the spring snowfall is light. The following table lists the potential income values arising from the three possible snow levels and Russell's three planting alternatives.

	Snowfall		
Alternative	*Light*	*Average*	*High*
Do not plant	−\$100,000	−\$10,000	−\$10,000
Plant oats	−20,000	30,000	30,000
Plant potatoes	−50,000	10,000	60,000

38. Without any information about what level of snowfall is likely, what alternative should Russell choose if he is risk-neutral and uses the *maximin* decision criterion?
39. Without any information about what level of snowfall is likely, what alternative should Russell choose if he is risk-neutral and uses the *maximax* decision criterion?
40. The long-range forecast from the National Weather Service indicates the precipitation forecast for the next 3 months as: P(light snow) = 0.5, P(average snow) = 0.3, P(heavy snow) = 0.2. On the basis of this information, and using the expected-value criterion, what alternative would you recommend for Russell?
41. Before making his decision, Russell constructs a risk-preference function. The following are several points on his curve.

Outcome	*Preference*
−\$75,000	0.00
0	0.58
10,000	0.62
40,000	0.78
100,000	1.00

Use these values to sketch the appropriate risk-preference curve for this problem and to construct a risk-preference table for the decision facing Russell.
42. Using the risk-preference table determined in Problem 41 and the probability assessments in Problem 40, choose the appropriate planting strategy for Russell, using the expected-risk preference criterion.
43. Russell Smith's neighbor has deep wells drilled on his farm. He is willing to sell Russell extra water, which will ensure normal water levels, if the wells do

not run dry. To use this potential water, Russell will have to install a temporary pipeline costing \$10,000. In addition, the extra water will cost \$15,000 and will be used only if snowfall is light or average. Russell assesses the probability the wells will not run dry as 75%. Draw the appropriate decision tree including this new alternative. Assess this decision tree assuming Russell is risk-neutral.

44. Use the decision tree from Problem 43 and the risk-preference curve determined in Problem 41 to decide whether Russell should arrange to purchase water from his neighbor.

45. In addition to considering purchasing water from his neighbor, Russell is also considering the alternative of buying drought insurance for the first time. The cost of this insurance will be \$5,000 and will pay off only if no water is received, starting in August. Russell estimates the payoff will be \$20,000 if he receives any insurance money. Add this new factor to the decision tree developed in Problem 43. Again, assuming Russell is a risk-neutral decision maker, recommend a course of action for him.

46. Use the decision tree from Problem 45 and the risk-preference curve determined in Problem 41 to recommend a course of action for Russell.

Problems 47–52 refer to the following situation.

Hatchman Electronics makes specialized fuel injection units for automobile engines. The company is presently completing its 5-year strategic plan. A major component in this plan involves analyzing the following situation.

Hatchman presently makes an injection unit that it sells to automobile manufacturers for \$200. The operating profit (revenue less direct manufacturing costs) for this unit is \$90. The company estimates the probability is 80% that demand for this product will continue, at the same price, for the next 5 years. If a competitor introduces a better unit, the selling price will be dropped to \$140 to maintain the company's market share. Hatchman Electronics is considering trying to develop an improved fuel injector. Whether the product is successful or not, the development costs will be amortized by adding \$20 to the cost of every injector sold for the next 5 years. If the development effort is successful, the improved unit will still be sold for \$200, but direct manufacturing costs will be reduced to \$70. The research and development department estimates the probability of the development effort being successful is 60%.

47. Develop a decision tree representing the Hatchman Electronics decision situation.

48. Assuming the Hatchman Electronics board of directors is willing to consider this problem from a risk-neutral perspective, should they decide to develop the new product?

49. Since the fuel injection unit is a high-volume product for Hatchman Electronics, the company may not be willing to analyze the decision from a risk-neutral perspective. Assume the preference function shown in Figure 20-21 applies to the decision. What is the best decision about producing the new product now?

FIGURE 20-21

Risk-Preference Curve for Hatchman Electronics

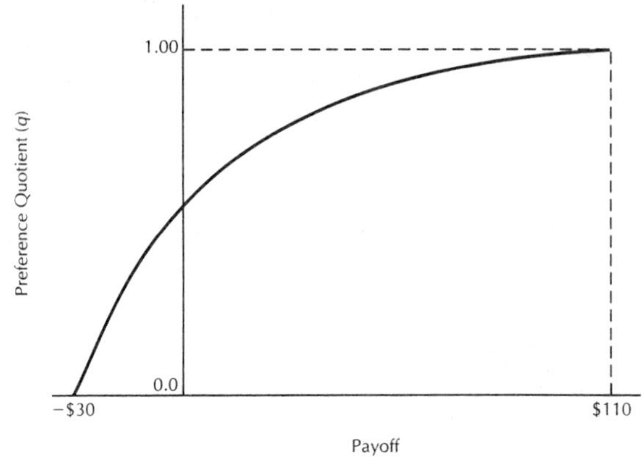

50. Hatchman Electronics has the option of contracting with Stewart Consultants to analyze the feasibility of developing the new fuel injection unit. The feasibility study will cost $5 million and will be added to the production cost of each of the 1 million units the company is planning to make over the next 5 years. If the study indicates the new development is feasible, the probability of the product being successfully developed will be increased to 90%. If the study indicates the new development is not feasible, the product may still be developed but the probability of its being successful drops to 20%. Hatchman's managers do not have enough information to speculate about the probability that the feasibility study will indicate a success; so, they assess each outcome—success and not a success—as equally likely. Develop the decision tree for this new situation.
51. Assuming the Hatchman Electronics board of directors is still willing to consider this problem from a risk-neutral perspective, should they hire Stewart Consultants? What is the new sequence of decisions that should be taken?
52. Hatchman's president has read that companies that take no risks do not remain competitive in today's environment. Put yourself in the president's position and develop a risk-preference function for the decision situation. What is the best decision about producing the new product now?

Problems 53–58 refer to the following situation.

The Grimm Group presents in-house training seminars to organizations throughout the United States. The company currently presents seminars on three topics: quality control, material management, and just-in-time (JIT) manufacturing. The quality control seminar costs each participant $500, and Ingrim's gross margin (revenue less direct expenses) is 40% of this amount. The material management seminar costs $450 for each attendee and also has a 40% gross margin; the JIT seminar costs $600 and has a 35% gross margin. After 5 years of expansion, attendance at the seminars has declined more than 10% in the past year. The revenues from the three operations last year were: quality control, $1,200,000; material management, $900,000; JIT, $1,400,000.

At the yearly forecasting meeting, Graciela Grimm, the company's founder, projects that if no changes are made in marketing philosophy, revenues will be stagnant this year. She is, however, considering two options that should increase demand for the three seminars. The first option is to incorporate a computer simulation game as part of each seminar. Projections indicate that adding this type of game will increase the demand for the quality control seminar by 10% and the demand for the other two seminars by 15%. Adding a game will increase the cost associated with each seminar participant by $50; but, because the market is very competitive, the company will have to hold the line on the price change. The second option is to offer 3-day training seminars on the same topics, but at 60% of the price of the 5-day seminars. Unfortunately, the cost of presenting the 3-day seminars will be reduced by only 20% from the cost of the original seminars. The president estimates the demand for the shorter seminars this year will generate revenues equal to 50% of the revenues realized from each 5-day seminar in the past year. Also, adding the shorter seminars will reduce the projected demand for the original seminars to 75% of last year's level.

53. Develop a decision tree describing the Grimm Group's decision situation.
54. Assuming President Grimm is risk-neutral for this decision, what alternative would you recommend?
55. Assume the president's attitude about risk can be represented by the preference curve developed for a previous project (Figure 20-22). What alternative would you recommend now?
56. An initial market survey of the acceptance of simulation games indicates they are so popular that there is a 70% chance the Grimm Group will be able to raise the price of the seminars by enough to maintain its previous margins

FIGURE 20-22

Risk-Preference Curve for the Grimm Group

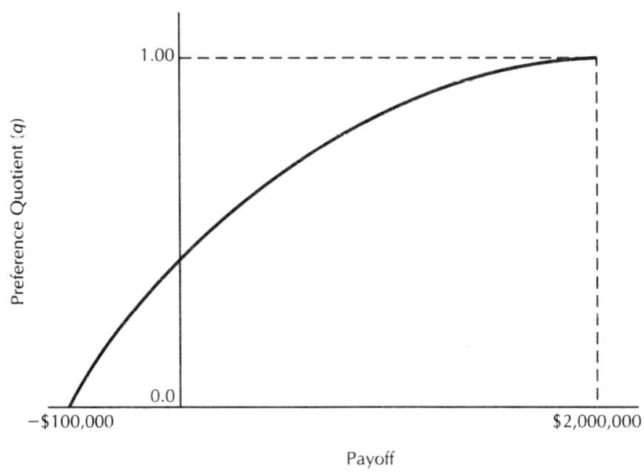

without affecting the demand. Incorporate this new information into your previous problem analysis.

57. Assume that Graciela Grimm is risk-neutral for the decision situation as amended by Problem 56. Now what alternative would you recommend?

58. Using Figure 20-22 to assess Grimm's attitude about risk, what alternative do you recommend as the decision for Problem 56?

CASES

20A Hadden Materials and Supplies, Inc.: Part 1

Mark Hadden and his son, Greg, began Hadden Materials and Supplies, Inc., in the mid-1980s. Both Mark and Greg had had successful careers with major U.S. corporations, but after several years of talking about it they came to the conclusion that they wanted to work together in their own business. They also concluded that they wanted to be in manufacturing, where they could take advantage of their previous experience and business contacts.

From the beginning, Mark has run the production shop and Greg has concentrated on sales. About 2 years ago, they got a contract to make an electronic component for natural gas heaters. At first they made this part exclusively for one company, but about 6 months ago they started making the same component for other heater manufacturers. The component is produced in large volume and sells for $30. The variable production cost per unit is $13, making this a very profitable product for the company.

However, until recently there was no way to determine whether a component would work properly until it had actually been installed in the heater unit. Whenever the heater manufacturer found a defect, Hadden Materials and Supplies would refund the full $30 plus pay a penalty of $10. Although the company has made major improvements in its quality control program, this particular component is very difficult to build and to have work properly. As a result, the defect rate has been approximately 25%.

A week ago, the company was approached by a representative of Tech-Notics, Inc., who said her company had a device for testing components like the one Hadden makes for gas heaters. By using this tester, Hadden could determine before shipping whether the component would work or not. This was one sales call that really drew Mark and Greg's attention. The sales representative agreed to bring a unit by for a trial the next morning. Greg called their largest customer and made some arrangements to "test the tester" at the customer's plant the next afternoon.

Over the next 2 days, Mark, Greg, and the Tech-Notics sales representative tested 400 components. Of these, 320 tested positive, indicating that they would turn out to be good; however, of the 320 that tested positive, seventy-two ended up actually being defective. In addition, of the components that got a negative reading, eight were found to be good. Although the testing device is not perfect, the Haddens were still encouraged.

The sales representative explained that her company preferred to lease the testers, with a financial arrangement that called for the lessor to pay $3 per test. (The tester had an automatic counter.) If the unit were sold outright, it would cost $6 million. Mark and Greg realized there was no way that they could afford to purchase the unit, so that option was immediately eliminated. However, they were interested in the lease plan and told the sales representative they would call her soon with their decision.

As Mark and Greg conferred over lunch, they estimated the heater component would remain in production for about 2 more years. During that time, they could expect orders for about 100,000 units. They also agreed that if they leased the tester, they would use it to test every component that they built. As Greg said, "Why should we lease it if we don't use it?" They also concluded that if an item tested negative, it would be scrapped and not shipped.

20B Hadden Materials and Supplies, Inc.: Part 2

About 2 hours after Mark Hadden had phoned the Tech-Notics sales representative to tell her of his company's tentative decision, he placed a call to Diane Rogers. Diane is a former colleague of Mark's who now serves as a consultant to manufacturing companies. After mark explained the details of the decision he and Greg had made, Diane asked whether they had considered their risk preferences in their analysis. Mark said that they thought they had, but he did not quite know what Diane was referring to.

Before long, Mark was offering to cover the expenses if Diane and Fred, her husband, would fly out for a long weekend—and if Diane would provide some advice on this decision. They agreed to get their work out of the way Friday evening and leave the rest of the weekend for some fun and relaxation.

Friday afternoon, after making sure that Diane and Fred had arrived and were settled into their hotel, Mark arranged to drive Diane to the plant to meet with Greg. As they discussed the decision situation, Diane made some notes. She remarked that it appeared Mark and Greg had not formally considered their preferences for risk; instead, they had conducted their analysis as if they were risk-neutral. She also noted that the decision regarding the tester should be analyzed as if only one component were being built instead of 100,000.

Diane suggested that together they try to develop a risk-preference function for this deal. First, she asked the partners to determine the highest possible addition and the biggest possible reduction in the company's net cash position that might result from the decision. Greg indicated that these ranged from a high of +$17 per unit to a low of −$26 per unit. Then Diane posed a series of questions, beginning with this one: "Suppose you are faced with an event that will give you a 50–50 chance at making $17 versus losing $26. Further, suppose that you will be forced to participate. Do you want to?"

Both Mark and Greg agreed that it did not seem like a very good deal. Diane then asked, "Suppose I will let you out of the deal for a fee. Would you pay me $20 right now to get out of the deal?"

FIGURE 20-23

Risk-Preference Curve for Hadden Materials and Supplies, Inc.

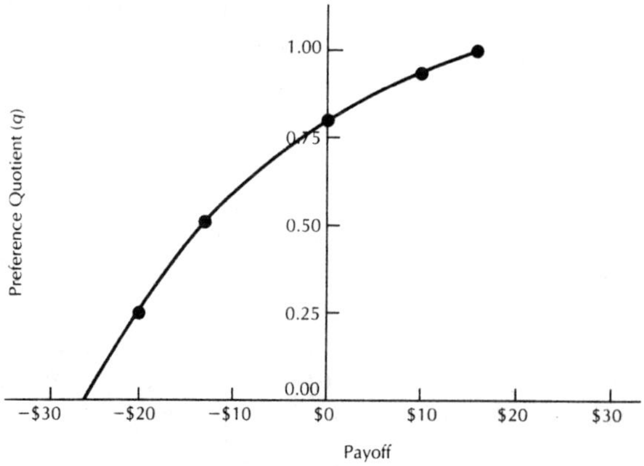

Mark and Greg conferred and decided that they would not pay $20, but they would pay $16 to get out of the deal. Diane wrote this down and continued asking similar questions until she finally announced, "Now we have enough information about your risk preferences to develop a risk-preference curve, which we can then use in your decision analysis."

The curve that Diane drew is shown in Figure 20-23. The group then set out to determine whether this finding would alter the decision Mark and Greg had made before conferring with Diane.

After making arrangements for an early tennis game Saturday morning, Mark asked Diane if she would take some time on Saturday to explain clearly what they had done this afternoon and why the results were the way they were, compared with the decision that Mark and Greg had reached earlier.

REFERENCES

Arrow, K. J. "Utilities, Attitudes, Choices: A Review Note." *Econometrica*. Vol. 26, 1958.

Baird, Bruce F. *Managerial Decision Making under Uncertainty*. New York: Wiley, 1989.

Bell, D. "Regret in Decision Making under Uncertainty." *Operations Research*. Vol. 30, 1982.

Brown, R. V., A. S. Kahr, and C. Peterson. *Decision Analysis for the Manager*. New York: Holt, 1974.

Bunn, D. W. *Applied Decision Analysis*. New York: McGraw-Hill, 1984.

Davidson, F. "Dimensions of Utility in a Regional Planning Context." *Decision Sciences*. January 1974.

Farquhar, P. "Utility Assessment Methods." *Management Science*. Vol. 30, 1984.

Felson, J. *Decision Making under Uncertainty*. New York: CBS Business and Professional Publishing, 1979.

Fishburn, P. C. *Utility Theory for Decision Making*. New York: Wiley, 1970.

Friedman, M., and L. J. Savage. "The Utility Analysis of Choices Involving Risk." *Journal of Political Economy*. August 1948.

Gregory, G. *Decision Analysis.* New York: Plenum, 1988.

Hammond, J. S. "Better Decisions with Preference Theory." *Harvard Business Review.* Vol. 45, November–December 1967.

Hespos, R. F., and P. A. Strassmann. "Stochastic Decision Trees for the Analysis of Investment Decisions." *Management Science.* Vol. 11, 1965.

Holloway, C. *Decision Making under Uncertainty: Models and Choices.* Englewood Cliffs, N.J.: Prentice-Hall, 1979.

Howard, R. A. "An Assessment of Decision Analysis." *Operations Research.* Vol. 28, 1980.

Keeney, R. L. "Decision Analysis: An Overview." *Operations Research.* Vol. 30, 1982.

Keeney, R. L., and H. Raiffa. *Decisions with Multiple Objectives: Preferences and Value Trade-offs.* New York: Wiley, 1976.

Lindley, D. V. *Making Decisions.* 2d ed. London: Wiley, 1985.

Raiffa, H. *Decision Analysis: Introductory Lectures on Choices under Uncertainty.* Reading, Mass.: Addison-Wesley, 1968.

Sampson, D. *Managerial Decision Analysis.* Homewood, Ill.: Irwin, 1988.

Schlaifer, R. *Analysis of Decisions under Uncertainty.* New York: McGraw-Hill, 1969.

Swalm, R. O. "Utility, Theory Insights into Risk Taking." *Harvard Business Review.* November–December 1966.

Thomas, H. "Strategic Decision Analysis: Applied Decision Analysis and Its Role in the Strategic Management Process." *Strategic Management Journal.* Vol. 5, 1984.

Appendices

APPENDIX A Binomial Distribution Table

$$P(X_1) = \frac{n!}{X_1!(n - X_1)!} p^{X_1}(q)^{n-X_1}$$

n = 1

X1	P=.01	P=.02	P=.03	P=.04	P=.05	P=.06	P=.07	P=.08	P=.09	P=.10	n−X1
0	.9900	.9800	.9700	.9600	.9500	.9400	.9300	.9200	.9100	.9000	1
1	.0100	.0200	.0300	.0400	.0500	.0600	.0700	.0800	.0900	.1000	0
	q=.99	q=.98	q=.97	q=.96	q=.95	q=.94	q=.93	q=.92	q=.91	q=.90	

X1	P=.11	P=.12	P=.13	P=.14	P=.15	P=.16	P=.17	P=.18	P=.19	P=.20	n−X1
0	.8900	.8800	.8700	.8600	.8500	.8400	.8300	.8200	.8100	.8000	1
1	.1100	.1200	.1300	.1400	.1500	.1600	.1700	.1800	.1900	.2000	0
	q=.89	q=.88	q=.87	q=.86	q=.85	q=.84	q=.83	q=.82	q=.81	q=.80	

X1	P=.21	P=.22	P=.23	P=.24	P=.25	P=.26	P=.27	P=.28	P=.29	P=.30	n−X1
0	.7900	.7800	.7700	.7600	.7500	.7400	.7300	.7200	.7100	.7000	1
1	.2100	.2200	.2300	.2400	.2500	.2600	.2700	.2800	.2900	.3000	0
	q=.79	q=.78	q=.77	q=.76	q=.75	q=.74	q=.73	q=.72	q=.71	q=.70	

X1	P=.31	P=.32	P=.33	P=.34	P=.35	P=.36	P=.37	P=.38	P=.39	P=.40	n−X1
0	.6900	.6800	.6700	.6600	.6500	.6400	.6300	.6200	.6100	.6000	1
1	.3100	.3200	.3300	.3400	.3500	.3600	.3700	.3800	.3900	.4000	0
	q=.69	q=.68	q=.67	q=.66	q=.65	q=.64	q=.63	q=.62	q=.61	q=.60	

X1	P=.41	P=.42	P=.43	P=.44	P=.45	P=.46	P=.47	P=.48	P=.49	P=.50	n−X1
0	.5900	.5800	.5700	.5600	.5500	.5400	.5300	.5200	.5100	.5000	1
1	.4100	.4200	.4300	.4400	.4500	.4600	.4700	.4800	.4900	.5000	0
	q=.59	q=.58	q=.57	q=.56	q=.55	q=.54	q=.53	q=.52	q=.51	q=.50	

n = 2

X1	P=.01	P=.02	P=.03	P=.04	P=.05	P=.06	P=.07	P=.08	P=.09	P=.10	n−X1
0	.9801	.9604	.9409	.9216	.9025	.8836	.8649	.8464	.8281	.8100	2
1	.0198	.0392	.0582	.0768	.0950	.1128	.1302	.1472	.1638	.1800	1
2	.0001	.0004	.0009	.0016	.0025	.0036	.0049	.0064	.0081	.0100	0
	q=.99	q=.98	q=.97	q=.96	q=.95	q=.94	q=.93	q=.92	q=.91	q=.90	

X1	P=.11	P=.12	P=.13	P=.14	P=.15	P=.16	P=.17	P=.18	P=.19	P=.20	n−X1
0	.7921	.7744	.7569	.7396	.7225	.7056	.6889	.6724	.6561	.6400	2
1	.1958	.2112	.2262	.2408	.2550	.2688	.2822	.2952	.3078	.3200	1
2	.0121	.0144	.0169	.0196	.0225	.0256	.0289	.0324	.0361	.0400	0
	q=.89	q=.88	q=.87	q=.86	q=.85	q=.84	q=.83	q=.82	q=.81	q=.80	

X1	P=.21	P=.22	P=.23	P=.24	P=.25	P=.26	P=.27	P=.28	P=.29	P=.30	n−X1
0	.6241	.6084	.5929	.5776	.5625	.5476	.5329	.5184	.5041	.4900	2
1	.3318	.3432	.3542	.3648	.3750	.3848	.3942	.4032	.4118	.4200	1
2	.0441	.0484	.0529	.0576	.0625	.0676	.0729	.0784	.0841	.0900	0
	q=.79	q=.78	q=.77	q=.76	q=.75	q=.74	q=.73	q=.72	q=.71	q=.70	

X1	P=.31	P=.32	P=.33	P=.34	P=.35	P=.36	P=.37	P=.38	P=.39	P=.40	n−X1
0	.4761	.4624	.4489	.4356	.4225	.4096	.3969	.3844	.3721	.3600	2
1	.4278	.4352	.4422	.4488	.4550	.4608	.4662	.4712	.4758	.4800	1
2	.0961	.1024	.1089	.1156	.1225	.1296	.1369	.1444	.1521	.1600	0
	q=.69	q=.68	q=.67	q=.66	q=.65	q=.64	q=.63	q=.62	q=.61	q=.60	

X1	P=.41	P=.42	P=.43	P=.44	P=.45	P=.46	P=.47	P=.48	P=.49	P=.50	n−X1
0	.3481	.3364	.3249	.3136	.3025	.2916	.2809	.2704	.2601	.2500	2
1	.4838	.4872	.4902	.4928	.4950	.4968	.4982	.4992	.4998	.5000	1
2	.1681	.1764	.1849	.1936	.2025	.2116	.2209	.2304	.2401	.2500	0
	q=.59	q=.58	q=.57	q=.56	q=.55	q=.54	q=.53	q=.52	q=.51	q=.50	

n = 3

X1	P=.01	P=.02	P=.03	P=.04	P=.05	P=.06	P=.07	P=.08	P=.09	P=.10	n−X1
0	.9703	.9412	.9127	.8847	.8574	.8306	.8044	.7787	.7536	.7290	3
1	.0294	.0576	.0847	.1106	.1354	.1590	.1816	.2031	.2236	.2430	2
2	.0003	.0012	.0026	.0046	.0071	.0102	.0137	.0177	.0221	.0270	1
3	.0000	.0000	.0000	.0001	.0001	.0002	.0003	.0005	.0007	.0010	0
	q=.99	q=.98	q=.97	q=.96	q=.95	q=.94	q=.93	q=.92	q=.91	q=.90	

X1	P=.11	P=.12	P=.13	P=.14	P=.15	P=.16	P=.17	P=.18	P=.19	P=.20	n−X1
0	.7050	.6815	.6585	.6361	.6141	.5927	.5718	.5514	.5314	.5120	3
1	.2614	.2788	.2952	.3106	.3251	.3387	.3513	.3631	.3740	.3840	2
2	.0323	.0380	.0441	.0506	.0574	.0645	.0720	.0797	.0877	.0960	1
3	.0013	.0017	.0022	.0027	.0034	.0041	.0049	.0058	.0069	.0080	0
	q=.89	q=.88	q=.87	q=.86	q=.85	q=.84	q=.83	q=.82	q=.81	q=.80	

X1	P=.21	P=.22	P=.23	P=.24	P=.25	P=.26	P=.27	P=.28	P=.29	P=.30	n−X1
0	.4930	.4746	.4565	.4390	.4219	.4052	.3890	.3732	.3579	.3430	3
1	.3932	.4015	.4091	.4159	.4219	.4271	.4316	.4355	.4386	.4410	2
2	.1045	.1133	.1222	.1313	.1406	.1501	.1597	.1693	.1791	.1890	1
3	.0093	.0106	.0122	.0138	.0156	.0176	.0197	.0220	.0244	.0270	0
	q=.79	q=.78	q=.77	q=.76	q=.75	q=.74	q=.73	q=.72	q=.71	q=.70	

X1	P=.31	P=.32	P=.33	P=.34	P=.35	P=.36	P=.37	P=.38	P=.39	P=.40	n−X1
0	.3285	.3144	.3008	.2875	.2746	.2621	.2500	.2383	.2270	.2160	3
1	.4428	.4439	.4444	.4443	.4436	.4424	.4406	.4382	.4354	.4320	2
2	.1989	.2089	.2189	.2289	.2389	.2488	.2587	.2686	.2783	.2880	1
3	.0298	.0328	.0359	.0393	.0429	.0467	.0507	.0549	.0593	.0640	0
	q=.69	q=.68	q=.67	q=.66	q=.65	q=.64	q=.63	q=.62	q=.61	q=.60	

X1	P=.41	P=.42	P=.43	P=.44	P=.45	P=.46	P=.47	P=.48	P=.49	P=.50	n−X1
0	.2054	.1951	.1852	.1756	.1664	.1575	.1489	.1406	.1327	.1250	3
1	.4282	.4239	.4191	.4140	.4084	.4024	.3961	.3894	.3823	.3750	2
2	.2975	.3069	.3162	.3252	.3341	.3428	.3512	.3594	.3674	.3750	1
3	.0689	.0741	.0795	.0852	.0911	.0973	.1038	.1106	.1176	.1250	0
	q=.59	q=.58	q=.57	q=.56	q=.55	q=.54	q=.53	q=.52	q=.51	q=.50	

n = 4

X1	P=.01	P=.02	P=.03	P=.04	P=.05	P=.06	P=.07	P=.08	P=.09	P=.10	n−X1
0	.9606	.9224	.8853	.8493	.8145	.7807	.7481	.7164	.6857	.6561	4
1	.0388	.0753	.1095	.1416	.1715	.1993	.2252	.2492	.2713	.2916	3
2	.0006	.0023	.0051	.0088	.0135	.0191	.0254	.0325	.0402	.0486	2
3	.0000	.0000	.0001	.0002	.0005	.0008	.0013	.0019	.0027	.0036	1
4	.0000	.0000	.0000	.0000	.0000	.0000	.0000	.0000	.0001	.0001	0
	q=.99	q=.98	q=.97	q=.96	q=.95	q=.94	q=.93	q=.92	q=.91	q=.90	

X1	P=.11	P=.12	P=.13	P=.14	P=.15	P=.16	P=.17	P=.18	P=.19	P=.20	n-X1
0	.6274	.5997	.5729	.5470	.5220	.4979	.4746	.4521	.4305	.4096	4
1	.3102	.3271	.3424	.3562	.3685	.3793	.3888	.3970	.4039	.4096	3
2	.0575	.0669	.0767	.0870	.0975	.1084	.1195	.1307	.1421	.1536	2
3	.0047	.0061	.0076	.0094	.0115	.0138	.0163	.0191	.0222	.0256	1
4	.0001	.0002	.0003	.0004	.0005	.0007	.0008	.0010	.0013	.0016	0
	q=.89	q=.88	q=.87	q=.86	q=.85	q=.84	q=.83	q=.82	q=.81	q=.80	

X1	P=.21	P=.22	P=.23	P=.24	P=.25	P=.26	P=.27	P=.28	P=.29	P=.30	n-X1
0	.3895	.3702	.3515	.3336	.3164	.2999	.2840	.2687	.2541	.2401	4
1	.4142	.4176	.4200	.4214	.4219	.4214	.4201	.4180	.4152	.4116	3
2	.1651	.1767	.1882	.1996	.2109	.2221	.2331	.2439	.2544	.2646	2
3	.0293	.0332	.0375	.0420	.0469	.0520	.0575	.0632	.0693	.0756	1
4	.0019	.0023	.0028	.0033	.0039	.0046	.0053	.0061	.0071	.0081	0
	q=.79	q=.78	q=.77	q=.76	q=.75	q=.74	q=.73	q=.72	q=.71	q=.70	

X1	P=.31	P=.32	P=.33	P=.34	P=.35	P=.36	P=.37	P=.38	P=.39	P=.40	n-X1
0	.2267	.2138	.2015	.1897	.1785	.1678	.1575	.1478	.1385	.1296	4
1	.4074	.4025	.3970	.3910	.3845	.3775	.3701	.3623	.3541	.3456	3
2	.2745	.2841	.2933	.3021	.3105	.3185	.3260	.3330	.3396	.3456	2
3	.0822	.0891	.0963	.1038	.1115	.1194	.1276	.1361	.1447	.1536	1
4	.0092	.0105	.0119	.0134	.0150	.0168	.0187	.0209	.0231	.0256	0
	q=.69	q=.68	q=.67	q=.66	q=.65	q=.64	q=.63	q=.62	q=.61	q=.60	

X1	P=.41	P=.42	P=.43	P=.44	P=.45	P=.46	P=.47	P=.48	P=.49	P=.50	n-X1
0	.1212	.1132	.1056	.0983	.0915	.0850	.0789	.0731	.0677	.0625	4
1	.3368	.3278	.3185	.3091	.2995	.2897	.2799	.2700	.2600	.2500	3
2	.3511	.3560	.3604	.3643	.3675	.3702	.3723	.3738	.3747	.3750	2
3	.1627	.1719	.1813	.1908	.2005	.2102	.2201	.2300	.2400	.2500	1
4	.0283	.0311	.0342	.0375	.0410	.0448	.0488	.0531	.0576	.0625	0
	q=.59	q=.58	q=.57	q=.56	q=.55	q=.54	q=.53	q=.52	q=.51	q=.50	

n = 5

X1	P=.01	P=.02	P=.03	P=.04	P=.05	P=.06	P=.07	P=.08	P=.09	P=.10	n-X1
0	.9510	.9039	.8587	.8154	.7738	.7339	.6957	.6591	.6240	.5905	5
1	.0480	.0922	.1328	.1699	.2036	.2342	.2618	.2866	.3086	.3280	4
2	.0010	.0038	.0082	.0142	.0214	.0299	.0394	.0498	.0610	.0729	3
3	.0000	.0001	.0003	.0006	.0011	.0019	.0030	.0043	.0060	.0081	2
4	.0000	.0000	.0000	.0000	.0000	.0001	.0001	.0002	.0003	.0004	1
5	.0000	.0000	.0000	.0000	.0000	.0000	.0000	.0000	.0000	.0000	0
	q=.99	q=.98	q=.97	q=.96	q=.95	q=.94	q=.93	q=.92	q=.91	q=.90	

X1	P=.11	P=.12	P=.13	P=.14	P=.15	P=.16	P=.17	P=.18	P=.19	P=.20	n-X1
0	.5584	.5277	.4984	.4704	.4437	.4182	.3939	.3707	.3487	.3277	5
1	.3451	.3598	.3724	.3829	.3915	.3983	.4034	.4069	.4089	.4096	4
2	.0853	.0981	.1113	.1247	.1382	.1517	.1652	.1786	.1919	.2048	3
3	.0106	.0134	.0166	.0203	.0244	.0289	.0338	.0392	.0450	.0512	2
4	.0007	.0009	.0012	.0017	.0022	.0028	.0035	.0043	.0053	.0064	1
5	.0000	.0000	.0000	.0001	.0001	.0001	.0001	.0002	.0002	.0003	0
	q=.89	q=.88	q=.87	q=.86	q=.85	q=.84	q=.83	q=.82	q=.81	q=.80	

X1	P=.21	P=.22	P=.23	P=.24	P=.25	P=.26	P=.27	P=.28	P=.29	P=.30	n-X1
0	.3077	.2887	.2707	.2536	.2373	.2219	.2073	.1935	.1804	.1681	5
1	.4090	.4072	.4043	.4003	.3955	.3898	.3834	.3762	.3685	.3601	4
2	.2174	.2297	.2415	.2529	.2637	.2739	.2836	.2926	.3010	.3087	3
3	.0578	.0648	.0721	.0798	.0879	.0962	.1049	.1138	.1229	.1323	2
4	.0077	.0091	.0108	.0126	.0146	.0169	.0194	.0221	.0251	.0283	1
5	.0004	.0005	.0006	.0008	.0010	.0012	.0014	.0017	.0021	.0024	0
	q=.79	q=.78	q=.77	q=.76	q=.75	q=.74	q=.73	q=.72	q=.71	q=.70	

X1	P=.31	P=.32	P=.33	P=.34	P=.35	P=.36	P=.37	P=.38	P=.39	P=.40	n−X1
0	.1564	.1454	.1350	.1252	.1160	.1074	.0992	.0916	.0845	.0778	5
1	.3513	.3421	.3325	.3226	.3124	.3020	.2914	.2808	.2700	.2592	4
2	.3157	.3220	.3275	.3323	.3364	.3397	.3423	.3441	.3452	.3456	3
3	.1418	.1515	.1613	.1712	.1811	.1911	.2010	.2109	.2207	.2304	2
4	.0319	.0357	.0397	.0441	.0488	.0537	.0590	.0646	.0706	.0768	1
5	.0029	.0034	.0039	.0045	.0053	.0060	.0069	.0079	.0090	.0102	0
	q=.69	q=.68	q=.67	q=.66	q=.65	q=.64	q=.63	q=.62	q=.61	q=.60	

X1	P=.41	P=.42	P=.43	P=.44	P=.45	P=.46	P=.47	P=.48	P=.49	P=.50	n−X1
0	.0715	.0656	.0602	.0551	.0503	.0459	.0418	.0380	.0345	.0312	5
1	.2484	.2376	.2270	.2164	.2059	.1956	.1854	.1755	.1657	.1562	4
2	.3452	.3442	.3424	.3400	.3369	.3332	.3289	.3240	.3185	.3125	3
3	.2399	.2492	.2583	.2671	.2757	.2838	.2916	.2990	.3060	.3125	2
4	.0834	.0902	.0974	.1049	.1128	.1209	.1293	.1380	.1470	.1563	1
5	.0116	.0131	.0147	.0165	.0185	.0206	.0229	.0255	.0282	.0313	0
	q=.59	q=.58	q=.57	q=.56	q=.55	q=.54	q=.53	q=.52	q=.51	q=.50	

n = 6

X1	P=.01	P=.02	P=.03	P=.04	P=.05	P=.06	P=.07	P=.08	P=.09	P=.10	n−X1
0	.9415	.8858	.8330	.7828	.7351	.6899	.6470	.6064	.5679	.5314	6
1	.0571	.1085	.1546	.1957	.2321	.2642	.2922	.3164	.3370	.3543	5
2	.0014	.0055	.0120	.0204	.0305	.0422	.0550	.0688	.0833	.0984	4
3	.0000	.0002	.0005	.0011	.0021	.0036	.0055	.0080	.0110	.0146	3
4	.0000	.0000	.0000	.0000	.0001	.0002	.0003	.0005	.0008	.0012	2
5	.0000	.0000	.0000	.0000	.0000	.0000	.0000	.0000	.0000	.0001	1
6	.0000	.0000	.0000	.0000	.0000	.0000	.0000	.0000	.0000	.0000	0
	q=.99	q=.98	q=.97	q=.96	q=.95	q=.94	q=.93	q=.92	q=.91	q=.90	

X1	P=.11	P=.12	P=.13	P=.14	P=.15	P=.16	P=.17	P=.18	P=.19	P=.20	n−X1
0	.4970	.4644	.4336	.4046	.3771	.3513	.3269	.3040	.2824	.2621	6
1	.3685	.3800	.3888	.3952	.3993	.4015	.4018	.4004	.3975	.3932	5
2	.1139	.1295	.1452	.1608	.1762	.1912	.2057	.2197	.2331	.2458	4
3	.0188	.0236	.0289	.0349	.0415	.0486	.0562	.0643	.0729	.0819	3
4	.0017	.0024	.0032	.0043	.0055	.0069	.0086	.0106	.0128	.0154	2
5	.0001	.0001	.0002	.0003	.0004	.0005	.0007	.0009	.0012	.0015	1
6	.0000	.0000	.0000	.0000	.0000	.0000	.0000	.0000	.0000	.0001	0
	q=.89	q=.88	q=.87	q=.86	q=.85	q=.84	q=.83	q=.82	q=.81	q=.80	

X1	P=.21	P=.22	P=.23	P=.24	P=.25	P=.26	P=.27	P=.28	P=.29	P=.30	n−X1
0	.2431	.2252	.2084	.1927	.1780	.1642	.1513	.1393	.1281	.1176	6
1	.3877	.3811	.3735	.3651	.3560	.3462	.3358	.3251	.3139	.3025	5
2	.2577	.2687	.2789	.2882	.2966	.3041	.3105	.3160	.3206	.3241	4
3	.0913	.1011	.1111	.1214	.1318	.1424	.1531	.1639	.1746	.1852	3
4	.0182	.0214	.0249	.0287	.0330	.0375	.0425	.0478	.0535	.0595	2
5	.0019	.0024	.0030	.0036	.0044	.0053	.0063	.0074	.0087	.0102	1
6	.0001	.0001	.0001	.0002	.0002	.0003	.0004	.0005	.0006	.0007	0
	q=.79	q=.78	q=.77	q=.76	q=.75	q=.74	q=.73	q=.72	q=.71	q=.70	

X1	P=.31	P=.32	P=.33	P=.34	P=.35	P=.36	P=.37	P=.38	P=.39	P=.40	n−X1
0	.1079	.0989	.0905	.0827	.0754	.0687	.0625	.0568	.0515	.0467	6
1	.2909	.2792	.2673	.2555	.2437	.2319	.2203	.2089	.1976	.1866	5
2	.3267	.3284	.3292	.3290	.3280	.3261	.3235	.3201	.3159	.3110	4
3	.1957	.2061	.2162	.2260	.2355	.2446	.2533	.2616	.2693	.2765	3
4	.0660	.0727	.0799	.0873	.0951	.1032	.1116	.1202	.1291	.1382	2
5	.0119	.0137	.0157	.0180	.0205	.0232	.0262	.0295	.0330	.0369	1
6	.0009	.0011	.0013	.0015	.0018	.0022	.0026	.0030	.0035	.0041	0
	q=.69	q=.68	q=.67	q=.66	q=.65	q=.64	q=.63	q=.62	q=.61	q=.60	

X1	P=.41	P=.42	P=.43	P=.44	P=.45	P=.46	P=.47	P=.48	P=.49	P=.50	n−X1
0	.0422	.0381	.0343	.0308	.0277	.0248	.0222	.0198	.0176	.0156	6
1	.1759	.1654	.1552	.1454	.1359	.1267	.1179	.1095	.1014	.0937	5
2	.3055	.2994	.2928	.2856	.2780	.2699	.2615	.2527	.2436	.2344	4
3	.2831	.2891	.2945	.2992	.3032	.3065	.3091	.3110	.3121	.3125	3

X1											n-X1
4	.1475	.1570	.1666	.1763	.1861	.1958	.2056	.2153	.2249	.2344	2
5	.0410	.0455	.0503	.0554	.0609	.0667	.0729	.0795	.0864	.0938	1
6	.0048	.0055	.0063	.0073	.0083	.0095	.0108	.0122	.0138	.0156	0
	q=.59	q=.58	q=.57	q=.56	q=.55	q=.54	q=.53	q=.52	q=.51	q=.50	

n = 7

X1	P=.01	P=.02	P=.03	P=.04	P=.05	P=.06	P=.07	P=.08	P=.09	P=.10	n-X1
0	.9321	.8681	.8080	.7514	.6983	.6485	.6017	.5578	.5168	.4783	7
1	.0659	.1240	.1749	.2192	.2573	.2897	.3170	.3396	.3578	.3720	6
2	.0020	.0076	.0162	.0274	.0406	.0555	.0716	.0886	.1061	.1240	5
3	.0000	.0003	.0008	.0019	.0036	.0059	.0090	.0128	.0175	.0230	4
4	.0000	.0000	.0000	.0001	.0002	.0004	.0007	.0011	.0017	.0026	3
5	.0000	.0000	.0000	.0000	.0000	.0000	.0000	.0001	.0001	.0002	2
6	.0000	.0000	.0000	.0000	.0000	.0000	.0000	.0000	.0000	.0000	1
7	.0000	.0000	.0000	.0000	.0000	.0000	.0000	.0000	.0000	.0000	0
	q=.99	q=.98	q=.97	q=.96	q=.95	q=.94	q=.93	q=.92	q=.91	q=.90	

X1	P=.11	P=.12	P=.13	P=.14	P=.15	P=.16	P=.17	P=.18	P=.19	P=.20	n-X1
0	.4423	.4087	.3773	.3479	.3206	.2951	.2714	.2493	.2288	.2097	7
1	.3827	.3901	.3946	.3965	.3960	.3935	.3891	.3830	.3756	.3670	6
2	.1419	.1596	.1769	.1936	.2097	.2248	.2391	.2523	.2643	.2753	5
3	.0292	.0363	.0441	.0525	.0617	.0714	.0816	.0923	.1033	.1147	4
4	.0036	.0049	.0066	.0086	.0109	.0136	.0167	.0203	.0242	.0287	3
5	.0003	.0004	.0006	.0008	.0012	.0016	.0021	.0027	.0034	.0043	2
6	.0000	.0000	.0000	.0000	.0001	.0001	.0001	.0002	.0003	.0004	1
7	.0000	.0000	.0000	.0000	.0000	.0000	.0000	.0000	.0000	.0000	0
	q=.89	q=.88	q=.87	q=.86	q=.85	q=.84	q=.83	q=.82	q=.81	q=.80	

X1	P=.21	P=.22	P=.23	P=.24	P=.25	P=.26	P=.27	P=.28	P=.29	P=.30	n-X1
0	.1920	.1757	.1605	.1465	.1335	.1215	.1105	.1003	.0910	.0824	7
1	.3573	.3468	.3356	.3237	.3115	.2989	.2860	.2731	.2600	.2471	6
2	.2850	.2935	.3007	.3067	.3115	.3150	.3174	.3186	.3186	.3177	5
3	.1263	.1379	.1497	.1614	.1730	.1845	.1956	.2065	.2169	.2269	4
4	.0336	.0389	.0447	.0510	.0577	.0648	.0724	.0803	.0886	.0972	3
5	.0054	.0066	.0080	.0097	.0115	.0137	.0161	.0187	.0217	.0250	2
6	.0005	.0006	.0008	.0010	.0013	.0016	.0020	.0024	.0030	.0036	1
7	.0000	.0000	.0000	.0000	.0001	.0001	.0001	.0001	.0002	.0002	0
	q=.79	q=.78	q=.77	q=.76	q=.75	q=.74	q=.73	q=.72	q=.71	q=.70	

X1	P=.31	P=.32	P=.33	P=.34	P=.35	P=.36	P=.37	P=.38	P=.39	P=.40	n-X1
0	.0745	.0672	.0606	.0546	.0490	.0440	.0394	.0352	.0314	.0280	7
1	.2342	.2215	.2090	.1967	.1848	.1732	.1619	.1511	.1407	.1306	6
2	.3156	.3127	.3088	.3040	.2985	.2922	.2853	.2778	.2698	.2613	5
3	.2363	.2452	.2535	.2610	.2679	.2740	.2793	.2838	.2875	.2903	4
4	.1062	.1154	.1248	.1345	.1442	.1541	.1640	.1739	.1838	.1935	3
5	.0286	.0326	.0369	.0416	.0466	.0520	.0578	.0640	.0705	.0774	2
6	.0043	.0051	.0061	.0071	.0084	.0098	.0113	.0131	.0150	.0172	1
7	.0003	.0003	.0004	.0005	.0006	.0008	.0009	.0011	.0014	.0016	0
	q=.69	q=.68	q=.67	q=.66	q=.65	q=.64	q=.63	q=.62	q=.61	q=.60	

X1	P=.41	P=.42	P=.43	P=.44	P=.45	P=.46	P=.47	P=.48	P=.49	P=.50	n-X1
0	.0249	.0221	.0195	.0173	.0152	.0134	.0117	.0103	.0090	.0078	7
1	.1211	.1119	.1032	.0950	.0872	.0798	.0729	.0664	.0604	.0547	6
2	.2524	.2431	.2336	.2239	.2140	.2040	.1940	.1840	.1740	.1641	5
3	.2923	.2934	.2937	.2932	.2918	.2897	.2867	.2830	.2786	.2734	4
4	.2031	.2125	.2216	.2304	.2388	.2468	.2543	.2612	.2676	.2734	3
5	.0847	.0923	.1003	.1086	.1172	.1261	.1353	.1447	.1543	.1641	2
6	.0196	.0223	.0252	.0284	.0320	.0358	.0400	.0445	.0494	.0547	1
7	.0019	.0023	.0027	.0032	.0037	.0044	.0051	.0059	.0068	.0078	0
	q=.59	q=.58	q=.57	q=.56	q=.55	q=.54	q=.53	q=.52	q=.51	q=.50	

n = 8

X1	P=.01	P=.02	P=.03	P=.04	P=.05	P=.06	P=.07	P=.08	P=.09	P=.10	n-X1
0	.9227	.8508	.7837	.7214	.6634	.6096	.5596	.5132	.4703	.4305	8
1	.0746	.1389	.1939	.2405	.2793	.3113	.3370	.3570	.3721	.3826	7

X1											n−X1
2	.0026	.0099	.0210	.0351	.0515	.0695	.0888	.1087	.1288	.1488	6
3	.0001	.0004	.0013	.0029	.0054	.0089	.0134	.0189	.0255	.0331	5
4	.0000	.0000	.0001	.0002	.0004	.0007	.0013	.0021	.0031	.0046	4
5	.0000	.0000	.0000	.0000	.0000	.0000	.0001	.0001	.0002	.0004	3
6	.0000	.0000	.0000	.0000	.0000	.0000	.0000	.0000	.0000	.0000	2
7	.0000	.0000	.0000	.0000	.0000	.0000	.0000	.0000	.0000	.0000	1
8	.0000	.0000	.0000	.0000	.0000	.0000	.0000	.0000	.0000	.0000	0
	q=.99	q=.98	q=.97	q=.96	q=.95	q=.94	q=.93	q=.92	q=.91	q=.90	

X1	P=.11	P=.12	P=.13	P=.14	P=.15	P=.16	P=.17	P=.18	P=.19	P=.20	n−X1
0	.3937	.3596	.3282	.2992	.2725	.2479	.2252	.2044	.1853	.1678	8
1	.3892	.3923	.3923	.3897	.3847	.3777	.3691	.3590	.3477	.3355	7
2	.1684	.1872	.2052	.2220	.2376	.2518	.2646	.2758	.2855	.2936	6
3	.0416	.0511	.0613	.0723	.0839	.0959	.1084	.1211	.1339	.1468	5
4	.0064	.0087	.0115	.0147	.0185	.0228	.0277	.0332	.0393	.0459	4
5	.0006	.0009	.0014	.0019	.0026	.0035	.0045	.0058	.0074	.0092	3
6	.0000	.0001	.0001	.0002	.0002	.0003	.0005	.0006	.0009	.0011	2
7	.0000	.0000	.0000	.0000	.0000	.0000	.0000	.0000	.0001	.0001	1
8	.0000	.0000	.0000	.0000	.0000	.0000	.0000	.0000	.0000	.0000	0
	q=.89	q=.88	q=.87	q=.86	q=.85	q=.84	q=.83	q=.82	q=.81	q=.80	

X1	P=.21	P=.22	P=.23	P=.24	P=.25	P=.26	P=.27	P=.28	P=.29	P=.30	n−X1
0	.1517	.1370	.1236	.1113	.1001	.0899	.0806	.0722	.0646	.0576	8
1	.3226	.3092	.2953	.2812	.2670	.2527	.2386	.2247	.2110	.1977	7
2	.3002	.3052	.3087	.3108	.3115	.3108	.3089	.3058	.3017	.2965	6
3	.1596	.1722	.1844	.1963	.2076	.2184	.2285	.2379	.2464	.25441	5
4	.0530	.0607	.0689	.0775	.0865	.0959	.1056	.1156	.1258	.1361	4
5	.0113	.0137	.0165	.0196	.0231	.0270	.0313	.0360	.0411	.0467	3
6	.0015	.0019	.0025	.0031	.0038	.0047	.0058	.0070	.0084	.0100	2
7	.0001	.0002	.0002	.0003	.0004	.0005	.0006	.0008	.0010	.0012	1
8	.0000	.0000	.0000	.0000	.0000	.0000	.0000	.0000	.0001	.0001	0
	q=.79	q=.78	q=.77	q=.76	q=.75	q=.74	q=.73	q=.72	q=.71	q=.70	

X1	P=.31	P=.32	P=.33	P=.34	P=.35	P=.36	P=.37	P=.38	P=.39	P=.40	n−X1
0	.0514	.0457	.0406	.0360	.0319	.0281	.0248	.0218	.0192	.0168	8
1	.1847	.1721	.1600	.1484	.1373	.1267	.1166	.1071	.0981	.0896	7
2	.2904	.2835	.2758	.2675	.2587	.2494	.2397	.2297	.2194	.2090	6
3	.2609	.2668	.2717	.2756	.2786	.2805	.2815	.2815	.2806	.2787	5
4	.1465	.1569	.1673	.1775	.1875	.1973	.2067	.2157	.2242	.2322	4
5	.0527	.0591	.0659	.0732	.0808	.0888	.0971	.1058	.1147	.1239	3
6	.0118	.0139	.0162	.0188	.0217	.0250	.0285	.0324	.0367	.0413	2
7	.0015	.0019	.0023	.0028	.0033	.0040	.0048	.0057	.0067	.0079	1
8	.0001	.0001	.0001	.0002	.0002	.0003	.0004	.0004	.0005	.0007	0
	q=.69	q=.68	q=.67	q=.66	q=.65	q=.64	q=.63	q=.62	q=.61	q=.60	

X1	P=.41	P=.42	P=.43	P=.44	P=.45	P=.46	P=.47	P=.48	P=.49	P=.50	n−X1
0	.0147	.0128	.0111	.0097	.0084	.0072	.0062	.0053	.0046	.0039	8
1	.0816	.0742	.0672	.0608	.0548	.0493	.0442	.0395	.0352	.0312	7
2	.1985	.1880	.1776	.1672	.1569	.1469	.1371	.1275	.1183	.1094	6
3	.2759	.2723	.2679	.2627	.2568	.2503	.2431	.2355	.2273	.2187	5
4	.2397	.2465	.2526	.2580	.2627	.2665	.2695	.2717	.2730	.2734	4
5	.1332	.1428	.1525	.1622	.1719	.1816	.1912	.2006	.2098	.2188	3
6	.0463	.0517	.0575	.0637	.0703	.0774	.0848	.0926	.1008	.1094	2
7	.0092	.0107	.0124	.0143	.0164	.0188	.0215	.0244	..0277	.0313	1
8	.0008	.0010	.0012	.0014	.0017	.0020	.0024	.0028	.0033	.0039	0
	q=.59	q=.58	q=.57	q=.56	q=.55	q=.54	q=.53	q=.52	q=.51	q=.50	

n = 9

X1	P=.01	P=.02	P=.03	P=.04	P=.05	P=.06	P=.07	P=.08	P=.09	P=.10	n−X1
0	.9135	.8337	.7602	.6925	.6302	.5730	.5204	.4722	.4279	.3874	9
1	.0830	.1531	.2116	.2597	.2985	.3292	.3525	.3695	.3809	.3874	8
2	.0034	.0125	.0262	.0433	.0629	.0840	.1061	.1285	.1507	.1722	7
3	.0001	.0006	.0019	.0042	.0077	.0125	.0186	.0261	.0348	.0446	6
4	.0000	.0000	.0001	.0003	.0006	.0012	.0021	.0034	.0052	.0074	5
5	.0000	.0000	.0000	.0000	.0000	.0001	.0002	.0003	.0005	.0008	4
6	.0000	.0000	.0000	.0000	.0000	.0000	.0000	.0000	.0000	.0001	3
7	.0000	.0000	.0000	.0000	.0000	.0000	.0000	.0000	.0000	.0000	2
8	.0000	.0000	.0000	.0000	.0000	.0000	.0000	.0000	.0000	.0000	1
9	.0000	.0000	.0000	.0000	.0000	.0000	.0000	.0000	.0000	.0000	0
	q=.99	q=.98	q=.97	q=.96	q=.95	q=.94	q=.93	q=.92	q=.91	q=.90	

X1	P=.11	P=.12	P=.13	P=.14	P=.15	P=.16	P=.17	P=.18	P=.19	P=.20	n-X1
0	.3504	.3165	.2855	.2573	.2316	.2082	.1869	.1676	.1501	.1342	9
1	.3897	.3884	.3840	.3770	.3679	.3569	.3446	.3312	.3169	.3020	8
2	.1927	.2119	.2295	.2455	.2597	.2720	.2823	.2908	.2973	.3020	7
3	.0556	.0674	.0800	.0933	.1069	.1209	.1349	.1489	.1627	.1762	6
4	.0103	.0138	.0179	.0228	.0283	.0345	.0415	.0490	.0573	.0661	5
5	.0013	.0019	.0027	.0037	.0050	.0066	.0085	.0108	.0134	.0165	4
6	.0001	.0002	.0003	.0004	.0006	.0008	.0012	.0016	.0021	.0028	3
7	.0000	.0000	.0000	.0000	.0000	.0001	.0001	.0001	.0002	.0003	2
8	.0000	.0000	.0000	.0000	.0000	.0000	.0000	.0000	.0000	.0000	1
9	.0000	.0000	.0000	.0000	.0000	.0000	.0000	.0000	.0000	.0000	0
	q=.89	q=.88	q=.87	q=.86	q=.85	q=.84	q=.83	q=.82	q=.81	q=.80	

X1	P=.21	P=.22	P=.23	P=.24	P=.25	P=.26	P=.27	P=.28	P=.29	P=.30	n-X1
0	.1199	.1069	.0952	.0846	.0751	.0665	.0589	.0520	.0458	.0404	9
1	.2867	.2713	.2558	.2404	.2253	.2104	.1960	.1820	.1685	.1556	8
2	.3049	.3061	.3056	.3037	.3003	.2957	.2899	.2831	.2754	.2668	7
3	.1891	.2014	.2130	.2238	.2336	.2424	.2502	.2569	.2624	.2668	6
4	.0754	.0852	.0954	.1060	.1168	.1278	.1388	.1499	.1608	.1715	5
5	.0200	.0240	.0285	.0335	.0389	.0449	.0513	.0583	.0657	.0735	4
6	.0036	.0045	.0057	.0070	.0087	.0105	.0127	.0151	.0179	.0210	3
7	.0004	.0005	.0007	.0010	.0012	.0016	.0020	.0025	.0031	.0039	2
8	.0000	.0000	.0001	.0001	.0001	.0001	.0002	.0002	.0003	.0004	1
9	.0000	.0000	.0000	.0000	.0000	.0000	.0000	.0000	.0000	.0000	0
	q=.79	q=.78	q=.77	q=.76	q=.75	q=.74	q=.73	q=.72	q=.71	q=.70	

X1	P=.31	P=.32	P=.33	P=.34	P=.35	P=.36	P=.37	P=.38	P=.39	P=.40	n-X1
0	.0355	.0311	.0272	.0238	.0207	.0180	.0156	.0135	.0117	.0101	9
1	.1433	.1317	.1206	.1102	.1004	.0912	.0826	.0747	.0673	.0605	8
2	.2576	.2478	.2376	.2270	.2162	.2052	.1941	.1831	.1721	.1612	7
3	.2701	.2721	.2731	.2729	.2716	.2693	.2660	.2618	.2567	.2508	6
4	.1820	.1921	.2017	.2109	.2194	.2272	.2344	.2407	.2462	.2508	5
5	.0818	.0904	.0994	.1086	.1181	.1278	.1376	.1475	.1574	.1672	4
6	.0245	.0284	.0326	.0373	.0424	.0479	.0539	.0603	.0671	.0743	3
7	.0047	.0057	.0069	.0082	.0098	.0116	.0136	.0158	.0184	.0212	2
8	.0005	.0007	.0008	.0011	.0013	.0016	.0020	.0024	.0029	.0035	1
9	.0000	.0000	.0000	.0001	.0001	.0001	.0001	.0002	.0002	.0003	0
	q=.69	q=.68	q=.67	q=.66	q=.65	q=.64	q=.63	q=.62	q=.61	q=.60	

X1	P=.41	P=.42	P=.43	P=.44	P=.45	P=.46	P=.47	P=.48	P=.49	P=.50	n-X1
0	.0087	.0074	.0064	.0054	.0046	.0039	.0033	.0028	.0023	.0020	9
1	.0542	.0484	.0431	.0383	.0339	.0299	.0263	.0231	.0202	.0176	8
2	.1506	.1402	.1301	.1204	.1110	.1020	.0934	.0853	.0776	.0703	7
3	.2442	.2369	.2291	.2207	.2119	.2027	.1933	.1837	.1739	.1641	6
4	.2545	.2573	.2592	.2601	.2600	.2590	.2571	.2543	.2506	.2461	5
5	.1769	.1863	.1955	.2044	.2128	.2207	.2280	.2347	.2408	.2461	4
6	.0819	.0900	.0983	.1070	.1160	.1253	.1348	.1445	.1542	.1641	3
7	.0244	.0279	.0318	.0360	.0407	.0458	.0512	.0571	.0635	.0703	2
8	.0042	.0051	.0060	.0071	.0083	.0097	.0114	.0132	.0153	.0176	1
9	.0003	.0004	.0005	.0006	.0008	.0009	.0011	.0014	.0016	.0020	0
	q=.59	q=.58	q=.57	q=.56	q=.55	q=.54	q=.53	q=.52	q=.51	q=.50	

n = 10

X1	P=.01	P=.02	P=.03	P=.04	P=.05	P=.06	P=.07	P=.08	P=.09	P=.10	n-X1
0	.9044	.8171	.7374	.6648	.5987	.5386	.4840	.4344	.3894	.3487	10
1	.0914	.1667	.2281	.2770	.3151	.3438	.3643	.3777	.3851	.3874	9
2	.0042	.0153	.0317	.0519	.0746	.0988	.1234	.1478	.1714	.1937	8
3	.0001	.0008	.0026	.0058	.0105	.0168	.0248	.0343	.0452	.0574	7
4	.0000	.0000	.0001	.0004	.0010	.0019	.0033	.0052	.0078	.0112	6
5	.0000	.0000	.0000	.0000	.0001	.0001	.0003	.0005	.0009	.0015	5
6	.0000	.0000	.0000	.0000	.0000	.0000	.0000	.0000	.0001	.0001	4
7	.0000	.0000	.0000	.0000	.0000	.0000	.0000	.0000	.0000	.0000	3
8	.0000	.0000	.0000	.0000	.0000	.0000	.0000	.0000	.0000	.0000	2
9	.0000	.0000	.0000	.0000	.0000	.0000	.0000	.0000	.0000	.0000	1
10	.0000	.0000	.0000	.0000	.0000	.0000	.0000	.0000	.0000	.0000	0
	q=.99	q=.98	q=.97	q=.96	q=.95	q=.94	q=.93	q=.92	q=.91	q=.90	

X1	P=.11	P=.12	P=.13	P=.14	P=.15	P=.16	P=.17	P=.18	P=.19	P=.20	n-X1
0	.3118	.2785	.2484	.2213	.1969	.1749	.1552	.1374	.1216	.1074	10
1	.3854	.3798	.3712	.3603	.3474	.3331	.3178	.3017	.2852	.2684	9
2	.2143	.2330	.2496	.2639	.2759	.2856	.2929	.2980	.3010	.3020	8
3	.0706	.0847	.0995	.1146	.1298	.1450	.1600	.1745	.1883	.2013	7
4	.0153	.0202	.0260	.0326	.0401	.0483	.0573	.0670	.0773	.0881	6
5	.0023	.0033	.0047	.0064	.0085	.0111	.0141	.0177	.0218	.0264	5
6	.0002	.0004	.0006	.0009	.0012	.0018	.0024	.0032	.0043	.0055	4
7	.0000	.0000	.0000	.0001	.0001	.0002	.0003	.0004	.0006	.0008	3
8	.0000	.0000	.0000	.0000	.0000	.0000	.0000	.0000	.0001	.0001	2
9	.0000	.0000	.0000	.0000	.0000	.0000	.0000	.0000	.0000	.0000	1
10	.0000	.0000	.0000	.0000	.0000	.0000	.0000	.0000	.0000	.0000	0
	q=.89	q=.88	q=.87	q=.86	q=.85	q=.84	q=.83	q=.82	q=.81	q=.80	

X1	P=.21	P=.22	P=.23	P=.24	P=.25	P=.26	P=.27	P=.28	P=.29	P=.30	n-X1
0	.0947	.0834	.0733	.0643	.0563	.0492	.0430	.0374	.0326	.0282	10
1	.2517	.2351	.2188	.2030	.1877	.1730	.1590	.1456	.1330	.1211	9
2	.3011	.2984	.2942	.2885	.2816	.2735	.2646	.2548	.2444	.2335	8
3	.2134	.2244	.2343	.2429	.2503	.2563	.2609	.2642	.2662	.2668	7
4	.0993	.1108	.1225	.1343	.1460	.1576	.1689	.1798	.1903	.2001	6
5	.0317	.0375	.0439	.0509	.0584	.0664	.0750	.0839	.0933	.1029	5
6	.0070	.0088	.0109	.0134	.0162	.0195	.0231	.0272	.0317	.0368	4
7	.0011	.0014	.0019	.0024	.0031	.0039	.0049	.0060	.0074	.0090	3
8	.0001	.0002	.0002	.0003	.0004	.0005	.0007	.0009	.0011	.0014	2
9	.0000	.0000	.0000	.0000	.0000	.0000	.0001	.0001	.0001	.0001	1
10	.0000	.0000	.0000	.0000	.0000	.0000	.0000	.0000	.0000	.0000	0
	q=.79	q=.78	q=.77	q=.76	q=.75	q=.74	q=.73	q=.72	q=.71	q=.70	

X1	P=.31	P=.32	P=.33	P=.34	P=.35	P=.36	P=.37	P=.38	P=.39	P=.40	n-X1
0	.0245	.0211	.0182	.0157	.0135	.0115	.0098	.0084	.0071	.0060	10
1	.1099	.0995	.0898	.0808	.0725	.0649	.0578	.0514	.0456	.0403	9
2	.2222	.2107	.1990	.1873	.1757	.1642	.1529	.1419	.1312	.1209	8
3	.2662	.2644	.2614	.2573	.2522	.2462	.2394	.2319	.2237	.2150	7
4	.2093	.2177	.2253	.2320	.2377	.2424	.2461	.2487	.2503	.2508	6
5	.1128	.1229	.1332	.1434	.1536	.1636	.1734	.1829	.1920	.2007	5
6	.0422	.0482	.0547	.0616	.0689	.0767	.0849	.0934	.1023	.1115	4
7	.0108	.0130	.0154	.0181	.0212	.0247	.0285	.0327	.0374	.0425	3
8	.0018	.0023	.0028	.0035	.0043	.0052	.0063	.0075	.0090	.0106	2
9	.0002	.0002	.0003	.0004	.0005	.0006	.0008	.0010	.0013	.0016	1
10	.0000	.0000	.0000	.0000	.0000	.0000	.0000	.0001	.0001	.0001	0
	q=.69	q=.68	q=.67	q=.66	q=.65	q=.64	q=.63	q=.62	q=.61	q=.60	

X1	P=.41	P=.42	P=.43	P=.44	P=.45	P=.46	P=.47	P=.48	P=.49	P=.50	n-X1
0	.0051	.0043	.0036	.0030	.0025	.0021	.0017	.0014	.0012	.0010	10
1	.0355	.0312	.0273	.0238	.0207	.0180	.0155	.0133	.0114	.0098	9
2	.1111	.1017	.0927	.0843	.0763	.0688	.0619	.0554	.0494	.0439	8
3	.2058	.1963	.1865	.1765	.1665	.1564	.1464	.1364	.1267	.1172	7
4	.2503	.2488	.2462	.2427	.2384	.2331	.2271	.2204	.2130	.2051	6
5	.2087	.2162	.2229	.2289	.2340	.2383	.2417	.2441	.2456	.2461	5
6	.1209	.1304	.1401	.1499	.1596	.1692	.1786	.1878	.1966	.2051	4
7	.0480	.0540	.0604	.0673	.0746	.0824	.0905	.0991	.1080	.1172	3
8	.0125	.0147	.0171	.0198	.0229	.0263	.0301	.0343	.0389	.0439	2
9	.0019	.0024	.0029	.0035	.0042	.0050	.0059	.0070	.0083	.0098	1
10	.0001	.0002	.0002	.0003	.0003	.0004	.0005	.0006	.0008	.0010	0
	q=.59	q=.58	q=.57	q=.56	q=.55	q=.54	q=.53	q=.52	q=.51	q=.50	

n = 11

X1	P=.01	P=.02	P=.03	P=.04	P=.05	P=.06	P=.07	P=.08	P=.09	P=.10	n-X1
0	.8953	.8007	.7153	.6382	.5688	.5063	.4501	.3996	.3544	.3138	11
1	.0995	.1798	.2433	.2925	.3293	.3555	.3727	.3823	.3855	.3835	10
2	.0050	.0183	.0376	.0609	.0867	.1135	.1403	.1662	.1906	.2131	9
3	.0002	.0011	.0035	.0076	.0137	.0217	.0317	.0434	.0566	.0710	8
4	.0000	.0000	.0002	.0006	.0014	.0028	.0048	.0075	.0112	.0158	7
5	.0000	.0000	.0000	.0000	.0001	.0002	.0005	.0009	.0015	.0025	6
6	.0000	.0000	.0000	.0000	.0000	.0000	.0000	.0001	.0002	.0003	5
7	.0000	.0000	.0000	.0000	.0000	.0000	.0000	.0000	.0000	.0000	4
8	.0000	.0000	.0000	.0000	.0000	.0000	.0000	.0000	.0000	.0000	3
9	.0000	.0000	.0000	.0000	.0000	.0000	.0000	.0000	.0000	.0000	2

10	.0000	.0000	.0000	.0000	.0000	.0000	.0000	.0000	.0000	.0000	1
11	.0000	.0000	.0000	.0000	.0000	.0000	.0000	.0000	.0000	.0000	0
	q=.99	q=.98	q=.97	q=.96	q=.95	q=.94	q=.93	q=.92	q=.91	q=.90	

X1	P=.11	P=.12	P=.13	P=.14	P=.15	P=.16	P=.17	P=.18	P=.19	P=.20	n-X1
0	.2775	.2451	.2161	.1903	.1673	.1469	.1288	.1127	.0985	.0859	11
1	.3773	.3676	.3552	.3408	.3248	.3078	.2901	.2721	.2541	.2362	10
2	.2332	.2507	.2654	.2774	.2866	.2932	.2971	.2987	.2980	.2953	9
3	.0865	.1025	.1190	.1355	.1517	.1675	.1826	.1967	.2097	.2215	8
4	.0214	.0280	.0356	.0441	.0536	.0638	.0748	.0864	.0984	.1107	7
5	.0037	.0053	.0074	.0101	.0132	.0170	.0214	.0265	.0323	.0388	6
6	.0005	.0007	.0011	.0016	.0023	.0032	.0044	.0058	.0076	.0097	5
7	.0000	.0001	.0001	.0002	.0003	.0004	.0006	.0009	.0013	.0017	4
8	.0000	.0000	.0000	.0000	.0000	.0000	.0001	.0001	.0001	.0002	3
9	.0000	.0000	.0000	.0000	.0000	.0000	.0000	.0000	.0000	.0000	2
10	.0000	.0000	.0000	.0000	.0000	.0000	.0000	.0000	.0000	.0000	1
11	.0000	.0000	.0000	.0000	.0000	.0000	.0000	.0000	.0000	.0000	0
	q=.89	q=.88	q=.87	q=.86	q=.85	q=.84	q=.83	q=.82	q=.81	q=.80	

X1	P=.21	P=.22	P=.23	P=.24	P=.25	P=.26	P=.27	P=.28	P=.29	P=.30	n-X1
0	.0748	.0650	.0564	.0489	.0422	.0364	.0314	.0270	.0231	.0198	11
1	.2187	.2017	.1854	.1697	.1549	.1408	.1276	.1153	.1038	.0932	10
2	.2907	.2845	.2768	.2680	.2581	.2474	.2360	.2242	.2121	.1998	9
3	.2318	.2407	.2481	.2539	.2581	.2608	.2619	.2616	.2599	.2568	8
4	.1232	.1358	.1482	.1603	.1721	.1832	.1937	.2035	.2123	.2201	7
5	.0459	.0536	.0620	.0709	.0803	.0901	.1003	.1108	.1214	.1321	6
6	.0122	.0151	.0185	.0224	.0268	.0317	.0371	.0431	.0496	.0566	5
7	.0023	.0030	.0039	.0050	.0064	.0079	.0098	.0120	.0145	.0173	4
8	.0003	.0004	.0006	.0008	.0011	.0014	.0018	.0023	.0030	.0037	3
9	.0000	.0000	.0001	.0001	.0001	.0002	.0002	.0003	.0004	.0005	2
10	.0000	.0000	.0000	.0000	.0000	.0000	.0000	.0000	.0000	.0000	1
11	.0000	.0000	.0000	.0000	.0000	.0000	.0000	.0000	.0000	.0000	0
	q=.79	q=.78	q=.77	q=.76	q=.75	q=.74	q=.73	q=.72	q=.71	q=.70	

X1	P=.31	P=.32	P=.33	P=.34	P=.35	P=.36	P=.37	P=.38	P=.39	P=.40	n-X1
0	.0169	.0144	.0122	.0104	.0088	.0074	.0062	.0052	.0044	.0036	11
1	.0834	.0744	.0662	.0587	.0518	.0457	.0401	.0351	.0306	.0266	10
2	.1874	.1751	.1630	.1511	.1395	.1284	.1177	.1075	.0978	.0887	9
3	.2526	.2472	.2408	.2335	.2254	.2167	.2074	.1977	.1876	.1774	8
4	.2269	.2326	.2372	.2406	.2428	.2438	.2436	.2423	.2399	.2365	7
5	.1427	.1533	.1636	.1735	.1830	.1920	.2003	.2079	.2148	.2207	6
6	.0641	.0721	.0806	.0894	.0985	.1080	.1176	.1274	.1373	.1471	5
7	.0206	.0242	.0283	.0329	.0379	.0434	.0494	.0558	.0627	.0701	4
8	.0046	.0057	.0070	.0085	.0102	.0122	.0145	.0171	.0200	.0234	3
9	.0007	.0009	.0011	.0015	.0018	.0023	.0028	.0035	.0043	.0052	2
10	.0001	.0001	.0001	.0001	.0002	.0003	.0003	.0004	.0005	.0007	1
11	.0000	.0000	.0000	.0000	.0000	.0000	.0000	.0000	.0000	.0000	0
	q=.69	q=.68	q=.67	q=.66	q=.65	q=.64	q=.63	q=.62	q=.61	q=.60	

X1	P=.41	P=.42	P=.43	P=.44	P=.45	P=.46	P=.47	P=.48	P=.49	P=.50	n-X1
0	.0030	.0025	.0021	.0017	.0014	.0011	.0009	.0008	.0006	.0005	11
1	.0231	.0199	.0171	.0147	.0125	.0107	.0090	.0076	.0064	.0054	10
2	.0801	.0721	.0646	.0577	.0513	.0454	.0401	.0352	.0308	.0269	9
3	.1670	.1566	.1462	.1359	.1259	.1161	.1067	.0976	.0888	.0806	8
4	.2321	.2267	.2206	.2136	.2060	.1978	.1892	.1801	.1707	.1611	7
5	.2258	.2299	.2329	.2350	.2360	.2359	.2348	.2327	.2296	.2256	6
6	.1569	.1664	.1757	.1846	.1931	.2010	.2083	.2148	.2206	.2256	5
7	.0779	.0861	.0947	.1036	.1128	.1223	.1319	.1416	.1514	.1611	4
8	.0271	.0312	.0357	.0407	.0462	.0521	.0585	.0654	.0727	.0806	3
9	.0063	.0075	.0090	.0107	.0126	.0148	.0173	.0201	.0233	.0269	2
10	.0009	.0011	.0014	.0017	.0021	.0025	.0031	.0037	.0045	.0054	1
11	.0001	.0001	.0001	.0001	.0002	.0002	.0002	.0003	.0004	.0005	0
	q=.59	q=.58	q=.57	q=.56	q=.55	q=.54	q=.53	q=.52	q=.51	q=.50	

n = 12

X1	P=.01	P=.02	P=.03	P=.04	P=.05	P=.06	P=.07	P=.08	P=.09	P=.10	n-X1
0	.8864	.7847	.6938	.6127	.5404	.4759	.4186	.3677	.3225	.2824	12
1	.1074	.1922	.2575	.3064	.3413	.3645	.3781	.3837	.3827	.3766	11
2	.0060	.0216	.0438	.0702	.0988	.1280	.1565	.1835	.2082	.2301	10

3	.0002	.0015	.0045	.0098	.0173	.0272	.0393	.0532	.0686	.0852	9
4	.0000	.0001	.0003	.0009	.0021	.0039	.0067	.0104	.0153	.0213	8
5	.0000	.0000	.0000	.0001	.0002	.0004	.0008	.0014	.0024	.0038	7
6	.0000	.0000	.0000	.0000	.0000	.0000	.0001	.0001	.0003	.0005	6
7	.0000	.0000	.0000	.0000	.0000	.0000	.0000	.0000	.0000	.0000	5
8	.0000	.0000	.0000	.0000	.0000	.0000	.0000	.0000	.0000	.0000	4
9	.0000	.0000	.0000	.0000	.0000	.0000	.0000	.0000	.0000	.0000	3
10	.0000	.0000	.0000	.0000	.0000	.0000	.0000	.0000	.0000	.0000	2
11	.0000	.0000	.0000	.0000	.0000	.0000	.0000	.0000	.0000	.0000	1
12	.0000	.0000	.0000	.0000	.0000	.0000	.0000	.0000	.0000	.0000	0
	q=.99	q=.98	q=.97	q=.96	q=.95	q=.94	q=.93	q=.92	q=.91	q=.90	

X1	P=.11	P=.12	P=.13	P=.14	P=.15	P=.16	P=.17	P=.18	P=.19	P=.20	n-X1
0	.2470	.2157	.1880	.1637	.1422	.1234	.1069	.0924	.0798	.0687	12
1	.3663	.3529	.3372	.3197	.3012	.2821	.2627	.2434	.2245	.2062	11
2	.2490	.2647	.2771	.2863	.2924	.2955	.2960	.2939	.2897	.2835	10
3	.1026	.1203	.1380	.1553	.1720	.1876	.2021	.2151	.2265	.2362	9
4	.0285	.0369	.0464	.0569	.0683	.0804	.0931	.1062	.1195	.1329	8
5	.0056	.0081	.0111	.0148	.0193	.0245	.0305	.0373	.0449	.0532	7
6	.0008	.0013	.0019	.0028	.0040	.0054	.0073	.0096	.0123	.0155	6
7	.0001	.0001	.0002	.0004	.0006	.0009	.0013	.0018	.0025	.0033	5
8	.0000	.0000	.0000	.0000	.0001	.0001	.0002	.0002	.0004	.0005	4
9	.0000	.0000	.0000	.0000	.0000	.0000	.0000	.0000	.0000	.0001	3
10	.0000	.0000	.0000	.0000	.0000	.0000	.0000	.0000	.0000	.0000	2
11	.0000	.0000	.0000	.0000	.0000	.0000	.0000	.0000	.0000	.0000	1
12	.0000	.0000	.0000	.0000	.0000	.0000	.0000	.0000	.0000	.0000	0
	q=.89	q=.88	q=.87	q=.86	q=.85	q=.84	q=.83	q=.82	q=.81	q=.80	

X1	P=.21	P=.22	P=.23	P=.24	P=.25	P=.26	P=.27	P=.28	P=.29	P=.30	n-X1
0	.0591	.0507	.0434	.0371	.0317	.0270	.0229	.0194	.0164	.0138	12
1	.1885	.1717	.1557	.1407	.1267	.1137	.1016	.0906	.0804	.0712	11
2	.2756	.2663	.2558	.2444	.2323	.2197	.2068	.1937	.1807	.1678	10
3	.2442	.2503	.2547	.2573	.2581	.2573	.2549	.2511	.2460	.2397	9
4	.1460	.1589	.1712	.1828	.1936	.2034	.2122	.2197	.2261	.2311	8
5	.0621	.0717	.0818	.0924	.1032	.1143	.1255	.1367	.1477	.1585	7
6	.0193	.0236	.0285	.0340	.0401	.0469	.0542	.0620	.0704	.0792	6
7	.0044	.0057	.0073	.0092	.0115	.0141	.0172	.0207	.0246	.0291	5
8	.0007	.0010	.0014	.0018	.0024	.0031	.0040	.0050	.0063	.0078	4
9	.0001	.0001	.0002	.0003	.0004	.0005	.0007	.0009	.0011	.0015	3
10	.0000	.0000	.0000	.0000	.0000	.0001	.0001	.0001	.0001	.0002	2
11	.0000	.0000	.0000	.0000	.0000	.0000	.0000	.0000	.0000	.0000	1
12	.0000	.0000	.0000	.0000	.0000	.0000	.0000	.0000	.0000	.0000	0
	q=.79	q=.78	q=.77	q=.76	q=.75	q=.74	q=.73	q=.72	q=.71	q=.70	

X1	P=.31	P=.32	P=.33	P=.34	P=.35	P=.36	P=.37	P=.38	P=.39	P=.40	n-X1
0	.0116	.0098	.0082	.0068	.0057	.0047	.0039	.0032	.0027	.0022	12
1	.0628	.0552	.0484	.0422	.0368	.0319	.0276	.0237	.0204	.0174	11
2	.1552	.1429	.1310	.1197	.1088	.0986	.0890	.0800	.0716	.0639	10
3	.2324	.2241	.2151	.2055	.1954	.1849	.1742	.1634	.1526	.1419	9
4	.2349	.2373	.2384	.2382	.2367	.2340	.2302	.2254	.2195	.2128	8
5	.1688	.1787	.1879	.1963	.2039	.2106	.2163	.2210	.2246	.2270	7
6	.0885	.0981	.1079	.1180	.1281	.1382	.1482	.1580	.1675	.1766	6
7	.0341	.0396	.0456	.0521	.0591	.0666	.0746	.0830	.0918	.1009	5
8	.0096	.0116	.0140	.0168	.0199	.0234	.0274	.0318	.0367	.0420	4
9	.0019	.0024	.0031	.0038	.0048	.0059	.0071	.0087	.0104	.0125	3
10	.0003	.0003	.0005	.0006	.0008	.0010	.0013	.0016	.0020	.0025	2
11	.0000	.0000	.0000	.0001	.0001	.0001	.0001	.0002	.0002	.0003	1
12	.0000	.0000	.0000	.0000	.0000	.0000	.0000	.0000	.0000	.0000	0
	q=.69	q=.68	q=.67	q=.66	q=.65	q=.64	q=.63	q=.62	q=.61	q=.60	

X1	P=.41	P=.42	P=.43	P=.44	P=.45	P=.46	P=.47	P=.48	P=.49	P=.50	n-X1
0	.0018	.0014	.0012	.0010	.0008	.0006	.0005	.0004	.0003	.0002	12
1	.0148	.0126	.0106	.0090	.0075	.0063	.0052	.0043	.0036	.0029	11
2	.0567	.0502	.0442	.0388	.0339	.0294	.0255	.0220	.0189	.0161	10
3	.1314	.1211	.1111	.1015	.0923	.0836	.0754	.0676	.0604	.0537	9
4	.2054	.1973	.1886	.1794	.1700	.1602	.1504	.1405	.1306	.1208	8
5	.2284	.2285	.2276	.2256	.2225	.2184	.2134	.2075	.2008	.1934	7
6	.1851	.1931	.2003	.2068	.2124	.2171	.2208	.2234	.2250	.2256	6
7	.1103	.1198	.1295	.1393	.1489	.1585	.1678	.1768	.1853	.1934	5
8	.0479	.0542	.0611	.0684	.0762	.0844	.0930	.1020	.1113	.1208	4
9	.0148	.0175	.0205	.0239	.0277	.0319	.0367	.0418	.0475	.0537	3
10	.0031	.0038	.0046	.0056	.0068	.0082	.0098	.0116	.0137	.0161	2
11	.0004	.0005	.0006	.0008	.0010	.0013	.0016	.0019	.0024	.0029	1
12	.0000	.0000	.0000	.0001	.0001	.0001	.0001	.0001	.0002	.0002	0
	q=.59	q=.58	q=.57	q=.56	q=.55	q=.54	q=.53	q=.52	q=.51	q=.50	

n = 13

X1	P=.01	P=.02	P=.03	P=.04	P=.05	P=.06	P=.07	P=.08	P=.09	P=.10	n-X1
0	.8775	.7690	.6730	.5882	.5133	.4474	.3893	.3383	.2935	.2542	13
1	.1152	.2040	.2706	.3186	.3512	.3712	.3809	.3824	.3773	.3672	12
2	.0070	.0250	.0502	.0797	.1109	.1422	.1720	.1995	.2239	.2448	11
3	.0003	.0019	.0057	.0122	.0214	.0333	.0475	.0636	.0812	.0997	10
4	.0000	.0001	.0004	.0013	.0028	.0053	.0089	.0138	.0201	.0277	9
5	.0000	.0000	.0000	.0001	.0003	.0006	.0012	.0022	.0036	.0055	8
6	.0000	.0000	.0000	.0000	.0000	.0001	.0001	.0003	.0005	.0008	7
7	.0000	.0000	.0000	.0000	.0000	.0000	.0000	.0000	.0000	.0001	6
8	.0000	.0000	.0000	.0000	.0000	.0000	.0000	.0000	.0000	.0000	5
9	.0000	.0000	.0000	.0000	.0000	.0000	.0000	.0000	.0000	.0000	4
10	.0000	.0000	.0000	.0000	.0000	.0000	.0000	.0000	.0000	.0000	3
11	.0000	.0000	.0000	.0000	.0000	.0000	.0000	.0000	.0000	.0000	2
12	.0000	.0000	.0000	.0000	.0000	.0000	.0000	.0000	.0000	.0000	1
13	.0000	.0000	.0000	.0000	.0000	.0000	.0000	.0000	.0000	.0000	0
	q=.99	q=.98	q=.97	q=.96	q=.95	q=.94	q=.93	q=.92	q=.91	q=.90	

X1	P=.11	P=.12	P=.13	P=.14	P=.15	P=.16	P=.17	P=.18	P=.19	P=.20	n-X1
0	.2198	.1898	.1636	.1408	.1209	.1037	.0887	.0758	.0646	.0550	13
1	.3532	.3364	.3178	.2979	.2774	.2567	.2362	.2163	.1970	.1787	12
2	.2619	.2753	.2849	.2910	.2937	.2934	.2903	.2848	.2773	.2680	11
3	.1187	.1376	.1561	.1737	.1900	.2049	.2180	.2293	.2385	.2457	10
4	.0367	.0469	.0583	.0707	.0838	.0976	.1116	.1258	.1399	.1535	9
5	.0082	.0115	.0157	.0207	.0266	.0335	.0412	.0497	.0591	.0691	8
6	.0013	.0021	.0031	.0045	.0063	.0085	.0112	.0145	.0185	.0230	7
7	.0002	.0003	.0005	.0007	.0011	.0016	.0023	.0032	.0043	.0058	6
8	.0000	.0000	.0001	.0001	.0001	.0002	.0004	.0005	.0008	.0011	5
9	.0000	.0000	.0000	.0000	.0000	.0000	.0000	.0001	.0001	.0001	4
10	.0000	.0000	.0000	.0000	.0000	.0000	.0000	.0000	.0000	.0000	3
11	.0000	.0000	.0000	.0000	.0000	.0000	.0000	.0000	.0000	.0000	2
12	.0000	.0000	.0000	.0000	.0000	.0000	.0000	.0000	.0000	.0000	1
13	.0000	.0000	.0000	.0000	.0000	.0000	.0000	.0000	.0000	.0000	0
	q=.89	q=.88	q=.87	q=.86	q=.85	q=.84	q=.83	q=.82	q=.81	q=.80	

X1	P=.21	P=.22	P=.23	P=.24	P=.25	P=.26	P=.27	P=.28	P=.29	P=.30	n-X1
0	.0467	.0396	.0334	.0282	.0238	.0200	.0167	.0140	.0117	.0097	13
1	.1613	.1450	.1299	.1159	.1029	.0911	.0804	.0706	.0619	.0540	12
2	.2573	.2455	.2328	.2195	.2059	.1921	.1784	.1648	.1516	.1388	11
3	.2508	.2539	.2550	.2542	.2517	.2475	.2419	.2351	.2271	.2181	10
4	.1667	.1790	.1904	.2007	.2097	.2174	.2237	.2285	.2319	.2337	9
5	.0797	.0909	.1024	.1141	.1258	.1375	.1489	.1600	.1705	.1803	8
6	.0283	.0342	.0408	.0480	.0559	.0644	.0734	.0829	.0928	.1030	7
7	.0075	.0096	.0122	.0152	.0186	.0226	.0272	.0323	.0379	.0442	6
8	.0015	.0020	.0027	.0036	.0047	.0060	.0075	.0094	.0116	.0142	5
9	.0002	.0003	.0005	.0006	.0009	.0012	.0015	.0020	.0026	.0034	4
10	.0000	.0000	.0001	.0001	.0001	.0002	.0002	.0003	.0004	.0006	3
11	.0000	.0000	.0000	.0000	.0000	.0000	.0000	.0000	.0000	.0001	2
12	.0000	.0000	.0000	.0000	.0000	.0000	.0000	.0000	.0000	.0000	1
13	.0000	.0000	.0000	.0000	.0000	.0000	.0000	.0000	.0000	.0000	0
	q=.79	q=.78	q=.77	q=.76	q=.75	q=.74	q=.73	q=.72	q=.71	q=.70	

X1	P=.31	P=.32	P=.33	P=.34	P=.35	P=.36	P=.37	P=.38	P=.39	P=.40	n-X1
0	.0080	.0066	.0055	.0045	.0037	.0030	.0025	.0020	.0016	.0013	13
1	.0469	.0407	.0351	.0302	.0259	.0221	.0188	.0159	.0135	.0113	12
2	.1265	.1148	.1037	.0933	.0836	.0746	.0663	.0586	.0516	.0453	11
3	.2084	.1981	.1874	.1763	.1651	.1538	.1427	.1317	.1210	.1107	10
4	.2341	.2331	.2307	.2270	.2222	.2163	.2095	.2018	.1934	.1845	9
5	.1893	.1974	.2045	.2105	.2154	.2190	.2215	.2227	.2226	.2214	8
6	.1134	.1239	.1343	.1446	.1546	.1643	.1734	.1820	.1898	.1968	7
7	.0509	.0583	.0662	.0745	.0833	.0924	.1019	.1115	.1213	.1312	6
8	.0172	.0206	.0244	.0288	.0336	.0390	.0449	.0513	.0582	.0656	5
9	.0043	.0054	.0067	.0082	.0101	.0122	.0146	.0175	.0207	.0243	4
10	.0008	.0010	.0013	.0017	.0022	.0027	.0034	.0043	.0053	.0065	3
11	.0001	.0001	.0002	.0002	.0003	.0004	.0006	.0007	.0009	.0012	2
12	.0000	.0000	.0000	.0000	.0000	.0000	.0001	.0001	.0001	.0001	1
13	.0000	.0000	.0000	.0000	.0000	.0000	.0000	.0000	.0000	.0000	0
	q=.69	q=.68	q=.67	q=.66	q=.65	q=.64	q=.63	q=.62	q=.61	q=.60	

X1	P=.41	P=.42	P=.43	P=.44	P=.45	P=.46	P=.47	P=.48	P=.49	P=.50	n-X1
0	.0010	.0008	.0007	.0005	.0004	.0003	.0003	.0002	.0002	.0001	13
1	.0095	.0079	.0066	.0054	.0045	.0037	.0030	.0024	.0020	.0016	12
2	.0395	.0344	.0298	.0256	.0220	.0188	.0160	.0135	.0114	.0095	11
3	.1007	.0913	.0823	.0739	.0660	.0587	.0519	.0457	.0401	.0349	10
4	.1750	.1653	.1553	.1451	.1350	.1250	.1151	.1055	.0962	.0873	9
5	.2189	.2154	.2108	.2053	.1989	.1917	.1838	.1753	.1664	.1571	8
6	.2029	.2080	.2121	.2151	.2169	.2177	.2173	.2158	.2131	.2095	7
7	.1410	.1506	.1600	.1690	.1775	.1854	.1927	.1992	.2048	.2095	6
8	.0735	.0818	.0905	.0996	.1089	.1185	.1282	.1379	.1476	.1571	5
9	.0284	.0329	.0379	.0435	.0495	.0561	.0631	.0707	.0788	.0873	4
10	.0079	.0095	.0114	.0137	.0162	.0191	.0224	.0261	.0303	.0349	3
11	.0015	.0019	.0024	.0029	.0036	.0044	.0054	.0066	.0079	.0095	2
12	.0002	.0002	.0003	.0004	.0005	.0006	.0008	.0010	.0013	.0016	1
13	.0000	.0000	.0000	.0000	.0000	.0000	.0001	.0001	.0001	.0001	0
	q=.59	q=.58	q=.57	q=.56	q=.55	q=.54	q=.53	q=.52	q=.51	q=.50	

n = 14

X1	P=.01	P=.02	P=.03	P=.04	P=.05	P=.06	P=.07	P=.08	P=.09	P=.10	n-X1
0	.8687	.7536	.6528	.5647	.4877	.4205	.3620	.3112	.2670	.2288	14
1	.1229	.2153	.2827	.3294	.3593	.3758	.3815	.3788	.3698	.3559	13
2	.0081	.0286	.0568	.0892	.1229	.1559	.1867	.2141	.2377	.2570	12
3	.0003	.0023	.0070	.0149	.0259	.0398	.0562	.0745	.0940	.1142	11
4	.0000	.0001	.0006	.0017	.0037	.0070	.0116	.0178	.0256	.0349	10
5	.0000	.0000	.0000	.0001	.0004	.0009	.0018	.0031	.0051	.0078	9
6	.0000	.0000	.0000	.0000	.0000	.0001	.0002	.0004	.0008	.0013	8
7	.0000	.0000	.0000	.0000	.0000	.0000	.0000	.0000	.0001	.0002	7
8	.0000	.0000	.0000	.0000	.0000	.0000	.0000	.0000	.0000	.0000	6
9	.0000	.0000	.0000	.0000	.0000	.0000	.0000	.0000	.0000	.0000	5
10	.0000	.0000	.0000	.0000	.0000	.0000	.0000	.0000	.0000	.0000	4
11	.0000	.0000	.0000	.0000	.0000	.0000	.0000	.0000	.0000	.0000	3
12	.0000	.0000	.0000	.0000	.0000	.0000	.0000	.0000	.0000	.0000	2
13	.0000	.0000	.0000	.0000	.0000	.0000	.0000	.0000	.0000	.0000	1
14	.0000	.0000	.0000	.0000	.0000	.0000	.0000	.0000	.0000	.0000	0
	q=.99	q=.98	q=.97	q=.96	q=.95	q=.94	q=.93	q=.92	q=.91	q=.90	

X1	P=.11	P=.12	P=.13	P=.14	P=.15	P=.16	P=.17	P=.18	P=.19	P=.20	n-X1
0	.1956	.1670	.1423	.1211	.1028	.0871	.0736	.0621	.0523	.0440	14
1	.3385	.3188	.2977	.2759	.2539	.2322	.2112	.1910	.1719	.1539	13
2	.2720	.2826	.2892	.2919	.2912	.2875	.2811	.2725	.2620	.2501	12
3	.1345	.1542	.1728	.1901	.2056	.2190	.2303	.2393	.2459	.2501	11
4	.0457	.0578	.0710	.0851	.0998	.1147	.1297	.1444	.1586	.1720	10
5	.0113	.0158	.0212	.0277	.0352	.0437	.0531	.0634	.0744	.0860	9
6	.0021	.0032	.0048	.0068	.0093	.0125	.0163	.0209	.0262	.0322	8
7	.0003	.0005	.0008	.0013	.0019	.0027	.0038	.0052	.0070	.0092	7
8	.0000	.0001	.0001	.0002	.0003	.0005	.0007	.0010	.0014	.0020	6
9	.0000	.0000	.0000	.0000	.0000	.0001	.0001	.0001	.0002	.0003	5
10	.0000	.0000	.0000	.0000	.0000	.0000	.0000	.0000	.0000	.0000	4
11	.0000	.0000	.0000	.0000	.0000	.0000	.0000	.0000	.0000	.0000	3
12	.0000	.0000	.0000	.0000	.0000	.0000	.0000	.0000	.0000	.0000	2
13	.0000	.0000	.0000	.0000	.0000	.0000	.0000	.0000	.0000	.0000	1
14	.0000	.0000	.0000	.0000	.0000	.0000	.0000	.0000	.0000	.0000	0
	q=.89	q=.88	q=.87	q=.86	q=.85	q=.84	q=.83	q=.82	q=.81	q=.80	

X1	P=.21	P=.22	P=.23	P=.24	P=.25	P=.26	P=.27	P=.28	P=.29	P=.30	n-X1
0	.0369	.0309	.0258	.0214	.0178	.0148	.0122	.0101	.0083	.0068	14
1	.1372	.1218	.1077	.0948	.0832	.0726	.0632	.0548	.0473	.0407	13
2	.2371	.2234	.2091	.1946	.1802	.1659	.1519	.1385	.1256	.1134	12
3	.2521	.2520	.2499	.2459	.2402	.2331	.2248	.2154	.2052	.1943	11
4	.1843	.1955	.2052	.2135	.2202	.2252	.2286	.2304	.2305	.2290	10
5	.0980	.1103	.1226	.1348	.1468	.1583	.1691	.1792	.1883	.1963	9
6	.0391	.0466	.0549	.0639	.0734	.0834	.0938	.1045	.1153	.1262	8
7	.0119	.0150	.0188	.0231	.0280	.0335	.0397	.0464	.0538	.0618	7
8	.0028	.0037	.0049	.0064	.0082	.0103	.0128	.0158	.0192	.0232	6
9	.0005	.0007	.0010	.0013	.0018	.0024	.0032	.0041	.0052	.0066	5
10	.0001	.0001	.0001	.0002	.0003	.0004	.0006	.0008	.0011	.0014	4
11	.0000	.0000	.0000	.0000	.0000	.0001	.0001	.0001	.0002	.0002	3
12	.0000	.0000	.0000	.0000	.0000	.0000	.0000	.0000	.0000	.0000	2
13	.0000	.0000	.0000	.0000	.0000	.0000	.0000	.0000	.0000	.0000	1
14	.0000	.0000	.0000	.0000	.0000	.0000	.0000	.0000	.0000	.0000	0
	q=.79	q=.78	q=.77	q=.76	q=.75	q=.74	q=.73	q=.72	q=.71	q=.70	

X1	P=.31	P=.32	P=.33	P=.34	P=.35	P=.36	P=.37	P=.38	P=.39	P=.40	n-X1
0	.0055	.0045	.0037	.0030	.0024	.0019	.0016	.0012	.0010	.0008	14
1	.0349	.0298	.0253	.0215	.0181	.0152	.0128	.0106	.0088	.0073	13
2	.1018	.0911	.0811	.0719	.0634	.0557	.0487	.0424	.0367	.0317	12
3	.1830	.1715	.1598	.1481	.1366	.1253	.1144	.1039	.0940	.0845	11
4	.2261	.2219	.2164	.2098	.2022	.1938	.1848	.1752	.1652	.1549	10
5	.2032	.2088	.2132	.2161	.2178	.2181	.2170	.2147	.2112	.2066	9
6	.1369	.1474	.1575	.1670	.1759	.1840	.1912	.1974	.2026	.2066	8
7	.0703	.0793	.0886	.0983	.1082	.1183	.1283	.1383	.1480	.1574	7
8	.0276	.0326	.0382	.0443	.0510	.0582	.0659	.0742	.0828	.0918	6
9	.0083	.0102	.0125	.0152	.0183	.0218	.0258	.0303	.0353	.0408	5
10	.0019	.0024	.0031	.0039	.0049	.0061	.0076	.0093	.0113	.0136	4
11	.0003	.0004	.0006	.0007	.0010	.0013	.0016	.0021	.0026	.0033	3
12	.0000	.0000	.0001	.0001	.0001	.0002	.0002	.0003	.0004	.0005	2
13	.0000	.0000	.0000	.0000	.0000	.0000	.0000	.0000	.0000	.0001	1
14	.0000	.0000	.0000	.0000	.0000	.0000	.0000	.0000	.0000	.0000	0
	q=.69	q=.68	q=.67	q=.66	q=.65	q=.64	q=.63	q=.62	q=.61	q=.60	

X1	P=.41	P=.42	P=.43	P=.44	P=.45	P=.46	P=.47	P=.48	P=.49	P=.50	n-X1
0	.0006	.0005	.0004	.0003	.0002	.0002	.0001	.0001	.0001	.0001	14
1	.0060	.0049	.0040	.0033	.0027	.0021	.0017	.0014	.0011	.0009	13
2	.0272	.0233	.0198	.0168	.0141	.0118	.0099	.0082	.0068	.0056	12
3	.0757	.0674	.0597	.0527	.0462	.0403	.0350	.0303	.0260	.0222	11
4	.1446	.1342	.1239	.1138	.1040	.0945	.0854	.0768	.0687	.0611	10
5	.2009	.1943	.1869	.1788	.1701	.1610	.1515	.1418	.1320	.1222	9
6	.2094	.2111	.2115	.2108	.2088	.2057	.2015	.1963	.1902	.1833	8
7	.1663	.1747	.1824	.1892	.1952	.2003	.2043	.2071	.2089	.2095	7
8	.1011	.1107	.1204	.1301	.1398	.1493	.1585	.1673	.1756	.1833	6
9	.0469	.0534	.0605	.0682	.0762	.0848	.0937	.1030	.1125	.1222	5
10	.0163	.0193	.0228	.0268	.0312	.0361	.0415	.0475	.0540	.0611	4
11	.0041	.0051	.0063	.0076	.0093	.0112	.0134	.0160	.0189	.0222	3
12	.0007	.0009	.0012	.0015	.0019	.0024	.0030	.0037	.0045	.0056	2
13	.0001	.0001	.0001	.0002	.0002	.0003	.0004	.0005	.0007	.0009	1
14	.0000	.0000	.0000	.0000	.0000	.0000	.0000	.0000	.0000	.0001	0
	q=.59	q=.58	q=.57	q=.56	q=.55	q=.54	q=.53	q=.52	q=.51	q=.50	

n = 15

X1	P=.01	P=.02	P=.03	P=.04	P=.05	P=.06	P=.07	P=.08	P=.09	P=.10	n-X1
0	.8601	.7386	.6333	.5421	.4633	.3953	.3367	.2863	.2430	.2059	15
1	.1303	.2261	.2938	.3388	.3658	.3785	.3801	.3734	.3605	.3432	14
2	.0092	.0323	.0636	.0988	.1348	.1691	.2003	.2273	.2496	.2669	13
3	.0004	.0029	.0085	.0178	.0307	.0468	.0653	.0857	.1070	.1285	12
4	.0000	.0002	.0008	.0022	.0049	.0090	.0148	.0223	.0317	.0428	11
5	.0000	.0000	.0001	.0002	.0006	.0013	.0024	.0043	.0069	.0105	10
6	.0000	.0000	.0000	.0000	.0000	.0001	.0003	.0006	.0011	.0019	9
7	.0000	.0000	.0000	.0000	.0000	.0000	.0000	.0001	.0001	.0003	8
	q=.99	q=.98	q=.97	q=.96	q=.95	q=.94	q=.93	q=.92	q=.91	q=.90	

X1	P=.11	P=.12	P=.13	P=.14	P=.15	P=.16	P=.17	P=.18	P=.19	P=.20	n-X1
0	.1741	.1470	.1238	.1041	.0874	.0731	.0611	.0510	.0424	.0352	15
1	.3228	.3006	.2775	.2542	.2312	.2090	.1878	.1678	.1492	.1319	14
2	.2793	.2870	.2903	.2897	.2856	.2787	.2692	.2578	.2449	.2309	13
3	.1496	.1696	.1880	.2044	.2184	.2300	.2389	.2452	.2489	.2501	12
4	.0555	.0694	.0843	.0998	.1156	.1314	.1468	.1615	.1752	.1876	11
5	.0151	.0208	.0277	.0357	.0449	.0551	.0662	.0780	.0904	.1032	10
6	.0031	.0047	.0069	.0097	.0132	.0175	.0226	.0285	.0353	.0430	9
7	.0005	.0008	.0013	.0020	.0030	.0043	.0059	.0081	.0107	.0138	8
8	.0001	.0001	.0002	.0003	.0005	.0008	.0012	.0018	.0025	.0035	7
9	.0000	.0000	.0000	.0000	.0001	.0001	.0002	.0003	.0005	.0007	6
10	.0000	.0000	.0000	.0000	.0000	.0000	.0000	.0000	.0001	.0001	5
	q=.89	q=.88	q=.87	q=.86	q=.85	q=.84	q=.83	q=.82	q=.81	q=.80	

X1	P=.21	P=.22	P=.23	P=.24	P=.25	P=.26	P=.27	P=.28	P=.29	P=.30	n-X1
0	.0291	.0241	.0198	.0163	.0134	.0109	.0089	.0072	.0059	.0047	15
1	.1162	.1018	.0889	.0772	.0668	.0576	.0494	.0423	.0360	.0305	14
2	.2162	.2010	.1858	.1707	.1559	.1416	.1280	.1150	.1029	.0916	13
3	.2490	.2457	.2405	.2336	.2252	.2156	.2051	.1939	.1821	.1700	12
4	.1986	.2079	.2155	.2213	.2252	.2273	.2276	.2262	.2231	.2186	11
5	.1161	.1290	.1416	.1537	.1651	.1757	.1852	.1935	.2005	.2061	10
6	.0514	.0606	.0705	.0809	.0917	.1029	.1142	.1254	.1365	.1472	9
7	.0176	.0220	.0271	.0329	.0393	.0465	.0543	.0627	.0717	.0811	8

X1											n-X1
8	.0047	.0062	.0081	.0104	.0131	.0163	.0201	.0244	.0293	.0348	7
9	.0010	.0014	.0019	.0025	.0034	.0045	.0058	.0074	.0093	.0116	6
10	.0002	.0002	.0003	.0005	.0007	.0009	.0013	.0017	.0023	.0030	5
11	.0000	.0000	.0000	.0001	.0001	.0002	.0002	.0003	.0004	.0006	4
12	.0000	.0000	.0000	.0000	.0000	.0000	.0000	.0000	.0001	.0001	3
	q=.79	q=.78	q=.77	q=.76	q=.75	q=.74	q=.73	q=.72	q=.71	q=.70	

X1	P=.31	P=.32	P=.33	P=.34	P=.35	P=.36	P=.37	P=.38	P=.39	P=.40	n-X1
0	.0038	.0031	.0025	.0020	.0016	.0012	.0010	.0008	.0006	.0005	15
1	.0258	.0217	.0182	.0152	.0126	.0104	.0086	.0071	.0058	.0047	14
2	.0811	.0715	.0627	.0547	.0476	.0411	.0354	.0303	.0259	.0219	13
3	.1579	.1457	.1338	.1222	.1110	.1002	.0901	.0805	.0716	.0634	12
4	.2128	.2057	.1977	.1888	.1792	.1692	.1587	.1481	.1374	.1268	11
5	.2103	.2130	.2142	.2140	.2123	.2093	.2051	.1997	.1933	.1859	10
6	.1575	.1671	.1759	.1837	.1906	.1963	.2008	.2040	.2059	.2066	9
7	.0910	.1011	.1114	.1217	.1319	.1419	.1516	.1608	.1693	.1771	8
8	.0409	.0476	.0549	.0627	.0710	.0798	.0890	.0985	.1082	.1181	7
9	.0143	.0174	.0210	.0251	.0298	.0349	.0407	.0470	.0538	.0612	6
10	.0038	.0049	.0062	.0078	.0096	.0118	.0143	.0173	.0206	.0245	5
11	.0008	.0011	.0014	.0018	.0024	.0030	.0038	.0048	.0060	.0074	4
12	.0001	.0002	.0002	.0003	.0004	.0006	.0007	.0010	.0013	.0016	3
13	.0000	.0000	.0000	.0000	.0001	.0001	.0001	.0001	.0002	.0003	2
	q=.69	q=.68	q=.67	q=.66	q=.65	q=.64	q=.63	q=.62	q=.61	q=.60	

X1	P=.41	P=.42	P=.43	P=.44	P=.45	P=.46	P=.47	P=.48	P=.49	P=.50	n-X1
0	.0004	.0003	.0002	.0002	.0001	.0001	.0001	.0001	.0000	.0000	15
1	.0038	.0031	.0025	.0020	.0016	.0012	.0010	.0008	.0006	.0005	14
2	.0185	.0156	.0130	.0108	.0090	.0074	.0060	.0049	.0040	.0032	13
3	.0558	.0489	.0426	.0369	.0318	.0272	.0232	.0197	.0166	.0139	12
4	.1163	.1061	.0963	.0869	.0780	.0696	.0617	.0545	.0478	.0417	11
5	.1778	.1691	.1598	.1502	.1404	.1304	.1204	.1106	.1010	.0916	10
6	.2060	.2041	.2010	.1967	.1914	.1851	.1780	.1702	.1617	.1527	9
7	.1840	.1900	.1949	.1987	.2013	.2028	.2030	.2020	.1997	.1964	8
8	.1279	.1376	.1470	.1561	.1647	.1727	.1800	.1864	.1919	.1964	7
9	.0691	.0775	.0863	.0954	.1048	.1144	.1241	.1338	.1434	.1527	6
10	.0288	.0337	.0390	.0450	.0515	.0585	.0661	.0741	.0827	.0916	5
11	.0091	.0111	.0134	.0161	.0191	.0226	.0266	.0311	.0361	.0417	4
12	.0021	.0027	.0034	.0042	.0052	.0064	.0079	.0096	.0116	.0139	3
13	.0003	.0004	.0006	.0008	.0010	.0013	.0016	.0020	.0026	.0032	2
14	.0000	.0000	.0001	.0001	.0001	.0002	.0002	.0003	.0004	.0005	1
15	.0000	.0000	.0000	.0000	.0000	.0000	.0000	.0000	.0000	.0000	0
	q=.59	q=.58	q=.57	q=.56	q=.55	q=.54	q=.53	q=.52	q=.51	q=.50	

n = 16

X1	P=.01	P=.02	P=.03	P=.04	P=.05	P=.06	P=.07	P=.08	P=.09	P=.10	n-X1
0	.8515	.7238	.6143	.5204	.4401	.3716	.3131	.2634	.2211	.1853	16
1	.1376	.2363	.3040	.3469	.3706	.3795	.3771	.3665	.3499	.3294	15
2	.0104	.0362	.0705	.1084	.1463	.1817	.2129	.2390	.2596	.2745	14
3	.0005	.0034	.0102	.0211	.0359	.0541	.0748	.0970	.1198	.1423	13
4	.0000	.0002	.0010	.0029	.0061	.0112	.0183	.0274	.0385	.0514	12
5	.0000	.0000	.0001	.0003	.0008	.0017	.0033	.0057	.0091	.0137	11
6	.0000	.0000	.0000	.0000	.0001	.0002	.0005	.0009	.0017	.0028	10
7	.0000	.0000	.0000	.0000	.0000	.0000	.0000	.0001	.0002	.0004	9
8	.0000	.0000	.0000	.0000	.0000	.0000	.0000	.0000	.0000	.0001	8
	q=.99	q=.98	q=.97	q=.96	q=.95	q=.94	q=.93	q=.92	q=.91	q=.90	

X1	P=.11	P=.12	P=.13	P=.14	P=.15	P=.16	P=.17	P=.18	P=.19	P=.20	n-X1
0	.1550	.1293	.1077	.0895	.0743	.0614	.0507	.0418	.0343	.0281	16
1	.3065	.2822	.2575	.2332	.2097	.1873	.1662	.1468	.1289	.1126	15
2	.2841	.2886	.2886	.2847	.2775	.2675	.2554	.2416	.2267	.2111	14
3	.1638	.1837	.2013	.2163	.2285	.2378	.2441	.2475	.2482	.2463	13
4	.0658	.0814	.0977	.1144	.1311	.1472	.1625	.1766	.1892	.2001	12
5	.0195	.0266	.0351	.0447	.0555	.0673	.0799	.0930	.1065	.1201	11
6	.0044	.0067	.0096	.0133	.0180	.0235	.0300	.0374	.0458	.0550	10
7	.0008	.0013	.0020	.0031	.0045	.0064	.0088	.0117	.0153	.0197	9
8	.0001	.0002	.0003	.0006	.0009	.0014	.0020	.0029	.0041	.0055	8
9	.0000	.0000	.0000	.0001	.0001	.0002	.0004	.0006	.0008	.0012	7
10	.0000	.0000	.0000	.0000	.0000	.0000	.0001	.0001	.0001	.0002	6
	q=.89	q=.88	q=.87	q=.86	q=.85	q=.84	q=.83	q=.82	q=.81	q=.80	

X1	P=.21	P=.22	P=.23	P=.24	P=.25	P=.26	P=.27	P=.28	P=.29	P=.30	n−X1
0	.0230	.0188	.0153	.0124	.0100	.0081	.0065	.0052	.0042	.0033	16
1	.0979	.0847	.0730	.0626	.0535	.0455	.0385	.0325	.0273	.0228	15
2	.1952	.1792	.1635	.1482	.1336	.1198	.1068	.0947	.0835	.0732	14
3	.2421	.2359	.2279	.2185	.2079	.1964	.1843	.1718	.1591	.1465	13
4	.2092	.2162	.2212	.2242	.2252	.2243	.2215	.2171	.2112	.2040	12
5	.1334	.1464	.1586	.1699	.1802	.1891	.1966	.2026	.2071	.2099	11
6	.0650	.0757	.0869	.0984	.1101	.1218	.1333	.1445	.1551	.1649	10
7	.0247	.0305	.0371	.0444	.0524	.0611	.0704	.0803	.0905	.1010	9
8	.0074	.0097	.0125	.0158	.0197	.0242	.0293	.0351	.0416	.0487	8
9	.0017	.0024	.0033	.0044	.0058	.0075	.0096	.0121	.0151	.0185	7
10	.0003	.0005	.0007	.0010	.0014	.0019	.0025	.0033	.0043	.0056	6
11	.0000	.0001	.0001	.0002	.0002	.0004	.0005	.0007	.0010	.0013	5
12	.0000	.0000	.0000	.0000	.0000	.0001	.0001	.0001	.0002	.0002	4
	q=.79	q=.78	q=.77	q=.76	q=.75	q=.74	q=.73	q=.72	q=.71	q=.70	

X1	P=.31	P=.32	P=.33	P=.34	P=.35	P=.36	P=.37	P=.38	P=.39	P=.40	n−X1
0	.0026	.0021	.0016	.0013	.0010	.0008	.0006	.0005	.0004	.0003	16
1	.0190	.0157	.0130	.0107	.0087	.0071	.0058	.0047	.0038	.0030	15
2	.0639	.0555	.0480	.0413	.0353	.0301	.0255	.0215	.0180	.0150	14
3	.1341	.1220	.1103	.0992	.0888	.0790	.0699	.0615	.0538	.0468	13
4	.1958	.1865	.1766	.1662	.1553	.1444	.1333	.1224	.1118	.1014	12
5	.2111	.2107	.2088	.2054	.2008	.1949	.1879	.1801	.1715	.1623	11
6	.1739	.1818	.1885	.1940	.1982	.2010	.2024	.2024	.2010	.1983	10
7	.1116	.1222	.1326	.1428	.1524	.1615	.1698	.1772	.1836	.1889	9
8	.0564	.0647	.0735	.0827	.0923	.1022	.1122	.1222	.1320	.1417	8
9	.0225	.0271	.0322	.0379	.0442	.0511	.0586	.0666	.0750	.0840	7
10	.0071	.0089	.0111	.0137	.0167	.0201	.0241	.0286	.0336	.0392	6
11	.0017	.0023	.0030	.0038	.0049	.0062	.0077	.0095	.0117	.0142	5
12	.0003	.0004	.0006	.0008	.0011	.0014	.0019	.0024	.0031	.0040	4
13	.0000	.0001	.0001	.0001	.0002	.0003	.0003	.0005	.0006	.0008	3
14	.0000	.0000	.0000	.0000	.0000	.0000	.0000	.0001	.0001	.0001	2
	q=.69	q=.68	q=.67	q=.66	q=.65	q=.64	q=.63	q=.62	q=.61	q=.60	

X1	P=.41	P=.42	P=.43	P=.44	P=.45	P=.46	P=.47	P=.48	P=.49	P=.50	n−X1
0	.0002	.0002	.0001	.0001	.0001	.0001	.0000	.0000	.0000	.0000	16
1	.0024	.0019	.0015	.0012	.0009	.0007	.0005	.0004	.0003	.0002	15
2	.0125	.0103	.0085	.0069	.0056	.0046	.0037	.0029	.0023	.0018	14
3	.0405	.0349	.0299	.0254	.0215	.0181	.0151	.0126	.0104	.0085	13
4	.0915	.0821	.0732	.0649	.0572	.0501	.0436	.0378	.0325	.0278	12
5	.1526	.1426	.1325	.1224	.1123	.1024	.0929	.0837	.0749	.0667	11
6	.1944	.1894	.1833	.1762	.1684	.1600	.1510	.1416	.1319	.1222	10
7	.1930	.1959	.1975	.1978	.1969	.1947	.1912	.1867	.1811	.1746	9
8	.1509	.1596	.1676	.1749	.1812	.1865	.1908	.1939	.1958	.1964	8
9	.0932	.1027	.1124	.1221	.1318	.1413	.1504	.1591	.1672	.1746	7
10	.0453	.0521	.0594	.0672	.0755	.0842	.0934	.1028	.1124	.1222	6
11	.0172	.0206	.0244	.0288	.0337	.0391	.0452	.0518	.0589	.0667	5
12	.0050	.0062	.0077	.0094	.0115	.0139	.0167	.0199	.0236	.0278	4
13	.0011	.0014	.0018	.0023	.0029	.0036	.0046	.0057	.0070	.0085	3
14	.0002	.0002	.0003	.0004	.0005	.0007	.0009	.0011	.0014	.0018	2
15	.0000	.0000	.0000	.0000	.0001	.0001	.0001	.0001	.0002	.0002	1
16	.0000	.0000	.0000	.0000	.0000	.0000	.0000	.0000	.0000	.0000	0
	q=.59	q=.58	q=.57	q=.56	q=.55	q=.54	q=.53	q=.52	q=.51	q=.50	

n = 17

X1	P=.01	P=.02	P=.03	P=.04	P=.05	P=.06	P=.07	P=.08	P=.09	P=.10	n−X1
0	.8429	.7093	.5958	.4996	.4181	.3493	.2912	.2423	.2012	.1668	17
1	.1447	.2461	.3133	.3539	.3741	.3790	.3726	.3582	.3383	.3150	16
2	.0117	.0402	.0775	.1180	.1575	.1935	.2244	.2492	.2677	.2800	15
3	.0006	.0041	.0120	.0246	.0415	.0618	.0844	.1083	.1324	.1556	14
4	.0000	.0003	.0013	.0036	.0076	.0138	.0222	.0330	.0458	.0605	13
5	.0000	.0000	.0001	.0004	.0010	.0023	.0044	.0075	.0118	.0175	12
6	.0000	.0000	.0000	.0000	.0001	.0003	.0007	.0013	.0023	.0039	11
7	.0000	.0000	.0000	.0000	.0000	.0000	.0001	.0002	.0004	.0007	10
8	.0000	.0000	.0000	.0000	.0000	.0000	.0000	.0000	.0000	.0001	9
	q=.99	q=.98	q=.97	q=.96	q=.95	q=.94	q=.93	q=.92	q=.91	q=.90	

X1	P=.11	P=.12	P=.13	P=.14	P=.15	P=.16	P=.17	P=.18	P=.19	P=.20	n−X1
0	.1379	.1138	.0937	.0770	.0631	.0516	.0421	.0343	.0278	.0225	17
1	.2898	.2638	.2381	.2131	.1893	.1671	.1466	.1279	.1109	.0957	16
2	.2865	.2878	.2846	.2775	.2673	.2547	.2402	.2245	.2081	.1914	15

X1											n−X1
3	.1771	.1963	.2126	.2259	.2359	.2425	.2460	.2464	.2441	.2393	14
4	.0766	.0937	.1112	.1287	.1457	.1617	.1764	.1893	.2004	.2093	13
5	.0246	.0332	.0432	.0545	.0668	.0801	.0939	.1081	.1222	.1361	12
6	.0061	.0091	.0129	.0177	.0236	.0305	.0385	.0474	.0573	.0680	11
7	.0012	.0019	.0030	.0045	.0065	.0091	.0124	.0164	.0211	.0267	10
8	.0002	.0003	.0006	.0009	.0014	.0022	.0032	.0045	.0062	.0084	9
9	.0000	.0000	.0001	.0002	.0003	.0004	.0006	.0010	.0015	.0021	8
10	.0000	.0000	.0000	.0000	.0000	.0001	.0001	.0002	.0003	.0004	7
11	.0000	.0000	.0000	.0000	.0000	.0000	.0000	.0000	.0000	.0001	6
	q=.89	q=.88	q=.87	q=.86	q=.85	q=.84	q=.83	q=.82	q=.81	q=.80	

X1	P=.21	P=.22	P=.23	P=.24	P=.25	P=.26	P=.27	P=.28	P=.29	P=.30	n−X1
0	.0182	.0146	.0118	.0094	.0075	.0060	.0047	.0038	.0030	.0023	17
1	.0822	.0702	.0597	.0505	.0426	.0357	.0299	.0248	.0206	.0169	16
2	.1747	.1584	.1427	.1277	.1136	.1005	.0883	.0772	.0672	.0581	15
3	.2322	.2234	.2131	.2016	.1893	.1765	.1634	.1502	.1372	.1245	14
4	.2161	.2205	.2228	.2228	.2209	.2170	.2115	.2044	.1961	.1868	13
5	.1493	.1617	.1730	.1830	.1914	.1982	.2033	.2067	.2083	.2081	12
6	.0794	.0912	.1034	.1156	.1276	.1393	.1504	.1608	.1701	.1784	11
7	.0332	.0404	.0485	.0573	.0668	.0769	.0874	.0982	.1092	.1201	10
8	.0110	.0143	.0181	.0226	.0279	.0338	.0404	.0478	.0558	.0644	9
9	.0029	.0040	.0054	.0071	.0093	.0119	.0150	.0186	.0228	.0276	8
10	.0006	.0009	.0013	.0018	.0025	.0033	.0044	.0058	.0074	.0095	7
11	.0001	.0002	.0002	.0004	.0005	.0007	.0010	.0014	.0019	.0026	6
12	.0000	.0000	.0000	.0001	.0001	.0001	.0002	.0003	.0004	.0006	5
13	.0000	.0000	.0000	.0000	.0000	.0000	.0000	.0000	.0001	.0001	4
	q=.79	q=.78	q=.77	q=.76	q=.75	q=.74	q=.73	q=.72	q=.71	q=.70	

X1	P=.31	P=.32	P=.33	P=.34	P=.35	P=.36	P=.37	P=.38	P=.39	P=.40	n−X1
0	.0018	.0014	.0011	.0009	.0007	.0005	.0004	.0003	.0002	.0002	17
1	.0139	.0114	.0093	.0075	.0060	.0048	.0039	.0031	.0024	.0019	16
2	.0500	.0428	.0364	.0309	.0260	.0218	.0182	.0151	.0125	.0102	15
3	.1123	.1007	.0898	.0795	.0701	.0614	.0534	.0463	.0398	.0341	14
4	.1766	.1659	.1547	.1434	.1320	.1208	.1099	.0993	.0892	.0796	13
5	.2063	.2030	.1982	.1921	.1849	.1767	.1677	.1582	.1482	.1379	12
6	.1854	.1910	.1952	.1979	.1991	.1988	.1970	.1939	.1895	.1839	11
7	.1309	.1413	.1511	.1602	.1685	.1757	.1818	.1868	.1904	.1927	10
8	.0735	.0831	.0930	.1032	.1134	.1235	.1335	.1431	.1521	.1606	9
9	.0330	.0391	.0458	.0531	.0611	.0695	.0784	.0877	.0973	.1070	8
10	.0119	.0147	.0181	.0219	.0263	.0313	.0368	.0430	.0498	.0571	7
11	.0034	.0044	.0057	.0072	.0090	.0112	.0138	.0168	.0202	.0242	6
12	.0008	.0010	.0014	.0018	.0024	.0031	.0040	.0051	.0065	.0081	5
13	.0001	.0002	.0003	.0004	.0005	.0007	.0009	.0012	.0016	.0021	4
14	.0000	.0000	.0000	.0001	.0001	.0001	.0002	.0002	.0003	.0004	3
15	.0000	.0000	.0000	.0000	.0000	.0000	.0000	.0000	.0000	.0001	2
	q=.69	q=.68	q=.67	q=.66	q=.65	q=.64	q=.63	q=.62	q=.61	q=.60	

X1	P=.41	P=.42	P=.43	P=.44	P=.45	P=.46	P=.47	P=.48	P=.49	P=.50	n−X1
0	.0001	.0001	.0001	.0001	.0000	.0000	.0000	.0000	.0000	.0000	17
1	.0015	.0012	.0009	.0007	.0005	.0004	.0003	.0002	.0002	.0001	16
2	.0084	.0068	.0055	.0044	.0035	.0028	.0022	.0017	.0013	.0010	15
3	.0290	.0246	.0207	.0173	.0144	.0119	.0097	.0079	.0064	.0052	14
4	.0706	.0622	.0546	.0475	.0411	.0354	.0302	.0257	.0217	.0182	13
5	.1276	.1172	.1070	.0971	.0875	.0784	.0697	.0616	.0541	.0472	12
6	.1773	.1697	.1614	.1525	.1432	.1335	.1237	.1138	.1040	.0944	11
7	.1936	.1932	.1914	.1883	.1841	.1787	.1723	.1650	.1570	.1484	10
8	.1682	.1748	.1805	.1850	.1883	.1903	.1910	.1904	.1886	.1855	9
9	.1169	.1266	.1361	.1453	.1540	.1621	.1694	.1758	.1812	.1855	8
10	.0650	.0733	.0822	.0914	.1008	.1105	.1202	.1298	.1393	.1484	7
11	.0287	.0338	.0394	.0457	.0525	.0599	.0678	.0763	.0851	.0944	6
12	.0100	.0122	.0149	.0179	.0215	.0255	.0301	.0352	.0409	.0472	5
13	.0027	.0034	.0043	.0054	.0068	.0084	.0103	.0125	.0151	.0182	4
14	.0005	.0007	.0009	.0012	.0016	.0020	.0026	.0033	.0041	.0052	3
15	.0001	.0001	.0001	.0002	.0003	.0003	.0005	.0006	.0008	.0010	2
16	.0000	.0000	.0000	.0000	.0000	.0000	.0001	.0001	.0001	.0001	1
17	.0000	.0000	.0000	.0000	.0000	.0000	.0000	.0000	.0000	.0000	0
	q=.59	q=.58	q=.57	q=.56	q=.55	q=.54	q=.53	q=.52	q=.51	q=.50	

n = 18

X1	P=.01	P=.02	P=.03	P=.04	P=.05	P=.06	P=.07	P=.08	P=.09	P=.10	n−X1
0	.8345	.6951	.5780	.4796	.3972	.3283	.2708	.2229	.1831	.1501	18
1	.1517	.2554	.3217	.3597	.3763	.3772	.3669	.3489	.3260	.3002	17

2	.0130	.0443	.0846	.1274	.1683	.2047	.2348	.2579	.2741	.2835	16
3	.0007	.0048	.0140	.0283	.0473	.0697	.0942	.1196	.1446	.1680	15
4	.0000	.0004	.0016	.0044	.0093	.0167	.0266	.0390	.0536	.0700	14
5	.0000	.0000	.0001	.0005	.0014	.0030	.0056	.0095	.0148	.0218	13
6	.0000	.0000	.0000	.0000	.0002	.0004	.0009	.0018	.0032	.0052	12
7	.0000	.0000	.0000	.0000	.0000	.0000	.0001	.0003	.0005	.0010	11
8	.0000	.0000	.0000	.0000	.0000	.0000	.0000	.0000	.0001	.0002	10
	q=.99	q=.98	q=.97	q=.96	q=.95	q=.94	q=.93	q=.92	q=.91	q=.90	

X1	P=.11	P=.12	P=.13	P=.14	P=.15	P=.16	P=.17	P=.18	P=.19	P=.20	n-X1
0	.1227	.1002	.0815	.0662	.0536	.0434	.0349	.0281	.0225	.0180	18
1	.2731	.2458	.2193	.1940	.1704	.1486	.1288	.1110	.0951	.0811	17
2	.2869	.2850	.2785	.2685	.2556	.2407	.2243	.2071	.1897	.1723	16
3	.1891	.2072	.2220	.2331	.2406	.2445	.2450	.2425	.2373	.2297	15
4	.0877	.1060	.1244	.1423	.1592	.1746	.1882	.1996	.2087	.2153	14
5	.0303	.0405	.0520	.0649	.0787	.0931	.1079	.1227	.1371	.1507	13
6	.0081	.0120	.0168	.0229	.0301	.0384	.0479	.0584	.0697	.0816	12
7	.0017	.0028	.0043	.0064	.0091	.0126	.0168	.0220	.0280	.0350	11
8	.0003	.0005	.0009	.0014	.0022	.0033	.0047	.0066	.0090	.0120	10
9	.0000	.0001	.0001	.0003	.0004	.0007	.0011	.0016	.0024	.0033	9
10	.0000	.0000	.0000	.0000	.0001	.0001	.0002	.0003	.0005	.0008	8
11	.0000	.0000	.0000	.0000	.0000	.0000	.0000	.0001	.0001	.0001	7
	q=.89	q=.88	q=.87	q=.86	q=.85	q=.84	q=.83	q=.82	q=.81	q=.80	

X1	P=.21	P=.22	P=.23	P=.24	P=.25	P=.26	P=.27	P=.28	P=.29	P=.30	n-X1
0	.0144	.0114	.0091	.0072	.0056	.0044	.0035	.0027	.0021	.0016	18
1	.0687	.0580	.0487	.0407	.0338	.0280	.0231	.0189	.0155	.0126	17
2	.1553	.1390	.1236	.1092	.0958	.0836	.0725	.0626	.0537	.0458	16
3	.2202	.2091	.1969	.1839	.1704	.1567	.1431	.1298	.1169	.1046	15
4	.2195	.2212	.2205	.2177	.2130	.2065	.1985	.1892	.1790	.1681	14
5	.1634	.1747	.1845	.1925	.1988	.2031	.2055	.2061	.2048	.2017	13
6	.0941	.1067	.1194	.1317	.1436	.1546	.1647	.1736	.1812	.1873	12
7	.0429	.0516	.0611	.0713	.0820	.0931	.1044	.1157	.1269	.1376	11
8	.0157	.0200	.0251	.0310	.0376	.0450	.0531	.0619	.0713	.0811	10
9	.0046	.0063	.0083	.0109	.0139	.0176	.0218	.0267	.0323	.0386	9
10	.0011	.0016	.0022	.0031	.0042	.0056	.0073	.0094	.0119	.0149	8
11	.0002	.0003	.0005	.0007	.0010	.0014	.0020	.0026	.0035	.0046	7
12	.0000	.0001	.0001	.0001	.0002	.0003	.0004	.0006	.0008	.0012	6
13	.0000	.0000	.0000	.0000	.0000	.0000	.0001	.0001	.0002	.0002	5
	q=.79	q=.78	q=.77	q=.76	q=.75	q=.74	q=.73	q=.72	q=.71	q=.70	

X1	P=.31	P=.32	P=.33	P=.34	P=.35	P=.36	P=.37	P=.38	P=.39	P=.40	n-X1
0	.0013	.0010	.0007	.0006	.0004	.0003	.0002	.0002	.0001	.0001	18
1	.0102	.0082	.0066	.0052	.0042	.0033	.0026	.0020	.0016	.0012	17
2	.0388	.0327	.0275	.0229	.0190	.0157	.0129	.0105	.0086	.0069	16
3	.0930	.0822	.0722	.0630	.0547	.0471	.0404	.0344	.0292	.0246	15
4	.1567	.1450	.1333	.1217	.1104	.0994	.0890	.0791	.0699	.0614	14
5	.1971	.1911	.1838	.1755	.1664	.1566	.1463	.1358	.1252	.1146	13
6	.1919	.1948	.1962	.1959	.1941	.1908	.1862	.1803	.1734	.1655	12
7	.1478	.1572	.1656	.1730	.1792	.1840	.1875	.1895	.1900	.1892	11
8	.0913	.1017	.1122	.1226	.1327	.1423	.1514	.1597	.1671	.1734	10
9	.0456	.0532	.0614	.0701	.0794	.0890	.0988	.1087	.1187	.1284	9
10	.0184	.0225	.0272	.0325	.0385	.0450	.0522	.0600	.0683	.0771	8
11	.0060	.0077	.0097	.0122	.0151	.0184	.0223	.0267	.0318	.0374	7
12	.0016	.0021	.0028	.0037	.0047	.0060	.0076	.0096	.0118	.0145	6
13	.0003	.0005	.0006	.0009	.0012	.0016	.0021	.0027	.0035	.0045	5
14	.0001	.0001	.0001	.0002	.0002	.0003	.0004	.0006	.0008	.0011	4
15	.0000	.0000	.0000	.0000	.0000	.0000	.0001	.0001	.0001	.0002	3
	q=.69	q=.68	q=.67	q=.66	q=.65	q=.64	q=.63	q=.62	q=.61	q=.60	

X1	P=.41	P=.42	P=.43	P=.44	P=.45	P=.46	P=.47	P=.48	P=.49	P=.50	n-X1
0	.0001	.0001	.0000	.0000	.0000	.0000	.0000	.0000	.0000	.0000	18
1	.0009	.0007	.0005	.0004	.0003	.0002	.0002	.0001	.0001	.0001	17
2	.0055	.0044	.0035	.0028	.0022	.0017	.0013	.0010	.0008	.0006	16
3	.0206	.0171	.0141	.0116	.0095	.0077	.0062	.0050	.0039	.0031	15
4	.0536	.0464	.0400	.0342	.0291	.0246	.0206	.0172	.0142	.0117	14
5	.1042	.0941	.0844	.0753	.0666	.0586	.0512	.0444	.0382	.0327	13
6	.1569	.1477	.1380	.1281	.1181	.1081	.0983	.0887	.0796	.0708	12
7	.1869	.1833	.1785	.1726	.1657	.1579	.1494	.1404	.1310	.1214	11
8	.1786	.1825	.1852	.1864	.1864	.1850	.1822	.1782	.1731	.1669	10
9	.1379	.1469	.1552	.1628	.1694	.1751	.1795	.1828	.1848	.1855	9
10	.0862	.0957	.1054	.1151	.1248	.1342	.1433	.1519	.1598	.1669	8
11	.0436	.0504	.0578	.0658	.0742	.0831	.0924	.1020	.1117	.1214	7
12	.0177	.0213	.0254	.0301	.0354	.0413	.0478	.0549	.0626	.0708	6

X1											n-X1
13	.0057	.0071	.0089	.0109	.0134	.0162	.0196	.0234	.0278	.0327	5
14	.0014	.0018	.0024	.0031	.0039	.0049	.0062	.0077	.0095	.0117	4
15	.0003	.0004	.0005	.0006	.0009	.0011	.0015	.0019	.0024	.0031	3
16	.0000	.0000	.0001	.0001	.0001	.0002	.0002	.0003	.0004	.0006	2
17	.0000	.0000	.0000	.0000	.0000	.0000	.0000	.0000	.0000	.0001	1
18	.0000	.0000	.0000	.0000	.0000	.0000	.0000	.0000	.0000	.0000	0
	q=.59	q=.58	q=.57	q=.56	q=.55	q=.54	q=.53	q=.52	q=.51	q=.50	

n = 19

X1	P=.01	P=.02	P=.03	P=.04	P=.05	P=.06	P=.07	P=.08	P=.09	P=.10	n-X1
0	.8262	.6812	.5606	.4604	.3774	.3086	.2519	.2051	.1666	.1351	19
1	.1586	.2642	.3294	.3645	.3774	.3743	.3602	.3389	.3131	.2852	18
2	.0144	.0485	.0917	.1367	.1787	.2150	.2440	.2652	.2787	.2852	17
3	.0008	.0056	.0161	.0323	.0533	.0778	.1041	.1307	.1562	.1796	16
4	.0000	.0005	.0020	.0054	.0112	.0199	.0313	.0455	.0618	.0798	15
5	.0000	.0000	.0002	.0007	.0018	.0038	.0071	.0119	.0183	.0266	14
6	.0000	.0000	.0000	.0001	.0002	.0006	.0012	.0024	.0042	.0069	13
7	.0000	.0000	.0000	.0000	.0000	.0001	.0002	.0004	.0008	.0014	12
8	.0000	.0000	.0000	.0000	.0000	.0000	.0000	.0001	.0001	.0002	11
	q=.99	q=.98	q=.97	q=.96	q=.95	q=.94	q=.93	q=.92	q=.91	q=.90	

X1	P=.11	P=.12	P=.13	P=.14	P=.15	P=.16	P=.17	P=.18	P=.19	P=.20	n-X1
0	.1092	.0881	.0709	.0569	.0456	.0364	.0290	.0230	.0182	.0144	19
1	.2565	.2284	.2014	.1761	.1529	.1318	.1129	.0961	.0813	.0685	18
2	.2854	.2803	.2708	.2581	.2428	.2259	.2081	.1898	.1717	.1540	17
3	.1999	.2166	.2293	.2381	.2428	.2439	.2415	.2361	.2282	.2182	16
4	.0988	.1181	.1371	.1550	.1714	.1858	.1979	.2073	.2141	.2182	15
5	.0366	.0483	.0614	.0757	.0907	.1062	.1216	.1365	.1507	.1636	14
6	.0106	.0154	.0214	.0288	.0374	.0472	.0581	.0699	.0825	.0955	13
7	.0024	.0039	.0059	.0087	.0122	.0167	.0221	.0285	.0359	.0443	12
8	.0004	.0008	.0013	.0021	.0032	.0048	.0068	.0094	.0126	.0166	11
9	.0001	.0001	.0002	.0004	.0007	.0011	.0017	.0025	.0036	.0051	10
10	.0000	.0000	.0000	.0001	.0001	.0002	.0003	.0006	.0009	.0013	9
11	.0000	.0000	.0000	.0000	.0000	.0000	.0001	.0001	.0002	.0003	8
	q=.89	q=.88	q=.87	q=.86	q=.85	q=.84	q=.83	q=.82	q=.81	q=.80	

X1	P=.21	P=.22	P=.23	P=.24	P=.25	P=.26	P=.27	P=.28	P=.29	P=.30	n-X1
0	.0113	.0089	.0070	.0054	.0042	.0033	.0025	.0019	.0015	.0011	19
1	.0573	.0477	.0396	.0326	.0268	.0219	.0178	.0144	.0116	.0093	18
2	.1371	.1212	.1064	.0927	.0803	.0692	.0592	.0503	.0426	.0358	17
3	.2065	.1937	.1800	.1659	.1517	.1377	.1240	.1109	.0985	.0869	16
4	.2196	.2185	.2151	.2096	.2023	.1935	.1835	.1726	.1610	.1491	15
5	.1751	.1849	.1928	.1986	.2023	.2040	.2036	.2013	.1973	.1916	14
6	.1086	.1217	.1343	.1463	.1574	.1672	.1757	.1827	.1880	.1916	13
7	.0536	.0637	.0745	.0858	.0974	.1091	.1207	.1320	.1426	.1525	12
8	.0214	.0270	.0334	.0406	.0487	.0575	.0670	.0770	.0874	.0981	11
9	.0069	.0093	.0122	.0157	.0198	.0247	.0303	.0366	.0436	.0514	10
10	.0018	.0026	.0036	.0050	.0066	.0087	.0112	.0142	.0178	.0220	9
11	.0004	.0006	.0009	.0013	.0018	.0025	.0034	.0045	.0060	.0077	8
12	.0001	.0001	.0002	.0003	.0004	.0006	.0008	.0012	.0016	.0022	7
13	.0000	.0000	.0000	.0000	.0001	.0001	.0002	.0002	.0004	.0005	6
14	.0000	.0000	.0000	.0000	.0000	.0000	.0000	.0000	.0001	.0001	5
	q=.79	q=.78	q=.77	q=.76	q=.75	q=.74	q=.73	q=.72	q=.71	q=.70	

X1	P=.31	P=.32	P=.33	P=.34	P=.35	P=.36	P=.37	P=.38	P=.39	P=.40	n-X1
0	.0009	.0007	.0005	.0004	.0003	.0002	.0002	.0001	.0001	.0001	19
1	.0074	.0059	.0046	.0036	.0029	.0022	.0017	.0013	.0010	.0008	18
2	.0299	.0249	.0206	.0169	.0138	.0112	.0091	.0073	.0058	.0046	17
3	.0762	.0664	.0574	.0494	.0422	.0358	.0302	.0253	.0211	.0175	16
4	.1370	.1249	.1131	.1017	.0909	.0806	.0710	.0621	.0540	.0467	15
5	.1846	.1764	.1672	.1572	.1468	.1360	.1251	.1143	.1036	.0933	14
6	.1935	.1936	.1921	.1890	.1844	.1785	.1714	.1634	.1546	.1451	13
7	.1615	.1692	.1757	.1808	.1844	.1865	.1870	.1860	.1835	.1797	12
8	.1088	.1195	.1298	.1397	.1489	.1573	.1647	.1710	.1760	.1797	11
9	.0597	.0687	.0782	.0880	.0980	.1082	.1182	.1281	.1375	.1464	10
10	.0268	.0323	.0385	.0453	.0528	.0608	.0694	.0785	.0879	.0976	9
11	.0099	.0124	.0155	.0191	.0233	.0280	.0334	.0394	.0460	.0532	8
12	.0030	.0039	.0051	.0066	.0083	.0105	.0131	.0161	.0196	.0237	7
13	.0007	.0010	.0014	.0018	.0024	.0032	.0041	.0053	.0067	.0085	6
14	.0001	.0002	.0003	.0004	.0006	.0008	.0010	.0014	.0018	.0024	5
15	.0000	.0000	.0000	.0001	.0001	.0001	.0002	.0003	.0004	.0005	4
16	.0000	.0000	.0000	.0000	.0000	.0000	.0000	.0000	.0001	.0001	3
	q=.69	q=.68	q=.67	q=.66	q=.65	q=.64	q=.63	q=.62	q=.61	q=.60	

X1	P=.41	P=.42	P=.43	P=.44	P=.45	P=.46	P=.47	P=.48	P=.49	P=.50	n-X1
0	.0000	.0000	.0000	.0000	.0000	.0000	.0000	.0000	.0000	.0000	19
1	.0006	.0004	.0003	.0002	.0002	.0001	.0001	.0001	.0001	.0000	18
2	.0037	.0029	.0022	.0017	.0013	.0010	.0008	.0006	.0004	.0003	17
3	.0144	.0118	.0096	.0077	.0062	.0049	.0039	.0031	.0024	.0018	16
4	.0400	.0341	.0289	.0243	.0203	.0168	.0138	.0113	.0092	.0074	15
5	.0834	.0741	.0653	.0572	.0497	.0429	.0368	.0313	.0265	.0222	14
6	.1353	.1252	.1150	.1049	.0949	.0853	.0761	.0674	.0593	.0518	13
7	.1746	.1683	.1611	.1530	.1443	.1350	.1254	.1156	.1058	.0961	12
8	.1820	.1829	.1823	.1803	.1771	.1725	.1668	.1601	.1525	.1442	11
9	.1546	.1618	.1681	.1732	.1771	.1796	.1808	.1806	.1791	.1762	10
10	.1074	.1172	.1268	.1361	.1449	.1530	.1603	.1667	.1721	.1762	9
11	.0611	.0694	.0783	.0875	.0970	.1066	.1163	.1259	.1352	.1442	8
12	.0283	.0335	.0394	.0458	.0529	.0606	.0688	.0775	.0866	.0961	7
13	.0106	.0131	.0160	.0194	.0233	.0278	.0328	.0385	.0448	.0518	6
14	.0032	.0041	.0052	.0065	.0082	.0101	.0125	.0152	.0185	.0222	5
15	.0007	.0010	.0013	.0017	.0022	.0029	.0037	.0047	.0059	.0074	4
16	.0001	.0002	.0002	.0003	.0005	.0006	.0008	.0011	.0014	.0018	3
17	.0000	.0000	.0000	.0000	.0001	.0001	.0001	.0002	.0002	.0003	2
	q=.59	q=.58	q=.57	q=.56	q=.55	q=.54	q=.53	q=.52	q=.51	q=.50	

n = 20

X1	P=.01	P=.02	P=.03	P=.04	P=.05	P=.06	P=.07	P=.08	P=.09	P=.10	n-X1
0	.8179	.6676	.5438	.4420	.3585	.2901	.2342	.1887	.1516	.1216	20
1	.1652	.2725	.3364	.3683	.3774	.3703	.3526	.3282	.3000	.2702	19
2	.0159	.0528	.0988	.1458	.1887	.2246	.2521	.2711	.2818	.2852	18
3	.0010	.0065	.0183	.0364	.0596	.0860	.1139	.1414	.1672	.1901	17
4	.0000	.0006	.0024	.0065	.0133	.0233	.0364	.0523	.0703	.0898	16
5	.0000	.0000	.0002	.0009	.0022	.0048	.0088	.0145	.0222	.0319	15
6	.0000	.0000	.0000	.0001	.0003	.0008	.0017	.0032	.0055	.0089	14
7	.0000	.0000	.0000	.0000	.0000	.0001	.0002	.0005	.0011	.0020	13
8	.0000	.0000	.0000	.0000	.0000	.0000	.0000	.0001	.0002	.0004	12
9	.0000	.0000	.0000	.0000	.0000	.0000	.0000	.0000	.0000	.0001	11
	q=.99	q=.98	q=.97	q=.96	q=.95	q=.94	q=.93	q=.92	q=.91	q=.90	

X1	P=.11	P=.12	P=.13	P=.14	P=.15	P=.16	P=.17	P=.18	P=.19	P=.20	n-X1
0	.0972	.0776	.0617	.0490	.0388	.0306	.0241	.0189	.0148	.0115	20
1	.2403	.2115	.1844	.1595	.1368	.1165	.0986	.0829	.0693	.0576	19
2	.2822	.2740	.2618	.2466	.2293	.2109	.1919	.1730	.1545	.1369	18
3	.2093	.2242	.2347	.2409	.2428	.2410	.2358	.2278	.2175	.2054	17
4	.1099	.1299	.1491	.1666	.1821	.1951	.2053	.2125	.2168	.2182	16
5	.0435	.0567	.0713	.0868	.1028	.1189	.1345	.1493	.1627	.1746	15
6	.0134	.0193	.0266	.0353	.0454	.0566	.0689	.0819	.0954	.1091	14
7	.0033	.0053	.0080	.0115	.0160	.0216	.0282	.0360	.0448	.0545	13
8	.0007	.0012	.0019	.0030	.0046	.0067	.0094	.0128	.0171	.0222	12
9	.0001	.0002	.0004	.0007	.0011	.0017	.0026	.0038	.0053	.0074	11
10	.0000	.0000	.0001	.0001	.0002	.0004	.0006	.0009	.0014	.0020	10
11	.0000	.0000	.0000	.0000	.0000	.0001	.0001	.0002	.0003	.0005	9
12	.0000	.0000	.0000	.0000	.0000	.0000	.0000	.0000	.0001	.0001	8
	q=.89	q=.88	q=.87	q=.86	q=.85	q=.84	q=.83	q=.82	q=.81	q=.80	

X1	P=.21	P=.22	P=.23	P=.24	P=.25	P=.26	P=.27	P=.28	P=.29	P=.30	n-X1
0	.0090	.0069	.0054	.0041	.0032	.0024	.0018	.0014	.0011	.0008	20
1	.0477	.0392	.0321	.0261	.0211	.0170	.0137	.0109	.0087	.0068	19
2	.1204	.1050	.0910	.0783	.0669	.0569	.0480	.0403	.0336	.0278	18
3	.1920	.1777	.1631	.1484	.1339	.1199	.1065	.0940	.0823	.0716	17
4	.2169	.2131	.2070	.1991	.1897	.1790	.1675	.1553	.1429	.1304	16
5	.1845	.1923	.1979	.2012	.2023	.2013	.1982	.1933	.1868	.1789	15
6	.1226	.1356	.1478	.1589	.1686	.1768	.1833	.1879	.1907	.1916	14
7	.0652	.0765	.0883	.1003	.1124	.1242	.1356	.1462	.1558	.1643	13
8	.0282	.0351	.0429	.0515	.0609	.0709	.0815	.0924	.1034	.1144	12
9	.0100	.0132	.0171	.0217	.0271	.0332	.0402	.0479	.0563	.0654	11
10	.0029	.0041	.0056	.0075	.0099	.0128	.0163	.0205	.0253	.0308	10
11	.0007	.0010	.0015	.0022	.0030	.0041	.0055	.0072	.0094	.0120	9
12	.0001	.0002	.0003	.0005	.0008	.0011	.0015	.0021	.0029	.0039	8
13	.0000	.0000	.0001	.0001	.0002	.0002	.0003	.0005	.0007	.0010	7
14	.0000	.0000	.0000	.0000	.0000	.0000	.0001	.0001	.0001	.0002	6
	q=.79	q=.78	q=.77	q=.76	q=.75	q=.74	q=.73	q=.72	q=.71	q=.70	

X1	P=.31	P=.32	P=.33	P=.34	P=.35	P=.36	P=.37	P=.38	P=.39	P=.40	n−X1
0	.0006	.0004	.0003	.0002	.0002	.0001	.0001	.0001	.0001	.0000	20
1	.0054	.0042	.0033	.0025	.0020	.0015	.0011	.0009	.0007	.0005	19
2	.0229	.0188	.0153	.0124	.0100	.0080	.0064	.0050	.0040	.0031	18
3	.0619	.0531	.0453	.0383	.0323	.0270	.0224	.0185	.0152	.0123	17
4	.1181	.1062	.0947	.0839	.0738	.0645	.0559	.0482	.0412	.0350	16
5	.1698	.1599	.1493	.1384	.1272	.1161	.1051	.0945	.0843	.0746	15
6	.1907	.1881	.1839	.1782	.1712	.1632	.1543	.1447	.1347	.1244	14
7	.1714	.1770	.1811	.1836	.1844	.1836	.1812	.1774	.1722	.1659	13
8	.1251	.1354	.1450	.1537	.1614	.1678	.1730	.1767	.1790	.1797	12
9	.0750	.0849	.0952	.1056	.1158	.1259	.1354	.1444	.1526	.1597	11
10	.0370	.0440	.0516	.0598	.0686	.0779	.0875	.0974	.1073	.1171	10
11	.0151	.0188	.0231	.0280	.0336	.0398	.0467	.0542	.0624	.0710	9
12	.0051	.0066	.0085	.0108	.0136	.0168	.0206	.0249	.0299	.0355	8
13	.0014	.0019	.0026	.0034	.0045	.0058	.0074	.0094	.0118	.0146	7
14	.0003	.0005	.0006	.0009	.0012	.0016	.0022	.0029	.0038	.0049	6
15	.0001	.0001	.0001	.0002	.0003	.0004	.0005	.0007	.0010	.0013	5
16	.0000	.0000	.0000	.0000	.0000	.0001	.0001	.0001	.0002	.0003	4
	q=.69	q=.68	q=.67	q=.66	q=.65	q=.64	q=.63	q=.62	q=.61	q=.60	

X1	P=.41	P=.42	P=.43	P=.44	P=.45	P=.46	P=.47	P=.48	P=.49	P=.50	n−X1
0	.0000	.0000	.0000	.0000	.0000	.0000	.0000	.0000	.0000	.0000	20
1	.0004	.0003	.0002	.0001	.0001	.0001	.0001	.0000	.0000	.0000	19
2	.0024	.0018	.0014	.0011	.0008	.0006	.0005	.0003	.0002	.0002	18
3	.0100	.0080	.0064	.0051	.0040	.0031	.0024	.0019	.0014	.0011	17
4	.0295	.0247	.0206	.0170	.0139	.0113	.0092	.0074	.0059	.0046	16
5	.0656	.0573	.0496	.0427	.0365	.0309	.0260	.0217	.0180	.0148	15
6	.1140	.1037	.0936	.0839	.0746	.0658	.0577	.0501	.0432	.0370	14
7	.1585	.1502	.1413	.1318	.1221	.1122	.1023	.0925	.0830	.0739	13
8	.1790	.1768	.1732	.1683	.1623	.1553	.1474	.1388	.1296	.1201	12
9	.1658	.1707	.1742	.1763	.1771	.1763	.1742	.1708	.1661	.1602	11
10	.1268	.1359	.1446	.1524	.1593	.1652	.1700	.1734	.1755	.1762	10
11	.0801	.0895	.0991	.1089	.1185	.1280	.1370	.1455	.1533	.1602	9
12	.0417	.0486	.0561	.0642	.0727	.0818	.0911	.1007	.1105	.1201	8
13	.0178	.0217	.0260	.0310	.0366	.0429	.0497	.0572	.0653	.0739	7
14	.0062	.0078	.0098	.0122	.0150	.0183	.0221	.0264	.0314	.0370	6
15	.0017	.0023	.0030	.0038	.0049	.0062	.0078	.0098	.0121	.0148	5
16	.0004	.0005	.0007	.0009	.0013	.0017	.0022	.0028	.0036	.0046	4
17	.0001	.0001	.0001	.0002	.0002	.0003	.0005	.0006	.0008	.0011	3
18	.0000	.0000	.0000	.0000	.0000	.0000	.0001	.0001	.0001	.0002	2
	q=.59	q=.58	q=.57	q=.56	q=.55	q=.54	q=.53	q=.52	q=.51	q=.50	

n = 25

X1	P=.01	P=.02	P=.03	P=.04	P=.05	P=.06	P=.07	P=.08	P=.09	P=.10	n−X1
0	.7778	.6035	.4670	.3604	.2774	.2129	.1630	.1244	.0946	.0718	25
1	.1964	.3079	.3611	.3754	.3650	.3398	.3066	.2704	.2340	.1994	24
2	.0238	.0754	.1340	.1877	.2305	.2602	.2770	.2821	.2777	.2659	23
3	.0018	.0118	.0318	.0600	.0930	.1273	.1598	.1881	.2106	.2265	22
4	.0001	.0013	.0054	.0137	.0269	.0447	.0662	.0899	.1145	.1384	21
5	.0000	.0001	.0007	.0024	.0060	.0120	.0209	.0329	.0476	.0646	20
6	.0000	.0000	.0001	.0003	.0010	.0026	.0052	.0095	.0157	.0239	19
7	.0000	.0000	.0000	.0000	.0001	.0004	.0011	.0022	.0042	.0072	18
8	.0000	.0000	.0000	.0000	.0000	.0001	.0002	.0004	.0009	.0018	17
9	.0000	.0000	.0000	.0000	.0000	.0000	.0000	.0001	.0002	.0004	16
10	.0000	.0000	.0000	.0000	.0000	.0000	.0000	.0000	.0000	.0001	15
	q=.99	q=.98	q=.97	q=.96	q=.95	q=.94	q=.93	q=.92	q=.91	q=.90	

X1	P=.11	P=.12	P=.13	P=.14	P=.15	P=.16	P=.17	P=.18	P=.19	P=.20	n−X1
0	.0543	.0409	.0308	.0230	.0172	.0128	.0095	.0070	.0052	.0038	25
1	.1678	.1395	.1149	.0938	.0759	.0609	.0486	.0384	.0302	.0236	24
2	.2488	.2283	.2060	.1832	.1607	.1392	.1193	.1012	.0851	.0708	23
3	.2358	.2387	.2360	.2286	.2174	.2033	.1874	.1704	.1530	.1358	22
4	.1603	.1790	.1940	.2047	.2110	.2130	.2111	.2057	.1974	.1867	21
5	.0832	.1025	.1217	.1399	.1564	.1704	.1816	.1897	.1945	.1960	20
6	.0343	.0466	.0606	.0759	.0920	.1082	.1240	.1388	.1520	.1633	19
7	.0115	.0173	.0246	.0336	.0441	.0559	.0689	.0827	.0968	.1108	18
8	.0032	.0053	.0083	.0123	.0175	.0240	.0318	.0408	.0511	.0623	17
9	.0007	.0014	.0023	.0038	.0058	.0086	.0123	.0169	.0226	.0294	16
10	.0001	.0003	.0006	.0010	.0016	.0026	.0040	.0059	.0085	.0118	15
11	.0000	.0001	.0001	.0002	.0004	.0007	.0011	.0018	.0027	.0040	14
12	.0000	.0000	.0000	.0000	.0001	.0002	.0003	.0005	.0007	.0012	13
13	.0000	.0000	.0000	.0000	.0000	.0000	.0001	.0001	.0002	.0003	12
14	.0000	.0000	.0000	.0000	.0000	.0000	.0000	.0000	.0000	.0001	11
	q=.89	q=.88	q=.87	q=.86	q=.85	q=.84	q=.83	q=.82	q=.81	q=.80	

X1	P=.21	P=.22	P=.23	P=.24	P=.25	P=.26	P=.27	P=.28	P=.29	P=.30	n−X1
0	.0028	.0020	.0015	.0010	.0008	.0005	.0004	.0003	.0002	.0001	25
1	.0183	.0141	.0109	.0083	.0063	.0047	.0035	.0026	.0020	.0014	24
2	.0585	.0479	.0389	.0314	.0251	.0199	.0157	.0123	.0096	.0074	23
3	.1192	.1035	.0891	.0759	.0641	.0537	.0446	.0367	.0300	.0243	22
4	.1742	.1606	.1463	.1318	.1175	.1037	.0906	.0785	.0673	.0572	21
5	.1945	.1903	.1836	.1749	.1645	.1531	.1408	.1282	.1155	.1030	20
6	.1724	.1789	.1828	.1841	.1828	.1793	.1736	.1661	.1572	.1472	19
7	.1244	.1369	.1482	.1578	.1654	.1709	.1743	.1754	.1743	.1712	18
8	.0744	.0869	.0996	.1121	.1241	.1351	.1450	.1535	.1602	.1651	17
9	.0373	.0463	.0562	.0669	.0781	.0897	.1013	.1127	.1236	.1336	16
10	.0159	.0209	.0269	.0338	.0417	.0504	.0600	.0701	.0808	.0916	15
11	.0058	.0080	.0109	.0145	.0189	.0242	.0302	.0372	.0450	.0536	14
12	.0018	.0026	.0038	.0054	.0074	.0099	.0130	.0169	.0214	.0268	13
13	.0005	.0007	.0011	.0017	.0025	.0035	.0048	.0066	.0088	.0115	12
14	.0001	.0002	.0003	.0005	.0007	.0010	.0015	.0022	.0031	.0042	11
15	.0000	.0000	.0001	.0001	.0002	.0003	.0004	.0006	.0009	.0013	10
16	.0000	.0000	.0000	.0000	.0000	.0001	.0001	.0002	.0002	.0004	9
17	.0000	.0000	.0000	.0000	.0000	.0000	.0000	.0000	.0001	.0001	8
	q=.79	q=.78	q=.77	q=.76	q=.75	q=.74	q=.73	q=.72	q=.71	q=.70	

X1	P=.31	P=.32	P=.33	P=.34	P=.35	P=.36	P=.37	P=.38	P=.39	P=.40	n−X1
0	.0001	.0001	.0000	.0000	.0000	.0000	.0000	.0000	.0000	.0000	25
1	.0011	.0008	.0006	.0004	.0003	.0002	.0001	.0001	.0001	.0000	24
2	.0057	.0043	.0033	.0025	.0018	.0014	.0010	.0007	.0005	.0004	23
3	.0195	.0156	.0123	.0097	.0076	.0058	.0045	.0034	.0026	.0019	22
4	.0482	.0403	.0334	.0274	.0224	.0181	.0145	.0115	.0091	.0071	21
5	.0910	.0797	.0691	.0594	.0506	.0427	.0357	.0297	.0244	.0199	20
6	.1363	.1250	.1134	.1020	.0908	.0801	.0700	.0606	.0520	.0442	19
7	.1662	.1596	.1516	.1426	.1327	.1222	.1115	.1008	.0902	.0800	18
8	.1680	.1690	.1681	.1652	.1607	.1547	.1474	.1390	.1298	.1200	17
9	.1426	.1502	.1563	.1608	.1635	.1644	.1635	.1609	.1567	.1511	16
10	.1025	.1131	.1232	.1325	.1409	.1479	.1536	.1578	.1603	.1612	15
11	.0628	.0726	.0828	.0931	.1034	.1135	.1230	.1319	.1398	.1465	14
12	.0329	.0399	.0476	.0560	.0650	.0745	.0843	.0943	.1043	.1140	13
13	.0148	.0188	.0234	.0288	.0350	.0419	.0495	.0578	.0667	.0760	12
14	.0057	.0076	.0099	.0127	.0161	.0202	.0249	.0304	.0365	.0434	11
15	.0019	.0026	.0036	.0048	.0064	.0083	.0107	.0136	.0171	.0212	10
16	.0005	.0008	.0011	.0015	.0021	.0029	.0039	.0052	.0068	.0088	9
17	.0001	.0002	.0003	.0004	.0006	.0009	.0012	.0017	.0023	.0031	8
18	.0000	.0000	.0001	.0001	.0001	.0002	.0003	.0005	.0007	.0009	7
19	.0000	.0000	.0000	.0000	.0000	.0000	.0001	.0001	.0002	.0002	6
	q=.69	q=.68	q=.67	q=.66	q=.65	q=.64	q=.63	q=.62	q=.61	q=.60	

X1	P=.41	P=.42	P=.43	P=.44	P=.45	P=.46	P=.47	P=.48	P=.49	P=.50	n−X1
0	.0000	.0000	.0000	.0000	.0000	.0000	.0000	.0000	.0000	.0000	25
1	.0000	.0000	.0000	.0000	.0000	.0000	.0000	.0000	.0000	.0000	24
2	.0003	.0002	.0001	.0001	.0001	.0000	.0000	.0000	.0000	.0000	23
3	.0014	.0011	.0008	.0006	.0004	.0003	.0002	.0001	.0001	.0001	22
4	.0055	.0042	.0032	.0024	.0018	.0014	.0010	.0007	.0005	.0004	21
5	.0161	.0129	.0102	.0081	.0063	.0049	.0037	.0028	.0021	.0016	20
6	.0372	.0311	.0257	.0211	.0172	.0138	.0110	.0087	.0068	.0053	19
7	.0703	.0611	.0527	.0450	.0381	.0319	.0265	.0218	.0178	.0143	18
8	.1099	.0996	.0895	.0796	.0701	.0612	.0529	.0453	.0384	.0322	17
9	.1442	.1363	.1275	.1181	.1084	.0985	.0886	.0790	.0697	.0609	16
10	.1603	.1579	.1539	.1485	.1419	.1342	.1257	.1166	.1071	.0974	15
11	.1519	.1559	.1583	.1591	.1583	.1559	.1521	.1468	.1404	.1328	14
12	.1232	.1317	.1393	.1458	.1511	.1550	.1573	.1581	.1573	.1550	13
13	.0856	.0954	.1051	.1146	.1236	.1320	.1395	.1460	.1512	.1550	12
14	.0510	.0592	.0680	.0772	.0867	.0964	.1060	.1155	.1245	.1328	11
15	.0260	.0314	.0376	.0445	.0520	.0602	.0690	.0782	.0877	.0974	10
16	.0113	.0142	.0177	.0218	.0266	.0321	.0382	.0451	.0527	.0609	9
17	.0042	.0055	.0071	.0091	.0115	.0145	.0179	.0220	.0268	.0322	8
18	.0013	.0018	.0024	.0032	.0042	.0055	.0071	.0090	.0114	.0143	7
19	.0003	.0005	.0007	.0009	.0013	.0017	.0023	.0031	.0040	.0053	6
20	.0001	.0001	.0001	.0002	.0003	.0004	.0006	.0009	.0012	.0016	5
21	.0000	.0000	.0000	.0000	.0001	.0001	.0001	.0002	.0003	.0004	4
22	.0000	.0000	.0000	.0000	.0000	.0000	.0000	.0000	.0000	.0001	3
	q=.59	q=.58	q=.57	q=.56	q=.55	q=.54	q=.53	q=.52	q=.51	q=.50	

n = 50

X1	P=.01	P=.02	P=.03	P=.04	P=.05	P=.06	P=.07	P=.08	P=.09	P=.10	n-X1
0	.6050	.3642	.2181	.1299	.0769	.0453	.0266	.0155	.0090	.0052	50
1	.3056	.3716	.3372	.2706	.2025	.1447	.0999	.0672	.0443	.0286	49
2	.0756	.1858	.2555	.2762	.2611	.2262	.1843	.1433	.1073	.0779	48
3	.0122	.0607	.1264	.1842	.2199	.2311	.2219	.1993	.1698	.1386	47
4	.0015	.0145	.0459	.0902	.1360	.1733	.1963	.2037	.1973	.1809	46
5	.0001	.0027	.0131	.0346	.0658	.1018	.1359	.1629	.1795	.1849	45
6	.0000	.0004	.0030	.0108	.0260	.0487	.0767	.1063	.1332	.1541	44
7	.0000	.0001	.0006	.0028	.0086	.0195	.0363	.0581	.0828	.1076	43
8	.0000	.0000	.0001	.0006	.0024	.0067	.0147	.0271	.0440	.0643	42
9	.0000	.0000	.0000	.0001	.0006	.0020	.0052	.0110	.0203	.0333	41
10	.0000	.0000	.0000	.0000	.0001	.0005	.0016	.0039	.0082	.0152	40
11	.0000	.0000	.0000	.0000	.0000	.0001	.0004	.0012	.0030	.0061	39
12	.0000	.0000	.0000	.0000	.0000	.0000	.0001	.0004	.0010	.0022	38
13	.0000	.0000	.0000	.0000	.0000	.0000	.0000	.0001	.0003	.0007	37
14	.0000	.0000	.0000	.0000	.0000	.0000	.0000	.0000	.0001	.0002	36
15	.0000	.0000	.0000	.0000	.0000	.0000	.0000	.0000	.0000	.0001	35
	q=.99	q=.98	q=.97	q=.96	q=.95	q=.94	q=.93	q=.92	q=.91	q=.90	

X1	P=.11	P=.12	P=.13	P=.14	P=.15	P=.16	P=.17	P=.18	P=.19	P=.20	n-X1
0	.0029	.0017	.0009	.0005	.0003	.0002	.0001	.0000	.0000	.0000	50
1	.0182	.0114	.0071	.0043	.0026	.0016	.0009	.0005	.0003	.0002	49
2	.0552	.0382	.0259	.0172	.0113	.0073	.0046	.0029	.0018	.0011	48
3	.1091	.0833	.0619	.0449	.0319	.0222	.0151	.0102	.0067	.0044	47
4	.1584	.1334	.1086	.0858	.0661	.0496	.0364	.0262	.0185	.0128	46
5	.1801	.1674	.1493	.1286	.1072	.0869	.0687	.0530	.0400	.0295	45
6	.1670	.1712	.1674	.1570	.1419	.1242	.1055	.0872	.0703	.0554	44
7	.1297	.1467	.1572	.1606	.1575	.1487	.1358	.1203	.1037	.0870	43
8	.0862	.1075	.1262	.1406	.1493	.1523	.1495	.1420	.1307	.1169	42
9	.0497	.0684	.0880	.1068	.1230	.1353	.1429	.1454	.1431	.1364	41
10	.0252	.0383	.0539	.0713	.0890	.1057	.1200	.1309	.1376	.1398	40
11	.0113	.0190	.0293	.0422	.0571	.0732	.0894	.1045	.1174	.1271	39
12	.0045	.0084	.0142	.0223	.0328	.0453	.0595	.0745	.0895	.1033	38
13	.0016	.0034	.0062	.0106	.0169	.0252	.0356	.0478	.0613	.0755	37
14	.0005	.0012	.0025	.0046	.0079	.0127	.0193	.0277	.0380	.0499	36
15	.0002	.0004	.0009	.0018	.0033	.0058	.0095	.0146	.0214	.0299	35
16	.0000	.0001	.0003	.0006	.0013	.0024	.0042	.0070	.0110	.0164	34
17	.0000	.0000	.0001	.0002	.0005	.0009	.0017	.0031	.0052	.0082	33
18	.0000	.0000	.0000	.0001	.0001	.0003	.0007	.0012	.0022	.0037	32
19	.0000	.0000	.0000	.0000	.0000	.0001	.0002	.0005	.0009	.0016	31
20	.0000	.0000	.0000	.0000	.0000	.0000	.0001	.0002	.0003	.0006	30
21	.0000	.0000	.0000	.0000	.0000	.0000	.0000	.0000	.0001	.0002	29
22	.0000	.0000	.0000	.0000	.0000	.0000	.0000	.0000	.0000	.0001	28
	q=.89	q=.88	q=.87	q=.86	q=.85	q=.84	q=.83	q=.82	q=.81	q=.80	

X1	P=.21	P=.22	P=.23	P=.24	P=.25	P=.26	P=.27	P=.28	P=.29	P=.30	n-X1
0	.0000	.0000	.0000	.0000	.0000	.0000	.0000	.0000	.0000	.0000	50
1	.0001	.0001	.0000	.0000	.0000	.0000	.0000	.0000	.0000	.0000	49
2	.0007	.0004	.0002	.0001	.0001	.0000	.0000	.0000	.0000	.0000	48
3	.0028	.0018	.0011	.0007	.0004	.0002	.0001	.0001	.0000	.0000	47
4	.0088	.0059	.0039	.0025	.0016	.0010	.0006	.0004	.0002	.0001	46
5	.0214	.0152	.0106	.0073	.0049	.0033	.0021	.0014	.0009	.0006	45
6	.0427	.0322	.0238	.0173	.0123	.0087	.0060	.0040	.0027	.0018	44
7	.0713	.0571	.0447	.0344	.0259	.0191	.0139	.0099	.0069	.0048	43
8	.1019	.0865	.0718	.0583	.0463	.0361	.0276	.0207	.0152	.0110	42
9	.1263	.1139	.1001	.0859	.0721	.0592	.0476	.0375	.0290	.0220	41
10	.1377	.1317	.1226	.1113	.0985	.0852	.0721	.0598	.0485	.0386	40
11	.1331	.1351	.1332	.1278	.1194	.1089	.0970	.0845	.0721	.0602	39
12	.1150	.1238	.1293	.1311	.1294	.1244	.1166	.1068	.0957	.0838	38
13	.0894	.1021	.1129	.1210	.1261	.1277	.1261	.1215	.1142	.1050	37
14	.0628	.0761	.0891	.1010	.1110	.1186	.1233	.1248	.1233	.1189	36
15	.0400	.0515	.0639	.0766	.0888	.1000	.1094	.1165	.1209	.1223	35
16	.0233	.0318	.0417	.0529	.0648	.0769	.0885	.0991	.1080	.1147	34

17	.0124	.0179	.0249	.0334	.0432	.0540	.0655	.0771	.0882	.0983	33
18	.0060	.0093	.0137	.0193	.0264	.0348	.0444	.0550	.0661	.0772	32
19	.0027	.0044	.0069	.0103	.0148	.0206	.0277	.0360	.0454	.0558	31
20	.0011	.0019	.0032	.0050	.0077	.0112	.0159	.0217	.0288	.0370	30
21	.0004	.0008	.0014	.0023	.0036	.0056	.0084	.0121	.0168	.0227	29
22	.0001	.0003	.0005	.0009	.0016	.0026	.0041	.0062	.0090	.0128	28
23	.0000	.0001	.0002	.0004	.0006	.0011	.0018	.0029	.0045	.0067	27
24	.0000	.0000	.0001	.0001	.0002	.0004	.0008	.0013	.0021	.0032	26
25	.0000	.0000	.0000	.0000	.0001	.0002	.0003	.0005	.0009	.0014	25
26	.0000	.0000	.0000	.0000	.0000	.0001	.0001	.0002	.0003	.0006	24
27	.0000	.0000	.0000	.0000	.0000	.0000	.0000	.0001	.0001	.0002	23
28	.0000	.0000	.0000	.0000	.0000	.0000	.0000	.0000	.0000	.0001	22
	q=.79	q=.78	q=.77	q=.76	q=.75	q=.74	q=.73	q=.72	q=.71	q=.70	

X1	P=.31	P=.32	P=.33	P=.34	P=.35	P=.36	P=.37	P=.38	P=.39	P=.40	n-X1
4	.0001	.0000	.0000	.0000	.0000	.0000	.0000	.0000	.0000	.0000	46
5	.0003	.0002	.0001	.0001	.0000	.0000	.0000	.0000	.0000	.0000	45
6	.0011	.0007	.0005	.0003	.0002	.0001	.0001	.0000	.0000	.0000	44
7	.0032	.0022	.0014	.0009	.0006	.0004	.0002	.0001	.0001	.0000	43
8	.0078	.0055	.0037	.0025	.0017	.0011	.0007	.0004	.0003	.0002	42
9	.0164	.0120	.0086	.0061	.0042	.0029	.0019	.0013	.0008	.0005	41
10	.0301	.0231	.0174	.0128	.0093	.0066	.0046	.0032	.0022	.0014	40
11	.0493	.0395	.0311	.0240	.0182	.0136	.0099	.0071	.0050	.0035	39
12	.0719	.0604	.0498	.0402	.0319	.0248	.0189	.0142	.0105	.0076	38
13	.0944	.0831	.0717	.0606	.0502	.0408	.0325	.0255	.0195	.0147	37
14	.1121	.1034	.0933	.0825	.0714	.0607	.0505	.0412	.0330	.0260	36
15	.1209	.1168	.1103	.1020	.0923	.0819	.0712	.0606	.0507	.0415	35
16	.1188	.1202	.1189	.1149	.1088	.1008	.0914	.0813	.0709	.0606	34
17	.1068	.1132	.1171	.1184	.1171	.1133	.1074	.0997	.0906	.0808	33
18	.0880	.0976	.1057	.1118	.1156	.1169	.1156	.1120	.1062	.0987	32
19	.0666	.0774	.0877	.0970	.1048	.1107	.1144	.1156	.1144	.1109	31
20	.0463	.0564	.0670	.0775	.0875	.0965	.1041	.1098	.1134	.1146	30
21	.0297	.0379	.0471	.0570	.0673	.0776	.0874	.0962	.1035	.1091	29
22	.0176	.0235	.0306	.0387	.0478	.0575	.0676	.0777	.0873	.0959	28
23	.0096	.0135	.0183	.0243	.0313	.0394	.0484	.0580	.0679	.0778	27
24	.0049	.0071	.0102	.0141	.0190	.0249	.0319	.0400	.0489	.0584	26
25	.0023	.0035	.0052	.0075	.0106	.0146	.0195	.0255	.0325	.0405	25
26	.0010	.0016	.0025	.0037	.0055	.0079	.0110	.0150	.0200	.0259	24
27	.0004	.0007	.0011	.0017	.0026	.0039	.0058	.0082	.0113	.0154	23
28	.0001	.0003	.0004	.0007	.0012	.0018	.0028	.0041	.0060	.0084	22
29	.0000	.0001	.0002	.0003	.0005	.0008	.0012	.0019	.0029	.0043	21
30	.0000	.0000	.0001	.0001	.0002	.0003	.0005	.0008	.0013	.0020	20
31	.0000	.0000	.0000	.0000	.0001	.0001	.0002	.0003	.0005	.0009	19
32	.0000	.0000	.0000	.0000	.0000	.0000	.0001	.0001	.0002	.0003	18
33	.0000	.0000	.0000	.0000	.0000	.0000	.0000	.0000	.0001	.0001	17
	q=.69	q=.68	q=.67	q=.66	q=.65	q=.64	q=.63	q=.62	q=.61	q=.60	

X1	P=.41	P=.42	P=.43	P=.44	P=.45	P=.46	P=.47	P=.48	P=.49	P=.50	n-X1
8	.0001	.0001	.0000	.0000	.0000	.0000	.0000	.0000	.0000	.0000	42
9	.0003	.0002	.0001	.0001	.0000	.0000	.0000	.0000	.0000	.0000	41
10	.0009	.0006	.0004	.0002	.0001	.0001	.0001	.0000	.0000	.0000	40
11	.0024	.0016	.0010	.0007	.0004	.0003	.0002	.0001	.0001	.0000	39
12	.0054	.0037	.0026	.0017	.0011	.0007	.0005	.0003	.0002	.0001	38
13	.0109	.0079	.0057	.0040	.0027	.0018	.0012	.0008	.0005	.0003	37
14	.0200	.0152	.0113	.0082	.0059	.0041	.0029	.0019	.0013	.0008	36
15	.0334	.0264	.0204	.0155	.0116	.0085	.0061	.0043	.0030	.0020	35
16	.0508	.0418	.0337	.0267	.0207	.0158	.0118	.0086	.0062	.0044	34
17	.0706	.0605	.0508	.0419	.0339	.0269	.0209	.0159	.0119	.0087	33
18	.0899	.0803	.0703	.0604	.0508	.0420	.0340	.0270	.0210	.0160	32
19	.1053	.0979	.0893	.0799	.0700	.0602	.0507	.0419	.0340	.0270	31
20	.1134	.1099	.1044	.0973	.0888	.0795	.0697	.0600	.0506	.0419	30
21	.1126	.1137	.1126	.1092	.1038	.0967	.0884	.0791	.0695	.0598	29
22	.1031	.1086	.1119	.1131	.1119	.1086	.1033	.0963	.0880	.0788	28
23	.0872	.0957	.1028	.1082	.1115	.1126	.1115	.1082	.1029	.0960	27
24	.0682	.0780	.0872	.0956	.1026	.1079	.1112	.1124	.1112	.1080	26
25	.0493	.0587	.0684	.0781	.0873	.0956	.1026	.1079	.1112	.1123	25
26	.0329	.0409	.0497	.0590	.0687	.0783	.0875	.0957	.1027	.1080	24
27	.0203	.0263	.0333	.0412	.0500	.0593	.0690	.0786	.0877	.0960	23

28	.0116	.0157	.0206	.0266	.0336	.0415	.0502	.0596	.0692	.0788	22
29	.0061	.0086	.0118	.0159	.0208	.0268	.0338	.0417	.0504	.0598	21
30	.0030	.0044	.0062	.0087	.0119	.0160	.0210	.0270	.0339	.0419	20
31	.0013	.0020	.0030	.0044	.0063	.0088	.0120	.0161	.0210	.0270	19
32	.0006	.0009	.0014	.0021	.0031	.0044	.0063	.0088	.0120	.0160	18
33	.0002	.0003	.0006	.0009	.0014	.0021	.0031	.0044	.0063	.0087	17
34	.0001	.0001	.0002	.0003	.0006	.0009	.0014	.0020	.0030	.0044	16
35	.0000	.0000	.0001	.0001	.0002	.0003	.0005	.0009	.0013	.0020	15
36	.0000	.0000	.0000	.0000	.0001	.0001	.0002	.0003	.0005	.0008	14
37	.0000	.0000	.0000	.0000	.0000	.0000	.0001	.0001	.0002	.0003	13
38	.0000	.0000	.0000	.0000	.0000	.0000	.0000	.0000	.0001	.0001	12
	q=.59	q=.58	q=.57	q=.56	q=.55	q=.54	q=.53	q=.52	q=.51	q=.50	

n = 100

X1	P=.01	P=.02	P=.03	P=.04	P=.05	P=.06	P=.07	P=.08	P=.09	P=.10	n-X1
0	.3660	.1326	.0476	.0169	.0059	.0021	.0007	.0002	.0001	.0000	100
1	.3697	.2707	.1471	.0703	.0312	.0131	.0053	.0021	.0008	.0003	99
2	.1849	.2734	.2252	.1450	.0812	.0414	.0198	.0090	.0039	.0016	98
3	.0610	.1823	.2275	.1973	.1396	.0864	.0486	.0254	.0125	.0059	97
4	.0149	.0902	.1706	.1994	.1781	.1338	.0888	.0536	.0301	.0159	96
5	.0029	.0353	.1013	.1595	.1800	.1639	.1283	.0895	.0571	.0339	95
6	.0005	.0114	.0496	.1052	.1500	.1657	.1529	.1233	.0895	.0596	94
7	.0001	.0031	.0206	.0589	.1060	.1420	.1545	.1440	.1188	.0889	93
8	.0000	.0007	.0074	.0285	.0649	.1054	.1352	.1455	.1366	.1148	92
9	.0000	.0002	.0023	.0121	.0349	.0687	.1040	.1293	.1381	.1304	91
10	.0000	.0000	.0007	.0046	.0167	.0399	.0712	.1024	.1243	.1319	90
11	.0000	.0000	.0002	.0016	.0072	.0209	.0439	.0728	.1006	.1199	89
12	.0000	.0000	.0000	.0005	.0028	.0099	.0245	.0470	.0738	.0988	88
13	.0000	.0000	.0000	.0001	.0010	.0043	.0125	.0276	.0494	.0743	87
14	.0000	.0000	.0000	.0000	.0003	.0017	.0058	.0149	.0304	.0513	86
15	.0000	.0000	.0000	.0000	.0001	.0006	.0025	.0074	.0172	.0327	85
16	.0000	.0000	.0000	.0000	.0000	.0002	.0010	.0034	.0090	.0193	84
17	.0000	.0000	.0000	.0000	.0000	.0001	.0004	.0015	.0044	.0106	83
18	.0000	.0000	.0000	.0000	.0000	.0000	.0001	.0006	.0020	.0054	82
19	.0000	.0000	.0000	.0000	.0000	.0000	.0000	.0002	.0009	.0026	81
20	.0000	.0000	.0000	.0000	.0000	.0000	.0000	.0001	.0003	.0012	80
21	.0000	.0000	.0000	.0000	.0000	.0000	.0000	.0000	.0001	.0005	79
22	.0000	.0000	.0000	.0000	.0000	.0000	.0000	.0000	.0000	.0002	78
23	.0000	.0000	.0000	.0000	.0000	.0000	.0000	.0000	.0000	.0001	77
24	.0000	.0000	.0000	.0000	.0000	.0000	.0000	.0000	.0000	.0000	76
	q=.99	q=.98	q=.97	q=.96	q=.95	q=.94	q=.93	q=.92	q=.91	q=.90	

X1	P=.11	P=.12	P=.13	P=.14	P=.15	P=.16	P=.17	P=.18	P=.19	P=.20	n-X1
0	.0000	.0000	.0000	.0000	.0000	.0000	.0000	.0000	.0000	.0000	100
1	.0001	.0000	.0000	.0000	.0000	.0000	.0000	.0000	.0000	.0000	99
2	.0007	.0003	.0001	.0000	.0000	.0000	.0000	.0000	.0000	.0000	98
3	.0027	.0012	.0005	.0002	.0001	.0000	.0000	.0000	.0000	.0000	97
4	.0080	.0038	.0018	.0008	.0003	.0001	.0001	.0000	.0000	.0000	96
5	.0189	.0100	.0050	.0024	.0011	.0005	.0002	.0001	.0000	.0000	95
6	.0369	.0215	.0119	.0063	.0031	.0015	.0007	.0003	.0001	.0001	94
7	.0613	.0394	.0238	.0137	.0075	.0039	.0020	.0009	.0004	.0002	93
8	.0881	.0625	.0414	.0259	.0153	.0086	.0047	.0024	.0012	.0006	92
9	.1112	.0871	.0632	.0430	.0276	.0168	.0098	.0054	.0029	.0015	91
10	.1251	.1080	.0860	.0637	.0444	.0292	.0182	.0108	.0062	.0034	90
11	.1265	.1205	.1051	.0849	.0640	.0454	.0305	.0194	.0118	.0069	89
12	.1160	.1219	.1165	.1025	.0838	.0642	.0463	.0316	.0206	.0128	88
13	.0970	.1125	.1179	.1130	.1001	.0827	.0642	.0470	.0327	.0216	87
14	.0745	.0954	.1094	.1143	.1098	.0979	.0817	.0641	.0476	.0335	86
15	.0528	.0745	.0938	.1067	.1111	.1070	.0960	.0807	.0640	.0481	85
16	.0347	.0540	.0744	.0922	.1041	.1082	.1044	.0941	.0798	.0638	84
17	.0212	.0364	.0549	.0742	.0908	.1019	.1057	.1021	.0924	.0789	83
18	.0121	.0229	.0379	.0557	.0739	.0895	.0998	.1033	.1000	.0909	82
19	.0064	.0135	.0244	.0391	.0563	.0736	.0882	.0979	.1012	.0981	81
20	.0032	.0074	.0148	.0258	.0402	.0567	.0732	.0870	.0962	.0993	80
21	.0015	.0039	.0084	.0160	.0270	.0412	.0571	.0728	.0859	.0946	79

22 .0007	.0019	.0045	.0094	.0171	.0282	.0420	.0574	.0724	.0849	78
23 .0003	.0009	.0023	.0052	.0103	.0182	.0292	.0427	.0576	.0720	77
24 .0001	.0004	.0011	.0027	.0058	.0111	.0192	.0301	.0433	.0577	76
25 .0000	.0002	.0005	.0013	.0031	.0064	.0119	.0201	.0309	.0439	75
26 .0000	.0001	.0002	.0006	.0016	.0035	.0071	.0127	.0209	.0316	74
27 .0000	.0000	.0001	.0003	.0008	.0018	.0040	.0076	.0134	.0217	73
28 .0000	.0000	.0000	.0001	.0004	.0009	.0021	.0044	.0082	.0141	72
29 .0000	.0000	.0000	.0000	.0002	.0004	.0011	.0024	.0048	.0088	71
30 .0000	.0000	.0000	.0000	.0001	.0002	.0005	.0012	.0027	.0052	70
31 .0000	.0000	.0000	.0000	.0000	.0001	.0002	.0006	.0014	.0029	69
32 .0000	.0000	.0000	.0000	.0000	.0000	.0001	.0003	.0007	.0016	68
33 .0000	.0000	.0000	.0000	.0000	.0000	.0000	.0001	.0003	.0008	67
34 .0000	.0000	.0000	.0000	.0000	.0000	.0000	.0001	.0002	.0004	66
35 .0000	.0000	.0000	.0000	.0000	.0000	.0000	.0000	.0001	.0002	65
36 .0000	.0000	.0000	.0000	.0000	.0000	.0000	.0000	.0000	.0001	64
37 .0000	.0000	.0000	.0000	.0000	.0000	.0000	.0000	.0000	.0000	63
q=.89	q=.88	q=.87	q=.86	q=.85	q=.84	q=.83	q=.82	q=.81	q=.80	

X1	P=.21	P=.22	P=.23	P=.24	P=.25	P=.26	P=.27	P=.28	P=.29	P=.30	n-X1
7	.0001	.0000	.0000	.0000	.0000	.0000	.0000	.0000	.0000	.0000	93
8	.0003	.0001	.0001	.0000	.0000	.0000	.0000	.0000	.0000	.0000	92
9	.0007	.0003	.0002	.0001	.0000	.0000	.0000	.0000	.0000	.0000	91
10	.0018	.0009	.0004	.0002	.0001	.0000	.0000	.0000	.0000	.0000	90
11	.0038	.0021	.0011	.0005	.0003	.0001	.0001	.0000	.0000	.0000	89
12	.0076	.0043	.0024	.0012	.0006	.0003	.0001	.0001	.0000	.0000	88
13	.0136	.0082	.0048	.0027	.0014	.0007	.0004	.0002	.0001	.0000	87
14	.0225	.0144	.0089	.0052	.0030	.0016	.0009	.0004	.0002	.0001	86
15	.0343	.0233	.0152	.0095	.0057	.0033	.0018	.0010	.0005	.0002	85
16	.0484	.0350	.0241	.0159	.0100	.0061	.0035	.0020	.0011	.0006	84
17	.0636	.0487	.0356	.0248	.0165	.0106	.0065	.0038	.0022	.0012	83
18	.0780	.0634	.0490	.0361	.0254	.0171	.0111	.0069	.0041	.0024	82
19	.0895	.0772	.0631	.0492	.0365	.0259	.0177	.0115	.0072	.0044	81
20	.0963	.0881	.0764	.0629	.0493	.0369	.0264	.0182	.0120	.0076	80
21	.0975	.0947	.0869	.0756	.0626	.0494	.0373	.0269	.0186	.0124	79
22	.0931	.0959	.0932	.0858	.0749	.0623	.0495	.0376	.0273	.0190	78
23	.0839	.0917	.0944	.0919	.0847	.0743	.0621	.0495	.0378	.0277	77
24	.0716	.0830	.0905	.0931	.0906	.0837	.0736	.0618	.0496	.0380	76
25	.0578	.0712	.0822	.0893	.0918	.0894	.0828	.0731	.0615	.0496	75
26	.0444	.0579	.0708	.0814	.0883	.0906	.0883	.0819	.0725	.0613	74
27	.0323	.0448	.0580	.0704	.0806	.0873	.0896	.0873	.0812	.0720	73
28	.0224	.0329	.0451	.0580	.0701	.0799	.0864	.0886	.0864	.0804	72
29	.0148	.0231	.0335	.0455	.0580	.0697	.0793	.0855	.0876	.0856	71
30	.0093	.0154	.0237	.0340	.0458	.0580	.0694	.0787	.0847	.0868	70
31	.0056	.0098	.0160	.0242	.0344	.0460	.0580	.0691	.0781	.0840	69
32	.0032	.0060	.0103	.0165	.0248	.0349	.0462	.0579	.0688	.0776	68
33	.0018	.0035	.0063	.0107	.0170	.0252	.0352	.0464	.0579	.0685	67
34	.0009	.0019	.0037	.0067	.0112	.0175	.0257	.0356	.0466	.0579	66
35	.0005	.0010	.0021	.0040	.0070	.0116	.0179	.0261	.0359	.0468	65
36	.0002	.0005	.0011	.0023	.0042	.0073	.0120	.0183	.0265	.0362	64
37	.0001	.0003	.0006	.0012	.0024	.0045	.0077	.0123	.0187	.0268	63
38	.0000	.0001	.0003	.0006	.0013	.0026	.0047	.0079	.0127	.0191	62
39	.0000	.0001	.0001	.0003	.0007	.0015	.0028	.0049	.0082	.0130	61
40	.0000	.0000	.0001	.0002	.0004	.0008	.0016	.0029	.0051	.0085	60
41	.0000	.0000	.0000	.0001	.0002	.0004	.0008	.0017	.0031	.0053	59
42	.0000	.0000	.0000	.0000	.0001	.0002	.0004	.0009	.0018	.0032	58
43	.0000	.0000	.0000	.0000	.0000	.0001	.0002	.0005	.0010	.0019	57
44	.0000	.0000	.0000	.0000	.0000	.0000	.0001	.0002	.0005	.0010	56
45	.0000	.0000	.0000	.0000	.0000	.0000	.0000	.0001	.0003	.0005	55
46	.0000	.0000	.0000	.0000	.0000	.0000	.0000	.0001	.0001	.0003	54
47	.0000	.0000	.0000	.0000	.0000	.0000	.0000	.0000	.0001	.0001	53
48	.0000	.0000	.0000	.0000	.0000	.0000	.0000	.0000	.0000	.0001	52
	q=.79	q=.78	q=.77	q=.76	q=.75	q=.74	q=.73	q=.72	q=.71	q=.70	

X1	P=.31	P=.32	P=.33	P=.34	P=.35	P=.36	P=.37	P=.38	P=.39	P=.40	n-X1
15	.0001	.0001	.0000	.0000	.0000	.0000	.0000	.0000	.0000	.0000	85
16	.0003	.0001	.0001	.0000	.0000	.0000	.0000	.0000	.0000	.0000	84
17	.0006	.0003	.0002	.0001	.0000	.0000	.0000	.0000	.0000	.0000	83

18	.0013	.0007	.0004	.0002	.0001	.0000	.0000	.0000	.0000	.0000	82
19	.0025	.0014	.0008	.0004	.0002	.0001	.0000	.0000	.0000	.0000	81
20	.0046	.0027	.0015	.0008	.0004	.0002	.0001	.0001	.0000	.0000	80
21	.0079	.0049	.0029	.0016	.0009	.0005	.0002	.0001	.0001	.0000	79
22	.0127	.0082	.0051	.0030	.0017	.0010	.0005	.0003	.0001	.0001	78
23	.0194	.0131	.0085	.0053	.0032	.0018	.0010	.0006	.0003	.0001	77
24	.0280	.0198	.0134	.0088	.0055	.0033	.0019	.0011	.0006	.0003	76
25	.0382	.0283	.0201	.0137	.0090	.0057	.0035	.0020	.0012	.0006	75
26	.0496	.0384	.0286	.0204	.0140	.0092	.0059	.0036	.0021	.0012	74
27	.0610	.0495	.0386	.0288	.0207	.0143	.0095	.0060	.0037	.0022	73
28	.0715	.0608	.0495	.0387	.0290	.0209	.0145	.0097	.0062	.0038	72
29	.0797	.0710	.0605	.0495	.0388	.0292	.0211	.0147	.0098	.0063	71
30	.0848	.0791	.0706	.0603	.0494	.0389	.0294	.0213	.0149	.0100	70
31	.0860	.0840	.0785	.0702	.0601	.0494	.0389	.0295	.0215	.0151	69
32	.0833	.0853	.0834	.0779	.0698	.0599	.0493	.0390	.0296	.0217	68
33	.0771	.0827	.0846	.0827	.0774	.0694	.0597	.0493	.0390	.0297	67
34	.0683	.0767	.0821	.0840	.0821	.0769	.0691	.0595	.0492	.0391	66
35	.0578	.0680	.0763	.0816	.0834	.0816	.0765	.0688	.0593	.0491	65
36	.0469	.0578	.0678	.0759	.0811	.0829	.0811	.0761	.0685	.0591	64
37	.0365	.0471	.0578	.0676	.0755	.0806	.0824	.0807	.0757	.0682	63
38	.0272	.0367	.0472	.0577	.0674	.0752	.0802	.0820	.0803	.0754	62
39	.0194	.0275	.0369	.0473	.0577	.0672	.0749	.0799	.0816	.0799	61
40	.0133	.0197	.0277	.0372	.0474	.0577	.0671	.0746	.0795	.0812	60
41	.0087	.0136	.0200	.0280	.0373	.0475	.0577	.0670	.0744	.0792	59
42	.0055	.0090	.0138	.0203	.0282	.0375	.0476	.0576	.0668	.0742	58
43	.0033	.0057	.0092	.0141	.0205	.0285	.0377	.0477	.0576	.0667	57
44	.0019	.0035	.0059	.0094	.0143	.0207	.0287	.0378	.0477	.0576	56
45	.0011	.0020	.0036	.0060	.0096	.0145	.0210	.0289	.0380	.0478	55
46	.0006	.0011	.0021	.0037	.0062	.0098	.0147	.0212	.0290	.0381	54
47	.0003	.0006	.0012	.0022	.0038	.0063	.0099	.0149	.0213	.0292	53
48	.0001	.0003	.0007	.0012	.0023	.0039	.0064	.0101	.0151	.0215	52
49	.0001	.0002	.0003	.0007	.0013	.0023	.0040	.0066	.0102	.0152	51
50	.0000	.0001	.0002	.0004	.0007	.0013	.0024	.0041	.0067	.0103	50
51	.0000	.0000	.0001	.0002	.0004	.0007	.0014	.0025	.0042	.0068	49
52	.0000	.0000	.0000	.0001	.0002	.0004	.0008	.0014	.0025	.0042	48
53	.0000	.0000	.0000	.0000	.0001	.0002	.0004	.0008	.0015	.0026	47
54	.0000	.0000	.0000	.0000	.0000	.0001	.0002	.0004	.0008	.0015	46
55	.0000	.0000	.0000	.0000	.0000	.0000	.0001	.0002	.0004	.0008	45
56	.0000	.0000	.0000	.0000	.0000	.0000	.0000	.0001	.0002	.0004	44
57	.0000	.0000	.0000	.0000	.0000	.0000	.0000	.0001	.0001	.0002	43
58	.0000	.0000	.0000	.0000	.0000	.0000	.0000	.0000	.0001	.0001	42
59	.0000	.0000	.0000	.0000	.0000	.0000	.0000	.0000	.0000	.0001	41
	q=.69	q=.68	q=.67	q=.66	q=.65	q=.64	q=.63	q=.62	q=.61	q=.60	

X1	P=.41	P=.42	P=.43	P=.44	P=.45	P=.46	P=.47	P=.48	P=.49	P=.50	n-X1
23	.0001	.0000	.0000	.0000	.0000	.0000	.0000	.0000	.0000	.0000	77
24	.0002	.0001	.0000	.0000	.0000	.0000	.0000	.0000	.0000	.0000	76
25	.0003	.0002	.0001	.0000	.0000	.0000	.0000	.0000	.0000	.0000	75
26	.0007	.0003	.0002	.0001	.0000	.0000	.0000	.0000	.0000	.0000	74
27	.0013	.0007	.0004	.0002	.0001	.0000	.0000	.0000	.0000	.0000	73
28	.0023	.0013	.0007	.0004	.0002	.0001	.0000	.0000	.0000	.0000	72
29	.0039	.0024	.0014	.0008	.0004	.0002	.0001	.0000	.0000	.0000	71
30	.0065	.0040	.0024	.0014	.0008	.0004	.0002	.0001	.0001	.0000	70
31	.0102	.0066	.0041	.0025	.0014	.0008	.0004	.0002	.0001	.0001	69
32	.0152	.0103	.0067	.0042	.0025	.0015	.0008	.0004	.0002	.0001	68
33	.0218	.0154	.0104	.0068	.0043	.0026	.0015	.0008	.0004	.0002	67
34	.0298	.0219	.0155	.0105	.0069	.0043	.0026	.0015	.0009	.0005	66
35	.0391	.0299	.0220	.0156	.0106	.0069	.0044	.0026	.0015	.0009	65
36	.0491	.0391	.0300	.0221	.0157	.0107	.0070	.0044	.0027	.0016	64
37	.0590	.0490	.0391	.0300	.0222	.0157	.0107	.0070	.0044	.0027	63
38	.0680	.0588	.0489	.0391	.0301	.0222	.0158	.0108	.0071	.0045	62
39	.0751	.0677	.0587	.0489	.0391	.0301	.0223	.0158	.0108	.0071	61
40	.0796	.0748	.0675	.0586	.0488	.0391	.0301	.0223	.0159	.0108	60
41	.0809	.0793	.0745	.0673	.0584	.0487	.0391	.0301	.0223	.0159	59
42	.0790	.0806	.0790	.0743	.0672	.0583	.0487	.0390	.0301	.0223	58
43	.0740	.0787	.0804	.0788	.0741	.0670	.0582	.0486	.0390	.0301	57
44	.0666	.0739	.0785	.0802	.0786	.0739	.0669	.0581	.0485	.0390	56
45	.0576	.0666	.0737	.0784	.0800	.0784	.0738	.0668	.0580	.0485	55
46	.0479	.0576	.0665	.0736	.0782	.0798	.0783	.0737	.0667	.0580	54
47	.0382	.0480	.0576	.0665	.0736	.0781	.0797	.0781	.0736	.0666	53
48	.0293	.0383	.0480	.0577	.0665	.0735	.0781	.0797	.0781	.0735	52
49	.0216	.0295	.0384	.0481	.0577	.0664	.0735	.0780	.0796	.0780	51
50	.0153	.0218	.0296	.0385	.0482	.0577	.0665	.0735	.0780	.0796	50
51	.0104	.0155	.0219	.0297	.0386	.0482	.0578	.0665	.0735	.0780	49
52	.0068	.0105	.0156	.0220	.0298	.0387	.0483	.0578	.0665	.0735	48
53	.0043	.0069	.0106	.0156	.0221	.0299	.0388	.0483	.0579	.0666	47
54	.0026	.0044	.0070	.0107	.0157	.0221	.0299	.0388	.0484	.0580	46

55	.0015	.0026	.0044	.0070	.0108	.0158	.0222	.0300	.0389	.0485	45
56	.0008	.0015	.0027	.0044	.0071	.0108	.0158	.0222	.0300	.0390	44
57	.0005	.0009	.0016	.0027	.0045	.0071	.0108	.0158	.0223	.0301	43
58	.0002	.0005	.0009	.0016	.0027	.0045	.0071	.0108	.0159	.0223	42
59	.0001	.0002	.0005	.0009	.0016	.0027	.0045	.0071	.0109	.0159	41
60	.0001	.0001	.0002	.0005	.0009	.0016	.0027	.0045	.0071	.0108	40
61	.0000	.0001	.0001	.0002	.0005	.0009	.0016	.0027	.0045	.0071	39
62	.0000	.0000	.0001	.0001	.0002	.0005	.0009	.0016	.0027	.0045	38
63	.0000	.0000	.0000	.0001	.0001	.0002	.0005	.0009	.0016	.0027	37
64	.0000	.0000	.0000	.0000	.0001	.0001	.0002	.0005	.0009	.0016	36
65	.0000	.0000	.0000	.0000	.0000	.0001	.0001	.0002	.0005	.0009	35
66	.0000	.0000	.0000	.0000	.0000	.0000	.0001	.0001	.0002	.0005	34
67	.0000	.0000	.0000	.0000	.0000	.0000	.0000	.0001	.0001	.0002	33
68	.0000	.0000	.0000	.0000	.0000	.0000	.0000	.0000	.0001	.0001	32
69	.0000	.0000	.0000	.0000	.0000	.0000	.0000	.0000	.0000	.0001	31
	q=.59	q=.58	q=.57	q=.56	q=.55	q=.54	q=.53	q=.52	q=.51	q=.50	

APPENDIX B Poisson Probability Distribution—Values of $P(X) = (\lambda t)^X e^{-\lambda t}/X!$

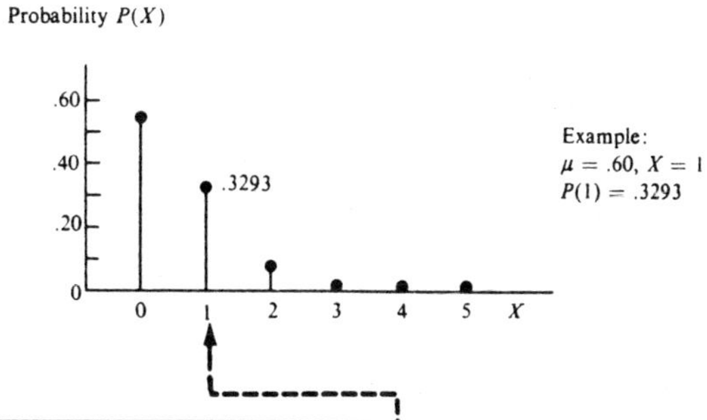

X_i	.005	.01	.02	.03	.04	.05	.06	.07	.08	.09
0	.9950	.9900	.9802	.9704	.9608	.9512	.9418	.9324	.9231	.9139
1	.0050	.0099	.0192	.0291	.0384	.0476	.0565	.0653	.0738	.0823
2	.0000	.0000	.0002	.0004	.0008	.0012	.0017	.0023	.0030	.0037
3	.0000	.0000	.0000	.0000	.0000	.0000	.0000	.0001	.0001	.0001

X_i	0.10	0.20	0.30	0.40	0.50	0.60	0.70	0.80	0.90	1.00
0	.9048	.8187	.7408	.6703	.6065	.5488	.4966	.4493	.4066	.3679
1	.0905	.1637	.2222	.2681	.3033	.3293	.3476	.3595	.3659	.3679
2	.0045	.0164	.0333	.0536	.0758	.0988	.1217	.1438	.1647	.1839
3	.0002	.0011	.0033	.0072	.0126	.0198	.0284	.0383	.0494	.0613
4	.0000	.0001	.0002	.0007	.0016	.0030	.0050	.0077	.0111	.0153
5	.0000	.0000	.0000	.0001	.0002	.0004	.0007	.0012	.0020	.0031
6	.0000	.0000	.0000	.0000	.0000	.0000	.0001	.0002	.0003	.0005
7	.0000	.0000	.0000	.0000	.0000	.0000	.0000	.0000	.0000	.0001

X_i	1.10	1.20	1.30	1.40	1.50	1.60	1.70	1.80	1.90	2.00
0	.3329	.3012	.2725	.2466	.2231	.2019	.1827	.1653	.1496	.1353
1	.3662	.3614	.3543	.3452	.3347	.3230	.3106	.2975	.2842	.2707
2	.2014	.2169	.2303	.2417	.2510	.2584	.2640	.2678	.2700	.2707
3	.0738	.0867	.0998	.1128	.1255	.1378	.1496	.1607	.1710	.1804
4	.0203	.0260	.0324	.0395	.0471	.0551	.0636	.0723	.0812	.0902
5	.0045	.0062	.0084	.0111	.0141	.0176	.0216	.0260	.0309	.0361
6	.0008	.0012	.0018	.0026	.0035	.0047	.0061	.0078	.0098	.0120
7	.0001	.0002	.0003	.0005	.0008	.0011	.0015	.0020	.0027	.0034
8	.0000	.0000	.0001	.0001	.0001	.0002	.0003	.0005	.0006	.0009
9	.0000	.0000	.0000	.0000	.0000	.0000	.0001	.0001	.0001	.0002

X_i	2.10	2.20	2.30	2.40	2.50	2.60	2.70	2.80	2.90	3.00
0	.1225	.1108	.1003	.0907	.0821	.0743	.0672	.0608	.0550	.0498
1	.2572	.2438	.2306	.2177	.2052	.1931	.1815	.1703	.1596	.1494
2	.2700	.2681	.2652	.2613	.2565	.2510	.2450	.2384	.2314	.2240
3	.1890	.1966	.2033	.2090	.2138	.2176	.2205	.2225	.2237	.2240
4	.0992	.1082	.1169	.1254	.1336	.1414	.1488	.1557	.1622	.1680
5	.0417	.0476	.0538	.0602	.0668	.0735	.0804	.0872	.0940	.1008
6	.0146	.0174	.0206	.0241	.0278	.0319	.0362	.0407	.0455	.0504
7	.0044	.0055	.0068	.0083	.0099	.0118	.0139	.0163	.0188	.0216
8	.0011	.0015	.0019	.0025	.0031	.0038	.0047	.0057	.0068	.0081
9	.0003	.0004	.0005	.0007	.0009	.0011	.0014	.0018	.0022	.0027
10	.0001	.0001	.0001	.0002	.0002	.0003	.0004	.0005	.0006	.0008
11	.0000	.0000	.0000	.0000	.0000	.0001	.0001	.0001	.0002	.0002
12	.0000	.0000	.0000	.0000	.0000	.0000	.0000	.0000	.0000	.0001

X_i	3.10	3.20	3.30	3.40	3.50	3.60	3.70	3.80	3.90	4.00
	λt									
0	.0450	.0408	.0369	.0334	.0302	.0273	.0247	.0224	.0202	.0183
1	.1397	.1304	.1217	.1135	.1057	.0984	.0915	.0850	.0789	.0733
2	.2165	.2087	.2008	.1929	.1850	.1771	.1692	.1615	.1539	.1465
3	.2237	.2226	.2209	.2186	.2158	.2125	.2087	.2046	.2001	.1954
4	.1734	.1781	.1823	.1858	.1888	.1912	.1931	.1944	.1951	.1954
5	.1075	.1140	.1203	.1264	.1322	.1377	.1429	.1477	.1522	.1563
6	.0555	.0608	.0662	.0716	.0771	.0826	.0881	.0936	.0989	.1042
7	.0246	.0278	.0312	.0348	.0385	.0425	.0466	.0508	.0551	.0595
8	.0095	.0111	.0129	.0148	.0169	.0191	.0215	.0241	.0269	.0298
9	.0033	.0040	.0047	.0056	.0066	.0076	.0089	.0102	.0116	.0132
10	.0010	.0013	.0016	.0019	.0023	.0028	.0033	.0039	.0045	.0053
11	.0003	.0004	.0005	.0006	.0007	.0009	.0011	.0013	.0016	.0019
12	.0001	.0001	.0001	.0002	.0002	.0003	.0003	.0004	.0005	.0006
13	.0000	.0000	.0000	.0000	.0001	.0001	.0001	.0001	.0002	.0002
14	.0000	.0000	.0000	.0000	.0000	.0000	.0000	.0000	.0000	.0001

X_i	4.10	4.20	4.30	4.40	4.50	4.60	4.70	4.80	4.90	5.00
	λt									
0	.0166	.0150	.0136	.0123	.0111	.0101	.0091	.0082	.0074	.0067
1	.0679	.0630	.0583	.0540	.0500	.0462	.0427	.0395	.0365	.0337
2	.1393	.1323	.1254	.1188	.1125	.1063	.1005	.0948	.0894	.0842
3	.1904	.1852	.1798	.1743	.1687	.1631	.1574	.1517	.1460	.1404
4	.1951	.1944	.1933	.1917	.1898	.1875	.1849	.1820	.1789	.1755
5	.1600	.1633	.1662	.1687	.1708	.1725	.1738	.1747	.1753	.1755
6	.1093	.1143	.1191	.1237	.1281	.1323	.1362	.1398	.1432	.1462
7	.0640	.0686	.0732	.0778	.0824	.0869	.0914	.0959	.1002	.1044
8	.0328	.0360	.0393	.0428	.0463	.0500	.0537	.0575	.0614	.0653
9	.0150	.0168	.0188	.0209	.0232	.0255	.0280	.0307	.0334	.0363
10	.0061	.0071	.0081	.0092	.0104	.0118	.0132	.0147	.0164	.0181
11	.0023	.0027	.0032	.0037	.0043	.0049	.0056	.0064	.0073	.0082
12	.0008	.0009	.0011	.0014	.0016	.0019	.0022	.0026	.0030	.0034
13	.0002	.0003	.0004	.0005	.0006	.0007	.0008	.0009	.0011	.0013
14	.0001	.0001	.0001	.0001	.0002	.0002	.0003	.0003	.0004	.0005
15	.0000	.0000	.0000	.0000	.0001	.0001	.0001	.0001	.0001	.0002

X_i	5.10	5.20	5.30	5.40	5.50	5.60	5.70	5.80	5.90	6.00
	λt									
0	.0061	.0055	.0050	.0045	.0041	.0037	.0033	.0030	.0027	.0025
1	.0311	.0287	.0265	.0244	.0225	.0207	.0191	.0176	.0162	.0149
2	.0793	.0746	.0701	.0659	.0618	.0580	.0544	.0509	.0477	.0446
3	.1348	.1293	.1239	.1185	.1133	.1082	.1033	.0985	.0938	.0892
4	.1719	.1681	.1641	.1600	.1558	.1515	.1472	.1428	.1383	.1339
5	.1753	.1748	.1740	.1728	.1714	.1697	.1678	.1656	.1632	.1606
6	.1490	.1515	.1537	.1555	.1571	.1584	.1594	.1601	.1605	.1606
7	.1086	.1125	.1163	.1200	.1234	.1267	.1298	.1326	.1353	.1377
8	.0692	.0731	.0771	.0810	.0849	.0887	.0925	.0962	.0998	.1033
9	.0392	.0423	.0454	.0486	.0519	.0552	.0586	.0620	.0654	.0688
10	.0200	.0220	.0241	.0262	.0285	.0309	.0334	.0359	.0386	.0413
11	.0093	.0104	.0116	.0129	.0143	.0157	.0173	.0190	.0207	.0225
12	.0039	.0045	.0051	.0058	.0065	.0073	.0082	.0092	.0102	.0113
13	.0015	.0018	.0021	.0024	.0028	.0032	.0036	.0041	.0046	.0052
14	.0006	.0007	.0008	.0009	.0011	.0013	.0015	.0017	.0019	.0022
15	.0002	.0002	.0003	.0003	.0004	.0005	.0006	.0007	.0008	.0009
16	.0001	.0001	.0001	.0001	.0001	.0002	.0002	.0002	.0003	.0003
17	.0000	.0000	.0000	.0000	.0000	.0001	.0001	.0001	.0001	.0001

	λt									
X_i	6.10	6.20	6.30	6.40	6.50	6.60	6.70	6.80	6.90	7.00
0	.0022	.0020	.0018	.0017	.0015	.0014	.0012	.0011	.0010	.0009
1	.0137	.0126	.0116	.0106	.0098	.0090	.0082	.0076	.0070	.0064
2	.0417	.0390	.0364	.0340	.0318	.0296	.0276	.0258	.0240	.0223
3	.0848	.0806	.0765	.0726	.0688	.0652	.0617	.0584	.0552	.0521
4	.1294	.1249	.1205	.1162	.1118	.1076	.1034	.0992	.0952	.0912
5	.1579	.1549	.1519	.1487	.1454	.1420	.1385	.1349	.1314	.1277
6	.1605	.1601	.1595	.1586	.1575	.1562	.1546	.1529	.1511	.1490
7	.1399	.1418	.1435	.1450	.1462	.1472	.1480	.1486	.1489	.1490
8	.1066	.1099	.1130	.1160	.1188	.1215	.1240	.1263	.1284	.1304
9	.0723	.0757	.0791	.0825	.0858	.0891	.0923	.0954	.0985	.1014
10	.0441	.0469	.0498	.0528	.0558	.0588	.0618	.0649	.0679	.0710
11	.0245	.0265	.0285	.0307	.0330	.0353	.0377	.0401	.0426	.0452
12	.0124	.0137	.0150	.0164	.0179	.0194	.0210	.0227	.0245	.0264
13	.0058	.0065	.0073	.0081	.0089	.0098	.0108	.0119	.0130	.0142
14	.0025	.0029	.0033	.0037	.0041	.0046	.0052	.0058	.0064	.0071
15	.0010	.0012	.0014	.0016	.0018	.0020	.0023	.0026	.0029	.0033
16	.0004	.0005	.0005	.0006	.0007	.0008	.0010	.0011	.0013	.0014
17	.0001	.0002	.0002	.0002	.0003	.0003	.0004	.0004	.0005	.0006
18	.0000	.0001	.0001	.0001	.0001	.0001	.0001	.0002	.0002	.0002
19	.0000	.0000	.0000	.0000	.0000	.0000	.0000	.0001	.0001	.0001

	λt									
	7.10	7.20	7.30	7.40	7.50	7.60	7.70	7.80	7.90	8.00
0	.0008	.0007	.0007	.0006	.0006	.0005	.0005	.0004	.0004	.0003
1	.0059	.0054	.0049	.0045	.0041	.0038	.0035	.0032	.0029	.0027
2	.0208	.0194	.0180	.0167	.0156	.0145	.0134	.0125	.0116	.0107
3	.0492	.0464	.0438	.0413	.0389	.0366	.0345	.0324	.0305	.0286
4	.0874	.0836	.0799	.0764	.0729	.0696	.0663	.0632	.0602	.0573
5	.1241	.1204	.1167	.1130	.1094	.1057	.1021	.0986	.0951	.0916
6	.1468	.1445	.1420	.1394	.1367	.1339	.1311	.1282	.1252	.1221
7	.1489	.1486	.1481	.1474	.1465	.1454	.1442	.1428	.1413	.1396
8	.1321	.1337	.1351	.1363	.1373	.1382	.1388	.1392	.1395	.1396
9	.1042	.1070	.1096	.1121	.1144	.1167	.1187	.1207	.1224	.1241
10	.0740	.0770	.0800	.0829	.0858	.0887	.0914	.0941	.0967	.0993
11	.0478	.0504	.0531	.0558	.0585	.0613	.0640	.0667	.0695	.0722
12	.0283	.0303	.0323	.0344	.0366	.0388	.0411	.0434	.0457	.0481
13	.0154	.0168	.0181	.0196	.0211	.0227	.0243	.0260	.0278	.0296
14	.0078	.0086	.0095	.0104	.0113	.0123	.0134	.0145	.0157	.0169
15	.0037	.0041	.0046	.0051	.0057	.0062	.0069	.0075	.0083	.0090
16	.0016	.0019	.0021	.0024	.0026	.0030	.0033	.0037	.0041	.0045
17	.0007	.0008	.0009	.0010	.0012	.0013	.0015	.0017	.0019	.0021
18	.0003	.0003	.0004	.0004	.0005	.0006	.0006	.0007	.0008	.0009
19	.0001	.0001	.0001	.0002	.0002	.0002	.0003	.0003	.0003	.0004
20	.0000	.0000	.0001	.0001	.0001	.0001	.0001	.0001	.0001	.0002
21	.0000	.0000	.0000	.0000	.0000	.0000	.0000	.0000	.0001	.0001

	λt									
X_i	8.10	8.20	8.30	8.40	8.50	8.60	8.70	8.80	8.90	9.00
0	.0003	.0003	.0002	.0002	.0002	.0002	.0002	.0002	.0001	.0001
1	.0025	.0023	.0021	.0019	.0017	.0016	.0014	.0013	.0012	.0011
2	.0100	.0092	.0086	.0079	.0074	.0068	.0063	.0058	.0054	.0050
3	.0269	.0252	.0237	.0222	.0208	.0195	.0183	.0171	.0160	.0150
4	.0544	.0517	.0491	.0466	.0443	.0420	.0398	.0377	.0357	.0337
5	.0882	.0849	.0816	.0784	.0752	.0722	.0692	.0663	.0635	.0607
6	.1191	.1160	.1128	.1097	.1066	.1034	.1003	.0972	.0941	.0911
7	.1378	.1358	.1338	.1317	.1294	.1271	.1247	.1222	.1197	.1171
8	.1395	.1392	.1388	.1382	.1375	.1366	.1356	.1344	.1332	.1318
9	.1256	.1269	.1280	.1290	.1299	.1306	.1311	.1315	.1317	.1318
10	.1017	.1040	.1063	.1084	.1104	.1123	.1140	.1157	.1172	.1186
11	.0749	.0776	.0802	.0828	.0853	.0878	.0902	.0925	.0948	.0970
12	.0505	.0530	.0555	.0579	.0604	.0629	.0654	.0679	.0703	.0728
13	.0315	.0334	.0354	.0374	.0395	.0416	.0438	.0459	.0481	.0504
14	.0182	.0196	.0210	.0225	.0240	.0256	.0272	.0289	.0306	.0324
15	.0098	.0107	.0116	.0126	.0136	.0147	.0158	.0169	.0182	.0194
16	.0050	.0055	.0060	.0066	.0072	.0079	.0086	.0093	.0101	.0109
17	.0024	.0026	.0029	.0033	.0036	.0040	.0044	.0048	.0053	.0058
18	.0011	.0012	.0014	.0015	.0017	.0019	.0021	.0024	.0026	.0029
19	.0005	.0005	.0006	.0007	.0008	.0009	.0010	.0011	.0012	.0014
20	.0002	.0002	.0002	.0003	.0003	.0004	.0004	.0005	.0005	.0006
21	.0001	.0001	.0001	.0001	.0001	.0002	.0002	.0002	.0002	.0003
22	.0000	.0000	.0000	.0000	.0001	.0001	.0001	.0001	.0001	.0001

	λt									
	9.10	9.20	9.30	9.40	9.50	9.60	9.70	9.80	9.90	10.00
0	.0001	.0001	.0001	.0001	.0001	.0001	.0001	.0001	.0001	.0000
1	.0010	.0009	.0009	.0008	.0007	.0007	.0006	.0005	.0005	.0005
2	.0046	.0043	.0040	.0037	.0034	.0031	.0029	.0027	.0025	.0023
3	.0140	.0131	.0123	.0115	.0107	.0100	.0093	.0087	.0081	.0076
4	.0319	.0302	.0285	.0269	.0254	.0240	.0226	.0213	.0201	.0189
5	.0581	.0555	.0530	.0506	.0483	.0460	.0439	.0418	.0398	.0378
6	.0881	.0851	.0822	.0793	.0764	.0736	.0709	.0682	.0656	.0631
7	.1145	.1118	.1091	.1064	.1037	.1010	.0982	.0955	.0928	.0901
8	.1302	.1286	.1269	.1251	.1232	.1212	.1191	.1170	.1148	.1126
9	.1317	.1315	.1311	.1306	.1300	.1293	.1284	.1274	.1263	.1251
10	.1198	.1210	.1219	.1228	.1235	.1241	.1245	.1249	.1250	.1251
11	.0991	.1012	.1031	.1049	.1067	.1083	.1098	.1112	.1125	.1137
12	.0752	.0776	.0799	.0822	.0844	.0866	.0888	.0908	.0928	.0948
13	.0526	.0549	.0572	.0594	.0617	.0640	.0662	.0685	.0707	.0729
14	.0342	.0361	.0380	.0399	.0419	.0439	.0459	.0479	.0500	.0521
15	.0208	.0221	.0235	.0250	.0265	.0281	.0297	.0313	.0330	.0347
16	.0118	.0127	.0137	.0147	.0157	.0168	.0180	.0192	.0204	.0217
17	.0063	.0069	.0075	.0081	.0088	.0095	.0103	.0111	.0119	.0128
18	.0032	.0035	.0039	.0042	.0046	.0051	.0055	.0060	.0065	.0071
19	.0015	.0017	.0019	.0021	.0023	.0026	.0028	.0031	.0034	.0037
20	.0007	.0008	.0009	.0010	.0011	.0012	.0014	.0015	.0017	.0019
21	.0003	.0003	.0004	.0004	.0005	.0006	.0006	.0007	.0008	.0009
22	.0001	.0001	.0002	.0002	.0002	.0002	.0003	.0003	.0004	.0004
23	.0000	.0001	.0001	.0001	.0001	.0001	.0001	.0001	.0002	.0002
24	.0000	.0000	.0000	.0000	.0000	.0000	.0000	.0001	.0001	.0001

X_1	λt 11.0	12.0	13.0	14.0	15.0	16.0	17.0	18.0	19.0	20.0
0	.0000	.0000	.0000	.0000	.0000	.0000	.0000	.0000	.0000	.0000
1	.0002	.0001	.0000	.0000	.0000	.0000	.0000	.0000	.0000	.0000
2	.0010	.0004	.0002	.0001	.0000	.0000	.0000	.0000	.0000	.0000
3	.0037	.0018	.0008	.0004	.0002	.0001	.0000	.0000	.0000	.0000
4	.0102	.0053	.0027	.0013	.0006	.0003	.0001	.0001	.0000	.0000
5	.0224	.0127	.0070	.0037	.0019	.0010	.0005	.0002	.0001	.0001
6	.0411	.0255	.0152	.0087	.0048	.0026	.0014	.0007	.0004	.0002
7	.0646	.0437	.0281	.0174	.0104	.0060	.0034	.0019	.0010	.0005
8	.0888	.0655	.0457	.0304	.0194	.0120	.0072	.0042	.0024	.0013
9	.1085	.0874	.0661	.0473	.0324	.0213	.0135	.0083	.0050	.0029
10	.1194	.1048	.0859	.0663	.0486	.0341	.0230	0150	.0095	.0058
11	.1194	.1144	.1015	.0844	.0663	.0496	.0355	.0245	.0164	.0106
12	.1094	.1144	.1099	.0984	.0829	.0661	.0504	.0368	.0259	.0176
13	.0926	.1056	.1099	.1060	.0956	.0814	.0658	.0509	.0378	.0271
14	.0728	.0905	.1021	.1060	.1024	.0930	.0800	.0655	.0514	.0387
15	.0534	.0724	.0885	.0989	.1024	.0992	.0906	.0786	.0650	.0516
16	.0367	.0543	.0719	.0866	.0960	.0992	.0963	.0884	.0772	.0646
17	.0237	.0383	.0550	.0713	.0847	.0934	.0963	.0936	.0863	.0760
18	.0145	.0256	.0397	.0554	.0706	.0830	.0909	.0936	.0911	.0844
19	.0084	.0161	.0272	.0409	.0557	.0699	.0814	.0887	.0911	.0888
20	.0046	.0097	.0177	.0286	.0418	.0559	.0692	.0798	.0866	.0888
21	.0024	.0055	.0109	.0191	.0299	.0426	.0560	.0684	.0783	.0846
22	.0012	.0030	.0065	.0121	.0204	.0310	.0433	.0560	.0676	.0769
23	.0006	.0016	.0037	.0074	.0133	.0216	.0320	.0438	.0559	.0669
24	.0003	.0008	.0020	.0043	.0083	.0144	.0226	.0329	.0442	.0557
25	.0001	.0004	.0010	.0024	.0050	.0092	.0154	.0237	.0336	.0446
26	.0000	.0002	·0005	.0013	.0029	.0057	.0101	.0164	.0246	.0343
27	.0000	.0001	.0002	.0007	.0016	.0034	.0063	.0109	.0173	.0254
28	.0000	.0000	.0001	.0003	.0009	.0019	.0038	.0070	.0117	.0181
29	.0000	.0000	.0001	.0002	.0004	.0011	.0023	.0044	.0077	.0125
30	.0000	.0000	.0000	.0001	.0002	.0006	.0013	.0026	.0049	.0083
31	.0000	.0000	.0000	.0000	.0001	.0003	.0007	.0015	.0030	.0054
32	.0000	.0000	.0000	.0000	.0001	.0001	.0004	.0009	.0018	.0034
33	.0000	.0000	.0000	.0000	.0000	.0001	.0002	.0005	.0010	.0020
34	.0000	.0000	.0000	.0000	.0000	.0000	.0001	.0002	.0006	.0012
35	.0000	.0000	.0000	.0000	.0000	.0000	.0000	.0001	.0003	.0007
36	.0000	.0000	.0000	.0000	.0000	.0000	.0000	.0001	.0002	.0004
37	.0000	.0000	.0000	.0000	.0000	.0000	.0000	.0000	.0001	.0002
38	.0000	.0000	.0000	.0000	.0000	.0000	.0000	.0000	.0000	.0001
39	.0000	.0000	.0000	.0000	.0000	.0000	.0000	.0000	.0000	.0001

Source: Stephen P. Shao. *Statistics for Business and Economics.* 3d ed. (Columbus, Ohio: Merrill Publishing Company, 1976), pp. 782–86. Used with permission.

APPENDIX C Standard Normal Distribution Table

To illustrate: 19.85% of the area under a normal curve lies between the mean, μ_x, and a point 0.52 standard deviation units away.

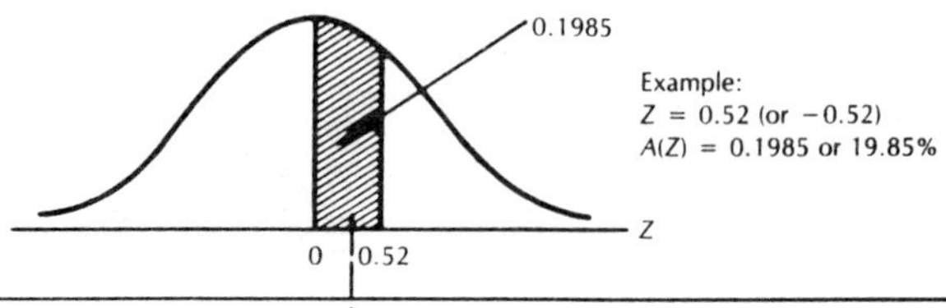

Z	.00	.01	.02	.03	.04	.05	.06	.07	.08	.09
0.0	.0000	.0040	.0080	.0120	.0160	.0199	.0239	.0279	.0319	.0359
0.1	.0398	.0438	.0478	.0517	.0557	.0596	.0636	.0675	.0714	.0753
0.2	.0793	.0832	.0871	.0910	.0948	.0987	.1026	.1064	.1103	.1141
0.3	.1179	.1217	.1255	.1293	.1331	.1368	.1406	.1443	.1480	.1517
0.4	.1554	.1591	.1628	.1664	.1700	.1736	.1772	.1808	.1844	.1879
0.5	.1915	.1950	.1985	.2019	.2054	.2088	.2123	.2157	.2190	.2224
0.6	.2257	.2291	.2324	.2357	.2389	.2422	.2454	.2486	.2517	.2549
0.7	.2580	.2611	.2642	.2673	.2704	.2734	.2764	.2794	.2823	.2852
0.8	.2881	.2910	.2939	.2967	.2995	.3023	.3051	.3078	.3106	.3133
0.9	.3159	.3186	.3212	.3238	.3264	.3289	.3315	.3340	.3365	.3389
1.0	.3413	.3438	.3461	.3485	.3508	.3531	.3554	.3577	.3599	.3621
1.1	.3643	.3665	.3686	.3708	.3729	.3749	.3770	.3790	.3810	.3830
1.2	.3849	.3869	.3888	.3907	.3925	.3944	.3962	.3980	.3997	.4015
1.3	.4032	.4049	.4066	.4082	.4099	.4115	.4131	.4147	.4162	.4177
1.4	.4192	.4207	.4222	.4236	.4251	.4265	.4279	.4292	.4306	.4319
1.5	.4332	.4345	.4357	.4370	.4382	.4394	.4406	.4418	.4429	.4441
1.6	.4452	.4463	.4474	.4484	.4495	.4505	.4515	.4525	.4535	.4545
1.7	.4554	.4564	.4573	.4582	.4591	.4599	.4608	.4616	.4625	.4633
1.8	.4641	.4649	.4656	.4664	.4671	.4678	.4686	.4693	.4699	.4706
1.9	.4713	.4719	.4726	.4732	.4738	.4744	.4750	.4756	.4761	.4767
2.0	.4772	.4778	.4783	.4788	.4793	.4798	.4803	.4808	.4812	.4817
2.1	.4821	.4826	.4830	.4834	.4838	.4842	.4846	.4850	.4854	.4857
2.2	.4861	.4864	.4868	.4871	.4875	.4878	.4881	.4884	.4887	.4890
2.3	.4893	.4896	.4898	.4901	.4904	.4906	.4909	.4911	.4913	.4916
2.4	.4918	.4920	.4922	.4925	.4927	.4929	.4931	.4932	.4934	.4936
2.5	.4938	.4940	.4941	.4943	.4945	.4946	.4948	.4949	.4951	.4952
2.6	.4953	.4955	.4956	.4957	.4959	.4960	.4961	.4962	.4963	.4964
2.7	.4965	.4966	.4967	.4968	.4969	.4970	.4971	.4972	.4973	.4974
2.8	.4974	.4975	.4976	.4977	.4977	.4978	.4979	.4979	.4980	.4981
2.9	.4981	.4982	.4982	.4983	.4984	.4984	.4985	.4985	.4986	.4986
3.0	.4987	.4987	.4987	.4988	.4988	.4989	.4989	.4989	.4990	.4990

APPENDIX D Values of *t* for Selected Probabilities

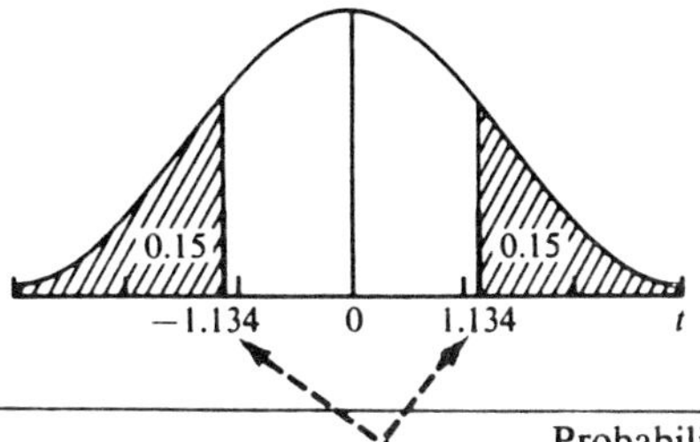

Example.
d.f. (Number of degrees of freedom) = 6:
One tail above $t = 1.134$ *or* below $t = -1.134$ represents 0.15 or 15% of the area under the curve. Two tails above $t = 1.134$ *and* below $t = -1.134$ represent 0.30 or 30%.

Probabilities
(or Areas Under *t*-Distribution Curve)

One tail	.45	.35	.25	.15	.10	.05	.025	.01	.005
Two tails	.90	.70	.50	.30	.20	.10	.05	.02	.01
Conf. Level	.10	.30	.50	.70	.80	.90	.95	.98	.99
d.f.	Values of *t*								
1	.158	.510	1.000	1.963	3.078	6.314	12.706	31.821	63.657
2	.142	.445	.816	1.386	1.886	2.920	4.303	6.965	9.925
3	.137	.424	.765	1.250	1.638	2.353	3.182	4.541	5.841
4	.134	.414	.741	1.190	1.533	2.132	2.776	3.747	4.604
5	.132	.408	.727	1.156	1.476	2.015	2.571	3.365	4.032
6	.131	.404	.718	**1.134**	1.440	1.943	2.447	3.143	3.707
7	.130	.402	.711	1.119	1.415	1.895	2.365	2.998	3.499
8	.130	.399	.706	1.108	1.397	1.860	2.306	2.896	3.355
9	.129	.398	.703	1.100	1.383	1.833	2.262	2.821	3.250
10	.129	.397	.700	1.093	1.372	1.812	2.228	2.764	3.169
11	.129	.396	.697	1.088	1.363	1.796	2.201	2.718	3.106
12	.128	.395	.695	1.083	1.356	1.782	2.179	2.681	3.055
13	.128	.394	.694	1.079	1.350	1.771	2.160	2.650	3.012
14	.128	.393	.692	1.076	1.345	1.761	2.145	2.624	2.977
15	.128	.393	.691	1.074	1.341	1.753	2.131	2.602	2.947
16	.128	.392	.690	1.071	1.337	1.746	2.120	2.583	2.921
17	.128	.392	.689	1.069	1.333	1.740	2.110	2.567	2.898
18	.127	.392	.688	1.067	1.330	1.734	2.101	2.552	2.878
19	.127	.391	.688	1.066	1.328	1.729	2.093	2.539	2.861
20	.127	.391	.687	1.064	1.325	1.725	2.086	2.528	2.845
21	.127	.391	.686	1.063	1.323	1.721	2.080	2.518	2.831
22	.127	.390	.686	1.061	1.321	1.717	2.074	2.508	2.819
23	.127	.390	.685	1.060	1.319	1.714	2.069	2.500	2.807
24	.127	.390	.685	1.059	1.318	1.711	2.064	2.492	2.797
25	.127	.390	.684	1.058	1.316	1.708	2.060	2.485	2.787
26	.127	.390	.684	1.058	1.315	1.706	2.056	2.479	2.779
27	.127	.389	.684	1.057	1.314	1.703	2.052	2.473	2.771
28	.127	.389	.683	1.056	1.313	1.701	2.048	2.467	2.763
29	.127	.389	.683	1.055	1.311	1.699	2.045	2.462	2.756
30	.127	.389	.683	1.055	1.310	1.697	2.042	2.457	2.750
40	.126	.388	.681	1.050	1.303	1.684	2.021	2.423	2.704
60	.126	.387	.679	1.046	1.296	1.671	2.000	2.390	2.660
120	.126	.386	.677	1.041	1.289	1.658	1.980	2.358	2.617
∞	.126	.385	.674	1.036	1.282	1.645	1.960	2.326	2.576

Source: Stephen P. Shao. *Statistics for Business and Economics.* 3d ed. (Columbus, Ohio: Merrill Publishing Company, 1976), p. 789. Used with permission.

APPENDIX E Values of χ^2 for Selected Probabilities

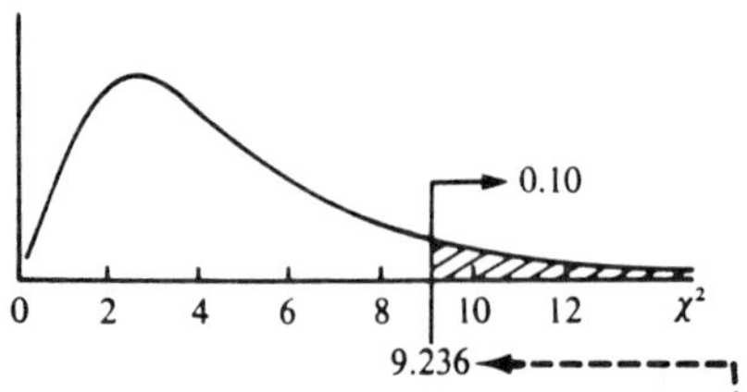

Example.
d.f. (Number of degrees of freedom) = 5:
The tail above $\chi^2 = 9.236$ represents 0.10 or 10% of the area under the curve.

	Probabilities (or Areas Under χ^2 Distribution Curve Above Given χ^2 Values)								
	.90	.70	.50	.30	.20	.10	.05	.02	.01
d.f	Values of χ^2								
1	.016	.148	.455	1.074	1.642	2.706	3.841	5.412	6.635
2	.211	.713	1.386	2.408	3.219	4.605	5.991	7.824	9.210
3	.584	1.424	2.366	3.665	4.642	6.251	7.815	9.837	11.345
4	1.064	2.195	3.357	4.878	5.989	7.779	9.488	11.668	13.277
5	1.610	3.000	4.351	6.064	7.289	**9.236**	11.070	13.388	15.086
6	2.204	3.828	5.348	7.231	8.558	10.645	12.592	15.033	16.812
7	2.833	4.671	6.346	8.383	9.803	12.017	14.067	16.622	18.475
8	3.490	5.527	7.344	9.524	11.030	13.362	15.507	18.168	20.090
9	4.168	6.393	8.343	10.656	12.242	14.684	16.919	19.679	21.666
10	4.865	7.267	9.342	11.781	13.442	15.987	18.307	21.161	23.209
11	5.578	8.148	10.341	12.899	14.631	17.275	19.675	22.618	24.725
12	6.304	9.034	11.340	14.011	15.812	18.549	21.026	24.054	26.217
13	7.042	9.926	12.340	15.119	16.985	19.812	22.362	25.472	27.688
14	7.790	10.821	13.339	16.222	18.151	21.064	23.685	26.873	29.141
15	8.547	11.721	14.339	17.322	19.311	22.307	24.996	28.259	30.578
16	9.312	12.624	15.338	18.418	20.465	23.542	26.296	29.633	32.000
17	10.085	13.531	16.338	19.511	21.615	24.769	27.587	30.995	33.409
18	10.865	14.440	17.338	20.601	22.760	25.989	28.869	33.346	34.805
19	11.651	15.352	18.338	21.689	23.900	27.204	30.144	33.687	36.191
20	12.443	16.266	19.337	22.775	25.038	28.412	31.410	35.020	37.566
21	13.240	17.182	20.337	23.858	26.171	29.615	32.671	36.343	38.932
22	14.041	18.101	21.337	24.939	27.301	30.813	33.924	37.659	40.289
23	14.848	19.021	22.337	26.018	28.429	32.007	35.172	38.968	41.638
24	15.659	19.943	23.337	27.096	29.553	33.196	36.415	40.270	42.980
25	16.473	20.867	24.337	28.172	30.675	34.382	37.652	41.566	44.314
26	17.292	21.792	25.336	29.246	31.795	35.563	38.885	42.856	45.642
27	18.114	22.719	26.336	30.319	32.912	36.741	40.113	44.140	46.963
28	18.939	23.647	27.336	31.391	34.027	37.916	41.337	45.419	48.278
29	19.768	24.577	28.336	32.461	35.139	39.087	42.557	46.693	49.588
30	20.599	25.508	29.336	33.530	36.250	40.256	43.773	47.962	50.892

Source: Stephen P. Shao. *Statistics for Business and Economics.* 3d ed. (Columbus, Ohio: Merrill Publishing Company, 1976), p. 790. Used with permission.

APPENDIX F Values of *F*

Upper 5% Probability (or 5% Area under *F*-Distribution Curve)

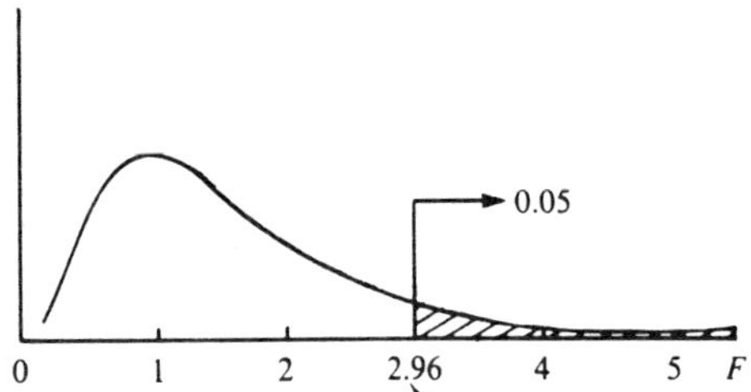

Example.
D_1 (degrees of freedom for numerator of F ratio) = 5,
D_2 (degrees of freedom for denominator) = 14:
The tail above $F = 2.96$ represents 0.05 or 5% of the area under the curve.

D_2 \ D_1	1	2	3	4	5	6	7	8	10	12
1	161	200	216	225	230	234	237	239	242	244
2	18.51	19.00	19.16	19.25	19.30	19.33	19.36	19.37	19.39	19.41
3	10.13	9.55	9.28	9.12	9.01	8.94	8.88	8.84	8.78	8.74
4	7.71	6.94	6.59	6.39	6.26	6.16	6.09	6.04	5.96	5.91
5	6.61	5.79	5.41	5.19	5.05	4.95	4.88	4.82	4.74	4.68
6	5.99	5.14	4.76	4.53	4.39	4.28	4.21	4.15	4.06	4.00
7	5.59	4.74	4.35	4.12	3.97	3.87	3.79	3.73	3.63	3.57
8	5.32	4.46	4.07	3.84	3.69	3.58	3.50	3.44	3.34	3.28
10	4.96	4.10	3.71	3.48	3.33	3.22	3.14	3.07	2.97	2.91
12	4.75	3.88	3.49	3.26	3.11	3.00	2.92	2.85	2.76	2.69
14	4.60	3.74	3.34	3.11	2.96	2.85	2.77	2.70	2.60	2.53
16	4.49	3.63	3.24	3.01	2.85	2.74	2.66	2.59	2.49	2.42
20	4.35	3.49	3.10	2.87	2.71	2.60	2.52	2.45	2.35	2.28
24	4.26	3.40	3.01	2.78	2.62	2.51	2.43	2.36	2.26	2.18
30	4.17	3.32	2.92	2.69	2.53	2.42	2.34	2.27	2.16	2.09
40	4.08	3.23	2.84	2.61	2.45	2.34	2.25	2.18	2.07	2.00
50	4.03	3.18	2.79	2.56	2.40	2.29	2.20	2.13	2.02	1.95
100	3.94	3.09	2.70	2.46	2.30	2.19	2.10	2.03	1.92	1.85
200	3.89	3.04	2.65	2.41	2.26	2.14	2.05	1.98	1.87	1.80
∞	3.84	2.99	2.60	2.37	2.21	2.09	2.01	1.94	1.83	1.75

D_2 \ D_1	14	16	20	24	30	40	50	100	200	∞
1	245	246	248	249	250	251	252	253	254	254
2	19.42	19.43	19.44	19.45	19.46	19.47	19.47	19.49	19.49	19.50
3	8.71	8.69	8.66	8.64	8.62	8.60	8.58	8.56	8.54	8.53
4	5.87	5.84	5.80	5.77	5.74	5.71	5.70	5.66	5.65	5.63
5	4.64	4.60	4.56	4.53	4.50	4.46	4.44	4.40	4.38	4.36
6	3.96	3.92	3.87	3.84	3.81	3.77	3.75	3.71	3.69	3.67
7	3.52	3.49	3.44	3.41	3.38	3.34	3.32	3.28	3.25	3.23
8	3.23	3.20	3.15	3.12	3.08	3.05	3.03	2.98	2.96	2.93
10	2.86	2.82	2.77	2.74	2.70	2.67	2.64	2.59	2.56	2.54
12	2.64	2.60	2.54	2.50	2.46	2.42	2.40	2.35	2.32	2.30
14	2.48	2.44	2.39	2.35	2.31	2.27	2.24	2.19	2.16	2.13
16	2.37	2.33	2.28	2.24	2.20	2.16	2.13	2.07	2.04	2.01
20	2.23	2.18	2.12	2.08	2.04	1.99	1.96	1.90	1.87	1.84
24	2.13	2.09	2.02	1.98	1.94	1.89	1.86	1.80	1.76	1.73
30	2.04	1.99	1.93	1.89	1.84	1.79	1.76	1.69	1.66	1.62
40	1.95	1.90	1.84	1.79	1.74	1.69	1.66	1.59	1.55	1.51
50	1.90	1.85	1.78	1.74	1.69	1.63	1.60	1.52	1.48	1.44
100	1.79	1.75	1.68	1.63	1.57	1.51	1.48	1.39	1.34	1.28
200	1.74	1.69	1.62	1.57	1.52	1.45	1.42	1.32	1.26	1.19
∞	1.69	1.64	1.57	1.52	1.46	1.40	1.35	1.24	1.17	1.00

Source: Reproduced by permission from *Statistical Methods*, 5th ed., by George W. Snedecor.

Upper 1% Probability (or 1% Area under *F*-Distribution Curve)

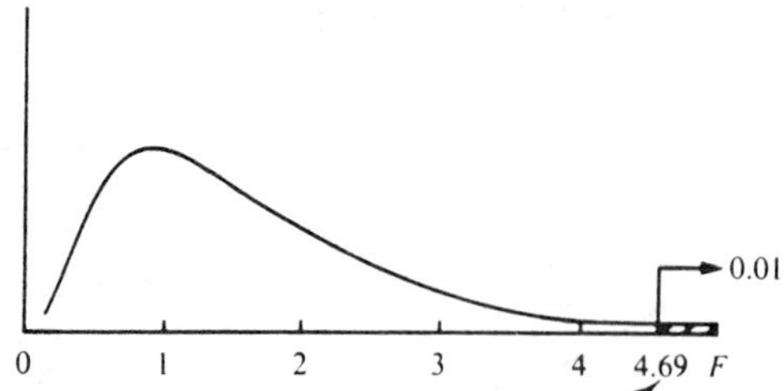

Example.
D_1 (degrees of freedom for numerator of F ratio) = 5,
D_2 (degrees of freedom for denominator) = **14**:
The tail above F = **4.69** represents 0.01 or 1% of the area under the curve.

D_2 \ D_1	1	2	3	4	5	6	7	8	10	12
1	4,052	4,999	5,403	5,625	5,764	5,859	5,928	5,981	6,056	6,106
2	98.49	99.00	99.17	99.25	99.30	99.33	99.34	99.36	99.40	99.42
3	34.12	30.82	29.46	28.71	28.24	27.91	27.67	27.49	27.23	27.05
4	21.20	18.00	16.69	15.98	15.52	15.21	14.98	14.80	14.54	14.37
5	16.26	13.27	12.06	11.39	10.97	10.67	10.45	10.27	10.05	9.89
6	13.74	10.92	9.78	9.15	8.75	8.47	8.26	8.10	7.87	7.72
7	12.25	9.55	8.45	7.85	7.46	7.19	7.00	6.84	6.62	6.47
8	11.26	8.65	7.59	7.01	6.63	6.37	6.19	6.03	5.82	5.67
10	10.04	7.56	6.55	5.99	5.64	5.39	5.21	5.06	4.85	4.71
12	9.33	6.93	5.95	5.41	5.06	4.82	4.65	4.50	4.30	4.16
14	8.86	6.51	5.56	5.03	4.69	4.46	4.28	4.14	3.94	3.80
16	8.53	6.23	5.29	4.77	4.44	4.20	4.03	3.89	3.69	3.55
20	8.10	5.85	4.94	4.43	4.10	3.87	3.71	3.56	3.37	3.23
24	7.82	5.61	4.72	4.22	3.90	3.67	3.50	3.36	3.17	3.03
30	7.56	5.39	4.51	4.02	3.70	3.47	3.30	3.17	2.98	2.84
40	7.31	5.18	4.31	3.83	3.51	3.29	3.12	2.99	2.80	2.66
50	7.17	5.06	4.20	3.72	3.41	3.18	3.02	2.88	2.70	2.56
100	6.90	4.82	3.98	3.51	3.20	2.99	2.82	2.69	2.51	2.36
200	6.76	4.71	3.88	3.41	3.11	2.90	2.73	2.60	2.41	2.28
∞	6.64	4.60	3.78	3.32	3.02	2.80	2.64	2.51	2.32	2.18

D_2 \ D_1	14	16	20	24	30	40	50	100	200	∞
1	6,142	6,169	6,208	6,234	6,258	6,286	6,302	6,334	6,352	6,366
2	99.43	99.44	99.45	99.46	99.47	99.48	99.48	99.49	99.49	99.50
3	26.92	26.83	26.69	26.60	26.50	26.41	26.35	26.23	26.18	26.12
4	14.24	14.15	14.02	13.93	13.83	13.74	13.69	13.57	13.52	13.46
5	9.77	9.68	9.55	9.47	9.38	9.29	9.24	9.13	9.07	9.02
6	7.60	7.52	7.39	7.31	7.23	7.14	7.09	6.99	6.94	6.88
7	6.35	6.27	6.15	6.07	5.98	5.90	5.85	5.75	5.70	5.65
8	5.56	5.48	5.36	5.28	5.20	5.11	5.06	4.96	4.91	4.86
10	4.60	4.52	4.41	4.33	4.25	4.17	4.12	4.01	3.96	3.91
12	4.05	3.98	3.86	3.78	3.70	3.61	3.56	3.46	3.41	3.36
14	3.70	3.62	3.51	3.43	3.34	3.26	3.21	3.11	3.06	3.00
16	3.45	3.37	3.25	3.18	3.10	3.01	2.96	2.86	2.80	2.75
20	3.13	3.05	2.94	2.86	2.77	2.69	2.63	2.53	2.47	2.42
24	2.93	2.85	2.74	2.66	2.58	2.49	2.44	2.33	2.27	2.21
30	2.74	2.66	2.55	2.47	2.38	2.29	2.24	2.13	2.07	2.01
40	2.56	2.49	2.37	2.29	2.20	2.11	2.05	1.94	1.88	1.81
50	2.46	2.39	2.26	2.18	2.10	2.00	1.94	1.82	1.76	1.68
100	2.26	2.19	2.06	1.98	1.89	1.79	1.73	1.59	1.51	1.43
200	2.17	2.09	1.97	1.88	1.79	1.69	1.62	1.48	1.39	1.28
∞	2.07	1.99	1.87	1.79	1.69	1.59	1.52	1.36	1.25	1.00

Source: Reproduced by permission from *Statistical Methods*, 5th ed., by George W. Snedecor. © 1956 by the Iowa State University Press.

APPENDIX G Distribution of the Studentized Range

$p = 0.95$

Percentage points of the Studentized range, $q = (x_{D_1} - x_1)/s_{D_2}$.

D_2 \ D_1	2	3	4	5	6	7	8	9	10
1	17·97	26·98	32·82	37·08	40·41	43·12	45·40	47·36	49·07
2	6·08	8·33	9·80	10·88	11·74	12·44	13·03	13·54	13·99
3	4·50	5·91	6·82	7·50	8·04	8·48	8·85	9·18	9·46
4	3·93	5·04	5·76	6·29	6·71	7·05	7·35	7·60	7·83
5	3·64	4·60	5·22	5·67	6·03	6·33	6·58	6·80	6·99
6	3·46	4·34	4·90	5·30	5·63	5·90	6·12	6·32	6·49
7	3·34	4·16	4·68	5·06	5·36	5·61	5·82	6·00	6·16
8	3·26	4·04	4·53	4·89	5·17	5·40	5·60	5·77	5·92
9	3·20	3·95	4·41	4·76	5·02	5·24	5·43	5·59	5·74
10	3·15	3·88	4·33	4·65	4·91	5·12	5·30	5·46	5·60
11	3·11	3·82	4·26	4·57	4·82	5·03	5·20	5·35	5·49
12	3·08	3·77	4·20	4·51	4·75	4·95	5·12	5·27	5·39
13	3·06	3·73	4·15	4·45	4·69	4·88	5·05	5·19	5·32
14	3·03	3·70	4·11	4·41	4·64	4·83	4·99	5·13	5·25
15	3·01	3·67	4·08	4·37	4·59	4·78	4·94	5·08	5·20
16	3·00	3·65	4·05	4·33	4·56	4·74	4·90	5·03	5·15
17	2·98	3·63	4·02	4·30	4·52	4·70	4·86	4·99	5·11
18	2·97	3·61	4·00	4·28	4·49	4·67	4·82	4·96	5·07
19	2·96	3·59	3·98	4·25	4·47	4·65	4·79	4·92	5·04
20	2·95	3·58	3·96	4·23	4·45	4·62	4·77	4·90	5·01
24	2·92	3·53	3·90	4·17	4·37	4·54	4·68	4·81	4·92
30	2·89	3·49	3·85	4·10	4·30	4·46	4·60	4·72	4·82
40	2·86	3·44	3·79	4·04	4·23	4·39	4·52	4·63	4·73
60	2·83	3·40	3·74	3·98	4·16	4·31	4·44	4·55	4·65
120	2·80	3·36	3·68	3·92	4·10	4·24	4·36	4·47	4·56
∞	2·77	3·31	3·63	3·86	4·03	4·17	4·29	4·39	4·47

D_2 \ D_1	11	12	13	14	15	16	17	18	19	20
1	50·59	51·96	53·20	54·33	55·36	56·32	57·22	58·04	58·83	59·56
2	14·39	14·75	15·08	15·38	15·65	15·91	16·14	16·37	16·57	16·77
3	9·72	9·95	10·15	10·35	10·52	10·69	10·84	10·98	11·11	11·24
4	8·03	8·21	8·37	8·52	8·66	8·79	8·91	9·03	9·13	9·23
5	7·17	7·32	7·47	7·60	7·72	7·83	7·93	8·03	8·12	8·21
6	6·65	6·79	6·92	7·03	7·14	7·24	7·34	7·43	7·51	7·59
7	6·30	6·43	6·55	6·66	6·76	6·85	6·94	7·02	7·10	7·17
8	6·05	6·18	6·29	6·39	6·48	6·57	6·65	6·73	6·80	6·87
9	5·87	5·98	6·09	6·19	6·28	6·36	6·44	6·51	6·58	6·64
10	5·72	5·83	5·93	6·03	6·11	6·19	6·27	6·34	6·40	6·47
11	5·61	5·71	5·81	5·90	5·98	6·06	6·13	6·20	6·27	6·33
12	5·51	5·61	5·71	5·80	5·88	5·95	6·02	6·09	6·15	6·21
13	5·43	5·53	5·63	5·71	5·79	5·86	5·93	5·99	6·05	6·11
14	5·36	5·46	5·55	5·64	5·71	5·79	5·85	5·91	5·97	6·03
15	5·31	5·40	5·49	5·57	5·65	5·72	5·78	5·85	5·90	5·96
16	5·26	5·35	5·44	5·52	5·59	5·66	5·73	5·79	5·84	5·90
17	5·21	5·31	5·39	5·47	5·54	5·61	5·67	5·73	5·79	5·84
18	5·17	5·27	5·35	5·43	5·50	5·57	5·63	5·69	5·74	5·79
19	5·14	5·23	5·31	5·39	5·46	5·53	5·59	5·65	5·70	5·75
20	5·11	5·20	5·28	5·36	5·43	5·49	5·55	5·61	5·66	5·71
24	5·01	5·10	5·18	5·25	5·32	5·38	5·44	5·49	5·55	5·59
30	4·92	5·00	5·08	5·15	5·21	5·27	5·33	5·38	5·43	5·47
40	4·82	4·90	4·98	5·04	5·11	5·16	5·22	5·27	5·31	5·36
60	4·73	4·81	4·88	4·94	5·00	5·06	5·11	5·15	5·20	5·24
120	4·64	4·71	4·78	4·84	4·90	4·95	5·00	5·04	5·09	5·13
∞	4·55	4·62	4·68	4·74	4·80	4·85	4·89	4·93	4·97	5·01

D_1: Size of sample from which range obtained. D_2: Degrees of freedom of independent s_{D_1}.

$p = 0.99$

D_2 \ D_1	2	3	4	5	6	7	8	9	10
1	90·03	135·0	164·3	185·6	202·2	215·8	227·2	237·0	245·6
2	14·04	19·02	22·29	24·72	26·63	28·20	29·53	30·68	31·69
3	8·26	10·62	12·17	13·33	14·24	15·00	15·64	16·20	16·69
4	6·51	8·12	9·17	9·96	10·58	11·10	11·55	11·93	12·27
5	5·70	6·98	7·80	8·42	8·91	9·32	9·67	9·97	10·24
6	5·24	6·33	7·03	7·56	7·97	8·32	8·61	8·87	9·10
7	4·95	5·92	6·54	7·01	7·37	7·68	7·94	8·17	8·37
8	4·75	5·64	6·20	6·62	6·96	7·24	7·47	7·68	7·86
9	4·60	5·43	5·96	6·35	6·66	6·91	7·13	7·33	7·49
10	4·48	5·27	5·77	6·14	6·43	6·67	6·87	7·05	7·21
11	4·39	5·15	5·62	5·97	6·25	6·48	6·67	6·84	6·99
12	4·32	5·05	5·50	5·84	6·10	6·32	6·51	6·67	6·81
13	4·26	4·96	5·40	5·73	5·98	6·19	6·37	6·53	6·67
14	4·21	4·89	5·32	5·63	5·88	6·08	6·26	6·41	6·54
15	4·17	4·84	5·25	5·56	5·80	5·99	6·16	6·31	6·44
16	4·13	4·79	5·19	5·49	5·72	5·92	6·08	6·22	6·35
17	4·10	4·74	5·14	5·43	5·66	5·85	6·01	6·15	6·27
18	4·07	4·70	5·09	5·38	5·60	5·79	5·94	6·08	6·20
19	4·05	4·67	5·05	5·33	5·55	5·73	5·89	6·02	6·14
20	4·02	4·64	5·02	5·29	5·51	5·69	5·84	5·97	6·09
24	3·96	4·55	4·91	5·17	5·37	5·54	5·69	5·81	5·92
30	3·89	4·45	4·80	5·05	5·24	5·40	5·54	5·65	5·76
40	3·82	4·37	4·70	4·93	5·11	5·26	5·39	5·50	5·60
60	3·76	4·28	4·59	4·82	4·99	5·13	5·25	5·36	5·45
120	3·70	4·20	4·50	4·71	4·87	5·01	5·12	5·21	5·30
∞	3·64	4·12	4·40	4·60	4·76	4·88	4·99	5·08	5·16

D_2 \ D_1	11	12	13	14	15	16	17	18	19	20
1	253·2	260·0	266·2	271·8	277·0	281·8	286·3	290·4	294·3	298·0
2	32·59	33·40	34·13	34·81	35·43	36·00	36·53	37·03	37·50	37·95
3	17·13	17·53	17·89	18·22	18·52	18·81	19·07	19·32	19·55	19·77
4	12·57	12·84	13·09	13·32	13·53	13·73	13·91	14·08	14·24	14·40
5	10·48	10·70	10·89	11·08	11·24	11·40	11·55	11·68	11·81	11·93
6	9·30	9·48	9·65	9·81	9·95	10·08	10·21	10·32	10·43	10·54
7	8·55	8·71	8·86	9·00	9·12	9·24	9·35	9·46	9·55	9·65
8	8·03	8·18	8·31	8·44	8·55	8·66	8·76	8·85	8·94	9·03
9	7·65	7·78	7·91	8·03	8·13	8·23	8·33	8·41	8·49	8·57
10	7·36	7·49	7·60	7·71	7·81	7·91	7·99	8·08	8·15	8·23
11	7·13	7·25	7·36	7·46	7·56	7·65	7·73	7·81	7·88	7·95
12	6·94	7·06	7·17	7·26	7·36	7·44	7·52	7·59	7·66	7·73
13	6·79	6·90	7·01	7·10	7·19	7·27	7·35	7·42	7·48	7·55
14	6·66	6·77	6·87	6·96	7·05	7·13	7·20	7·27	7·33	7·39
15	6·55	6·66	6·76	6·84	6·93	7·00	7·07	7·14	7·20	7·26
16	6·46	6·56	6·66	6·74	6·82	6·90	6·97	7·03	7·09	7·15
17	6·38	6·48	6·57	6·66	6·73	6·81	6·87	6·94	7·00	7·05
18	6·31	6·41	6·50	6·58	6·65	6·73	6·79	6·85	6·91	6·97
19	6·25	6·34	6·43	6·51	6·58	6·65	6·72	6·78	6·84	6·89
20	6·19	6·28	6·37	6·45	6·52	6·59	6·65	6·71	6·77	6·82
24	6·02	6·11	6·19	6·26	6·33	6·39	6·45	6·51	6·56	6·61
30	5·85	5·93	6·01	6·08	6·14	6·20	6·26	6·31	6·36	6·41
40	5·69	5·76	5·83	5·90	5·96	6·02	6·07	6·12	6·16	6·21
60	5·53	5·60	5·67	5·73	5·78	5·84	5·89	5·93	5·97	6·01
120	5·37	5·44	5·50	5·56	5·61	5·66	5·71	5·75	5·79	5·83
∞	5·23	5·29	5·35	5·40	5·45	5·49	5·54	5·57	5·61	5·65

Source: Reprinted with permission from E. S. Pearson and H. O. Hartley, *Biometrika Tables for Statisticians* (New York: Cambridge University Press, 1954).

APPENDIX H Random Number Table

1260	5529	9540	3569	8381	9742	2590	2516	4243	8130
8979	2446	7606	6948	4519	2636	6655	1166	2096	1137
5470	0061	1760	5993	4319	0825	6874	3753	8362	1237
9733	0297	0804	4942	7694	9340	2502	3597	7691	5000
7492	6719	6816	7567	0364	2306	2217	5626	6526	6166
3715	2248	2337	6530	1660	7441	1598	0477	6620	1250
9491	4842	6210	9140	0180	5935	7218	4966	0537	4416
5192	7719	0654	4428	9771	4677	3291	4459	7432	2054
1714	3725	9397	9648	2550	0704	1239	5263	1601	5177
1052	8415	3686	4239	3272	7135	5768	8718	7582	8366
6998	3891	9352	6056	3621	5395	4551	4017	2405	0831
4216	4724	2898	1050	2164	8020	5274	6688	8636	2438
7115	2637	3828	0810	4598	2329	7953	4913	0033	2661
6647	4252	1869	9634	1341	7958	9460	1712	6060	0638
3475	2925	5097	8258	8343	7264	3295	8021	6318	0454
0415	1533	7670	0618	5193	9291	2205	2046	0890	6997
7064	4946	2618	7116	3784	2007	2326	4361	4695	8612
9772	4445	0343	5238	0317	7531	5916	8229	3296	2321
5365	4306	4036	9873	9669	8505	8675	3116	1484	9975
6395	4681	9319	6908	8154	5415	5728	1593	9452	8213
1554	0411	3436	1101	0966	5188	0225	5615	8568	5169
6745	7372	6984	0228	1920	6710	3459	0663	1407	9211
2217	3801	5860	1673	0264	6911	7623	7137	0774	5898
9255	9297	4305	5060	8312	9192	6016	7238	5193	4908
1615	9761	5744	2733	5314	6985	6670	0975	5487	6107
6679	4951	5716	5889	4413	1513	5023	7313	0317	0517
5221	3207	0351	2452	1072	3830	5518	5972	6111	9352
7720	5131	4867	6501	6970	4075	4869	4798	7104	5342
2767	6055	2801	7033	5305	9382	2354	4135	5975	7830
9202	6815	8211	5274	2303	1437	8995	2514	6515	0049
9359	2754	8587	2790	9524	5068	1230	4165	7025	4365
1078	7661	0999	4413	3446	2971	7576	3385	3308	0557
5732	4853	2025	1145	9743	8646	4918	3674	8049	1622
1596	0578	1493	4681	3806	8837	4241	4123	6513	3083
0602	8144	8976	9195	9012	7700	1708	5724	0315	8032
3624	8592	7942	4289	0736	4986	4839	4507	4997	7407
9328	3001	1462	1101	0804	9724	4082	2384	9631	8334
1981	1295	1963	3391	5757	4403	5857	4329	3682	3823
6001	4295	1488	6702	9954	6980	4027	8492	8195	7934
3743	0097	4798	6390	6465	6449	7990	3774	3577	3895

3343	6936	1449	2915	6668	8543	3147	1442	6022	0056
9208	3820	5165	3445	2642	2910	8336	1244	6346	0487
4581	3768	1559	7558	6660	0116	7949	5609	2887	4156
3206	5146	7191	8420	2319	4650	3734	0501	0739	2025
5662	8315	4226	8395	2931	1812	3575	9341	5894	3691
4631	6278	9444	4058	0505	4449	5959	7483	8641	1311
1046	6653	8333	5813	6586	9820	0190	9214	1947	9677
5231	2788	7198	5904	8370	8347	6599	7304	6430	3495
5349	6641	3234	8692	4424	9179	2767	9517	1173	4160
8363	9625	3329	5262	5360	8181	9298	6629	2433	9414
5967	1261	2470	8867	1962	1630	8360	6024	6232	8386
6716	3916	8712	6673	1156	0001	6760	6287	4546	5743
0323	3514	8550	3709	6614	5764	0600	7444	2795	4426
1765	0918	8972	9924	5941	0331	6909	4872	5693	8957
4345	6886	2032	4817	2725	9471	2443	9532	4770	1271
9614	8571	2174	0071	7824	0504	9600	6414	5734	1371
1291	8246	5019	6559	5051	5265	1184	9030	6689	2776
3867	3915	8311	2430	1235	7283	6481	2012	8487	0226
1056	1880	3610	7796	7192	6663	5810	3512	1572	2921
1691	2237	6713	4048	8865	5794	3419	4372	6996	8342
7920	8490	2822	2647	1700	5335	0732	9987	7501	1223
1646	4251	7732	2136	4339	0331	9293	1061	2663	4821
7928	2575	2139	2825	3806	2082	9285	7640	6166	5758
3563	9078	1979	1141	7911	6981	0183	7479	1146	8949
6546	3459	3824	2151	3313	0178	9143	7854	3935	7300
8315	8778	1296	3434	9420	3622	3521	0807	5719	7764
8442	4933	8173	6427	4354	3523	3492	2816	9191	6261
7446	1576	2520	6120	8546	3146	6084	1260	3737	1333
2619	1261	2028	7505	0710	4589	9632	2347	1975	6839
0814	8542	1526	1202	8091	9441	0456	0603	8297	1412

Source: Reprinted from Richard J. Hopeman, *Production and Operations Management*, 4th ed. (Columbus, Ohio: Merrill Publishing Company, 1980), 569–70. Used with permission.

APPENDIX I Durbin–Watson Test Bounds

Level of Significance $\alpha = 0.05$

	$p-1=1$		$p-1=2$		$p-1=3$		$p-1=4$		$p-1=5$	
n	d_L	d_U	d_L	d_U	d_L	d_U	d_L	d_U	d_L	d_U
15	1.08	1.36	0.95	1.54	0.82	1.75	0.69	1.97	0.56	2.21
16	1.10	1.37	0.98	1.54	0.86	1.73	0.74	1.93	0.62	2.15
17	1.13	1.38	1.02	1.54	0.90	1.71	0.78	1.90	0.67	2.10
18	1.16	1.39	1.05	1.53	0.93	1.69	0.82	1.87	0.71	2.06
19	1.18	1.40	1.08	1.53	0.97	1.68	0.86	1.85	0.75	2.02
20	1.20	1.41	1.10	1.54	1.00	1.68	0.90	1.83	0.79	1.99
21	1.22	1.42	1.13	1.54	1.03	1.67	0.93	1.81	0.83	1.96
22	1.24	1.43	1.15	1.54	1.05	1.66	0.96	1.80	0.86	1.94
23	1.26	1.44	1.17	1.54	1.08	1.66	0.99	1.79	0.90	1.92
24	1.27	1.45	1.19	1.55	1.10	1.66	1.01	1.78	0.93	1.90
25	1.29	1.45	1.21	1.55	1.12	1.66	1.04	1.77	0.95	1.89
26	1.30	1.46	1.22	1.55	1.14	1.65	1.06	1.76	0.98	1.88
27	1.32	1.47	1.24	1.56	1.16	1.65	1.08	1.76	1.01	1.86
28	1.33	1.48	1.26	1.56	1.18	1.65	1.10	1.75	1.03	1.85
29	1.34	1.48	1.27	1.56	1.20	1.65	1.12	1.74	1.05	1.84
30	1.35	1.49	1.28	1.57	1.21	1.65	1.14	1.74	1.07	1.83
31	1.36	1.50	1.30	1.57	1.23	1.65	1.16	1.74	1.09	1.83
32	1.37	1.50	1.31	1.57	1.24	1.65	1.18	1.73	1.11	1.82
33	1.38	1.51	1.32	1.58	1.26	1.65	1.19	1.73	1.13	1.81
34	1.39	1.51	1.33	1.58	1.27	1.65	1.21	1.73	1.15	1.81
35	1.40	1.52	1.34	1.58	1.28	1.65	1.22	1.73	1.16	1.80
36	1.41	1.52	1.35	1.59	1.29	1.65	1.24	1.73	1.18	1.80
37	1.42	1.53	1.36	1.59	1.31	1.66	1.25	1.72	1.19	1.80
38	1.43	1.54	1.37	1.59	1.32	1.66	1.26	1.72	1.21	1.79
39	1.43	1.54	1.38	1.60	1.33	1.66	1.27	1.72	1.22	1.79
40	1.44	1.54	1.39	1.60	1.34	1.66	1.29	1.72	1.23	1.79
45	1.48	1.57	1.43	1.62	1.38	1.67	1.34	1.72	1.29	1.78
50	1.50	1.59	1.46	1.63	1.42	1.67	1.38	1.72	1.34	1.77
55	1.53	1.60	1.49	1.64	1.45	1.68	1.41	1.72	1.38	1.77
60	1.55	1.62	1.51	1.65	1.48	1.69	1.44	1.73	1.41	1.77
65	1.57	1.63	1.54	1.66	1.50	1.70	1.47	1.73	1.44	1.77
70	1.58	1.64	1.55	1.67	1.52	1.70	1.49	1.74	1.46	1.77
75	1.60	1.65	1.57	1.68	1.54	1.71	1.51	1.74	1.49	1.77
80	1.61	1.66	1.59	1.69	1.56	1.72	1.53	1.74	1.51	1.77
85	1.62	1.67	1.60	1.70	1.57	1.72	1.55	1.75	1.52	1.77
90	1.63	1.68	1.61	1.70	1.59	1.73	1.57	1.75	1.54	1.78
95	1.64	1.69	1.62	1.71	1.60	1.73	1.58	1.75	1.56	1.78
100	1.65	1.69	1.63	1.72	1.61	1.74	1.59	1.76	1.57	1.78

Level of Significance $\alpha = 0.01$

n	$p-1=1$		$p-1=2$		$p-1=3$		$p-1=4$		$p-1=5$	
	d_L	d_U	d_L	d_U	d_L	d_U	d_L	d_U	d_L	d_U
15	0.81	1.07	0.70	1.25	0.59	1.46	0.49	1.70	0.39	1.96
16	0.84	1.09	0.74	1.25	0.63	1.44	0.53	1.66	0.44	1.90
17	0.87	1.10	0.77	1.25	0.67	1.43	0.57	1.63	0.48	1.85
18	0.90	1.12	0.80	1.26	0.71	1.42	0.61	1.60	0.52	1.80
19	0.93	1.13	0.83	1.26	0.74	1.41	0.65	1.58	0.56	1.77
20	0.95	1.15	0.86	1.27	0.77	1.41	0.68	1.57	0.60	1.74
21	0.97	1.16	0.89	1.27	0.80	1.41	0.72	1.55	0.63	1.71
22	1.00	1.17	0.91	1.28	0.83	1.40	0.75	1.54	0.66	1.69
23	1.02	1.19	0.94	1.29	0.86	1.40	0.77	1.53	0.70	1.67
24	1.04	1.20	0.96	1.30	0.88	1.41	0.80	1.53	0.72	1.66
25	1.05	1.21	0.98	1.30	0.90	1.41	0.83	1.52	0.75	1.65
26	1.07	1.22	1.00	1.31	0.93	1.41	0.85	1.52	0.78	1.64
27	1.09	1.23	1.02	1.32	0.95	1.41	0.88	1.51	0.81	1.63
28	1.10	1.24	1.04	1.32	0.97	1.41	0.90	1.51	0.83	1.62
29	1.12	1.25	1.05	1.33	0.99	1.42	0.92	1.51	0.85	1.61
30	1.13	1.26	1.07	1.34	1.01	1.42	0.94	1.51	0.88	1.61
31	1.15	1.27	1.08	1.34	1.02	1.42	0.96	1.51	0.90	1.60
32	1.16	1.28	1.10	1.35	1.04	1.43	0.98	1.51	0.92	1.60
33	1.17	1.29	1.11	1.36	1.05	1.43	1.00	1.51	0.94	1.59
34	1.18	1.30	1.13	1.36	1.07	1.43	1.01	1.51	0.95	1.59
35	1.19	1.31	1.14	1.37	1.08	1.44	1.03	1.51	0.97	1.59
36	1.21	1.32	1.15	1.38	1.10	1.44	1.04	1.51	0.99	1.59
37	1.22	1.32	1.16	1.38	1.11	1.45	1.06	1.51	1.00	1.59
38	1.23	1.33	1.18	1.39	1.12	1.45	1.07	1.52	1.02	1.58
39	1.24	1.34	1.19	1.39	1.14	1.45	1.09	1.52	1.03	1.58
40	1.25	1.34	1.20	1.40	1.15	1.46	1.10	1.52	1.05	1.58
45	1.29	1.38	1.24	1.42	1.20	1.48	1.16	1.53	1.11	1.58
50	1.32	1.40	1.28	1.45	1.24	1.49	1.20	1.54	1.16	1.59
55	1.36	1.43	1.32	1.47	1.28	1.51	1.25	1.55	1.21	1.59
60	1.38	1.45	1.35	1.48	1.32	1.52	1.28	1.56	1.25	1.60
65	1.41	1.47	1.38	1.50	1.35	1.53	1.31	1.57	1.28	1.61
70	1.43	1.49	1.40	1.52	1.37	1.55	1.34	1.58	1.31	1.61
75	1.45	1.50	1.42	1.53	1.39	1.56	1.37	1.59	1.34	1.62
80	1.47	1.52	1.44	1.54	1.42	1.57	1.39	1.60	1.36	1.62
85	1.48	1.53	1.46	1.55	1.43	1.58	1.41	1.60	1.39	1.63
90	1.50	1.54	1.47	1.56	1.45	1.59	1.43	1.61	1.41	1.64
95	1.51	1.55	1.49	1.57	1.47	1.60	1.45	1.62	1.42	1.64
100	1.52	1.56	1.50	1.58	1.48	1.60	1.46	1.63	1.44	1.65

Source: J. Durbin and G. S. Watson, "Testing for Serial Correlation in Least Squares Regression, II," *Biometrika* 38 (1951), 159–78. Reprinted with permission.

APPENDIX J Lilliefors Test Statistic

	$p = .80$	.85	.90	.95	.99
Sample size $n = 4$	.300	.319	.352	.381	.417
5	.285	.299	.315	.337	.405
6	.265	.277	.294	.319	.364
7	.247	.258	.276	.300	.348
8	.233	.244	.261	.285	.331
9	.223	.233	.249	.271	.311
10	.215	.224	.239	.258	.294
11	.206	.217	.230	.249	.284
12	.199	.212	.223	.242	.275
13	.190	.202	.214	.234	.268
14	.183	.194	.207	.227	.261
15	.177	.187	.201	.220	.257
16	.173	.182	.195	.213	.250
17	.169	.177	.189	.206	.245
18	.166	.173	.184	.200	.239
19	.163	.169	.179	.195	.235
20	.160	.166	.174	.190	.231
25	.142	.147	.158	.173	.200
30	.131	.136	.133	.161	.187
Over 30	$\frac{.736}{\sqrt{n}}$	$\frac{.768}{\sqrt{n}}$	$\frac{.805}{\sqrt{n}}$	$\frac{.886}{\sqrt{n}}$	$\frac{1.031}{\sqrt{n}}$

The entries in this table are the approximate quantiles, w_p, of the Lilliefors test statistic, T_2. Reject H_0 at the level α if T_2 exceeds $w_{1-\alpha}$ for the particular sample size n.

From Table 1 of "On the Kolmogorov–Smirnov Test for Normality with Mean and Variance Unknown," by H. W. Lilliefors, *Journal of the American Statistical Association* **62** (1967): 399–402. Reprinted by permission.

APPENDIX K Critical Values of *r* in the Runs Test

a. Lower Tail: Too Few Runs

n_1 \ n_2	2	3	4	5	6	7	8	9	10	11	12	13	14	15	16	17	18	19	20
2											2	2	2	2	2	2	2	2	2
3					2	2	2	2	2	2	2	2	2	3	3	3	3	3	3
4				2	2	2	3	3	3	3	3	3	3	3	4	4	4	4	4
5			2	2	3	3	3	3	3	4	4	4	4	4	4	4	5	5	5
6		2	2	3	3	3	3	4	4	4	4	5	5	5	5	5	5	6	6
7		2	2	3	3	3	4	4	5	5	5	5	5	6	6	6	6	6	6
8		2	3	3	3	4	4	5	5	5	6	6	6	6	6	7	7	7	7
9		2	3	3	4	4	5	5	5	6	6	6	7	7	7	7	8	8	8
10		2	3	3	4	5	5	5	6	6	7	7	7	7	8	8	8	8	9
11		2	3	4	4	5	5	6	6	7	7	7	8	8	8	9	9	9	9
12	2	2	3	4	4	5	6	6	7	7	7	8	8	8	9	9	9	10	10
13	2	2	3	4	5	5	6	6	7	7	8	8	9	9	9	10	10	10	10
14	2	2	3	4	5	5	6	7	7	8	8	9	9	9	10	10	10	11	11
15	2	3	3	4	5	6	6	7	7	8	8	9	9	10	10	11	11	11	12
16	2	3	4	4	5	6	6	7	8	8	9	9	10	10	11	11	11	12	12
17	2	3	4	4	5	6	7	7	8	9	9	10	10	11	11	11	12	12	13
18	2	3	4	5	5	6	7	8	8	9	9	10	10	11	11	12	12	13	13
19	2	3	4	5	6	6	7	8	8	9	10	10	11	11	12	12	13	13	13
20	2	3	4	5	6	6	7	8	9	9	10	10	11	12	12	13	13	13	14

b. Upper Tail: Too Many Runs

n_1 \ n_2	2	3	4	5	6	7	8	9	10	11	12	13	14	15	16	17	18	19	20
2																			
3																			
4				9	9														
5			9	10	10	11	11												
6			9	10	11	12	12	13	13	13	13								
7				11	12	13	13	14	14	14	14	15	15	15					
8				11	12	13	14	14	15	15	16	16	16	16	17	17	17	17	17
9					13	14	14	15	16	16	16	17	17	18	18	18	18	18	18
10					13	14	15	16	16	17	17	18	18	18	19	19	19	20	20
11					13	14	15	16	17	17	18	19	19	19	20	20	20	21	21
12					13	14	16	16	17	18	19	19	20	20	21	21	21	22	22
13						15	16	17	18	19	19	20	20	21	21	22	22	23	23
14						15	16	17	18	19	20	20	21	22	22	23	23	23	24
15						15	16	18	18	19	20	21	22	22	23	23	24	24	25
16							17	18	19	20	21	21	22	23	23	24	25	25	25
17							17	18	19	20	21	22	23	23	24	25	25	26	26
18							17	18	19	20	21	22	23	24	25	25	26	26	27
19							17	18	20	21	22	23	23	24	25	26	26	27	27
20							17	18	20	21	22	23	24	25	25	26	27	27	28

Adapted from Frieda S. Swed and C. Eisenhart, "Tables for testing randomness of grouping in a sequence of alternatives," *Ann. Math. Statist.* 14 (1943): 83–86, with the permission of the publisher.

APPENDIX L Critical Values of T in the Wilcoxon Matched-Pairs Signed-Ranks Test

N	Level of significance for one-tailed test		
	.025	.01	.005
	Level of significance for two-tailed test		
	.05	.02	.01
6	0	—	—
7	2	0	—
8	4	2	0
9	6	3	2
10	8	5	3
11	11	7	5
12	14	10	7
13	17	13	10
14	21	16	13
15	25	20	16
16	30	24	20
17	35	28	23
18	40	33	28
19	46	38	32
20	52	43	38
21	59	49	43
22	66	56	49
23	73	62	55
24	81	69	61
25	89	77	68

Adapted from Table I of F. Wilcoxon, *Some Rapid Approximate Statistical Procedures* (New York: American Cyanamid Company, 1949), 13, with the permission of the publisher.

APPENDIX M Mann–Whitney U Test Probabilities

$n_2 = 3$

U \ n_1	1	2	3
0	.250	.100	.050
1	.500	.200	.100
2	.750	.400	.200
3		.600	.350
4			.500
5			.650

$n_2 = 4$

U \ n_1	1	2	3	4
0	.200	.067	.028	.014
1	.400	.133	.057	.029
2	.600	.267	.114	.057
3		.400	.200	.100
4		.600	.314	.171
5			.429	.243
6			.571	.343
7				.443
8				.557

$n_2 = 5$

U \ n_1	1	2	3	4	5
0	.167	.047	.018	.008	.004
1	.333	.095	.036	.016	.008
2	.500	.190	.071	.032	.016
3	.667	.286	.125	.056	.028
4		.429	.196	.095	.048
5		.571	.286	.143	.075
6			.393	.206	.111
7			.500	.278	.155
8			.607	.365	.210
9				.452	.274
10				.548	.345
11					.421
12					.500
13					.579

$n_2 = 6$

U \ n_1	1	2	3	4	5	6
0	.143	.036	.012	.005	.002	.001
1	.286	.071	.024	.010	.004	.002
2	.428	.143	.048	.019	.009	.004
3	.571	.214	.083	.033	.015	.008
4		.321	.131	.057	.026	.013
5		.429	.190	.086	.041	.021
6		.571	.274	.129	.063	.032
7			.357	.176	.089	.047
8			.452	.238	.123	.066
9			.548	.305	.165	.090
10				.381	.214	.120
11				.457	.268	.155
12				.545	.331	.197
13					.396	.242
14					.465	.294
15					.535	.350
16						.409
17						.469
18						.531

$n_2 = 7$

U \ n_1	1	2	3	4	5	6	7
0	.125	.028	.008	.003	.001	.001	.000
1	.250	.056	.017	.006	.003	.001	.001
2	.375	.111	.033	.012	.005	.002	.001
3	.500	.167	.058	.021	.009	.004	.002
4	.625	.250	.092	.036	.015	.007	.003
5		.333	.133	.055	.024	.011	.006
6		.444	.192	.082	.037	.017	.009
7		.556	.258	.115	.053	.026	.013
8			.333	.158	.074	.037	.019
9			.417	.206	.101	.051	.027
10			.500	.264	.134	.069	.036
11			.583	.324	.172	.090	.049
12				.394	.216	.117	.064
13				.464	.265	.147	.082
14				.538	.319	.183	.104
15					.378	.223	.130
16					.438	.267	.159
17					.500	.314	.191
18					.562	.365	.228
19						.418	.267
20						.473	.310
21						.527	.355
22							.402
23							.451
24							.500
25							.549

$n_2 = 8$

U \ n_1	1	2	3	4	5	6	7	8	t	Normal
0	.111	.022	.006	.002	.001	.000	.000	.000	3.308	.001
1	.222	.044	.012	.004	.002	.001	.000	.000	3.203	.001
2	.333	.089	.024	.008	.003	.001	.001	.000	3.098	.001
3	.444	.133	.042	.014	.005	.002	.001	.001	2.993	.001
4	.556	.200	.067	.024	.009	.004	.002	.001	2.888	.002
5		.267	.097	.036	.015	.006	.003	.001	2.783	.003
6		.356	.139	.055	.023	.010	.005	.002	2.678	.004
7		.444	.188	.077	.033	.015	.007	.003	2.573	.005
8		.556	.248	.107	.047	.021	.010	.005	2.468	.007
9			.315	.141	.064	.030	.014	.007	2.363	.009
10			.387	.184	.085	.041	.020	.010	2.258	.012
11			.461	.230	.111	.054	.027	.014	2.153	.016
12			.539	.285	.142	.071	.036	.019	2.048	.020
13				.341	.177	.091	.047	.025	1.943	.026
14				.404	.217	.114	.060	.032	1.838	.033
15				.467	.262	.141	.076	.041	1.733	.041
16				.533	.311	.172	.095	.052	1.628	.052
17					.362	.207	.116	.065	1.523	.064
18					.416	.245	.140	.080	1.418	.078
19					.472	.286	.168	.097	1.313	.094
20					.528	.331	.198	.117	1.208	.113
21						.377	.232	.139	1.102	.135
22						.426	.268	.164	.998	.159
23						.475	.306	.191	.893	.185
24						.525	.347	.221	.788	.215
25							.389	.253	.683	.247
26							.433	.287	.578	.282
27							.478	.323	.473	.318
28							.522	.360	.368	.356
29								.399	.263	.396
30								.439	.158	.437
31								.480	.052	.481
32								.520		

Reproduced from H. B. Mann and D. R. Whitney, "On a test of whether one of two random variables is stochastically larger than the other," *Ann. Math Statist.* 18 (1947): 52–54, with the permission of the publisher.

APPENDIX N Mann–Whitney *U* Test Critical Values

Critical Values of U for a One-tailed Test at $\alpha = 0.001$ or for a Two-tailed Test at $\alpha = 0.002$

n_1 \ n_2	9	10	11	12	13	14	15	16	17	18	19	20
1												
2												
3									0	0	0	0
4		0	0	0	1	1	1	2	2	3	3	3
5	1	1	2	2	3	3	4	5	5	6	7	7
6	2	3	4	4	5	6	7	8	9	10	11	12
7	3	5	6	7	8	9	10	11	13	14	15	16
8	5	6	8	9	11	12	14	15	17	18	20	21
9	7	8	10	12	14	15	17	19	21	23	25	26
10	8	10	12	14	17	19	21	23	25	27	29	32
11	10	12	15	17	20	22	24	27	29	32	34	37
12	12	14	17	20	23	25	28	31	34	37	40	42
13	14	17	20	23	26	29	32	35	38	42	45	48
14	15	19	22	25	29	32	36	39	43	46	50	54
15	17	21	24	28	32	36	40	43	47	51	55	59
16	19	23	27	31	35	39	43	48	52	56	60	65
17	21	25	29	34	38	43	47	52	57	61	66	70
18	23	27	32	37	42	46	51	56	61	66	71	76
19	25	29	34	40	45	50	55	60	66	71	77	82
20	26	32	37	42	48	54	59	65	70	76	82	88

Critical Values of U for a One-tailed Test at $\alpha = 0.01$ or for a Two-tailed Test at $\alpha = 0.02$

n_1 \ n_2	9	10	11	12	13	14	15	16	17	18	19	20
1												
2					0	0	0	0	0	0	1	1
3	1	1	1	2	2	2	3	3	4	4	4	5
4	3	3	4	5	5	6	7	7	8	9	9	10
5	5	6	7	8	9	10	11	12	13	14	15	16
6	7	8	9	11	12	13	15	16	18	19	20	22
7	9	11	12	14	16	17	19	21	23	24	26	28
8	11	13	15	17	20	22	24	26	28	30	32	34
9	14	16	18	21	23	26	28	31	33	36	38	40
10	16	19	22	24	27	30	33	36	38	41	44	47
11	18	22	25	28	31	34	37	41	44	47	50	53
12	21	24	28	31	35	38	42	46	49	53	56	60
13	23	27	31	35	39	43	47	51	55	59	63	67
14	26	30	34	38	43	47	51	56	60	65	69	73
15	28	33	37	42	47	51	56	61	66	70	75	80
16	31	36	41	46	51	56	61	66	71	76	82	87
17	33	38	44	49	55	60	66	71	77	82	88	93
18	36	41	47	53	59	65	70	76	82	88	94	100
19	38	44	50	56	63	69	75	82	88	94	101	107
20	40	47	53	60	67	73	80	87	93	100	107	114

Critical Values of U for a One-tailed Test at $\alpha = 0.025$ or for a Two-tailed Test at $\alpha = 0.05$

n_1 \ n_2	9	10	11	12	13	14	15	16	17	18	19	20
1												
2	0	0	0	1	1	1	1	1	2	2	2	2
3	2	3	3	4	4	5	5	6	6	7	7	8
4	4	5	6	7	8	9	10	11	11	12	13	13
5	7	8	9	11	12	13	14	15	17	18	19	20
6	10	11	13	14	16	17	19	21	22	24	25	27
7	12	14	16	18	20	22	24	26	28	30	32	34
8	15	17	19	22	24	26	29	31	34	36	38	41
9	17	20	23	26	28	31	34	37	39	42	45	48
10	20	23	26	29	33	36	39	42	45	48	52	55
11	23	26	30	33	37	40	44	47	51	55	58	62
12	26	29	33	37	41	45	49	53	57	61	65	69
13	28	33	37	41	45	50	54	59	63	67	72	76
14	31	36	40	45	50	55	59	64	67	74	78	83
15	34	39	44	49	54	59	64	70	75	80	85	90
16	37	42	47	53	59	64	70	75	81	86	92	98
17	39	45	51	57	63	67	75	81	87	93	99	105
18	42	48	55	61	67	74	80	86	93	99	106	112
19	45	52	58	65	72	78	85	92	99	106	113	119
20	48	55	62	69	76	83	90	98	105	112	119	127

Critical Values of U for a One-tailed Test at $\alpha = 0.05$ or for a Two-tailed Test at $\alpha = 0.10$

n_2 \ n_1	9	10	11	12	13	14	15	16	17	18	19	20
1											0	0
2	1	1	1	2	2	2	3	3	3	4	4	4
3	3	4	5	5	6	7	7	8	9	9	10	11
4	6	7	8	9	10	11	12	14	15	16	17	18
5	9	11	12	13	15	16	18	19	20	22	23	25
6	12	14	16	17	19	21	23	25	26	28	30	32
7	15	17	19	21	24	26	28	30	33	35	37	39
8	18	20	23	26	28	31	33	36	39	41	44	47
9	21	24	27	30	33	36	39	42	45	48	51	54
10	24	27	31	34	37	41	44	48	51	55	58	62
11	27	31	34	38	42	46	50	54	57	61	65	69
12	30	34	38	42	47	51	55	60	64	68	72	77
13	33	37	42	47	51	56	61	65	70	75	80	84
14	36	41	46	51	56	61	66	71	77	82	87	92
15	39	44	50	55	61	66	72	77	83	88	94	100
16	42	48	54	60	65	71	77	83	89	95	101	107
17	45	51	57	64	70	77	83	89	96	102	109	115
18	48	55	61	68	75	82	88	95	102	109	116	123
19	51	58	65	72	80	87	94	101	109	116	123	130
20	54	62	69	77	84	92	100	107	115	123	130	138

Adapted and abridged from Tables 1, 3, 5, and 7 of D. Auble, "Extended tables for the Mann–Whitney statistic," *Bulletin of the Institute of Educational Research at Indiana University* **1**, No. 2 (1953) with the permission of the publisher.

Answers to Selected Problems

Chapter 2

7. a. 8 classes, $20 width
   b.

Balance	*Frequency*
$ 0.00–$ 19.99	15
20.00– 39.99	11
40.00– 59.99	8
60.00– 79.99	9
80.00– 99.99	8
100.00– 119.99	4
120.00– 139.99	2
140.00– 159.99	3

9. 0.083, 0.292, 0.250, 0.125, 0.083, 0.083, 0.083

19. a. 9
    b. For check numbers: Calculated width, 381.56; more convenient width, 400. For amount: Calculated width, 11.647; more convenient width, 12.

Chapter 3

1. Mean = 16.4376; median = 16; mode = 16

3. Mean = 16.881; median = 17.26; no mode

5. Range = 15. For population: Variance = 19.621; standard deviation = 4.43. For sample: Variance = 20.929; standard deviation = 4.57.

7. Mean = 16.881; standard deviation = 4.07. Within one standard deviation: 60% of actual values; within two standard deviations: 100% of actual values; within three standard deviations: 100% of actual values.

9. Mean = 14.11; median = 13.83

11. Mean = 51.82; median = 33.75; variance = 1,999.72; standard deviation = 44.72

13. 20.91

15. Set A

23. a. 15.3 b. 14.5 c. 12 d. 25.69474, 5.069 e. Increases the mean f. Median

25. a. 70.425 b. 70 c. 70 d. 37.8916, 6.1556

29. Pine: Mean = 1.93; standard deviation = 1.28. Redwood: Mean = 1.3; standard deviation = 1.06. Cedar: Mean = 2.43; standard deviation = 1.46.

31. a. 41.26 b. 39.5 c. 240.69, 15.51

d.

Class	*f*	*M*
15 and under 25	10	20
25 and under 35	10	30
35 and under 45	11	40
45 and under 55	8	50
55 and under 65	5	60
65 and under 75	5	70
75 and under 85	1	80

f. 41.4 g. 39.55 h. 281.67, 16.78

33. a. Seed type C
b. $CV_A = 18.18$; $CV_B = 26.79$; $CV_C = 25$; seed type A

35. CV of height = 3.6; CV of weight = 6.78

Chapter 4

1. 30,240
3. 630,630
5. 10
7. a. 0.056 b. 0.167 c. 0.111 d. 0.028 e. 0.019 f. 0.019
9. a. 0.4 b. 0.4 c. 0.04 d. 0.6 e. 0.66 f. 0
11. a. 0.007 b. 0.115 c. 0.082 d. 0.0063
21. a. 0.49 b. 0.4 c. 0.11
25. a. 12 b. 1,056
27. 6,435
29. 462
31. a. 56 b. 336
33. Not independent
35. 0.26272
37. a. 0.44 b. 0.194 c. 0.927
39. a. 0.596 b. 0.087 c. Not independent
41. a. Tennis; P (tennis|Jones wins) = 0.727, P(golf|Jones wins) = 0.273
b. Tennis

Chapter 5

1. Mean = 3; standard deviation = 1.254
3. Mean = expected value = 23.50; variance = 37.75; standard deviation = 6.144
5. a. 0.11, 0.10, 0.20, 0.275, 0.14, 0.10, 0.025, 0.05
b. 2.885
c. 1.773
d. Between 0 and 6.431 calls
11. Mean = 1.8; standard deviation = 1.24
15. a. 0.0 b. 0.0 c. 0.0099 d. 0.0199
17. Mean = 22.5; standard deviation = 3.969
19. Mean = 175; variance = 52.5; standard deviation = 7.246; CV = 4.14
23. 0.6244
25. a. 0.0355 b. 0.0218 c. 0.0709
27. 0.1356
29. a. 0.7166 b. 0.4529 c. 0.4392
31. Mean = 10; standard deviation = 3.1623
33. More than 100
41. a. 1.1 b. 0.943 c. $7.29
43. a. $E(X) = 750$; $E(Y) = 100$
b. $SD(X) = 844.1$; $SD(Y) = 717.64$
c. $CV(X) = 112.5$; $CV(Y) = 717.6$
45. b. 3.5 c. 0.00243
47. b. 0.087 c. 1.9998
49. a. 0.2396
51. a. 0.4168 b. 0.4168 c. 0.0002
53. b. 0.0021 c. 0.0061
55. a. 40 b. 80 c. $1.80 d. 4
57. P(equally composed) = 0.476; P(all one party) = 0.0476
59. P(4 good) = 0.1667; P(3 bad) = 0.033
61. 0.0816
63. 0.0076
65. a. 0.0067 b. 0.0317
67. a. 0.0009 b. 0.0267 c. 6 mistakes
69. a. 0.1512 b. 0.6472 c. 0.7149
71. b. 2.6 c. Variance = 2.6; standard deviation = 1.612 d. 0.0055

Chapter 6

1. a. 40 b. 11.55 c. 0.25 d. 0
3. a. 11.5 b. 0.714 c. 2.021
5. b. 10,000 c. 1,154.7 d. 11,600
7. a. 0.3707 b. 0.6293 c. 0.2514 d. 0.1846
9. a. 0.1762 b. 0.3446 c. 0.4401 d. 0.0548
11. 7.46
13. 0.5398
15. 0.8212
17. a. 10 b. 3.13 c. 0.7372
23. b. 0.2222 c. 0.4444 d. 4.75 e. 1.299
25. 0.000000016
27. 4.2
29. a. 0.0228 b. 0.9544 c. 0.25 d. 0.0062, 0.9876, 0.25
31. a. 0.6554 b. 0.5478 c. 0.3967 d. 0.7339
33. a. 10 feet 5.4675 inches b. 0.892
35. P(more than 74) = 0.1271; P(more than 90) = 0.011
37. 76
39. a. P(between 5.85 and 6.15) = 0.8664 b. Standard deviation should be 0.058
41. a. 0.0078 b. $P(70) = 0$ c. 2,000
43. a. 0.9956 b. 0.5160

Chapter 7

1. a. Mean = 27.375; standard deviation = 7.78 b. 70
3. a. 14,322.71 b. 35
5. a. Mean = 245.5; standard deviation = 93.85 b. 120
7. a. 58 b. 3.33 c. 2.236
9. a. 0.5 b. 0.86
11. Mean = 36.7; standard deviation = 0.94
13. a. 0.1469 b. 0.3156 c. 0.3212 d. 0.6995
15. a. 0.0038 b. 0.9982
17. a. 400 b. 0.4 c. 0.015 d. 0.9082 e. 0.0038 f. 0.7258 g. 0.1587
49. Mean = 45; standard deviation = 3.13
57. 1.195
61. 0
65. 0.2389
67. a. 0.2643 b. 0.3752
69. a. 0.1112 b. 0.2483
71. a. 0 b. 0 c. 0.0119, not in adjustment
73. 0
75. 0, 0

Chapter 8

1. a. 571.28 ____ 588.72 b. 569.61 ____ 590.39
3. a. 171 b. 385
5. 1,209,067.53 ____ 1,297,932.469
7. a. 1.131 ____ 1.269 b. 1.142 ____ 1.258
9. 85
11. a. 0.131 ____ 0.219 b. 0.122 ____ 0.228
13. 601
17. 0.0815 ____ 0.1435
19. 0.569 ____ 0.681
21. a. −16.56 ____ −13.44 b. −17.21 ____ −12.79
23. a. −0.044 ____ 0.104 b. −0.058 ____ 0.118
25. −0.0436 ____ 0.0348
27. 1.6376 ____ 3.3624
37. 14,000.97 ____ 14,409.03
39. −0.0449 ____ 0.0209
41. a. 0.232 ____ 0.768
43. Additional sample size = 8,375; total added cost = $14,656.25
45. a. 2.893 ____ 5.107

47. **a.** 0.2082 ____ 0.3178
b. 0.2414 ____ 0.3206

51. 0.588 ____ 0.732

53. **a.** 0.820 ____ 0.926 **b.** 4,269

55. **a.** 53.76 ____ 59.84
b. 145,220.93 ____ 161,499.07

57. 335, 753

59. 8.428 ____ 9.072

61. 98

63. **a.** 26,855
b. 26,453.08 ____ 27,256.92
c. 26,517.68 ____ 27,192.32

65. For 95% confidence:
−0.0045 ____ 0.0445

67. **a.** Sample 3 largest; sample 1 smallest
b. 97.4% confidence **c.** Sample 3
d. Sample 1: 4.17; sample 2: 4.13; sample 3: 2.78; sample size = 240
e. Sample 1

Chapter 9

1. **a.** Reject H_0 if $Z > 1.645$ or if $\overline{X} >$ 205.23
b. $Z = 1.41$; accept H_0

3. **a.** Reject H_0 if $Z < -1.645$
b. $Z = -0.98$; accept H_0

5. **a.** Reject H_0 if $\overline{X} < 4{,}394.07$ or $\overline{X} >$ 4,505.93
b. $\overline{X} = 4{,}475.60$; accept H_0

7. **a.** H_0: $\mu = 24$; H_A: $\mu \neq 24$
b. Reject H_0 if $Z < -1.96$ or $Z > 1.96$; $Z = 4.57$, reject H_0

9. **a.** Beta = 0.6480
b. Reject H_0 if $\overline{X} > 1{,}205.20$; $\overline{X} =$ 1,201.3; accept H_0

11. **a.** Beta = 0.9192
b. Reject H_0 if $\overline{X} < 4{,}317.1$; $\overline{X} = 4{,}337.5$; accept H_0

13. **a.** Beta = 0.0129
b. Reject H_0 if $\overline{X} < 17.49$; $\overline{X} = 17.4$; reject H_0

15. **a.** 2,771
b. Reject H_0 if $\overline{X} > 2{,}002.5$

17. **a.** 39
b. Reject H_0 if $\overline{X} < 1{,}966.83$

19. **a.** H_0: $\mu \geq 1$; H_A: $\mu < 1$
b. 68
c. Reject H_0 if $\overline{X} < 0.95$; accept H_0

27. Sample size = 4; reject H_0 if $\overline{X} < 2.52$; reject H_0; Type I error

29. **a.** H_0: $\mu \geq 20$; H_A: $\mu < 20$
b. Reject H_0 if $\overline{X} < 19.92$
c. Beta = 0
d. Beta = 0.121

31. **a.** H_0: $\mu \leq 10$; H_A: $\mu > 10$
b. Accept H_0

35. **a.** H_0: $\mu \geq 40$; H_A: $\mu < 40$
b. Reject H_0

37. **a.** H_0: $\mu = 417$; H_A: $\mu \neq 417$
c. Accept H_0

41. **a.** H_0: $\mu \geq 50$; H_A: $\mu < 50$
b. Reject H_0 if $\overline{X} < 47.208$; accept H_0

43. **a.** H_0: $\mu \geq 10$; H_A: $\mu < 10$
b. Reject H_0 if $\overline{X} < 9.541$
c. Reject H_0

45. Reject H_0 if $\overline{X} < 9.479$; accept H_0

47. **a.** H_0: $\mu \geq 5$; H_A: $\mu < 5$
b. Reject H_0 if $Z < -1.645$; $Z = -2.3$; reject H_0

49. H_0: $\mu \leq 60$; H_A: $\mu > 60$; reject H_0 if $Z > 1.645$; $Z = -26.35$; accept H_0

51. **a.** H_0: $\mu \geq 900$; H_A: $\mu < 900$
b. Reject H_0 if $\overline{X} < 866.95$
c. 0.6217
d. 0.5636

53. **a.** H_0: $\mu \geq 52$; H_A: $\mu < 52$
b. Reject H_0 if $Z < -1.28$; $Z = -44.72$; reject H_0

55. **a.** H_0: $\mu \geq 3.4$; H_A: $\mu < 3.4$
b. Reject H_0 if $Z < -1.645$; $Z = -8.49$; reject H_0
c. $Z = -2.4$; reject H_0
d. $Z = -2.25$; reject H_0

57. a. H_0: $\mu = 16.2$; H_A: $\mu \neq 16.2$; reject H_0 if $Z < -1.96$ or $Z > 1.96$; $Z = 2.48$; reject H_0
    b. $Z = 6.40$; reject H_0

Chapter 10

1. Reject H_0 if $Z > 1.645$; $Z = 0.675$; accept H_0
3. Reject H_0 if $\hat{p} < 0.12$ or $\hat{p} > 0.28$; $\hat{p} = 0.225$; accept H_0
5. H_0: $p \geq 0.4$; H_A: $p < 0.4$; reject H_0 if $\hat{p} < 0.319$; $\hat{p} = 0.38$; accept H_0
7. a. Reject H_0 if $Z < -1.96$ or $Z > 1.96$
   b. $Z = 8.43$; reject H_0
9. a. Reject H_0 if $Z < -1.96$ or $Z > 1.96$
   b. $Z = -22.69$; reject H_0
11. a. Reject H_0 if $Z > 1.645$
    b. $Z = 0.99$; accept H_0
13. a. H_0: $\mu_1 - \mu_2 \geq 0$; H_A: $\mu_1 - \mu_2 < 0$
    b. Reject H_0 if $Z < -1.28$; $Z = -1.89$; reject H_0
15. Reject H_0 if $Z < -1.645$ or $Z > 1.645$; $Z = -1.81$; reject H_0
17. Reject H_0 if $Z > 2.05$; $Z = 2.41$; reject H_0
19. H_0: $p_1 - p_2 = 0$; H_A: $p_1 - p_2 \neq 0$; reject H_0 if $Z < -1.96$ or $Z > 1.96$; $Z = 4.48$; reject H_0
21. a. J, $n = 80$
    b. Reject if number of defects ≥ 6
23. H_0: $p_1 \leq p_2$; H_A: $p_1 > p_2$; reject H_0 if $Z > 1.645$; $Z = -1.72$; accept H_0
25. a. H_0: $p \geq 0.75$; H_A: $p < 0.75$
    b. Reject H_0 if $\hat{p} < 0.717$; $\hat{p} = 0.919$; accept H_0
27. a. H_0: $p \leq 0.2$; H_A: $p > 0.2$
    b. Reject H_0 if $\hat{p} > 0.232$; $\hat{p} = 0.384$; reject H_0
29. a. H_0: $p \geq 0.5$; H_A: $p < 0.5$
    b. Reject H_0 if $\hat{p} < 0.44$
    c. $\hat{p} = 0.47$; accept H_0
31. H_0: $p \geq 0.25$; H_A: $p < 0.25$; reject H_0 if $\hat{p} < 0.179$; $\hat{p} = 0.2$; accept H_0
33. a. H_0: $p \geq 0.35$; H_A: $p < 0.35$
    b. Reject H_0 if $\hat{p} < 0.315$; $\hat{p} = 0.42$; accept H_0
35. a. H_0: $p_1 \leq p_2$; H_A: $p_1 > p_2$
    c. Reject H_0 if $Z > 2.05$; $Z = 0.203$; accept H_0
37. a. H_0: $\mu_1 - \mu_2 \geq 0.4$; H_A: $\mu_1 - \mu_2 < 0.4$
    b. Reject H_0 if $Z < -1.645$; $Z = 2.66$; accept H_0
39. H_0: $p \geq 0.5$; H_A: $p < 0.5$; reject H_0 if $\hat{p} < 0.432$; $\hat{p} = 0.477$; accept H_0
41. a. H_0: $\mu_B \geq \mu_S$; H_A: $\mu_B < \mu_S$
    b. Reject H_0 if $Z < -2.33$; $Z = -1.55$; accept H_0
    c. Reject H_0 if $Z < -1.28$; $Z = -1.55$; reject H_0

Chapter 11

1. a. 3.106 b. 1.833 c. 2.080 d. 1.734
3. −1.12
7. a. 112.752 ____ 134.248
   b. 114.759 ____ 132.241
9. a. 3.637 ____ 4.823
   b. 3.779 ____ 4.681
11. 2.629 ____ 4.271
13. Mean = 2.1; standard deviation = 1.969; 0.692 ____ 3.508
15. a. 36.15 b. 14.37 ____ 57.93
17. a. −0.476 ____ 1.176
19. −12.814 ____ 4.814
21. −1.055 ____ 1.331
25. −43.22 ____ −5.78
27. Reject H_0 if $t < -1.316$; $t = -0.72$; accept H_0
29. Reject H_0 if $t < -2.086$ or $t > 2.086$; $t = -5.34$; reject H_0
31. Reject H_0 if $t > 2.528$; $t = 0.302$; accept H_0

33. H_0: $\mu_1 - \mu_2 = 0$; H_A: $\mu_1 - \mu_2 \neq 0$; reject H_0 if $t < -1.833$ or $t > 1.833$; $t = -0.084$; accept H_0

35. H_0: $\mu_1 - \mu_2 = 0$; H_A: $\mu_1 - \mu_2 \neq 0$; reject H_0 if $t < -2.477$ or $t > 2.477$; $t = -0.06$; accept H_0

37. −0.439 ____ 0.559

41. H_0: $\mu_1 \leq \mu_2$; H_A: $\mu_1 > \mu_2$; reject H_0 if $t > 1.383$; $t = 0.671$; accept H_0

43. **a.** −0.83 ____ 2.164
b. −1.243 ____ 2.577
d. −2.35 ____ 3.67

45. **a.** −6.558 ____ 3.758

47. **a.** H_0: $\mu \geq 40$; H_A: $\mu < 40$
c. Reject H_0 if $T < -1.895$; $t = -3.48$; reject H_0

49. **a.** H_0: $\mu_1 - \mu_2 \leq 0$; H_A: $\mu_1 - \mu_2 > 0$
b. Reject H_0 if $t > 2.457$; $t = 1.24$; accept H_0

53. **a.** 1.021 ____ 1.379
c. 0.984 ____ 1.416

55. H_0: $\mu \geq 6$; H_A: $\mu < 6$; reject H_0 if $t < -1.711$; $t = 1.66$; accept H_0

57. **a.** H_0: $\mu_1 - \mu_2 = 0$; H_A: $\mu_1 - \mu_2 \neq 0$
b. Reject H_0 if $t < -1.796$ or $t > 1.796$; $t = -0.419$; accept H_0

59. H_0: $\mu_1 = \mu_2$; H_A: $\mu_1 \neq \mu_2$; reject H_0 if $t < -1.711$ or $t > 1.711$; $t = 2.738$; reject H_0

61. −2.448 ____ 5.848

63. **a.** H_0: $\mu \leq 1{,}000$; H_A: $\mu > 1{,}000$; reject H_0 if $t > 1.895$; $t = 1.535$; accept H_0

65. 487.988 ____ 499.012

67. **a.** 108.33 **b.** −19.927 ____ 236.587

69. **b.** −7.651 ____ 11.207

71. H_0: $\mu_1 - \mu_2 = 0$; H_A: $\mu_1 - \mu_2 \neq 0$; reject H_0 if $t < -2.447$ or $t > 2.447$; $t = -0.248$; accept H_0

Chapter 12

1. 16.919

3. 26.171

5. **a.** Reject H_0 if $\chi^2 > 16.919$; $\chi^2 = 11.025$; accept H_0
b. Reject H_0 if $\chi^2 > 39.087$; $\chi^2 = 39.15$; reject H_0

7. **a.** Reject H_0 if $\chi^2 > 18.549$; $\chi^2 = 16$; accept H_0
b. Reject H_0 if $\chi^2 > 42.557$; $\chi^2 = 50.75$; reject H_0

9. **a.** H_0: $\sigma^2 \leq 64$; H_A: $\sigma^2 > 64$
b. Reject H_0 if $\chi^2 > 21.064$
c. $\chi^2 = 23.23$; reject H_0

11. **a.** 3.62 **b.** 3.11 **c.** 3.05

13. **a.** Reject H_0 if $F > 2.86$
b. $F = 1.20$; accept H_0

15. **a.** Reject H_0 if $F < 3.23$
b. $F = 2.16$; reject H_0

17. **a.** H_0: $\sigma_1^2 \leq \sigma_2^2$; H_A: $\sigma_1^2 > \sigma_2^2$
b. Reject H_0 if $F > 1.98$; $F = 3.48$; reject H_0
c. H_0: $\mu_1 - \mu_2 = 0$; H_A: $\mu_1 - \mu_2 \neq 0$; reject H_0 if $t < -2.021$ or $t > 2.021$; $t = 6.133$; reject H_0

19. **b.** 317.73
c. 163.72
d. Reject H_0 if $F > 3.16$; $F = 11.64$; reject H_0

21. **b.** Reject H_0 if $F > 5.49$; $F = 7.42$; reject H_0

25. **b.** 183
c. 89.44
d. Reject H_0 if $F > 3.68$; $F = 15.35$; reject H_0
e. T range = 3.657; difference 1 & 2: 7.33; difference 2 & 3: 6.00; difference 1 & 3: 1.33

27. **b.** 1,178
c. 3,148
d. Reject H_0 if $F > 6.93$; $F = 2.25$; accept H_0

29. Reject H_0 if $F > 3.68$; $F = 22.33$; reject H_0; T range = 7.60; difference 1 & 2: 13.16; difference 2 & 3: 6.00; difference 1 & 3: 19.16

31. **b.** TSS = 1,494.88; SSBL = 63.38; SSB = 1,274.13; SSW = 157.37

c. F between groups = 56.70; F between blocks = 1.21; differences: 3.50, 6.87, 12.87, 10.37, 16.37, 6.00; LSD = 2.846

33. b. F between groups = 11.9; F between blocks = 2.6

41. H_0: $\sigma^2 \le 0.0016$; H_A: $\sigma^2 > 0.0016$; reject H_0 if $\chi^2 > 30.144$; $\chi^2 = 44.186$; reject H_0

43. H_0: $\sigma^2 \le 9$; H_A: $\sigma^2 > 9$; reject H_0 if $\chi^2 > 14.684$; $\chi^2 = 27.04$; reject H_0.
H_0: $\mu = 36$; H_A: $\mu \ne 36$; reject H_0 if $t < -1.833$ or $t > 1.833$; $t = 0.608$; accept H_0.

45. H_0: $\sigma_1^2 = \sigma_2^2$; H_A: $\sigma_1^2 \ne \sigma_2^2$; reject H_0 if $F > 2.58$; $F = 1.44$; accept H_0.
Reject H_0 if $F > 3.77$; accept H_0.
H_0: $\mu_1 - \mu_2 = 0$; H_A: $\mu_1 - \mu_2 \ne 0$; reject H_0 if $t < -2.056$ or $t > 2.056$; $t = -0.632$; accept H_0.

47. a. H_0: $\sigma_1^2 \le \sigma_2^2$; H_A: $\sigma_1^2 > \sigma_2^2$
b. Reject H_0 if $F > 2.28$; $F = 1.45$; accept H_0

49. H_0: $\sigma_1^2 = \sigma_2^2$; H_A: $\sigma_1^2 \ne \sigma_2^2$; reject H_0 if $F > 4.85$; $F = 2.61$; accept H_0

51. Reject H_0 if $F > 8.105$; $F = 7.359$; accept H_0

53. Reject H_0 if $F > 4.43$; $F = 59.4$; reject H_0

55. a. Reject H_0 if $t < -2.12$ or $t > 2.12$; $t = 1.16$; accept H_0
b. Reject H_0 if $F > 4.49$; $F = 1.35$; accept H_0

57. Reject H_0 if $F > 3.55$; $F = 9$; reject H_0

59. a. Reject H_0 if $F > 5.39$; $F = 22.31$; reject H_0
b. Differences: 4,400, 1,800, 2,600; T range = 2,086.52

61. a. Reject H_0 if $F > 3.49$; $F = 10.36$; reject H_0
b. Differences: 2.16, 4.94, 2.78; T range = 2.76

63. a. Reject H_0 if $F > 3.685$; $F = 5.28$; reject H_0
b. Differences: $8.92 < 10.29$; $12.75 > 11.67$; $3.83 < 12.30$

65. a. Reject H_0 if $F > 2.92$; $F = 6.53$; reject H_0
b. Differences: $1.19 < 2.19$; $1.68 < 2.04$; $0.71 < 2.10$; $0.49 < 1.84$; $1.9 > 1.89$; $2.39 > 1.72$

67. a. Reject H_0 if $F > 3.1$; $F = 7.66$; reject H_0

69. F between blocks = 10.95

71. F between groups = 6.22; F between blocks = 30.69; Differences: 8.4, 98.8, 0.7, 90.4, 7.7, 98.1; LSD = 57.26

Chapter 13

7. b. 0.9239
c. Reject H_0 if $t < -2.306$ or $t > 2.306$; $t = 6.8295$; reject H_0

9. b. Reject H_0 if $t < -1.697$ or $t > 1.697$; $t = 7.3030$; reject H_0

13. b. −0.8290; reject H_0 if $t < -2.365$ or $t > 2.365$; $t = -3.9219$; reject H_0
c. $\hat{Y} = 19.7547 - 0.0835X$

15. b. −0.5411; reject H_0 if $t < -2.262$ or $t > 2.262$; $t = -1.9303$; accept H_0
c. $\hat{Y} = 5.1568 - 0.0751X$
d. SSE = 12.8580; SS(Y variable) = 18.1819; SS(Residuals) = 0.0001

17. a. Reject H_0 if $t < -2.069$ or $t > 2.069$; $t = 2.0744$; reject H_0

19. b. Reject H_0 if $t < -2.01$ or $t > 2.01$; $t = -3.2436$; reject H_0

21. a. Reject H_0 if $t < -2.069$ or $t > 2.069$; $t = 13.4259$; reject H_0
c. 122.6548 ______ 167.3452

23. b. −16.3916 ______ −3.8488

25. a. 7,400
b. 7,399.3714 ______ 7,400.6286
c. 7,397.2636 ______ 7,402.7364

27. a. 1,242.1440
b. 36,315.7411 ______ 36,324.2589
c. 36,307.2234 ______ 36,332.7766

41. 0.0002884 ____ 0.000768

43. b. 0.891
  c. Reject H_0 if $t < -2.12$ or $t > 2.12$; $t = 7.85$; reject H_0

45. For $\alpha = 0.10$: Reject H_0 if $t < -1.701$ or $t > 1.701$; $t = 4.78$; reject H_0

47. b. 0.951; reject H_0 if $t < -2.306$ or $t >$ 2.306; $t = 8.7$; reject H_0
  c. $\hat{Y} = 10.482 + 2.154X$

53. a. 0.0002558 ____ 0.0003442
  c. Reject H_0 if $F > 3.94$; $F = 182$; reject H_0

55. b. $\hat{Y} = 1{,}219.803 - 9.12X$
  c. −22.73 ____ 4.49
  d. Reject H_0 if $t < -1.833$ or $t > 1.833$; $t = -1.23$; accept H_0

57. a. Reject H_0 if $t < -1.96$ or $t > 1.96$; $t = 54.05$; reject H_0
  b. 2.91 ____ 3.57

59. 3.436 ____ 3.492

61. a. $\hat{Y} = -19.4 + 2.90X$; reject H_0 if $t <$ -2.120 or $t > 2.120$; $t = 16.89$; reject H_0

63. a. $\hat{Y} = 66.7 + 10.6X$; reject H_0 if $t <$ -1.782 or $t > 1.782$; $t = 7.88$; reject H_0

Chapter 14

1. Reject H_0 if $t < -2.262$ or $t > 2.262$; (Y, X_1): $t = 2.12$; (Y, X_2): $t = 2.91$; (Y, X_3): $t = 1.83$; (X_1, X_2): $t = 2.55$; (X_1, X_3): $t = 0.81$; (X_2, X_3): $t = 0.09$

3. a. $-476 + 0.742X_1 + 1.31X_2 + 0.119X_3$
  b. 0.735
  c. Reject H_0 if $F > 4.35$; $F = 6.461$; reject H_0
  d. X_2, X_3
  e. 0.621

5. Reject H_0 if $t < -2.145$ or $t > 2.145$; (Y, X_1): $t = 6.01$; (Y, X_2): $t = 1.70$; (Y, X_3): $t = 2.80$; (Y, X_4): $t = -2.03$; (X_1, X_2): $t = 1.12$; (X_1, X_3): $t = 2.65$; (X_1, X_4): $t = -1.31$; (X_2, X_3): $t = 1.65$; (X_2, X_4): $t = -1.87$; (X_3, X_4): $t = -2.46$

7. a. $14{,}133 + 63.2X_1 + 10.1X_2 + 31.5X_3 - 55.5X_4$
  b. 0.775
  c. Reject H_0 if $F > 3.36$; $F = 9.45$; reject H_0
  d. X_1
  e. 0.693
  f. X_1: 30.27 ____ 96.03;
  X_2: −21.40 ____ 41.60;
  X_3: −358.30 ____ 421.30;
  X_4: −192.12 ____ 81.20

9. 3

13. b. $-1{,}012.1 + 69.1X_1$
  c. $-586.256 + 22.861X_1 + 2{,}302.267X_2 + 1{,}869.813X_3$; Reject H_0 if $F > 4.35$; $F = 5.393$; reject H_0
  d. $-586.256 + 22.861X_2$

15. a. X_1 b. No other variables entered
  c. $11{,}392.04318 + 72.2163X_1$
  d. Reject H_0 if $F > 4.60$; $F = 36.07$; reject H_0.
  Reject H_0 if $t < -2.16$ or $t > 2.16$; $t = 6.006$; reject H_0.

33. $A_L = -0.5139$; $A_H = 0.5139$

37. Reject H_0 if $t < -2.201$ or $t > 2.201$; t for X_1: 1.99; t for X_2: 0.86; t for X_3: 1.52; accept H_0 for all variables

41. Reject H_0 if $t < -2.16$ or $t > 2.16$; t for (Y, X_1): 2.877; t for (Y, X_2): 1.371; t for (Y, X_3): 2.85; t for (Y, X_4): 2.00

43. 0.844; reject H_0 if $F > 3.48$; $F = 13.607$; reject H_0

45. Reject H_0 if $t < -2.228$ or $t > 2.228$; t for X_1: 4.422; t for X_2: −0.788; t for X_3: 3.581; t for X_4: 2.581

47. Reject H_0 if $t < -2.160$ or $t > 2.160$; t for (Y, X_5): 7.266; t for (Y, X_6): 3.171

49. Reject H_0 if $F > 3.58$; $F = 9.125$; reject H_0

51. $-100{,}834 + 94.8X_1 - 347X_2 + 1X_3 + 1{,}043X_4 + 0.837X_5 + 596X_6$

53. Reject H_0 if $t < -2.069$ or $t > 2.069$; t for $(Y, X_1) = -2.12$; t for (Y, X_2): 2.47;

t for (Y, X_3): -1.21; t for (X_1, X_2): 0.246; t for (X_1, X_3): 2.79; t for (X_2, X_3): 1.35

55. Reject H_0 if $F > 4.26$; $F = 6.14$; reject H_0
59. Reject H_0 if $t < -2.08$ or $t > 2.08$; t for β_1: -1.6555; t for β_2: 3.132; t for β_3: -1.163.
Reject H_0 if $F > 3.07$; $F = 5.33$; reject H_0.

Chapter 15

3. -0.5485
5. Reject H_0 if $\phi_{cal} < \dfrac{-Z_{.05}}{\sqrt{n}}$; $-0.5485 < -0.1163$; reject H_0
7. 0.1679; reject H_0 if $\phi_{cal} > \dfrac{-Z_{.05}}{\sqrt{n}}$; $0.1679 > 0.05228$; reject H_0
9. Reject H_0 if $\chi^2 > 26.296$; $\chi^2 = 17.5467$; accept H_0
11. Reject H_0 if $\chi^2 > 9.488$; $\chi^2 = 2.35$; accept H_0
13. Reject H_0 if $\chi^2 > 21.026$; $\chi^2 = 28.44$; reject H_0
15. Reject H_0 if $\chi^2 > 15.507$; $\chi^2 = 61.5267$; reject H_0
17. Reject H_0 if $\chi^2 > 9.488$; $\chi^2 = 6.372$; accept H_0
19. Reject H_0 if $0.075 > w_p$; $w_p = .19$; accept H_0
25. Reject H_0 if $\chi^2 > 11.34$; $\chi^2 = 6.625$; accept H_0
27. Reject H_0 if $\chi^2 > 4.605$; $\chi^2 = 404.336$; reject H_0
29. Reject H_0 if $\chi^2 > 11.07$; $\chi^2 = 41.74$; reject H_0
31. Reject H_0 if $\chi^2 > 11.07$; $\chi^2 = 80.944$; reject H_0
33. **b.** Reject H_0 if $\chi^2 > 3.84$; $\chi^2 = 3.338$; accept H_0
    c. Reject H_0 if $Z < -1.96$ or $Z > 1.96$; $Z = -1.828$; accept H_0

Chapter 16

1. **a.** 11
   b. Reject H_0 if $r \leq 6$ or $r \geq 16$; $r = 11$; accept H_0
3. Reject H_0 if $Z < -1.645$ or $Z > 1.645$; $Z = -13.4128$; reject H_0
5. **a.** Reject H_0 if $t < -2.074$ or $t > 2.074$; $t = 1.27$; accept H_0
   b. Reject H_0 if $U \leq 37$; $U = 51$; accept H_0
7. p-value = .319; accept H_0
9. Reject H_0 if $T \leq 4$; $T = 14$; accept H_0
11. **b.** Reject H_0 if $Z < -1.96$ or $Z > 1.96$; $Z = 0.9409$; accept H_0
13. **b.** Reject H_0 if $H > 5.991$; $H = 5.416$; accept H_0
15. $H = 66.26$
17. **a.** -0.3
    b. Reject H_0 if $t < -2.262$ or $t > 2.262$; $t = -0.943$; accept H_0
23. Reject H_0 if $U \leq 30$; $U = 14$; reject H_0
25. Reject H_0 if $t < -1.734$ or $t > 1.734$; $t = 0.066$; accept H_0
27. Reject H_0 if $U \leq 24$; $U = 58$; accept H_0
29. $\alpha = 0.10$; reject H_0 if $\chi^2 > 4.61$; $H = 5.803$; reject H_0
31. **b.** Reject H_0 if $t < -2.228$ or $t > 2.228$; $t = -2.485$; reject H_0
35. **c.** Reject H_0 if $t < -2.306$ or $t > 2.306$; $t = 3.02$; reject H_0
37. Reject H_0 if $r \leq 3$ or $r \geq 11$; $r = 4$; accept H_0
39. **b.** Reject H_0 if $Z < -1.96$ or $Z > 1.96$; $Z = 4.178$; reject H_0
41. Reject H_0 if $t < -2.16$ or $t > 2.16$; $t = 4.706$; reject H_0
43. **c.** Reject H_0 if $T \leq 8$; $T = 17$; accept H_0

Chapter 17

5. a. $101 + 1.98X$ b. 0.633
7. Ratio to trend: 0.977, 1.004, 0.940, 0.966, 1.019, 1.041, 1.004, 1.005, 1.076, 1.007, 0.947, 1.009, 1.049, 1.049, 0.977, 0.925; normalized average seasonal index, Qtr. 1: 103.1; Qtr. 2: 102.6; Qtr. 3: 96.7; Qtr. 4: 97.6
9. Norm. avg. seas. index (Jan–Dec): 88.3, 85.6, 89.6, 99.1, 101.0, 93.3, 98.2, 103.1, 107.3, 102.4, 113.3, 118.8
11. Norm. avg. seas. index (Qtr. 1–4): 101.5, 92.1, 107.9, 98.5; $\hat{Y} = 222.375 + 1.353X$; $R^2 = 0.117$
13. Index numbers: 100.00, 116.49, 122.16, 131.44, 143.30, 144.85, 154.64, 165.98, 174.23, 181.96, 186.08, 200.52, 209.79
15. Radio index numbers: 100.00, 103.33, 110.00, 115.33, 120.67, 126.67, 132.00; newspaper index numbers: 100.00, 105.00, 115.00, 130.00, 145.00, 160.00, 165.00
17. Laspeyres index: 100.00, 104.59, 113.78, 126.43, 139.08, 151.89, 156.97
19. 9.88, 10.14, 10.49, 11.78, 11.90, 12.48
29. $\hat{Y} = 115{,}423.56 + 20{,}359t^2$; $R^2 = 0.972$; $t = 21.89$
31. $\hat{Y} = -1.4 + 1.5308t$; $R^2 = 0.939$; reject H_0 if $t < -2.228$ or $t > 2.228$; $t = 12.43$; reject H_0
33. $\hat{Y} = 23.43513 - 0.12157t$; $R^2 = 0.257$; reject H_0 if $t < -2.201$ or $t > 2.201$; $t = -5.184$; reject H_0
41. Company 1: 100, 109.15, 132.26, 141.68, 161.84, 174.29, 190.96; Company 2: 100, 104.52, 114.37, 122.16, 140.71
43. Labor index: 100, 101.99, 107.96, 111.94, 119.40, 121.89, 124.88, 124.63, 123.88, 118.41, 120.40; Materials index: 100, 105.16, 108.82, 109.46, 110.11, 111.18, 111.94, 115.48, 114.84, 116.34, 116.13
45. Paasche index: 100, 105.16, 108.82, 109.46, 110.11, 111.19, 111.94, 115.49, 114.84, 116.35, 116.13
47. Unweighted aggregate index: 100, 112.70, 126.98, 146.03, 165.08, 176.19, 188.89, 206.35
49. Paasche index: 100, 113.55, 129.68, 149.68, 169.68, 181.29, 194.84, 213.55

Chapter 18

5. $\hat{Y} = 243.875 + 5.463t$; $R^2 = 0.905$; forecast: 336.75, 342.21, 347.68, 353.14
7. Forecast: 343.98, 348.72, 314.36, 352.65; $\hat{Y} = 242.4847 + 5.6362t$; $R^2 = 0.94$
9. a. $\hat{Y} = 54.837 + 0.663t$; $R^2 = 0.57$; forecast: 93.46, 94.10, 94.73, 95.36, 96.00, 96.63, 97.26, 97.90, 98.53, 99.16; 99.79, 100.43
   b. Norm. avg. seas. index (Jan–Dec): 0.9589, 0.8831, 0.8880, 0.9928, 1.0274, 0.9244, 0.9776, 1.0172, 1.0489, 1.0040, 1.1116, 1.1661; forecast: 88.07, 81.62, 82.59, 92.92, 96.76, 87.61, 93.22, 97.59, 101.25, 97.50, 108.60, 114.61; $\hat{Y} = 56.088 + 0.586t$; $R^2 = 0.663$
11. a. First-order lag: $49.966 + 0.84357Y_{t-1}$, $R^2 = 0.866$; second-order lag: $91.8097 + 0.714629Y_{t-2}$, $R^2 = 0.706$; third-order lag: $97.049 + 0.7157Y_{t-3}$, $R^2 = 0.716$; fourth-order lag: $83.65979 + 0.782542Y_{t-4}$, $R^2 = 0.794$
   b. Fourth-order lag
   c. 338.77, 343.46, 334.86, 329.38
13. a. One-period lag: $16.75220 + 0.790257Y_{t-1}$, $R^2 = 0.751$; twelve-period lag: $46.441 + 0.457159Y_{t-12}$, $R^2 = 0.603$
   b. Twelve-period lag
15. a. 132.5 b. 133.3 c. 129.64 d. 139.33 e. Weighted moving average

25. a. 3,506,000 b. 3,286,003
    c. 4,068,983 d. Double exponential model

27. a. 20,775,000 b. 18,671,111
    c. 23,421,900 d. Double exponential model

29. a. 2,817.50 b. 2,817.06 c. 2,809.69
    d. Single exponential model

31. 1,437.6; MSE = 125,192.9; MAD = 307.7857

33. c. Norm. avg. seas. index (Qtr 1–4): 80.57189, 109.3428, 103.4445, 106.6408
    d. Forecast: 1,455.1, 2,022.4, 1,958.3, 2,065.4; $\hat{Y} = 1{,}064.59 + 43.611t$; $R^2 = 0.916$

35. a. $\hat{Y} = 781.04 + 0.4844Y_{t-1}$; $R^2 = 0.2645$
    b. $\hat{Y} = -74.295 + 0.9333Y_{t-4}$; $R^2 = 0.9337$
    c. Four-period lagged autoregressive model

39. 303.4; MSE = 9,625.22; MAD = 77.77

41. c. Norm. avg. seas. index (Qtr 1–4): 74.05257, 89.64874, 128.5465, 107.7521
    d. Forecast: 257.22, 341.41, 501.33, 430.08; $\hat{Y} = 215.987 + 9.158t$; $R^2 = 0.646$

43. a. $\hat{Y} = 158.267 + 0.4980Y_{t-1}$; $R^2 = 0.2202$
    b. $\hat{Y} = -37.66364 + 1.279Y_{t-4}$; $R^2 = 0.8999$
    c. Four-period lagged autoregressive model

Chapter 19

1. 20; maximum payoff = 15
3.

Order Size	$E(X)$
15	10
16	10.85
17	11.40
18	11.35
19	10.10
20	8.40

Order 17 books

5. 500; payoff = 500
7. 2 lots, expected payoff = 60
9. Buy no lots; expected values = 0
11. 200; maximum payoff = 3,000
13. Keep for two years, then sell if no increase in demand; expected value = \$57,000
15. Expand; expected value = \$34,500
17. Build the large resort; expected value = \$1.95 million
29. Revenues = \$10,000; Costs = \$3,872; sign contract
31. 60,000; expected payoff = \$6,760,000
33. 6; expected payoff = 144,000
35. \$60,000 home: maximin—3, \$0; maximax—6, 72
    \$100,000 home: maximin—0, \$0; maximax—6, 168
37. 5; expected payoff = \$1,250,000
41. Option 2: 4, expected payoff = \$580,000; Option 3: 3, expected payoff = \$840,000
43. 1,500, expected payoff = \$4,312.50
45. 4, expected payoff = \$9.50
47. Accept offer; expected payoff = \$47,280
49. Open market; expected cost = \$27,360
51. Sell independent; expected revenue = \$1,128,000
53. Still sell independently
57. Lease cost sunk cost, no impact on decision

Chapter 20

1. $P(A|D) = 0.5$; $P(B|D) = 0.5$; equally likely
3. $P(A|D) = 0.476$; $P(B|D) = 0.143$;

$P(C|D) = 0.381$; plant A: \$4,760; plant B: \$1,430; plant C: \$3,810

5. $P(N|D) = 0.79$; $P(O|D) = 0.21$; new grower
7. Gamble 1: RP = −\$4,000; gamble 2: RP = −\$1,500; gamble 3: RP = −\$8,500; risk seeking
9. **b.** Indifferent between alternative with \$4,500 premium (EV = \$17,000) and no insurance (EV = \$17,000)
   c. \$10,000 premium insurance policy; expected preference quotient = 0.964
21. $P(A|D) = 0.521$; $P(B|D) = 0.375$; $P(C|D) = 0.104$; plant A: \$208,400; plant B: \$150,000; plant C: \$41,600
23. **b.** Do not install; expected payoff = 0
25. 0.647
27. Posterior probabilities: 0.0120, 0.9880
29. **a.** Go ahead with service; highest expected payoff with service = \$400,000
    b. Posterior probabilities: 0.0017, 0.1418, 0.5692, 0.2874
    c. Proceed; expected payoff = \$1,284,500
31. Posterior probabilities: good, .0257; fair, 0.9383; poor, 0.0360
33. $P(\text{fair}) = 99.99\%$
35. Lease; expected payoff = \$75,000
37. Lease; expected payoff = \$80,010
39. Plant potatoes
43. Plant potatoes, buy water; expected payoff = \$20,500
45. Install pipe, plant potatoes, buy water, expected payoff = \$20,500
49. Do not develop model; expected preference = 0.872
51. Do not sign contract, develop improved model; expected payoff = \$85.20
55. Add three-day version
57. Add the game

Index